ALIENATION

The Cultural Climate of Modern Man

EDITED WITH INTRODUCTIONS BY

GERALD SYKES

VOLUME II

GEORGE BRAZILLER   NEW YORK

Copyright © 1964, by Gerald Sykes

Published simultaneously in Canada by
Ambassador Books, Limited, Toronto

All rights reserved
For information, address the publisher,
George Braziller, Inc.
215 Park Avenue South, New York 3

Library of Congress Catalog Card Number: 64-23164

FIRST PRINTING

PRINTED IN THE UNITED STATES OF AMERICA

For copyright information and credits for selections in this volume,
see Acknowledgments, volume 1, p. iii

CONTENTS

189688

VOLUME I

BOOK ONE: VICTIMS

This Neutrality Toward Death

I Watched Them Disappear

Public Smile, Private Blank

Those of the Inhabitants of Sodom Who Were Spared

BOOK TWO: PERSPECTIVES

CONTENTS

VOLUME II

BOOK THREE: DIALOGUES

The New Art Is Not Accessible to Every Man

Nevertheless He Was in Reality a Wolf

Vassal, Slave, Inferior

Lend a Myth to God

BOOK FOUR: SURVIVORS

A Necrophilous and Senseless Cry

An Earthly Story With a Hellish Meaning

This Is All Very Baffling to Man

Primary Words Are Spoken From the Being

Just Ease These Darbies at the Wrist

ALIENATION
The Cultural Climate of Modern Man

Gabriel Marcel

THE DECLINE OF WISDOM

THE LIMITATIONS OF INDUSTRIAL CIVILISATION

Industrial civilisation: the meaning of the words seems obvious, but I think only because they evoke a set of images and ready-made ideas. The moment we say 'industrial civilisation' we see factories, smoke, slums, suburbs, what have you, and all the commonplaces about mechanisation spring into our minds; 'Mechanisation means progress', or 'Mechanisation is a scourge' and so on. But none of it is enough to enable us to form even a preliminary concept.

The trouble (as I have had occasion to say in a lecture I gave in Florence) is that the notion of civilisation itself has its ambiguities, and the idea of industrial civilisation, seemingly more exact, cannot help being affected by them. In principle, or rather at first, 'civilisation' meant the state of civilised man as against a state of being primitive—savagery, barbarism; this is an idea we already find in the philosophy of the Greeks, particularly of Aristotle, and which, after suffering a number of mishaps, reappeared in force in the humanism of the Renaissance. Perhaps we should note that its apparent obviousness and brilliance dimmed in proportion as the accent was placed upon original sin and its to some extent irreparable consequences.

In the eighteenth century, however, at least in J. J. Rousseau's writings, it was confronted with a form of nature worship which pin-pointed its corruption; while in the nineteenth century, on the contrary, the West, fascinated by the progress of science and technics, seized on the idea of civilisation as the reward of the fullest development of man's rational faculties. For positivism and all the schools of thought connected with it, civilisation was the triumph of enlightened order over confusion, violence and disorder. The optimists of a hundred years ago even thought of it as the means to universal peace, implying the gradual substitution of right for might and bringing with it not only generally increased well-being, but as a corollary the harmonious development of the sciences and the arts.

It would be difficult for us after the events of the past half-century to share this optimism and in particular to see why man's growing mastery over nature should go hand in hand with the triumph of right. In any case, the development of historical science and sociology has in the meantime given rise to a very different conception. In place of the over-all and in many ways confused notion of civilisation as a whole there has grown up the idea of civilisations which are not only distinct but alto-gether separate and irreducible to one another's terms, civilisations which may co-exist, though not without friction, but which are ever in danger of replacing one another in circumstances which are always tragic.

It became more and more evident, especially in the light of ethnologi-cal discoveries, that those whom the civilised had presumptuously label-led savages had their own civilisation with its perfectly recognisable structure and cohesion.

It is tempting to say that in view of all this there came about a dissociation between the ideas of civilisation and value which in the global concept had been inseparable. Actually I do not believe that this can ever be absolute; it would be more true to say that with the develop-ment of a pluralist and historicist theory of civilisations, values came to be *relativised*—if I may be forgiven so barbarous a term. However you define it, a civilisation implies beliefs—that is to say, values; what is dangerous is to assert *a priori* that these values are necessarily those which rationalist European thought, starting with the Greeks, has at-tempted to define as universals. Not that I would say that such a reduc-tion is necessarily impossible, only that it would need the utmost caution.

Can any of this help us to see a little further into what 'industrial civilisation' means?

Obviously it is quite different from a rural civilisation, for example. We have only to think of England to see how these two sorts of civilisa-tion were able to co-exist for a very long time, even in juxtaposition; nor can it be said that their co-existence has now ended, though everything goes to show that industrial civilisation is predominating and this in cir-cumstances which can easily be defined.

What is also evident is that each of these civilisations forms around a particular way of life, and above all that each of these ways of living be-longs to its own particular environment.

I have been greatly struck by what Georges Friedmann has to say about what he calls the technical environment as against the natural environment.

THE TECHNICAL ENVIRONMENT.

In the natural environment man is present in his work. 'The span of work is as yet no bigger than that of man's natural movements in their technical capacity. The tools which *homo faber* uses in his natural en-

vironment may be complex but their interposition between his hand or
foot and the material on which he is at work does not mean that his part
in production is eliminated. On the contrary, they humanise production
further since they make it possible to manufacture something to which
the craftsman, who completes the work himself, brings greater continuity
and precision, carrying out his plan and giving it the harmony of a
finished whole. In such a profession as medicine this fullness of human
presence is still noticeable'.

The natural environment as such is a climate of presence and sympathy. In it 'a life rich in direct understanding, in presence, is combined
with the spread of craftsmanship and the beginnings of industry'.

Nothing more different from this could be found than the technical
environment which, as such, is artificial and inhuman in the strongest
sense, even where everything has been done to improve the material
conditions of work. 'In this milieu', says Georges Friedmann, 'boredom is
the worker's mate, the only possible escape is on the side of man'; and
Georges Naval, the author of *Traveaux* and *Parcours,* who has been
through this experience, writes:

> In the world of the factory all that there remains of nature is man, the
> companion, the fellow being. If you were alone in it you would die. No
> trees, no plants, no dogs. Everything you touch is hard, dense; next to it
> the soft stuff of which your hand is made seems very fragile. In that fluid
> world of metal it is reassuring to meet a comrade.

Georges Friedmann comments that so long as this world is still frequented by men, by comrades, there is a chance of conquering it, of
moulding it to the ends of culture and dignity. Nothing could be more
true, I think, but we must still ask ourselves on what terms this comradeship can remain genuine. It stares us in the face that it is in grave
danger of being impaired by the intrusion of politics, or if you like of
propaganda.

The moment men are brought in whose function is to pass on slogans,
a milieu which was still living and charged with currents of friendship
and even genuine brotherhood is in danger of being frozen, or to put it
in another way, of turning into a field for the transmission of quite different currents, which are inhuman and magnetised by the ends purely of
domination.

A question which arises here is whether people whose training has been
almost exclusively technical are not much more susceptible to this kind
of propaganda than those who have received what at the beginning of
this century was still called a general culture. Not that I would suggest
a return to the teaching of the classics as it was conceived at the end
of the nineteenth and the beginning of the twentieth centuries; but it

seems that a counterweight to the growing technical trend in education needs to be invented.

A strictly complementary aspect of industrial civilisation is brought to light in this fine passage by Spengler which occurs in the last chapter of his *Decline of the West*:[1]

Then followed . . . the discovery of the steam engine. . . . Till then nature had rendered services, but now she was tied to the yoke as *a slave*, and her work was as though in contempt measured by a standard of horse-power. We advanced from the muscle-force of the Negro, which was set to work in organised routines, to the organic reserves of the Earth's crust, where the life-forces of millennia lay stored as coal; and today we cast our eyes on inorganic nature, where water-forces are already being brought in to supplement coal. As the horse-powers run to millions and milliards, the numbers of the population increase and increase, on a scale that no other Culture ever thought possible. This growth is a *product of the Machine*, which insists on being used and directed, and to that end centuples the forces of each individual. For the sake of the machine, human life becomes precious. *Work* becomes the great word of ethical thinking; in the eighteenth century it loses its derogatory implication in all languages. The machine works and forces the man to cooperate. The entire Culture reaches a degree of activity such that the earth trembles under it.

And what now develops, in the space of hardly a century, is a drama of such greatness that the men of a future Culture, with other souls and other passions, will hardly be able to resist the conviction that 'in those days' nature herself was tottering. The politics stride over cities and peoples; even the economics, deeply as they bite into the destinies of the plant and animal worlds, merely touch the fringe of life and efface themselves. But this technique will leave traces of its heyday behind it when all else is lost and forgotten. For this Faustian passion has altered the Face of the Earth.

This is the outward- and upward-straining life-feeling—true descendant, therefore, of the Gothic—as expressed in Goethe's Faust monologue when the steam-engine was yet young. The intoxicated soul wills to fly above space and Time. An ineffable longing tempts Man to indefinable horizons. He would free himself from the earth, rise into the infinite, leave the Bonds of the body, and circle in the universe of space amongst the stars. That which the glowing and soaring inwardness of St. Bernard sought at the beginning, that which Grünewald and Rembrandt conceived in their backgrounds, and Beethoven in the trans-earthly tones of his last quartets, comes back now in the intellectual intoxication of the inventions that crowd one upon another. Hence the fanastic traffic that crosses the continents in a few days, that puts itself across oceans in floating cities, that bores through mountains, rushes about in subterranean labyrinths, uses the steam-engine till its last possibilities have been exhausted, and then passes on to the gas-engine, and finally raises itself above the roads and railways and flies in the air; hence it is that the spoken word is sent in one moment over all the oceans; hence comes the ambition to break all records and beat all dimensions, to build giant halls for giant machines, vast ships and bridge-spans, buildings that deliriously scrape the clouds, fabulous forces pressed together to a focus to obey the hand of a child, stamping and quivering and droning works of steel and glass in which tiny man moves as unlimited monarch and, at the last, feels nature as beneath him.

And these machines become in their forms less and ever less human, more ascetic, mystic, esoteric. They weave the earth over with an infinite web of subtle forces, currents, and tensions. Their bodies become ever more and more immaterial, ever less noisy. The wheels, rollers, and levers are vocal no more. All that matters withdraws itself into the interior. Man has felt the machine to be devilish, and rightly. It signifies in the eyes of the believer the deposition of God. It delivers sacred Causality over to man and by him, with a sort of foreseeing omniscience, is set in motion, silent and irresistible.

The expression 'Faustian passion' may be surprising, but its use is justified by certain texts in Act IV of the Second Faust. 'The earthly sphere', declares Faust, 'is still big enough, I find, for big actions whose success may light up the world. I feel in myself a great strength ready to be used with courage.' And a little further he speaks to the Emperor of 'spirits silently at work in the depths of unfathomable abysses, decomposing and combining rich emanations into rare, metallic gases and ceaselessly inventing new things'. So I think it is legitimate to keep Spengler's expression and to describe the values of industrial civilisation as Faustian. Perhaps by exploring this notion and by linking it with that of the industrial environment, we may have a chance to discover the limits of this civilisation.

There is every evidence that there is in it a fundamental paradox.

THE CHARACTERISTICS OF TECHNICAL PROGRESS

It is evident that the mastery of the forces of nature by means of increasingly elaborate technical processes is a liberation which should be welcomed as such; but it is no less true that, for reasons which must be examined, this liberation is in danger of being itself turned into a slavery. It is in this contradiction that the drama of industrial civilisation lies. Going back to the ambiguity I mentioned at the beginning, I would say that, again for the same reasons, this particular civilisation is in danger of developing *against* certain universal values which would seem to be a part of civilisation in general.

But here we must be very careful. In his valuable book[2] on Work and Civilisation, M. Hyacinthe Dubreuil very properly and forcefully denounces the judgments which intellectuals often make upon realities of which they have no experience. I believe his criticism to be fully justified and I am most anxious, in what follows, to avoid any such mistake.

'Literature which attacks technical progress and machinery and turns them into a sort of monster', writes M. Dubreuil, 'is a waste of time. It is a case of mistaken identity; for although if work is badly done, somebody is responsible, the villain is not the lifeless machine but man who has decided to use it wrongly.'

I should like to distinguish between these two statements. The first is perfectly correct: it is ridiculous to denounce technical progress as such (I will come back to this point, for I am anxious not to leave the slightest ambiguity). The second assertion seems to me, however, to imply an over-simplification and I would even say a mistake: man has not 'decided' to use the lifeless machine wrongly; the truth is infinitely more complex, as we shall see.

As to the absurdity of condemning technical progress in itself, I think it is possible to establish certain principles which it would be hard to dispute. To start with a definition, let us say simply that a technique is a specialised and rationally elaborated form of knowledge, and let us add that the techniques we are concerned with here are all skills which contribute to the transformation of the world. They all offer certain basic characteristics which it would be difficult to overstress.

(1) They are specialised and, almost always, within their own specialised field they tend to give rise to new forms of specialisation.

(2) They are perfectible.

(3) And they are transmissible. Indeed, the more rationalised they are, the more easily can they be transmitted.

What does run the danger of getting lost is what craftsmen call a knack, something that can only be passed on by example if at all, and not by any theoretical training or instruction. Again, certain empirical recipes may have been lost because they were never, properly speaking, fixed. But a technique such as we conceive it today is transmissible by definition.

The perfectibility of techniques should also be emphasised, and we must note particularly that in this field perfectibility has an exact and univocal meaning. If in fact one technical process is better than another it is because it improves output or makes it possible to produce the same amount in less time or at less cost (in either case production is by definition improved). What is interesting from the philosophical point of view is that in this technical domain alone the word progress has kept the fullness of its meaning. To see the truth of this we have only to take a look at the fog in which it wraps itself the moment it is applied, say, to morals or to institutions. The reason is that the criteria applicable to ethics, politics or indeed aesthetics can not have the same precision as they have in the field of technics. I believe this to be a most important point, and I think that if the theories of progress current since the eighteenth century and particularly since Condorcet have been so deceptive this may largely be due to the neglect of its basic truth. It could be shown, I think, that if there is such a thing as social progress it is to the extent that there exist social techniques.

But after all the essential questions are those which have to do with human happiness, or shall we say contentment on the one hand and with spiritual quality on the other. And it has yet to be shown that the progress of social techniques as such is sufficient either to increase contentment or to develop spiritual quality. Only the most rudimentary psychology could induce us without further argument to believe it does.

THE POSITIVE VALUE OF TECHNICAL PROGRESS

I have blamed myself recently, particularly when I was lecturing in South America, with not having perhaps brought out sufficiently in my writings what I would call the positive value of technical progress. I am not thinking only of its usefulness—only a lunatic would deny that—but of something more than mere utility. There is no doubt that in applying a technique which he has mastered the technician experiences a joy which is not only basically innocent, but even noble. It is a joy which is bound up with the consciousness of power over inanimate things, that is to say, over a reality which is subordinate and is in a sense meant to be controlled by man.

It is true that things offer a resistance, but it is, as it were, the resistance of inertia which it is good to overcome. Moreover, it can only be overcome by means which have an extreme precision. The value of a technique is that of the precision with which it is applied, and we must remember the connection between precision and intellectual honesty.

A link notion—and it already bears an ethical or at least pre-ethical character—is that of accuracy. No technician can do without the virtue of accuracy: in his world inaccuracy is always punished and the punishment is sometimes terrible. Hence the awareness of responsibility which he incessantly carries with him.

At the same time this awareness has to be of a particularly subtle kind. It must not invade the foreground of his consciousness but must remain on its outer fringes. A surgeon performing an operation cannot forget his responsibility for a moment, but it must not weigh on him to the point of being an obsession: it is not on this that he must focus or even concentrate his mind but on his task; responsibility is rather the spirit in which his task is carried out or the light in which he sees it, and this is the very light of his sense of accuracy and precision.

And, again, there is the purity and soundness of the joy which goes with technical research when it results in a discovery. I am inclined to think that what is positive in all this is that the technician is not thinking of himself, but of his task, and here again there is the saving virtue of precision. It is true, of course, that the technician is a man and that it is natural for him to think of the personal advantage his success may bring him, but this consideration is, as it were, collateral; his research work in itself holds no room for vanity, for the time being at any rate it literally drives it out. In this the technician differs from the intellectual or the artist; in a sense his work is necessarily more pure, it leaves literally no place for ambition or flattery.

Alain distinguishes between human attitudes involved in actions applied to things and those applied to people. It is indeed far simpler for an action to be pure if it bears on things, while to act on people, or to be more accurate, to bring to bear on them the techniques which are rightly applicable to things is, we shall see, an abuse pregnant with the gravest consequences.

THE EFFECT OF TECHNICAL PROGRESS ON MAN

All this brings us to the second of M. Dubreuil's assertions, the one concerning the wrong use of the machine. I have already said that I disagree with it.

We might say, using Christian terms—and these terms are urged on us not only by faith but also by reflection—that it is in the nature of techniques to lead the mind into temptation. But we must immediately qualify this statement. It would obviously be absurd to think of techniques as wielding power in their own right; it is always a being who leads into temptation.

I do not, of course, intend to go into the problem of daemonology, although it undoubtedly arises on the fringes of our enquiry. All we have to ask ourselves here, and this without trespassing beyond experience, is what the notion of temptation means and in what circumstances it may become active. My view is that it is invariably bound up with power. The moment that we are endowed with power of whatever sort we are exposed to the temptation of abusing it. How are we to account for this fact which is so intimately part of our way of being?—I think that it is nearly always a phenomenon which could be compared to vertigo—vertigo being the impulse to 'let oneself go to' something.

What I mean is this. The exercise of any sort of power should by rights be accompanied by the exercise of control over this power itself—this is a sort of 'power at one remove'. But in practice such concomitance of strength and control over that strength is by no means inevitable. We find, on the contrary, that the more suddenly power is acquired—or at any rate the less the conditions of its acquisition are like those of natural growth—the more does it tend to behave as a *parvenu*: like a self-made man who believes (always quite wrongly) that he is in no man's debt, it rejects, as though it were an unwarrantable intrusion or encroachment, any form of limitation or control over itself.

This being said, my suggestion that it is in the nature of techniques to lead the mind into temptation simply amounts to this: a man who has mastered one or more techniques tends in principle to distrust what is alien to these techniques; or rather, he will at a pinch admit the validity of this or that other technique he has only heard of or knows only at second hand; but he will usually be most unwilling to accept the idea that a meta-technical activity may have value. But in respect of technical power which is immediate, what I have called power at one remove is necessarily meta-technical. Indeed it is these powers at one remove which, in a technical civilisation, are most likely to be discredited.

But let us not forget that the activity among all others which can most truly be described as power at one remove is reflection. And in fact, everything goes to show that in a civilisation of this sort the importance of reflection will be minimised if not denied. Already we see logico-mathematical neo-positivism, a philosophy which denies the role of reflection altogether, gradually invading England and a part of the United States; to the philosophers of this school, the idea of a philosophy of reflection is utterly alien, they almost put it aside as a sort of mysticism.

At this point our analysis must be taken a step further. Whence does reflection spring? I mean true reflection which on no account must be confused with some kind of ratiocination. I once wrote in *Being and Having,* 'Power at one remove is nourished by a blindfolded intuition; this intuition is something that I am, not something that I have', and it belongs to philosophical thought to retrieve it and, as it were, to make it articulate.

But let us not linger in this abstract realm. The more the world I dwell in is alive, the more generously it is watered by life, the more my intuition —and I would really prefer to call it my participation—will be rich and substantial at its source. But does this not bring us back to the difference between natural and technical environment? For there is no doubt that the technical environment is the poorest possible in life, the furthest possible removed from nature. While in the natural environment, as Friedmann writes, 'the whole of human life and in particular the whole life of work is woven through and through by those rhythms which, flowing from generation to generation, have been gradually formed and established in the society to which they so intimately belong'.

I would not in the least suggest our indulging in some sort of pseudo-romantic hankering after a lost paradise, a paradise whose undoubted benefits, we may be sure, were balanced by terrible disadvantages. All I am trying to show is that although we cannot speak, like M. Dubreuil, of unwillingness or of ill will on the part of man, technical development does, taken in itself, tend to create a world which is singularly barren and as a result unfavourable to the use of powers at one remove; and let us note that these powers correspond fairly closely to what in other ages was known as wisdom.

As a simple illustration of what I mean by a barren world, take the family and the danger it runs in a technical milieu where the women work as well as men, the children are virtually left to themselves and there often arises between them and their parents a sort of mutual hostility. When I spoke of a world which is generously watered by life I was thinking particularly of the benefits of a strongly established family.

But what is it that wisdom as such is normally called upon to oppose? It stands over against *hybris*, pride. Where the counterweight to pride is lacking, the techniques left, as it were, to their own weight, are moreover burdened by the weight of pride which in no sense belongs to them. For once again, it is not that the techniques have an intrinsic reality; they are only given a specious reality through a vice of abstraction in the one who uses them, takes his pleasure in them and lastly becomes their slave.

To put it differently, techniques tend to become the dynamic line-aments of an abstract world in which the intellect is the more at ease the more it is specialised. Actually, this mental agility is the result of a train-ing of which the value, I repeat, is not disputable. But this training im-plies no contact at any point with an environment which is concrete and, as it were, not altogether explicitly definable; in this it is the opposite of organic growth, and I am not thinking only of the growth of the body, but of a feeling, a belief, of the becoming of the imagination in all its forms.

THE ABSTRACT CHARACTER OF INDUSTRIAL ENVIRONMENT

By an odd coincidence, I have just read the following passage in a book by Helmuth Gollwitzer[3] which contains one of the most objective criticisms I have ever come across of Soviet man:

This system neither recognises any subject as confronting it nor as a result does it allow the development of any such subjects, whether individuals or groups, and this means exactly that here nothing is allowed to grow. If life is unfettered growth in conformity with its own laws, this is surely the gravest accusation that can be brought. And indeed, for the life of the community, both the spiritual and the economic consequences of this fact are terrible. There is room for nothing but pre-established plans and manufactured objects: anything that grows is suspect.

It can of course be objected that what is true of the Soviet world is not necessarily true of industrial civilisation in general, but is this not perhaps merely because in other countries that civilisation has not yet unfolded all its implications? Thus in the United States, the logic of technocracy sometimes comes up against a sentimentality which can be almost childish, while on other occasions it goes hand in hand with a confused religiosity. But what matters to us is to discover what this logic really is and the ways in which it shows itself.

There are two points which seem to me of the highest importance.

Firstly, there is a danger of the technical environment becoming for us the pattern of the universe, that is to say, the categories of its particular structure being claimed to be valid for an objective conception of the world.

And note that this is not a matter of interpretation only; the interpretation becomes embodied, it seeks to reconstitute the world, moulding it to its own image. Never shall I forget my impression on first coming to a country such as Venezuela, where I had the feeling that what had been a landscape was being turned into a builder's yard. There you may witness the kind of planned sectioning and cutting up which I would venture to call sacrilegious. I had this feeling most strongly in Rio de Janeiro, where the hills were going to be levelled without the slightest consideration for the reality of the original site. This is something very significant; whereas in the past a city moulded itself on the natural structure or pre-structure, as it were fulfilling it, we are likely to see larger and larger agglomerations piling up without the slightest regard for the natural pre-formation. There is not the least hesitation in doing violence to nature to carry out an abstract plan.

These words, abstract, abstraction, keep coming back, and this cannot be helped because it is just the crux of it. But we must try to understand the reason for this predominance in the industrial world of the abstract, the planned, the organised, the dissected. It is a difficult question because the causes and conditions are so tangled up that we cannot be sure of discovering all at once which of them is the key to all the others. It is likely anyway that here, as so often, the categories of cause and effect have to be transcended and the vicious circle is the rule. Mass production on a scale which was inconceivable in the past is of course related to the existence of the masses whose needs must be satisfied and for the satisfaction of those needs an individualised economy is inadequate.

But these masses are not only at the beginning, but at the end; I mean that they are themselves—as masses—partly the result of mass production and its consequences in every economic field. There is also the fact that big industry tends itself to create the needs which it later claims to satisfy. And no doubt it must be added that this whole process becomes increasingly inevitable as time goes on, or if you prefer, *it tends to create its own inevitability.*

So far as I can see (but I must again stress that my lack of competence forbids me to speak categorically) we are confronted by an enormous system which consolidates itself more and more, so that it is less easy to see the logical possibility of anything altering it in principle. 'Logical', I said, but history is there to show us how inadequate are such logical, rational considerations. The mysterious role of crises, catastrophes, even natural upheavals may be to bring into play compensating elements, which act, however, in ways that confound our reason.

THE PROCESS OF DEHUMANISATION AND THE TECHNICALITY OF KNOWLEDGE

It is of course an absurd illusion to think that by means of some sort of world planning these calamities can be kept permanently at bay.

But there is something more important still. It is impossible for man not to consider himself as part of this cosmos—or of this a-cosmos—planned and dissected by the technicians; as a result, he inevitably becomes a target for those techniques which, in principle, are legitimately applicable only to the outward world. There are already countless instances of this in the fields of experimental psychology, psychiatry and so on.

One of the most characteristic of them is the incredible development of the use of tests in America and in the Americanised countries. There are, of course, certain fields where their use is altogether justified; I would say that such a field is that of motor-sensory behaviour; it is perfectly proper to determine by means of tests whether a given person is fit to exercise certain well defined functions directly related to such activity —to be a pilot or a truck driver, for instance. But the more we leave this field for that of the intelligence properly so called, that is to say, of understanding and *a fortiori* of affectivity, the objection to the use of tests is grave, even decisive.

Experimentation, if we reflect upon it, should as such be handled warily; but the striking fact is that, for the reasons I have given, it is reflection which is simply set aside in these Americanised countries. I have had a recent confirmation of it in talking with a Swedish psychologist who told me that he had literally discovered since he came to France the limitations of certain techniques which were sanctioned in his own country without the slightest warning as to the conditions in which they could be suitably applied.

But we must see that as soon as the technical environment has become the predominating, general, normal environment, it is strictly normal for such techniques to become generalised and to proliferate. This is one more victory for abstraction, the individual being now a unit whom it is possible and right to deal with as with all the other units in his category.

And what becomes of the distinction between the normal and the abnormal? It will almost inevitably be interpreted in a behaviourist sense. It is normal for the individual placed in such and such conditions to react in a given way and any anomaly is a failure to adapt himself. The end of it, almost certainly, is what I would call a general *pragmatisation* of human beings and relations, as indeed we see in America and Americanised countries such as Sweden. The astonishingly high incidence of psychosis in these countries is enough to show that the system which they seem to have adopted involves a tragic oversight of certain deep human exigencies, and this is perhaps the more convincing because these are countries which are prosperous and where all the basic needs seem generally speaking to be satisfied. But the ravages caused in them by boredom, sexual immorality and drunkenness are, as it were, irrefutable symptoms of a deep-seated lesion, of what I would indeed prefer to call a sin against life itself.

But make no mistake—that sin is most intimately bound up with a certain technical representation of the world. I would say that as a result of the act by which man projects upon the world the light of a knowledge which is technicalised, an increasingly monstrous image of the world and of himself is thrown back at him—an image which is ever more distorted and ever less decypherable.

Is this not indeed perhaps the unrecognisable image which so often faces us in modern art? In general, the consequences of all this are incalculable, particularly in what relates to self-knowledge. The Socratic axiom implied the idea of an identity between the knower and the known, and this idea was at the basis of traditional philosophy until Hegel. But now, following upon the hyperbolic development of technics, a development of which the so-called acceleration of history is perhaps in some ways only a corollary, the truth of this postulate is increasingly put in doubt. As a result the subject tends less and less to be treated as a subject and is consequently less and less respected. Hence that spreading violation of privacy which is one of the most horrifying features of the modern world, whose worst excesses in this direction show themselves in literature.

It might at least be thought that, as a beneficent counterpart to all this, the new skills might strengthen man's hold on his earthly habitation; unfortunately experience belies it, and the reason is doubtless that in such a world the very idea of taking root ends by seeming contradictory. What we said of agglomerations replacing cities is relevant: an agglomeration is, as it were, the very *embodiment of uprootedness*.

In such a world the mass transfers of populations which have taken place in the totalitarian countries should no longer be considered an anomaly. On the contrary, they may well become the rule once the vital link is broken between man and his environment and people are seen as mere units of production—as machines which are needed here or there for reasons connected with the general economy and whose feelings are of not the slightest interest. Indeed, perhaps it would be best so to train these men-machines that their needs and feelings would become atrophied and in the end vanish!

I remember once being told by someone who was dealing with the terrible problem of Displaced Persons that some country or other only wanted people who could makes shoes! The entity one-who-can-make-shoes is substituted for the concrete reality of so-and-so, married to such and such a person and father of such and such a child.

This indeed is again the sin against life understood in its deepest sense. Life is no longer, as it were, conceived except in bio-sociological terms, that is to say, as a process whose physico-chemical conditions are claimed to be strictly and objectively definable and which exists in view of a given task which relates to the collectivity.

Here again the wildest excesses of the totalitarian régimes seem only to be the ultimate expression of a monstrous logic, the logic of dehumanisation. It is easy enough to show that its hallmark is always that of the will to power. And no doubt we shall always feel the need to find a scapegoat in whom to localise that will. Indeed it is quite possible that at the outset, some one person hungering for domination helped to launch this terrifying venture. But it must not be forgotten that by now the system is endowed with its own power of self-consolidation, which incidentally is the crowning absurdity, since it may in the end involve us in the sacrifice of all, certainly not for all but precisely for no one— an immense holocaust to nothingness.

But how should we not see in all this a huge inverted caricature of what the Christian can only call the plan of salvation? I have said inverted for if on the one side sacrifice is the very expression of love, on the other it is the manifestation of a devitalised rationality which is already turning human beings into robots. But this glaring opposition can only be seen at the furthest limit, because undeniably, so long as this enormous process of dehumanisation is still on its way, it involves qualities which are genuinely spiritual, especially generosity, although of that generosity it tends, by the strangest paradox, to dry up the springs and as it were to preclude the very possibility. Thus I do not hesitate to say that, if we could discover what this process is at bottom and in principle, putting aside the illusions and misconceptions which it encourages and exploits, we would see that it cannot be considered as anything except basically daemoniac.

REMEDIES FOR THE DEHUMANISATION OF THE WORLD

So I do no violence to my argument if I say that the world is in need of exorcism. But this is obviously a misleading term and I have in mind no sort of magic formulae. The only genuinely exorcising power is that of love, and even then love needs to be incarnate.

But as we have known for twenty centuries, such an incarnation, if it can take place at all, can only do so at the humblest level. There must be a Bethlehem of reflection and fervour and this I see as the only genuine hearth and nourishment for thought anxious to avoid at all cost falling into ideology or still worse into foolish sentimentality.

But nothing I have said should make us forget the considerations we started from. It would indeed be to fall under the joint spells of sentimentalism and ideology to hope for some sort of Gandhi revolution and a return to a pre-technical age. The burden of technics has been assumed by man and he can no longer put it down because he finds it heavy. The consequences of such an abdication would be catastrophic. Just as in becoming de-Christianised humanity tends to fall far below the level of pre-Christian civilisation, so in giving up what must after all be called the conquests of science it would fall into the lowest degradation.

So the problem—and of course, here we can only state it—is only to know how we may struggle efficaciously against the weight by which in a technical age man is dragged down into the excesses of technocracy. If the word liberty, today so dishonoured, still has any meaning, it is strictly applicable to this act. But clearly, it is not just a question of putting on a brake: no genuine action can be merely negative. It is a question of mobilising such forces as are capable of effectively opposing this immense drift; that these forces are spiritual nobody will deny; but spiritual is another word which is frequently misinterpreted and misspent. What I think we need today is to react with our whole strength against that dissociation of life from spirit which a bloodless rationalism has brought about.

This does not mean that we should go back to some sort of false romanticism—I must admit that I find traces of it even in Bergson. Perhaps the most important task on the plane of speculation is to deepen once again the notion of life itself in the light of the highest and most genuine religious thought. I have had occasion recently to observe that in Germany some such new development seems to be taking place, in profound reaction against the aberrations which have for so long disfigured the very image of that country.

But it must be added at once that this development, which can only take place on the highest levels of spirituality and reflective thought, can never reach the fullness of its authenticity and value unless it has its counterpart in the sphere of action, and it is here that the need for humility can be plainly seen. For to have exorcising power, action must be on the level of good will, that is to say, love of one's neighbour. It is impossible, I think, to condemn too mercilessly the illusion of achieving anything by introducing into spirituality the sort of planning operations which can only act against the spirit.

I have spoken of meta-technical activities; the proper place of meta-technics is at the juncture of the spiritual and the vital, in a mysterious region which is also that of the *charismata*.

Like all other religious terms without exception, the term charismata can mislead, perhaps by evoking some absurd imagery of kindly spells cast by personages muffled in priestly robes. The simplest is to go back to the etymology. Charisma means gift, a gift of love which itself is gift.

It is in gift, that is to say in grace, that there assuredly lies the only principle capable of breaking, I will not say the world of the techniques in so far as they are admirable means to be used for the good of all, but those superstructures which threaten in the long run to stifle their beneficent power, because they are ordained to the triumph of pride which ultimately encompasses the destruction of the proud.

NOTES

1. Allen and Unwin, 1926.
2. *Travail et Civilisation*, 1953, Plon, Paris.
3. *Und Führer Woher du Nicht Willst*, Munich, Kaiser Verlag, 1953.

E. E. Cummings

i their son

from *i—six nonlectures*

You will perhaps pardon me, as a nonlecturer, if I begin my second nonlecture with an almost inconceivable assertion: I was born at home.

For the benefit of those of you who can't imagine what the word "home" implies, or what a home could possibly have been like, I should explain that the idea of home is the idea of privacy. But again—what is privacy? You probably never heard of it. Even supposing that (from time to time) walls exist around you, those walls are no longer walls; they are merest pseudosolidities, perpetually penetrated by the perfectly predatory collective organs of sight and sound. Any apparent somewhere which you may inhabit is always at the mercy of a ruthless and omnivorous everywhere. The notion of a house, as one single definite particular and unique place to come into, from the anywhereish and everywhereish world outside—that notion must strike you as fantastic. You have been brought up to believe that a house, or a universe, or a you, or any other object, is only seemingly solid: really (and you are realists, whom nobody and nothing can deceive) each seeming solidity is a collection of large holes—and, in the case of a house, the larger the holes the better; since the principal function of a modern house is to admit whatever might otherwise remain outside. You haven't the least or feeblest conception of being here, and now, and alone, and yourself. Why (you ask) should anyone want to be here, when (simply by pressing a button) anyone can be in fifty places at once? How could anyone want to be now, when anyone can go whening all over creation at the twist of a knob? What could induce anyone to desire aloneness, when billions of soi-disant dollars are mercifully squandered by a good and great government lest anyone anywhere should ever for a single instant be alone? As for being yourself—why on earth should you be yourself; when instead of being yourself you can be a hundred, or a thousand, or a hundred thousand thousand, other people? The very thought of being oneself in an epoch of interchangeable selves must appear supremely ridiculous.

Fine and dandy; but, so far as I am concerned, poetry and every other art was and is and forever will be strictly and distinctly a question of individuality. If poetry were anything—like dropping an atombomb—

which anyone did, anyone could become a poet merely by doing the necessary anything; whatever that anything might or might not entail. But (as it happens) poetry is being, not doing. If you wish to follow, even at a distance, the poet's calling (and here, as always, I speak from my own totally biased and entirely personal point of view) you've got to come out of the measurable doing universe into the immeasurable house of being. I am quite aware that, wherever our socalled civilization has slithered, there's every reward and no punishment for unbeing. But if poetry is your goal, you've got to forget all about punishments and all about rewards and all about selfstyled obligations and duties and responsibilities etcetera ad infinitum and remember one thing only: that it's you—nobody else—who determine your destiny and decide your fate. Nobody else can be alive for you; nor can you be alive for anybody else. Toms can be Dicks and Dicks can be Harrys, but none of them can ever be you. There's the artist's responsibility; and the most awful responsibility on earth. If you can take it, take it—and be. If you can't, cheer up and go about other people's business; and do (or undo) till you drop.

My own home faced the Cambridge world as a finely and solidly constructed mansion, preceded by a large oval lawn and ringed with an imposing white-pine hedge. Just in front of the house itself stood two huge appletrees; and faithfully, every spring, these giants lifted their worlds of fragrance toward the room where I breathed and dreamed. Under one window of this room flourished (in early summer) a garden of magnificent roses; the gift of my parents' dear friend "stubby" Child —who (I learned later) baptized me and who (I still later discovered) was the Child of English And Scottish Ballads. As a baby, I sported a white sweater; on which my mother had embroidered a red H, for Harvard.

Our nearest neighbor, dwelling (at a decent distance) behind us, was Roland Thaxter; primarily the father of my loveliest playmate and ultimately the professor of cryptogamic botany. To our right, on Irving Street, occurred professors James and Royce and Warren; to our left, on Scott Street, transpired professor of economics Taussig. Somewhat back of the Taussig house happened professor Lanman—"known and loved throughout India" as my mother would say, with a pensive smile. She had been slightly astonished by an incident which embellished her official introduction to Mr and Mrs Lanman: the celebrated Sanscrit scholar having, it seems, seized his would-be interlocutor's hand, yanked her aside, and violently whispered "do you see anything peculiar about my wife?"—then (without giving my mother time to reply) "she has new shoes on" professor Lanman hissed "and they hurt her!" I myself experienced astonishment when first witnessing a spectacle which frequently thereafter repeated itself at professor Royce's gate. He came rolling peacefully forth, attained the sidewalk, and was about to turn right and wander up Irving, when Mrs Royce shot out of the house with a piercing cry "Josie! Josie!" waving something stringlike in her dexter fist. Mr Royce politely paused, allowing his spouse to catch up with him; he then shut both eyes, while she snapped around his collar a narrow necktie possessing a permanent bow; his eyes thereupon opened, he bowed, she smiled, he advanced, she retired, and the scene was over. As for professor Taussig, he had a cocker spaniel named Hamlet; and the Taussig family always put Hamlet out when they played their pianola —no doubt the first law of economics—but Hamlet's hearing was excellent, and he yodelled heartrendingly as long as the Hungarian Rhapsody persisted. Genial professor Warren's beautiful wife (whose own beautiful name was Salomé Machado) sometimes came to call on my maternal grandmother; and Salomé always brought her guitar. I remember sitting spellbound on our upstairs porch among appleblossoms, one heavenly spring afternoon, adoring the quick slim fingers of Salomé Machado's exquisite left hand—and I further remember how, as Salomé sang and played, a scarlet tanager alighted in the blossoms; and listened, and disappeared.

One of the many wonderful things about a home is that it can be as lively as you please without ever becoming public. The big Cambridge house was in this respect, as in all other respects, a true home. Although I could be entirely alone when I wished, a varied social life awaited me whenever aloneness palled. A father and mother—later, a sister—two successive grandmothers and an aunt (all three of whom sang, or played the piano, or did both, extremely well) and one uncle, plus three or four hearty and jovial servants, were at my almost unlimited disposal. The servants—and this strikes me as a more than important point—very naturally enjoyed serving: for they were not ignobly irresponsible impersons, they were not shamelessly overpaid and mercilessly manipulated anonymities, they were not pampered and impotent particles of a greedy and joyless collective obscenity. In brief: they were not slaves. Actually, these good and faithful servants (of whom I speak) were precisely everything which no slave can ever be—they were alive; they were loved and loving human beings. From them, a perfect ignoramus could and did learn what any unworld will never begin to begin to so much as suspect: that slavery, and the only slavery, is service without love.

After myself and my father and mother, I loved most dearly my mother's brother George. He was by profession a lawyer, by inclination a bon vivant, and by nature a joyous human being. When this joyous human being wasn't toiling in his office, or hobnobbing with socalled swells at the Brookline country club, he always became my playfellow. No more innocently goodhearted soul ever kissed the world goodnight; but when it came to literature, bloodthirsty was nothing to him. And (speaking of bloodthirstiness) I here devoutly thank a beneficent Providence for allowing me to live my childhood and my boyhood and even my youth without ever once glimpsing that typical item of an era of at least penultimate confusion—the uncomic nonbook. No paltry supermen, no shadowy space-cadets, no trifling hyperjunglequeens and pantless pantherwomen insulted my virginal imagination. I read or was read, at an early age, the most immemorial myths, the wildest wild animal stories, lots of Scott and quantities of Dickens (including the immortal Pickwick Papers) Robinson Crusoe and The Swiss Family Robinson, Gulliver's Travels, Twenty Thousand Leagues Under the Sea, poetry galore, The Holy Bible, and The Arabian Nights. One city winter I floated through chivalry with Mallory and Froissart: the following country summer—we had by then acquired a farm—I dressed as a Red Indian, slept in a teepee, and almost punctured our best Jersey cow with a random arrow; in emulation of the rightful inhabitants of my wrongful native land.

A gruesome history of the Tower Of London had been conscientiously compiled by a prominent British prelate, endowed with what would now be termed sadistic trends; and suddenly this fearful opus burgeoned in our midst. Every night after dinner, if George were on deck, he would rub his hands and wink magnificently in my direction and call to my maiden aunt "Jane, let's have some ruddy gore!" whereupon Jane would protestingly join us in the parlor; and George would stealthily produce the opus; and she would blushfully read; and I would cling to the sofa in exquisite terror. We also read—for sheer relaxation—Lorna Doone (with whom I fell sublimely in love) and Treasure Island (as a result of which, the blind pirate Pew followed me upstairs for weeks; while for months, if not years, onelegged John Silver stood just behind me as my trembling fingers fumbled the electric light chain).

Out of Brookline's already mentioned country club, I readily conjured a gorgeous and dangerous play-world: somewhat resembling the three ring circus of the five Ringling brothers; and dedicated by dashing gentlemen to fair ladies and fine horses and other entrancing symbols of luxurious living. George had not been born into this fashionable cosmos, but he loved it so much that he learned to smoke cigars: and if he hadn't learned anything, the cosmos would certainly have welcomed him for his own abundant self's sake. His own abundant self wrote vers de société; which he recited at orgies or banquets—I was never sure which—but also, for my benefit, chez lui. And no sooner had George discovered my liking for verse than he presented me with an inestimable treasure entitled The Rhymester—opening which totally unostentatious masterpiece, I entered my third poetic period.

Poetic period number one had been nothing if not individualistic; as two almost infantile couplets, combining fearless expression with keen observation, amply testify. The first of these primeval authenticities passionately exclaims

O,the pretty birdie,O;
with his little toe,toe,toe!

while the second mercilessly avers

there was a little farder
and he made his mudder harder

—but, alas! a moribund mental cloud soon obscured my vital psychic sky. The one and only thing which mattered about any poem (so ran my second poetic period's credo) was what the poem said; its socalled meaning. A good poem was a poem which did good, and a bad poem was a poem which didn't: Julia Ward Howe's Battle Hymn Of The Republic being a good poem because it helped free the slaves. Armed with this ethical immutability, I composed canticles of comfort on behalf of the griefstricken relatives of persons recently deceased; I implored healthy Christians to assist poor-whites afflicted with The Curse Of The Worm (short for hookworm); and I exhorted right-minded patriots to abstain from dangerous fireworks on the 4th of July. Thus it will be seen that, by the year 1900, one growing American boy had reached exactly that stage of "intellectual development" beyond which every ungrowing Marxist adult of today is strictly forbidden, on pain of physical disappearance, ever to pass.

The Rhymester diverted my eager energies from what to how: from substance to structure. I learned that there are all kinds of intriguing verse-forms, chiefly French; and that each of these forms can and does exist in and of itself, apart from the use to which you or I may not or may put it. A rondel is a rondel, irrespective of any idea which it may be said to embody; and whatever a ballade may be about, it is always a ballade—never a villanelle or a rondeau. With this welcome revelation, the mental cloud aforesaid ignominiously dissolved; and my psychic sky joyfully reappeared, more vital even than before.

One ever memorable day, our ex-substantialist (deep in structural meditation) met head-on professor Royce; who was rolling peacefully home from a lecture. "Estlin" his courteous and gentle voice hazarded "I understand that you write poetry." I blushed. "Are you perhaps" he inquired, regarding a particular leaf of a particular tree "acquainted with the sonnets of Dante Gabriel Rossetti?" I blushed a different blush and shook an ignorant head. "Have you a moment?" he shyly suggested, less than half looking at me; and just perceptibly appended "I rather imagine you might enjoy them." Shortly thereafter, sage and ignoramus were sitting opposite each other in a diminutive study (marvellously smelling of tobacco and cluttered with student notebooks of a menacing bluish shade)—the ignoramus listening, enthralled; the sage intoning, lovingly and beautifully, his favorite poems. And very possibly (although I don't, as usual, know) that is the reason—or more likely the unreason —I've been writing sonnets ever since.

En route to a university whose name begins with H, our unhero attended four Cambridge schools: the first, private—where everybody was extraordinarily kind; and where (in addition to learning nothing) I burst into tears and nosebleeds—the other three, public; where I flourished like the wicked and learned what the wicked learned, and where almost nobody cared about somebody else. Two figures emerge from this almost: a Miss Maria Baldwin and a Mr Cecil Derry. Miss Baldwin, the dark lady mentioned in my first nonlecture (and a lady if ever a lady existed) was blessed with a delicious voice, charming manners, and a deep understanding of children. Never did any demidivine dictator more gracefully and easily rule a more unruly and less graceful populace. Her very presence emanated an honor and a glory: the honor of spiritual freedom—no mere freedom from—and the glory of being, not (like most extant mortals) really undead, but actually alive. From her I marvellingly learned that the truest power is gentleness. Concerning Mr Derry, let me say only that he was (and for me will always remain) one of those blessing and blessed spirits who deserve the name of teacher: predicates who are utterly in love with their subject; and who, because they would gladly die for it, are living for it gladly. From him I learned (and am still learning) that gladness is next to godliness. He taught me Greek. This may be as apt a moment as any to state that in the world of my boyhood—long, long ago; before time was space and Oedipus was a complex and religion was the opiate of the people and pigeons had learned to play pingpong—social stratification not merely existed but luxuriated. All women were not, as now, ladies; a gentleman was a gentleman; and a mucker (as the professional denizens of Irving and Scott streets knew full well: since their lofty fragment of Cambridge almost adjoined plebeian Somerville) was a mucker. Being myself a professor's (& later a clergyman's) son, I had every socalled reason to accept these conventional distinctions without cavil; yet for some unreason I didn't. The more implacably a virtuous Cambridge drew me toward what might have been her bosom, the more sure I felt that soi-disant respectability comprised nearly everything which I couldn't respect, and the more eagerly I explored sinful Somerville. But while sinful Somerville certainly possessed a bosom (in fact, bosoms) she also possessed fists which hit below the belt and arms which threw snowballs containing small rocks. Little by little and bruise by teacup, my doubly disillusioned spirit made an awe-inspiring discovery; which (on more than several occasions) has prevented me from wholly misunderstanding socalled humanity: the discovery, namely, that all groups, gangs, and collectivities—no matter how apparently disparate—are fundamentally alike; and that what makes any world go round is not the trivial difference between a Somerville and a Cambridge, but the immeasurable difference between either of them and individuality. Whether this discovery is valid for you, I can't pretend to say: but I can and do say, without pretending, that it's true for me—inasmuch as I've found (and am still finding) authentic individuals in the most varied environments conceivable. Nor will anything ever persuade me that, by turning Somerville into Cambridge or Cambridge into Somerville or both into neither, anybody can make an even slightly better world. Better worlds (I suggest) are born, not made; and their birthdays are the birthdays of individuals. Let us pray always for individuals; never for worlds. "He who would do good to another" cries the poet and painter William Blake "must do it in Minute Particulars"—and probably many of you are familiar with this greatly pitying line. But I'll wager that not three of you could quote me the line which follows it

General Good is the plea of the scoundrel, hypocrite & flatterer

for that deeply terrible line spells the doom of all unworlds; whatever their slogans and their strategies, whoever their heroes or their villains.

Only a butterfly's glide from my home began a mythical domain of semiwilderness; separating cerebral Cambridge and orchidaceous Somerville. Deep in this magical realm of Between stood a palace, containing

Harvard University's far-famed Charles Eliot Norton: and lowly folk, who were neither professors nor professors' children, had nicknamed the district Norton's Woods. Here, as a very little child, I first encountered that mystery who is Nature; here my enormous smallness entered Her illimitable being; and here someone actually infinite or impossibly alive—someone who might almost (but not quite) have been myself— wonderingly wandered the mortally immortal complexities of Her beyond imagining imagination

O sweet spontaneous
earth how often have
the
doting

    fingers of
prurient philosophers pinched
and
poked

thee
,has the naughty thumb
of science prodded
thy

    beauty   .how
often have religions taken
thee upon their scraggy knees
squeezing and

buffeting thee that thou mightest conceive
gods
    (but
true

to the incomparable
couch of death thy
rhythmic
lover

    thou answerest

them only with

        spring)

—later, this beyond imagining imagination revealed a not believably mountaining ocean, at Lynn; and, in New Hampshire, oceaning miraculously mountains. But the wonder of my first meeting with Herself is with me now; and also with me is the coming (obedient to Her each resurrection) of a roguish and resistless More Than Someone: Whom my deepest selves unfailingly recognized, though His disguise protected him from all the world

in Just-
spring   when the world is mud-
luscious the little
lame balloonman
whistles   far   and wee

and eddyandbill come
running from marbles and
piracies and it's
spring

when the world is puddle-wonderful

the queer
old balloonman whistles
far   and   wee
and bettyandisbel come dancing

from hop-scotch and jump-rope and

it's
spring
and
    the

            goat-footed

balloonMan   whistles
far
and
wee

this Turbulent Individual Incognito must have rendered his disciple even less law-abiding than usual; for I vividly remember being chased (with two charming little girls) out of the tallest and thickest of several palatial lilac bushes: our pursuer being a frantic scarecrow-demon masquerading as my good friend Bernard Magrath, professor Charles Eliot Norton's gifted coachman. But why not? Then it was spring; and in spring anything may happen.

Absolutely anything.

In honor of which truth (and in recognition of the fact that, as recent events have shown, almost anything can happen in November) let me now present, without socalled criticism or comment, five springtime celebrations which I love even more than if they were my own—first, a poem by Thomas Nashe; second, the opening of Chaucer's Canterbury Tales; third, a chorus from Atalanta in Calydon by Swinburne; fourth, a rondel by Charles d'Orléans; and finally, a song by Shakespeare. Item: if these celebrations don't sing (instead of speaking) for themselves, please blame me; not them.

Spring, the sweete spring, is the yeres pleasant King,
Then bloomes eche thing, then maydes daunce in a ring,
Cold doeth not sting, the pretty birds doe sing,
Cuckow, jugge, jugge, pu we, to witta woo.

The Palme and May make countrey houses gay,
Lambs friske and play, the Shepherds pype all day,
And we heare aye birds tune this merry lay,
Cuckow, jugge, jugge, pu we, to witta woo.

The fields breathe sweete, the dayzies kisse our feete,
Young lovers meete, old wives a sunning sit;
In every streete, these tunes our eares doe greete,
Cuckow, jugge, jugge, pu we, too witta woo.
    Spring, the sweete spring.

    Whan that Aprille with his shoures sote
The droghte of Marche hath perced to the rote,
And bathed every veyne in swich licour,
Of which vertu engendred is the flour;
Whan Zephirus eek with his swete breeth
Inspired hath in every holt and heeth
The tendre croppes, and the yonge sonne
Hath in the Ram his halfe cours y-ronne,
And smale fowles maken melodye,
That slepen al the night with open yë,
(So priketh hem nature in hir corages):

Than longen folk to goon on pilgrimages
(And palmers for to seken straunge strondes)
To ferne halwes, couthee in sondry londes;
And specially, from every shires ende
Of Engelond, to Caunterbury they wende,
The holy blisful martir for to seke,
That hem hath holpen, whan that they were seke.

When the hounds of spring are on winter's traces,
   The mother of months in meadow or plain
Fills the shadows and windy places
   With lisp of leaves and ripple of rain;
And the brown bright nightingale amorous
Is half assuaged for Itylus,
For the Thracian ships and the foreign faces.
   The tongueless vigil, and all the pain.

Come with bows bent and with emptying of quivers,
   Maiden most perfect, lady of light,
With a noise of winds and many rivers,
   With a clamour of waters, and with might;
Bind on thy sandals, O thou most fleet,
Over the splendour and speed of thy feet;
For the faint east quickens, the wan west shivers,
   Round the feet of the day and the feet of the night.

Where shall we find her, how shall we sing to her,
   Fold our hands round her knees, and cling?
O that man's heart were as fire and could spring to her,
   Fire, or the strength of the streams that spring!
For the stars and the winds are unto her
As raiment, as songs of the harp-player;
For the risen stars and the fallen cling to her,
   And the southwest-wind and the west-wind sing.

For winter's rains and ruins are over,
   And all the season of snows and sins;
The days dividing lover and lover,
   The light that loses, the night that wins;
And time remember'd is grief forgotten,
And frosts are slain and flowers begotten,
And in green underwood and cover
   Blossom by blossom the Spring begins.

The full streams feed on flower of rushes,
 Ripe grasses trammel a travelling foot,
The faint fresh flame of the young year flushes
 From leaf to flower and flower to fruit;
And fruit and leaf are as gold and fire,
And the oat is heard above the lyre,
And the hoofed heel of a satyr crushes
 The chestnut-husk at the chestnut-root.

And Pan by noon and Bacchus by night,
 Fleeter of foot than the fleet-foot kid,
Follows with dancing and fills with delight
 The Mæned and the Bassarid;
And soft as lips that laugh and hide
The laughing leaves of the trees divide,
And screen from seeing and leave in sight
 The god pursuing, the maiden hid.

The ivy falls with the Bacchanal's hair
 Over her eyebrows hiding her eyes;
The wild vine slipping down leaves bare
 Her bright breast shortening into sighs;
The wild vine slips with the weight of its leaves,
But the berried ivy catches and cleaves
To the limbs that glitter, the feet that scare
 The wolf that follows, the fawn that flies.

Le temps a laissié son manteau
De vent, de froidure et de pluye,
Et s'est vestu de brouderie
De souleil luisant cler et beau.

Il n'y a beste ne oyseau
Qu'en son jargon ne chante ou crie;
Le temps a laissié son manteau
De vent, de froidure et de pluye.

Rivière, fontaine et ruisseau
Portent, en livrée jolie,
Gouttes d'argen d'or faverie,
Chascun s'abille de nouveau;
Le temps a laissié son manteau
De vent, de froidure et de pluye.

It was a Lover and his lasse,
　With a hay, and a ho, and a hey nonino:
That o'er the greene corne field did passe,
　In the spring time, the onely pretty ring time,
When Birds do sing, hay ding a ding, ding.
Sweet Lovers love the spring.

Betweene the acres of the Rie,
　With a hey, and a ho, and a hey nonino:
These prettie Countryfolk would lie,
　In the spring time, the onely pretty ring time,
When the Birds do sing, hey ding a ding, ding.
Sweet Lovers love the spring.

This Carroll they began that houre,
　With a hey, and a ho, and a hey nonino:
How that a life was but a Flower,
　In the spring time, the onely pretty ring time,
When Birds do sing, hey ding a ding, ding.
Sweet Lovers love the spring.

And therefore take the present time
　With a hey, and a ho, and a hey nonino:
For love is crowned with the prime,
　In the spring time, the onely pretty ring time,
When Birds do sing, hey ding a ding, ding.
Sweet Lovers love the spring.

Robert Price

THE HIDDEN AIRDROME

Go bedizened
in a bracelet of enemy teeth,
gold crosses in your ears
and your holy number;

Join with the waiting
on the bed of fragile sand
turned down
in the GI moonlight;

Run your finger
round the superb rim,
relax back upon
the tufted grass;

Guard through the branches
for the airway
by which Jehovah
will come to rob you.

WE MUST WEAR OUT OUR SOULS IN SUBTLE SCHEMES

Charles Baudelaire

LA MORT DES ARTISTES

Combien faut-il de fois secourer mes grelots
Et baiser ton front bas, morne caricature?
Pour piquer dans le but, de mystique nature,
Combien, ô mon carquois, perdre de javelots?

Nous userons notre âme en de subtils complots,
Et nous démolirons mainte lourde armature,
Avant de contempler la grande Créature
Dont l'infernal désir nous remplit de sanglots!

Il en est qui jamais n'ont connu leur Idole,
Et ces sculpteurs damnes et marqués d'un affront,
Qui vont se martelant la poitrine et le front,

N'ont qu'un espoir, étrange et sombre Capitole!
C'est que la Mort, planant comme un soleil nouveau,
Fera s'épanouir les fleurs de leur cerveau!

THE DEATH OF ARTISTS

How often must I shake my bells and kiss
Your low forehead, O dismal Caricature?
How many arrows must I shoot amiss
Before I strike the target's mystic lure?

We must wear out our souls in subtle schemes,
We must dismantle many a scaffolding,
Before we know the Creature of our dreams
That fills our hearts with sobs and sorrowing.

Some never know the Idol of their soul;
Like sculptors damned and branded for disgrace
Who hammer upon their own breast and face,

They have *one* hope—their somber Capitol!
That Death may rise, a sun of another kind,
And bring to bloom the flowers of their mind.

Stendhal

THE LIFE OF HENRI BRULARD

I found myself this morning, the 16th of October 1832, at San Pietro in Montorio, on the Janiculum, at Rome. There was a splendid sun; a light and almost imperceptible sirocco was wafting a few little white clouds over the Alban Mount; the air was full of delightful warmth; I was glad to be alive. I clearly made out Frascati and Castle Gandolfo, which are four leagues from here, and the Villa Aldobrandini, where there is the sublime fresco of Judith by Domenichino. I can see perfectly the white wall marking the repairs finally effected by Prince F. Borghese, the same whom I saw at Wagram as colonel of the Cuirassier regiment the day my friend M. de M— had his leg shot away. Much farther off I perceive the rock of Palestrina and the white masonry of Castle San Pietro, which was once its citadel. Below the wall against which I am leaning are the great orange trees of the Cappucini garden, then the Tiber and the Priory of Malta, and a little beyond, to the right, the tomb of Cecilia Metella, San Paolo, and the Pyramid of Cestius. Facing me I see Santa Maria Maggiore and the long lines of the Palace of Monte-Cavallo. All ancient and modern Rome, from the old Appian Way, with its ruined tombs and aqueducts, to the magnificent gardens of the Pincio, laid out by the French, lies unfolded to the view.

This place, I said to myself, musing, has not its like in the world; and, do what I would, the old Rome prevailed over the modern; all my memories of Livy came thronging back to me. To the left of the convent, on the Alban Mount, I perceived the Fields of Hannibal.

What a splendid view! It is here, then, that Raphael's *Transfiguration* was admired for two and a half centuries. How different from the dismal gallery of gray marble where it is now buried in the depths of the Vatican! And so for two hundred and fifty years that masterpiece was here, two hundred and fifty years! . . .

Ah! in three months' time I shall be fifty. Is it really possible? 1783, '93, 1803, I count it all over on my fingers . . . and 1833, fifty. Is it really possible! Fifty! I am going to turn fifty. And I sang the air by Grétry: "When a man is fifty years old."

This unexpected discovery did not annoy me, I had just meditated on Hannibal and the Romans. Greater men than I are dead and gone! . . . After all, I said to myself, I have not filled up my life badly. Filled up!

Ah! I mean to say that chance has not given me too many misfortunes, for can I in the least be said to have directed my life?

And to be on the point of falling in love with Mlle de Grisheim! What could I hope from a young lady of noble family, the daughter of a general in favor two months before the Battle of Jena! Brichaud was quite right when he said to me, in his usual cynical way: "When a man loves a woman, he says to himself: 'What do I want to do with her?' "

I sat down on the steps of San Pietro, and there I mused for an hour or two on this idea: I shall soon be fifty, it is high time that I got to know myself. What I have been, what I am, I should really find it hard to say.

I am taken for a very witty and unfeeling man, a Lovelace even, and I see that I have spent most of my time in unhappy love-affairs. I was madly in love with Mlle Kably, Mlle de Grisheim, Mme de Diphortz, Métilde, and I never possessed them; and several of these loves lasted for three or four years. Métilde entirely filled my life from 1818 to 1824. And I am not yet cured, I added, after dreaming for a good quarter of an hour, perhaps, of nothing but her. Did she love me?

My heart was deeply touched and moved to prayer and ecstasy. And Menti, in what grief was I plunged when she left me! At this point I shivered at the thought of the 15th of September 1826 at San Remo, on my return from England. What a year I spent from the 15th of September 1826 to the 15th of September 1827! On the day of this dread anniversary I was at the island of Ischia. And I noticed a distinct improvement: instead of letting my thoughts dwell directly on my unhappiness, as I had done some months before, I now thought only of the memory of the wretched state into which I had sunk, for instance, in October 1826. This observation consoled me greatly.

What have I really been, then? I shall never know. To what friend, however enlightened he may be, can I appeal? M. di Fiore himself could not give me an opinion. To what friend have I ever spoken a word about the sorrow love has caused me?

And it is a singular and most unfortunate fact, I said to myself this morning, but my victories (as I used to call them then, my head being full of military matters) did not bring me a pleasure even half as great as the deep sorrow caused me by my defeats.

The amazing victory over Menti did not give me a pleasure comparable to the hundredth part of the pain which she gave me by leaving me for M. de Bospier.

Was it that I had a depressing personality? . . . And here, as I could not tell what to say, I began again, without thinking, to admire the sublime aspect of the ruins of Rome and its modern grandeur: opposite me the Coliseum; and, beneath my feet, the Farnese Palace, with its beautiful arcaded loggia full of modern works; the Corsini Palace, too, beneath my feet.

Have I been a clever man? Have I had any talent for anything? M. Daru[1] used to say that I was crassly ignorant; yes, but it was Besançon who told me this, and the gaiety of my character made Besançon, that morose ex-secretary-general, very jealous. But was my character gay?

In the end I did not come down from the Janiculum until the light evening mist warned me that I should soon be overtaken by that nasty, unhealthy cold which falls suddenly the moment after sundown in this country. I hurried back to the Palazzo Conti (Piazza Minerva). I felt harassed. I was wearing a pair of white trousers of an English stuff; and I wrote inside, on the band: "16 October 1832, I am going to be fifty," contracted like this, so that it should not be understood: Imgo ingt obef if ty.

In the evening, on returning rather bored from the ambassador's reception, I said to myself: I ought to write my life; then perhaps, at last, when it is finished, I should know what I have been, whether gay or sad, a clever man or a fool, brave or timid; and finally, whether the sum total be happy or unhappy, I shall be able to make di Fiore read this manuscript.

The idea is inviting. Yes, but that frightful quantity of *I's* and *me's!* They would be enough to put the most kind-hearted reader into a bad temper. With these *I's* and *me's* it would be, allowing for the difference of talent, like M. de Chateaubriand, that king of egotists. *De je mis avec moi tu fais le récidive.*[3] I say this line to myself every time I read a page of his. One might, it is true, use the third person in writing; *he did, he said*; yes, but then how record the inner movements of the soul? It is on this point especially that I should like to consult di Fiore.

I do not resume till the 23rd of November 1835. This same idea of writing my life came to me lately during my journey to Ravenna; to tell the truth, I have had it in mind many times since 1832, but I have always been discouraged by that terrible difficulty of the *I's* and *me's* which will make the author odious; I do not feel that I have enough talent to get round it. To tell the truth, I am anything but sure that I have enough talent to be read. I sometimes find great pleasure in writing, that is all.

If there is another world, I shall not fail to go and see Montesquieu; if he says to me: "My poor fellow, you had no talent whatsoever," I shall be annoyed, but not at all surprised. I often feel this: what eye can see itself? It is less than three years since I discovered the wherefore of this.

I can see clearly that many writers who enjoy a great reputation are detestable. What it would be a blasphemy to say today of M. de

Chateaubriand (a sort of Balzac) will be a truism in 1880. I have never changed my opinion of this Balzac; when it appeared, toward 1803, Chateaubriand's *Génie* seemed to me ridiculous. But is feeling the faults of another the same thing as possessing talent? I notice that the worst painters see each other's faults very well: M. Ingres is quite right in what he says against M. Gros, and M. Gros against M. Ingres (I choose those who will perhaps still be talked about in 1935).

Such are the arguments which reassured me with regard to these Memoirs. Suppose that I go on with this manuscript and that once it is written I do not burn it; I shall leave it, not to a friend, who might become a religious fanatic, or sell himself to a party, like that young dupe Thomas Moore. I will leave it to a bookseller, to M. Levavasseur for instance (Place Vendôme, Paris):

Very well, then, here is our bookseller who, after my death, receives a great bound volume of this vile writing. He will have a little of it copied, and will read it; if it strikes him as boring, if M. de Stendhal is no longer heard of, he will leave the rigmarole alone, and it will be found again perhaps two hundred years later, like the memoirs of Benvenuto Cellini.

If he prints it and it bores people, it will be talked about thirty years after just as the poem *La Navigation,* by that spy Esménard, which was so often the subject of conversation at M. Daru's luncheons in 1802, is talked about now. And even that spy was, as it seems to me, the censor or director of all the newspapers, which puffed him outrageously every week. He was the Salvandy[4] of his time, even more impudent, if possible, but with far more ideas.

So my Confessions will have ceased to exist thirty years after they are printed, if the *I's* and *me's* bore my readers too much; and yet I shall have had the pleasure of writing them, and of making a thorough examination of my conscience. . . . Moreover, if they are a success, I stand the chance of being read in 1900 by such spirits as I love, the Mme Rolands, the Mélanie Guilberts, the . . .[5]

For instance, today, the 24th of November 1835, I have just got back from the Sistine Chapel, where I did not enjoy myself at all, though I was provided with a good glass for seeing the vault and Michelangelo's *Last Judgment;* but I had committed an excess in coffee-drinking at the Caetanis' the day before yesterday (it was the fault of a machine brought from London by Michelangelo Caetani), and this had given me neuralgia. The machine was too perfect. This too excellent coffee was a bill of exchange drawn on my future happiness in favor of the present moment; it has brought back my old neuralgia, and I have been to the Sistine Chapel like a sheep, *id est*, with no pleasure: my imagination could not once spread its wings. I admired the gold brocade drapery painted in fresco at the side of the throne, I mean to say the Pope's great walnut armchair. This drapery bears the name of Sixtus IV, Pope *(Sixtus IIII, Papa),* and one could touch it with one's hand. It is two feet from one's eyes, and still produces an illusion after three hundred and fifty-four years.

Being no good for anything, not even for writing the official letters which are my professional duty, I have had a fire lit, and I am writing this, I hope without lying, with no illusions about myself, but with pleasure, like a letter to a friend. What will this friend's ideas be in 1880? How different from ours! Today these two ideas: *the most rascally of kings* and *hypocritical Tartar,* applied to two names which I dare not write,[6] would be, in the eyes of three quarters of my acquaintances, an enormous imprudence, an enormity.

In 1880 these judgments will be truisms which even the Kératrys of the age will no longer dare to repeat. This is something new for me; to talk to people whose cast of mind, species of education, prejudices, and religion are totally unknown to one. What an encouragement to be truthful, and simply truthful!—that is the only thing that lasts. Benvenuto was truthful, and one follows him with pleasure, as if he had written yesterday; whereas one skips the pages of that Jesuit Marmontel, although he takes every possible pains not to offend, like a regular Academician. At Leghorn I refused to buy his Memoirs, at twenty sous a volume—I who adore that kind of writing.

But how many precautions are necessary to prevent oneself from lying!

For instance, at the beginning of the first chapter there is something which may seem like tall talk. No, reader, I was not a soldier at Wagram in 1809.

You must know that forty-five years before your time it was the fashion to have been a soldier under Napoleon. So today, in 1835, it is a lie quite worth writing if one gives it to be understood indirectly, and without an absolute lie (in the manner of the Jesuits), that one was a soldier at Wagram.

The fact is that I was quartermaster and sub-lieutenant in the 6th Dragoons when this regiment arrived in Italy in May 1800, I believe; and that I resigned my commission at the time of the short peace of 1803.[7] I was bored to death with my fellow officers, and thought nothing could be so pleasant as to live in Paris like a philosopher (that was the phrase I used to use to myself then), on the hundred and fifty francs a month which my father gave me. I supposed that after his death I should have twice as much, or double that again; with the passion for knowledge which then burned within me, it was far too much.

I did not become a colonel, as I should have done with the powerful protection of the Comte Daru, my cousin; but I have been much happier, I think. I soon gave up thinking about studying and imitating M. de Turenne; this idea had been my unvarying aim during the three years that I was a dragoon. It was sometimes rivaled by another: to write comedies like Molière and live with an actress. At that time I had already an invincible aversion from respectable women and the hypocrisy which they find indispensable. My colossal laziness won the day. Once in Paris, I passed six whole months without visiting my family (the Messieurs Daru, Mme Le Brun, M. and Mme de Baure); every day I would say: "Tomorrow." I passed two years like this, on the fifth floor of a house in the rue D'Angiviller, with a fine view of the colonnade of the Louvre, reading La Bruyère, Montaigne and J.-J. Rousseau, whose turgidity soon offended me. It is here that my character was formed. I also read the tragedies of Alfieri a great deal, forcing myself to take pleasure in them. I revered Cabanis, Tracy, and J.-B. Say; I often read Cabanis, whose vague style distressed me. I lived, as solitary and mad as a Spaniard, a thousand miles away from real life. The good Father Jeki, an Irishman, gave me lessons in English, but I made no progress; I was madly enthusiastic about *Hamlet*.

But I am letting myself be carried away, I am wandering from the point, I shall be unintelligible if I do not follow the sequence of time; and, besides, the circumstances will not come back to me so well.

Well, then, at Wagram in 1809 I was not a soldier, but, on the contrary, an assistant to the Commissaries of War, a position in which my cousin M. Daru had placed me, so as to "remove me from vice," to use the expression of my family. For my solitude in the rue D'Angiviller had ended in living at Marseilles for a year with a charming actress, a woman of superior feelings, to whom I never gave a penny.

In the first place, for the capital reason that my father still gave me a hundred and fifty francs a month, on which I had to live, and at Marseilles, in 1805, this allowance was very irregularly paid.

But I am wandering from the point again. In October 1806, after Jena, I was assistant to the Commissaries of War, a position scorned by the soldiers; in 1810, on August 3, I became a minor official, an "auditor," of the Council of State, and a few days later inspector-general of the Crown Furnishing Department. I was in favor, not with the master (Napoleon did not talk to madmen like me), but I was highly approved by that best of men the Duke of Friuli (Duroc). But I am wandering from the point.

I fell with Napoleon in April 1814. I came to Italy to live as I had done in the rue D'Angiviller. In 1821 I left Milan with despair in my soul, on account of Métilde, and thinking seriously of blowing out my brains. At first everything bored me in Paris; later on, I wrote to distract my mind. Métilde died, so it was useless to return to Milan. I had become perfectly happy; that is saying too much—but, at any rate, quite passably happy—in 1830, when I wrote *Le Rouge et le Noir*.

I was overjoyed at the July Days.[8] I saw the firing under the colonnade of the Théâtre-Français, with very little danger to myself. I shall never forget that fine sunny day, and my first sight of the tricolor flag, on the 29th or 30th, toward eight o'clock, after sleeping in the house of Commander Pinto, whose niece was frightened. On the 25th of September I was appointed consul at Trieste by M. Molé,[9] whom I had never seen. From Trieste I came in 1831 to Città-Vecchia and Rome, where I am still, and where I am bored for lack of the opportunity to exchange ideas with anyone. From time to time I feel the need of conversation in the evening with intelligent people, and in the absence of this I feel as if I were stifled.

Such, then, are the main divisions of my story: born in 1783, a dragoon in 1800, a student from 1803 to 1806. In 1806 assistant to the Commissaries of War, and commissariat officer at Brunswick. In 1809 making returns of the wounded at Essling or Wagram, going on missions along the Danube, on its snow-covered banks, at Linz and Passau, in love with Mme Petit, and, in order to see her, asking to go to Spain. On the 3rd of August 1810, appointed by her (it amounted to that) to a minor position in the Council of State. This life of high favor and expense brings me to Moscow, makes me commissariat officer at Sagan, in Silesia, and causes my fall in April 1814. Would anyone believe it? To me, personally, my fall was a pleasure.

After my fall[10] I was a student, a writer, madly in love, publishing my *History of Painting in Italy* in 1817; my father becomes an Ultra,[11] is ruined, and dies in 1819, I believe; I return to Paris in June 1821. I am in despair on account of Métilde; she dies, I had rather she were dead than unfaithful, I write, it consoles me, I am happy. In 1830, in September, I return to the administrative career in which I am still occupied, regretting my life as a writer on the third floor of the Hôtel de Valois, No. 71 rue de Richelieu.

I have been a wit since the winter of 1826; before that I was silent out of laziness. I am taken, I believe, for the gayest and most unfeeling of men; it is true that I have never said a single word about the women I have loved. In this respect I have experienced all the symptoms of the melancholy temperament described by Cabanis.[12] I have had very little success.

But the other day, musing about life on the solitary road above the Alban Lake, I found that my life could be summed up by the following names, whose initials I wrote in the dust, like Zadig, with my stick, seated on the little bench behind the stations of the Calvary of the Minori Menzati, erected by the brother of Urban VIII, Barberini, beside those two beautiful trees enclosed by a little round wall:

Virginie (Kably), Angela (Pietragrua), Adèle (Rebuffel), Mélanie (Guilbert), Mina (de Grisheim), Alexandrine (Petit), Angelina, whom I never loved (Bereyter), Angela (Pietragrua), Métilde (Dembowski), Clémentine, Giulia. And finally, for a month at most, Mme Azur, whose Christian name I have forgotten, and yesterday, imprudently, Amalia (B.).

Most of these charming creatures did not honor me with their favors; but they have literally filled my life. After them came my works. In reality I have not been ambitious, but in 1811 I thought myself ambitious.

The habitual state of my life has been that of an unsuccessful lover, fond of music and painting—I mean to say, enjoying the productions of these arts but not practicing them unskillfully. I have sought with an exquisite sensibility the sight of beautiful landscapes; it is with that one aim that I have traveled. The landscapes were like a bow which played upon my soul; and views mentioned by nobody, the line of rocks on the way to Arbois, I think, as one approaches it from Dôle by the high road, are for me a tangible and obvious image of the soul of Métilde. I see that dreaming is what I have preferred to everything, even to a reputation for wit. It was only in 1826 that I took enough trouble to assume the profession of improvising in dialogue for the benefit of the society in which I happened to be; and it was because of the despair in which I had passed the first months of that fatal year.

I learned lately, by reading it in a book (the letters of Victor Jacquemont, the Indian explorer), that it had been possible for someone to think me brilliant. A few years before, I had seen almost the same thing in a book by Lady Morgan, which was then the fashion. I had forgotten this fine quality, which has made me so many enemies. (It was perhaps only the appearance of this quality, and the enemies were people too common to be judges of what was brilliant; for instance, how can a man like the Comte d'Argout be a judge of brilliancy? A man whose happiness lies in reading two or three duodecimo volumes every day of some novel written for housemaids. How should M. de Lamartine be a judge of wit? In the first place, he has none, and in the second place, he too devours two volumes a day of the dullest works. Saw him at Florence in 1824 or 1826.)

The great drawback of being clever is that one has to keep one's eyes fixed on the semi-idiots who surround one, and to let one's mind be colored by their undistinguished sensations. My fault is to fasten upon the person least incapable of imagination and to become unintelligible to the rest, who are perhaps all the better pleased.

Since I have been in Rome I am not witty so often as once a week, and even then barely for five minutes; I had rather dream. These people have not enough understanding of the subtleties of the French language to feel the subtleties of my observations; they must have the coarse wit of a bagman; just like melodrama, which delights them (witness Michelangelo Caetani) and is their daily bread. The sight of its success freezes me. I cannot condescend to talk to people who have applauded melodrama. I see all the nothingness of vanity.

It was two months ago, then, in September 1835, while I was musing upon writing these Memoirs, on the shore of the Alban Lake (two hundred feet above the level of the lake) that I wrote in the dust, like Zadig, these initials:

$$\text{a}\quad \text{d}\qquad \text{i}\quad \text{l}\quad \text{ine}\quad \text{pg}\quad \text{de}\qquad \text{r}$$
$$\text{V. A . A . M. M . A . A . A . M . C. G . A .}$$
$$1\qquad\quad 2\qquad\quad 3\qquad\qquad\quad 4\quad 5\quad 6$$

(Mme Azur, whose Christian name I have forgotten).

I was musing profoundly upon these names and the amazing follies and sillinesses which they made me commit (I mean amazing to me, not to the reader; besides, I do not repent of them).

The fact is that I have possessed only six of the women whom I have loved.

The greatest passion must be disputed between Mélanie, Alexandrine, Métilde, and Clémentine. Clémentine is the one who caused me the greatest suffering by leaving me. But is this suffering to be compared to that occasioned by Métilde, who would not say that she loved me?

With all of these, and with several others, I have always been a child; and so I have had very little success. But in spite of this, they have filled my life with great passions, and have left me memories which charm me, some of them after twenty-four years, like the memory of the Madonna del Monte, at Varese, in 1811. I have never been a man of pleasure— not sufficiently so. My thoughts were full of the woman I loved, and of nothing else; and when I was not in love I was musing on the spectacle of human things, or reading with delight Montesquieu or Walter Scott. And that is "cause why," as children say, I am so far from being blasé about their cunning tricks and little graces that, at the age of fifty-two, as I write this, I am still under the charm of a long gossip which Amalia had with me yesterday at the Teatro Valle.

In order to consider them as philosophically as possible, and so to try and divest them of the aureole which makes my head dizzy, dazzles me, and deprives me of the faculty of seeing clearly, I will classify these ladies (mathematical term) according to their various qualities. To begin with their usual passion then—namely, vanity—I will say that two of them were countesses and one a baroness.

The richest was Alexandrine Petit; she and her husband spent a good eighty thousand francs a year. The poorest was Mina de Grisheim, the youngest daughter of a general with no fortune, the favorite of a fallen prince, whose pay supported the whole family; or Mlle Bereyter, an actress at the Opera Bouffe.

I try to make an abstraction of the charm, the dazzling quality of events, by considering them in this military fashion. It is my sole expedient for arriving at the truth about a subject on which I can converse with nobody. Owing to the shamefacedness of the melancholy temperament (Cabanis), I have always been incredibly, insanely discreet on this point. In intelligence Clémentine surpassed all the others. Métilde surpassed them in the Spanish nobility of her sentiments; Giulia, it seems to me, in force of character, although at first sight she appeared the weakest; Angela P. was a sublime woman of pleasure in the Italian fashion, like Lucrezia Borgia, and Mme Azur a woman of pleasure, but not sublime, like the Du Barry.

I was never in trouble about money except twice, at the end of 1805 and up to August 1806, when my father ceased sending me money—without giving me notice, that was the trouble; once he was five months without paying my allowance of a hundred and fifty francs. Hence the great times of poverty which I shared with the Viscount; he received his allowance punctually, but regularly gambled it all away the day he received it.

In 1829 and 1830 I was in difficulties more owing to carelessness and imprudence than to actual lack of means, for I went on three or four journeys, to Italy, England, and Barcelona, and at the end of this period I owed only four hundred francs.

My greatest money difficulties led me to the unpleasant step of borrowing a hundred francs, or sometimes two hundred, from M. Beau. I returned them after a month or two; and in the end, in September 1830, I owed four hundred francs to my tailor, Michel. Those who know the way of living among young men of my time will consider this very moderate. From 1800 to 1830 I had not owed a penny to my tailor, Léger, nor to his successor, Michel (22, rue Vivienne).

My friends at that date, 1830, Messieurs de Mareste and Colomb, were friends of a singular kind; they would no doubt have taken active steps to save me from any great danger, but when I went out in a new coat they would have given twenty francs, especially the former, to see somebody throw a glass of dirty water over me. (Except the Vicomte de Barral and Bigillion, of Saint-Ismier, I have never had any friends in my whole life who were not of that sort.)

They were good fellows, highly prudent, who had got together a salary or an income of twelve thousand or fifteen thousand francs by assiduous toil or skillfulness, and could not bear to see me gay, careless, and happy with a pen and a blank notebook, living on not more than four thousand or five thousand francs. They would have been a hundred times fonder of me if they had seen me unhappy and sad at having only half or a third of their income; me, who had perhaps shocked them a little in the old days, when I had a coachman, two horses, a *calèche,* and a cabriolet; for my luxury had risen to these heights in the days of the Emperor. At that time I was ambitious, or thought I was; what hampered me in this supposition was the fact that I did not know what to desire. I was ashamed of being in love with the Countess Al. Petit, I had as my kept mistress Mlle A. Bereyter, an actress at the Opera Bouffe, I lunched at the Café Hardy, I was full of an incredible activity, I came back from Saint-Cloud to Paris on purpose to hear an act of the *Matrimonio Segreto* at the Odéon (Mme Barilli, Barilli, Tachinardi, Mme Festa, Mlle Bereyter). My cabriolet used to wait at the door of the Café Hardy; that was what my brother-in-law never forgave me.

All this might be mistaken for silly conceit, and yet it was not that. I tried to enjoy life and action, but I made no attempt to display a greater enjoyment or activity than really existed. M. Prunelle, the doctor and wit, whose rational mind I liked greatly (a horribly ugly man, since celebrated as a venal deputy and mayor of Lyons toward 1833), and who was an acquaintance of mine in those days, said of me: "He was an arrant coxcomb." This judgment was echoed by my acquaintances. Perhaps, indeed, they were right.

My excellent middle-class brother-in-law, M. Périer-Lagrange (a retired merchant who was gradually ruining himself by agriculture, without knowing it, near La Tour-du-Pin), when he lunched with me at the Café Hardy and saw me ordering the waiters about sharply (for, with all the duties which I had to perform, I was often in a hurry), was delighted because these waiters made some joke among themselves which implied that I was a conceited ass; but it did not annoy me at all. I have always, as if by instinct (an instinct thoroughly confirmed since then by the Chambers), had a profound contempt for the middle classes.

All the same, I divined that it was only in the middle classes that there were to be found energetic men of the stamp of my cousin Rebuffel (a merchant in the rue Saint-Denis), Father Ducros, librarian of the city of Grenoble, the incomparable Gros (of the rue Saint-Laurent), a geometer of the highest order and my master (unknown to my male relations, for he was a Jacobin, and my family were bigoted Ultras). These three men possessed all my esteem and all my affection, in so far as my respect for them and the difference of age could admit of those relations which lead to love. I was even, with them, the same as I was later with those whom I loved too much: dumb, motionless, stupid, unlovable, and sometimes giving offense by reason of my very devotion and selflessness. Self-love, self-interest, my very self, disappeared in the presence of the person I loved. I became absorbed into that person. What, then, was not my state when that person was a worthless woman, like Mme Pietragrua? But I am always anticipating. Shall I have the courage to write these Confessions intelligibly? I ought to be telling a story, and I am writing a commentary on events which are very detailed, but, precisely on account of their microscopic proportions, require to be told very clearly. What patience will you need, my reader!

And so, in my opinion, energy was to be found, even in my eyes (in 1811), only in that class which has to struggle with real necessities.

My friends of noble family—MM. Raymond de Berenger (killed at Lützen), Saint-Ferréol, Sinard (a bigotedly religious man who died young), Gabriel Du B—— (a bit of a cheat, or a shameless borrower, now a peer of France and Ultra to the very depths of his soul), M. de Monval—always seemed to me to have a singular quality, an alarming respect for conventional observances (for instance, Sinard). They were always seeking after "the best tone," "the right thing," as we used to say at Grenoble in 1793. But I was far from sharing these views very definitely. It is less than a year since my conception of nobility became finally complete. Instinctively, my life in the moral sphere has been passed in a close consideration of five or six principal ideas, and in trying to see the truth about them.

Raymond de Berenger was an excellent fellow and a real example of the maxim *noblesse oblige;* whereas Monval (who died about 1829 at Grenoble, a colonel and generally despised) was the ideal of a deputy of the Center. All this could already be seen quite clearly when these gentlemen were fifteen years old, about 1798.

It is only while writing them down, in 1835, that I see the truth clearly about most of these things, so completely have they been enveloped up to now in the halo of youth, which arises from the extreme acuteness of our sensations.

It is by dint of employing the methods of philosophy—for instance, by dint of classifying the friends of my youth by genera, as M. Adrien de Jussieu does for his plants (in botany)—that I seek to attain the truth which eludes me. I perceive that what I took for high mountains in 1800 were for the most part nothing but molehills; but this is a discovery which I did not make till very late.

I see that I was like a nervous horse, and it is to a remark made to me by M. de Tracy (the famous Comte Destutt de Tracy, a peer of France and a member of the French Academy, and, best of all, the originator of the law of the 3rd Prairial [May 22] on the Central Schools), it is to a remark made to me by M. de Tracy that I owe this discovery.

I must give an example. For a trifle, for instance a door half open at night, I would imagine to myself two armed men lying in wait to prevent me from reaching a window which looked onto a passage where I could see my mistress. It was an illusion which a wise man, like my friend Abraham Constantin, would not have had. But in a few seconds' time (four or five at the most) the sacrifice of my life was made and perfected and I rushed like a hero on my two enemies, who turned into a half-open door.

Less than two months ago something of this kind happened to me again, but in the moral sphere. The sacrifice had been made, and all the necessary courage had been forthcoming, when twenty hours afterward I perceived, on re-reading a hastily read letter (from M. Herrard), that it was an illusion. I always read very fast what is painful to me.

And so, by classifying my life like a collection of plants, I found the following:

Childhood, early education, from 1786 to 1800.	15 years
Military service, from 1800 to 1803.	3 years
Second part of education, ridiculous love-affairs with Mlle Adèle Clozel and her mother, who annexed her daughter's lover. Life in the rue D'Angiviller. Lastly, my beautiful life at Marseilles with Mélanie, from 1803 to 1805.	2 years
Return to Paris, end of my education.	1 year
Official life under Napoleon, from 1806 to the end of 1814 (from October 1806 to his abdication in 1814).	7½ years
My adhesion, in the same number of the *Moniteur* as that in which was announced the abdication of Napoleon. Travels, great and terrible loves, consolation found in writing books, from 1814 to 1830.	15½ years
Second period of official life, from 15th of September 1830 up to the present quarter of an hour.	5 years

I made my entry into society in the drawing-room of Mme de Vaulserre, a bigot with an odd face and a receding chin, a daughter of the Baron des Adrets and a friend of my mother's. This was probably about 1794. I had a passionate temperament, and the shyness described by Cabanis. I was extremely affected by the beautiful arms of Mlle Bonne de Saint-Vallier, I think; I see the face and the beautiful arms, but the name is uncertain: perhaps it was Mlle de Lavalette. M. de Saint-Ferréol, of whom I have never heard since, was my enemy and rival, and M. de Sinard, a mutual friend, pacified us. All this happened in a magnificent ground-floor apartment opening onto the garden of Des

Adrets' mansion, now destroyed and become the dwelling of a middle-class family, in the rue Neuve at Grenoble. At the same period began my passionate admiration for Father Ducros (a secularized Franciscan friar, a man of the highest merit, at least so it appears to me). I had as my intimate friend my grandfather, M. Henri Gagnon, a doctor of medicine.

After all these general observations, I will now be born.

NOTES

1. M. Daru: Stendhal's cousin, the Count Daru, who, as chief commissary of war, organized Masséna's Army of Switzerland in 1799, the Army of Reserve for North Italy, and, after 1803, Napoleon's Grand Army. In 1811 he became Secretary of State; in 1813, Minister for War. In Ch. XXXVI and following, Stendhal gives his impressions of Daru and his family.

2. Besançon: his friend the Baron de Mareste, so nicknamed by Stendhal because he had been secretary-general of the prefecture of Doubs, the chief town of which is Besançon.

3. "Backsliding once again, you join the *I's* and *me's*."

4. Salvandy: a moderate liberal publicist who served the Duc Decazes, Louis XVIII's liberal minister, and after 1830 became a conservative minister under Louis Philippe. Stendhal's objection to him and his literary style is no doubt chiefly due to political reasons.

5. Unfinished in the original French.

6. *"The most rascally of kings* and *hypocritical Tartar"*: Louis Philippe and Nicholas I of Russia. As a servant and admirer of Napoleon, Stendhal hated Louis Philippe; Nicholas I he hated as the "tyrant" who was responsible for crushing the liberties of Poland.

7. "The short peace": the Peace of Amiens, concluded between Napoleon and Great Britain in March 1802; it lasted till May 1803.

8. July Days: the revolution of July 1830, which excluded from the throne Charles X, the last legitimate King of France, and placed on the throne Louis Philippe, with the parliamentary title of "King of the French."

9. Molé: Minister for Foreign Affairs during the early months of Louis Philippe's reign, and later Prime Minister, 1836–39.

10. "My fall in April 1814": at the abdication of Napoleon, which took place April 11, 1814, after the Allies had entered Paris.

11. Ultra: the name given to the extreme reactionary party in the *Chambre introuvable* after the restoration of Louis XVIII, because they were "more royalist than the King"; they were violently Catholic, and identified the interests of "the altar and the throne."

12. Cabanis (1757–1808): French physiologist, whose treatise on the *Relations between the Physical and Moral Nature of Man* expounds a materialist philosophy which had considerable influence at the time when Stendhal was young.

William Blake

PROVERBS OF HELL

In seed time learn, in harvest teach, in winter enjoy.
Drive your cart and your plough over the bones of the dead.
The road of excess leads to the palace of wisdom.
Prudence is a rich, ugly old maid courted by Incapacity.
He who desires but acts not, breeds pestilence.
The cut worm forgives the plough.
Dip him in the river who loves water.
A fool sees not the same tree that a wise man sees.
He whose face gives no light, shall never become a star.
Eternity is in love with the productions of time.
The busy bee has no time for sorrow.
The hours of folly are measur'd by the clock; but of wisdom, no clock
can measure.
All wholesome food is caught without a net or a trap.
Bring out number, weight, and measure in a year of dearth.
No bird soars too high, if he soars with his own wings.
A dead body revenges not injuries.
The most sublime act is to set another before you.
If the fool would persist in his folly he would become wise.
Folly is the cloak of knavery.
Shame is Pride's cloak.
Prisons are built with stones of Law, brothels with bricks of Religion.
The pride of the peacock is the glory of God.
The lust of the goat is the bounty of God.
The wrath of the lion is the wisdom of God.
The nakedness of woman is the work of God.
Excess of sorrow laughs. Excess of joy weeps.
The roaring of lions, the howling of wolves, the raging of the stormy
sea, and the destructive sword are portions of eternity too great for the
eye of man.
The fox condemns the trap, not himself.
Joys impregnate. Sorrows bring forth.
Let man wear the fell of the lion, woman the fleece of the sheep.
The bird a nest, the spider a web, man friendship.

The selfish, smiling fool, and the sullen, frowning fool shall be both thought wise, that they may be a rod.

What is now proved was once only imagin'd.

The rat, the mouse, the fox, the rabbit watch the roots; the lion, the tiger, the horse, the elephant watch the fruits.

The cistern contains: the fountain overflows.

One thought fills immensity.

Always be ready to speak your mind, and a base man will avoid you.

Everything possible to be believ'd is an image of truth.

The eagle never lost so much time as when he submitted to learn of the crow.

The fox provides for himself; but God provides for the lion.

Think in the morning. Act in the noon. Eat in the evening. Sleep in the night.

He who has suffer'd you to impose on him, knows you.

As the plough follows words, so God rewards prayers.

The tigers of wrath are wiser than the horses of instruction.

Expect poison from the standing water.

You never know what is enough unless you know what is more than enough.

Listen to the fool's reproach! it is a kingly title!

The eyes of fire, the nostrils of air, the mouth of water, the beard of earth.

The weak in courage is strong in cunning.

The apple tree never asks the beech how he shall grow; nor the lion, the horse, how he shall take his prey.

The thankful receiver bears a plentiful harvest.

If others had not been foolish, we should be so.

The soul of sweet delight can never be defil'd.

When thou seest an eagle, thou seest a portion of Genius; lift up thy head!

As the caterpillar chooses the fairest leaves to lay her eggs on, so the priest lays his curse on the fairest joys.

To create a little flower is the labour of ages.

Damn braces. Bless relaxes.

The best wine is the oldest, the best water the newest.

Prayers plough not! Praises reap not!

Joys laugh not! Sorrows weep not!

The head Sublime, the heart Pathos, the genitals Beauty, the hands and feet Proportion.

As the air to a bird or the sea to a fish, so is contempt to the contemptible.

The crow wish'd everything was black, the owl that everything was white.

Exuberance is Beauty.

If the lion was advised by the fox, he would be cunning.

Improvement makes straight roads; but the crooked roads without improvement are roads of Genius.

Sooner murder an infant in its cradle than nurse unacted desires.

Where man is not, nature is barren.

Truth can never be told so as to be understood, and not be believ'd.

Enough! or Too much.

William Shakespeare

HAMLET

Enter HAMLET, *reading.*

Oh, give me leave;

Polonius. How does my good Lord Hamlet?

Hamlet. Well, God-a-mercy.

Pol. Do you know me, my lord?

Ham. Excellent well; you are a fishmonger.

Pol. Not I, my lord.

Ham. Then I would you were so honest a man.

Pol. Honest, my lord?

Ham. Ay, sir; to be honest, as this world goes, is to be one man picked out of ten thousand.

Pol. That's very true, my lord.

Ham. For if the sun breed maggots in a dead dog, being a good kissing carrion,—Have you a daughter?

Pol. I have, my lord.

Ham. Let her not walk i' the sun; conception is a blessing; but not as your daughter may conceive:—Friend, look to 't.

Pol. How say you that? [*Aside*] Still harping on my daughter; yet he knew me not at first; he said I was a fishmonger; he is far gone, far gone; and truly in my youth I suffered much extremity for love; very near this. I'll speak to him again.—What do you read, my lord?

Ham. Words, words, words.

Pol. What is the matter, my lord?

Ham. Between who?

Pol. I mean, the matter that you read, my lord.

Ham. Slanders, sir; for the satirical rogue says here that old men have grey beards, that their faces are wrinkled, their eyes purging thick amber and plum-tree gum, and that they have a plentiful lack of wit, together with most weak hams; all which, sir, though I most powerfully and potently believe, yet I hold it not honesty to have it thus set down; for you yourself, sir, should be old as I am, if like a crab you could go backward.

Pol. [*Aside*] Though this be madness, yet there is method in't.— Will you walk out of the air, my lord?

Ham. Into my grave?

Pol. Indeed, that is out o' the air.—[*Aside*] How pregnant some-times his replies are! a happiness that often madness hits on, which reason and sanity could not so prosperously be delivered of. I will leave him, and suddenly contrive the means of meeting between him and my daughter.—My honourable lord, I will most humbly take my leave of you.

Ham. You cannot, sir, take from me any thing that I will more willingly part withal; except my life, except my life, except my life.

Pol. Fare you well, my lord.

Ham. These tedious old fools!

Enter ROSENCRANTZ *and* GUILDENSTERN.

Pol. You go to seek the Lord Hamlet; there he is.

Ros. [*To Polonius*] God save you, sir! [*Exit Polonius.*]

Guil. My honoured lord!

Ros. My most dear lord!

Ham. My excellent good friends! How dost thou, Guildenstern?—Ah, Rosencrantz? Good lads, how do ye both?

Ros. As the indifferent children of the earth.

Guil. Happy, in that we are not over-happy;
On Fortune's cap we are not the very button.

Ham. Nor the soles of her shoe?

Ros. Neither, my lord.

Ham. Then you live about her waist, or in the middle of her favours?

Guil. 'Faith, her privates we.

Ham. In the secret parts of Fortune? Oh, most true; she is a strum-pet. What's the news?

Ros. None, my lord, but that the world's grown honest.

Ham. Then is Doomsday near; but your news is not true. Let me question more in particular; what have you, my good friends, deserved at the hands of Fortune, that she sends you to prison hither?

Guil. Prison, my lord?

Ham. Denmark's a prison.

Ros. Then is the world one.

Ham. A goodly one; in which there are many confines, wards, and dungeons; Denmark being one o' the worst.

Ros. We think not so, my lord.

Ham. Why, then 'tis none to you; for there is nothing either good or bad, but thinking makes it so; to me it is a prison.

Ros. Why, then your ambition makes it one; 'tis too narrow for your mind.

Ham.   O God, I could be bounded in a nut-shell, and count myself a king of infinite space, were it not that I have bad dreams.

Guil.   Which dreams, indeed, are ambition; for the very substance of the ambitious is merely the shadow of a dream.

Ham.   A dream itself is but a shadow.

Ros.   Truly, and I hold ambition of so airy and light a quality that it is but a shadow's shadow.

Ham.   Then are our beggars bodies, and our monarchs and outstretched heroes the beggars' shadows. Shall we to the court? for, by my fay, I cannot reason.

Ros. Guil.   We'll wait upon you.

Ham.   No such matter; I will not sort you with the rest of my servants; for, to speak to you like an honest man, I am most dreadfully attended. But, in the beaten way of friendship, what make you at Elsinore?

Ros.   To visit you, my lord; no other occasion.

Ham.   Beggar that I am, I am even poor in thanks; but I thank you; and sure, dear friends, my thanks are too dear a halfpenny. Were you not sent for? Is it your own inclining? Is it a free visitation? Come, deal justly with me; come, come; nay, speak.

Guil.   What should we say, my lord?

Ham.   Why, any thing, but to the purpose. You were sent for; and there is a kind of confession in your looks, which your modesties have not craft enough to colour. I know the good king and queen have sent for you.

Ros.   To what end, my lord?

Ham.   That you must teach me. But let me conjure you, by the rights of our fellowship, by the consonancy of our youth, by the obligation of our ever-preserved love, and by what more dear a better proposer could charge you withal, be even and direct with me, whether you were sent for, or no.

Ros.   [*Aside to Guil.*] What say you?

Ham.   [*Aside*] Nay, then I have an eye of you.—If you love me, hold not off.

Guil.   My lord, we were sent for.

Ham.   I will tell you why; so shall my anticipation prevent your discovery, and your secrecy to the king and queen moult no feather. I have of late,—but wherefore I know not,—lost all my mirth, forgone all custom of exercises; and indeed it goes so heavily with my disposition that this goodly frame, the earth, seems to me a sterile promontory; this most excellent canopy, the air, look you, this brave o'erhanging firmament, this majestical roof fretted with golden fire,—why, it appears no other thing to me than a foul and pestilent congregation of vapours. What a piece of work is man! how noble in reason! how infinite in faculty! in form and moving, how express and admirable! in action, how like an angel! in apprehension, how like a god! the beauty of the world! the paragon of animals! And yet, to me, what is this quintessence of dust? man delights not me; no, nor woman neither, though by your smiling you seem to say so.

Ros.   My lord, there was no such stuff in my thoughts.

Ham.   Why did you laugh, then, when I said 'man delights not me'?

Ros.   To think, my lord, if you delight not in man, what lenten entertainment the players shall receive from you; we coted them on the way; and hither are they coming, to offer you service.

Ham.   He that plays the king shall be welcome; his majesty shall have tribute of me; the adventurous knight shall use his foil and target; the lover shall not sigh gratis; the humorous man shall end his part in peace; the clown shall make those laugh whose lungs are tickle o' the sere, and the lady shall say her mind freely, or the blank verse shall halt for't. What players are they?

Ros.   Even those you were wont to take such delight in, the tragedians of the city.

Ham.   How chances it they travel? their residence, both in reputation and profit, was better both ways.

Ros.   I think their inhibition comes by the means of the late innovation.

Ham.   Do they hold the same estimation they did when I was in the city? are they so followed?

Ros.   No, indeed, they are not.

Ham.   How comes it? do they grow rusty?

Ros.   Nay, their endeavour keeps in the wonted pace; but there is, sir, an aerie of children, little eyases, that cry out on the top of question and are most tyrannically clapped for't; these are now the fashion, and so berattle the common stages—so they call them—that many wearing rapiers are afraid of goose-quills, and dare scarce come thither.

Ham.   What, are they children? who maintains 'em? how are they escoted? Will they pursue the quality no longer than they can sing? will they not say afterwards, if they should grow themselves to common players,—as it is most like, if their means are no better,—their writers do them wrong, to make them exclaim against their own succession?

Ros.   Faith, there has been much to-do on both sides, and the nation holds it no sin to tarre them to controversy; there was for a while no money bid for argument, unless the poet and the player went to cuffs in the question.

Ham.   Is't possible.

Guil. Oh, there has been much throwing about of brains.

Ham. Do the boys carry it away?

Ros. Ay, that they do, my lord; Hercules and his load too.

Ham. It is not very strange; for my uncle is king of Denmark, and those that would make mows at him while my father lived give twenty, forty, fifty, a hundred ducats a-piece, for his picture in little. 'Sblood, there is something in this more than natural, if philosophy could find it out.

[*Flourish of trumpets within.*]

Guil. There are the players.

Ham. Gentlemen, you are welcome to Elsinore. Your hands, come; the appurtenance of welcome is fashion and ceremony; let me comply with you in this garb, lest my extent to the players, which, I tell you, must show fairly outwards, should more appear like entertainment than yours. You are welcome; but my uncle-father and aunt-mother are deceived.

Guil. In what, my dear lord?

Ham. I am but mad north-north-west; when the wind is southerly, I know a hawk from a handsaw.

Enter POLONIUS.

Pol. Well be with you, gentlemen!

Ham. Hark you, Guildenstern;—and you too;—at each ear a hearer: that great baby you see there is not yet out of his swaddling clouts.

Ros. Happily he's the second time come to them; for, they say, an old man is twice a child.

Ham. I will prophesy he comes to tell me of the players; mark it.— You say right, sir; o' Monday morning; 'twas so, indeed.

Pol. My lord, I have news to tell you.

Ham. My lord, I have news to tell you. When Roscius was an actor in Rome,—

Pol. The actors are come hither, my lord.

Ham. Buz, buz!

Pol. Upon my honour,—

Ham. Then came each actor on his ass,—

Pol. The best actors in the world, either for tragedy, comedy, history, pastoral, pastoral-comical, historical-pastoral, tragical-historical, tragical-comical-historical-pastoral, scene individable, or poem unlimited; Seneca cannot be too heavy, nor Plautus too light. For the law of writ and the liberty, these are the only men.

Ham. O Jephthah, judge of Israel, what a treasure hadst thou!

Pol. What treasure had he, my lord?

Ham. **Why,**

> 'One fair daughter, and no more,
> The which he loved passing well.'

Pol. [*Aside*] Still on my daughter.

Ham. Am I not i' the right, old Jephthah?

Pol. If you call me Jephthah, my lord, I have a daughter that I love
passing well.

Ham. Nay, that follows not.

Pol. What follows, then, my lord?

Ham. **Why,**

> 'As by lot, God wot,'

and then, you know,

> 'It came to pass, as most like it was,'—

the first row of the pious chanson will show you more; for look, where
my abridgements come.—

Enter four or five PLAYERS.

You are welcome, masters; welcome all. I am glad to see ye well. Welcome, good friends.—O, my old friend! Thy face is valanced since I saw
thee last; comest thou to beard me in Denmark?—What, my young lady
and mistress! By'r lady, your ladyship is nearer to heaven than when I saw
you last, by the altitude of a chopine. Pray God, your voice, like a piece
of uncurrent gold, be not cracked within the ring.—Masters, you are
all welcome. We'll e'en to 't like French falconers, fly at any thing we
see; we'll have a speech straight; come, give us a taste of your quality;
come, a passionate speech.

First Play. What speech, my good lord?

Ham. I heard thee speak me a speech once, but it was never acted;
or, if it was, not above once; for the play, I remember, pleased not the
million; 'twas caviare to the general; but it was,—as I received it, and
others, whose judgements in such matters cried in the top of mine,—an
excellent play, well digested in the scenes, set down with as much modesty
as cunning. I remember, one said there were no sallets in the lines to make
the matter savoury, nor no matter in the phrase that might indict the
author of affection; but called it an honest method, as wholesome as
sweet, and by very much more handsome than fine. One speech in it I
chiefly loved; 'twas Æneas's tale to Dido; and thereabout of it especially,
where he speaks of Priam's slaughter. If it live in your memory, begin
at this line; let me see, let me see;

> 'The rugged Pyrrhus, like th' Hyrcanian beast,'—

'tis not so; it begins with 'Pyrrhus.'

> 'The rugged Pyrrhus,—he whose sable arms,
> 'Black as his purpose, did the night resemble

'When he lay couched in the ominous horse,—
'Hath now this dread and black complexion smear'd
'With heraldry more dismal; head to foot
'Now is he total gules; horridly trick'd
'With blood of fathers, mothers, daughters, sons,
'Baked and impasted with the parching streets,
'That lend a tyrannous and damned light
'To their lord's murder; roasted in wrath and fire,
'And thus o'er-sized with coagulate gore,
'With eyes like carbuncles, the hellish Pyrrhus
'Old grandsire Priam seeks.'
So, proceed you.

Pol. 'Fore God, my lord, well spoken, with good accent and good discretion.

First Play.   'Anon he finds him
'Striking too short at Greeks; his antique sword,
'Rebellious to his arm, lies where it falls,
'Repugnant to command; unequal match'd,
'Pyrrhus at Priam drives; in rage strikes wide;
'But with the whiff and wind of his fell sword
'The unnerved father falls. Then senseless Ilium,
'Seeming to feel this blow, with flaming top
'Stoops to his base, and with a hideous crash
'Takes prisoner Pyrrhus' ear; for, lo! his sword,
'Which was declining on the milky head
'Of reverend Priam, seem'd i' the air to stick;
'So, as a painted tyrant, Pyrrhus stood,
'And, like a neutral to his will and matter,
'Did nothing.
'But as we often see, against some storm,
'A silence in the heavens, the rack stand still,
'The bold winds speechless and the orb below
'As hush as death, anon the dreadful thunder
'Doth rend the region; so after Pyrrhus' pause
'Aroused vengeance sets him a new a-work;
'And never did the Cyclops' hammers fall
'On Mars his armour, forged for proof eterne,
'With less remorse than Pyrrhus' bleeding sword
'Now falls on Priam.
'Out, out, thou strumpet, Fortune! All you gods,
'In general synod take away her power;
'Break all the spokes and fellies from her wheel,
'And bowl the round nave down the hill of heaven

'As low as to the fiends!'

Pol.   This is too long.

Ham.   It shall to the barber's, with your beard.—Prithee, say on;
he's for a jig or a tale of bawdy, or he sleeps; say on; come to Hecuba.

First Play.   'But who, O, who had seen the mobled queen,—'

Ham.   'The mobled queen?'

Pol.   That's good; 'mobled queen' is good.

First Play.   'Run barefoot up and down, threatening the flames
   'With bisson rheum; a clout about that head
   'Where late the diadem stood; and for a robe,
   'About her lank and all o'er-teemed loins,
   'A blanket, in the alarm of fear caught up;
   'Who this had seen, with tongue in venom steep'd,
   ''Gainst Fortune's state would treason have pronounced;
   'But if the gods themselves did see her then,
   'When she saw Pyrrhus make malicious sport
   'In mincing with his sword her husband's limbs,
   'The instant burst of clamour that she made,—
   'Unless things mortal move them not at all,—
   'Would have made milch the burning eyes of heaven
   'And passion in the gods.'

Pol.   Look, whether he has not turned his colour and has tears in's
eyes.—Pray you, no more.

Ham.   'Tis well; I'll have thee speak out the rest soon.—Good my
lord, will you see the players well bestowed? Do you hear, let them be
well used, for they are the abstracts and brief chronicles of the time;
after your death you were better have a bad epitaph than their ill report
while you live.

Pol.   My lord, I will use them according to their desert.

Ham.   God's bodykins, man, much better! Use every man after his
desert, and who should 'scape whipping? Use them after your own
honour and dignity; the less they deserve, the more merit is in your
bounty. Take them in.

Pol.   Come, sirs.

Ham.   Follow him, friends; we'll hear a play to-morrow.

   [*Exit Polonius with all the Players but the First.*]
—Dost thou hear me, old friend; can you play *The Murder of Gonzago?*

First Play.   Ay, my lord.

Ham.   We'll ha't to-morrow night. You could, for a need, study a
speech of some dozen or sixteen lines, which I would set down and insert
in't, could you not?

First Play.   Ay, my lord.

Ham.   Very well. Follow that lord; and look you mock him not.

[*Exit First Player.*]—My good friends, I'll leave you till night; you are welcome to Elsinore.

 Ros. Good my lord.

 Ham. Ay, so, God be wi' ye! [*Exeunt Rosencrantz and Guildenstern.*] —Now I am alone.

Oh what a rogue and peasant slave am I!
Is it not monstrous that this player here,
But in a fiction, in a dream of passion,
Could force his soul so to his own conceit
That from her working all his visage wann'd;
Tears in his eyes, distraction in's aspect,
A broken voice, and his whole function suiting
With forms to his conceit? And all for nothing!
For Hecuba?
What's Hecuba to him, or he to Hecuba,
That he should weep for her? What would he do,
Had he the motive and the cue for passion
That I have? He would drown the stage with tears
And cleave the general ear with horrid speech,
Make mad the guilty and appal the free,
Confound the ignorant, and amaze indeed
The very faculties of eyes and ears.
Yet I,
A dull and muddy-mettled rascal, peak,
Like John-a-dreams, unpregnant of my cause,
And can say nothing; no, not for a king,
Upon whose property and most dear life
A damn'd defeat was made. Am I a coward?
Who calls me villain? breaks my pate across?
Plucks off my beard, and blows it in my face?
Tweaks me by the nose? gives me the lie i' the throat,
As deep as to the lungs? who does me this?
Ha!
'Swounds, I should take it; for it cannot be
But I am pigeon-liver'd, and lack gall
To make oppression bitter; or ere this
I should have fatted all the region kites
With this slave's offal; bloody, bawdy villain!
Remorseless, treacherous, lecherous, kindless villain!
O, vengeance!
Why, what an ass am I! This is most brave,
That I, the son of a dear father murder'd,
Prompted to my revenge by heaven and hell,

Must, like a whore, unpack my heart with words,
And fall a-cursing, like a very drab,
A scullion!
Fie upon 't! foh! About, my brain! Hum, I have heard
That guilty creatures, sitting at a play,
Have, by the very cunning of the scene,
Been struck so to the soul that presently
They have proclaim'd their malefactions;
For murder, though it have no tongue, will speak
With most miraculous organ. I'll have these players
Play something like the murder of my father
Before mine uncle; I'll observe his looks;
I'll tent him to the quick; if he but blench,
I know my course. The spirit that I have seen
May be the devil; and the devil hath power
To assume a pleasing shape; yea, and perhaps
Out of my weakness and my melancholy,
As he is very potent with such spirits,
Abuses me to damn me. I'll have grounds
More relative than this. The play's the thing
Wherein I'll catch the conscience of the king.   [Exit.]

St. John of the Cross

THE DARK NIGHT OF THE SOUL

BOOK I

THE PASSIVE NIGHT OF SENSE

THE NECESSITY OF THIS NIGHT FOR BEGINNERS IN CONTEMPLATION

Souls begin to enter the dark night when God is drawing them out of
the state of beginners, which is that of those who meditate on the spiritual
road, and is leading them into that of proficients, the state of contempla-
tives, that, having passed through it, they may arrive at the state of the
perfect, which is that of the divine union with God.

GENERAL IMPERFECTIONS OF BEGINNERS
LOVE OF CONSOLATIONS

Such souls delight to spend many hours, and perhaps whole nights, in
prayer; their pleasures are penances, their joy in fasting, and their consolations lie in the use of the sacraments and in speaking of divine things.
For many persons, spirituality consists in remaining faithful to practices
thus understood; and, not without good effect, they put into them all the
care and all the diligence necessary. Nevertheless, in the true spiritual
sense, what they do is very weak and very imperfect. They are drawn to
these things and to their spiritual exercises by the comfort and satisfaction
they find therein. . . . In these very spiritual works themselves they commit faults and fall into many imperfections.

SPIRITUAL IMPERFECTIONS OF BEGINNERS
I. PRIDE

When beginners become aware of their own fervour and diligence in
their spiritual works and devotional exercises, this prosperity of theirs
gives rise to secret pride—though holy things tend of their own nature
to humility—because of their imperfections; and the issue is that they
conceive a certain satisfaction in the contemplation of their works and
of themselves. From the same source, too, proceeds that empty eagerness

which they display to some extent, and occasionally very much, in speaking before others of the spiritual life, and sometimes as teachers rather than learners. They condemn others in their heart when they see that they are not devout in their way. Sometimes also they say it in words, showing themselves herein to be like the Pharisee, who in the act of prayer boasted of his own works and despised the Publican.

Some of them go so far as to desire none should be thought good but themselves, and, so, at all times both in word and deed fall into condemnation and detraction of others. They are occasionally desirous that others should perceive their spirituality and devotion, and for that end they give outward tokens by movements, sighs and divers ceremonies; sometimes, too, they fall into certain trances in public rather than in private —whereto Satan contributes—and are pleased when others are witnesses of them.

They are ashamed to confess their sins plainly, lest their confessors should think less of them, so they go about palliating them, that they may not seem so bad; which is excusing rather than accusing themselves. Sometimes they go to a stranger to confess their sins that their usual confessor may think they are not sinners, but good people.

Scarcely anyone can be found who, in his first fervours, did not fall into some of these faults.

But those who at this time are going on to perfection proceed in a very different way, and in a very different temper of mind: they grow and are built up in humility.

For the greater their fervour, the more numerous their good works; and the keener the pleasure therein, the more they perceive—for they humble themselves—how much is that which God deserves at their hands, and how little is all they can do for Him; thus the more they do, the less are they satisfied. They have a great desire to speak of their shortcomings and sins, which they would rather have known than their virtues. When they fall into any imperfection they bear up under it with humility, in meekness of spirit, in loving fear of God, and hoping in Him. But the souls who in the beginning travel thus towards perfection are, as I said, few, yea, very few.

II. SPIRITUAL AVARICE

Many a beginner also falls at times into great spiritual avarice. Scarcely anyone is contented with that measure of the spirit which God gives; they are very disconsolate and querulous because they do not find the comfort they desire in spiritual things. Many are never satisfied with listening to spiritual counsels and precepts, with reading books which treat of their state; and they spend more time in this than in doing their duty, having no regard to that mortification, and perfection of interior poverty of spirit to which they ought to apply themselves. Besides, they load themselves with images, rosaries, and crucifixes, curious and costly.

III. TENDENCY TO SENSUALITY

Very often, in the midst of their spiritual exercises, and when they cannot help themselves, the impure movements and disturbances of sensuality are felt; and sometimes even when the mind is absorbed in prayer, or when they are receiving the sacraments of penance and the eucharist. These movements, not being in their power, proceed from one of three sources.

(i.) They proceed occasionally—though but rarely, and in persons of delicate constitutions—from sensible sweetness in spiritual things. For when sense and spirit are both delighted together, the whole nature of man is moved in that delectation according to its measure and character. For then the spirit, that is, the higher part of our nature, is moved to delight itself in God; and sensuality, which is the lower part, is moved towards sensible gratification, because it knows, and admits, of none other, and therefore is moved to what lies nearest to it, namely, sensual pleasure. And so it happens that the soul is in spirit praying, and on the other hand in the senses troubled, to its great disgust, with the rebellious movements and disturbances of the flesh passively; this happens often at the moment of communion.

(ii.) Satan, in order to disquiet the soul during prayer, or when preparing for it, causes these filthy movements of our lower nature, and these, when in any degree admitted, are injury enough. Some persons not only relax in their prayers through fear of these movements, which is the object of Satan when he undertakes to assail them, but even abandon them altogether, for they imagine that they are more liable to these assaults during prayer than at other times. This is certainly true; for the devil then assails them more than at other times, that they may cease from prayer. He represents before them then, most vividly, the most foul and filthy images.

(iii.) The third source of these depraved movements which war against the soul is usually the fear of them.

Some souls are so sensitive that they never experience spiritual fervour or consolation in prayer without the spirit of luxury intruding.

Sometimes, spiritual persons, when either speaking of spiritual things, or doing good works, display a certain energy or boldness towards persons whom they may call to mind or encounter, making before these a display of a certain measure of vain joy.

Some, too, form spiritual friendships with others, the source of which is luxury, and not spirituality. We may know it to be so by observing whether the remembrance of that affection increases our recollection and love of God, or brings remorse of conscience. When this affection is purely spiritual, the love of God grows with it, and the more we think of it the more we think of God, and the greater our longing for Him; for the one grows with the other.

When the soul enters the dark night, these affections are ruled by reason; that night strengthens and purifies the affection which is according to God, and removes, destroys, or mortifies the other. In the beginning both are by it put out of sight, as I shall explain hereafter.

IV. ANGER

When spiritual things give beginners no more sweetness and delight, they naturally become peevish, and in that bitterness of spirit prove a burden to themselves in all they do; trifles make them angry, and they are at times intolerable to all about them. This happens generally after great sweetness in prayer; and so, when that sensible sweetness is past, their natural temper is soured and rendered morose. They are like a babe weaned from the breast, which he found so sweet. When this natural feeling of displeasure is not permitted to grow, there is no sin, but only imperfection, which will have to be purged away in the severity and aridities of the dark night.

There are other spiritual persons, too, among these who fall into another kind of spiritual anger. They are angry with other people for their faults, with a sort of unquiet zeal, and watch them; they are occasionally moved to blame them, and even do so in anger, constituting themselves guardians of virtue. All this is contrary to spiritual meekness.

Others, again, seeing their own imperfections, become angry with themselves with an impatience that is not humble. They are so impatient with their shortcomings as if they would be saints in one day. . . . There is no perfect remedy for this but in the dark night. There are, however, some people who are so patient, and who advance so slowly in their spiritual progress, that God wishes they were not so patient.

V. SPIRITUAL GLUTTONY

There is scarcely one among beginners, however good his progress, who, in the matter of this sin, does not fall into some of the many imperfections to which beginners are liable, because of that sweetness which in the beginning they find in spiritual exercises.

For, allured by the delights they then experience, some of them kill themselves by penances, and others weaken themselves by fasting. They take upon themselves more than they can bear, without rule or advice; they try to conceal their austerities from those whom they are bound to obey, and some even venture to practise them though commanded to abstain.

There are also unreasonable people who undervalue submission and obedience, which is the penance of the reason and judgment, and therefore a more acceptable and sweet sacrifice unto God than all the acts of bodily penance.

And these beginners conduct themselves in the same way when they are praying; they imagine that the whole business of prayer consists in sensible devotion, and this they strive to obtain with all their might, wearying out their brains and perplexing all the faculties of their souls. When they miss that sensible devotion, they are cast down, thinking they have done nothing. For this reason, it is most necessary that they should enter into the dark night that they may be cleansed from this childishness.

The perfection and value of things consist not in the multitude thereof, but in our knowing how to deny ourselves in them.

VI. ENVY AND SLOTH

Many are often vexed because of other men's goodness. They are sensibly afflicted when others outstrip them on the spiritual road, and will not endure to hear them praised. They become fretful over other men's virtues, and are sometimes unable to refrain from contradiction when they are commended; they depreciate them as much as they can, looking on them with an evil eye.

As to spiritual sloth, beginners are wont to find their most spiritual occupations irksome, and avoid them as repugnant to their taste.

NEED FOR THE DARK NIGHT

In this night God weans beginners from the breasts of sweetness, in pure aridities and interior darkness, cleanses them from all imperfections and childish ways, and by ways most different makes them grow in virtue. For after all the exertions of beginners to mortify themselves in their actions and passions, their success will not be perfect, or even great, until God Himself shall do it for them in the purgation of the dark night.[1]

WHAT THE DARK NIGHT IS

By the dark night I mean contemplation. It produces in spiritual men two sorts of darkness or purgations conformable to the two divisions of man's nature into sensual and spiritual. Thus the first night, or sensual purgation, wherein the soul is purified or detached, will be of the senses, subjecting them to the spirit. The other is that night or spiritual purgation wherein the soul is purified and detached in the spirit, and which subdues and disposes it for union with God in love. The night of sense is common, and the lot of many: these are the beginners, of whom I shall first speak. The spiritual night is the portion of very few; and they are those who have made some progress, exercised therein, of whom I shall speak hereafter.

I may pass on to treat more at large of spiritual night; for of that very little has been said, either by word of mouth or in writing, and little is known of it even by experience.

RECOLLECTION IS FAVOURABLE TO THE DARK NIGHT

Recollected persons enter the dark night sooner than others, after they have begun their spiritual course; because they are kept at a greater distance from the occasions of falling away, and because they correct more quickly their worldly desires, which is necessary in order to begin to enter the blessed night of sense.

THREE SIGNS OF THE PASSIVE NIGHT OF THE SENSES

The first is this: when we find no comfort in the things of God, and none also in created things.

It is probable that this dryness is not the result of sins or of imperfections recently committed; for if it were, we should feel some inclination or desire for other things than those of God.

Inasmuch as this absence of pleasure in the things of heaven and of earth may proceed from bodily indisposition or a melancholy temperament, which frequently cause dissatisfaction with all things, the second test and condition become necessary.

The second test and condition of this purgation are that the memory dwells ordinarily upon God with a painful anxiety and carefulness, the soul thinks it is not serving God, but going backwards, because it is no longer conscious of any sweetness in the things of God. In that case it is clear that his weariness of spirit and aridity are not the results of weakness and lukewarmness; for the peculiarity of lukewarmness is the want of earnestness in, and of interior solicitude for, the things of God.

The cause of this dryness is that God is transferring to the spirit the goods and energies of the senses, which, being now unable to assimilate them, become dry, parched up, and empty; for the sensual nature of man is helpless in those things which belong to the spirit simply. Thus the spirit having tasted, the flesh shrinks and fails.

The substantial nature of its interior food, which is the commencement of contemplation, is dim and dry to the senses. This contemplation is in general secret, and unknown to him who is admitted into it, and with the aridity and emptiness which it produces in the senses, it makes the soul long for solitude and quiet, without the power of reflecting on anything distinctly, or even desiring to do so.

CONDUCT: PASSIVITY

Now, if they who are in this state knew how to be quiet, to disregard every interior and exterior work,—to be without solicitude about anything—they would have, in this tranquility, a sense of their most delicate interior nourishment. This is so delicate that, in general, it eludes our perceptions if we make any special effort to feel it, for, as I am saying, it does its work when the soul is most tranquil and free; it is like the air which vanishes when we shut our hands to grasp it. If the soul will do anything in its own strength, it will hinder rather than aid God's work.

It was far otherwise once. The reason is this: God is now working in the soul, in the state of contemplation, that is, when it advances from meditation to the state of proficients, in such a way as to seem to have bound up all the interior faculties, leaving no help in the understanding, no sweetness in the will, no reflections in the memory. Therefore, at this time, all that the soul can do of itself ends, as I have said, in disturbing the peace and the work of God in the spirit amid the dryness of sense. This peace, being spiritual and delicate, effects a work that is quiet and delicate, unobtrusive and satisfactory, pacific and utterly alien from the former delights, which were perceptible and sensible.

The third sign we have for ascertaining whether this dryness be the purgation of sense, is inability to meditate and make reflections, and to excite the imagination, as before, notwithstanding all the efforts we may make; for God begins now to communicate Himself, no longer through the channel of sense, as formerly, in consecutive reflections, by which we arranged and divided our knowledge, but in pure spirit, which admits not of successive reflections, and in the act of pure contemplation, to which neither the interior nor the exterior senses of our lower nature can ascend. Hence it is that the fancy and the imagination cannot help or suggest any reflections, nor use them ever afterwards.

As soon as we enter upon this state, the inability to make our meditations continually grows. It is true that this purgation at first is not continuous in some persons, for they are not altogether without sensible sweetness and comfort—their weakness renders their rapid weaning inexpedient—nevertheless, it grows upon them more and more, and the operations of sense diminish, if they are going on to perfection. They, however, who are not walking in the way of contemplation, meet with a very different treatment, for the night of aridities is not continuous with them, they are sometimes in it, and sometimes not; they are at one time unable to meditate, and at another able as before.

God leads these persons into this night only to try them and to humble them, and to correct their desires, that they may not grow up spiritual gluttons, and not for the purpose of leading them into the way of the spirit, which is contemplation. God does not raise to contemplation every one that is tried in the way of the spirit, nor even half of them, and He knoweth the reason. Hence it is that these persons are never wholly weaned from the breasts of meditations and reflections, but only, as I have said, at intervals and at certain seasons.

CONDUCT IN THE NIGHT OF THE SENSES
PASSAGE TO CONTEMPLATION

During the aridities of the night of sense—when God effects the change of which I have spoken, drawing the soul out of the way of sense into that of the spirit, from meditation to contemplation, where it is helpless in the things of God, so far as its own powers are concerned, spiritual persons have to endure great afflictions, not so much because of aridity, but because they are afraid that they will be lost on this road; thinking that they are spiritually ruined, and that God has forsaken them, because they find no help or consolation in holy things. Under these circumstances, they weary themselves, and strive, as they were wont, to fix the powers of the soul with some satisfaction upon some matter of meditation, imagining when they cannot do this, and are conscious of the effort, that they are doing nothing. This they do not without great dislike and inward unwillingness on the part of the soul, which enjoys its state of quietness and rest, the faculties not being at work.

In thus turning away from this state they make no progress in the other, because, by exerting their own spirit, they lose that spirit which they had, that of tranquility and peace.

THE NEED OF A GOOD DIRECTOR

Under these circumstances, if they meet with no one who understands the matter, these persons fall away, and abandon the right road; or become weak, or at least put hindrances in the way of their further advancement, because of the great efforts they make to proceed in their former way of meditation, fatiguing their natural powers beyond measure. They think that their state is the result of negligence or of sin.

MEDITATION SHOULD BE ABANDONED

The conduct to be observed in the night of sense is this: in nowise have recourse to meditations, for, as I have said, the time is now past, let the soul be quiet and at rest, though they may think they are doing nothing, that they are losing time, and that their lukewarmness is the reason of their unwillingness to employ their thoughts. They will do enough if they keep patience, and persevere in prayer; all they have to do is to keep their soul free, unembarrassed, and at rest from all thoughts and all knowledge, not anxious about their meditation,[2] contenting themselves simply with directing their attention lovingly and calmly towards God; and all this without anxiety or effort, or desire to feel and taste His presence. For all such efforts disquiet the soul, and distract it from the calm repose and sweet tranquillity of contemplation to which they are now admitted.

And though they may have many scruples that they are wasting time, and that it may be better for them to betake themselves to some other good work, seeing that in prayer and meditation they are become helpless; yet let them be patient with themselves, and remain quiet, for that which they are uneasy about is their own satisfaction and liberty of spirit.

When the soul interiorly rests, every action and passion, or consideration at that time, will distract and disturb it, and make it feel the dryness and emptiness of sense. The more it strives to find help in affections and knowledge, the more will it feel the deficiency which cannot now be supplied in that way. It is therefore expedient for the soul which is in this condition not to be troubled because its faculties have become useless, yea, rather it should desire that they may become so quickly; for by not hindering the operation of infused contemplation, to which God is now admitting it, the soul is refreshed in peaceful abundance, and set on fire with the spirit of love, which this contemplation, dim and secret, induces and establishes within it.

FIRST IMPRESSIONS: ANXIOUS LOVE AND FEAR OF GOD

The burning fire of love, in general, is not felt at first, for it has not begun to burn, either because of our natural impurity, or because the soul, not understanding its own state, has not given it a peaceful rest within. Sometimes, however, whether it be so or not, a certain longing after God begins to be felt; and the more it grows, the more the soul feels itself touched and inflamed with the love of God, without knowing or understanding how or whence that love comes, except that at times this burning so inflames it that it longs earnestly after God.

This love, in general, is not felt at first, but only the dryness and emptiness of which I am speaking: and then, instead of love, which is afterwards enkindled, what the soul feels in the dryness and the emptiness of its faculties is a general painful anxiety about God, and a certain painful misgiving that it is not serving Him. But a soul anxious and afflicted for His sake is a sacrifice not a little pleasing unto God. Secret contemplation keeps the soul in this state of anxiety, until, in the course of time, having purged the sensual nature of man, in some degree, of its natural forces and affections by means of the aridities it occasions, it shall have kindled within it this divine love. But in the meantime, like a sick man in the hands of his physician, all it has to do, in the dark night and dry purgation of the desire, is to suffer, healing its many imperfections.

THE NARROW GATE

The narrow gate is this night of sense. The soul detaches itself from sense that it may enter on it, basing itself on faith, which is a stranger to all sense, that it may afterwards travel along the straight road of that other night—the night of the spirit, by which it advances towards God in most pure faith, which is the means of union with Him.

THE ADVANTAGES OF THE NIGHT OF THE SENSES

The spirit, being emptied and dried of all sensible sweetness, is given the bread of infused contemplation.

Of these, the first is the knowledge of self and its own vileness. By contrasting the abundance of satisfaction in former times and by the difficulty which good works now present to it, the soul is brought to a knowledge of its own vileness and misery, which in the season of prosperity it saw not.

It possesses and retains that excellent and necessary virtue of self-knowledge, counting itself for nothing, and having no satisfaction in itself, because it sees that of itself it does and can do nothing.

The soul learns to commune with God with more respect and reverence. . . . We learn how reverently and discreetly in spiritual detachment we are to converse with God. When the desires are quelled, and sensible joy and consolation withdrawn, the understanding remains free and clear for the reception of the truth.

"In a desert land, and inaccessible, and without water; so in the holy have I appeared to Thee, that I might see Thy strength and Thy glory." The Psalmist does not say here—and it is worthy of observation—that his previous sweetness and delight were any dispositions or means whereby he might come to the knowledge of the glory of God, but rather that it was through an aridity and emptying of the powers of sense, spoken of here as the barren and dry land.

Moreover, he does not say that his reflections and meditations on divine things, with which he was once familiar, had led him to the knowledge and contemplation of God's power, but, rather, his inability to meditate on God, to form reflections by the help of his imagination; that is the inaccessible land.

SPIRITUAL HUMILITY

The soul, seeing itself parched and miserable, does not, even for a moment, think itself better than others. Out of this grows the love of our neighbour. . . . The soul sees nothing but its own misery, which it keeps so constantly before its eyes that it can look upon nothing else.

In this state, too, men are submissive and obedient in the spiritual way, for when they see their own wretchedness they not only listen to instruction, but desire to have it from anyone who will guide their steps and tell them what they ought to do.

MOMENTS OF ILLUMINATION

Sometimes, and even quite often, in the midst of aridities and hardship, God communicates to the soul, when it least expects it, spiritual sweetness, most pure love, and spiritual knowledge of the most exalted kind, of greater worth and profit than any of which it had previous experience, though at first the soul may not think so, for the spiritual influence now communicated is most delicate, and imperceptible by sense.

THAT WHICH DOMINATES

The fear of God and the desire to please Him increase in this arid night.

When the house of sensuality is at rest, that is, when the passions are mortified and concupiscence is quenched, the soul begins to set out on the way of the spirit, the way of those who progress and of proficients, which is also called the illuminative way.

THE DEVIL

Progress towards the night of the spirit is attended with heavy trials and temptations of sense of long continuance, in some longer than in others; for to some is sent the angel of Satan, the spirit of impurity, to buffet them with horrible and violent temptations of the flesh, to trouble their minds with filthy thoughts, and their imaginations with representations of sin most vividly depicted; which, at times, becomes an affliction more grievous than death.

At other times this night is attended by the spirit of blasphemy; the thoughts and conceptions are overrun with intolerable blasphemies, which now and then are suggested to the imagination with such violence as almost to break forth in words; this, too, is a heavy affliction.

Again, another hateful spirit, called by the prophet "the spirit of giddiness," is suffered to torment them. This spirit so clouds their judgment that they are filled with a thousand scruples and perplexities so embarrassing that they can never satisfy themselves about them, nor submit their judgment therein to the counsel and direction of others.

DURATION OF THE PURIFICATION

These trials are measured by the divine will, and are proportioned to the imperfections, many or few, to be purged away: and also to the degree of union in love to which God intends to raise the soul: that is the measure of its humiliations, both in their intensity and duration.

Those who are strong and more able to bear suffering, are purified in more intense trials, and in less time. But those who are weak are purified very slowly, with weak temptations, and the night of their purgation is long: their senses are refreshed from time to time lest they should fall away; these, however, come late to the pureness of their perfection in this life, and some of them never. These persons are not clearly in the purgative night, nor clearly out of it; for though they make no progress, yet in order that they may be humble and know themselves, God tries them for a season in aridities and temptations, and visits them with His consolations at intervals lest they should become fainthearted, and seek for comfort in the ways of the world.

NOTES

1. "Without contemplation one will never make much progress in virtue, and one will never be much use in helping the progress of others. One never will get quite free from one's weaknesses and imperfections. One will be always attached to earth, and one will never rise much above the feelings of nature. One will never be able to serve God with perfection. But with contemplation one will do more, both for oneself and for others, in a month, than one could do without it in ten years. It produces acts of excellence detached from the impurities of nature, very sublime acts of love of God such as can rarely be made without this gift; and finally it perfects faith and all the other virtues, lifting them to the highest degree to which it is possible to rise."—P. LALLEMANT, S.J., *Doctrine Spirituelle: VIIe Principe,* Ch. IV.

2. "As to God, we shall never attain to Him but by the complete repose of the faculties of the intellect, no longer perceiving either deification, nor life, nor substance which holds any exact comparison with this primal cause, supereminently raised above all things."—DIONYSIUS: *Divine Names,* Chapter II.

Plato

THE REPUBLIC

BOOK VII

And now, I said, let me show in a figure how far our nature is enlightened or unenlightened:—Behold! human beings living in an underground den, which has a mouth open towards the light and reaching all along the den; here they have been from their childhood, and have their legs and necks chained so that they can not move, and can only see before them, being prevented by the chains from turning round their heads. Above and behind them a fire is blazing at a distance, and between the fire and the prisoners there is a raised way; and you will see, if you look, a low wall built along the way, like the screen which marionette players have in front of them, over which they show the puppets.

I see.

And do you see, I said, men passing along the wall carrying all sorts of vessels, and statues and figures of animals made of wood and stone and various materials, which appear over the wall? Some of them are talking, others silent.

You have shown me a strange image, and they are strange prisoners.

Like ourselves, I replied; and they see only their own shadows, or the shadows of one another, which the fire throws on the opposite wall of the cave?

True, he said; how could they see anything but the shadows if they were never allowed to move their heads?

And of the objects which are being carried in like manner they would only see the shadows?

Yes, he said.

And if they were able to converse with one another, would they not suppose that they were naming what was actually before them?[1]

Very true.

And suppose further that the prison had an echo which came from the other side, would they not be sure to fancy when one of the passers-by spoke that the voice which they heard came from the passing shadow?

No question, he replied.

To them, I said, the truth would be literally nothing but the shadows of the images.

That is certain.

And now look again, and see what will naturally follow if the prisoners are released and disabused of their error. At first, when any of them is liberated and compelled suddenly to stand up and turn his neck round and walk and look towards the light, he will suffer sharp pains; the glare will distress him, and he will be unable to see the realities of which in his former state he had seen the shadows; and then conceive some one saying to him, that what he saw before was an illusion, but that now, when he is approaching nearer to being and his eye is turned towards more real existence, he has a clearer vision,—what will be his reply? And you may further imagine that his instructor is pointing to the objects as they pass and requiring him to name them,—will he not be perplexed? Will he not fancy that the shadows which he formerly saw are truer than the objects which are now shown to him?

Far truer.

And if he is compelled to look straight at the light, will he not have a pain in his eyes which will make him turn away to take refuge in the objects of vision which he can see, and which he will conceive to be in reality clearer than the things which are now being shown to him?

True, he said.

And suppose once more, that he is reluctantly dragged up a steep and rugged ascent, and held fast until he is forced into the presence of the sun himself, is he not likely to be pained and irritated? When he approaches the light his eyes will be dazzled, and he will not be able to see anything at all of what are now called realities.

Not all in a moment, he said.

He will require to grow accustomed to the sight of the upper world. And first he will see the shadows best, next the reflections of men and other objects in the water, and then the objects themselves; then he will gaze upon the light of the moon and the stars and the spangled heaven; and he will see the sky and the stars by night better than the sun or the light of the sun by day?

Certainly.

Last of all he will be able to see the sun, and not mere reflections of him in the water, but he will see him in his own proper place, and not in another; and he will contemplate him as he is.

Certainly.

He will then proceed to argue that this is he who gives the season and the years, and is the guardian of all that is in the visible world, and in a certain way the cause of all things which he and his fellows have been accustomed to behold?

Clearly, he said, he would first see the sun and then reason about him.

And when he remembered his old habitation, and the wisdom of the den and his fellow-prisoners, do you not suppose that he would felicitate himself on the change, and pity them?

Certainly, he would.

And if they were in the habit of conferring honors among themselves on those who were quickest to observe the passing shadows and to remark which of them went before, and which followed after, and which were together; and who were therefore best able to draw conclusions as to the future, do you think that he would care for such honors and glories, or envy the possessors of them? Would he not say with Homer,

"Better to be the poor servant of a poor master,"

and to endure anything, rather than think as they do and live after their manner?

Yes, he said, I think that he would rather suffer anything than entertain these false notions and live in this miserable manner.

Imagine once more, I said, such an one coming suddenly out of the sun to be replaced in his old situation; would he not be certain to have his eyes full of darkness?

To be sure, he said.

And if there were a contest, and he had to compete in measuring the shadows with the prisoners who had never moved out of the den, while his sight was still weak, and before his eyes had become steady (and the time which would be needed to acquire this new habit of sight might be very considerable), would he not be ridiculous? Men would say of him that up he went and down he came without his eyes; and that it was better not even to think of ascending; and if any one tried to loose another and lead him up to the light, let them only catch the offender, and they would put him to death.

No question, he said.

This entire allegory, I said, you may now append, dear Glaucon, to the previous argument; the prison-house is the world of sight, the light of the fire is the sun, and you will not misapprehend me if you interpret the journey upwards to be the ascent of the soul into the intellectual world according to my poor belief, which, at your desire, I have expressed— whether rightly or wrongly God knows. But, whether true or false, my opinion is that in the world of knowledge the idea of good appears last of all, and is seen only with an effort; and, when seen, is also inferred to be the universal author of all things beautiful and right, parent of light and of the lord of light in this visible world, and the immediate source of reason and truth in the intellectual; and that this is the power upon which he who would act rationally either in public or private life must have his eye fixed.

I agree, he said, as far as I am able to understand you.

Moreover, I said, you must not wonder that those who attain to this beatific vision are unwilling to descend to human affairs; for their souls are ever hastening into the upper world where they desire to dwell; which desire of theirs is very natural, if our allegory may be trusted.

Yes, very natural.

And is there anything surprising in one who passes from divine contemplations to the evil state of man, misbehaving himself in a ridiculous manner; if, while his eyes are blinking and before he has become accustomed to the surrounding darkness, he is compelled to fight in courts of law, or in other places, about the images or the shadows of images of justice, and is endeavoring to meet the conceptions of those who have never yet seen absolute justice?

Anything but surprising, he replied.

Any one who has common sense will remember that the bewilderments of the eyes are of two kinds, and arise from two causes, either from coming out of the light or from going into the light, which is true of the mind's eye, quite as much as of the bodily eye; and he who remembers this when he sees any one whose vision is perplexed and weak, will not be too ready to laugh; he will first ask whether that soul of man has come out of the brighter life, and is unable to see because unaccustomed to the dark, or having turned from darkness to the day is dazzled by excess of light. And he will count the one happy in his condition and state of being, and he will pity the other; or, if he have a mind to laugh at the soul which comes from below into the light, there will be more reason in this than in the laugh which greets him who returns from above out of the light into the den.

That, he said, is a very just distinction.

But then, if I am right, certain professors of education must be wrong when they say that they can put a knowledge into the soul which was not there before, like sight into blind eyes.

They undoubtedly say this, he replied.

Whereas, our argument shows that the power and capacity of learning exists in the soul already; and that just as the eye was unable to turn from darkness to light without the whole body, so too the instrument of knowledge can only by the movement of the whole soul be turned from the world of becoming into that of being, and learn by degrees to endure the sight of being, and of the brightest and best of being, or in other words, of the good.

Very true.

And must there not be some art which will effect conversion in the easiest and quickest manner; not implanting the faculty of sight, for that exists already, but has been turned in the wrong direction, and is looking away from the truth?

Yes, he said, such an art may be presumed.

And whereas the other so-called virtues of the soul seem to be akin to bodily qualities, for even when they are not originally innate they can be implanted later by habit and exercise, the virtue of wisdom more than anything else contains a divine element which always remains, and by this conversion is rendered useful and profitable; or, on the other hand, hurtful and useless. Did you never observe the narrow intelligence flashing from the keen eye of a clever rogue—how eager he is, how clearly his paltry soul sees the way to his end; he is the reverse of blind, but his keen eyesight is forced into the service of evil, and he is mischievous in proportion to his cleverness?

Very true, he said.

But what if there had been a circumcision of such natures in the days of their youth; and they had been severed from those sensual pleasures, such as eating and drinking, which, like leaden weights, were attached to them at their birth, and which drag them down and turn the vision of their souls upon the things that are below—if, I say, they had been released from these impediments and turned in the opposite direction, the very same faculty in them would have seen the truth as keenly as they see what their eyes are turned to now.

Very likely.

Yes, I said; and there is another thing which is likely, or rather a necessary inference from what has preceded, that neither the uneducated and uninformed of the truth, nor yet those who never make an end of their education, will be able ministers of State; not the former, because they have no single aim of duty which is the rule of all their actions, private as well as public; nor the latter, because they will not act at all except upon compulsion, fancying that they are already dwelling apart in the islands of the blest.

Very true, he replied.

Then, I said, the business of us who are the founders of the State will be to compel the best minds to attain that knowledge which we have already shown to be the greatest of all—they must continue to ascend until they arrive at the good; but when they have ascended and seen enough we must not allow them to do as they do now.

What do you mean?

I mean that they remain in the upper world: but this must not be allowed; they must be made to descend again among the prisoners in the den, and partake of their labors and honors, whether they are worth having or not.

But is not this unjust? he said; ought we to give them a worse life, when they might have a better?

You have again forgotten, my friend, I said, the intention of the legislator, who did not aim at making any one class in the State happy above the rest; the happiness was to be in the whole State, and he held the citizens together by persuasion and necessity, making them benefactors of the State, and therefore benefactors of one another; to this end he created them, not to please themselves, but to be his instruments in binding up the State.

True, he said, I had forgotten.

Observe, Glaucon, that there will be no injustice in compelling our philosophers to have a care and providence of others; we shall explain to them that in other States, men of their class are not obliged to share in the toils of politics: and this is reasonable, for they grow up at their own sweet will, and the government would rather not have them. Being self-taught, they can not be expected to show any gratitude for a culture which they have never received. But we have brought you into the world to be rulers of the hive, kings of yourselves and of the other citizens, and have educated you far better and more perfectly than they have been educated, and you are better able to share in the double duty. Wherefore each of you, when his turn comes, must go down to the general underground abode, and get the habit of seeing in the dark. When you have acquired the habit, you will see ten thousand times better than the inhabitants of the den, and you will know what the several images are, and what they represent, because you have seen the beautiful and just and good in their truth. And thus our State, which is also yours, will be a reality, and not a dream only, and will be administered in a spirit unlike that of other States, in which men fight with one another about shadows only and are distracted in the struggle for power, which in their eyes is a great good. Whereas the truth is that the State in which the rulers are most reluctant to govern is always the best and most quietly governed, and the State in which they are most eager, the worst.

Quite true, he replied.

And will our pupils, when they hear this, refuse to take their turn at the toils of State, when they are allowed to spend the greater part of their time with one another in the heavenly light?

Impossible, he answered; for they are just men, and the commands which we impose upon them are just; there can be no doubt that every one of them will take office as a stern necessity, and not after the fashion of our present rulers of State.

Yes, my friend, I said; and there lies the point. You must contrive for your future rulers another and a better life than that of a ruler, and then you may have a well-ordered State; for only in the State which offers this, will they rule who are truly rich, not in silver and gold, but in virtue and wisdom, which are the true blessings of life. Whereas if they go to the administration of public affairs, poor and hungering after their own private advantage, thinking that hence they are to snatch the chief good, order there can never be; for they will be fighting about office, and the civil and domestic broils which thus arise will be the ruin of the rulers themselves and of the whole State.

Most true, he replied.

And the only life which looks down upon the life of political ambition is that of true philosophy. Do you know of any other?

Indeed, I do not, he said.

And those who govern ought not to be lovers of the task? For, if they are, there will be rival lovers, and they will fight.

No question.

Who then are those whom we shall compel to be guardians? Surely they will be the men who are wisest about affairs of State, and by whom the State is best administered, and who at the same time have other honors and another and better life than that of politics?

They are the men, and I will choose them, he replied.

NOTE

1. Reading παρόντα.

BOOK THREE

DIALOGUES

*Alienation is felt most keenly by those unsolaced by institutional sup-
port. Since Nietzsche's announcement that God is dead, and Freud's
dismissal of religion as an infantile illusion, intellectuals have been more
aware of their "occupational" aloneness than ever. Whitehead has replied by defining religion as what a man does with his solitariness. Meanwhile most intellectuals have sought institutional support—in parties,
businesses, or academies.*

*The theme of aloneness-versus-safety runs through the ensuing dia-
logues. Is art being revivified or dehumanized? Apollinaire says one thing;
Ortega says another. Meanwhile practising artists raise the question of
how much inspiration can be found by the unaided individual talent, and
how much must draw upon other forces, historical, social or archetypal.
If the destruction of artistic language has coincided, as Eliade says, with
psychoanalysis, what must be done to find a new mythology that will
sustain the new artist? Must he subject himself to scientific disciplines
of the psychoanalytic kind, or can he safely continue in carefree ignorance of his true motivations and his true relationship to myth? Is Beckett
a dead-end or a fresh beginning? Has an advance-guard academy been
erected on the achievements of the recent past that blocks literary fulfilment in our own time? Has the aestheticism of connoisseurs become
a greater source of illusion, among intellectuals, than religion?*

*In one way or another such questions run through these variations
on a theme.*

THE NEW ART IS NOT ACCESSIBLE TO EVERY MAN

José Ortega y Gasset

THE DEHUMANIZATION OF ART

ARTISTIC ART

If the new art is not accessible to every man this implies that its impulses are not of a generically human kind. It is an art not for men in general but for a special class of men who may not be better but who evidently are different.

One point must be clarified before we go on. What is it the majority of people call aesthetic pleasure? What happens in their minds when they "like" a work of art; for instance, a theatrical performance? The answer is easy. A man likes a play when he has become interested in the human destinies presented to him, when the love and hatred, the joys and sorrows of the personages so move his heart that he participates in it all as though it were happening in real life. And he calls a work "good" if it succeeds in creating the illusion necessary to make the imaginary personages appear like living persons. In poetry he seeks the passion and pain of the man behind the poet. Paintings attract him if he finds on them figures of men or women whom it would be interesting to meet.

A landscape is pronounced "pretty" if the country it represents deserves for its loveliness or its grandeur to be visited on a trip.

It thus appears that to the majority of people aesthetic pleasure means a state of mind which is essentially undistinguishable from their ordinary behavior. It differs merely in accidental qualities, being perhaps less utilitarian, more intense, and free from painful consequences. But the object towards which their attention and, consequently, all their other mental activities are directed is the same as in daily life: people and passions. By art they understand a means through which they are brought in contact with interesting human affairs. Artistic forms proper—figments, fantasy—are tolerated only if they do not interfere with the perception of human forms and fates. As soon as purely aesthetic elements predominate and the story of John and Mary grows elusive, most people feel out of their depth and are at a loss what to make of the scene, the book, or the painting. As they have never practiced any other attitude but the practical one in which a man's feelings are aroused and he is emotionally involved, a work that does not invite sentimental intervention leaves them without a cue.

Now, this is a point which has to be made perfectly clear. Not only is grieving and rejoicing at such human destinies as a work of art presents or narrates a very different thing from true artistic pleasure, but preoccupation with the human content of the work is in principle incompatible with aesthetic enjoyment proper.

We have here a very simple optical problem. To see a thing we must adjust our visual apparatus in a certain way. If the adjustment is inadequate the thing is seen indistinctly or not at all. Take a garden seen through a window. Looking at the garden we adjust our eyes in such a way that the ray of vision travels through the pane without delay and rests on the shrubs and flowers. Since we are focusing on the garden and our ray of vision is directed toward it, we do not see the window but look clear through it. The purer the glass, the less we see it. But we can also deliberately disregard the garden and, withdrawing the ray of vision, detain it at the window. We then lose sight of the garden; what we still behold of it is a confused mass of color which appears pasted to the pane. Hence to see the garden and to see the windowpane are two incompatible operations which exclude one another because they require different adjustments.

Similarly a work of art vanishes from sight for a beholder who seeks in it nothing but the moving fate of John and Mary or Tristan and Isolde and adjusts his vision to this. Tristan's sorrows are sorrows and can evoke compassion only in so far as they are taken as real. But an object of art is artistic only in so far as it is not real. In order to enjoy Titian's portrait of Charles the Fifth on horseback we must forget that this is Charles the Fifth in person and see instead a portrait—that is, an image, a fiction. The portrayed person and his portrait are two entirely different things; we are interested in either one or the other. In the first case we "live" with Charles the Fifth, in the second we look at an object of art.

But not many people are capable of adjusting their perceptive apparatus to the pane and the transparency that is the work of art. Instead they look right through it and revel in the human reality with which the work deals. When they are invited to let go of this prey and to direct their attention to the work of art itself they will say that they cannot see such a thing, which indeed they cannot, because it is all artistic transparency and without substance.

During the nineteenth century artists proceeded in all too impure a fashion. They reduced the strictly aesthetic elements to a minimum and let the work consist almost entirely in a fiction of human realities. In this sense all normal art of the last century must be called realistic. Beethoven and Wagner were realistic, and so was Chateaubriand as well as Zola. Seen from the vantage-point of our day Romanticism and Naturalism draw closer together and reveal their common realistic root.

Works of this kind are only partially works of art, or artistic objects. Their enjoyment does not depend upon our power to focus on transparencies and images, a power characteristic of the artistic sensibility; all they require is human sensibility and willingness to sympathize with our neighbor's joys and worries. No wonder that nineteenth century art has been so popular; it is made for the masses inasmuch as it is not art but an extract from life. Let us remember that in epochs with two different types of art, one for minorities and one for the majority, the latter has always been realistic.[1]

I will not now discuss whether pure art is possible. Perhaps it is not; but as the reasons that make me inclined to think so are somewhat long and difficult the subject better be dropped. Besides, it it not of major importance for the matter in hand. Even though pure art may be impossible there doubtless can prevail a tendency toward a purification of art. Such a tendency would effect a progressive elimination of the human, all too human, elements predominant in romantic and naturalistic production. And in this process a point can be reached in which the human content has grown so thin that it is negligible. We then have an art which can be comprehended only by people possessed of the peculiar gift of artistic sensibility—an art for artists and not for the masses, for "quality" and not for hoi polloi.

That is why modern art divides the public into two classes, those who understand it and those who do not understand it—that is to say, those who are artists and those who are not. The new art is an artistic art.

I do not propose to extol the new way in art or to condemn the old. My purpose is to characterize them as the zoologist characterizes two contrasting species. The new art is a world-wide fact. For about twenty years now the most alert young people of two successive generations— in Berlin, Paris, London, New York, Rome, Madrid—have found themselves faced with the undeniable fact that they have no use for traditional art; moreover, that they detest it. With these young people one can do one of two things: shoot them, or try to understand them. As soon as one decides in favor of the latter it appears that they are endowed with a perfectly clear, coherent, and rational sense of art. Far from being a whim, their way of feeling represents the inevitable and fruitful result of all previous artistic achievement. Whimsical, arbitrary, and consequently unprofitable it would be to set oneself against the new style and obstinately remain shut up in old forms that are exhausted and the worse for wear. In art, as in morals, what ought to be done does not depend on our personal judgment; we have to accept the imperative imposed by the time. Obedience to the order of the day is the most hopeful choice open to the individual. Even so he may achieve nothing; but he is much more likely to fail if he insists on composing another Wagnerian opera, another naturalistic novel.

In art repetition is nothing. Each historical style can engender a certain number of different forms within a generic type. But there always comes a day when the magnificent mine is worked out. Such, for instance, has been the fate of the romantico-naturalistic novel and theater. It is a naïve error to believe that the present infecundity of these two genres is due to lack of talent. What happens is that the possible combinations within these literary forms are exhausted. It must be deemed fortunate that this situation coincides with the emergence of a new artistic sensibility capable of detecting other untouched veins.

When we analyze the new style we find that it contains certain closely connected tendencies. It tends (1) to dehumanize art, (2) to avoid living forms, (3) to see to it that the work of art is nothing but a work of art, (4) to consider art as play and nothing else, (5) to be essentially ironical, (6) to beware of sham and hence to aspire to scrupulous realization, (7) to regard art as a thing of no transcending consequence.

In the following I shall say a few words about each of these features of modern art.

A FEW DROPS OF PHENOMENOLOGY

A great man is dying. His wife is by his bedside. A doctor takes the dying man's pulse. In the background two more persons are discovered:

a reporter who is present for professional reasons, and a painter whom mere chance has brought here. Wife, doctor, reporter, and painter witness one and the same event. Nonetheless, this identical event—a man's death—impresses each of them in a different way. So different indeed that the several aspects have hardly anything in common. What this scene means to the wife who is all grief has so little to do with what it means to the painter who looks on impassively that it seems doubtful whether the two can be said to be present at the same event.

It thus becomes clear that one and the same reality may split up into many diverse realities when it is beheld from different points of view. And we cannot help asking ourselves: Which of all these realities must then be regarded as the real and authentic one? The answer, no matter how we decide, cannot but be arbitrary. Any preference can be founded on caprice only. All these realities are equivalent, each being authentic for its corresponding point of view. All we can do is to classify the points of view and to determine which among them seems, in a practical way, most normal or most spontaneous. Thus we arrive at a conception of reality that is by no means absolute, but at least practical and normative.

As for the points of view of the four persons present at the death bed, the clearest means of distinguishing them is by measuring one of their dimensions, namely the emotional distance between each person and the event they all witness. For the wife of the dying man the distance shrinks to almost nothing. What is happening so tortures her soul and absorbs her mind that it becomes one with her person. Or to put it inversely, the wife is drawn into the scene, she is part of it. A thing can be seen, an event can be observed, only when we have separated it from ourselves and it has ceased to form a living part of our being. Thus the wife is not present at the scene, she is in it. She does not behold it, she "lives" it.

The doctor is several degrees removed. To him this is a professional case. He is not drawn into the event with the frantic and blinding anxiety of the poor woman. However it is his bounden duty as a doctor to take a serious interest, he carries responsibility, perhaps, his professional honor is at stake. Hence he too, albeit in a less integral and less intimate way, takes part in the event. He is involved in it not with his heart but with the professional portion of his self. He too "lives" the scene although with an agitation originating not in the emotional center, but in the professional surface, of his existence.

When we now put ourselves in the place of the reporter we realize that we have traveled a long distance away from the tragic event. So far indeed that we have lost all emotional contact with it. The reporter, like the doctor, has been brought here for professional reasons and not out of a spontaneous human interest. But while the doctor's profession requires him to interfere, the reporter's requires him precisely to stay aloof; he has to confine himself to observing. To him the event is a mere scene, a pure spectacle on which he is expected to report in his newspaper column. He takes no feeling part in what is happening here, he is emotionally free, an outsider. He does not "live" the scene, he observes it. Yet he observes it with a view to telling his readers about it. He wants to interest them, to move them, and if possible to make them weep as though they each had been the dying man's best friend. From his schooldays he remembers Horace's recipe: *"Si vis me flere dolendum est primum ipsi tibi"*—if you want me to weep you must first grieve yourself.

Obedient to Horace the reporter is anxious to pretend emotion, hoping that it will benefit his literary performance. If he does not "live" the scene he at least pretends to "live" it.

The painter, in fine, completely unconcerned, does nothing but keep his eyes open. What is happening here is none of his business; he is, as it were, a hundred miles removed from it. His is a purely perceptive attitude; indeed, he fails to perceive the event in its entirety. The tragic inner meaning escapes his attention which is directed exclusively toward the visual part—color values, lights, and shadows. In the painter we find a maximum of distance and a minimum of feeling intervention.

The inevitable dullness of this analysis will, I hope, be excused if it now enables us to speak in a clear and precise way of a scale of emotional distances between ourselves and reality. In this scale, the degree of closeness is equivalent to the degree of feeling participation; the degree of remoteness, on the other hand, marks the degree to which we have freed ourselves from the real event, thus objectifying it and turning it into a theme of pure observation. At one end of the scale the world—persons, things, situations—is given to us in the aspect of "lived" reality; at the other end we see everything in the aspect of "observed" reality.

At this point we must make a remark that is essential in aesthetics and without which neither old art nor new art can be satisfactorily analyzed. Among the diverse aspects of reality we find one from which all the others derive and which they all presuppose: "lived" reality. If nobody had ever "lived" in pure and frantic abandonment a man's death, the doctor would not bother, the readers would not understand the reporter's pathos, and the canvas on which the painter limned a person on a bed surrounded by mourning figures would be meaningless. The same holds for any object, be it a person, a thing, or a situation. The primal aspect of an apple is that in which I see it when I am about to eat it. All its other possible forms—when it appears, for instance, in a Baroque ornament, or on a still life of Cézanne's, or in the eternal metaphor of a girl's apple cheeks—preserve more or less that original aspect. A painting or a poem without any vestiges of "lived" forms would be unintelligible, i.e., nothing—as a discourse is nothing whose every word is emptied of its customary meaning.

That is to say, in the scale of realities "lived" reality holds a peculiar primacy which compels us to regard it as "the" reality. Instead of "lived" reality we may say "human" reality. The painter who impassively witnesses the death-scene appears "inhuman." In other words, the human point of view is that in which we "live" situations, persons, things. And, vice versa, realities—a woman, a countryside, an event—are human when they present the aspect in which they are usually "lived."

As an example, the importance of which will appear later, let us mention that among the realities which constitute the world are our ideas. We use our ideas in a "human" way when we employ them for thinking things. Thinking of Napoleon, for example, we are normally concerned with the great man of that name. A psychologist, on the other hand, adopts an unusual, "inhuman" attitude when he forgets about Napoleon and, prying into his own mind, tries to analyze his idea of Napoleon as such idea. His perspective is the opposite of that prevailing in spontaneous life. The idea, instead of functioning as the means to think an object with, is itself made the object and the aim of thinking. We shall soon see the unexpected use which the new art has made of this "inhuman" inversion.

FIRST INSTALLMENT ON THE DEHUMANIZATION OF ART

With amazing swiftness modern art has split up into a multitude of divergent directions. Nothing is easier than to stress the differences. But such an emphasis on the distinguishing and specific features would be pointless without a previous account of the common fund that in a varying and sometimes contradictory manner asserts itself throughout modern art. Did not Aristotle already observe that things differ in what they have in common? Because all bodies are colored we notice that they are differently colored. Species are nothing if not modifications of a genus, and we cannot understand them unless we realize that they draw, in their several ways, upon a common patrimony.

I am little interested in special directions of modern art and, but for a few exceptions, even less in special works. Nor do I, for that matter, expect anybody to be particularly interested in my valuation of the new artistic produce. Writers who have nothing to convey but their praise or dispraise of works of art had better abstain from writing. They are unfit for this arduous task.

The important thing is that there unquestionably exists in the world a new artistic sensibility.[2] Over against the multiplicity of special directions and individual works, the new sensibility represents the generic fact and the source, as it were, from which the former spring. This sensibility it is worth while to define. And when we seek to ascertain the most general and most characteristic feature of modern artistic production we come upon the tendency to dehumanize art. After what we have said above, this formula now acquires a tolerably precise meaning.

Let us compare a painting in the new style with one of, say, 1860. The simplest procedure will be to begin by setting against one another the objects they represent: a man perhaps, a house, or a mountain. It then appears that the artist of 1860 wanted nothing so much as to give to the objects in his picture the same looks and airs they possess outside it when they occur as parts of the "lived" or "human" reality. Apart from this he may have been animated by other more intricate aesthetic ambitions, but what interests us is that his first concern was with securing this likeness. Man, house, mountain are at once recognized, they are our good old friends; whereas on a modern painting we are at a loss to recognize them. It might be supposed that the modern painter has failed to achieve resemblance. But then some pictures of the 1860's are "poorly" painted, too, and the objects in them differ considerably from the corresponding objects outside them. And yet, whatever the differences, the very blunders of the traditional artist point toward the "human" object; they are downfalls on the way toward it and somehow equivalent to the orienting words "This is a cock" with which Cervantes lets the painter Orbanejo enlighten his public. In modern paintings the opposite happens. It is not that the painter is bungling and fails to render the natural (natural = human) thing because he deviates from it, but that these deviations point in a direction opposite to that which would lead to reality.

Far from going more or less clumsily toward reality, the artist is seen going against it. He is brazenly set on deforming reality, shattering its human aspect, dehumanizing it. With the things represented on traditional paintings we could have imaginary intercourse. Many a young Englishman has fallen in love with Gioconda. With the objects of modern pictures no intercourse is possible. By divesting them of their aspect of "lived" reality the artist has blown up the bridges and burned the ships that could have taken us back to our daily world. He leaves us locked up in an abstruse universe, surrounded by objects with which human dealings are inconceivable, and thus compels us to improvise other forms of intercourse completely distinct from our ordinary ways with things. We must invent unheard-of-gestures to fit those singular figures. This new way of life which presupposes the annulment of spontaneous life is precisely what we call understanding and enjoyment of art. Not that this life lacks sentiments and passions, but those sentiments and passions evidently belong to a flora other than that which covers the hills and dales of primary and human life. What those ultra-objects[3] evoke in our inner artist are secondary passions, specifically aesthetic sentiments.

It may be said that, to achieve this result, it would be simpler to dismiss human forms—man, house, mountain—altogether and to construct entirely original figures. But, in the first place, this is not feasible.[4] Even in the most abstract ornamental line a stubborn reminiscence lurks of certain "natural" forms. Secondly—and this is the crucial point—the art of which we speak is inhuman not only because it contains no things human, but also because it is an explicit act of dehumanization. In his escape from the human world the young artist cares less for the *"terminus ad quem,"* the startling fauna at which he arrives, than for the *"terminus a quo,"* the human aspect which he destroys. The question is not to paint something altogether different from a man, a house, a mountain, but to paint a man who resembles a man as little as possible; a house that preserves of a house exactly what is needed to reveal the metamorphosis; a cone miraculously emerging—as the snake from his slough—from what used to be a mountain. For the modern artist, aesthetic pleasure derives from such a triumph over human matter. That is why he has to drive home the victory by presenting in each case the strangled victim.

It may be thought a simple affair to fight shy of reality, but it is by no means easy. There is no difficulty in painting or saying things which make no sense whatever, which are unintelligible and therefore nothing. One only needs to assemble unconnected words or to draw random lines.[5] But to construct something that is not a copy of "nature" and yet possesses substance of its own is a feat which presupposes nothing less than genius.

"Reality" constantly waylays the artist to prevent his flight. Much cunning is needed to effect the sublime escape. A reversed Odysseus, he must free himself from his daily Penelope and sail through reefs and rocks to Circe's Faery. When, for a moment, he succeeds in escaping the perpetual ambush, let us not grudge him a gesture of arrogant triumph, a St. George gesture with the dragon prostrate at his feet.

INVITATION TO UNDERSTANDING

The works of art that the nineteenth century favored invariably contain a core of "lived" reality which furnishes the substance, as it were, of the aesthetic body. With this material the aesthetic process works, and its working consists in endowing the human nucleus with glamour and dignity. To the majority of people this is the most natural and the only possible setup of a work of art. Art is reflected life, nature seen through a temperament, representation of human destinies, and so on. But the fact is that our young artists, with no less conviction, maintain the opposite. Must the old always have the last word today while tomorrow infallibly the young win out? For one thing, let us not rant and rave. *"Dove si grida,"* Leonardo da Vinci warns us, *"no é vera scienza." "Neque lugere neque indignari sed intelligere,"* recommends Spinoza. Our firmest convictions are apt to be the most suspect, they mark our limits and our bonds. Life is a petty thing unless it is moved by the indomitable urge to extend its boundaries. Only in proportion as we are desirous of living more do we really live. Obstinately to insist on carrying on within the same familiar horizon betrays weakness and a decline of vital energies. Our horizon is a biological line, a living part of our organism. In times of fullness of life it expands, elastically moving in unison almost with our breathing. When the horizon stiffens it is because it has become fossilized and we are growing old.

It is less obvious than academicians assume that a work of art must consist of human stuff which the Muses comb and groom. Art cannot be reduced to cosmetics. Perception of "lived" reality and perception of artistic form, as I have said before, are essentially incompatible because they call for a different adjustment of our perceptive apparatus. An art that requires such a double seeing is a squinting art. The nineteenth century was remarkably cross-eyed. That is why its products, far from representing a normal type of art, may be said to mark a maximum aberration in the history of taste. All great periods of art have been careful not to let the work revolve about human contents. The imperative of unmitigated realism that dominated the artistic sensibility of the last century must be put down as a freak in aesthetic evolution. It thus appears that the new inspiration, extravagant though it seems, is merely returning, at least in one point, to the royal road of art. For this road is called "will to style." But to stylize means to deform reality, to derealize; style involves dehumanization. And vice versa, there is no other means of stylizing except by dehumanizing. Whereas realism, exhorting the artist faithfully to follow reality, exhorts him to abandon style. A Zurbarán enthusiast, groping for the suggestive word, will declare that the works of this painter have "character." And character and not style is distinctive of the works of Lucas and Sorolla, of Dickens and Galdós. The eighteenth century, on the other hand, which had so little character was a past master of style.

MORE ABOUT THE DEHUMANIZATION OF ART

The young set has declared taboo any infiltration of human contents into art. Now, human contents, the component elements of our daily world, form a hierarchy of three ranks. There is first the realm of persons, second that of living beings, lastly there are the inorganic things. The veto of modern art is more or less apodictic according to the rank the respective object holds in this hierarchy. The first stratum, as it is most human, is most carefully avoided.

This is clearly discernible in music and in poetry. From Beethoven to Wagner music was primarily concerned with expressing personal feelings. The composer erected great structures of sound in which to accommodate his autobiography. Art was, more or less, confession. There existed no way of aesthetic enjoyment except by contagion. "In music," Nietzsche declared, "the passions enjoy themselves." Wagner poured into *Tristan and Isolde* his adultery with Mathilde Wesendonck, and if we want to enjoy this work we must, for a few hours, turn vaguely adulterous ourselves. That darkly stirring music makes us weep and tremble and melt away voluptuously. From Beethoven to Wagner all music is melodrama.

And that is unfair, a young artist would say. It means taking advantage of a noble weakness inherent in man which exposes him to infection from his neighbor's joys and sorrows. Such an infection is no mental phenomenon; it works like a reflex in the same way as the grating of a knife upon glass sets the teeth on edge. It is an automatic effect, nothing else. We must distinguish between delight and titillation. Romanticism hunts with a decoy, it tampers with the bird's fervor in order to riddle him with the pellets of sounds. Art must not proceed by psychic contagion, for psychic contagion is an unconscious phenomenon, and art ought to be full clarity, high noon of the intellect. Tears and laughter are, aesthetically, frauds. The gesture of beauty never passes beyond smiles, melancholy or delighted. If it can do without them, better still. *"Toute maîtrise jette le froid"* (Mallarmé).

There is, to my mind, a good deal of truth in the young artist's verdict. Aesthetic pleasure must be a seeing pleasure. For pleasures may be blind or seeing. The drunken man's happiness is blind. Like everything in the world it has a cause, the alcohol; but it has no motive. A man who has won at sweepstakes is happy too, but in a different manner; he is happy "about" something. The drunken man's merriment is hermetically enclosed in itself, he does not know why he is happy. Whereas the joy of the winner consists precisely in his being conscious of a definite fact that motivates and justifies his contentment. He is glad because he is aware of an object that is in itself gladdening. His is a happiness with eyes and which feeds on its motive, flowing, as it were, from the object to the subject.[6]

Any phenomenon that aspires to being mental and not mechanical must bear this luminous character of intelligibility, of motivation. But the pleasure aroused by romantic art has hardly any connection with its content. What has the beauty of music—something obviously located without and beyond myself in the realm of sound—what has the beauty of music to do with that melting mood it may produce in me? Is not this a thorough confusion? Instead of delighting in the artistic object people delight in their own emotions, the work being only the cause and the alcohol of their pleasure. And such a *quid pro quo* is bound to happen whenever art is made to consist essentially in an exposition of "lived" realities. "Lived" realities are too overpowering not to evoke a sympathy which prevents us from perceiving them in their objective purity.

Seeing requires distance. Each art operates a magic lantern that removes and transfigures its objects. On its screen they stand aloof, inmates of an inaccessible world, in an absolute distance. When this derealization is lacking, an awkward perplexity arises: we do not know whether to "live" the things or to observe them.

Madame Tussaud's comes to mind and the peculiar uneasiness aroused by dummies. The origin of this uneasiness lies in the provoking ambiguity with which wax figures defeat any attempt at adopting a clear and consistent attitude toward them. Treat them as living beings, and they will sniggeringly reveal their waxen secret. Take them for dolls, and they seem to breathe in irritated protest. They will not be reduced to mere objects. Looking at them we suddenly feel a misgiving: should it not be they who are looking at us? Till in the end we are sick and tired of those hired corpses. Wax figures are melodrama at its purest.

The new sensibility, it seems to me, is dominated by a distaste for human elements in art very similar to the feelings cultured people have-always experienced at Madame Tussaud's, while the mob has always been delighted by that gruesome waxen hoax. In passing we may here ask ourselves a few impertinent questions which we have no intention to answer now. What is behind this disgust at seeing art mixed up with life? Could it be disgust for the human sphere as such, for reality, for life? Or is it rather the opposite: respect for life and unwillingness to confuse it with art, so inferior a thing as art? But what do we mean by calling art an inferior function—divine art, glory of civilization, *fine fleur* of culture, and so forth? As we were saying, these questions are impertinent; let us dismiss them.

In Wagner, melodrama comes to a peak. Now, an artistic form, on reaching its maximum, is likely to topple over into its opposite. And thus we find that in Wagner the human voice has already ceased to be the protagonist and is drowned in the cosmic din of the orchestra. However, a more radical change was to follow. Music had to be relieved of private sentiments and purified in an exemplary objectification. This was the deed of Debussy. Owing to him, it has become possible to listen to music serenely, without swoons and tears. All the various developments in the art of music during these last decades move on the ground of the new ultraworldly world conquered by the genius of Debussy. So decisive is this conversion of the subjective attitude into the objective that any subsequent differentiations appear comparatively negligible.[7] Debussy dehumanized music, that is why he marks a new era in the art of music.

The same happened in poetry. Poetry had to be disencumbered. Laden with human matter it was dragging along, skirting the ground and bumping into trees and house tops like a deflated balloon. Here Mallarmé was the liberator who restored to the lyrical poem its ethereal quality and ascending power. Perhaps he did not reach the goal himself. Yet it was he who gave the decisive order: shoot ballast.

For what was the theme of poetry in the romantic century? The poet informed us prettily of his private upper-middle-class emotions, his major and minor sorrows, his yearnings, his religious or political pre-occupations, and, in case he was English, his reveries behind his pipe. In one way or another, his ambition was to enhance his daily existence. Thanks to personal genius, a halo of finer substance might occasionally surround the human core of the poem—as for instance in Baudelaire. But this splendor was a by-product. All the poet wished was to be human.

"And that seems objectionable to a young man?" somebody who has ceased to be one asks with suppressed indignation. "What does he want the poet to be? A bird, an ichthyosaurus, a dodecahedron?"

I can't say. However, I believe that the young poet when writing poetry simply wishes to be a poet. We shall yet see that all new art (like new science, new politics—new life, in sum) abhors nothing so much as blurred borderlines. To insist on neat distinctions is a symptom of mental honesty. Life is one thing, art is another—thus the young set think or at least feel—let us keep the two apart. The poet begins where the man ends. The man's lot is to live his human life, the poet's to invent what is nonexistent. Herein lies the justification of the poetical profession. The poet aggrandizes the world by adding to reality, which is there by itself, the continents of his imagination. Author derives from *auctor,* he who augments. It was the title Rome bestowed upon her generals when they had conquered new territory for the City.

Mallarmé was the first poet in the nineteenth century who wanted to be nothing but a poet. He "eschewed"—as he said himself—"the ma-terials offered by nature" and composed small lyrical objects distinct from the human fauna and flora. This poetry need not be "felt." As it contains nothing human, it contains no cue for emotion either. When a woman is mentioned it is "the woman no one"; when an hour strikes it is "the hour not marked on dials." Proceeding by negatives, Mallarmé's verse muffles all vital resonance and presents us with figures so extramundane that merely looking at them is delight. Among such creatures, what business has the poor face of the man who officiates as poet? None but to disappear, to vanish and to become a pure nameless voice breathing into the air the words—those true protagonists of the lyrical pursuit. This pure and nameless voice, the mere acoustic carrier of the verse, is the voice of the poet who has learned to extricate himself from the surrounding man.

Wherever we look we see the same thing: flight from the human person. The methods of dehumanization are many. Those employed today may differ vastly from Mallarmé's; in fact, I am well aware that his pages are still reached by romantic palpitations. Yet just as modern music belongs to a historical unity that begins with Debussy, all new poetry moves in the direction in which Mallarmé pointed. The landmarks of these two names seem to me essential for charting the main line of the new style above the indentations produced by individual inspirations.

It will not be easy to interest a person under thirty in a book that under the pretext of art reports on the doings of some men and women. To him, such a thing smacks of sociology or psychology. He would accept it gladly if issues were not confused and those facts were told him in sociological and psychological terms. But art means something else to him.

Poetry has become the higher algebra of metaphors.

NOTES

1. For instance in the Middle Ages. In accordance with the division of society in the two strata of noblemen and commoners, there existed an aristocratic art which was "conventional" and "idealistic," and a popular art which was realistic and satirical.

2. This new sensibility is a gift not only of the artist proper but also of his audience. When I said above that the new art is an art for artists I understood by "artists" not only those who produce this art but also those who are capable of perceiving purely artistic values.

3. "Ultraism" is one of the most appropriate names that have been coined to denote the new sensibility.

4. An attempt has been made in this extreme sense—in certain works by Picasso—but it has failed signally.

5. This was done by the Dadaistic hoax. It is interesting to note again (see the above footnote) that the very vagaries and abortive experiments of the new art derive with a certain cogency from its organic principle, thereby giving ample proof that modern art is a unified and meaningful movement.

6. Causation and motivation are two completely different relations. The causes of our states of consciousness are not present in these states; science must ascertain them. But the motive of a feeling, of a volition, of a belief forms part of the act itself. Motivation is a conscious relation.

7. A more detailed analysis of Debussy's significance with respect to romantic music may be found in the author's above quoted essay "Musicalia."

Guillaume Apollinaire

THE NEW SPIRIT AND THE POETS

The new spirit which will dominate the entire world has nowhere come to light in poetry as it has in France. The strong intellectual discipline which the French have always imposed on themselves permits them, as well as their spiritual kin, to have a conception of life, of the arts and of letters, which, without being simply the recollection of antiquity, is also not the counterpart of romantic prettiness.

The new spirit which is making itself heard strives above all to inherit from the classics a sound good sense, a sure critical spirit, perspectives on the universe and on the soul of man, and the sense of duty which lays bare our feelings and limits or rather contains their manifestations.

It strives further to inherit from the romantics a curiosity which will incite it to explore all the domains suitable for furnishing literary subject matter which will permit life to be exalted in whatever form it occurs.

To explore truth, to search for it, as much in the ethnic domain, for example, as in that of the imagination—those are the principal characteristics of the new spirit.

This tendency, moreover, has always had its bold proponents, although they were unaware of it; for a long time it has been taking shape and making progress.

However, this is the first time that it has appeared fully conscious of itself. Up to now the literary field has been kept within narrow limits. One wrote in prose or one wrote in verse. In prose, rules of grammar established the form.

As for poetry, rimed versification was the only rule, which underwent periodical attacks, but which was never shaken.

Free verse gave wings to lyricism; but it was only one stage of the exploration that can be made in the domain of form.

The investigations of form have subsequently assumed a great importance. Is it not understandable?

How could the poet not be interested in these investigations which can lead to new discoveries in thought and lyricism?

Assonance, alliteration as well as rime are conventions, each of which has its merits.

Typographical artifices worked out with great audacity have the advantage of bringing to life a visual lyricism which was almost unknown before our age. These artifices can still go much further and achieve the synthesis of the arts, of music, painting, and literature.

That is only one search for attaining new and perfectly legitimate expressions.

Who would dare to say that rhetorical exercises, the variations on the theme of: *I die of thirst beside the fountain* did not have a determining influence on Villon? Who would dare to say the investigations of form of the rhetoricians and of the Marotic[1] school did not serve to purify the French style up to its flowering in the seventeenth century?

It would have been strange if in an epoch when the popular art *par excellence,* the cinema, is a book of pictures, the poets had not tried to compose pictures for meditative and refined minds which are not content with the crude imaginings of the makers of films. These last will become more perceptive, and one can predict the day when, the photograph and the cinema having become the only form of publication in use, the poet will have a freedom heretofor unknown.

One should not be astonished if, with only the means they have now at their disposal, they set themselves to preparing this new art (vaster than the plain art of words) in which, like conductors of an orchestra of unbelievable scope, they will have at their disposition the entire world, its noises and its appearances, the thought and language of man, song, dance, all the arts and all the artifices, still more mirages than Morgan could summon up on the hill of Gibel, with which to compose the visible and unfolded book of the future.

But generally you will not find in France the "words at liberty" which have been reached by the excesses of the Italian and Russian futurists, the extravagant offspring of the new spirit, for France abhors disorder. She returns willingly to principles, but she has a horror of chaos.

We can hope, then, in regard to what constitutes the material and the manner of art, for a liberty of unimaginable opulence. Today the poets are serving their apprenticeship to this encyclopaedic liberty. In the realm of inspiration, their liberty can not be less than that of a daily newspaper which on a single sheet treats the most diverse matters and ranges over the most distant countries. One wonders why the poet should not have at least an equal freedom, and should be restricted, in an era of the telephone, the wireless, and aviation, to a greater cautiousness in confronting space.

The rapidity and simplicity with which minds have become accustomed to designating by a single word such complex beings as a crowd, a nation, the universe, do not have their modern counterpart in poetry. Poets are filling the gap, and their synthetic poems are creating new entities which have a plastic value as carefully composed as that of collective terms.

Man has familiarised himself with those formidable beings which we know as machines, he has explored the domain of the infinitely small, and new domains open up for the activity of his imagination: that of the infinitely large and that of prophecy.

Do not believe that this new spirit is complicated, slack, artificial, and frozen. In keeping with the very order of nature, the poet puts aside any high-flown purpose. There is no longer any Wagnerianism in us, and the young authors have cast far away all the enchanted clothing of the mighty romanticism of Germany and Wagner, just as they have rejected the rustic tinsel of our early evaluations of Jean-Jacques Rousseau.

I do not believe that social developments will ever go so far that one will not be able to speak of national literature. On the contrary, however far one advances on the path of new freedoms, they will only reinforce most of the ancient disciplines and bring out new ones which will not be less demanding than the old. This is why I think that, whatever happens, art increasingly has a country. Furthermore, poets must always express a milieu, a nation; and artists, just as poets, just as philosophers, form a social estate which belongs doubtless to all humanity, but as the expression of a race, of one given environment.

Art will only cease being national the day that the whole universe, living in the same climate, in houses built in the same style, speaks the same language with the same accent—that is to say never. From ethnic and national differences are born the variety of literary expressions, and it is that very variety which must be preserved.

A cosmopolitan lyric expression would only yield shapeless works without character or individual structure, which would have the value of the commonplaces of international parliamentary rhetoric. And notice that the cinema, which is the perfect cosmopolitan art, already shows ethnic differences immediately apparent to everyone, and film enthusiasts immediately distinguish between an American and an Italian film. Likewise the new spirit, which has the ambition of manifesting a universal spirit and which does not intend to limit its activity, is none the less, and claims to respect the fact, a particular and lyric expression of the French nation, just as the classic spirit is, *par excellence,* a sublime expression of the same nation.

It must not be forgotten that it is perhaps more dangerous for a nation to allow itself to be conquered intellectually than by arms. That is why the new spirit asserts above all an order and a duty which are the great classic qualities manifested by French genius; and to them it adds liberty. This liberty and this order, which combine in the new spirit, are its characteristic and its strength.

However, this synthesis of the arts which has been consummated in our time, must not degenerate into confusion. That is to say that it would be, if not dangerous, at least absurd, for example to reduce poetry to a sort of imitative harmony which would not have the excuse of exactness.

One is right to imagine that imitative harmony can play a rôle, but it will be the basis only of an art in which machinery plays a part; for example, a poem or a symphony composed on a phonograph might well consist of noises artistically chosen and lyrically blended or juxtaposed; whereas, for my part, I think it wrong that a poem should be composed simply of the imitation of a noise to which no lyric, tragic, or pathetic meaning can be attached. And if a few poets devote themselves to this game, it should be regarded only as an exercise, a sort of rough notation of what they will include in a finished work. The "brekeke koax" of Aristophanes' *Frogs* is nothing if one separates it from the work in which it takes on all its comic and satiric meaning. The prolonged " i i i i " sounds, lasting a whole line, of Francis Jammes' bird are a sorry harmony if they are detached from the poem to whose total fantasy they give precision.

When a modern poet notes in several lines the throbbing sound of an airplane, it must be regarded above all as the desire of the poet to accustom his sensibility to reality. His passion for truth impels him to take almost scientific notes which, if he wishes to present them as poems, have the faults of being *trompe-oreilles* so to speak, to which actuality will always be superior.

On the other hand, if he wants for example to amplify the art of the dance and attempt a choreography whose buffoons would not restrict themselves to *entrechats* but would utter cries setting off the harmony with an imitative novelty, that is a search which is not absurd, whose popular origins are found in all peoples among whom war dances, for example, are almost always embellished with savage cries.

To come back to the concern with truth and the verisimilitude which rules all investigation, all attempts, all efforts of the new spirit, it must be added that there is no ground for astonishment if a certain number or even a great many of them remain sterile for the moment and sink into ridicule. The new spirit is full of dangers and snares.

All that, however, belongs to the spirit of today, and to condemn categorically these trials and efforts would be to make an error of the kind which, rightly or wrongly, is attributed to M. Thiers in declaring that the railroads were only a scientific game and that the world could not produce enough iron to build rails from Paris to Marseilles.

The new spirit, therefore, admits even hazardous literary experience, and those experiences are at times anything but lyric. This is why lyricism is only one domain of the new spirit in today's poetry, which often contents itself with experiments and investigations without concerning itself over giving them lyric significance. They are materials which the poet amasses, which the new spirit amasses, and these materials will form a basis of truth whose simplicity and modesty must never give pause, for their consequences can be very great things.

At a later date, those who study the literary history of our time will be amazed that, like the alchemists, the dreamers and poets devoted themselves, without even the pretext of a philosopher's stone, to inquiries and to notations which exposed them to the ridicule of their contemporaries, of journalists and of snobs.

But their inquiries will be useful; they will be the foundation of a new realism which will perhaps not be inferior to that so poetic and learned realism of ancient Greece.

With Alfred Jarry, moreover, we have seen laughter rise from the lower region where it was writhing, to furnish the poet with a totally new lyricism. Where is the time when Desdemona's handkerchief seemed to be an inadmissible ridiculousness? Today even ridicule is sought after, it must be seized upon and it has its place in poetry because it is a part of life in the same way as heroism and all that formerly nourished a poet's enthusiasm.

The romantics have tried to give to things of rude appearance a horrible or tragic meaning. It would be better to say that they only worked for the benefit of what is horrible. They wanted to establish the horrible much more than the melancholy. The new spirit does not seek to transform ridicule; it conserves for it a rôle which is not without flavour. Likewise it does not seem to give a sense of nobility to the horrible. It leaves it horrible and does not debase the noble. *It is not a decorative art. Nor is it an impressionist art.* It is every study of exterior and interior nature, it is all eagerness for truth.

Even if it is true that there is nothing new under the sun, *the new spirit does not refrain from discovering new profundities in all this that is not new under the sun.* Good sense is its guide, and this guide leads it into corners, if not new, at least unknown.

But is there nothing new under the sun? It remains to be seen.

What! My head has been X-rayed. I have seen, while I live, my own cranium, and that would be nothing new?

Solomon spoke for the Queen of Sheba, no doubt, and he liked novelty so well that his concubines were without number.

The air is filled with strangely human birds. Machines, the daughters of man and having no mother, live a life from which passion and feeling are absent, and would that be nothing new?

Wise men ceaselessly investigate new universes which are discovered at every crossroads of matter, and there is nothing new under the sun? For the sun perhaps. But for men!

There are a thousand natural combinations which have not yet been composed. Men will conceive them and use them to good purpose, composing thus with nature that supreme art which is life. These new combinations, these new works—they are the art of life, which is called progress. In this sense, progress exists. But if it is held to consist in an eternal becoming, a sort of messianism as appalling as the fable of Tantalus, Sisyphus, and the Danaidae, then Solomon was right over all the prophets of Israel.

What is new exists without being progress. Everything is in the effect of surprise. The new spirit depends equally on surprise, on what is most vital and new in it. *Surprise is the greatest source of what is new*. It is by surprise, by the important position that has been given to surprise, that the new spirit distinguishes itself from all the literary and artistic movements which have preceded it.

In this respect, it detaches itself from all of them and belongs only to our time.

We have established it on the solid basis of good sense and of experience, which have induced us to accept things and feelings only according to truth, and it is according to truth that we admit them, not seeking at all to make sublime what is naturally ridiculous or *vice versa*. And from these truths surprise is most often the result, since they run counter to commonly held opinion. Many of these truths have not been examined; it is enough to unveil them to cause surprise.

One can likewise express a supposed truth so as to cause surprise, simply because no one has yet dared to present it thus. But a supposed truth is not opposed by good sense, without which it would no longer be truth, even supposed truth. That is why I imagine that, if women could bear no more children, men could make them, and why in showing it to be so I express a literary truth which could only be termed a fable outside of literature, and I thus cause surprise. But my supposed truth is no more extraordinary or unbelievable than those of the Greeks, which show Minerva coming armed out of the head of Jupiter.

Insofar as airplanes did not fill the sky, the fable of Icarus was only a supposed truth. Today, it is no longer a fable. And our inventors have accustomed us to greater prodigies than that which consists in delegating to men the function which women have of bearing children. I should say further that, these fables having been even more than realized, it is up to the poet to imagine new ones which inventors can in turn realize.

The new spirit requires that these prophetic ventures be accepted. It is why you will find traces of prophecy in most works conceived in the new spirit. The divine games of life and imagination give free rein to a totally new poetic activity.

It is that poetry and creation are one and the same; only that man can be called poet who invents, who creates insofar as a man can create. The poet is he who discovers new joys, even if they are hard to bear. One can be a poet in any field: it is enough that one be adventuresome and pursue any new discovery.

The richest domain being the imagination, the least known, whose extent is infinite, it is not astonishing that the name of poet has been particularly reserved for those who look for the new joys which mark out the enormous spaces of the imagination.

The least fact is for a poet the postulate, the point of departure for an unknown immensity where the fires of joy flame up in multiple meanings.

There is no need, in undertaking discovery, to choose with the reassuring support of any rules, even those decreed by taste, a quality classified as sublime. One can begin with an everyday event: a dropped handkerchief can be for the poet the lever with which to move an entire universe. It is well known how much an apple's fall meant to Newton when he saw it, and that scholar can thus be called a poet. That is why the poet today scorns no movement in nature, and his mind pursues discovery just as much in the most vast and evasive syntheses: crowds, nebulae, oceans, nations, as in apparently simple facts: a hand which searches a pocket, a match which lights by scratching, the cries of animals, the odor of gardens after rain, a flame which is born on the hearth. Poets are not simply men devoted to the beautiful. They are also and especially devoted to truth, in so far as the unknown can be penetrated, so much that the unexpected, the surprising, is one of the principal sources of poetry today. And who would dare say that, for those who are worthy of joy, what is new is not beautiful? Others will soon busy themselves about discrediting this sublime novelty, after which it can enter the domain of reason, but only within those limits in which the poets, the sole dispensers of the true and the beautiful, have advanced it.

The poet, by the very nature of his explorations, is isolated in the new world into which he enters the first, and the only consolation which is left to him is that, since men must live in the end by truths in spite of the falsehoods with which they pad them, the poet alone sustains the life whereby humanity finds these truths. This is why modern poets are above all singers of a constantly new truth. And their task is infinite; they have surprised you and will surprise you again. They are already imagining schemes more profound than those which created with Machiavellian astuteness the useful and frightful symbol of money.

Those who imagined the fable of Icarus, so marvellously realized today, will find others. They will carry you, living and awake, into a nocturnal world sealed with dreams. Into universes which tremble ineffably above our heads. Into those nearer and further universes which gravitate to the same point of infinity as what we carry within us. And more marvels than those which have been born since the birth of the most ancient among us, will make the contemporary inventions of which we are so proud seem pale and childish.

Poets will be charged finally with giving by means of lyric teleologies and arch-lyric alchemies a constantly purer meaning to the idea of divinity, which is so alive within us, which is perpetual renewal of ourselves, that eternal creation, that endless rebirth by which we live.

As far as we know, there are scarcely any poets today outside the French language.

All the other languages seem to keep silent so that the universe may hear the voices of the new French poets.

The entire world looks toward this light which alone illuminates the darkness which surrounds us.

Here, however, these voices which are being raised scarcely make themselves heard.

Modern poets, creators, inventors, prophets; they ask that what they say be examined in the light of the greatest good of the group to which they belong. They turn toward Plato and beg him, if he would banish them from the Republic, at least to hear them first.

France, the guardian of the whole secret of civilization, a secret only because of the imperfection of those who strive to divine it, has for this very reason become for the greater part of the world a seminary of poets and artists who daily increase the patrimony of civilization.

And through the truth and the joy they spread, they will make this civilization, if not adaptable to any nation whatever, at least supremely agreeable to all.

The French bring poetry to all people:

To Italy, where the example of French poetry has given inspiration to a superb young nationalist school of boldness and patriotism.

To England, where lyricism is insipid, and practically exhausted.

To Spain and especially in Catalonia, where the whole of an ardent young generation, which has already produced painters who are an honor to two nations, follows with attention the productions of our poets.

To Russia, where the imitation of French lyrics has at times given way to an even greater effort, as will astonish no one.

To Latin America, where the young poets write impassioned commentaries on their French predecessors.

To North America, to which in recognition of Edgar Poe and Walt Whitman, French missionaries are carrying during the war the fertile elements destined to nourish a new production of which we have as yet no idea, but which will doubtless not be inferior to those two great pioneers of poetry.

France is full of schools which protect and carry on the lyric spirit, groups in which boldness is taught; however, one remark must be made: poetry derives first of all from the people in whose language it is expressed.

The poetic schools, before throwing themselves into heroic adventures or distant apostleships, must mould, strengthen, clarify, enlarge, immortalize, and sing the greatness of the country which gave birth to them, of the country which has nourished and instructed them, so to speak, with what is most healthy and with what is purest and best in her blood and substance.

Has modern French poetry done for France all that it could?

Has it always been, in France, as active, as zealous as it has been elsewhere?

Contemporary literary history is enough to suggest these questions, and to answer them one would have to be able to calculate what national and promising tendencies the new spirit carries within it.

The new spirit is above all the enemy of estheticism, of formulae, and of cultism. It attacks no school whatever, for it does not wish to be a school, but rather one of the great currents of literature encompassing all schools since symbolism and naturalism. It fights for the reestablishment of the spirit of initiative, for the clear understanding of its time, and for the opening of new vistas on the exterior and interior universes which are not inferior to those which scientists of all categories discover ever day and from which they extract endless marvels.

Marvels impose on us the duty not to allow the poetic imagination and subtlety to lag behind that of workers who are improving the machine. Already, scientific language is out of tune with that of the poets. It is an intolerable state of affairs. Mathematicians have the right to say that their dreams, their preoccupations, often outdistance by a hundred cubits the crawling imaginations of poets. It is up to the poets to decide if they will not resolutely embrace the new spirit, outside of which only three doors remain open: that of pastiche, that of satire, and that of lamentation, however sublime it be.

Can poetry be forced to establish itself outside of what surrounds it, to ignore the magnificent exuberance of life which the activities of men are adding to nature and which allow the world to be mechanized in an incredible fashion?

The new spirit is of the very time in which we are living, a time rich in surprises. The poets wish to master prophecy, that spirited mare that has never been tamed.

And finally they want, one day, to mechanize poetry as the world has been mechanized. They want to be the first to provide a totally new lyricism for these new means of expression which are giving impetus to art—the phonograph and the cinema. They are still only at the stage of incunabula. But wait, the prodigies will speak for themselves and the new spirit which fills the universe with life will manifest itself formidably in literature, in the arts, and in everything that is known.

NOTE
1. From the French Poet Clement Marot (1495–1544).

Mircea Eliade

MYTH AND REALITY

THE "END OF THE WORLD" IN MODERN ART

Western societies have nothing comparable to the optimism shown by Communist eschatology and the primitive millennialisms. On the contrary, today there is an ever more intense fear of a catastrophic End of the World brought about by thermonuclear weapons. In the thought of the West this End will be total and final; it will not be followed by a new Creation of the World. We cannot here undertake a systematic analysis of the many and various expressions of atomic fear in the modern world. But other Western cultural phenomena seem to us significant for our investigation. Since the beginning of the century the plastic arts, as well as literature and music, have undergone such radical transformations that it has been possible to speak of a "destruction of the language of art." Beginning in painting, this destruction of language has spread to poetry, to the novel, and just recently, with Ionesco, to the theater. In some cases there is a real annihilation of the established artistic Universe. Looking at some recent canvases, we get the impression that the artist wished to make *tabula rasa* of the entire history of painting. There is more than a destruction, there is a reversion to Chaos, to a sort of primordial *massa confusa*. Yet at the same time, contemplating such works, we sense that the artist is searching for something that he has not yet expressed. He had to make a clean sweep of the ruins and trash accumulated by the preceding plastic revolutions; he had to reach a germinal mode of matter, so that he could begin the history of art over again from zero. Among many modern artists we sense that the "destruction of the plastic language" is only the first phase of a more complex process and that the re-creation of a new Universe must necessarily follow.

In modern art the nihilism and pessimism of the first revolutionaries and demolishers represent attitudes that are already outmoded. Today no great artist believes in the degeneration and imminent disappearance of his art. From this point of view the modern artists' attitude is like that of the "primitives"; they have contributed to the destruction of the World—that is, to the destruction of *their* World, their artistic Universe —in order to create another. But this cultural phenomenon is of the utmost importance, for it is primarily the artists who represent the genuine creative forces of a civilization or a society. Through their creation the artists anticipate what is to come—sometimes one or two generations later—in other sectors of social and cultural life.

It is significant that the destruction of artistic languages has coincided with the rise of psychoanalysis. Depth psychology has given currency to the interest in origins, an interest that is so typical of the man of the archaic societies. It would be intensely interesting to study the process of re-evaluation undergone by the myth of the End of the World in contemporary art. We should see that artists, far from being the neurotics they are often said to be, are, on the contrary, more healthy psychically than many modern men. They have understood that a true new beginning can come only after a real End. And, the first among moderns, the artists have set themselves to destroying *their* World in order to re-create an artistic Universe in which man can at once live and contemplate and dream. . . .

MYTHS OF THE ELITE

Less attention has been paid to what could be called the myths of the elite, especially those crystallized around artistic creation and its cultural and social repercussions. These myths, be it said, have succeeded in imposing themselves far beyond the closed corporation of the initiate, principally because of the inferiority complex that now afflicts both the public and official art circles. The aggressive incomprehension of the public, of critics, and of the official representatives of art toward a Rimbaud or a Van Gogh, the disastrous consequences—especially for collectors and museums—produced by indifference toward innovating movements, from impressionism to cubism and surrealism, have been hard lessons for the critics and the public as well as for art dealers, museum directors, and collectors. Today their only fear is not to be advanced enough and hence not to be in time to recognize genius in a work that is at first sight unintelligible. Perhaps never before in history has the artist been so certain that the more daring, iconoclastic, absurd, and inaccessible he is, the more he will be recognized, praised, spoiled, idolatrized. In some countries the result has even been an academicism in reverse, the academicism of the "avant-garde"—to such a point that any artistic experience that makes no concessions to this new conformism is in danger of being stifled or ignored.

The myth of the damned artist, which obsessed the nineteenth century, is outmoded today. Especially in the United States, but also in Western Europe, audacity and defiance have long since ceased to be harmful to an artist. On the contrary, he is asked to conform to his mythical image, that is, to be strange, irreducible, and to "produce something new." It is the absolute triumph of the permanent revolution in art. "Anything goes" is no longer an adequate formulation: now every novelty is considered a stroke of genius beforehand and put on the same plane as the innovations of a Van Gogh or a Picasso, even if the artist only mutilates a poster or signs a sardine tin.

The significance of this cultural phenomenon is the greater because, perhaps for the first time in the history of art, there is no longer any tension between artists, critics, collectors, and the public. They are all in agreement always, and long before a new work is created or an unknown artist discovered. The one thing that matters is not to have to say later that one did not understand the importance of a new artistic experience.

We cannot, of course, here analyze the mythology of the modern elites in all its manifestations. We shall confine ourselves to a few remarks. First of all, we may note the redeeming function of "difficulty," especially as found in works of modern art. If the elite revel in *Finnegans Wake,* or in atonal music, or in *tachisme,* it is also because such works represent closed worlds, hermetic universes that cannot be entered except by overcoming immense difficulties, like the initiatory ordeals of the archaic and traditional societies. On the one hand, one has the experience of an "initiation," an experience that has almost vanished from the modern World; on the other hand, one proclaims to the "others" (i.e., the "mass") that one belongs to a select minority—not, as once, to an aristocracy (for modern elites lean toward the left), but to a gnosis that has the advantage of being at once spiritual and secular in that it opposes both official values and the traditional churches. Through their cult of extravagant originality, of difficulty, of incomprehensibility, the elites advertise their escape from the banal universe of their parents while at the same time revolting against certain contemporary philosophies of despair.

Basically, being fascinated by the difficulty, not to say the incomprehensibility, of works of art expresses the desire to discover a new, secret, hitherto unknown meaning for the World and human life. One dreams of being "initiated" and thereby made able to understand the occult meaning of all these destructions of artistic languages, these "original" experiences that, at first sight, no longer seem to have anything in common with art. The torn posters, the empty, scorched, slashed canvases, the "art objects" that explode on opening day, the improvised plays in which the actors' speeches are drawn by lot—*all this must have a meaning,* just as certain incomprehensible words in *Finnegans Wake* come to be fraught with many meanings and values and with a strange beauty for the initiate when he discovers that they are derived from modern Greek or Swahili words disfigured by aberrant consonants, and enriched by secret allusions to possible puns when they are spoken aloud and very fast.

To be sure, all the genuine revolutionary experiences of modern art reflect certain aspects of the contemporary spiritual crisis or at least of the crisis in artistic knowledge and creation. But what concerns our investigation is the fact that the "elites" find in the extravagance and unintelligibility of modern works the opportunity for an initiatory gnosis. It is a "new World" being built up from ruins and enigmas, an almost private World, which one would like to keep for oneself and a very few initiates. But the prestige of difficulty and incomprehensibility is such that, very soon, the "public" too is conquered and proclaims its total acceptance of the elite's discoveries.

The destruction of artistic languages was accomplished by cubism, dadaism and surrealism, by atonality and "musique concrète," by James Joyce, Becket, and Ionesco. Only the epigones are left furiously demolishing what has already been demolished. For, as we pointed out in an earlier chapter, the genuine creators are not willing to take their stand on ruins. Everything leads us to believe that the reduction of "artistic Universes" to the primordial state of *materia prima* is only a phase in a more complex process; just as in the cyclic conceptions of the archaic and traditional societies "Chaos," the regression of all forms to the indistinction of the *materia prima,* is followed by a new Creation, which can be homologized with a cosmogony.

We cannot here develop and refine these few observations, for the crisis in the modern arts is only of subsidiary concern to our study. Yet we must dwell for a moment on the situation and the role of literature, especially of epic literature, for it is not unrelated to mythology and mythical behavior. We do not intend to discuss the "origins" of epic literature; it is well known that, like the other literary genres, the epic and the novel continue mythological narrative, though on a different plane and in pursuit of different ends. In both cases it is a question of telling a significant story, of relating a series of dramatic events that took place in a more or less fabulous past. There is no need to go over the long and complex process that transformed some particular "mythological material" into the "subject" of an epic. What we consider important is the fact that in modern societies the prose narrative, especially the novel, has taken the place of the recitation of myths in traditional and popular societies. More than this—it is possible to dissect out the "mythical" structure of certain modern novels, in other words, to show the literary survival of great mythological themes and characters. (This is true especially in regard to the initiatory theme, the theme of the ordeals of the Hero-Redeemer and his battles with monsters, the mythologies of Woman and of Wealth.) From this point of view we could say, then, that the modern passion for the novel expresses the desire to hear the greatest possible number of "mythological stories" desacralized or simply camouflaged under "profane" forms.

No less significant is the fact that people feel the need to read "histories" and narratives that could be called paradigmatic, since they proceed in accordance with a traditional model. Whatever the gravity of the present crisis of the novel, it is none the less true that the need to find one's way into "foreign" Universes and to follow the complications of a "story" seems to be consubstantial with the human condition and hence irreducible. It is a difficult need to define, being at once desire to communicate with "others," with "strangers," and share in their dramas and hopes, and at the same time the need to know what *can have taken place*. It is hard to conceive of a human being who is not fascinated by "narrative," that is, by a recounting of significant events, by what has happened to men endowed with the "twofold reality" of literary characters (for, on the one hand, they reflect the historical and psychological reality of members of a modern society and, on the other, they possess all the magical power of an imaginary creation).

But it is especially the "escape from Time" brought about by reading —most effectively by novel reading—that connects the function of literature with that of mythologies. To be sure, the time that one "lives" when reading a novel is not the time that a member of a traditional society recovers when he listens to a myth. But in both cases alike, one "escapes" from historical and personal time and is submerged in a time that is fabulous and trans-historical. The reader is confronted with a strange, imaginary time, whose rhythms vary indefinitely, for each narrative has its own time that is peculiar to it and to it alone. The novel does not have access to the primordial time of myths, but in so far as he tells a credible story, the novelist employs a time that is *seemingly historical* yet is condensed or prolonged, a time, then, that has at its command all the freedoms of imaginary worlds.

More strongly than any of the other arts, we feel in literature a revolt against historical time, the desire to attain to other temporal rhythms than that in which we are condemned to live and work. One wonders whether the day will come when this desire to transcend one's own time —personal, historical time—and be submerged in a "strange" time, whether ecstatic or imaginary, will be completely rooted out. As long as it persists, we can say that modern man preserves at least some residues of "mythological behavior." Traces of such a mythological behavior can also be deciphered in the desire to rediscover the intensity with which one experienced or knew something *for the first time;* and also in the desire to recover the distant past, the blissful period of the "beginnings."

Here too, as we might expect, there is always the struggle against Time, the hope to be freed from the weight of "dead Time," of the Time that crushes and kills.

Alfred Jarry

UBU ROI

ACT I

SCENE 1

Père Ubu, Mère Ubu.

PÈRE UBU   Shittr![1]

MÈRE UBU   Oh! That's a nice way to talk. Père Ubu, ye are a bloody great oaf.

PÈRE UBU   Why don't I bash your brains in, Mère Ubu?

MÈRE UBU   It's not me you ought to do in, Père Ubu, it's someone else.

PÈRE UBU   By my green candle, I don't understand.

MÈRE UBU   Well, Père Ubu, are ye content with your lot?

PÈRE UBU   By my green candle, shittr, Madame, certainly I am content. I could be content with less; I'm a captain of dragoons, I'm King Venceslas' confidential officer, I've been decorated with the Order of Red Eagle of Poland, I'm ex-King of Aragon; what more do you want?

MÈRE UBU   What! When you've been King of Aragon, you're satisfied to lead to the Reviews a paltry fifty flunkeys armed with nothing but cabbage-cutters—when you could make the crown of Poland succeed the crown of Aragon on your noddle?

PÈRE UBU   Mm? Mère Ubu, I don't understand a word of what you're saying.

MÈRE UBU   How stupid you are!

PÈRE UBU   By my green candle, King Venceslas is still very much alive; and even supposing he dies, hasn't he got hordes of children?

MÈRE UBU   Who's stopping you from slaughtering the whole family and putting yourself in their place?

PÈRE UBU   Oh! Mère Ubu, you insult me, and you'll find yourself in the stewpan in a minute.

MÈRE UBU   Huh! you poor fish, if I found myself in the stewpan, who'd mend the seats of your breeches?

PÈRE UBU   Well, what of it? Isn't my arse the same as anyone else's?

MÈRE UBU   If I were you, what I'd want to do with my arse would be to install it on a throne. You could increase your fortune indefinitely, have sausages whenever you liked, and ride through the streets in a carriage.

PÈRE UBU   If I were King, I'd have a big headpiece made like the one I had in Aragon which those louts of Spaniards stole from me in such a shameless manner.

MÈRE UBU   And you could get yourself an umbrella and a great big cloak that would come right down to your feet.

PÈRE UBU   Ah! I yield to temptation. Clod of a shittr, shittr of a clod, if ever I meet him on a dark night he'll go through a bad quarter of an hour.

MÈRE UBU   Oh good, Père Ubu, now you're a real man.

PÈRE UBU   Oh no, though! I, a captain of dragoons, slay the king of Poland! I'd rather die.

MÈRE UBU   (*aside*) Oh shittr! (*aloud*) Then are you going to stay as poor as a rat, Père Ubu?

PÈRE UBU   Gadzookers, by my green candle, I prefer to be as poor as a skinny, honest rat than as rich as a vicious, fat cat.

MÈRE UBU   And the cape? and the umbrella? and the great big cloak?

PÈRE UBU   And what of them, Mère Ubu?

(*He goes off banging the door.*)

MÈRE UBU   Fart, shittr, it's hard to get him moving, but fart, shittr, I reckon I've shaken him all the same. Thanks to God and myself, in a week, maybe, I'll be Queen of Poland.

SCENE 2

The scene represents a room in Père Ubu's house, where a magnificent meal is prepared.

Père Ubu, Mère Ubu

MÈRE UBU   Huh! our guests are extremely late.

PÈRE UBU   Yes, by my green candle. I'm starving. Mère Ubu, you're exceeding ugly today. Is it because we have visitors?

MÈRE UBU   (*shrugging her shoulders*) shittr!

PÈRE UBU (*seizing a roast chicken*)   Look here, I'm hungry, I'm going to take a bite of this bird. It's a chicken I believe. It's not bad.

MÈRE UBU   What are you doing, you ass? What will our guests have to eat?

PÈRE UBU   Oh, there'll be enough for them. I won't touch anything else. Mère Ubu, go over to the window and see if our guests are coming.

MÈRE UBU (*going over*)   I can't see anything.

(*In the meantime Père Ubu pinches a fillet of veal.*)

MÈRE UBU   Ah! here comes Captain Bordure with his partisans. But what are you eating, Père Ubu?

PÈRE UBU   Nothing, a bit of veal.

MÈRE UBU   Oh the veal, the veal, vile creature! He ate the veal! Help!

PÈRE UBU   By my green candle, I'll tear your eyes out.

SCENE 3

Père Ubu, Mère Ubu, Captain Bordure and his partisans.

MÈRE UBU   Good day, gentlemen, we were awaiting you impatiently. Sit down.

CAPT. BORDURE   Good day, Madame. But where on earth is Père Ubu?

PÈRE UBU   Here I am! here I am! Damn it, by my green candle, I'm fat enough, I should have thought.

CAPT. BORDURE   Good day, Père Ubu. Sit down, my men.

(*They all sit down.*)

PÈRE UBU   Phew! a bit more and I'd have stove in my chair.

CAPT. BORDURE   Well, Mère Ubu, what are you giving us today that's good?

MÈRE UBU   Here's the menu.

PÈRE UBU   Oh, I'm interested in that.

MÈRE UBU   Soupe polonaise, rastron ribs, veal, chicken, dog pie, turkeys' rumps, charlotte russe.

PÈRE UBU   Hey, that's enough, I should think. Is there any more?

MÈRE UBU (*continuing*)   Ice pudding, salad, fruit, dessert, boiled beef, jerusalem artichokes, cauliflower à la shittr.

PÈRE UBU   Huh! do you think I'm the Emperor of Orient that you spend such a lot?

MÈRE UBU   Don't listen to him, he's an imbecile.

PÈRE UBU   Ah! I'll sharpen my teeth on your calves.

MÈRE UBU   Have your dinner instead, Père Ubu. Here's some polonaise.

PÈRE UBU   Hell, it's awful.

CAPT. BORDURE   It's certainly not very nice.

MÈRE UBU   Bunch of crooks, what do you want, then?

PÈRE UBU (*striking his forehead*)   Oh, I've got an idea. I'll be back in a minute.

(*He goes off.*)

MÈRE UBU   Gentlemen, let's try some veal.

CAPT. BORDURE   It's very good, I've finished.

MÈRE UBU   Now for the rumps.

CAPT. BORDURE   Exquisite, exquisite! Long live Mère Ubu.

ALL   Long live Mère Ubu.

PÈRE UBU (*coming back*)   And you'll soon be saying long live Père Ubu.
(*He has a lavatory brush in his hand and throws it on to the festive board.*)

MÈRE UBU   Blockhead, what are you doing?

PÈRE UBU   Taste it.

(*Several taste it and are poisoned.*)

PÈRE UBU   Mère Ubu, pass me the rastron cutlets so that I can serve them.

MÈRE UBU   Here you are.

PÈRE UBU   Outside, everyone! Captain Bordure, I want to talk to you.

THE OTHERS   Hey, we haven't had anything to eat.

PÈRE UBU   What d'you mean, you haven't had anything to eat? Out you go, everybody. Stay here, Bordure.

(*No one budges.*)

PÈRE UBU   Haven't you gone yet? By my green candle, I'll do you in with rastron ribs.

(*He begins to throw them.*)

ALL   Oo! Ouch! Help! Defend yourselves! Murder! I'm dead!

PÈRE UBU   Shittr, shittr, shittr! Outside! I'm cleverer than I thought!

ALL   Every man for himself! Lousy Père Ubu! traitor and mean skunk!

PÈRE UBU   Ah! They've gone. I can breathe, but I've had a rotten dinner. Come on, Bordure.

SCENE 4

Mère Ubu, Père Ubu, Captain Bordure.

PÈRE UBU   Well, Captain, did you have a good dinner?

CAPT. BORDURE   Very good, Monsieur, except for the shittr.

PÈRE UBU   Huh! The shittr wasn't bad.

MÈRE UBU   *Chacun à son gout.*

PÈRE UBU   Captain Bordure, I've decided to make you Duke of Lithuania.

CAPT. BORDURE   What? I thought you were very badly off, Père Ubu.

PÈRE UBU   In a few days, if you choose, I shall reign over Poland.

CAPT. BORDURE   Are you going to kill Venceslas?

PÈRE UBU   This fellow's no fool, he's guessed.

CAPT. BORDURE   If it's a question of killing Venceslas, I'm on. I'm his mortal enemy, and I'll answer for my men.

PÈRE UBU (*throwing himself on him and kissing him*)   Oh, oh, I'm very fond of you, Bordure.

CAPT. BORDURE   Pooh, you stink, Père Ubu. Don't you ever wash?

PÈRE UBU   Sometimes.

MÈRE UBU   Never!

PÈRE UBU   I'll tread on your toes.

MÈRE UBU   Big shittr!

PÈRE UBU   Well, Bordure, I've done with you. But, by my green candle, I swear by Mère Ubu to make you Duke of Lithuania.

MÈRE UBU   But . . .

PÈRE UBU   Be quiet, my sweet child.

   (*They go out.*)

SCENE 5

Père Ubu, Mère Ubu, a messenger.

PÈRE UBU   Monsieur, what do you want? Go away, you bore me.

MESSENGER   Monsieur, you are summoned to the King's presence.

PÈRE UBU   Oh shittr! gadzookers! by my green candle, I am discovered. I'll lose my head! Alas! Alack!

MÈRE UBU   What a feeble man! And there's not much time.

PÈRE UBU   Ah! I've got an idea. I'll say that it was Mère Ubu and Bordure.

MÈRE UBU   Oh! Fat P.U., if you do that . . .

PÈRE UBU   Now! I'll go this minute.

   (*He goes out.*)

MÈRE UBU (*running after him*)   Hi! Père Ubu, Père Ubu, I'll give you some grub.

   (*She goes out.*)

PÈRE UBU (*off*)   Oh! Shittr! You're a grub yourself.

SCENE 6

King Venceslas, surrounded by his officers; Bordure; the king's sons: Boleslas, Ladislas, Bougrelas; then Père Ubu.

PÈRE UBU (*entering*)   Oh! you know, it wasn't me, it was Mère Ubu and Bordure.

THE KING   What's the matter, Père Ubu?

CAPT. BORDURE   He's had too much to drink.

THE KING   Like me this morning.

PÈRE UBU   Yes, I'm boozed, it's because I've drunk too much French wine.

THE KING   Père Ubu, I want to recognise your numerous services as

Captain of Dragoons, and I am making you Count of Sandomir as from today.

PÈRE UBU Oh Monsieur Venceslas, I don't know how to thank you.

THE KING Don't thank me, Père Ubu, and be present tomorrow morning at the great Review.

PÈRE UBU I'll be there, but be good enough to accept this little toy whistle.

(*He presents the King with a toy whistle.*)

THE KING What do you expect me to do with a toy whistle at my age? I'll give it to Bougrelas.

BOUGRELAS What an ass that Père Ubu is.

PÈRE UBU Now I'll bugger off.

(*As he turns round he falls down.*)

Oh! Ow! Help! By my green candle, I've ruptured my intestine and busted my dungzine.

THE KING (*picking him up*) Père Ubu, hast hurt thyself?

PÈRE UBU Yes indeed I have, and I shall certainly pass away. What will happen to Mère Ubu?

THE KING We shall provide for her.

PÈRE UBU Your kindness knows no bounds. (*He goes out*) Yes but, King Venceslas, you won't be any the less slaughtered, you know.

SCENE 7

UBU'S HOUSE

Giron, Pile, Cotice, Père Ubu, Mère Ubu, Conspirators, Soldiers, Capt. Bordure.

PÈRE UBU Well, my good friends, it's high time to decide on our plans for the conspiracy. Let's hear everybody's views. First of all I'll tell you mine, if you'll allow me.

CAPT. BORDURE Go ahead, Père Ubu.

PÈRE UBU Well then, my friends, in my opinion we should simply poison the King by sticking some arsenic in his lunch. When he starts stuffing himself he'll fall down dead, and then I'll be King.

ALL Pooh, what a lousy beast.

PÈRE UBU So what? Doesn't that suit you? Then let Bordure say what he thinks.

CAPT. BORDURE I think we should give him a terrific blow with a sword and split him open from head to middle.

ALL Yes, that's noble and gallant.

PÈRE UBU And what if he starts kicking you? I remember now that when there's a Review on he wears iron shoes that hurt very badly. If I had any sense I'd go off and denounce you to get myself out of this dirty business, and I reckon he'd give me some cash, as well.

MÈRE UBU Oh the traitor, the coward, the villain and mean skunk.

ALL Down with Père Ubu!

PÈRE UBU Hey, gentlemen, keep quiet if you don't want to be put in my pocket. Anyway, I agree to expose myself for you. So you, Bordure, make yourself responsible for splitting open the King.

CAPT. BORDURE Wouldn't it be better if we all threw ourselves on him at once, bawling and shouting? We might be able to get the troops on our side that way.

PÈRE UBU Well, this is what we'll do, then. I'll try and tread on his toes, he'll kick out at me, I'll say SHITTR to him and at this signal you'll throw yourselves on him.

MÈRE UBU Yes, and as soon as he's dead you'll take his sceptre and crown.

CAPT. BORDURE And I'll go off with my men in pursuit of the royal family.

PÈRE UBU Yes, and I specially recommend young Bougrelas to you.
(*They go out.*)

PÈRE UBU (*running after them and making them come back*) Gentlemen, we have forgotten an indispensable ceremony; we must swear to fight gallantly.

CAPT. BORDURE But how can we? We haven't got a priest.

PÈRE UBU Mère Ubu will stand in for one.

ALL All right, so be it!

PÈRE UBU Then you swear to kill the King properly?

ALL Yes, we swear. Long live Père Ubu!

NOTE

1. *"Merde!"* in the original.

Samuel Beckett

WAITING FOR GODOT

VLADIMIR: *(to Pozzo).* Tell him to think.

POZZO: Give him his hat.

VLADIMIR: His hat?

POZZO: He can't think without his hat.

VLADIMIR: *(to Estragon).* Give him his hat.

ESTRAGON: Me! After what he did to me! Never!

VLADIMIR: I'll give it to him.

He does not move.

ESTRAGON: *(to Pozzo).* Tell him to go and fetch it.

POZZO: It's better to give it to him.

VLADIMIR: I'll give it to him.

He picks up the hat and tenders it at arm's length to Lucky, who does not move.

POZZO: You must put it on his head.

ESTRAGON: *(to Pozzo).* Tell him to take it.

POZZO: It's better to put it on his head.

VLADIMIR: I'll put it on his head.

He goes round behind Lucky, approaches him cautiously, puts the hat on his head and recoils smartly. Lucky does not move. Silence.

ESTRAGON: What's he waiting for?

POZZO: Stand back! *(Vladimir and Estragon move away from Lucky. Pozzo jerks the rope. Lucky looks at Pozzo.)* Think, pig! *(Pause. Lucky begins to dance.)* Stop! *(Lucky stops.)* Forward! *(Lucky advances.)* Stop! *(Lucky stops.)* Think! Silence.*

LUCKY: On the other hand with regard to—

POZZO: Stop! *(Lucky stops.)* Back! *(Lucky moves back.)* Stop! *(Lucky stops.)* Turn! *(Lucky turns towards auditorium.)* Think!

During Lucky's tirade the others react as follows.

1) Vladimir and Estragon all attention, Pozzo dejected and disgusted.

2) Vladimir and Estragon begin to protest, Pozzo's sufferings increase.

3) Vladimir and Estragon attentive again, Pozzo more and more agitated and groaning.
4) Vladimir and Estragon protest violently. Pozzo jumps up, pulls on the rope. General outcry. Lucky pulls on the rope, staggers, shouts his text. All three throw themselves on Lucky who struggles and shouts his text.

LUCKY: Given the existence as uttered forth in the public works of Puncher and Wattmann of a personal God quaquaquaqua with white beard quaquaquaqua outside time without extension who from the heights of divine apathia divine athambia divine aphasia loves us dearly with some exceptions for reasons unknown but time will tell and suffers like the divine Miranda with those who for reasons unknown but time will tell are plunged in torment plunged in fire whose fire flames if that continues and who can doubt it will fire the firmament that is to say blast hell to heaven so blue still and calm so calm with a calm which even though intermittent is better than nothing but not so fast and considering what is more that as a result of the labors left unfinished crowned by the Acacacacademy of Anthropopopometry of Essy-in-Possy of Testew and Cunard it is established beyond all doubt all other doubt than that which clings to the labors of men that as a result of the labors unfinished of Testew and Cunard it is established as hereinafter but not so fast for reasons unknown that as a result of the public works of Puncher and Wattmann it is established beyond all doubt that in view of the labors of Fartov and Belcher left unfinished for reasons unknown of Testew and Cunard left unfinished it is established what many deny that man in Possy of Testew and Cunard that man in Essy that man in short that man in brief in spite of the strides of alimentation and defecation wastes and pines wastes and pines and concurrently simultaneously what is more for reasons unknown in spite of the strides of physical culture the practice of sports such as tennis football running cycling swimming flying floating riding gliding conating camogie skating tennis of

all kinds dying flying sports of all sorts autumn
summer winter winter tennis of all kinds hockey of
all sorts penicilline and succedanea in a word I
resume flying gliding golf over nine and eighteen
holes tennis of all sorts in a word for reasons
unknown in Feckham Peckham Fulham Clapham
namely concurrently simultaneously what is more
for reasons unknown but time will tell fades away
I resume Fulham Clapham in a word the dead
loss per head since the death of Bishop Berkeley
being to the tune of one inch four ounce per head
approximately by and large more or less to the
nearest decimal good measure round figures stark
naked in the stockinged feet in Connemara in a
word for reasons unknown no matter what matter
the facts are there and considering what is more
much more grave that in the light of the labors
lost of Steinweg and Peterman it appears what is
more much more grave that in the light the light
the light of the labors lost of Steinweg and
Peterman that in the plains in the mountains by
the seas by the rivers running water running fire
the air is the same and then the earth namely the
air and then the earth in the great cold the great
dark the air and the earth abode of stones in the
great cold alas alas in the year of their Lord six
hundred and something the air the earth the sea
the earth abode of stones in the great deeps the
great cold on sea on land and in the air I resume
for reasons unknown in spite of the tennis the
facts are there but time will tell I resume alas
alas on on in short in fine on on abode of stones
who can doubt it I resume but not so fast I
resume the skull fading fading fading and
concurrently simultaneously what is more for
reasons unknown in spite of the tennis on on the
beard the flames the tears the stones so blue so
calm alas alas on on the skull the skull the skull
the skull in Connemara in spite of the tennis the
labors abandoned left unfinished graver still
abode of stones in a word I resume alas alas
abandoned unfinished the skull the skull in
Connemara in spite of the tennis the skull alas the

stones Cunard (*mêlée, final vociferations*) tennis
. . . the stones . . . so calm . . . Cunard . . .
unfinished . . .

POZZO: His hat!

*Vladimir seizes Lucky's hat. Silence of Lucky. He falls.
Silence. Panting of the victors.*

ESTRAGON: Avenged!

Vladimir examines the hat, peers inside it.

POZZO: Give me that! (*He snatches the hat from Vladimir, throws
it on the ground, tramples on it.*) There's an end to his
thinking!

Eugène Ionesco

THE BALD SOPRANO

MR. SMITH: Well, we're sorry to see you go.

MRS. SMITH: You have been very entertaining.

MRS. MARTIN: Thanks to you, we have passed a truly Cartesian quarter of an hour.

FIRE CHIEF [*moving towards the door, then stopping*]: Speaking of that—the bald soprano? [*General silence, embarrassment.*]

MRS. SMITH: She always wears her hair in the same style.

FIRE CHIEF: Ah! Then goodbye, ladies and gentlemen.

MR. MARTIN: Good luck, and a good fire!

FIRE CHIEF: Let's hope so. For everybody.

[*Fire Chief exits. All accompany him to the door and then return to their seats.*]

MRS. MARTIN: I can buy a pocketknife for my brother, but you can't buy Ireland for your grandfather.

MR. SMITH: One walks on his feet, but one heats with electricity or coal.

MR. MARTIN: He who sells an ox today, will have an egg tomorrow.

MRS. SMITH: In real life, one must look out of the window.

MRS. MARTIN: One can sit down on a chair, when the chair doesn't have any.

MR. SMITH: One must always think of everything.

MR. MARTIN: The ceiling is above, the floor is below.

MRS. SMITH: When I say yes, it's only a manner of speaking.

MRS. MARTIN: To each his own.

MR. SMITH: Take a circle, caress it, and it will turn vicious.

MRS. SMITH: A schoolmaster teaches his pupils to read, but the cat suckles her young when they are small.

MRS. MARTIN: Nevertheless, it was the cow that gave us tails.

MR. SMITH: When I'm in the country, I love the solitude and the quiet.

MR. MARTIN: You are not old enough yet for that.

MRS. SMITH: Benjamin Franklin was right; you are more nervous than he.

MRS. MARTIN: What are the seven days of the week?

MR. SMITH: Monday, Tuesday, Wednesday, Thursday, Friday, Saturday, Sunday.[1]

MR. MARTIN: Edward is a clerck; his sister Nancy is a typist, and his brother William a shop-assistant.[2]

MRS. SMITH: An odd family!

MRS. MARTIN: I prefer a bird in the bush to a sparrow in a barrow.

MR. SMITH: Rather a steak in a chalet than gristle in a castle.

MR. MARTIN: An Englishman's home is truly his castle.

MRS. SMITH: I don't know enough Spanish to make myself understood.

MRS. MARTIN: I'll give you my mother-in-law's slippers if you'll give me your husband's coffin.

MR. SMITH. I'm looking for a monophysite priest to marry to our maid.

MR. MARTIN: Bread is a staff, whereas bread is also a staff, and an oak springs from an oak every morning at dawn.

MRS. SMITH: My uncle lives in the country, but that's none of the midwife's business.

MR. MARTIN: Paper is for writing, the cat's for the rat. Cheese is for scratching.

MRS. SMITH: The car goes very fast, but the cook beats batter better.

MR. SMITH: Don't be turkeys; rather kiss the conspirator.

MR. MARTIN: Charity begins at home.[3]

MRS. SMITH: I'm waiting for the aqueduct to come and see me at my windmill.

MR. MARTIN: One can prove that social progress is definitely better with sugar.

MR. SMITH: To hell with polishing!

[*Following this last speech of Mr. Smith's, the others are silent for a moment, stupefied. We sense that there is a certain nervous irritation. The strokes of the clock are more nervous too. The speeches which follow must be said, at first, in a glacial, hostile tone. The hostility and the nervousness increase. At the end of this scene, the four characters must be standing very close to each other, screaming their speeches, raising their fists, ready to throw themselves upon each other.*]

MR. MARTIN: One doesn't polish spectacles with black wax.

MRS. SMITH: Yes, but with money one can buy anything.

MR. MARTIN: I'd rather kill a rabbit than sing in the garden.

MR. SMITH: Cockatoos, cockatoos, cockatoos, cockatoos, cockatoos, cockatoos, cockatoos, cockatoos, cockatoos, cockatoos.

MRS. SMITH: Such caca, such caca, such caca, such caca, such caca, such caca, such caca, such caca, such caca.

MR. MARTIN: Such cascades of cacas, such cascades of cacas, such cascades of cacas, such cascades of cacas, such cascades of cacas, such cascades of cacas, such cascades of cacas, such cascades of cacas.

MR. SMITH: Dogs have fleas, dogs have fleas.

MRS. MARTIN: Cactus, coccyx! crocus! cockaded! cockroach!

MRS. SMITH: Incasker, you incask us.

MR. MARTIN: I'd rather lay an egg in a box than go and steal an ox.

MRS. MARTIN [*opening her mouth very wide*]: Ah! oh! ah! oh! Let me gnash my teeth.

MR. SMITH: Crocodile!

MR. MARTIN: Let's go and slap Ulysses.

MR. SMITH: I'm going to live in my cabana among my cacao trees.

MRS. MARTIN: Cacao trees on cacao farms don't bear coconuts, they yield cocoa! Cacao trees on cacao farms don't bear coconuts, they yield cocoa! Cacao trees on cacao farms don't bear coconuts, they yield cocoa.

MRS. SMITH: Mice have lice, lice haven't mice.

MRS. MARTIN: Don't ruche my brooch!

MR. MARTIN: Don't smooch the brooch!

MR. SMITH: Groom the goose, don't goose the groom.

MRS. MARTIN: The goose grooms.

MRS. SMITH: Groom your tooth.

MR. MARTIN: Groom the bridegroom, groom the bridegroom.

MR. SMITH: Seducer seduced!

MRS. MARTIN: Scaramouche!

MRS. SMITH: Sainte-Nitouche!

MR. MARTIN: Go take a douche.

MR. SMITH: I've been goosed.

MRS. MARTIN: Sainte-Nitouche stoops to my cartouche.

MRS. SMITH: "Who'd stoop to blame? . . . and I never choose to stoop."

MR. MARTIN: Robert!

MR. SMITH: Browning!

MRS. MARTIN, MR. SMITH: Rudyard.

MRS. SMITH, MR. MARTIN: Kipling.

MRS. MARTIN, MR. SMITH: Robert Kipling!

MRS. SMITH, MR. MARTIN: Rudyard Browning.*

MRS. MARTIN: Silly gobblegobblers, silly gobblegobblers.

MR. MARTIN: Marietta, spot the pot!

MRS. SMITH: Krishnamurti, Krishnamurti, Krishnamurti!

* Translator's note: in the French text these speeches read as follows:
MME SMITH.—N'y touchez pas, elle est brisée.
M. MARTIN.—Sully!
M. SMITH.—Prudhomme!
MME MARTIN, M. SMITH.—François.
MME SMITH, M. MARTIN.—Coppée.
MME MARTIN, M. SMITH.—Copée Sully!
MME SMITH, M. MARTIN.—Prudhomme François.

MR. SMITH: The pope elopes! The pope's got no horoscope. The horoscope's bespoke.

MRS. MARTIN: Bazaar, Balzac, bazooka!

MR. MARTIN: Bizarre, beaux-arts, brassieres!

MR. SMITH: A, e, i, o, u, a, e, i, o, u, a, e, i, o, u, i!

MRS. MARTIN: B, c, d, f, g, l, m, n, p, r, s, t, v, w, x, z!

MR. MARTIN: From sage to stooge, from stage to serge!

MRS. SMITH [*imitating a train*]: Choo, choo, choo, choo, choo, choo, choo, choo, choo, choo, choo!

MR. SMITH: It's!

MRS. MARTIN: Not!

MR. MARTIN: That!

MRS. SMITH: Way!

MR. SMITH: It's!

MRS. MARTIN: O!

MR. MARTIN: Ver!

MRS. SMITH: Here!

[*All together, completely infuriated, screaming in each others' ears. The light is extinguished. In the darkness we hear, in an increasingly rapid rhythm:*]

ALL TOGETHER: It's not that way, it's over here; it's not that way, it's over here, it's not that way, it's over here, it's not that way, it's over here!⁴

[*The words cease abruptly. Again, the lights come on. Mr. and Mrs. Martin are seated like the Smiths at the beginning of the play. The play begins again with the Martins, who say exactly the same lines as the Smiths in the first scene, while the curtain softly falls.*]

NOTES

1. In English in the original.—Translator's note.
2. *Ibid.*
3. *Ibid.*
4. When produced some of the speeches in this last scene were cut or shuffled. Moreover, the final beginning again, if one can call it that, still involved the Smiths, since the author did not have the inspired idea of substituting the Martins for the Smiths until after the hundredth performance.

T. S. Eliot

THE CLASSICS AND THE MAN OF LETTERS

Not very long ago, an eminent author, in the course of expressing his views about the future of education after this war, went a little out of his way to declare that in the new order there would still be a place for Greek. He qualified this concession, however, by explaining that the study of Greek was a field of scholarship of equal dignity with Egyptology, and several other specialized studies which he named, and that the opportunity to pursue these studies should, in any liberal society, be provided for the few who were particularly drawn to them. I read this in one of the periodicals which are found in the waiting-rooms of certain experts in applied science; and having neglected to make a note of the passage before being summoned to my professional appointment, I cannot quote chapter and verse, and therefore withhold the name of the author. But this statement, made without irony and wholly in a spirit of enlightened generosity, started the train of thought which I propose to continue here. I am grateful to the writer for having suggested to my mind the only possible role in which I can present myself on this occasion. In my earlier years I obtained, partly by subtlety, partly by effrontery, and partly by accident, a reputation amongst the credulous for learning and scholarship, of which (having no further use for it) I have since tried to disembarrass myself. Better to confess one's weaknesses, when they are certain to be revealed sooner or later, than to leave them to be exposed by posterity: though it is, I have discovered, easier in our times to acquire an undeserved reputation for learning than to get rid of it: but that is neither here nor there. My point is that if I made those claims for the classics which can only be supported by the erudition of the scholar, or those which can only be pleaded by what we now call the education*ist*, I might jeopardize the cause: for there are far better scholars than I, who attach less importance to the study of Latin and Greek than I do, and there are teachers who can demonstrate the impracticability of the studies which I should like to promote. But if I present the defence of the classics merely from the point of view of the man of letters, I am on safer ground: and I think you will agree that the claim to be a man of letters is, after all, a modest pretension. I must, however, begin by explaining why I have used this rather indefinite term, and what I mean by it.

If I were more specific, and spoke of 'the poet', 'the novelist', 'the dramatist', or 'the critic', I should suggest to your minds a number of particular considerations which would distract your attention from the view of literature as a whole which I wish to keep before us in the present context. Take, for instance, the term 'poet' and the objections which it would immediately evoke. We are commonly inclined to assume that the creation of literature, and poetry especially, depends simply upon the unpredictable appearance from time to time of writers of genius; that genius cannot be brought into the world at will, that when it does appear it is likely to break every rule, that no system of education can foster it, and no system of education can stifle it. If we look at literature as merely a succession of great writers, instead of looking at the literature of one European language as something which forms a significant whole in itself, and a significant part in the literature of Europe, this is the view we are likely to take. Taking this view, we look at each great writer by himself; and looking at him by himself, we are unlikely to believe that he would have been a greater writer, or an inferior writer, if he had had a different kind of education. The defects of a great writer's background are inextricably confused with its advantages; just as the shortcomings of his character are indissolubly associated with his shining virtues, and his material difficulties with his success. Can we regret, for instance, that François Villon did not choose to mix with more respectable society, or that Robert Burns did not have the same schooling as Dr. Johnson? The life of a man of genius, viewed in relation to his writing, comes to take a pattern of inevitability, and even his disabilities will seem to have stood him in good stead.

This way of looking at a great poet or novelist or dramatist, is half of the truth: it is what we find when we look at one writer after another, without balancing this point of view by the imaginative grasp of a national literature as a whole. I wanted to make it clear that I do not pretend that a classical education is essential for the writer of genius: and unless I can suggest to your minds that a great literature is more than the sum of a number of great writers, that it has a character of its own, much of my contention will be misunderstood. It is because I do not want to concentrate your attention upon the man of genius that I have used the term 'man of letters'. This includes men of the second or third, or lower ranks as well as the greatest; and these secondary writers provide collectively, and individually in varying degrees, an important part of the environment of the great writer, as well as his first audience, his first appreciators, his first critical correctors—and perhaps his first detractors. The continuity of a literature is essential to its greatness; it is very largely the function of secondary writers to preserve this continuity, and to provide a body of writing which is not necessarily read by posterity, but which plays a great part in forming the link between those writers who continue to be read. This continuity is largely unconscious, and only visible in historical retrospect: I need only refer you for evidence to the monumental, though brief, essay by Professor R. W. Chambers on *The Continuity of English Prose.* And it is within this continuity, and within this environment, that, for my present purpose, individual authors have to be considered. When we look at them in this way, we can see that, among the great, even some of the most formal and correct have been also innovators and even rebels, and that even some of the most revolutionary have carried on the work of those from whose influence they rebelled.

It would be easy, indeed, to muster an army of great names, of men who have become great writers with very little educational advantage. Bunyan and Abraham Lincoln are only two among the names more frequently cited. These men, and others, learned how to use the English language very largely from the English Bible: and it is the tritest commonplace that a knowledge of the Bible, Shakespeare and Bunyan (I might add the Book of Common Prayer) could teach a man of genius, or a man of first-rate ability short of genius, all that he needs in order to write English well. But I would remark first, that it is by no means irrelevant that the translators of that English Bible were great scholars in their time as well as great stylists; and we have to ask, not merely what had Shakespeare and Bunyan read, but what had the English authors read whose works nourished Shakespeare and Bunyan? And I would remark next, that the education given to Shakespeare, or Bunyan, or Lincoln, would be about the most difficult kind to get to-day. It would be much more reasonable to expect to find a poet with the learning of a Ben Jonson or a Milton than either a poet or prose writer who had had the advantages of Shakespeare or Bunyan. No schoolmaster could afford the reputation of sending his pupils forth as illfurnished as these men were. And there is too much to read, for anybody to be expected to master, and to believe in, a few authors; apart from the fact that out of school there is every pressure to write badly, to talk incoherently, and to think confusedly.

It should be apparent at this point, that our primary concern in considering the education of the man of letters, is not the amount of learning which a man acquires, the number of years during which he is subjected to the educational process, or the degree of scholastic distinction which he attains: what is of prime importance is the type of education within which his schooling falls. The most instructive contrast of degree of education within the same type is that provided by Shakespeare and Milton, our two greatest poets. We can say of Shakespeare, that never has a man turned so little knowledge to such great account;

we must couple Milton with Dante, in saying that never has a poet possessed of such great learning so completely justified the acquistion of it. Shakespeare's education, what he had of it, belongs in the same tradition as that of Milton: it was essentially a classical education. The significance of a type of education may lie almost as much in what it omits as in what it includes. Shakespeare's classical knowledge appears to have been derived largely from translations. But he lived in a world in which the wisdom of the ancients was respected, and their poetry admired and enjoyed; he was less well educated than many of his colleagues, but his was education of the same kind—and it is almost more important, for a man of letters, that his associates should be well educated than that he should be well educated himself. The stand-ards and the values were there; and Shakespeare himself had that ability, which is not native to everyone, to extract the utmost possible from translations. In these two advantages he had what mattered most.

If Shakespeare's knowledge was fragmentary and second-hand, that of Milton was comprehensive and direct. A lesser poet, with the learning and the tastes of Milton, would have been in danger of becoming a mere pedant in verse. An understanding of Milton's poetry requires some acquaintance with several subjects none of which is very much in favour to-day: a knowledge of the Bible, not necessarily in Hebrew and Greek, but certainly in English; a knowledge of classical literature, mythology, and history, of Latin syntax and versification and of Christian theology. Some knowledge of Latin is necessary, not only for understanding what Milton is talking about, but much more for understanding his style and his music. It is not that Milton's vocabulary is excessively weighted with Latin words: there was more of that in the previous century. An acquaintance with Latin is necessary if we are to understand, and to accept, the involutions of his sentence structure, and if we are to hear the complete music of his verse. The present generation may miss, what we cannot expect from Milton, the colloquial style, the sound of the conversational voice, the range of mood and emotion which requires a more homely diction for its expression; it may sometimes find his syntax tortured. Milton has been reproached, and there is some truth behind the reproach, for writing English like a dead language: I think it was Landor who said so, and Landor is a critic to be treated with respect. Milton's was certainly a style fatal to imitators: that is just as true of the style of James Joyce, and the influence of a great writer upon other writers can neither add to nor detract from his title to honour. The point is that Milton's Latinism is essential to his greatness, and that I have only chosen him as the extreme example of English poetry in general. You may write English poetry without knowing any Latin; I am not so sure whether without Latin you can wholly understand it. I believe, and have said elsewhere, that the rich possibilities of English verse—possibilities still unexhausted—owe much to the variety of racial strains bringing in a variety of speech and verse rhythms; and that English verse also owes much to the fact that Greek for three hundred years, and Latin for longer than that, have gone to its formation. And what I have said of verse can be applied to prose also, though perhaps with less compulsion: can we really enter into the style of Clarendon unless we have at least a smattering of Tacitus, or the style of Gibbon unless we have some awareness of the immense power upon him of the classical and post-classical chroniclers, the patristic and post-patristic theologians, who provided him with his material?

If a classical education is the background for English literature in the past, we are justified in affirming not merely that a good knowledge of Latin (if not of Greek) should be expected of those who teach English literature, but that some knowledge of Latin should be expected of those who study it. This is not quite the direction, however, which I propose to pursue. I am not here concerned with the teaching of literature, but with teaching only in relation to those who are going to write it. For many generations the classics provided the basis of the education of the people from whom the majority of our men of letters have sprung: which is far from saying that the majority of our men of letters have been recruited from any limited social class. This common basis of education has, I believe, had a great part in giving English letters of the past that unity which gives us the right to say that we have not only produced a succession of great writers, but a literature, and a literature which is a distinguished part of a recognizable entity called European Literature. We are then justified in inquiring what is likely to happen, to our language and our literature, when the connection between the classics and our own literature is completely broken, when the classical scholar is as completely specialized as the Egyptologist, and when the poet or the critic whose mind and taste have been exercised on Latin and Greek literature will be more exceptional than the dramatist who has prepared himself for his task in the theatre by a close study of optical, electrical and acoustical physics? You have the option of welcoming the change as the dawn of emancipation, or of deploring it as the twilight of literature; but at least you must agree that we might expect it to mark some great difference between the literature of the past and that of the future—perhaps so great as to be the transition from an old language to a new one.

In the past twenty years I have observed what seems to me a deterioration in the middle literary stratum, and notably in the standards and the scholarship which are wanted for literary criticism. Lest you judge too hastily that this complaint is merely the creak of rheumatic middle age, I will quote a representative of a younger literary generation than my own, Mr. Michael Roberts:

'By the summer of 1939 there were only two serious literary papers in England: an admirable quarterly called *Scrutiny*, with a small circulation, and *The Times Literary Supplement*, which, like the more serious libraries, had fewer readers in 1938 than in 1922. The notion of quality became submerged in the idea that "it's all a matter of taste", and the untutored taste of the individual was tempered only by the fear of being excessively eccentric or excessively conventional. One ingenious publisher succeeded in making the best of both worlds, by advertising "A Novel for a Few People. 20th Thousand".'

The reasons for such a decline are no doubt complex, and I am not going to suggest that this is all due to the neglect of classical studies, or that a revival of these studies would be enough to stem the current. But the disappearance of any common background of instruction, any common body of literary and historical knowledge, any common acquaintance with the foundations of English literature, has probably made it easier for writers to comply with the pressure of tendencies for which they were not responsible. One function of criticism—I am not thinking of the great critics or the classics of criticism, but rather of the hebdomadary reviewer, formerly anonymous, who has now more often the publicity of signature, though seldom the satisfaction of higher pay—one function of criticism is to act as a kind of cog regulating the rate of change of literary taste. When the cog sticks, and reviewers remain fast in the taste of a previous generation, the machine needs to be ruthlessly dismantled and reassembled; when it slips, and the reviewer accepts novelty as a sufficient criterion of excellence, the machine needs to be stopped and tightened up. The effect of either fault in the machine is to cause a division between those who see no good in anything that is new, and those who see no good in anything else: the antiquation of the old, and the eccentricity and even charlatanism of the new, are both thereby accelerated. The effect of this failure of criticism is to place the serious writer in a dilemma: either to write for too large a public or to write for too small a public. And the curious result of either choice, is to place a premium on the ephemeral. The novelty of a work of imagination which is only popular, and has nothing really new in it, soon wears off: for a later generation will prefer the original to the copy, when both belong to the past. And the novelty of anything that is merely new produces only a momentary shock: the same work will not produce the same shock twice, but must be followed by something newer.

The charge has been brought against the more original literature of our time, that it has been written for a small and exclusive audience—

an audience not small and exclusive because it was the best, but because (so it has been alleged) it consisted of perverse, eccentric, or anti-social people with their snobbish parasites. This appears to be an accusation which the most dissimilar groups can concur in bringing: the conservative who regard anything new as anarchic, and the radical who regard anything they do not understand as undemocratic. With the political passions enlisted for the support of these judgments I am not here concerned. My point is that this is a consequence, not of individual aberrancy—though it creates a situation in which the sham can easily pass, for a time and with some readers, as genuine—but of social disintegration: in the literary aspect, of critical decay. It arises from the lack of continuous communication, of the artist with his friends and fellow artists and the small number of keen amateurs of the arts, with a larger public educated in the same way, of taste cultivated upon the literature of the past but ready to accept what is good in the present when that is brought to their notice, and so with the world at large. If an author's first discriminating readers are themselves isolated from the larger world, their influence upon him may be unbalanced: their taste is in danger of yielding to their group prejudice and fancy, and they may easily succumb to the temptation of overvaluing the achievement of their members and favourite authors.

It is one thing to pass these strictures upon the present condition of literature, or to voice forebodings of its diminished future, and quite another to put forward positive suggestions about the type of education most profitable for the man of letters, and the way in which it could be fitted in to the general educational scheme. In concern with education we are attentive to the problems of the child and the adolescent; very largely to the average or the mediocre child; very largely to the child whose educational opportunities have heretofore been meagre. When we think of the larger pattern we are apt to think (quite rightly) in terms of the production of good citizens. The question I leave with you is the question whether we think the maintenance of the greatness of our literature a matter of sufficient importance to be taken account of, in our educational planning, at all? and even if we agree about its importance, whether education can take any reponsibility for it? The answer may be, No. But the question must be asked, and the answer must not be a hasty answer. The right answer can only come after some very hard thinking, and thinking with very wide scope, by many people. I would not dissimulate the difficulty. The problem of training an adequate supply of good scientists, in various departments, is one very much with us; it is, I imagine, one much more readily capable of solution than is my problem. But I do not think that it would seem so much more soluble, were it not that we all recognize, under the pressure of material evidence, its necessity; and I think that agreement on the importance of a problem makes the solution of it much more likely.

I can see that the proper training of a man with the scientific bent, even now when the ramifications of the sciences are so extensive and the knowledge to be assimilated in any branch of science so vast, is more readily susceptible of precise determination. So, for that matter, is the training for any other art than that of letters. The painter, the sculptor, the architect, the musician, though they may have more difficulty in scraping a living, or in combining the pursuit of their art with an unrelated stipendiary job, all have a much more definite technique to master than that of the writer. Their essential training is more technical; the subjects which they must learn are more clearly indicated; and they do not need that varied general culture without which the man of letters is ill-equipped. Another difference, not unconnected with the foregoing, is that literary ability does not, with any certainty, manifest itself so early, or with such precise confidence of its goal, as does a bent towards another art. A desire to express oneself in verse is (or so my experience inclines me to believe) a trait of the majority of Anglo-Saxons of both sexes at some stage of their development: it may even persist long after the lack of vocation is patent to everyone except the authors themselves. When a schoolboy composes good verses, we are justified in expecting that he will, in later life, excel in some pursuit or other—but that pursuit may take him very far from poetry or letters—it may lead toward the bar or the episcopal bench. The truly literary mind is likely to develop slowly; it needs a more comprehensive and more varied diet, a more miscellaneous knowledge of facts, a greater experience of men and of ideas, than the mind required for the practice of the other arts. It therefore presents a more baffling educational problem. In saying this, I am not arrogating any pre-eminence for the art of letters itself: I am merely pointing out a difference in the preparation.

I should like to make clear at this point that there are several arguments in favour of the classical education with which, however cogent and sufficient, I am not here concerned. Into the question whether all children, whatever their destination, should be taught elementary Latin, and perhaps Greek—the question whether it is desirable, and then whether it is practicable—I shall not venture. I would only remark that the question of the age up to which all children should have the same education, and the question of the common element in all education up to a later stage, is a very important one even from the point of view of the man of letters: for upon this depends the possibility of a general audience, the possibility both of the author's being able to communicate with people in all walks of life, and of their being able to understand each other. I would also observe in passing, that to postpone the introduction to Latin to the age at which a boy appears to be more gifted for languages than for other studies is to postpone it too long— apart from my belief that it would be most desirable for everyone to possess some knowledge of Latin even if none of Greek. I am not here interested, however, in the advocacy of the study of these two languages as 'mental discipline'. I think that the defence of any study purely as 'discipline' in the modern sense can be maintained too obstinately: I have, for instance, heard compulsory chapel defended, by an unbeliever, on the ground that it was good for boys to have a duty which they dis- liked so much. The defence of 'discipline' in the abstract, the belief that any 'mental discipline' carried out in the right way and far enough will produce an abstract 'educated man', seems to have some relation to the egalitarian tendencies of the nineteenth century which extended to sub- jects of study the name ideal of equality held for the human beings who might study them. A *disciple*, at any rate, is surely a willing pupil, and one who attaches himself to a master voluntarily, because he believes in the value of the subject which the master professes and believes that that master is qualified to give him the initiation he wants. Discipleship, that is, starts by a valuation—by the desire to attain to some particular knowledge or proficiency, not by the desire for training in the abstract followed by the judgement that this subject of study will provide it. For my purpose it is the value of the subject that is in question, not the incidental and necessary 'discipline' by which its command is at- tained. And as I am not considering discipline in the abstract, so I am not considering 'education' in the abstract, or the somewhat barren question of the definition of the abstract 'educated man'.

For my purposes, also, the distinction between 'vocational' and 'cultural' education is of little use: apart from the disadvantage that 'vocational' is apt to connote merely a salary and a pension, and 'cul- tural' to connote an 'education for leisure' which is either a refined hedonism or a skill to practise harmless hobbies. The writer, *qua* writer, seldom draws a salary, and he has no problem of occupying a sup- posed leisure. Everything may be grist to his mill, and the more knowl- edge of every kind that he can assimilate the better: the serious dis- tinction, for him, is between the subjects which he should be taught, and the subjects which he should acquire by himself. His business is com- munication through language; when he is an imaginative writer, he is en- gaged in the most difficult form of communication, where precision is of the utmost importance, a precision which cannot be given before- hand but has to be found in every new phrase. In order to understand language in the way in which the man of letters should understand it, we must know the various purposes for which language has been used;

and that involves some knowledge of the subjects for the communication of which men have used language in the past: notably of history, for you cannot understand the literature of the past without some knowledge of the conditions under which it was written, and the sort of people who wrote it; of logic, for that is an investigation of the anatomy of thought in language; of philosophy, for that is the attempt to use language in the most abstract way possible.

Into this already formidable programme we have to introduce at some stage at least one modern foreign language as well as our own language and the classics. It should be a major language with a parallel development to our own, and with a flourishing contemporary literature; for we are greatly helped to develop objectivity of taste if we can appreciate the work of foreign authors, living in the same world as ourselves, and expressing their vision of it in another great language. The possession of several foreign languages is of course better than of one alone; but it is impossible to understand the language, the literature and the people of more than one foreign country equally well. In our time, the most important foreign language, for the man of letters, has been French: and I need not remind you that for French a knowledge of Latin is still more important, and a knowledge of Greek hardly less important, than for English. For a man of very exceptional linguistic ability, who was not already sunk beneath the burden of the acquirements I recommend, I believe that an acquaintance with some great and more remote language might be a very valuable addition; Hebrew suggests itself, but both for extreme difference of structure and intellectual dignity a very good choice would be Chinese: but to mention this is to scan the very horizon of possibility.

All these branches of learning have to be acquired through teachers; and there does not appear to be much space left in the curriculum for scientific subjects. I am assuming however that my excellent man of letters will have had (what I did not attain) enough training at school in the language of mathematics not to be completely baffled when he attempts, by himself, to understand the general significance of some scientific discovery. The only reason of universal applicability, why he could not acquire more detailed scientific knowledge in his formal education, is the very obvious one that there was not time: for I have allowed for some hours to be spent in eating, sleeping, social ritual, conviviality, worship, athletic activities and physical training. It is most desirable that he should be able, throughout his life, to take an interest in subjects in which he has not been trained; for, as I have suggested, to a person of some power of imagination almost anything can be of use. It is sometimes suggested that the wonders of science provide nourishment for the imagination. I am sure they can: but I think a distinction should be drawn between the imagination of a great scientist, arriving at a discovery on the basis of observed phenomena the significance of which had escaped other equally well trained and informed scientists, and the imagination of a Lucretius, or even a Shelley, informing their scientific knowledge with an emotional life with which the scientist, as such, has no concern.

I have not, as you see, been urging the claims of 'cultural', or general, education against specialized; for, in its way, the education of the man of letters must be itself specialized and 'vocational'. But we have to face one more difficulty. I have made clear that I am not attempting to legislate for the man of genius, but for the environment of men of letters into which he will be born or find his way. But on the other hand you cannot draw a sharp line between the man of letters and his audience, between the critic in print and the critic in conversation. Nobody suffers more from being limited to the society of his own profession than does the writer: it is still worse when his audience is composed chiefly of other writers or would-be writers. He needs a small public of substantially the same education as himself, as well as the same tastes; a larger public with some common background with him; and finally he should have something in common with everyone who has intelligence and sensibility and can read his language. The problem of the survival of English literature, therefore, brings us to the problem of the need for unity in education, the need for some unification which will not be to the detriment of any of the branches of learning and investigation, scientific or humanistic. This problem, so much greater than any problem of administration, organization, or curricular devices, because it is a spiritual problem, because its solution involves not merely planning, but *growing* a pattern of values, is so vast a problem that it is not one for the educational specialist alone, but for all who are concerned with the structure of society. It is one with which I have no more to do here than to show my awareness of it. My only contribution is to proclaim that the future of English Literature will be deeply affected by the way in which we solve, or fail to solve this problem.

My particular thesis has been that the maintenance of classical education is essential to the maintenance of the continuity of English Literature. How, and by what adaptation to the necessary, the desirable and the inevitable, the place for the classics in education is to be found is not a subject on which I have the right to claim your attention. But I am sure that this is one important line of defence of the classics. The standards of the highest scholarship have to be kept up, and the work of research honoured: it is necessary that the prestige of the great scholar should not be allowed to dwindle. That there will continue to be a place for the great scholar—without whom the whole fabric of classical education crumbles—I do not doubt: what is less certain is that in the future he will be discovered young enough to be given the proper training; and that he will be allowed any greater role than that of preparing a few younger men to carry on his work, without prospect of wider influence. The second group is that of non-professional scholarship and of scholarship in other fields in which an accurate knowledge of the classical languages is, or should be required; it includes not only the theologians and the historians, but the clergy and ministry, the teachers of modern language and literature, and the literary critics. For the last of these, certainly, it should hardly be enough that he should have spent some years at school in acquiring the languages, if he never afterwards opens a text: he must have the literature accessible and operative in his taste and judgement; he must be able to enjoy it. But the maintenance of these types of scholarship is not enough or even possible unless some knowledge of the civilizations of Greece and Rome, some respect for their achievements, some understanding of their historical relation to our own, and some acquaintance with their literature and their wisdom *in translation* can be cultivated among a very much larger number of people: among those who (like myself) have not remembered enough to read the originals with ease, and among those who have never studied the languages at all. A limited preserve of scholarship will be ineffectual unless a much wider respect for, and appreciation of the relevance of, the subject-matter of this scholarship can be disseminated amongst those who will never be given the first-hand knowledge.

My assertions about the dependence of English Literature upon the Latin and Greek literatures, will, I am aware, have no persuasive influence whatever upon several classes of people. There are those who do not believe that literature is a matter of any great importance, and those who, while conceding a certain value to the literature of the past, do not consider it of great importance that English Literature should continue to take a front rank. There are those who acknowledge the importance of literature, but do not believe that one type of education or another will make much difference to its further survival. There are those who, immersed perhaps in the immense difficulties of providing some sort of education or other to the whole of the nation, consider this extra problem less urgent, or complain that they have so many other things to think of that it is more than can be coped with. And finally, there are those who want so new a world that they even welcome the prospect of a breach of continuity. And in many minds, no doubt, all of these attitudes can co-exist in a half-formed state; now one, now another, presenting itself in consciousness.

To attempt to confute all these objections would be an impertinence in the present company, and some of them come much more within the province of those who have had life-long experience of the class-room and the council chamber. My appeal can only address itself to those who already accept the contention that the preservation of a living literature is more than a matter of interest only to amateurs of verse and readers of novels; and who see in it the preservation of developed speech, and of civilization against barbarism. They will be those also who appreciate the need, if the present chaos is ever to be reduced to order, of something more than an administrative or an economic unification—the need of a cultural unification in diversity of Europe, and who believe that a new unity can only grow on the old roots: the Christian Faith, and the classical languages which Europeans inherit in common. These roots are, I think inextricably intertwined. I should not care to risk the heresy, upon which some religious-political writers have appeared to verge, of regarding Christianity as a European, rather than a universal Faith: I do not wish to be accused of inventing a new heresy to the effect that salvation depends upon getting a first in classics. But the culture of Europe, such as it is, is a Christian culture; and conversely, the traditional religious faith of Europe, including Britain, cannot preserve its intellectual vigour unless a high standard of Latin and Greek scholarship is maintained amongst its teachers. But these considerations are beyond the mandate which I have assumed for this occasion. And I do not wish to leave you with the impression that I am asking too much of formal education, either in the sphere of religion or in that of literature: I am quite aware that an educational system cannot of itself bring about either great faith or great literature: it is truer to say that our education is not so much the generator of our culture as the offspring of it. But those who care for the preservation, the extension and the advancement of our culture cannot fail to interest themselves, however unqualified they may be to pass judgement, in our classical heritage.

Virgil Thomson

SHADES OF POETS DEAD AND GONE

From *The State of Music*

Poetry is the oldest of the arts and the most respected. The musical tradition we practice has scarcely a thousand years. Architecture, sculpture, and decorative design have passed since ancient times through so many esthetic revolutions that very little is left in them of any authoritative tradition. Improvisational one-man easel-painting in oil (painting as we know it) dates barely from the seventeenth century.

Poetry, as we know it, goes straight back to the Greeks and to the Hebrew children. There has been no interruption for twenty-five hundred years in the transmission of its technical procedures, no hiatus in the continuity of its comprehension by the literate classes of Europe. It has survived changes in religion, political revolutions, the birth and death of languages. Its classic masters enjoy a prestige scarcely exceded by that of the Holy Evangelists. By populace and scholars alike they are admired above confessors and martyrs, priests, prophets, historians, psychologists, romancers, and ethical guides, and far above statesmen or soldiers, orators or newshawks. For they and their heirs are the recognized masters of the most puissant of all instruments, the word.

The poetic prestige remains, but the poetic function has contracted. As champions of the arts of love, poets made war for centuries on the Christian Church and won. As analysts of its motivations and as experts of amorous device, they were the undisputed masters of that subject till Sigmund Freud, a nerve doctor, beat them at it in our own day. (Karl Marx, a nineteenth-century economist, had already beaten them at social analysis and at political prophecy.) With love now the specialty (in every aspect) of the medical profession, with government (both past and future) better understood by sectarian political groups and better explained by journalists, with dramaturgy better practiced in Hollywood and Joinville, and storytelling done more convincingly by the writers of police-fiction, what is there left for the poet to do that might even partially justify his hereditary prestige?

He could retreat into "pure" poetry, of course; and he often tries to. Much good may it do him. Because the sorry truth is there is no such refuge. In recent years the poets have talked a good deal about "purity." I am not sure what they mean by "pure" poetry, unless they mean poetry without a subject-matter; and that means exactly nothing.

Music and painting can exist perfectly well without a subject-matter, at least without any obvious or stated subject-matter. Painting of this kind is called "abstract." Musicians used to distinguish between "program" music and "absolute" music. The latter term meant music without a literary text or any specific illustrative intention, that is to say, instrumental music of an introspective nature. Neither "abstract" painting nor "absolute" music is any "purer" than any other kind of painting or music, and no painter or musician ever pretends it is. It is merely more obscure. When painters speak of "purity of line," they mean a complete lack of obscurity. When they speak of a "pure" color, they mean a shade that is unequivocal. Say an artist's intentions are "pure," if you must. That means he is not commercial-minded. The word *pure* cannot possibly have any meaning when applied to the content or structure of literature. Poetry could be pure only if it could be devoid of meaning, which it can't. You can make nonsense poetry, certainly; you can dissociate and reassociate words. But you cannot take the meanings out of words; you simply can't. You can only readjust their order. And nobody can or ever does write poetry without a subject.

What subjects, then, are available to the poet today? Practically none. Money, political events, heroism, science, mathematical logic, crime, the libido, the sexual variations, the limits of personality, the theory of revolution: the incidents of all these are more graphically recited by journalists, the principles better explained by specialists. There really isn't much left for the heirs of Homer and Shakespeare to do but to add their case-histories to the documentation of introspective psychology by the practice of automatic writing. Highly trained in linguistics (though the philologists are not bad at that either) and wearing the mantle of the Great Tradition, admired unreasonably and feared not unreasonably (for they are desperate men), they still have, as poets, no civil status, no social function, no serious job to do, and no income.

They haven't even any audience to speak of. For some time now they have been depending mainly on one another for applause. Hence the pretentiousness and the high intellectual tone of all they write. I mean that for fifty years poetry has mostly been read by other poets, and that for a good thirty years now has mostly been written to be read by other poets.

The impasse is complete. Contemporary civilization has no place for the poet save one of mere honor. Science, learning, journalism, fiction, religion, magic, and politics, all his ancient bailiwicks, are closed to him formally and completely. He is allowed to render small services to these now and then as a disseminator of existing knowledge. He is always regarded, however, by the specialists as a possible betrayer; and consequently at no time is he allowed to speak of such subjects with any but a temporarily delegated authority.

His lot is a tragic one. Nothing is left him of his art but an epigone's skill and some hereditary prestige. This last is still large enough to give him face in front of his co-citizens and to keep up the recruiting. It doesn't pay anything at all, of course. It won't buy a beer, a bus-fare, or a contraceptive. Nor does it prevent the darkest despair from seizing him when he is alone.

The prestige of classic poetry is enough to explain the market among cultured women for poets as lovers. I use the word market deliberately, because in these love affairs a certain amount of money nearly always changes hands. The poet who has no job and no private resources is a liability on his intimates. If he has a job, he is usually too busy working at it to take on seriously a love affair with a woman of leisure. If he has money from home, he always keeps somebody else or spends it on riotous living. Any independent woman who gets involved with a poet had better figure that he is going to cost her something sooner or later, if only for bailing him out of night-courts.

For poets live high. When one is as poor as they, budgets make no sense and economies make no sense. Nothing makes any sense but basic luxury—eating well, drinking well, and making love. Independent and well-to-do women whose sex-mechanisms are excited by intellectual conversation are very useful indeed to poetry, provided they don't go motherly. (Poets don't care much for maternal types and they have a horror of fatherhood.) They serve the poet as muse, audience, and patroness all in one as long as they last. This isn't long usually. They get scared off by the violence of it all, as well as by the expense.

Everything the poet does is desperate and excessive. He eats like a pig; he starves like a professional beauty; he tramps; he bums; he gets arrested; he steals; he absconds; he blackmails; he dopes; he acquires every known vice and incurable disease, not the least common of which is solitary dipsomania.

All this after twenty-five, to be sure. Up to that age he is learning his art. There is available a certain amount of disinterested subvention for expansive lyrical poetry, the poetry of adolescence and early manhood. But nobody can make a grown-up career out of a facility for lyrical expansiveness. That kind of effusion is too intense, too intermittent. The mature nervous system won't stand it. At about twenty-six, the poets start looking around for some subject-matter outside themselves, something that will justify sustained execution while deploying to advantage all their linguistic virtuosity.

There is no such subject-matter available. Their training has unfitted them for the rendering of either those religious-political-and-epic or those humane-philosophical-and-dramatic subjects that were formerly the special domain of poetry. They are like certain scions of ancient families who have been brought up to look and act like aristocrats but who don't know beans about government. They even write more like heirs of the great dead than like creators of living literature. Their minds are full of noble-sounding words and a complete incomprehension of everything that takes place beyond the rise and fall of their own libidos. They cannot observe; they cannot even use words and syntax objectively. They are incurably egocentric.

This explains the high mortality, both literary and physiological, that takes place among poets around the age of thirty. Faced with a cultural as well as an economic impasse, some hang on just long enough to finish a few extended but essentially lyrical works conceived in the midtwenties and then die of drink, dope, tuberculosis, or even plain suicide. Others, especially in England, become journalistic correspondents at twenty-six. The French tend toward the civil and consular services. Americans become pedagogues or reporters. A few marry rich widows. This last solution need not be counted as a literary mortality, because it is rarely permanent. It does get the poet over some difficult years of transition, however, without forcing him into drugs or invalidism; so that when the lady sees financial ruin approaching, the poet can and most frequently does start a new literary life, this time as a prose author with an objective method and a recognizable integration to his time and society.

For the poet who insists on remaining a poet, there is a compromise formula. He must manage to get through his youth either with a small patrimony or with enough health left to allow him to work at a regular job of some kind, preferably not connected with literature. In this case he usually settles down in the thirties to steady domesticity with a woman approaching (though never topping) his own social class and disappears into the landscape of ordinary modern life, carefully budgeting his leisure, his income, and his alcoholic intake. He keeps up his poetic correspondence (one of the strange things about poets is the way they keep warm by writing to one another all over the world) and occasionally takes part in esthetic controversy, all the while laying regularly but slowly his poetic eggs and publishing them in book form at three-to-five-year intervals. These eggs are called "poems of some length," and they essay to treat of historical or sociological subject-matter in the epic style. The manner is always essentially lyrical, however; and since lyricism without youth, without expansiveness, and without heat is a pretty sad affair, the best that can be said of these estimable efforts is that they are "the work of a mature talent," that they are "masterly," that they show a "profound feeling" for something or other. The fact remains that they are fairly ineffectual and are less read, on the whole, than his youthful works. An edition of five hundred to two thousand copies is disposed of, with luck, to libraries and bibliophiles, both of these last being collectors of poetry for its prestige-value. Sometimes the edition doesn't sell at all, in which case the publisher puts down his loss to prestige-advertising. Most publishers do a few such volumes a year, because they think it a good idea to have some poetry in the catalogue. You never know.

These middle-aged poets are just as charming as ever and much easier for peaceable persons to go about with than the young ones, because their habits are not such a strain on one's vitality. They are busy men with always time for a chat. They love to do you favors. They are good fathers, faithful husbands, and superb hosts. Once in a while they go out on an all-night binge; and their wives don't really mind, because a binge makes hubby feel like a dangerous fellow again. It builds him up to himself. And at no risk. Because he never does anything on these nights-out but sit with a crony and talk.

Poets at any age make sound friends. They are always helping you out of jams. They give you money. They respect your working hours but don't scold you when you don't work. They practice conversation as an art and friendship as a religion. I like too their violence, their fist-fights with cops, their Parisian literary wars. The displays of pure bitterness that one observes among them in England I find less invigorating, because the intensity of these seems to be due not so much to professional disagreement as to that exercise of social hatred within one's own class that seems to be the characteristic and special quality of British life just now.

I like their human warmth, their copious hospitality (however poor they may be), their tolerance about morals and their intolerance about ideas, their dignified resignation at all times. I even like their wives and their animals (for they mostly have wives and they all have cats or dogs or horses). Mostly I like their incredible and immutable loyalties. They are the last of honor and chivalry. They may be sordid sots or peaceful papas or gigolos on a leash. They imagine themselves to be knights-errant jousting before the Courts of Love. And they act accordingly, observing incomprehensibly delicate scruples, maintaining till death principles and refinements of principles that reason, common sense, and social convention have long since discarded as absurd. I knew a poet once who refused to salt his food when dining at a certain house, because, intending later to make love to the hostess, he would have considered it a breach of his obligation as a guest to attempt any violation of his host's home-life after having "eaten his salt." He was remembering, no doubt, some Arabic or medieval saw. He was not remembering that the "salt" of the precept could only have nowadays a symbolic meaning and that the food he partook of had already been salted in cooking anyway.

I like also their preoccupation with religion, the black arts, and psychoanalysis, and their complete inability to practice any of these consistently, even in an amateur way. They could, of course, if they were not, at the same time, so egocentric and so responsible to a tradition. Anybody can be clairvoyant or perform a miracle or two here and there who really wants to and who isn't afraid of the techniques. Unfortunately the techniques are all extremely dangerous to handle. That these techniques occasionally work there is, I think, no question. Illnesses, accidents, cures, and suicides, the favorable or unfavorable outcome of amorous projects and business deals, even the finding of lost objects, can be and every day are effected from a distance by interested outsiders. Prophecy is extensively carried on today through the techniques of numerology and of astrological calculation. A more active interference in other people's affairs is operated by the employment of three different kinds of technique. The hocus-pocus of medieval black art is far from uncommon, as are also the rituals of voodoo and fetich. Prayer, incantation, and trance are even commoner. Willful exploitations of animal magnetism, of psychological domination, and of euphoric states are the bases of organized religions practicing openly. These last means are employed quite frankly in every domain of modern life, even (and by both sides) in class warfare. Organized salesmanship depends on little else, as do equally the morales of citizen armies and of militant political parties.

The poets seldom succumb to the temptation of tampering with any of these techniques, though they are not infrequently the victims of such practice by members of their own households. They don't do it themselves because the practice of poetry is exactly contrary in method to the exertion of secret or of psychological influences. Poetry is practiced today and, so far as I know, is only practiced in the manner that used to be called the tradition of Humane Letters, which is to say that it is written by one man to be read by all men and that it makes to him who reads it exactly whatever sense it would make to any other disinterested reader. Its vocabulary consists of neutral dictionary words. Magic practices, on the other hand, require the use of an emotional and hermetic vocabulary comprehensible in its full meaning only to initiates and hence effective psychologically far beyond the dictionary meanings of the words used or the normal significance of the gestures that accompany them. For all his egocentricity, the poet is not anti-social. The practice of magic, by whatever technique, is extremely anti-social, because all the techniques of it depend for their working on the breakdown of somebody's personality.

Now the barriers of personality are the highest product of culture and of biological evolution. Their erection is the *modus operandi,* and the interplay of persons and groups around them is the unique end of what almost anybody means by civilization. Naturally their destruction is anti-social and anti-cultural. And just as naturally, the poets, being the direct heirs of the oldest tradition of thought in civilization, are more aware than most men of the existence of anti-cultural practices and of the danger to all concerned of any self-indulgence in that direction.

Organized religions and organized devotion to revolutionary political ideals are rarely in the long run anti-social, though I would not say so much for high-powered salesmanship. The poet's objection to organized religions is that they are all in opposition to the intellectual tradition; they are the enemies of poetry and humane letters. And so are all enterprises that keep large groups of people united by the exploitation of animal magnetism (read "sex-appeal"), mental domination, and euphoric states. Such enterprises are, by definition, not anti-social if a large number of people is involved. They are simply anti-cultural. They may be aimed at an admirable end, and they are very tempting indeed if they seem to be about to effect political changes of a collectivist nature. But no matter how eager your poet may be to aid in the achievement of the desired end, he views with alarm any means of doing so that might render those left alive after the achieving of it mentally unfit to enjoy the thing achieved. His greatest value in revolutionary movements, for instance, is his annoyance-value, his incessant and tiresome insistence on the maintenance at all times of the full intellectual paraphernalia.

Laymen are likely to think the poets are just being fanciful when they talk about magic and sorcery. This is not so. They are talking very good sense indeed, though their terminology may be antiquated. As a matter of fact, they are the only group of men in the world that has any profound prescience about the unchaining of the dark forces that has taken place in our century. Their chief utility to us all is that they help us to fight those dark forces by the only effective means there is or ever has been. I mean the light of reason, the repitition of sage precept, and the continual application to all the dilemmas of human life of the ancient and unalterable principles of disinterested thought.

It seemed a few years ago as if psychiatry might be about to provide a bulwark against obscurantism. The number of psychiatrists and psychoanalysts who have themselves fallen for the delights of mental domination, who, by inducting their patients into a state of euphoria through which no reality can pierce, have covered up their failure to produce in

these an integrated and realistic attitude toward society, the number,
I say, of such physicians is too large. As venal a branch of science as
that cannot be counted a bulwark of civilization. No doubt the material
handled is dangerous. For the subconscious can only be plumbed by
breaking down all personal barriers; there cannot be left even the cur-
tained impersonality of the confessional. The slightest misstep in the
handling of this doctor-patient intimacy produces a permanent enslave-
ment of the patient and another scar on the already hard-boiled crust
of the doctor's sensitivity. Let us charitably call such physicians "martyrs to science," like those laboratory-men who lose hands finger by
finger working with radium. The intimacy of psychoanalysis is very
much like radium, in fact, and like black magic too. It works, of course.
But many a body and many a soul gets burned to a crisp in the process.

Poets are always getting burned; but mostly it is only their bodies that
suffer, as anybody's body does who fans his youth into a flame. They
rarely get burned by poetry. For the material of poetry is words, and
words themselves are neutral. They only give off light. They never give
off heat unless arranged in formulas. Poets hate formulas.

This is what Parisian literary wars are mostly about. They are attacks
on formulas that have become powerful within the profession. The
clearest statement of principle goes bad if it is repeated too often. It
ceases to be a statement and becomes a slogan. It loses its clear meaning
and takes on psychological power. The literary mind considers (and
rightly) that any statement which carries more power than meaning is
evil. War is therefore declared on the author of the statement in point,
by another author, usually on some pretext of personal prestige. As
the war goes on from wisecrack to manifesto to calumny, authors get
involved who don't even know the original belligerents or the incidents
of provocation. Everybody calls everybody else horrid names and a
great deal of wit is unleashed. Then it all dies down and everybody makes
up. But the formula, having now been subjected both to the light of
reason and to all the thirty-two positions of ridicule, is no longer any
good to anybody. Analysis and laughter have broken its back. The
Demon is foiled. Demagogy is frustrated. Poetry is thereupon vigorous
again and abundant till the next time a formula starts to rear its Sacred
Head.

When I speak of statements that have more power than meaning, I am
not referring to hermetic poetry, obscure poetry, or ordinary nonsense.
These are not meaningless matters. On the contrary, they are over-full
of meaning. Some poets wish to mean so many things at once that they
can only write at all by the technique of multiple meaning, the most
ancient of all poetic techniques, by the way, and newly come again to
favor through the prestige of the physical sciences, which have made

spectacular advance in our century by means of the dissociationist discipline. There is non-Aristotelian poetry just as there is non-Euclidian geometry. You cannot subject poetry to the conventions of common sense. Not, at least, if you want it to mean anything more than journalism does. There is that kind of verse, of course, too; and it sells extremely well; but it is journalistic verse for vulgar usage, fake folklore. I might cite Kipling, Edgar Guest, R. W. Service, and E. A. Robinson as successful practitioners of it. It bears the same relation to poetry that *Mighty Lak' a Rose* does to music. Nobody in the profession takes it any more seriously than that. William Blake, Mallarmé, Gertrude Stein, and Lewis Carroll, on the other hand, however hermetic, however obscure or nonsensical, are taken very seriously indeed by the profession. They are taken as a bitter potion by many, but they are taken and taken seriously by everybody, however little any given poet may enjoy their competition. Even the plain public knows them for original masters.

There is no way out of the poet's plight. The best he can do for the present is to write poetry as if nobody were listening (a supposition not far from the truth) and to occupy the rest of the day as best he can. Earning money by writing poetry is out of the question, unless he can adapt himself to the theater, which it is not easy for him to do. The real difficulty about writing poetry is filling up the other twenty-three and a half hours a day. For, compared with the laboriousness of music writing and oil painting, there is very little real work involved in poetical composition. Lengthy reflection is involved and mental discipline and the nervous intensity of occasional concentration. But none of these takes time out of a man's life. The mind prepares itself in secret, underneath life's surface occupations. Putting down the result on paper is no job at all compared to the stroke-by-stroke improvisation of an oil-painting or the note-by-note inditing of a musical score.

If the poet works at a regular job, he hasn't got enough time to shake around and keep his ideas in solution. He crystallizes. If he doesn't work at a regular job, he has too much leisure to spend and no money. He gets into debt and bad health, eats on his own soul. It is very much too bad that his working-life includes so little of sedative routine.

I have mentioned the theater as a possible outlet for poetry and as a source of financial intake for the poet. For fifty years the poets and the theater people have been flirting with one another. In the great times of poetry they did more than that, of course; but even still some poet every now and then writes a playable play in verse. In our own day E. E. Cummings, T. S. Eliot, W. H. Auden, and Bert Brecht have held the attention of theater audiences that did not consist of other poets. On the whole, however, your modern poet conceives his art as a solo performance. He despises interpreters and relinquishes with great reluctance the splendid isolation of print. Also, theater people themselves, although less devoted than poets imagine to the vulgar or naturalistic style, are nevertheless a bit suspicious of the modern poet's hermetism. The poet, of course, is suspicious of everything that has to do with money-making. (Poor child, he has rarely made any since Tennyson.) Also, his confirmed egocentricity makes it difficult for him to render character objectively, which it is necessary for him to do if the poetic theater is to be anything more than a morality-play or a cerebral revue.

The musical theater, the opera, he approaches with more good will than he does the spoken theater, though he is not too happy even there about sharing honors with a composer. I realize that the composer usually hogs the show, sometimes deliberately; but still it is not certain that a loyal collaboration with composers and singers would always leave the poet in second place. It most certainly would not if the art of intoned heroic declamation ever got revived. Such a revival would be necessary if tragedy were to become popular again in our ultra-musical age. And the rebirth of a popular taste for tragedy is not at all inconceivable in a world where moral elegance, economic determinism, and personal defeat are about the only aspects under which the interplay between character and social forces can be described convincingly.

Let me sum up by repeating. That music is an island, like Ceylon or Tahiti, or perhaps even more like England, which Bossuet called "the most famous island in the world." That the waters around it are teeming with digestible fish that travel in schools and are known as painters. That swimming around among these at high speed and spouting as they go are prehistoric monsters called poets, who terrify all living things, fish and islanders alike. That these monsters are quite tame, however, in spite of their furious airs, and that since they have no industrial value just now, and since their presence offers no real danger to musical life or to the fishing industry (for they attack only one another), they are allowed to survive and are occasionally given food. Indeed, their evolutions offer a spectacle that is considered by the islanders to be not only picturesque but salutary, instructive, and grand.

Nikolai V. Gogol

THE OVERCOAT

In the department of ——, but it is better not to mention the department. The touchiest things in the world are departments, regiments, courts
of justice, in a word, all branches of public service. Each individual nowadays thinks all society insulted in his person. Quite recently, a complaint
was received from a district chief of police in which he plainly demonstrated that all the imperial institutions were going to the dogs, and that
the Czar's sacred name was being taken in vain; and in proof he appended to the complaint a romance, in which the district chief of police
is made to appear about once in every ten pages, and sometimes in a
downright drunken condition. Therefore, in order to avoid all unpleasant-
ness, it will be better to designate the department in question, as a certain
department.

So, in a certain department there was a certain official—not a very
notable one, it must be allowed—short of stature, somewhat pock-
marked, red-haired, and mole-eyed, with a bald forehead, wrinkled
cheeks, and a complexion of the kind known as sanguine. The St. Petersburg climate was responsible for this. As for his official rank—with us
Russians the rank comes first—he was what is called a perpetual titular
councillor, over which, as is well known, some writers make merry and
crack their jokes, obeying the praiseworthy custom of attacking those
who cannot bite back.

His family name was Bashmachkin. This name is evidently derived
from bashmak (shoe); but, when, at what time, and in what manner,
is not known. His father and grandfather, and all the Bashmachkins, always wore boots, which were resoled two or three times a year. His name
was Akaky Akakiyevich. It may strike the reader as rather singular and
far-fetched; but he may rest assured that it was by no means far-fetched,
and that the circumstances were such that it would have been impossible
to give him any other.

This was how it came about.

Akaky Akakiyevich was born, if my memory fails me not, in the
evening on the 23rd of March. His mother, the wife of a Government
official, and a very fine woman, made all due arrangements for having the
child baptised. She was lying on the bed opposite the door; on her right
stood the godfather, Ivan Ivanovich Eroshkin, a most estimable man,

who served as the head clerk of the senate; and the godmother, Arina Semyonovna Bielobrinshkova, the wife of an officer of the quarter, and a woman of rare virtues. They offered the mother her choice of three names, Mokiya, Sossiya, or that the child should be called after the martyr Khozdazat. "No," said the good woman, "all those names are poor." In order to please her, they opened the calendar at another place; three more names appeared, Triphily, Dula, and Varakhasy. "This is awful," said the old woman. "What names! I truly never heard the like. I might have put up with Varadat or Varukh, but not Triphily and Varakhasy!" They turned to another page and found Pavsikakhy and Vakhtisy. "Now I see," said the old woman, "that it is plainly fate. And since such is the case, it will be better to name him after his father. His father's name was Akaky, so let his son's name be Akaky too." In this manner he became Akaky Akakiyevich. They christened the child, whereat he wept, and made a grimace, as though he foresaw that he was to be a titular councillor.

In this manner did it all come about. We have mentioned it in order that the reader might see for himself that it was a case of necessity, and that it was utterly impossible to give him any other name.

When and how he entered the department, and who appointed him, no one could remember. However much the directors and chiefs of all kinds were changed, he was always to be seen in the same place, the same attitude, the same occupation—always the letter-copying clerk—so that it was afterwards affirmed that he had been born in uniform with a bald head. No respect was shown him in the department. The porter not only did not rise from his seat when he passed, but never even glanced at him, any more than if a fly had flown through the reception-room. His superiors treated him in coolly despotic fashion. Some insignificant assistant to the head clerk would thrust a paper under his nose without so much as saying, "Copy," or, "Here's an interesting little case," or anything else agreeable, as is customary amongst well-bred officials. And he took it, looking only at the paper, and not observing who handed it to him, or whether he had the right to do so; simply took it, and set about copying it.

The young officials laughed at and made fun of him, so far as their official wit permitted; told in his presence various stories concocted about him, and about his landlady, an old woman of seventy; declared that she beat him; asked when the wedding was to be; and strewed bits of paper over his head, calling them snow. But Akaky Akakiyevich answered not a word, any more than if there had been no one there besides himself. It even had no effect upon his work. Amid all these annoyances he never made a single mistake in a letter. But if the joking became wholly unbearable, as when they jogged his head, and prevented his attending to his work, he would exclaim:

"Leave me alone! Why do you insult me?"

And there was something strange in the words and the voice in which they were uttered. There was in it something which moved to pity; so much so that one young man, a newcomer, who, taking pattern by the others, had permitted himself to make sport of Akaky, suddenly stopped short, as though all about him had undergone a transformation, and presented itself in a different aspect. Some unseen force repelled him from the comrades whose acquaintance he had made, on the supposition that they were decent, well-bred men. Long afterwards, in his gayest moments, there recurred to his mind the little official with the bald forehead, with his heart-rending words, "Leave me alone! Why do you insult me?" In these moving words, other words resounded—"I am thy brother." And the young man covered his face with his hand; and many a time afterwards, in the course of his life, shuddered at seeing how much inhumanity there is in man, how much savage coarseness is concealed beneath refined, cultured, worldly refinement, and even, O God! in that man whom the world acknowledges as honourable and upright.

It would be difficult to find another man who lived so entirely for his duties. It is not enough to say that Akaky laboured with zeal; no, he laboured with love. In his copying, he found a varied and agreeable employment. Enjoyment was written on his face; some letters were even favourites with him; and when he encountered these, he smiled, winked, and worked with his lips, till it seemed as though each letter might be read in his face, as his pen traced it. If his pay had been in proportion to his zeal, he would, perhaps, to his great surprise, have been made even a councillor of state. But he worked, as his companions, the wits, put it, like a horse in a mill.

However, it would be untrue to say that no attention was paid to him. One director being a kindly man, and desirous of rewarding him for his long service, ordered him to be given something more important than mere copying. So he was ordered to make a report of an already concluded affair, to another department; the duty consisting simply in changing the heading and altering a few words from the first to the third person. This caused him so much toil, that he broke into a perspiration, rubbed his forehead, and finally said, "No, give me rather something to copy." After that they let him copy on forever.

Outside this copying, it appeared that nothing existed for him. He gave no thought to his clothes. His uniform was not green, but a sort of rusty-meal colour. The collar was low, so that his neck, in spite of the fact that it was not long, seemed inordinately so as it emerged from it, like the necks of the plaster cats which pedlars carry about on their heads. And something was always sticking to his uniform, either a bit of hay or some trifle. Moreover, he had a peculiar knack, as he walked along the street, of arriving beneath a window just as all sorts of rubbish was being flung out of it; hence he always bore about on his hat scraps of melon rinds, and other such articles. Never once in his life did he give heed to what was going on every day in the street; while it is well known that his young brother officials trained the range of their glances till they could see when any one's trouser-straps came undone upon the opposite sidewalk, which always brought a malicious smile to their faces. But Akaky Akakiyevich saw in all things the clean, even strokes of his written lines; and only when a horse thrust his nose, from some unknown quarter, over his shoulder, and sent a whole gust of wind down his neck from his nostrils, did he observe that he was not in the middle of a line, but in the middle of the street.

On reaching home, he sat down at once at the table, sipped his cabbage-soup up quickly, and swallowed a bit of beef with onions, never noticing their taste, and gulping down everything with flies and anything else which the Lord happened to send at the moment. When he saw that his stomach was beginning to swell, he rose from the table, and copied papers which he had brought home. If there happened to be none, he took copies for himself, for his own gratification, especially if the document was noteworthy, not on account of its style, but of its being addressed to some distinguished person.

Even at the hour when the grey St. Petersburg sky had quite disappeared, and all the official world had eaten or dined, each as he could, in accordance with the salary he received and his own fancy; when all were resting from the department jar of pens, running to and fro, for their own and other people's indispensable occupations, and from all the work that an uneasy man makes willingly for himself, rather than what is necessary; when officials hasten to dedicate to pleasure the time which is left to them, one bolder than the rest going to the theatre; another, into the street looking under the bonnets; another wasting his evening in compliments to some pretty girl, the star of a small official circle; another—and this is the common case of all—visiting his comrades on the third or fourth floor, in two small rooms with an ante-room or kitchen, and some pretensions to fashion, such as a lamp or some other trifle which has cost many a sacrifice of dinner or pleasure trip; in a word, at the hour when all officials disperse among the contracted quarters of their friends, to play whist, as they sip their tea from glasses with a kopek's worth of sugar, smoke long pipes, relate at time some bits of gossip which a Russian man can never, under any circumstances, refrain from, and when there is nothing else to talk of, repeat eternal anecdotes about the commandant to whom they had sent word that the tails of the horses on the Falconet Monument had been cut off; when all strive to divert themselves, Akaky Akakiyevich indulged in no kind of diversion. No one could even say that he had seen him at any kind of evening party. Having written to his heart's content, he lay down to sleep, smiling at the thought of the coming day—of what God might send him to copy on the morrow.

Thus flowed on the peaceful life of the man, who, with a salary of four hundred rubles, understood how to be content with his lot; and thus it would have continued to flow on, perhaps, to extreme old age, were it not that there are various ills strewn along the path of life for titular councillors as well as for private, actual, court, and every other species of councillor, even to those who never give any advice or take any themselves.

There exists in St. Petersburg a powerful foe of all who receive a salary of four hundred rubles a year, or thereabouts. This foe is no other than the Northern cold, although it is said to be very healthy. At nine o'clock in the morning, at the very hour when the streets are filled with men bound for the various official departments, it begins to bestow such powerful and piercing nips on all noses impartially, that the poor officials really do not know what to do with them. At an hour when the foreheads of even those who occupy exalted positions ache with the cold, and tears start to their eyes, the poor titular councillors are sometimes quite unprotected. Their only salvation lies in traversing as quickly as possible, in their thin little cloaks, five or six streets, and then warming their feet in the porter's room, and so thawing all their talents and qualifications for official service, which had become frozen on the way.

Akaky Akakiyevich had felt for some time that his back and shoulders were paining with peculiar poignancy, in spite of the fact that he tried to traverse the distance with all possible speed. He began finally to wonder whether the fault did not lie in his cloak. He examined it thoroughly at home, and discovered that in two places, namely, on the back and shoulders, it had become thin as gauze. The cloth was worn to such a degree that he could see throught it, and the lining had fallen into pieces. You must know that Akaky Akakiyevich's cloak served as an object of ridicule to the officials. They even refused it the noble name of cloak, and called it a cape. In fact, it was of singular make, its collar diminishing year by year to serve to patch its other parts. The patching did not exhibit great skill on the part of the tailor, and was, in fact, baggy and ugly. Seeing how the matter stood, Akaky Akakiyevich decided that it would be necessary to take the cloak to Petrovich, the tailor, who lived somewhere on the fourth floor up a dark staircase, and who, in spite of his having but one eye and pock-marks all over his face, busied himself with considerable success in repairing the trousers and coats of officials and others; that is to say, when he was sober and not nursing some other scheme in his head.

It is not necessary to say much about this tailor, but as it is the custom to have the character of each personage in a novel clearly defined there is no help for it, so here is Petrovich the tailor. At first he was called only Grigory, and was some gentleman's serf. He commenced calling himself Petrovich from the time when he received his free papers, and further began to drink heavily on all holidays, at first on the great ones, and then on all church festivals without discrimination, wherever a cross stood in the calendar. On this point he was faithful to ancestral custom; and when quarrelling with his wife, he called her a low female and a German. As we have mentioned his wife, it will be necessary to say a word or two about her. Unfortunately, little is known of her beyond the fact that Petrovich had a wife, who wore a cap and a dress, but could not lay claim to beauty, at least, no one but the soldiers of the guard even looked under her cap when they met her.

Ascending the staircase which led to Petrovich's room—which staircase was all soaked with dish-water and reeked with the smell of spirits which affects the eyes, and is an inevitable adjunct to all dark stairways in St. Petersburg houses—ascending the stairs, Akaky Akakiyevich pondered how much Petrovich would ask, and mentally resolved not to give more than two rubles. The door was open, for the mistress, in cooking some fish, had raised such a smoke in the kitchen that not even the beetles were visible. Akaky Akakiyevich passed through the kitchen unperceived, even by the housewife, and at length reached a room where he beheld Petrovich seated on a large unpainted table, with his legs tucked under him like a Turkish pasha. His feet were bare, after the fashion of tailors as they sit at work; and the first thing which caught the eye was his thumb, with a deformed nail thick and strong as a turtle's shell. About Petrovich's neck hung a skein of silk and thread, and upon his knees lay some old garment. He had been trying unsuccessfully for three minutes to thread his needle, and was enraged at the darkness and even at the thread, growling in a low voice, "It won't go through, the barbarian! you pricked me, you rascal!"

Akaky Akakiyevich was vexed at arriving at the precise moment when Petrovich was angry. He liked to order something of Petrovich when he was a little downhearted, or, as his wife expressed it, "when he had settled himself with brandy, the one-eyed devil!" Under such circumstances Petrovich generally came down in his price very readily, and even bowed and returned thanks. Afterwards, to be sure, his wife would come, complaining that her husband had been drunk, and so had fixed the price too low; but, if only a ten-kopek piece were added then the matter would be settled. But now it appeared that Petrovich was in a sober condition, and therefore rough, taciturn, and inclined to demand, Satan only knows what price. Akaky Akakiyevich felt this, and would gladly have beat a retreat, but he was in for it. Petrovich screwed up his one eye very intently at him, and Akaky Akakiyevich involuntarily said, "How do you do, Petrovich?"

"I wish you a good morning, sir," said Petrovich squinting at Akaky Akakiyevich's hands, to see what sort of booty he had brought.

"Ah! I—to you, Petrovich, this—" It must be known that Akaky Akakiyevich expressed himself chiefly by prepositions, adverbs, and scraps of phrases which had no meaning whatever. If the matter was a very difficult one, he had a habit of never completing his sentences, so that frequently, having begun a phrase with the words, "This, in fact, is quite—" he forgot to go on, thinking he had already finished it.

"What is it?" asked Petrovich, and with his one eye scanned Akaky Akakiyevich's whole uniform from the collar down to the cuffs, the back, the tails and the buttonholes, all of which were well known to him, since they were his own handiwork. Such is the habit of tailors; it is the first thing they do on meeting one.

"But I, here, this—Petrovich—a cloak, cloth—here you see, everywhere, in different places, it is quite strong—it is a little dusty and looks old, but it is new, only here in one place it is a little—on the back, and here on one of the shoulders, it is a little worn, yes, here on this shoulder it is a little—do you see? That is all. And a little work—"

Petrovich took the cloak, spread it out, to begin with, on the table, looked at it hard, shook his head, reached out his hand to the window-sill for his snuff-box, adorned with the portrait of some general, though what general is unknown, for the place where the face should have been had been rubbed through by the finger and a square bit of paper had been pasted over it. Having taken a pinch of snuff, Petrovich held up the cloak, and inspected it against the light, and again shook his head. Then he turned it, lining upwards, and shook his head once more. After which he again lifted the general-adorned lid with its bit of pasted paper, and having stuffed his nose with snuff, closed and put away the snuff-box, and said finally, "No, it is impossible to mend it. It is a wretched garment!"

Akaky Akakiyevich's heart sank at these words.

"Why is it impossible, Petrovich?" he said, almost in the pleading voice of a child. "All that ails it is, that it is worn on the shoulders. You must have some pieces——"

"Yes, patches could be found, patches are easily found," said Petrovich, "but there's nothing to sew them to. The thing is completely rotten. If you put a needle to it—see, it will give way."

"Let it give way, and you can put on another patch at once."

"But there is nothing to put the patches on to. There's no use in strengthening it. It is too far gone. It's lucky that it's cloth, for, if the wind were to blow, it would fly away."

"Well, strengthen it again. How this, in fact——"

"No," said Petrovich decisively, "there is nothing to be done with it. It's a thoroughly bad job. You'd better, when the cold winter weather comes on, make yourself some gaiters out of it, because stockings are not warm. The Germans invented them in order to make more money." Petrovich loved on all occasions to have a fling at the Germans. "But it is plain you must have a new cloak."

At the word "new" all grew dark before Akaky Akakiyevich's eyes, and everything in the room began to whirl round. The only thing he saw clearly was the general with the paper face on the lid of Petrovich's snuff-box. "A new one?" said he, as if still in a dream. "Why, I have no money for that."

"Yes, a new one," said Petrovich, with barbarous composure.

"Well, if it came to a new one, how—it——"

"You mean how much would it cost?"

"Yes."

"Well, you would have to lay out a hundred and fifty or more," said Petrovich, and pursed up his lips significantly. He liked to produce powerful effects, liked to stun utterly and suddenly, and then to glance sideways to see what face the stunned person would put on the matter.

"A hundred and fifty rubles for a cloak!" shrieked poor Akaky Akakiyevich, perhaps for the first time in his life, for his voice had always been distinguished for softness.

"Yes, sir," said Petrovich, "for any kind of cloak. If you have a marten fur on the collar, or a silk-lined hood, it will mount up to two hundred."

"Petrovich, please," said Akaky Akakiyevich in a beseeching tone, not hearing, and not trying to hear, Petrovich's words, and disregarding all his "effects," "some repairs, in order that it may wear yet a little longer."

"No, it would only be a waste of time and money," said Petrovich. And Akaky Akakiyevich went away after these words, utterly discouraged. But Petrovich stood for some time after his departure, with significantly compressed lips, and without betaking himself to his work, satisfied that he would not be dropped, and an artistic tailor employed.

Akaky Akakiyevich went out into the street as if in a dream. "Such an affair!" he said to himself. "I did not think it had come to—" and then after a pause, he added, "Well, so it is! see what it has come to at last! and I never imagined that it was so!" Then followed a long silence, after which he exclaimed, "Well, so it is! see what already—nothing unexpected that—it would be nothing—what a strange circumstance!" So saying, instead of going home, he went in exactly the opposite direction without suspecting it. On the way, a chimney-sweep bumped up against him, and blackened his shoulder, and a whole hatful of rubbish landed on him from the top of a house which was building. He did not notice it, and only when he ran against a watchman, who, having planted his halberd beside him, was shaking some snuff from his box into his horny hand, did he recover himself a little, and that because the watchman said, "Why are you poking yourself into a man's very face? Haven't you the pavement?" This caused him to look about him, and turn towards home.

There only, he finally began to collect his thoughts, and to survey his position in its clear and actual light, and to argue with himself, sensibly and frankly, as with a reasonable friend, with whom one can discuss private and personal matters. "No," said Akaky Akakiyevich, "it is impossible to reason with Petrovich now. He is that—evidently, his wife has been beating him. I'd better go to him on Sunday morning. After Saturday night he will be a little cross-eyed and sleepy, for he will want to get drunk, and his wife won't give him any money, and at such a time, a ten-kopek piece in his hand will—he will become more fit to reason with, and then the cloak and that——" Thus argued Akaky Akakiyevich with himself, regained his courage, and waited until the first Sunday, when, seeing from afar that Petrovich's wife had left the house, he went straight to him.

Petrovich's eye was indeed very much askew after Saturday. His head drooped, and he was very sleepy; but for all that, as soon as he knew what it was a question of, it seemed as though Satan jogged his memory. "Impossible," said he. "Please to order a new one." Thereupon Akaky Akakiyevich handed over the ten-kopek piece. "Thank you, sir. I will drink your good health," said Petrovich. "But as for the cloak, don't trouble yourself about it; it is good for nothing. I will make you a capital new one, so let us settle about it now."

Akaky Akakiyevich was still for mending it, but Petrovich would not hear of it, and said, "I shall certainly have to make you a new one, and you may depend upon it that I shall do my best. It may even be, as the fashion goes, that the collar can be fastened by silver hooks under a flap."

Then Akaky Akakiyevich saw that it was impossible to get along without a new cloak, and his spirit sank utterly. How, in fact, was it to be done? Where was the money to come from? He must have some new trousers, and pay a debt of long standing to the shoemaker for putting new tops to his old boots, and he must order three shirts from the seamstress, and a couple of pieces of linen. In short, all his money must be spent. And even if the director should be so kind as to order him to receive forty-five or even fifty rubles instead of forty, it would be a mere nothing, a mere drop in the ocean towards the funds necessary for a cloak, although he knew that Petrovich was often wrongheaded enough to blurt out some outrageous price, so that even his own wife could not refrain from exclaiming, "Have you lost your senses, you fool?" At one time he would not work at any price, and now it was quite likely that he had named a higher sum than the cloak would cost.

But although he knew that Petrovich would undertake to make a cloak for eighty rubles, still, where was he to get the eighty rubles from? He might possibly manage half. Yes, half might be procured, but where was the other half to come from? But the reader must first be told where the first half came from.

Akaky Akakiyevich had a habit of putting, for every ruble he spent, a groschen into a small box, fastened with lock and key, and with a slit in the top for the reception of money. At the end of every half-year he counted over the heap of coppers, and changed it for silver. This he had done for a long time, and in the course of years, the sum had mounted up to over forty rubles. Thus he had one half on hand. But where was he to find the other half? Where was he to get another forty rubles from? Akaky Akakiyevich thought and thought, and decided that it would be necessary to curtail his ordinary expenses, for the space of one year at least, to dispense with tea in the evening, to burn no candles, and, if there was anything which he must do, to go into his landlady's room, and work by her light. When he went into the street, he must walk as lightly as he could, and as cautiously, upon the stones, almost upon tiptoe, in order not to wear his heels down in too short a time. He must give the laundress as little to wash as possible; and, in order not to wear out his clothes, he must take them off as soon as he got home, and wear only his cotton dressing-gown, which had been long and carefully saved.

To tell the truth, it was a little hard for him at first to accustom himself to these deprivations. But he got used to them at length, after a fashion, and all went smoothly. He even got used to being hungry in the evening, but he made up for it by treating himself, so to say, in spirit, by bearing ever in mind the idea of his future cloak. From that time forth, his existence seemed to become, in some way, fuller, as if he were married, or as if some other man lived in him, as if, in fact, he were not alone, and some pleasant friend had consented to travel along life's path with him, the friend being no other than the cloak, with thick wadding and a strong lining incapable of wearing out. He became more lively, and even his character grew firmer, like that of a man who has made up his mind, and set himself a goal. From his face and gait, doubt and indecision, all hesitating and wavering disappeared of themselves. Fire gleamed in his eyes, and occasionally the boldest and most daring ideas flitted through his mind. Why not, for instance, have marten fur on the collar? The thought of this almost made him absent-minded. Once, in copying a letter, he nearly made a mistake, so that he exclaimed almost aloud, "Ugh!" and crossed himself. Once, in the course of every month, he had a conference with Petrovich on the subject of the cloak, where it would be better to buy the cloth, and the colour, and the price. He always returned home satisfied, though troubled, reflecting that the time would come at last when it could all be bought, and then the cloak made.

The affair progressed more briskly than he had expected. For beyond all his hopes, the director awarded neither forty nor forty-five rubles for Akaky Akakiyevich's share, but sixty. Whether he suspected that Akaky Akakiyevich needed a cloak, or whether it was merely chance, at all events, twenty extra rubles were by this means provided. This circumstance hastened matters. Two or three months more of hunger and Akaky Akakiyevich had accumulated about eighty rubles. His heart, generally so quiet, began to throb. On the first possible day, he went shopping in company with Petrovich. They bought some very good cloth, and at a reasonable rate too, for they had been considering the matter for six months, and rarely let a month pass without their visiting the shops to enquire prices. Petrovich himself said that no better cloth could be had. For lining, they selected a cotton stuff, but so firm and thick, that Petrovich declared it to be better than silk, and even prettier and more glossy. They did not buy the marten fur, because it was, in fact, dear, but in its stead, they picked out the very best of cat-skin which could be found in the shop, and which might, indeed, be taken for marten at a distance.

Petrovich worked at the cloak two whole weeks, for there was a great deal of quilting; otherwise it would have been finished sooner. He charged twelve rubles for the job, it could not possibly have been done for less. It was all sewed with silk, in small, double seams, and Petrovich went over each seam afterwards with his own teeth, stamping in various patterns.

It was—it is difficult to say precisely on what day, but probably the most glorious one in Akaky Akakiyevich's life, when Petrovich at length brought home the cloak. He brought it in the morning, before the hour when it was necessary to start for the department. Never did a cloak arrive so exactly in the nick of time, for the severe cold had set in, and it seemed to threaten to increase. Petrovich brought the cloak himself as befits a good tailor. On his countenance was a significant expression, such as Akaky Akakiyevich had never beheld there. He seemed fully sensible that he had done no small deed, and crossed a gulf separating tailors who put in linings, and execute repairs, from those who make new things. He took the cloak out of the pocket-handerchief in which he had brought it. The handkerchief was fresh from the laundress, and he put it in his pocket for use. Taking out the cloak, he gazed proudly at it, held it up with both hands, and flung it skilfully over the shoulders of Akaky Akakiyevich. Then he pulled it and fitted it down behind with his hand, and he draped it around Akaky Akakiyevich without buttoning it. Akaky Akakiyevich, like an experienced man, wished to try the sleeves. Petrovich helped him on with them, and it turned out that the sleeves were satisfactory also. In short, the cloak appeared to be perfect, and most seasonable. Petrovich did not neglect to observe that it was only because he lived in a narrow street, and had no signboard, and had known Akaky Akakiyevich so long, that he had made it so cheaply; but that if he had been in business on the Nevsky Prospect, he would have charged seventy-five rubles for the making alone. Akaky Akakiyevich did not care to argue this point with Petrovich. He paid him, thanked him, and set out at once in his new cloak for the department. Petrovich followed him, and pausing in the street, gazed long at the cloak in the distance, after which he went to one side expressly to run through a crooked alley, and emerge again into the street beyond to gaze once more upon the cloak from another point, namely, directly in front.

Meantime Akaky Akakiyevich went on in holiday mood. He was conscious every second of the time that he had a new cloak on his shoulders, and several times he laughed with internal satisfaction. In fact, there were two advantages, one was its warmth, the other its beauty. He saw nothing of the road, but suddenly found himself at the department. He took off his cloak in the ante-room, looked it over carefully, and confided it to the special care of the attendant. It is impossible to say precisely how it was that every one in the department knew at once that Akaky Akakiyevich had a new cloak, and that the "cape" no longer existed. All rushed at the same moment into the ante-room to inspect it. They congratulated him, and said pleasant things to him, so that he began at first to smile, and then to grow ashamed. When all surrounded him, and said that the new cloak must be "christened," and that he must at least give them all a party, Akaky Akakiyevich lost his head completely, and did not know where he stood, what to answer, or how to get out of it. He stood blushing all over for several minutes, trying to assure them with great simplicity that it was not a new cloak, that it was in fact the old "cape."

At length one of the officials, assistant to the head clerk, in order to show that he was not at all proud, and on good terms with his inferiors, said:

"So be it, only I will give the party instead of Akaky Akakiyevich; I invite you all to tea with me to-night. It just happens to be my name-day too."

The officials naturally at once offered the assistant clerk their congratulations, and accepted the invitation with pleasure. Akaky Akakiye-vich would have declined; but all declared that it was discourteous, that it was simply a sin and a shame, and that he could not possibly refuse. Besides, the notion became pleasant to him when he recollected that he should thereby have a chance of wearing his new cloak in the evening also.

That whole day was truly a most triumphant festival for Akaky Akakiyevich. He returned home in the most happy frame of mind, took off his cloak, and hung it carefully on the wall, admiring afresh the cloth and the lining. Then he brought out his old, worn-out cloak, for comparison. He looked at it, and laughed, so vast was the difference. And long after dinner he laughed again when the condition of the "cape" recurred to his mind. He dined cheerfully, and after dinner wrote nothing, but took his ease for a while on the bed, until it got dark. Then he dressed himself leisurely, put on his cloak, and stepped out into the street.

Where the host lived, unfortunately we cannot say. Our memory begins to fail us badly. The houses and streets in St. Petersburg have become so mixed up in our head that it is very difficult to get anything out of it again in proper form. This much is certain, that the official lived in the best part of the city; and therefore it must have been anything but near to Akaky Akakiyevich's residence. Akaky Akakiyevich was first obliged to traverse a kind of wilderness of deserted, dimly-lighted streets. But in proportion as he approached the official's quarter of the city, the streets became more lively, more populous, and more brilliantly illuminated. Pedestrians began to appear; handsomely dressed ladies were more frequently encountered; the men had otter skin collars to their coats; shabby sleigh-men with their wooden, railed sledges stuck over with brassheaded nails, became rarer; whilst on the other hand, more and more drivers in red velvet caps, lacquered sledges and bear-skin coats began to appear, and carriages with rich hammer-cloths flew swiftly through the streets, their wheels scrunching the snow.

Akaky Akakiyevich gazed upon all this as upon a novel sight. He had not been in the streets during the evening for years. He halted out of curiosity before a shop-window, to look at a picture representing a handsome woman, who had thrown off her shoe, thereby baring her whole foot in a very pretty way; whilst behind her the head of a man with whiskers and a handsome moustache peeped through the doorway of another room. Akaky Akakiyevich shook his head, and laughed, and then went on his way. Why did he laugh? Either because he had met with a thing utterly unknown, but for which every one cherishes, nevertheless, some sort of feeling, or else he thought, like many officials, "Well, those French! What is to be said? If they do go in for anything of that sort, why——" But possibly he did not think at all.

Akaky Akakiyevich at length reached the house in which the head clerk's assistant lodged. He lived in fine style. The staircase was lit by a lamp, his apartment being on the second floor. On entering the vestibule, Akaky Akakiyevich beheld a whole row of goloshes on the floor. Among them, in the centre of the room, stood a samovar, humming and emitting clouds of steam. On the walls hung all sorts of coats and cloaks, among which there were even some with beaver collars, or velvet facings. Beyond, the buzz of conversation was audible, and became clear and loud, when the servant came out with a trayful of empty glasses, cream-jugs and sugar-bowls. It was evident that the officials had arrived long before, and had already finished their first glass of tea.

Akaky Akakiyevich, having hung up his own cloak, entered the inner room. Before him all at once appeared lights, officials, pipes, and card-tables, and he was bewildered by a sound of rapid conversation rising from all the tables, and the noise of moving chairs. He halted very awkwardly in the middle of the room, wondering what he ought to do. But they had seen him. They received him with a shout, and all thronged at once into the ante-room, and there took another look at his cloak. Akaky Akakiyevich, although somewhat confused, was frank-hearted, and could not refrain from rejoicing when he saw how they praised his cloak. Then, of course, they all dropped him and his cloak, and returned, as was proper, to the tables set out for whist.

All this, the noise, the talk, and the throng of people, was rather overwhelming to Akaky Akakiyevich. He simply did not know where he stood, or where to put his hands, his feet, and his whole body. Finally he sat down by the players, looked at the cards, gazed at the face of one and another, and after a while began to gape, and to feel that it was wearisome, the more so, as the hour was already long past when he usually went to bed. He wanted to take leave of the host, but they would not let him go, saying that he must not fail to drink a glass of champagne, in honour of his new garment. In the course of an hour, supper, consisting of vegetable salad, cold veal, pastry, confectioner's pies, and champagne, was served. They made Akaky Akakiyevich drink two glasses of champagne, after which he felt things grow livelier.

Still, he could not forget that it was twelve o'clock, and that he should have been at home long ago. In order that the host might not think of some excuse for detaining him, he stole out of the room quickly, sought out, in the ante-room, his cloak, which, to his sorrow, he found lying on the floor, brushed it, picked off every speck upon it, put it on his shoulders, and descended the stairs to the street.

In the street all was still bright. Some petty shops, those permanent clubs of servants and all sorts of folks, were open. Others were shut, but, nevertheless, showed a streak of light the whole length of the door-crack, indicating that they were not yet free of company, and that probably some domestics, male and female, were finishing their stories and conversations, whilst leaving their masters in complete ignorance as to their whereabouts. Akaky Akakiyevich went on in a happy frame of mind. He even started to run, without knowing why, after some lady, who flew past like a flash of lightning. But he stopped short, and went on very quietly as before, wondering why he had quickened his pace. Soon there spread before him those deserted streets which are not cheerful in the daytime, to say nothing of the evening. Now they were even more dim and lonely. The lanterns began to grow rarer, oil, evidently, had been less liberally supplied. Then came wooden houses and fences. Not a soul anywhere; only the snow sparkled in the streets, and mournfully veiled the low-roofed cabins with their closed shutters. He approached the spot where the street crossed a vast square with houses barely visible on its farther side, a square which seemed a fearful desert.

Afar, a tiny spark glimmered from some watchman's-box, which seemed to stand on the edge of the world. Akaky Akakiyevich's cheerfulness diminished at this point in a marked degree. He entered the square, not without an involuntary sensation of fear, as though his heart warned him of some evil. He glanced back, and on both sides it was like a sea about him. "No, it is better not to look," he thought, and went on, closing his eyes. When he opened them, to see whether he was near the end of the square, he suddenly beheld, standing just before his very nose, some bearded individuals, of precisely what sort, he could not make out. All grew dark before his eyes, and his heart throbbed.

"Of course, the cloak is mine!" said one of them in a loud voice, seizing hold of his collar. Akaky Akakiyevich was about to shout "Help!" when the second man thrust a fist, about the size of an official's head, at his very mouth, muttering, "Just you dare to scream!"

Akaky Akakiyevich felt them strip off his cloak, and give him a kick. He fell headlong upon the snow, and felt no more.

In a few minutes he recovered consciousness, and rose to his feet, but no one was there. He felt that it was cold in the square, and that his cloak was gone. He began to shout, but his voice did not appear to reach the outskirts of the square. In despair, but without ceasing to shout, he started at a run across the square, straight towards the watch-box, beside which stood the watchman, leaning on his halberd, and apparently curious to know what kind of a customer was running towards him shouting. Akaky Akakiyevich ran up to him, and began in a sobbing voice to shout that he was asleep, and attended to nothing, and did not see when a man was robbed. The watchman replied that he had seen two men stop him in the middle of the square, but supposed that they were friends of his, and that, instead of scolding vainly, he had better go to the police on the morrow, so that they might make a search for whoever had stolen the cloak.

Akaky Akakiyevich ran home and arrived in a state of complete disorder, his hair which grew very thinly upon his temples and the back of his head all tousled, his body, arms and legs, covered with snow. The old woman, who was mistress of his lodgings, on hearing a terrible knocking, sprang hastily from her bed, and, with only one shoe on, ran to open the door, pressing the sleeve of her chemise to her bosom out of modesty. But when she had opened it, she fell back on beholding Akaky Akakiyevich in such a condition. When he told her about the affair, she clasped her hands, and said that he must go straight to the district chief of police, for his subordinate would turn up his nose, promise well, and drop the matter there. The very best thing to do, therefore, would be to go to the district chief, whom she knew, because Finnish Anna, her former cook, was now nurse at his house. She often saw him passing the house, and he was at church every Sunday, praying, but at the same time gazing cheerfully at everybody; so that he must be a good man, judging from all appearances. Having listened to this opinion, Akaky Akakiyevich betook himself sadly to his room. And how he spent the night there, any one who can put himself in another's place may readily imagine.

Early in the morning, he presented himself at the district chief's, but was told the official was asleep. He went again at ten and was again informed that he was asleep. At eleven, and they said, "The superintendent is not at home." At dinner time, and the clerks in the ante-room would not admit him on any terms, and insisted upon knowing his business. So that at last, for once in his life, Akaky Akakiyevich felt an inclination to show some spirit, and said curtly that he must see the chief in person, that they ought not to presume to refuse him entrance, that he came from the department of justice, and that when he complained of them, they would see.

The clerks dared make no reply to this, and one of them went to call the chief, who listened to the strange story of the theft of the coat. Instead of directing his attention to the principal points of the matter, he began to question Akaky Akakiyevich. Why was he going home so late? Was he in the habit of doing so, or had he been to some disorderly house? So that Akaky Akakiyevich got thoroughly confused, and left him, without knowing whether the affair of his cloak was in proper train or not.

All that day, for the first time in his life, he never went near the department. The next day he made his appearance, very pale, and in his old cape, which had become even more shabby. The news of the robbery of the cloak touched many, although there were some officials present who never lost an opportunity, even such a one as the present, of ridiculing Akaky Akakiyevich. They decided to make a collection for him on the spot, but the officials had already spent a great deal in subscribing for the director's portrait, and for some book, at the suggestion of the head of that division, who was a friend of the author; and so the sum was trifling.

One of them, moved by pity, resolved to help Akaky Akakiyevich with some good advice, at least, and told him that he ought not to go to the police, for although it might happen that a police-officer, wishing to win the approval of his superiors, might hunt up the cloak by some means, still, his cloak would remain in the possession of the police if he did not offer legal proof that it belonged to him. The best thing for him, therefore, would be to apply to a certain prominent personage; since this prominent personage, by entering into relation with the proper persons, could greatly expedite the matter.

As there was nothing else to be done, Akaky Akakiyevich decided to go to the prominent personage. What was the exact official position of the prominent personage, remains unknown to this day. The reader must know that the prominent personage had but recently become a prominent personage, having up to that time been only an insignificant person. Moreover, his present position was not considered prominent in comparison with others still more so. But there is always a circle of people to whom what is insignificant in the eyes of others, is important enough. Moreover, he strove to increase his importance by sundry devices. For instance, he managed to have the inferior officials meet him on the staircase when he entered upon his service; no one was to presume to come directly to him, but the strictest etiquette must be observed; the collegiate recorder must make a report to the government secretary, the government secretary to the titular councillor, or whatever other man was proper, and all business must come before him in this manner. In Holy Russia, all is thus contaminated with the love of imitation; every man imitates and copies his superior. They even say that a certain titular councillor, when promoted to the head of some small separate office, immediately partitioned off a private room for himself, called it the audience chamber, and posted at the door a lackey with red collar and braid, who grasped the handle of the door, and opened to all comers, though the audience chamber would hardly hold an ordinary writing table.

The manners and customs of the prominent personage were grand and imposing, but rather exaggerated. The main foundation of his system was strictness. "Strictness, strictness, and always strictness!" he generally said; and at the last word he looked significantly into the face of the person to whom he spoke. But there was no necessity for this, for the halfscore of subordinates, who formed the entire force of the office, were properly afraid. On catching sight of him afar off, they left their work, and waited, drawn up in line, until he had passed through the room. His ordinary converse with his inferiors smacked of sternness, and consisted chiefly of three phrases: "How dare you?" "Do you know whom you are speaking to?" "Do you realise who is standing before you?"

Otherwise he was a very kind-hearted man, good to his comrades, and ready to oblige. But the rank of general threw him completely off his balance. On receiving any one of that rank, he became confused, lost his way, as it were, and never knew what to do. If he chanced to be amongst his equals, he was still a very nice kind of man, a very good fellow in many respects, and not stupid, but the very moment that he found himself in the society of people but one rank lower than himself, he became silent. And his situation aroused sympathy, the more so, as he felt himself that he might have been making an incomparably better use of his time. In his eyes, there was sometimes visible a desire to join some interesting conversation or group, but he was kept back by the thought, "Would it not be a very great condescension on his part? Would it not be familiar? And would he not thereby lose his importance?" And in consequence of such reflections, he always remained in the same dumb state, uttering from time to time a few monosyllabic sounds, and thereby earning the name of the most wearisome of men.

To this prominent personage Akaky Akakiyevich presented himself, and this at the most unfavourable time for himself, though opportune for the prominent personage. The prominent personage was in his cabinet, conversing very gaily with an old acquaintance and companion of his childhood, whom he had not seen for several years, and who had just arrived, when it was announced to him that a person named Bashmachkin had come. He asked abruptly, "Who is he?"—"Some official," he was informed. "Ah, he can wait! This is no time for him to call," said the important man.

It must be remarked here that the important man lied outrageously. He had said all he had to say to his friend long before, and the conversation had been interspersed for some time with very long pauses, during which they merely slapped each other on the leg, and said, "You think so, Ivan Abramovich!" "Just so, Stepan Varlamovich!" Nevertheless, he ordered that the official should be kept waiting, in order to show his friend, a man who had not been in the service for a long time, but had lived at home in the country, how long officials had to wait in his ante-room.

At length, having talked himself completely out, and more than that, having had his fill of pauses, and smoked a cigar in a very comfortable arm-chair with reclining back, he suddenly seemed to recollect, and said to the secretary, who stood by the door with papers of reports, "So it seems that there is an official waiting to see me. Tell him that he may come in." On perceiving Akaky Akakiyevich's modest mien and his worn uniform, he turned abruptly to him, and said, "What do you want?" in a curt hard voice, which he had practised in his room in private, and before the looking-glass, for a whole week before being raised to his present rank.

Akaky Akakiyevich, who was already imbued with a due amount of fear, became somewhat confused, and as well as his tongue would permit, explained, with a rather more frequent addition than usual of the word "that" that his cloak was quite new, and had been stolen in the most inhuman manner; that he had applied to him, in order that he might, in some way, by his intermediation—that he might enter into correspondence with the chief of police, and find the cloak.

For some inexplicable reason, this conduct seemed familiar to the prominent personage.

"What, my dear sir!" he said abruptly, "are you not acquainted with etiquette? To whom have you come? Don't you know how such matters are managed? You should first have presented a petition to the office. It would have gone to the head of the department, then to the chief of the division, then it would have been handed over to the secretary, and the secretary would have given it to me."

"But, your excellency," said Akaky Akakiyevich, trying to collect his small handful of wits, and conscious at the same time that he was perspiring terribly, "I, your excellency, presumed to trouble you because secretaries—are an untrustworthy race."

"What, what, what!" said the important personage. "Where did you get such courage? Where did you get such ideas? What impudence towards their chiefs and superiors has spread among the young generation!" The prominent personage apparently had not observed that Akaky Akakiyevich was already in the neighbourhood of fifty. If he could be called a young man, it must have been in comparison with some one who was seventy. "Do you know to whom you are speaking? Do you realise who is standing before you? Do you realise it? Do you realise it, I ask you!" Then he stamped his foot, and raised his voice to such a pitch that it would have frightened even a different man from Akaky Akakiyevich.

Akaky Akakiyevich's senses failed him. He staggered, trembled in every limb, and, if the porters had not run in to support him, would have fallen to the floor. They carried him out insensible. But the prominent personage, gratified that the effect should have surpassed his expectations, and quite intoxicated with the thought that his word could even deprive a man of his senses, glanced sideways at his friend in order to see how he looked upon this, and perceived, not without satisfaction, that his friend was in a most uneasy frame of mind, and even beginning on his part, to feel a trifle frightened.

Akaky Akakiyevich could not remember how he descended the stairs, and got into the street. He felt neither his hands nor feet. Never in his life had he been so rated by any high official, let alone a strange one. He went staggering on through the snow-storm, which was blowing in the streets, with his mouth wide open. The wind, in St. Petersburg fashion, darted upon him from all quarters, and down every cross-street. In a twinkling it had blown a quinsy into his throat, and he reached home unable to utter a word. His throat was swollen, and he lay down on his bed. So powerful is sometimes a good scolding!

The next day a violent fever developed. Thanks to the generous assistance of the St. Petersburg climate, the malady progressed more rapidly than could have been expected, and when the doctor arrived, he found, on feeling the sick man's pulse, that there was nothing to be done, except to prescribe a poultice, so that the patient might not be left entirely without the beneficent aid of medicine. But at the same time, he predicted his end in thirty-six hours. After this he turned to the landlady, and said, "And as for you, don't waste your time on him. Order his pine coffin now, for an oak one will be too expensive for him."

Did Akaky Akakiyevich hear these fatal words? And if he heard them, did they produce any overwhelming effect upon him? Did he lament the bitterness of his life?—We know not, for he continued in a delirious condition. Visions incessantly appeared to him, each stranger than the other. Now he saw Petrovich, and ordered him to make a cloak, with some traps for robbers, who seemed to him to be always under the bed; and he cried every moment to the landlady to pull one of them from under his coverlet. Then he inquired why his old mantle hung before him when he had a new cloak. Next he fancied that he was standing before the prominent person, listening to a thorough setting-down and saying, "Forgive me, your excellency!" but at last he began to curse, uttering the most horrible words, so that his aged landlady crossed herself, never in her life having heard anything of the kind from him, and more so, as these words followed directly after the words "your excellency." Later on he talked utter nonsense, of which nothing could be made, all that was evident being that these incoherent words and thoughts hovered ever about one thing, his cloak.

At length poor Akaky Akakiyevich breathed his last. They sealed up neither his room nor his effects, because, in the first place, there were no heirs, and, in the second, there was very little to inherit beyond a bundle of goosequills, a quire of white official paper, three pairs of socks, two or three buttons which had burst off his trousers, and the mantle already known to the reader. To whom all this fell, God knows. I confess that the person who told me this tale took no interest in the matter. They carried Akaky Akakiyevich out, and buried him.

And St. Petersburg was left without Akaky Akakiyevich, as though he had never lived there. A being disappeared, who was protected by none, dear to none, interesting to none, and who never even attracted to himself the attention of those students of human nature who omit no opportunity of thrusting a pin through a common fly and examining it under the microscope. A being who bore meekly the jibes of the department, and went to his grave without having done one unusual deed, but to whom, nevertheless, at the close of his life, appeared a bright visitant in the form of a cloak, which momentarily cheered his poor life, and upon him, thereafter, an intolerable misfortune descended, just as it descends upon the heads of the mighty of this world!

Several days after his death, the porter was sent from the department to his lodgings, with an order for him to present himself there immediately, the chief commanding it. But the porter had to return unsuccessful, with the answer that he could not come; and to the question, "Why?" replied, "Well, because he is dead! he was buried four days ago." In this manner did they hear of Akaky Akakiyevich's death at the department. And the next day a new official sat in his place, with a handwriting by no means so upright, but more inclined and slanting.

But who could have imagined that this was not really the end of Akaky Akakiyevich, that he was destined to raise a commotion after death, as if in compensation for his utterly insignificant life? But so it happened, and our poor story unexpectedly gains a fantastic ending.

A rumour suddenly spread through St. Petersburg, that a dead man had taken to appearing on the Kalinkin Bridge, and its vicinity, at night in the form of an official seeking a stolen cloak, and that, under the pretext of its being the stolen cloak, he dragged, without regard to rank or calling, every one's cloak from his shoulders, be it catskin, beaver, fox, bear, sable, in a word, every sort of fur and skin which men adopted for their covering. One of the department officials saw the dead man with his own eyes, and immediately recognised in him Akaky Akakiyevich. This, however, inspired him with such terror, that he ran off with all his might, and therefore did not scan the dead man closely, but only saw how the latter threatened him from afar with his finger. Constant complaints poured in from all quarters, that the backs and shoulders, not only of titular but even of court councillors, were exposed to the danger of a cold, on account of the frequent dragging off of their cloaks.

Arrangements were made by the police to catch the corpse, alive or dead, at any cost, and punish him as an example to others, in the most severe manner. In this they nearly succeeded, for a watchman, on guard in Kirinshkin Lane, caught the corpse by the collar on the very scene of his evil deeds, when attempting to pull off the frieze cloak of a retired musician. Having seized him by the collar, he summoned, with a shout, two of his comrades, whom he enjoined to hold him fast, while he himself felt for a moment in his boot, in order to draw out his snuff-box, and refresh his frozen nose. But the snuff was of a sort which even a corpse could not endure. The watchman having closed his right nostril with his finger, had no sooner succeeded in holding half a handful up to the left, than the corpse sneezed so violently that he completely filled the eyes of all three. While they raised their hands to wipe them, the dead man vanished completely, so that they positively did not know whether they had actually had him in their grip at all. Thereafter the watchmen conceived such a terror of dead men that they were afraid even to seize the living, and only screamed from a distance. "Hey, there! go your way!" So the dead official began to appear even beyond the Kalinkin Bridge, causing no little terror to all timid people.

But we have totally neglected that certain prominent personage who may really be considered as the cause of the fantastic turn taken by this true history. First of all, justice compels us to say, that after the departure of poor, annihilated Akaky Akakiyevich, he felt something like remorse. Suffering was unpleasant to him, for his heart was accessible to many good impulses, in spite of the fact that his rank often prevented his showing his true self. As soon as his friend had left his cabinet, he began to think about poor Akaky Akakiyevich. And from that day forth, poor Akaky Akakiyevich, who could not bear up under an official reprimand, recurred to his mind almost every day. The thought troubled him to such an extent, that a week later he even resolved to send an official to him, to learn whether he really could assist him. And when it was reported to him that Akaky Akakiyevich had died suddenly of fever, he was startled, hearkened to the reproaches of his conscience, and was out of sorts for the whole day.

Wishing to divert his mind in some way and drive away the disagreeable impression, he set out that evening for one of his friends' houses, where he found quite a large party assembled. What was better, nearly every one was of the same rank as himself, so that he need not feel in the least constrained. This had a marvellous effect upon his mental state. He grew expansive, made himself agreeable in conversation, in short, he passed a delightful evening. After supper he drank a couple of glasses of champagne—not a bad recipe for cheerfulness, as every one knows. The champagne inclined him to various adventures, and he determined not to return home, but to go and see a certain well-known lady, of

German extraction, Karolina Ivanovna, a lady, it appears, with whom he was on a very friendly footing.

It must be mentioned that the prominent personage was no longer a young man, but a good husband and respected father of a family. Two sons, one of whom was already in the service, and a good-looking, sixteen-year-old daughter, with a slightly arched but pretty little nose, came every morning to kiss his hand and say, *"Bon jour, papa."* His wife, a still fresh and good-looking woman, first gave him her hand to kiss, and then, reversing the procedure, kissed his. But the prominent personage, though perfectly satisfied in his domestic relations, considered it stylish to have a friend in another quarter of the city. This friend was scarcely prettier or younger than his wife; but there are such puzzles in the world, and it is not our place to judge them. So the important personage descended the stairs, stepped into his sledge, said to the coachman, "To Karolina Ivanovna's," and, wrapping himself luxuriously in his warm cloak, found himself in that delightful frame of mind than which a Russian can conceive nothing better, namely, when you think of nothing yourself, yet when the thoughts creep into your mind of their own accord, each more agreeable than the other, giving you no trouble either to drive them away, or seek them. Fully satisfied, he recalled all the gay features of the evening just passed and all the mots which had made the little circle laugh. Many of them he repeated in a low voice, and found them quite as funny as before; so it is not surprising that he should laugh heartily at them. Occasionally, however, he was interrupted by gusts of wind, which, coming suddenly, God knows whence or why, cut his face, drove masses of snow into it, filled out his cloak-collar like a sail, or suddenly blew it over his head with supernatural force, and thus caused him constant trouble to disentangle himself.

Suddenly the important personage felt some one clutch him firmly by the collar. Turning round, he perceived a man of short stature, in an old, worn uniform, and recognised, not without terror, Akaky Akaki-yevich. The official's face was white as snow, and looked just like a corpse's. But the horror of the important personage transcended all bounds when he saw the dead man's mouth open, and heard it utter the following remarks, while it breathed upon him the terrible odour of the grave: "Ah, here you are at last! I have you, that—by the collar! I need your cloak. You took no trouble about mine, but reprimanded me. So now give up your own."

The pallid prominent personage almost died of fright. Brave as he was in the office and in the presence of inferiors generally, and although, at the sight of his manly form and appearance, every one said, "Ugh! how much character he has!" at this crisis, he, like many possessed of an heroic exterior, experienced such terror, that, not without cause, he began to fear an attack of illness. He flung his cloak hastily from his shoulders and shouted to his coachman in an unnatural voice, "Home at full speed!" The coachman, hearing the tone which is generally employed at critical moments, and even accompanied by something much more tangible, drew his head down between his shoulders in case of an emergency, flourished his whip, and flew on like an arrow. In a little more than six minutes the prominent personage was at the entrance of his own house. Pale, thoroughly scared, and cloakless, he went home instead of to Karolina Ivanovna's, reached his room somehow or other, and passed the night in the direst distress; so that the next morning over their tea, his daughter said, "You are very pale to-day, papa." But papa remained silent, and said not a word to any one of what had happened to him, where he had been, or where he had intended to go.

This occurrence made a deep impression upon him. He even began to say, "How dare you? Do you realise who is standing before you?" less frequently to the under-officials, and, if he did utter the words, it was only after first having learned the bearings of the matter. But the most noteworthy point was, that from that day forward the apparition of the dead official ceased to be seen. Evidently the prominent personage's cloak just fitted his shoulders. At all events, no more instances of his dragging cloaks from people's shoulders were heard of. But many active and solicitous persons could by no means reassure themselves, and asserted that the dead official still showed himself in distant parts of the city.

In fact, one watchman in Kolomen saw with his own eyes the apparition come from behind a house. But the watchman was not a strong man, so he was afraid to arrest him, and followed him in the dark, until, at length, the apparition looked round, paused, and inquired, "What do you want?" at the same time showing such a fist as is never seen on living men. The watchman said, "Nothing," and turned back instantly. But the apparition was much too tall, wore huge moustaches, and, directing its steps apparently towards the Obukhov Bridge, disappeared in the darkness of the night.

Tommaso Landolfi

GOGOL'S WIFE

At this point, confronted with the whole complicated affair of Nikolai Vassilevitch's wife, I am overcome by hesitation. Have I any right to disclose something which is unknown to the whole world, which my unforgettable friend himself kept hidden from the world (and he had his reasons), and which I am sure will give rise to all sorts of malicious and stupid misunderstandings? Something, moreover, which will very probably offend the sensibilities of all sorts of base, hypocritical people, and possibly of some honest people too, if there are any left? And finally, have I any right to disclose something before which my own spirit recoils, and even tends toward a more or less open disapproval?

But the fact remains that, as a biographer, I have certain firm obligations. Believing as I do that every bit of information about so lofty a genius will turn out to be of value to us and to future generations, I cannot conceal something which in any case has no hope of being judged fairly and wisely until the end of time. Moreover, what right have we to condemn? Is it given to us to know, not only what intimate needs, but even what higher and wider ends may have been served by those very deeds of a lofty genius which perchance may appear to us vile? No indeed, for we understand so little of these privileged natures. "It is true," a great man once said, "that I also have to pee, but for quite different reasons."

But without more ado I will come to what I know beyond doubt, and can prove beyond question, about this controversial matter, which will now—I dare to hope—no longer be so. I will not trouble to recapitulate what is already known of it, since I do not think this should be necessary at the present stage of development of Gogol studies.

Let me say it at once: Nikolai Vassilevitch's wife was not a woman. Nor was she any sort of human being, nor any sort of living creature at all, whether animal or vegetable (although something of the sort has sometimes been hinted). She was quite simply a balloon. Yes, a balloon; and this will explain the perplexity, or even indignation of certain biographers who were also the personal friends of the Master, and who complained that, although they often went to his house, they never saw her and "never even heard her voice." From this they deduced all sorts of dark and disgraceful complications—yes, and criminal ones too. No, gentlemen, everything is always simpler than it appears. You did not hear her voice simply because she could not speak, or to be more exact, she could only speak in certain conditions as we shall see. And it was always, except once, in a tête-à-tête with Nikolai Vassilevitch. So let us not waste time with any cheap or empty refutations but come at once to as exact and complete a description as possible of the being or object in question.

Gogol's so-called wife was an ordinary dummy made of thick rubber, naked at all seasons, buff in tint, or as is more commonly said, flesh-colored. But since women's skins are not all of the same color, I should specify that hers was a light-colored, polished skin, like that of certain brunettes. It, or she, was, it is hardly necessary to add, of feminine sex. Perhaps I should say at once that she was capable of very wide altera-tions of her attributes without, of course, being able to alter her sex itself. She could sometimes appear to be thin, with hardly any breasts and with narrow hips more like a young lad than a woman, and at other times to be excessively well-endowed or—let us not mince matters—fat. And she often changed the color of her hair, both on her head and elsewhere on her body, though not necessarily at the same time. She could also seem to change in all sorts of other tiny particulars, such as the position of moles, the vitality of the mucous membranes and so forth. She could even to a certain extent change the very color of her skin. One is faced with the necessity of asking oneself who she really was, or whether it would be proper to speak of a single "person"—and in fact we shall see that it would be imprudent to press this point.

The cause of these changes, as my readers will already have under-stood, was nothing else but the will of Nikolai Vassilevitch himself. He would inflate her to a greater or lesser degree, would change her wig and her other tufts of hair, would grease her with ointments and touch her up in various ways so as to obtain more or less the type of woman which suited him at that moment. Following the natural inclinations of his fancy, he even amused himself sometimes by producing grotesque or monstrous forms; as will be readily understood, she became deformed when inflated beyond a certain point or if she remained below a certain pressure.

But Gogol soon tired of these experiments, which he held to be "after all, not very respectful" to his wife, whom he loved in his own way—however inscrutable it may remain to us. He loved her, but which of these incarnations, we may ask ourselves, did he love? Alas, I have already indicated that the end of the present account will furnish some sort of an answer. And how can I have stated above that it was Nikolai Vassilevitch's will which ruled that woman? In a certain sense, yes, it is true; but it is equally certain that she soon became no longer his slave but his tyrant. And here yawns the abyss, or if you prefer it, the Jaws of Tartarus. But let us not anticipate.

I have said that Gogol obtained with his manipulations *more or less* the type of woman which he needed from time to time. I should add that when, in rare cases, the form he obtained perfectly incarnated his desire, Nikolai Vassilevitch fell in love with it "exclusively," as he said in his own words, and that this was enough to render "her" stable for a certain time—until he fell out of love with "her." I counted no more than three or four of these violent passions—or, as I suppose they would be called today, infatuations—in the life (dare I say in the conjugal life?) of the great writer. It will be convenient to add here that a few years after what one may call his marriage, Gogol had even given a name to his wife. It was Caracas, which is, unless I am mistaken, the capital of Venezuela. I have never been able to discover the reason for this choice: great minds are so capricious!

Speaking only of her normal appearance, Caracas was what is called a fine woman—well built and proportioned in every part. She had every smallest attribute of her sex properly disposed in the proper location. Particularly worthy of attention were her genitals organs (if the adjective is permissible in such a context). They were were formed by means of ingenious folds in the rubber. Nothing was forgotten, and their operation was tendered easy by various devices, as well as by the internal pressure of the air.

Caracas also had a skeleton, even though a rudimentary one. Perhaps it was made of whalebone. Special care had been devoted to the construction of the thoracic cage, of the pelvic basin and of the cranium. The first two systems were more or less visible in accordance with the thickness of the fatty layer, if I may so describe it, which covered them. It is a greaty pity that Gogol never let me know the name of the creator of such a fine piece of work. There was an obstinancy in his refusal which was never quite clear to me.

Nikolai Vassilevitch blew his wife up through the anal sphincter with a pump of his own invention, rather like those which you hold down with your two feet and which are used today in all sorts of mechanical workshops. Situated in the anus was a little one-way valve, or whatever the correct technical description would be, like the mitral valve of the heart, which, once the body was inflated, allowed more air to come in but none to go out. To deflate, one unscrewed a stopper in the mouth, at the back of the throat.

And that, I think, exhausts the description of the most noteworthy peculiarities of this being. Unless perhaps I should mention the splendid rows of white teeth which adorned her mouth and the dark eyes which, in spite of their immobility, perfectly simulated life. Did I say simulate?

Good heavens, simulate is not the word! Nothing seems to be the word, when one is speaking of Caracas! Even these eyes could undergo a change of color, by means of a special process to which, since it was long and tiresome, Gogol seldom had recourse. Finally, I should speak of her voice, which it was only once given to me to hear. But I cannot do that without going more fully into the relationship between husband and wife, and in this I shall no longer be able to answer to the truth of everything with absolute certitude. On my conscience I could not—so confused, both in itself and in my memory, is that which I now have to tell.

Here, then, as they occur to me, are some of my memories.

The first and, as I said, the last time I ever heard Caracas speak to Nikolai Vassilevitch was one evening when we were absolutely alone. We were in the room where the woman, if I may be allowed the expression, lived. Entrance to this room was strictly forbidden to everybody. It was furnished more or less in the Oriental manner, had no windows and was situated in the most inaccessible part of the house. I did know that she could talk, but Gogol had never explained to me the circumstances under which this happened. There were only the two of us, or three, in there. Nikolai Vassilevitch and I were drinking vodka and discussing Butkov's novel. I remember that we left this topic, and he was maintaining the necessity for radical reforms in the laws of inheritance. We had almost forgotten her. It was then that, with a husky and submissive voice, like Venus on the nuptial couch, she said point-blank: "I want to go poo-poo."

I jumped, thinking I had misheard, and looked across at her. She was sitting on a pile of cushions against the wall; that evening she was a soft, blonde beauty, rather well-covered. Her expression seemed commingled of shrewdness and slyness, childishness and irresponsibility. As for Gogol, he blushed violently and, leaping on her, stuck two fingers down her throat. She immediately began to shrink and to turn pale; she took on once again that lost and astonished air which was especially hers, and was in the end reduced to no more than a flabby skin on a perfunctory bony armature. Since, for practical reasons which will readily be divined, she had an extraordinary flexible backbone, she folded up almost in two, and for the rest of the evening she looked up at us from where she had slithered to the floor, in utter abjection.

All Gogol said was: "She only does it for a joke, or to annoy me, because as a matter of fact she does not have such needs." In the presence of other people, that is to say of me, he generally made a point of treating her with a certain disdain.

We went on drinking and talking, But Nikolai Vassilevitch seemed very much disturbed and absent in spirit. Once he suddenly interrupted what he was saying, seized my hand in his and burst into tears. "What can I do now?" he exclaimed. "You understand, Foma Paskalovitch, that I loved her?"

It is necessary to point out that it was impossible, except by a miracle, ever to repeat any of Caracas' forms. She was a fresh creation every time, and it would have been wasted effort to seek to find again the exact proportions, the exact pressure, and so forth, of a former Caracas. Therefore the plumpish blonde of that evening was lost to Gogol from that time forth forever; this was in fact the tragic end of one of those few loves of Nikolai Vassilevitch, which I described above. He gave me no explanation; he sadly rejected my proffered comfort, and that evening we parted early. But his heart had been laid bare to me in that outburst. He was no longer so reticent with me, and soon had hardly any secrets left. And this, I may say in parenthesis, caused me very great pride.

It seems that things had gone well for the "couple" at the beginning of their life together. Nikolai Vassilevitch had been content with Caracas and slept regularly with her in the same bed. He continued to observe this custom till the end, saying with a timid smile that no companion could be quieter or less importunate than she. But I soon began to doubt this, especially judging by the state he was sometimes in when he woke up. Then, after several years, their relationship began strangely to deteriorate.

All this, let it be said once and for all, is no more than a schematic attempt at an explanation. About that time the woman actually began to show signs of independence or, as one might say, of autonomy. Nikolai Vassilevitch had the extraordinary impression that she was acquiring a personality of her own, indecipherable perhaps, but still distinct from his, and one which slipped through his fingers. It is certain that some sort of continuity was established between each of her appearances—between all those brunettes, those blondes, those redheads and auburn-headed girls, between those plump, those slim, those dusky or snowy or golden beauties, there was a certain something in common. At the beginning of this chapter I cast some doubt on the propriety of considering Caracas as a unitary personality; nevertheless I myself could not quite, whenever I saw her, free myself of the impression that, however unheard of it may seem, this was fundamentally the same woman. And it may be that this was why Gogol felt he had to give her a name.

An attempt to establish in what precisely subsisted the common attributes of the different forms would be quite another thing. Perhaps it was no more and no less than the creative afflatus of Nikolai Vassilevitch himself. But no, it would have been too singular and strange if he had been so much divided off from himself, so much averse to himself. Because whoever she was, Caracas was a disturbing presence and even—it is better to be quite clear—a hostile one. Yet neither Gogol nor I ever succeeded in formulating a remotely tenable hypothesis as to her true nature; when I say formulate, I mean in terms which would be at once rational and accessible to all. But I cannot pass over an extraordinary event which took place at this time.

Caracas fell ill of a shameful disease—or rather Gogol did—though he was not then having, nor had he ever had, any contact with other women. I will not even try to describe how this happened, or where the filthy complaint came from; all I know is that it happened. And that my great, unhappy friend would say to me: "So Foma Paskalovitch, you see what lay at the heart of Caracas; it was the spirit of syphilis."

Sometimes he would even blame himself in a quite absurd manner; he was always prone to self-accusation. This incident was a real catastrophe as far as the already obscure relationship between husband and wife, and the hostile feelings of Nikolai Vassilevitch himself, were concerned. He was compelled to undergo long-drawn-out and painful treatment—the treatment of those days—and the situation was aggravated by the fact that the disease in the woman did not seem to be easily curable. Gogol deluded himself for some time that, by blowing his wife up and down and furnishing her with the most widely divergent aspects, he could obtain a woman immune from the contagion, but he was forced to desist when no results were forthcoming.

I shall be brief, seeking not to tire my readers, and also because what I remember seems to become more and more confused. I shall therefore hasten to the tragic conclusion. As to this last, however, let there be no mistake. I must once again make it clear that I am very sure of my ground. I was an eyewitness. Would that I had not been!

The years went by. Nikolai Vassilevitch's distaste for his wife became stronger, though his love for her did not show any signs of diminishing. Toward the end, aversion and attachment struggled so fiercely with each other in his heart that he became quite stricken, almost broken up. His restless eyes, which habitually assumed so many different expressions and sometimes spoke so sweetly to the heart of his interlocutor, now almost always shone with a fevered light, as if he were under the effect of a drug. The strangest impulses arose in him, accompanied by the most senseless fears. He spoke to me of Caracas more and more often, accusing her of unthinkable and amazing things. In these regions I could not follow him, since I had but a sketchy acquaintance with his wife, and hardly any intimacy—and above all since my sensibility was so limited compared with his. I shall accordingly restrict myself to reporting some of his accusations, without reference to my personal impressions.

"Believe it or not, Foma Paskalovitch," he would, for example, often to me: "Believe it or not, *she's aging!*" Then, unspeakably moved, he would, as was his way, take my hands in his. He also accused Caracas of giving herself up to solitary pleasures, which he had expressly forbidden. He even went so far as to charge her with betraying him, but the things he said became so extremely obscure that I must excuse myself from any further account of them.

One thing that appears certain is that toward the end Caracas, whether aged or not, had turned into a bitter creature, querulous, hypocritical and subject to religious excess. I do not exclude the possibility that she may have had an influence on Gogol's moral position during the last period of his life, a position which is sufficiently well known. The tragic climax came one night quite unexpectedly when Nikolai Vassilevitch and I were celebrating his silver wedding—one of the last evenings we were to spend together. I neither can nor should attempt to set down what it was that led to his decision, at a time when to all appearances he was resigned to tolerating his consort. I know not what new events had taken place that day. I shall confine myself to the facts; my readers must make what they can of them.

That evening Nikolai Vassilevitch was unusually agitated. His distaste for Caracas seemed to have reached an unprecedented intensity. The famous "pyre of vanities"—the burning of his manuscripts—had already taken place; I should not like to say whether or not at the instigation of his wife. His state of mind had been further inflamed by other causes. As to his physical condition, this was ever more pitiful, and strengthened my impression that he took drugs. All the same, he began to talk in a more or less normal way about Belinsky, who was giving him some trouble with his attacks on the *Selected Correspondence*. Then suddenly, tears rising to his eyes, he interrupted himself and cried out: "No. No. It's too much, too much. I can't go on any longer," as well as other obscure and disconnected phrases which he would not clarify. He seemed to be talking to himself. He wrung his hands, shook his head, got up and sat down again after having taken four or five anxious steps round the room. When Caracas appeared, or rather when we went in to her later in the evening in her Oriental chamber, he controlled himself no longer and began to behave like an old man, if I may so express myself, in his second childhood, quite giving way to his absurd impulses. For instance, he kept nudging me and winking and senselessly repeating: "There she is, Foma Paskalovitch; there she is!" Meanwhile she seemed to look up at us with a disdainful attention. But behind these "mannerisms" one could feel in him a real repugnance, a repugnance which had, I suppose, now reached the limits of the endurable. Indeed . . .

After a certain time Nikolai Vassilevitch seemed to pluck up courage. He burst into tears, but somehow they were more manly tears. He wrung his hands again, seized mine in his, and walked up and down, muttering: "That's enough! We can't have any more of this. This is an unheard of thing. How can such a thing be happening to me? How can a man be expected to put up with *this?*"

He then leapt furiously upon the pump, the existence of which he seemed just to have remembered, and, with it in his hand, dashed like a whirlwind to Caracas. He inserted the tube in her anus and began to inflate her. . . . Weeping the while, he shouted like one possessed: "Oh, how I love her, how I love her, my poor, poor darling! . . . But she's going to burst! Unhappy Caracas, most pitiable of God's creatures! But die she must!"

Caracas was swelling up. Nikolai Vassilevitch sweated, wept and pumped. I wished to stop him but, I know not why, I had not the courage. She began to become deformed and shortly assumed the most monstrous aspect; and yet she had not given any signs of alarm—she was used to these jokes. But when she began to feel unbearably full, or perhaps when Nikolai Vassilevitch's intentions became plain to her, she took on an expression of bestial amazement, even a little beseeching, but still without losing that disdainful look. She was afraid, she was even committing herself to his mercy, but still she could not believe in the immediate approach of her fate; she could not believe in the frightful audacity of her husband. He could not see her face because he was behind her. But I looked at her with fascination, and did not move a finger.

At last the internal pressure came through the fragile bones at the base of her skull, and printed on her face an indescribable rictus. Her belly, her thighs, her lips, her breasts and what I could see of her buttocks had swollen to incredible proportions. All of a sudden she belched, and gave a long hissing groan; both these phenomena one could explain by the increase in pressure, which had suddenly forced a way out through the valve in her throat. Then her eyes bulged frantically, threatening to jump out of their sockets. Her ribs flared wide apart and were no longer attached to the sternum, and she resembled a python digesting a donkey. A donkey, did I say? An ox! An elephant! At this point I believed her already dead, but Nikolai Vassilevitch, sweating, weeping and repeating: "My dearest! My beloved! My best!" continued to pump.

She went off unexpectedly and, as it were, all of a piece. It was not one part of her skin which gave way and the rest which followed, but her whole surface at the same instant. She scattered in the air. The pieces fell more or less slowly, according to their size, which was in no case above a very restricted one. I distinctly remember a piece of her cheek, with some lip attached, hanging on the corner of the mantelpiece. Nikolai Vassilevitch stared at me like a madman. Then he pulled himself together and, once more with furious determination, he began carefully to collect those poor rags which once had been the shining skin of Caracas, and all of her.

"Good-by, Caracas," I thought I heard him murmur, "Good-by! You were too pitiable!"And then suddenly and quite audibly: "The fire! The fire! She too must end up in the fire." He crossed himself—with his left hand, of course. Then, when he had picked up all those shriveled rags, even climbing on the furniture so as not to miss any, he threw them straight on the fire in the hearth, where they began to burn slowly and with an excessively unpleasant smell. Nikolai Vassilevitch, like all Russians, had a passion for throwing important things in the fire.

Red in the face, with an inexpressible look of despair, and yet of sinister triumph too, he gazed on the pyre of those miserable remains. He had seized my arm and was squeezing it convulsively. But those traces of what had once been a being were hardly well alight when he seemed yet again to pull himself together, as if he were suddenly remembering something or taking a painful decision. In one bound he was out of the room.

A few seconds later I heard him speaking to me through the door in a broken, plaintive voice: "Foma Paskalovitch, I want you to promise not to look. *Golubchik,* promise not to look at me when I come in."

I don't know what I answered, or whether I tried to reassure him in any way. But he insisted, and I had to promise him, as if he were a child, to hide my face against the wall and only turn round when he said I might. The door then opened violently and Nikolai Vassilevitch burst into the room and ran to the fireplace.

And here I must confess my weakness, though I consider it justified by the extraordinary circumstances. I looked round before Nikolai Vassilevitch told me I could; it was stronger than me. I was just in time to see him carrying something in his arms, something which he threw on the fire with all the rest, so that it suddenly flared up. At that, since the desire to *see* had entirely mastered every other thought in me, I dashed to the fireplace. But Nikolai Vassilevitch placed himself between me and it and pushed me back with a strength of which I had not believed him capable. Meanwhile the object was burning and giving off clouds of smoke. And before he showed any sign of calming down there was nothing left but a heap of silent ashes.

The true reason why I wished to see was because I had already glimpsed. But it was only a glimpse, and perhaps I should not allow myself to introduce even the slightest element of uncertainty into this true story. And yet, an eyewitness account is not complete without a mention of that which the witness knows with less than complete certainty. To cut a long story short, that something was a baby. Not a flesh and blood baby, of course, but more something in the line of a rubber doll or a model. Something, which, to judge by its appearance, could have been called *Caracas' son.*

Was I mad too? That I do not know, but I do know that this was what I saw, not clearly, but with my own eyes. And I wonder why it was that when I was writing this just now I didn't mention that when Nikolai Vassilevitch came back into the room he was muttering between his clenched teeth: "Him too! Him too!"

And that is the sum of my knowledge of Nikolai Vassilevitch's wife. In the next chapter I shall tell what happened to him afterwards, and that will be the last chapter of his life. But to give an interpretation of his feelings for his wife, or indeed for anything, is quite another and more difficult matter, though I have attempted it elsewhere in this volume, and refer the reader to that modest effort. I hope I have thrown sufficient light on a most controversial question and that I have unveiled the mystery, if not of Gogol, then at least of his wife. In the course of this I have implicitly given the lie to the insensate accusation that he ill-treated or even beat his wife, as well as other like absurdities. And what else can be the goal of a humble biographer such as the present writer but to serve the memory of that lofty genius who is the object of his study?

VLADIMIR NABOKOV

NIKOLAI GOGOL

The Apotheosis of a Mask

1

". . . A certain man who was, I daresay, not very remarkable: short
he was and somewhat pox-marked and somewhat on the carroty side,
and somewhat even blear-eyed and a little bald in front, with sym-
metrically wrinkled cheeks and the kind of complexion termed hemor-
rhoidal . . .

". . . His name was Bashmachkin. Already the name itself clearly shows
that it had formerly come from *bashmak*—a shoe. But when, and at what
time had it come from "shoe," this is totally unknown. All of them—the
father and the grandfather, and even the brother-in-law—absolutely all
the Bashmachkins—used to wear boots which they re-soled not more
often than three times a year."

2

Gogol was a strange creature, but genius is always strange; it is only
your healthy second-rater who seems to the grateful reader to be a wise
old friend, nicely developing the reader's own notions of life. Great
literature skirts the irrational. *Hamlet* is the wild dream of a neurotic
scholar. Gogol's *The Overcoat* is a grotesque and grim nightmare making
black holes in the dim pattern of life. The superficial reader of that
story will merely see in it the heavy frolics of an extravagant buffoon; the
solemn reader will take for granted that Gogol's prime intention was to
denounce the horrors of Russian bureaucracy. But neither the person
who wants a good laugh, nor the person who craves for books "that
make one think," will understand what *The Overcoat* is really about.
Give me a creative reader; this is a tale for him.

Steady Pushkin, matter-of-fact Tolstoy, restrained Chekhov have all
had their moments of irrational insight which simultaneously blurred the
sentence and disclosed a secret meaning worth the sudden focal shift.
But with Gogol this shifting is the very basis of his art, so that whenever

he tried to write in the round hand of literary tradition and to treat rational ideas in a logical way, he lost all trace of talent. When, as in his immortal *The Overcoat,* he really let himself go and pottered happily on the brink of his private abyss, he became the greatest artist that Russia has yet produced.

The sudden slanting of the rational plane of life may be accomplished of course in many ways, and every great writer has his own method. With Gogol it was a combination of two movements: a jerk and a glide. Imagine a trap-door that opens under your feet with absurd suddenness, and a lyrical gust that sweeps you up and then lets you fall with a bump into the next trap-hole. The absurd was Gogol's favourite muse—but when I say "the absurd," I do not mean the quaint or the comic. The absurd has as many shades and degrees as the tragic has, and moreover, in Gogol's case, it borders upon the latter. It would be wrong to assert that Gogol placed his characters in absurd situations. You cannot place a man in an absurd situation if the whole world he lives in is absurd; you cannot do this if you mean by "absurd" something provoking a chuckle or a shrug. But if you mean the pathetic, the human condition, if you mean all such things that in less weird worlds are linked up with the loftiest aspirations, the deepest sufferings, the strongest passions then, of course, the necessary breach is there, and a pathetic human, lost in the midst of Gogol's nightmarish, irresponsible world, would be "absurd," by a kind of secondary contrast.

On the lid of the tailor's snuff-box there was "the portrait of a General; I do not know what general because the tailor's thumb had made a hole in the general's face and a square of paper had been gummed over the hole." Thus with the absurdity of Akaky Akakiyevich Bashmachkin. We did not expect that, amid the whirling masks, one mask would turn out to be a real face, or at least the place where that face ought to be. The essence of mankind is irrationally derived from the chaos of fakes which form Gogol's world. Akaky Akakyevich, the hero of *The Overcoat,* is absurd *because* he is pathetic, *because* he is human and *because* he has been engendered by those very forces which seem to be in such contrast to him.

He is not merely human and pathetic. He is something more, just as the background is not mere burlesque. Somewhere behind the obvious contrast there is a subtle genetic link. His being discloses the same quiver and shimmer as does the dream world to which he belongs. The allusions to something else behind the crudely painted screens are so artistically combined with the superficial texture of the narration that civic-minded Russians have missed them completely. But a creative reading of Gogol's story reveals that here and there in the most innocent descriptive passage, this or that word, sometimes a mere adverb or a preposition, for instance the word "even" or "almost," is inserted in such a way as to make the harmless sentence explode in a wild display of nightmare fireworks; or else the passage that had started in a rambling colloquial manner all of a sudden leaves the tracks and swerves into the irrational where it really belongs; or again, quite as suddenly, a door bursts open and a mighty wave of foaming poetry rushes in only to dissolve in bathos, or to turn into its own parody, or to be checked by the sentence breaking and reverting to a conjuror's patter, that patter which is such a feature of Gogol's style. It gives one the sensation of something ludicrous and at the same time stellar, lurking constantly around the corner—and one likes to recall that the difference between the comic side of things, and their cosmic side, depends upon one sibilant.

3

So what is that queer world, glimpses of which we keep catching through the gaps of the harmless-looking sentences? It is in a way the *real* one but it looks wildly absurd to us, accustomed as we are to the stage setting that screens it. It is from these glimpses that the main character of *The Overcoat,* the meek little clerk, is formed, so that he embodies the spirit of that secret but real world which breaks through Gogol's style. He is that meek little clerk, a ghost, a visitor from some tragic depths who by chance happened to assume the disguise of a petty official. Russian progressive critics sensed in him the image of the underdog and the whole story impressed them as a social protest. But it is something much more than that. The gaps and black holes in the texture of Gogol's style imply flaws in the texture of life itself. Something is very wrong and all men are mild lunatics engaged in pursuits that seem to them very important while an absurdly logical force keeps them at their futile jobs—this is the real "message" of the story. In this world of utter futility, of futile humility and futile domination, the highest degree that passion, desire, creative urge can attain is a new cloak which both tailors and customers adore on their knees. I am not speaking of the moral point or the moral lesson. There can be no moral lesson in such a world because there are no pupils and no teachers: this world *is* and it excludes everything that might destroy it, so that any improvement, any struggle, any moral purpose or endeavour, are as utterly impossible as changing the course of a star. It is Gogol's world and as such wholly different from Tolstoy's world, or Pushkin's, or Chekhov's or my own. But after reading Gogol one's eyes may become gogolised and one is apt to see bits of his world in the most unexpected places. I have visited many countries, and something like Akaky Akakiyevich's overcoat has been the passionate dream of this or that chance acquaintance who never had heard about Gogol.

4

The plot of *The Overcoat* is very simple. A poor little clerk makes a great decision and orders a new overcoat. The coat while in the making becomes the dream of his life. On the very first night that he wears it he is robbed of it on a dark street. He dies of grief and his ghost haunts the city. This is all in the way of plot, but of course the *real* plot (as always with Gogol) lies in the style, in the inner structure of this transcendental anecedote. In order to appreciate it at its true worth one must perform a kind of mental somersault so as to get rid of conventional values in literature and follow the author along the dream road of his superhuman imagination. Gogol's world is somewhat related to such conceptions of modern physics as the "Concertina Universe" or the "Explosion Universe"; it is far removed from the comfortably revolving clockwork worlds of the last century. There is a curvature in literary style as there is curvature in space—but few are the Russian readers who do care to plunge into Gogol's magic chaos head first, with no restraint or regret. The Russian who thinks Turgenev was a great writer, and bases his notion of Pushkin upon Chaïkovsky's vile libretti, will merely paddle into the gentlest wavelets of Gogol's mysterious sea and limit his reaction to an enjoyment of what he takes to be whimsical humour and colourful quips. But the diver, the seeker for black pearls, the man who prefers the monsters of the deep to the sunshades on the beach, will find in *The Overcoat* shadows linking our state of existence to those other states and modes which we dimly apprehend in our rare moments of irrational perception. The prose of Pushkin is three-dimensional; that of Gogol is four-dimensional, at least. He may be compared to his contemporary, the mathematician Lobachevsky, who blasted Euclid and discovered a century ago many of the theories which Einstein later developed. If parallel lines do not meet it is not because meet they cannot, but because they have other things to do. Gogol's art as disclosed in *The Overcoat* suggests that parallel lines not only may meet, but that they can wriggle and get most extravagantly entangled, just as two pillars reflected in water indulge in the most wobbly contortions if the necessary ripple is there. Gogol's genius is exactly that ripple—two and two make five, if not the square root of five, and it all happens quite naturally in Gogol's world, where neither rational mathematics nor indeed any of our pseudophysical agreements with ourselves can be seriously said to exist.

5

The clothing process indulged in by Akaky Akakiyevich, the making and the putting on of the cloak, is really his *disrobing* and his gradual reversion to the stark nakedness of his own ghost. From the very beginning of the story he is in training for his supernaturally high jump—and such harmless-looking details as his tiptoeing in the streets to spare his shoes or his not quite knowing whether he is in the middle of the street or in the middle of the sentence; these details gradually dissolve the clerk Akaky Akakiyevich so that towards the end of the story his ghost seems to be the most tangible, the most real part of his being. The account of his ghost haunting the streets of St. Petersburg in search of the cloak of which he had been robbed and finally appropriating that of a high official who had refused to help him in his misfortune—this account, which to the unsophisticated may look like an ordinary ghost story, is transformed towards the end into something for which I can find no precise epithet. It is both an apotheosis and a *dégringolade*. Here it is:—

"The Important Person almost died of fright. In his office and generally in the presence of subordinates he was a man of strong character, and whoever glanced at his manly appearance and shape used to imagine his kind of temper with something of a shudder; at the present moment however he (as happens in the case of many people of prodigiously powerful appearance) experienced such terror that, not without reason, he *even* expected to have a fit of some sort. He *even* threw off his cloak of his own accord and then exhorted the coachman in a wild voice to take him home and drive like mad. Upon hearing tones which were generally used at critical moments and were *even* [notice the recurrent use of this word] accompanied by something far more effective, the coachman thought it wiser to draw his head in; he lashed at the horses, and the carriage sped like an arrow. Six minutes later, or a little more [according to Gogol's special timepiece] the Important Person was already at the porch of his house. Pale, frightened and cloakless, instead of arriving at Caroline Ivanovna's [a woman he kept] he had thus come home; he staggered to his bedroom and spent an exceedingly troubled night, so that next morning, at breakfast, his daughter said to him straightaway: 'You are quite pale to-day, papa.' But papa kept silent and [now comes the parody of a Bible parable!] he told none of what had befallen him, nor where he had been, nor whither he had wished to go. The whole occurrence made a very strong impression on him [here begins the downhill slide, that spectacular bathos which Gogol uses for his particular needs]. Much more seldom *even* did he address to his subordinates the words 'How dare you?—Do you know to whom you are speaking?'—or at least if he did talk that way it was not till he had first listened to what they had to tell. But still more remarkable was the fact that from that time on the ghostly clerk quite ceased to appear: evidently the Important Person's overcoat fitted him well; at least no more did one hear of over-coats being snatched from people's shoulders. However, many active and vigilant persons refused to be appeased and kept asserting that in remote parts of the city the ghostly clerk still showed himself. And indeed a suburban policeman saw with his own eyes [the downward slide from the moralistic note to the grotesque is now a tumble] a ghost appear from behind a house. But being by nature somewhat of a weakling (so that once, an ordinary full-grown young pig which had rushed out of some private house knocked him off his feet to the great merriment of a group of cab drivers from whom he demanded, and obtained, as a penalty for this derision, ten coppers from each to buy himself snuff), he did not venture to stop the ghost but just kept on walking behind it in the dark-ness, until the ghost suddenly turned, stopped and inquired: "What d'you want, you?'—and showed a fist of a size rarely met with *even* among the living. 'Nothing,' answered the sentinel and proceeded to go back at once. That ghost, however, was a much taller one and had a huge moustache. It was heading apparently towards Obukhov Bridge and presently dis-appeared completely in the darkness of the night."

The torrent of "irrelevant" details (such as the bland assumption that "full-grown young pigs" commonly occur in private houses) produces such a hypnotic effect that one almost fails to realise one simple thing (and that is the beauty of the final stroke). A piece of most important information, the main structural idea of the story is here deliberately masked by Gogol (because all reality is a mask). The man taken for Akaky Akakiyevich's cloakless ghost is actually the man who stole his cloak. But Akaky Akakiyevich's ghost existed solely on the strength of his lacking a cloak, whereas now the policeman, lapsing into the queerest paradox of the story, mistakes for this ghost just the very person who was its antithesis, the man who had stolen the cloak. Thus the story describes a full circle: a vicious circle as all circles are, despite their posing as apples, or planets, or human faces.

So to sum up: the story goes this way: mumble, mumble, lyrical wave, mumble, lyrical wave, mumble, lyrical wave, mumble, fantastic climax, mumble, mumble, and back into the chaos from which they all had derived. At this super-high level of art, literature is of course not con-cerned with pitying the underdog or cursing the upper-dog. It appeals to that secret depth of the human soul where the shadows of other worlds pass like the shadows of nameless and soundless ships.

6

As one or two patient readers may have gathered by now, this is really the only appeal that interests me. My purpose in jotting these notes on Gogol has, I hope, become perfectly clear. Bluntly speaking, it amounts to the following: if you expect to find out something about Russia, if you are eager to know why the blistered Germans bungled their blitz, if you are interested in "ideas" and "facts" and "messages," keep away from Gogol. The awful trouble of learning Russian in order to read him will not be repaid in your kind of hard cash. Keep away, keep away. He has nothing to tell you. Keep off the tracks. High tension. Closed for the duration. Avoid, refrain, don't. I would like to have here a full list of all possible interdictions, vetoes and threats. Hardly necessary of course—as the wrong sort of reader will certainly never get as far as this. But I do welcome the right sort—my brothers, my doubles. My brother is playing the organ. My sister is reading. She is my aunt. You will first learn the alphabet, the labials, the linguals, the dentals, the letters that buzz, the drone and the bumblebee, and the Tse-tse Fly. One of the vowels will make you say "Ugh!" You will feel mentally stiff and bruised after your first declension of personal pronouns. I see, however, no other way of getting to Gogol (or to any other Russian writer for that matter). His work, as all great literary achievements, is a phenomenon of language and not one of ideas. "Gaw-gol," not "Go-gall." The final "l" is a soft dissolving "l" which does not exist in English. One cannot hope to understand an author if one cannot even pronounce his name. My translations of various passages are the best my poor vocabulary could afford, but even had they been as perfect as those which I hear with my innermost ear, without being able to render their intonation, they still would not replace Gogol. While trying to convey my attitude towards his art I have not produced any tangible proofs of its peculiar existence. I can only place my hand on my heart and affirm that I have not imagined Gogol. He really wrote, he really lived.

Gogol was born on the 1st of April, 1809. According to his mother (who, of course, made up the following dismal anecdote) a poem he had written at the age of five was seen by Kapnist, a well-known writer of sorts. Kapnist embraced the solemn urchin and said to the glad parents: "He will become a writer of genius if only destiny gives him a good Christian for teacher and guide." But the other thing—his having been born on the 1st of April—is true.

NEVERTHELESS HE WAS IN REALITY A WOLF

Hermann Hesse

STEPPENWOLF

TREATISE ON THE STEPPENWOLF

There was once a man, Harry, called the Steppenwolf. He went on two legs, wore clothes and was a human being, but nevertheless he was in reality a wolf of the Steppes. He had learned a good deal of all that people of a good intelligence can, and was a fairly clever fellow. What he had not learned, however, was this: to find contentment in himself and his own life. The cause of this apparently was that at the bottom of his heart he knew all the time (or thought he knew) that he was in reality not a man, but a wolf of the Steppes. Clever men might argue the point whether he truly was a wolf, whether, that is, he had been changed, before birth perhaps, from a wolf into a human being, or had been given the soul of a wolf, though born as a human being; or whether, on the other hand, this belief that he was a wolf was no more than a fancy or a disease of his. It might, for example, be possible that in his childhood he was a little wild and disobedient and disorderly, and that those who brought him up had declared a war of extinction against the beast in him; and precisely this had given him the idea and the belief that he was in fact actually a beast with only a thin covering of the human. On this point one could speak at length and entertainingly, and indeed write a book about it. The Steppenwolf, however, would be none the better for it, since for him it was all one whether the wolf had been bewitched or beaten into him, or whether it was merely an idea of his own. What others chose to think about it or what he chose to think himself was no good to him at all. It left the wolf inside him just the same.

And so the Steppenwolf had two natures, a human and a wolfish one. This was his fate, and it may well be that it was not a very exceptional one. There must have been many men who have had a good deal of the dog or the fox, of the fish or the serpent in them without experiencing any extraordinary difficulties on that account. In such cases, the man and the fish lived on together and neither did the other any harm. The one even helped the other. Many a man indeed has carried this condition to such enviable lengths that he has owed his happiness more to the fox or the ape in him than to the man. So much for common knowledge. In the case of Harry, however, it was just the opposite. In him the man and the wolf did not go the same way together, but were in continual and deadly enmity. One existed simply and solely to harm the other, and when there are two in one blood and in one soul who are at deadly enmity, then life fares ill. Well, to each his lot, and none is light.

Now with our Steppenwolf it was so that in his conscious life he lived now as a wolf, now as a man, as indeed the case is with all mixed beings. But, when he was a wolf, the man in him lay in ambush, ever on the watch to interfere and condemn, while at those times that he was man the wolf did just the same. For example, if Harry, as man, had a beautiful thought, felt a fine and noble emotion, or performed a so-called good act, then the wolf bared his teeth at him and laughed and showed him with bitter scorn how laughable this whole pantomime was in the eyes of a beast, of a wolf who knew well enough in his heart what suited him, namely, to trot alone over the Steppes and now and then to gorge himself with blood or to pursue a female wolf. Then, wolfishly seen, all human activities became horribly absurd and misplaced, stupid and vain. But it was exactly the same when Harry felt and behaved as a wolf and showed others his teeth and felt hatred and enmity against all human beings and their lying and degenerate manners and customs. For then the human part of him lay in ambush and watched the wolf, called him brute and beast, and spoiled and embittered for him all pleasure in his simple and healthy and wild wolf's being.

Thus it was then with the Steppenwolf, and one may well imagine that Harry did not have an exactly pleasant and happy life of it. This does not mean, however, that he was unhappy in any extraordinary degree (although it may have seemed so to himself all the same, inasmuch as every man takes the sufferings that fall to his share as the greatest). That cannot be said of any man. Even he who has no wolf in him, may be none the happier for that. And even the unhappiest life has its sunny moments and its little flowers of happiness between sand and stone. So it was, then, with the Steppenwolf too. It cannot be denied that he was generally very unhappy; and he could make others unhappy also, that is, when he loved them or they him. For all who got to love him, saw always only the one side in him. Many loved him as a refined and clever and interesting man, and were horrified and disappointed when they had come upon the wolf in him. And they had to because Harry wished, as every sentient being does, to be loved as a whole and therefore it was just with those whose love he most valued that he could least of all conceal and belie the wolf. There were those, however, who loved precisely the wolf in him, the free, the savage, the untamable, the dangerous and strong, and these found it peculiarly disappointing and deplorable when suddenly the wild and wicked wolf was also a man, and had hankerings after goodness and refinement, and wanted to hear Mozart, to read poetry and to cherish human ideals. Usually these were the most disappointed and angry of all; and so it was that the Steppenwolf brought his own dual and divided nature into the destinies of others besides himself whenever he came into contact with them.

Now, whoever thinks that he knows the Steppenwolf and that he can imagine to himself his lamentably divided life is nevertheless in error. He does not know all by a long way. He does not know that, as there is no rule without an exception and as one sinner may under certain circumstances be dearer to God than ninety and nine righteous persons, with Harry too there were now and then exceptions and strokes of good luck, and that he could breathe and think and feel sometimes as the wolf, sometimes as the man, clearly and without confusion of the two; and even on very rare occasions, they made peace and lived for one another in such fashion that not merely did one keep watch whilst the other slept but each strengthened and confirmed the other. In the life of this man, too, as well as in all things else in the world, daily use and the accepted and common knowledge seemed sometimes to have no other aim than to be arrested now and again for an instant, and broken through, in order to yield the place of honor to the exceptional and miraculous. Now whether these short and occasional hours of happiness balanced and alleviated the lot of the Steppenwolf in such a fashion that in the upshot happiness and suffering held the scales even, or whether perhaps the short but intense happiness of those few hours outweighed all suffering and left a balance over is again a question over which idle persons may meditate to their hearts' content. Even the wolf brooded often over this, and those were his idle and unprofitable days.

In this connection one thing more must be said. There are a good many people of the same kind as Harry. Many artists are of his kind. These persons all have two souls, two beings within them. There is God and the devil in them; the mother's blood and the father's; the capacity for happiness and the capacity for suffering; and in just such a state of enmity and entanglement towards and within each other as were the wolf and man in Harry. And these men, for whom life has no repose, live at times in their rare moments of happiness with such strength and indescribable beauty, the spray of their moment's happiness is flung so high and dazzlingly over the wide sea of suffering, that the light of it, spreading its radiance, touches others too with its enchantment. Thus, like a precious, fleeting foam over the sea of suffering arise all those works of art, in which a single individual lifts himself for an hour so high above his personal destiny that his happiness shines like a star and appears to all who see it as something eternal and as a happiness of their own. All these men, whatever their deeds and works may be, have really no life; that is to say, their lives are not their own and have no form. They are not heroes, artists or thinkers in the same way that other men are judges, doctors, shoemakers, or schoolmasters. Their life consists of a perpetual tide, unhappy and torn with pain, terrible and meaningless, unless one is ready to see its meaning in just those rare experiences, acts, thoughts and works that shine out above the chaos of such a life. To such men the desperate and horrible thought has come that perhaps the whole of human life is but a bad joke, a violent and ill-fated abortion of the primal mother, a savage and dismal catastrophe of nature. To them, too, however, the other thought has come that man is perhaps not merely a half-rational animal but a child of the gods and destined to immortality.

Men of every kind have their characteristics, their features, their virtues and vices and their deadly sins. Prowling about at night was one of the Steppenwolf's favorite tendencies. The morning was a wretched time of day for him. He feared it and it never brought him any good. On no morning of his life had he ever been in good spirits nor done any good before midday, nor ever had a happy idea, nor devised any pleasure for himself or others. By degrees during the afternoon he warmed and became alive, and only towards evening, on his good days, was he productive, active and, sometimes, aglow with joy. With this was bound up his need for loneliness and independence. There was never a man with a deeper and more passionate craving for independence than he. In his youth when he was poor and had difficulty in earning his bread, he preferred to go hungry and in torn clothes rather than endanger his narrow limit of independence. He never sold himself for money or an easy life or to women or to those in power; and had thrown away a hundred times what in the world's eyes was his advantage and happiness in order to safeguard his liberty. No prospect was more hateful and distasteful to him than that he should have to go to an office and conform to daily and yearly routine and obey others. He hated all kinds of offices, governmental or commercial, as he hated death, and his worst nightmare was confinement in barracks. He contrived, often at great sacrifice, to avoid all such predicaments. It was here that his strength and his virtue rested. On this point he could neither be bent nor bribed. Here his character was firm and indeflectable. Only, through this virtue, he was bound the closer to his destiny of suffering. It happened to him as it does to all; what he strove for with the deepest and most stubborn instinct of his being fell to his lot, but more than is good for men. In the beginning his dream and his happiness, in the end it was his bitter fate. The man of power is ruined by power, the man of money by money, the submissive man by subservience, the pleasure seeker by pleasure. He achieved his aim. He was ever more independent. He took orders from no man and ordered his ways to suit no man. Independently and alone, he decided what to do and to leave undone. For every strong man attains to that which a genuine impulse bids him seek. But in the midst of the freedom he had attained Harry suddenly became aware that his freedom was a death and that he stood alone. The world in an uncanny fashion left him in peace. Other men concerned him no longer. He was not even concerned about himself. He began to suffocate slowly in the more and more rarefied atmosphere of remoteness and solitude. For now it was his wish no longer, nor his aim, to be alone and independent, but rather his lot and his sentence. The magic wish had been fulfilled and could not be cancelled, and it was no good now to open his arms with longing and goodwill to welcome the bonds of society. People left him alone now. It was not, however, that he was an object of hatred and repugnance. On the contrary, he had many friends. A great many people liked him. But it was no more than sympathy and friendliness. He received invitations, presents, pleasant letters; but no more. No one came near to him. There was no link left, and no one could have had any part in his life even had anyone wished it. For the air of lonely men surrounded him now, a still atmosphere in which the world around him slipped away, leaving him incapable of relationship, an atmosphere against which neither will nor longing availed. This was one of the significant earmarks of his life.

Another was that he was numbered among the suicides. And here it must be said that to call suicides only those who actually destroy themselves is false. Among these, indeed, there are many who in a sense are suicides only by accident and in whose being suicide has no necessary place. Among the common run of men there are many of little personality and stamped with no deep impress of fate, who find their end in suicide without belonging on that account to the type of the suicide by inclination; while on the other hand, of those who are to be counted as suicides by the very nature of their beings are many, perhaps a majority, who never in fact lay hands on themselves. The "suicide," and Harry was one, need not necessarily live in a peculiarly close relationship to death. One may do this without being a suicide. What is peculiar to the suicide is that his ego, rightly or wrongly, is felt to be an extremely dangerous, dubious, and doomed germ of nature; that he is always in his own eyes exposed to an extraordinary risk, as though he stood with the slightest foothold on the peak of a crag whence a slight push from without or an instant's weakness from within suffices to precipitate him into the void. The line of fate in the case of these men is marked by the belief they have that suicide is their most probable manner of death. It might be presumed that such temperaments, which usually manifest themselves in early youth and persist through life, show a singular defect of vital force. On the contrary, among the "suicides" are to be found unusually tenacious and eager and also hardy natures. But just as there are those who at the least indisposition develop a fever, so do those whom we call suicides, and who are always very emotional and sensitive, develop at the least shock the notion of suicide. Had we a science with the courage and authority to concern itself with mankind, instead of with the mechanism merely of vital phenomena, had we something of the nature of an anthropology, or a psychology, these matters of fact would be familiar to every one.

What was said above on the subject of suicides touches obviously nothing but the surface. It is psychology, and, therefore, partly physics. Metaphysically considered, the matter has a different and a much clearer aspect. In this aspect suicides present themselves as those who are overtaken by the sense of guilt inherent in individuals, those souls that find the aim of life not in the perfecting and molding of the self, but in liberating themselves by going back to the mother, back to God, back to the all. Many of these natures are wholly incapable of ever having recourse to real suicide, because they have a profound consciousness of the sin of doing so. For us they are suicides nonetheless; for they see death and not life as the releaser. They are ready to cast themselves away in surrender, to be extinguished and to go back to the beginning.

As every strength may become a weakness (and under some circumstances must) so, on the contrary, may the typical suicide find a strength and a support in his apparent weakness. Indeed, he does so more often than not. The case of Harry, the Steppenwolf, is one of these. As thousands of his like do, he found consolation and support, and not merely the melancholy play of youthful fancy, in the idea that the way to death was open to him at any moment. It is true that with him, as with all men of his kind, every shock, every pain, every untoward predicament at once called forth the wish to find an escape in death. By degrees, however, he fashioned for himself out of this tendency a philosophy that was actually serviceable to life. He gained strength through familiarity with the thought that the emergency exit stood always open, and became curious, too, to taste his suffering to the dregs. If it went too badly with him he could feel sometimes with a grim malicious pleasure: "I am curious to see all the same just how much a man can endure. If the limit of what is bearable is reached, I have only to open the door to escape." There are a great many suicides to whom this thought imparts an uncommon strength.

On the other hand, all suicides have the responsibility of fighting against the temptation of suicide. Every one of them knows very well in some corner of his soul that suicide, though a way out, is rather a mean and shabby one, and that it is nobler and finer to be conquered by life than to fall by one's own hand. Knowing this, with a morbid conscience whose source is much the same as that of the militant conscience of so-called self-contented persons, the majority of suicides are left to a protracted struggle against their temptation. They struggle as the kleptomaniac against his own vice. The Steppenwolf was not unfamiliar with this struggle. He had engaged in it with many a change of weapons. Finally, at the age of forty-seven or thereabouts, a happy and not unhumorous idea came to him from which he often derived some amusement. He appointed his fiftieth birthday as the day on which he might allow himself to take his own life. On this day, according to his mood, so he agreed with himself, it should be open to him to employ the emergency exit or not. Let happen to him what might, illness, poverty, suffering and bitterness, there was a time-limit. It could not extend beyond these few years, months, days whose number daily diminished. And in fact he bore much adversity, which previously would have cost him severer and longer tortures and shaken him perhaps to the roots of his being, very much more easily. When for any reason it went particularly badly with him, when peculiar pains and penalties were added to the desolateness and loneliness and savagery of his life, he could say to his tormentors: "Only wait, two years and I am your master." And with this he cherished the thought of the morning of his fiftieth birthday. Letters of congratulation would arrive, while he, relying on his razor, took leave of all his pains and closed the door behind him. Then gout in the joints, depression of spirits, and all pains of head and body could look for another victim.

It still remains to elucidate the Steppenwolf as an isolated phenomenon, in his relation, for example, to the bourgeois world, so that his symptoms may be traced to their source. Let us take as a starting point, since it offers itself, his relation to the bourgeoisie.

To take his own view of the matter, the Steppenwolf stood entirely outside the world of convention, since he had neither family life nor social ambitions. He felt himself to be single and alone, whether as a queer fellow and a hermit in poor health, or as a person removed from the common run of men by the prerogative of talents that had something of genius in them. Deliberately, he looked down upon the ordinary man and was proud that he was not one. Nevertheless his life in many aspects was thoroughly ordinary. He had money in the bank and supported poor relations. He was dressed respectably and inconspicuously, even though without particular care. He was glad to live on good terms with the police and the tax collectors and other such powers. Besides this, he was secretly and persistently attracted to the little bourgeois world, to those quiet and respectable homes with tidy gardens, irreproachable stair-cases and their whole modest air of order and comfort. It pleased him to set himself outside it, with his little vices and extravagances, as a queer fellow or a genius, but he never had his domicile in those provinces of life where the bourgeoisie had ceased to exist. He was not at ease with violent and exceptional persons or with criminals and outlaws, and he took up his abode always among the middle classes, with whose habits and standards and atmosphere he stood in a constant relation, even though it might be one of contrast and revolt. Moreover, he had been brought up in a provincial and conventional home and many of the notions and much of the examples of those days had never left him. In theory he had nothing whatever against the servant class, yet in practice it would have been beyond him to take a servant quite seriously as his equal. He was capable of loving the political criminal, the revolutionary or intellectual seducer, the outlaw of state and society, as his brother, but as for theft and robbery, murder and rape, he would not have known how to deplore them otherwise than in a thoroughly bourgeois manner.

In this way he was always recognising and affirming with one half of himself, in thought and act, what with the other half he fought against and denied. Brought up, as he was, in a cultivated home in the approved manner, he never tore part of his soul loose from its conventionalities even after he had long since individualised himself to a degree beyond its scope and freed himself from the substance of its ideals and beliefs.

Now what we call "bourgeois," when regarded as an element always to be found in human life, is nothing else than the search for a balance. It is the striving after a mean between the countless extremes and opposites that arise in human conduct. If we take any one of these coupled opposites, such as piety and profligacy, the analogy is immediately comprehensible. It is open to a man to give himself up wholly to spiritual views, to seeking after God, to the ideal of saintliness. On the other hand, he can equally give himself up entirely to the life of instinct, to the lusts of the flesh, and so direct all his efforts to the attainment of momentary pleasures. The one path leads to the saint, to the martyrdom of the spirit and surrender to God. The other path leads to the profligate, to the martyrdom of the flesh, the surrender to corruption. Now it is between the two, in the middle of the road, that the bourgeois seeks to walk. He will never surrender himself either to lust or to asceticism. He will never be a martyr or agree to his own destruction. On the contrary, his ideal is not to give up but to maintain his own identity. He strives neither for the saintly nor its opposite. The absolute is his abhorrence. He may be ready to serve God, but not by giving up the fleshpots. He is ready to be virtuous, but likes to be easy and comfortable in this world as well. In short, his aim is to make a home for himself between two extremes in a temperate zone without violent storms and tempests; and in this he succeeds though it be at the cost of that intensity of life and feeling which an extreme life affords. A man cannot live intensely except at the cost of the self. Now the bourgeois treasures nothing more highly than the self (rudimentary as his may be). And so at the cost of intensity he achieves his own preservation and security. His harvest is a quiet mind which he prefers to being possessed by God, as he does comfort to pleasure, convenience to liberty, and a pleasant temperature to that deathly inner consuming fire. The bourgeois is consequently by nature a creature of weak impulses, anxious, fearful of giving himself away and easy to rule. Therefore, he has substituted majority for power, law for force, and the polling booth for responsibility.

It is clear that this weak and anxious being, in whatever numbers he exists, cannot maintain himself, and that qualities such as his can play no other rôle in the world than that of a herd of sheep among free roving wolves. Yet we see that, though in times when commanding natures are uppermost, the bourgeois goes at once to the wall, he never goes under; indeed at times he even appears to rule the world. How is this possible? Neither the great numbers of the herd, nor virtue, nor comon sense, nor organization could avail to save it from destruction. No medicine in the world can keep a pulse beating that from the outset was so weak. Nevertheless the bourgeoisie prospers. Why?

The answer runs: Because of the Steppenwolves. In fact, the vital force of the bourgeoisie resides by no means in the qualities of its normal members, but in those of its extremely numerous "outsiders" who by virtue of the extensiveness and elasticity of its ideals it can embrace. There is always a large number of strong and wild natures who share the life of the fold. Our Steppenwolf, Harry, is a characteristic example. He who is developed far beyond the level possible to the bourgeois, he who knows the bliss of meditation no less than the gloomy joys of hatred and self-hatred, he who despises law, virtue and common sense, is nevertheless captive to the bourgeoisie and cannot escape it. And so all through the mass of the real bourgeoisie are interposed numerous layers of humanity, many thousands of lives and minds, every one of whom, it is true, would have outgrown it and have obeyed the call to unconditioned life, were they not fastened to it by sentiments of their childhood and infected for the most part with its less intense life; and so they are kept lingering, obedient and bound by obligation and service. For with the bourgeoisie the opposite of the formula for the great is true: He who is not against me is with me.

If we now pause to test the soul of the Steppenwolf, we find him distinct from the bourgeois in the higher development of his individuality —for all extreme individuation turns against itself, intent upon its own destruction. We see that he had in him strong impulses both to be a saint and a profligate; and yet he could not, owing to some weakness or inertia, make the plunge into the untrammelled realms of space. The parent constellation of the bourgeoisie binds him with its spell. This is his place in the universe and this his bondage. Most intellectuals and most artists belong to the same type. Only the strongest of them force their way through the atmosphere of the bourgeois earth and attain to the cosmic. The others all resign themselves or make compromises. Despising the bourgeoisie, and yet belonging to it, they add to its strength and glory; for in the last resort they have to share their beliefs in order to live. The lives of these infinitely numerous persons make no claim to the tragic; but they live under an evil star in a quite considerable affliction; and in this hell their talents ripen and bear fruit. The few who break free seek their reward in the unconditioned and go down in splendor. They wear the thorn crown and their number is small. The others, however, who remain in the fold and from whose talents the bourgeoisie reaps much gain, have a third kingdom left open to them, an imaginary and yet a sovereign world, humor. The lone wolves who know no peace, these victims of unceasing pain to whom the urge for tragedy has been denied and who can never break through the starry space, who feel themselves summoned thither and yet cannot survive in its atmosphere—for them is reserved, provided suffering has made their spirits tough and elastic enough, a way of reconcilement and an escape into humor. Humor has always something bourgeois in it, although the true bourgeois is incapable of understanding it. In its imaginary realm the intricate and many-faceted ideal of all Steppenwolves finds its realisation. Here it is possible not only to extol the saint and the profligate in one breath and to make the poles meet, but to include the bourgeois, too, in the same affirmation. Now it is possible to be possessed by God and to affirm the sinner, and vice versa, but it is not possible for either saint or sinner (or for any other of the unconditioned) to affirm as well that lukewarm mean, the bourgeois. Humor alone, that magnificent discovery of those who are cut short in their calling to highest endeavor, those who falling short of tragedy are yet as rich in gifts as in affliction, humor alone (perhaps the most inborn and brilliant achievement of the spirit) attains to the impossible and brings every aspect of human existence within the rays of its prism. To live in the world as though it were not the world, to respect the law and yet to stand above it, to have possessions as though "one possessed nothing," to renounce as though it were no renunciation, all these favorite and often formulated propositions of an exalted worldly wisdom, it is in the power of humor alone to make efficacious.

And supposing the Steppenwolf were to succeed, and he has gifts and resources in plenty, in decocting this magic draught in the sultry mazes of his hell, his rescue would be assured. Yet there is much lacking. The possibility, the hope only are there. Whoever loves him and takes his part may wish him this rescue. It would, it is true, keep him forever tied to the bourgeois world, but his suffering would be bearable and productive. His relation to the bourgeois world would lose its sentimentality both in its love and in its hatred, and his bondage to it would cease to cause him the continual torture of shame.

To attain to this, or, perhaps it may be, to be able at last to dare the leap into the unknown, a Steppenwolf must once have a good look at himself. He must look deeply into the chaos of his own soul and plumb its depths. The riddle of his existence would then be revealed to him at once in all its changelessness, and it would be impossible for him ever after to escape first from the hell of the flesh to the comforts of a sentimental philosophy and then back to the blind orgy of his wolfishness. Man and wolf would then be compelled to recognise one another without the masks of false feeling and to look one another straight in the eye. Then they would either explode and separate forever, and there would be no more Steppenwolf, or else they would come to terms in the dawning light of humor.

It is possible that Harry will one day be led to this latter alternative. It is possible that he will learn one day to know himself. He may get hold of one of our little mirrors. He may encounter the Immortals. He may find in one of our magic theaters the very thing that is needed to free his neglected soul. A thousand such possibilities await him. His fate brings them on, leaving him no choice; for those outside of the bourgeoisie live in the atmosphere of these magic possibilities. A mere nothing suffices—and the lightning strikes.

And all this is very well known to the Steppenwolf, even though his eye may never fall on this fragment of his inner biography. He has a suspicion of his allotted place in the world, a suspicion of the Immortals, a suspicion that he may meet himself face to face; and he is aware of the existence of that mirror in which he has such bitter need to look and from which he shrinks in such deathly fear.

For the close of our study there is left one last fiction, a fundamental delusion to make clear. All interpretation, all psychology, all attempts to make things comprehensible, require the medium of theories, mythologies and lies; and a self-respecting author should not omit, at the close of an exposition, to dissipate these lies so far as may be in his power. If I say "above" or "below," that is already a statement that requires explanation, since an above and a below exist only in thought, only as abstractions. The world itself knows nothing of above or below.

So too, to come to the point, is the Steppenwolf a fiction. When Harry feels himself to be a were-wolf, and chooses to consist of two hostile and opposed beings, he is merely availing himself of a mythological simplification. He is no were-wolf at all, and if we appeared to accept without scrutiny this lie which he invented for himself and believes in, and tried to regard him literally as a two-fold being and a Steppenwolf, and so designated him, it was merely in the hope of being more easily understood with the assistance of a delusion, which we must now endeavor to put in its true light.

The division into wolf and man, flesh and spirit, by means of which Harry tries to make his destiny more comprehensible to himself is a very great simplification. It is a forcing of the truth to suit a plausible, but erroneous, explanation of that contradiction which this man discovers in himself and which appears to himself to be the source of his by no means negligible sufferings. Harry finds in himself a human being, that is to say, a world of thoughts and feelings, of culture and tamed or sublimated nature, and besides this he finds within himself also a wolf, that is to say, a dark world of instinct, of savagery and cruelty, of unsublimated or raw nature. In spite of this apparently clear division of his being between two spheres, hostile to one another, he has known happy moments now and then when the man and the wolf for a short while were reconciled with one another. Suppose that Harry tried to ascertain in any single moment of his life, any single act, what part the man had in it and what part the wolf, he would find himself at once in a dilemma, and his whole beautiful wolf-theory would go to pieces. For there is not a single human being, not even the primitive Negro, not even the idiot, who is so conveniently simple that his being can be explained as the sum of two or three principal elements; and to explain so complex a man as Harry by the artless division into wolf and man is a hopelessly childish attempt. Harry consists of a hundred or a thousand selves, not of two. His life oscillates, as everyone's does, not merely between two poles, such as the body and the spirit, the saint and the sinner, but between thousand and thousands.

We need not be surprised that even so intelligent and educated a man as Harry should take himself for a Steppenwolf and reduce the rich and complex organism of his life to a formula so simple, so rudimentary and primitive. Man is not capable of thought in any high degree, and even the most spiritual and highly cultivated of men habitually sees the world and himself through the lenses of delusive formulas and artless simplifications—and most of all himself. For it appears to be an inborn and imperative need of all men to regard the self as a unit. However often and however grievously this illusion is shattered, it always mends again. The judge who sits over the murderer and looks into his face, and at one moment recognizes all the emotions and potentialities and possibilities of the murderer in his own soul and hears the murderer's voice as his own, is at the next moment one and indivisible as the judge, and scuttles back into the shell of his cultivated self and does his duty and condemns the murderer to death. And if ever the suspicion of their manifold being dawns upon men of unusual powers and of unusually delicate perceptions, so that, as all genius must, they break through the illusion of the unity of the personality and perceive that the self is made up of a bundle of selves, they have only to say so and at once the majority puts them under lock and key, calls science to aid, establishes schizomania and protects humanity from the necessity of hearing the cry of truth from the lips of these unfortunate persons. Why then waste words, why utter a thing that every thinking man accepts as self-evident, when the mere utterance of it is a breach of taste? A man, therefore, who gets so far as making the supposed unity of the self two-fold is already almost a genius, in any case a most exceptional and interesting person. In reality, however, every ego, so far from being a unity is in the highest degree a manifold world, a constellated heaven, a chaos of forms, of states and stages, of inheritances and potentialities. It appears to be a necessity as imperative as eating and breathing for everyone to be forced to regard this chaos as a unity and to speak of his ego as though it were a one-fold and clearly detached and fixed phenomenon. Even the best of us shares the delusion.

The delusion rests simply upon a false analogy. As a body everyone is single, as a soul never. In literature, too, even in its ultimate achievement, we find this customary concern with apparently whole and single personalities. Of all literature up to our days the drama has been the most highly prized by writers and critics, and rightly, since it offers (or might offer) the greatest possibilities of representing the ego as a manifold entity, but for the optical illusion which makes us believe that the characters of the play are one-fold entities by lodging each one in an undeniable body, singly, separately and once and for all. An artless esthetic criticism, then, keeps its highest praise for this so-called character-drama in which each character makes his appearance unmistakably as a separate and single entity. Only from afar and by degrees the suspicion dawns here and there that all this is perhaps a cheap and superficial esthetic philosophy, and that we make a mistake in attributing to our great dramatists those magnificent conceptions of beauty that come to us from antiquity. These conceptions are not native to us, but are merely picked up at second hand, and it is in them, with their common source in the visible body, that the origin of the fiction of an ego, an individual, is really to be found. There is no trace of such a notion in the poems of ancient India. The heroes of the epics of India are not individuals, but whole reels of individualities in a series of incarnations. And in modern times there are poems, in which, behind the veil of a concern with individuality and character that is scarcely, indeed, in the author's mind, the motive is to present a manifold activity of soul. Whoever wishes to recognize this must resolve once and for all not to regard the characters of such a poem as separate beings, but as the various facets and aspects of a higher unity, in my opinion, of the poet's soul. If "Faust" is treated in this way, Faust, Mephistopheles, Wagner and the rest form a unity and a supreme individuality; and it is in this higher unity alone, not in the several characters, that something of the true nature of the soul is revealed. When Faust, in a line immortalized among schoolmasters and greeted with a shudder of astonishment by the Philistine, says: "Two souls, alas, do dwell within my breast!" he has forgotten Mephisto and a whole crowd of other souls that he has in his breast likewise. The Steppenwolf, too, believes that he bears two souls (wolf and man) in his breast and even so finds his breast disagreeably cramped because of them. The breast and the body are indeed one, but the souls that dwell in it are not two, nor five, but countless in number. Man is an onion made up of a hundred integuments, a texture made up of many threads. The ancient Asiatics knew this well enough, and in the Buddhist Yoga an exact technique was devised for unmasking the illusion of the personality. The human merry-go-round sees many changes: the illusion that cost India the efforts of thousands of years to unmask is the same illusion that the West has labored just as hard to maintain and strengthen.

If we consider the Steppenwolf from this standpoint it will be clear to us why he suffered so much under his ludicrous dual personality. He believes, like Faust, that two souls are far too many for a single breast and must tear the breast asunder. They are on the contrary far too few, and Harry does shocking violence to his poor soul when he endeavors to apprehend it by means of so primitive an image. Although he is a most cultivated person, he proceeds like a savage that cannot count further than two. He calls himself part wolf, part man, and with that he thinks he has come to an end and exhausted the matter. With the "man" he packs in everything spiritual and sublimated or even cultivated to be found in himself, and with the wolf all that is instinctive, savage and chaotic. But things are not so simple in life as in our thoughts, nor so rough and ready as in our poor idiotic language; and Harry lies about himself twice over when he employs this niggardly wolf-theory. He assigns, we fear, whole provinces of his soul to the "man" which are a long way from being human, and parts of his being to the wolf that long ago have left the wolf behind.

Like all men Harry believes that he knows very well what man is and yet does not know at all, although in dreams and other states not subject to control he often has his suspicions. If only he might not forget them, but keep them, as far as possible at least, for his own. Man is not by any means of fixed and enduring form (this, in spite of suspicions to the contrary on the part of their wise men, was the ideal of the ancients). He is much more an experiment and a transition. He is nothing else than the narrow and perilous bridge between nature and spirit. His innermost destiny drives him on to the spirit and to God. His innermost longing draws him back to nature, the mother. Between the two forces his life hangs tremulous and irresolute. "Man," whatever people think of him, is never anything more than a temporary bourgeois compromise. Convention rejects and bans certain of the more naked instincts, a little consciousness, morality and debestialization is called for, and a modicum of spirit is not only permitted but even thought necessary. The "man" of this concordat, like every other bourgeois ideal, is a compromise, a timid and artlessly sly experiment, with the aim of cheating both the angry primal mother Nature and the troublesome primal father Spirit of their pressing claims, and of living in a temperate zone between the two of them. For this reason the bourgeois today burns as heretics and hangs as criminals those to whom he erects monuments tomorrow.

That man is not yet a finished creation but rather a challenge of the spirit; a distant possibility dreaded as much as it is desired; that the way towards it has only been covered for a very short distance and with terrible agonies and ecstasies even by those few for whom it is the scaffold today and the monument tomorrow—all this the Steppenwolf, too, suspected. What, however, he calls the "man" in himself, as opposed to the wolf, is to a great extent nothing else than this very same average man of the bourgeois convention.

As for the way to true manhood, the way to the immortals, he has, it is true, an inkling of it and starts upon it now and then for a few hesitating steps and pays for them with much suffering and many pangs of loneliness. But as for striving with assurance, in response to that supreme demand, towards the genuine manhood of the spirit, and going the one narrow way to immortality, he is deeply afraid of it. He knows too well that it leads to still greater sufferings, to proscription, to the last renunciation, perhaps to the scaffold, and even though the enticement of immortality lies at the journey's end, he is still unwilling to suffer all these sufferings and to die all these deaths. Though the goal of manhood is better known to him than to the bourgeois, still he shuts his eyes. He is resolved to forget that the desperate clinging to the self and the desperate clinging to life are the surest way to eternal death, while the power to die, to strip one's self naked, and the eternal surrender of the self bring immortality with them. When he worships his favorites among the immortals, Mozart, perchance, he always looks at him in the long run through bourgeois eyes. His tendency is to explain Mozart's perfected being, just as a schoolmaster would, as a supreme and special gift rather than as the outcome of his immense powers of surrender and suffering, of his indifference to the ideals of the bourgeois, and of his patience under that last extremity of loneliness which rarifies the atmosphere of the bourgeois world to an ice-cold ether, around those who suffer to become men, that loneliness of the Garden of Gethsemane.

This Steppenwolf of ours has always been aware of at least the Faustian two-fold nature within him. He has discovered that the one-fold of the body is not inhabited by a one-fold of the soul, and that at best he is only at the beginning of a long pilgrimage towards this ideal harmony. He would like either to overcome the wolf and become wholly man or to renounce mankind and at last to live wholly a wolf's life. It may be presumed that he has never carefully watched a real wolf. Had he done so he would have seen, perhaps, that even animals are not undivided in spirit. With them, too, the well-knit beauty of the body hides a being of manifold states and strivings. The wolf, too, has his abysses. The wolf, too, suffers. No, back to nature is a false track that leads nowhere but to suffering and despair. Harry can never turn back again and become wholly wolf, and could he do so he would find that even the wolf is not of primeval simplicity, but already a creature of manifold complexity. Even the wolf has two, and more than two, souls in his wolf's breast, and he who desires to be a wolf falls into the same forgetfulness as the man who sings: "If I could be a child once more!" He who sentimentally sings of blessed childhood is thinking of the return to nature and innocence and the origin of things, and has quite forgotten that these blessed children are beset with conflict and complexities and capable of all suffering.

There is, in fact, no way back either to the wolf or to the child. From the very start there is no innocence and no singleness. Every created thing, even the simplest, is already guilty, already multiple. It has been thrown into the muddy stream of being and may never more swim back again to its source. The way to innocence, to the uncreated and to God leads on, not back, not back to the wolf or to the child, but ever further into sin, ever deeper into human life. Nor will suicide really solve your problem, unhappy Steppenwolf. You will, instead, embark on the longer and wearier and harder road of life. You will have to multiply many times your two-fold being and complicate your complexities still further. Instead of narrowing your world and simplifying your soul, you will have to absorb more and more of the world and at last take all of it up in your painfully expanded soul, if you are ever to find peace. This is the road that Buddha and every great man has gone, whether consciously or not, insofar as fortune favored his quest. All births mean separation from the All, the confinement within limitation, the separation from God, the pangs of being born ever anew. The return into the All, the dissolution of painful individuation, the reunion with God means the expansion of the soul until it is able once more to embrace the All.

We are not dealing here with man as he is known to economics and statistics, as he is seen thronging the streets by the million, and of whom no more account can be made than of the sand of the sea or the spray of its waves. We are not concerned with the few millions less or more. They are a stock-in-trade, nothing else. No, we are speaking of man in the highest sense, of the end of the long road to true manhood, of kingly men, of the immortals. Genius is not so rare as we sometimes think; nor, certainly, so frequent as may appear from history books or, indeed, from the newspapers. Harry has, we should say, genius enough to attempt the quest of true manhood instead of discoursing pitifully about his stupid Steppenwolf at every difficulty encountered.

It is as much a matter for surprise and sorrow that men of such possibilities should fall back on Steppenwolves and "Two souls, alas!" as that they reveal so often that pitiful love for the bourgeoisie. A man who can understand Buddha and has an intuition of the heaven and hell of humanity ought not to live in a world ruled by "common sense" and democracy and bourgeois standards. It is only from cowardice that he lives in it; and when its dimensions are too cramping for him and the bourgeois parlor too confining, he lays it at the wolf's door, and refuses to see that the wolf is as often as not the best part of him. All that is wild in himself he calls wolf and considers it wicked and dangerous and the bugbear of all decent life. He cannot see, even though he thinks himself an artist and possessed of delicate perceptions, that a great deal else exists in him besides and behind the wolf. He cannot see that not all that bites is wolf and that fox, dragon, tiger, ape and bird of paradise are there also. And he cannot see that this whole world, this Eden and its manifestations of beauty and terror, of greatness and meanness, of strength and tenderness is crushed and imprisoned by the wolf legend just as the real man in him is crushed and imprisoned by that sham existence, the bourgeois.

Man designs for himself a garden with a hundred kinds of trees, a thousand kinds of flowers, a hundred kinds of fruit and vegetables. Suppose, then, that the gardener of this garden knew no other distinction than between edible and inedible, nine-tenths of this garden would be useless to him. He would pull up the most enchanting flowers and hew down the noblest trees and even regard them with a loathing and envious eye. This is what the Steppenwolf does with the thousand flowers of his soul. What does not stand classified as either man or wolf he does not see at all. And consider all that he imputes to "man"! All that is cowardly and apish, stupid and mean—while to the wolf, only because he has not succeeded in making himself its master, is set down all that is strong and noble.

Now we bid Harry good-by and leave him to go on his way alone. Were he already among the immortals—were he already there at the goal to which his difficult path seems to be taking him, with what amazement he would look back to all this coming and going, all this indecision and wild zig-zag trail. With what a mixture of encouragement and blame, pity and joy, he would smile at this Steppenwolf.

C. P. Cavafy

AS MUCH AS YOU CAN

And if you cannot make your life as you want it,
at least try this
as much as you can: do not disgrace it
in the crowding contact with the world,
in the many movements and all the talk.

Do not disgrace it by taking it,
dragging it around often and exposing it
to the daily folly
of relationships and associations,
till it becomes like an alien burdensome life.

Arthur Rimbaud

A SEASON IN HELL

Ah! cette vie de mon enfance, la grande route par tous les temps, sobre surnaturellement, plus désintéressé que le meilleur des mendiants, fier de n'avoir ni pays, ni amis, quelle sottise c'était.—Et je m'en aperçois seulement!

—J'ai eu raison de mépriser ces bonshommes qui ne perdraient pas l'occasion d'une caresse, parasites de la propreté et de la santé de nos femmes, aujourd'hui qu'elles sont si peu d'accord avec nous.

J'ai eu raison dans tous mes dédains: puisque je m'évade!

Je m'évade?

Je m'explique.

Hier encore, je soupirais: "Ciel! sommes-nous assez de damnés ici-bas! Moi, j'ai tant de temps déjà dans leur troupe! Je les connais tous. Nous nous reconnaissons toujours; nous nous dégoûtons. La charité nous est inconnue. Mais nous sommes polis; nos relations avec le monde sont très convenables." Est-ce étonnant? Le monde! les marchands, les naïfs!— Nous ne sommes pas déshonorés.—Mais les élus, comment nous recevraient-ils? Or il y a des gens hargneux et joyeux, de faux élus, puisqu'il nous faut de l'audace ou de l'humilité pour les arborer. Ce sont les seuls élus. Ce ne sont pas des bénisseurs!

M'étant retrouvé deux sous de raison,—ça passe vite!—je vois que mes malaises viennent de ne m'être pas figuré assez tôt que nous sommes à l'Occident. Les marais occidentaux! Non que je croie la lumière altérée, la forme exténuée, le mouvement égaré . . . Bon! voici que mon esprit veut absolument se charger de tous les développements cruels qu'a subis l'esprit depuis la fin de l'Orient . . . Il en veut, mon esprit!

. . . Mes deux sous de raison sont finis!—L'esprit est autorité, il veut que je sois en Occident. Il faudrait le faire taire pour conclure comme je voulais.

J'envoyais au diable les palmes des martyres, les rayons de l'art, l'orgueil des inventeurs, l'ardeur des pillards; je retournais à l'Orient et à la sagesse première et éternelle.—Il paraît que c'est un rêve de paresse grossière!

Pourtant, je ne songeais guère au plaisir d'échapper aux souffrances modernes. Je n'avais pas en vue la sagesse bâtarde du Coran.—Mais n'y

THE IMPOSSIBLE

Ah, the life of my childhood, the highway in all kinds of weather, the time when I was supernaturally solemn, more impartial than the best of beggars, proud to have neither country nor friends, what nonsense it was.—And I am just barely aware of the fact now!

—I was right to despise the fatheads who never miss a chance at a kiss, the parasites of the cleanliness and the health of our women, today when they are so little in accord with us.

I was right in all my scorn: for I am running away!

Running away?

I'll explain.

Just yesterday I was sighing to myself: "My God! Are there enough of us damned down here? I myself have already spent so much time in their company. I know them all. We always recognize each other; we disgust each other. Good will is unknown to us. But we are polite; our relations with the world are quite as they should be." Is this astonishing? The world! Merchants, simpletons!—We are not disgraced.—But the chosen ones, how would they receive us? Now there are surly people and joyous people, people falsely chosen, since we need audacity or humility in order to approach them. They alone are chosen. They are not sanctimonious!

Having regained reason—two cents' worth—it went quickly enough! —I see that my discomforts come from my failure to understand soon enough that we are of the Western World. The marshes of the West! Not that I think the light is spoiled, the form worn out, the movement misguided . . . Good! My spirit now wants to take upon itself completely all the cruel stages which the human spirit has passed through since the end of the Orient . . . My spirit demands this!

. . . My two cents' worth of reason is spent!—The spirit is in command and wants me to be a Western man. It will have to keep quiet if I am to end up as I wanted to.

I said to the devil with the palms of martyrs, the radiance of art, the pride of inventors, the energy of pirates; I returned to the Orient, to the primal and eternal wisdom.—It seems that this is a coarse and lazy dream!

a-t-il pas un supplice réel en ce que, depuis cette déclaration de la science, le christianisme, l'homme *se joue,* se prouve les évidences, se gonfle du plaisir de répéter ces preuves, et ne vit que comme cela? Torture subtile, niaise; source de mas divagations spirituelles. La nature pourrait s'ennuyer, peut-être! M. Prudhomme est né avec le Christ.

N'est-ce-pas parce que nous cultivons la brume? Nous mangeons la fièvre avec nos légumes aqueux. Et l'ivrognerie! et le tabac! et l'ignorance! et les dévouements!—Tout cela est-il assez loin de la pensée, de la sagesse de l'Orient, la patrie primitive? Pourquoi un monde moderne, si de pareils poisons s'inventent!

Les gens d'Eglise diront: C'est compris. Mais vous voulez parler de l'Eden. Rien pour vous dans l'histoire des peuples orientaux.—C'est vrai; c'est à l'Eden que je songeais! Qu'est-ce que c'est pour mon rêve, cette pureté des races antiques!

Les philosophes: Le monde n'a pas d'âge. L'humanité se déplace, simplement. Vous êtes en Occident, mais libre d'habiter dans votre Orient, quelque ancien qu'il vous le faille,—et d'y habiter bien. Ne soyez pas un vaincu. Philosophes, vous êtes de votre Occident.

Mon esprit, prends garde. Pas de partis de salut violents. Exerce-toi!—Ah! la science ne va pas assez vite pour nous!

—Mais je m'aperçois que mon esprit dort.

S'il était bien éveillé toujours à partir de ce moment, nous serions bientôt à la vérité, qui peut-être nous entoure avec ses anges pleurant! . . . —S'il avait été éveillé jusqu'à ce moment-ci, c'est que je n'aurais pas cédé aux instincts délétères, à une époque immémoriale! . . .—S'il avait toujours été bien éveillé, je voguerais en pleine sagesse! . . .

O pureté! pureté!

C'est cette minute d'éveil qui m'a donné la vision de la pureté!—Par l'esprit on va à Dieu!

Déchirante infortune!

Nevertheless, the pleasure of evading the tortures of modern life scarcely occurred to me. I was not thinking of the bastard wisdom of the Koran.—But isn't it actually torture that since this declaration of science, Christianity, man *makes believe,* convinces himself of his evidence, prides himself on the pleasure of repeating these proofs, and lives only like that. A subtle and ridiculous torture, and the source of my spiritual wanderings. Perhaps nature might get bored with herself! Mr. Stuffed Shirt was born with Christ.

Isn't this because we cultivate the fog? We eat fever with our watery vegetables. And drunkenness! and tobacco! and ignorance! and prayers! —Is all that far enough from the thought and wisdom of the Orient, the primitive fatherland? Why have a modern world, if such poisons are fermented?

The clergy will say: why, of course. Why, you mean Eden. There's nothing for you in the history of the Oriental peoples.—That's right; it's of Eden I was thinking! What has the purity of ancient races to do with my dream?

The philosophers will say: The world has no particular age. Humanity shifts about, that's all. You are in the West, but free to live in your Orient, as old a one as you need,—and to live comfortably there. Don't be a defeatist.—Philosophers, you're Western men and you talk like it.

Take care, my spirit. No violent decisions for salvation. Watch out!— Ah, science doesn't go quickly enough for us.

—But I see that my spirit is asleep.

If my spirit were always wide-awake from this moment on, we would soon arrive at the truth, which perhaps even now surrounds us with her angels, weeping! . . . If it had been awake up until now, I would not have given in to degenerate instincts, to a forgotten epoch! . . . If it had always been wide-awake, I would be sailing in full wisdom! . . .

O purity! purity!

It is this moment of waking which has given me the vision of purity!— By the spirit one attains God!

Heart-rending misfortune!

Enid Starkie

ARTHUR RIMBAUD

At the time when Rimbaud went to Paris in the autumn of 1871, Verlaine was living with his wife's parents in the Rue Nicolet in Montmartre. He had lost his Civil Service appointment on account of his suspected sympathy with the Commune; but it is probable that his dismissal, or rather non-reappointment, by the new régime, was in part due to his inefficiency and to his intemperate habits. During the disturbed period of the war and the revolution he had slipped back into his bachelor way of life and taken once more to drink. It had been to remove him from the temptations of such associations that his mother had married him to Mathilde Mauté de Fleurville. Now that he was earning nothing his own private income, added to the marriage portion of his young wife, was no longer sufficient to keep them in bourgeois comfort, especially since Mathilde was expecting a baby. The young couple therefore went to live with the Mauté de Fleurville, who owned a small *hôtel* and garden in a quiet street in Montmartre.

Mathilde Verlaine was glad to return once more to what she still regarded as her home, for she much preferred the leisured ease of her parents' house to her more bohemian life with her husband. With naïve pride she expatiates in her memoirs on the splendour of the house, the two large reception rooms and the dining-room on the ground floor, all opening on to the trim garden, her parents' rooms on the first floor and that of her half-brother Charles, while the second floor was given over to the 'jeune ménage'. The house contained as well a library and a guest-room.

The Mauté de Fleurville came of respectable moneyed bourgeois stock who had no legitimate claim to nobility. They had amassed a fortune, probably in business, though this is nowhere stated, and, as was frequently the case in the Second Empire, had then added the 'particule' to their name to give it the appearance of the nobility which they considered fitting to their fortune. As a young man M. Mauté de Fleurville had taken his degree in law at the University of Paris, but he never practised his profession, and his daughter was deeply offended when Lepelletier once described the father-in-law of his friend Verlaine as a former 'notaire'. Her father, she proudly declared, never earned any money in his life, 'il n'a jamais rien fait que vivre selon ses goûts'. After the war and the Commune, he lived in ease and respectability with his wife and family in their comfortable home in Montmartre.

Madame Mauté de Fleurville prided herself on her acquaintance with art and on her association with those who produced it. Her son by her first marriage, Charles de Sivry, was a composer of light music who enjoyed some fame in his own day, and she herself was a well-known music teacher. At this time, in 1871, young Claude Debussy was her pupil. She was proud to think that her son-in-law, Paul Verlaine, was highly spoken of in the best literary circles of the day as a poet with a future, for she had heard him praised by well-established Parnassian poets and Academicians—she was a believer in those to whom honours had been awarded. She had been pleased to give her only daughter to so eminent a man of letters and had been willing to overlook the lapses of which she had been informed, considering them to be merely the inevitable wild oats of a young Parisian, such as could, with firmness, be eradicated after marriage. She liked to think of herself as a patron of the arts, as an encourager and discoverer of unknown and young talent. She listened with great interest when Paul Verlaine spoke of the bright new star which was rising on the distant provincial horizon of literature. She thought that here was her chance of staking out her claim before anyone else heard of this young poet, and in imagination she already saw herself pointing out to future admiring audiences the famous poet, Arthur Rimbaud, whom she had rescued from great poverty and obscurity, and who had made his début from her house. He was said by her son-in-law to show promise of surpassing even Victor Hugo. It was she who suggested that Paul should invite his young friend to stay at her house, but little did she know what a monster she was introducing into the family nest. She was told that he was young and she expected to see a youth with the Botticelli angel face of Alfred de Musset as a young man. The Romantic movement had given the general public very definite ideas of what the appearance of a poet should be. Well known were the pictures of Chateaubriand looking out to sea with dreaming eyes and wind-swept locks curling round his nobel brow. Well known too were the God-like grace of the young Lamartine and the austere distinction of de Vigny. But most beloved of all was Alfred de Musset's picture in his Renaissance page costume.

Madame Mauté de Fleurville did not hope that a contemporary poet could rival these gods of her youth, but she expected him at least to seem *distingué*. Even if he could not look, like Hérédia, a Spanish grandee, he could at least look a respectable schoolmaster like Mallarmé. It would never have entered her head that anyone of note could look as Rimbaud had looked the first time she set eyes on him; she could never have believed that anyone who looked like that could ever come to any good. She had only seen such men lounging on the seats in the boulevards, especially since the war, when the police had become so lax. No one like that had certainly ever entered her house.

Rimbaud's visit was a disaster from the very beginning. Verlaine and Charles Cros had gone to the station to meet him, but through some mistake they had missed him. To a country-bred lad like Rimbaud the walk meant nothing, and finding no one to meet him he set off on foot for Montmartre and arrived alone, hot and dusty, to the consternation of Madame Mauté de Fleurville and her daughter. Mathilde never forgot the amazement both she and her mother had felt when the country youth was shown into the drawing-room where they were sitting waiting for him to arrive with Verlaine, and wondering what he would be like. Now they saw a coarse young peasant, with rough hands and a face red from exposure to wind and sun. He was at this time just beginning to shoot up and his old clothes of the previous year were by now too small; the sleeves did not cover his knobbly wrists and the trousers, the famous slate-blue trousers, did not reach the coarse blue cotton socks hand-knitted by his mother. He was, moreover, extremely dirty and untidy; his hair was standing on end as if it had never been brushed, and what looked like a dirty string slung round his collar, served as a tie. Worst of all he had arrived without any kind of luggage whatsoever, no tooth-brush, no hairbrush, no change of linen.

Rimbaud had always possessed an uncanny, animal-like sensitivity to atmosphere and now he was quick to feel the impression that he was making. He sensed immediately, beneath the mannered politeness of mother and daughter, the hostility and the disapproval. In such cases he always became surly and silent, hiding his emotion beneath insolence. The two women were trying to entertain him, or, more correctly, trying, under great difficulties, to fulfil what they considered the social obligations of gentlefolk—they cared little whether their guest was entertained or not—when Verlaine and Cros arrived back from the station.

Verlaine too could not disguise the astonishment he felt on seeing a mere boy sitting in the drawing-room, when he had expected to find a man of over twenty, someone nearer his own age. Suddenly he saw a leggy boy with wild hair and the awkward movements of a growing youth who has not yet learnt what to do with his unwieldy limbs, and who cannot control his cracked voice. But above the scraggy and clumsy body of an adolescent not yet fully grown he saw a child's face, round-cheeked and rosy, with the purest and most piercing blue eyes he had ever encountered. He insists on the good looks of Rimbaud at this time and describes his extreme beauty of face at the age of sixteen. It appears to have been only prejudice and antipathy which made Mathilde Verlaine and so many others describe him as coarse and ugly.

The first dinner was a complete fiasco. Madame Verlaine and Madame Mauté de Fleurville paralysed Rimbaud with their bright, meaningless conversation, and he was, moreover, unused to the company of women. They darted endless and pointless questions at him concerning his journey and his future plans; and from the height of Parisian condescension, asked for his opinion of French provincial life. Rimbaud's views on this subject would in any case not have been mentionable in polite society. Charles de Sivry's brittle Parisian chatter also irritated him and soon he made no further attempt to hide his contempt of his hosts. In more propitious circumstances he would have found Charles Cros sympathetic but he was now ill at ease and bewildered, and he was still further discomfited when Cros fired questions at him concerning his aesthetic principles and his literary doctrine, and when he openly analysed his work. Rimbaud was tired and in a state of confusion, and he never was at the best of times a fluent conversationalist; now he lapsed into gloomy silence and remained tongue-tied, answering only in monosyllables the questions good-naturedly put to him. He gave the impression of surliness and ill-temper, but in truth he was more deeply sunk in misery and distress, more profoundly disappointed, than he had ever been in his life.

Looking back on the evening later, Verlaine could never remember more than one remark which Rimbaud had made, and this had no bearing on literature. There was present in the room during the meal a little dog, Madame Mauté de Fleurville's most treasured possession, a pampered and spoilt little darling but good-humoured and well-behaved, and it ran from one person to another begging for scraps of food, soliciting affection and caresses. Rimbaud, whom its antics soon began to irritate, looked down at the pretty creature and said in tones of the deepest contempt: 'Les chiens, ce sont des libéraux!'

As the meal progressed Rimbaud became more awkward and insolent. Before dinner was over and coffee served, to the horror of the ladies, he drew his filthy pipe from his pocket, crossed his legs and, leaning his elbows on the table just as if he were in a low pub, moodily puffed his evil-smelling tobacco smoke over the dinner-table.

The evening which was to stretch out indefinitely with stimulating literary conversation, ended early. Madame Mauté de Fleurville, alleging that Rimbaud must be feeling tired after his journey, and would not wish to remain up chatting, gave the signal for withdrawal not long after the meal had ended.

Rimbaud's visit never recovered from the failure of the first evening, and he made no further efforts to ingratiate himself with his hostess; in fact he did all he could to outrage her feelings by his expressions of opinion and by his conduct. He was determined that if she thought badly of him she should have ample grounds for this view. One day Verlaine on returning home found his friend smoking and sunning himself as he lay stretched in the October sun on the gravelled path that led to the house. He could be seen by every passer-by and the inhabitants of that respectable neighbourhood stood staring in at him in great amazement. There ensued much talk in the district about Madame Mauté de Fleurville's strange guest and all agreed that it was indeed curious that she should permit her son-in-law to consort with such a wild hooligan. And the gossip spread and developed through all the *loges de concierge* of the quarter.

Madame Mauté de Fleurville was firmly of the opinion that Arthur Rimbaud was depraving her son-in-law, reading him into debauch and inciting him to open rebellion. In this she was unjust, for Verlaine had, to a certain extent, escaped from the meshes of conjugal discipline before the coming of Rimbaud to Paris. He was after all ten years older than his young friend; he had knocked about the Latin Quarter since his adolescence; as a youth he was alleged to have practised sodomy and he was already a confirmed drunkard by the time of his marriage with Mathilde Mauté de Fleurville. At first, carried away by the new delights of married life with a wife only just seventeen, he had settled down temporarily under the stern discipline of his father-in-law. But conjugal respectability had begun to pall before he met Rimbaud, especially latterly, when the delicate health of his pregnant wife deprived his sensual nature of the physical joys which, hitherto, had made his bondage bearable. It would be nearer the truth to say that it was he who helped Rimbaud to reach the 'dérèglement de tous les sens' which was the latter's aim. There is no doubt that Rimbaud was an apt pupil who encouraged his elder and, driving him on to further deeds of daring, incited him most outrageous conduct and that he would no longer have to face alone the disapproval of his stern mother-in-law, that it was Rimbaud indeed who now received the brunt of disapprobation.

On 30 October 1871 George Verlaine was born and for three whole days after that everything went well. Verlaine was all that a proud young father should be. He returned every day for dinner and spent the evening with his wife. Then, on the fourth day, his good resolutions broke down under the strain of his model behaviour. He remained out until two o'clock in the morning and returned home in a state of advanced intoxication. Alcohol, and especially absinthe, was always poison to him; he came back in a nasty frame of mind and threatened all those whom he encountered. He went straight to his wife's room and when she begged him to retire to his he refused. The monthly nurse began to grow frightened and threatened to summon the parents for help, but Mathilde did not wish them to be called. Next, in spite of all remonstrances, he lay down on his wife's bed, fully dressed as he was, with his boots still on his feet and his hat on his head; he lay with his head to the foot of the bed and placed his muddy feet on the pillow close to Mathilde's face, and in this manner soon fell into a drunken sleep. Next morning, when Madame Mauté de Fleurville came to see her daughter, she was horrified at the sight of her son-in-law still lying there fast asleep and fully dressed, and Mathilde adds that her mother, in spite of her usual kindness, was indignant.

In the meantime, however, old Mauté de Fleurville returned home from his shooting party in the country and the strong man immediately put down his foot, with all the pother that always arises when the masculine head of the house takes action. In violent terms he demanded what the women of the house had been about in permitting such conduct to continue and said that he would not endure the presence of this interloper in his house one moment longer. He informed his son-in-law that he must, forthwith, find another abode for his undesirable friend.

When Rimbaud had departed, Mathilde entered the guestroom to have it set to rights and she found, to her amazement and revulsion, little insects crawling over the pillow, which she had never seen before, but her mother, apparently more experienced, informed her that these were lice. She told her husband what she had found, hoping to disgust him with his friend, but Paul only burst out laughing in her face and said that Rimbaud liked to keep such parasites in his hair to have them handy to throw on the priests whom he passed in the streets.

Rimbaud, however, had not waited to be turned out by Mauté de Fleurville, or for Verlaine to find him other lodgings. He fled, of his own accord, without telling anyone where he was going—this was easy since he had no possessions except the clothes on his back. But Verlaine felt responsible for him and his kind heart was troubled to think of his young friend alone and friendless in Paris without any means of subsistence, and he looked for him everywhere that he could think of, but did not succeed in finding him. It was only some weeks later that he met him by chance in the street and he was then startled by the change in him. His appearance of bucolic health had completely vanished and he was pale and hollow-cheeked, in rags and covered with vermin. Since he had left Montmartre he had tried to obtain work, but in vain; he had done any odd job that he could pick up in order not to starve; amongst other things he had peddled rings for keys in the streets. He had lived in the state of destitution which he had known during his previous visit. Moved to tears by the sight of his poverty, Verlaine gave him a square meal and then brought him to Charles Cros and André Gill, who were to look after him until some permanent arrangement could be made. Verlaine next approached Théodore de Banville, whose kindness and generosity to unknown and struggling artists was proverbial. Banville remembered the name of the young poet who had written to him on two occasions from Charleville and he rented for him an unfurnished attic in the house in which he himself lived, in the Rue de Buci, off the Boulevard Saint-Germain; this his mother furnished with the things most urgently needed. Ever since his earliest years, Madame de Banville had carefully tended her only son, encouraging and fostering his poetic talent, and priding herself that in so doing she was a better and more understanding mother than the mother of his unfortunate friend, Charles Baudelaire. Théodore was now close on fifty, one of the best considered poets of the day, and she still looked after him with the same jealous and sympathetic care. Thinking of his early years, her heart was touched at the sight of the young poet from the provinces, a mere child, who had come far from his own mother's care, without a penny in his pocket, to fight his way in the heartless town of Paris.

She and her son provided him with a roof over his head, but it was Charles Cros who fed him—as is learnt from the unpublished letter to Pradelle, in the Bérès documents, dated 6 November 1871. Eventually several men of letters subscribed the sum of three francs a day for his current expenses. On this he would not certainly grow rich or self-indulgent, but he would, at least, not starve.

Rimbaud did not, however, remain long in the Rue de Buci. It is alleged that the neighbours complained to Banville of his guest's conduct, and that as a result of this he was requested to leave the house. It is said that when he first went to his new room in his verminous, filthy clothes, he could not bear the thought of defiling so fresh and clean a lodging. He then undressed and, to the horror of the people living on the opposite side of the street, stood naked at the open window to fling the bundle of dirty clothes into the thoroughfare below.

It is here, we are told, that he wrote *Les Chercheuses de Poux,* inspired by an event of the previous year. In spite of the subject-matter, the extreme loveliness of the lines has an evocative power which suggests a poem by Baudelaire:

> Quand le front de l'enfant, plein de rouges tourmentes,
> Implore l'essaim blanc des rêves indistincts,
> Il vient près de son lit deux grandes soeurs charmantes
> Avec de frêles doigts aux ongles argentins.
>
> Elles assoient l'enfant auprès d'une croisée
> Grande ouverte où l'air bleu baigne un fouillis de fleurs
> Et dans ses lourds cheveux où tombe la rosée,
> Promènent leurs doigts fins, terribles et charmeurs.

Il écoute chanter leurs haleines craintives
Qui fleurent de longs miels végétaux et rosés
Et qu'interrompt parfois un sifflement, salives
Reprises sur la lèvre ou désirs de baisers.

Il entend leurs cils noirs battant sous les silences
Parfumés; et leurs doigts électriques et doux
Font crépiter, parmi ses grises indolences,
Sous leurs ongles royaux la mort des petits poux.

Voilà que monte en lui le vin de la Paresse,
Soupir d'harmonica qui pourrait délirer;
L'enfant se sent, selon la lenteur des caresses,
Sourdre et mourir sans cesse un désir de pleurer.

After leaving the Rue de Buci, Rimbaud camped for a time with the composer Cabaner, sleeping on his sofa. Cabaner used to live in the Hôtel des Etrangers, in the Rue Racine near the Odéon, and he was the vaguest and most absent-minded of creatures who never knew or minded how many people made use of his room for a night's shelter. He thought of nothing beyond his art and he had only been very dimly conscious of the siege of Paris by the Prussians. When the second siege started, that by the Versaillais, he said: 'What! are the Germans at it again?' Then, noticing amazement and disgust on the faces of those who were listening to him, he quickly corrected himself, saying: 'Goodness! It has lasted so long that I thought it must be some other country by now.'

He was a man of emaciated, almost diaphanous appearance, whose face seemed to consist solely in a soft, flowing beard and a pair of large, dreamy eyes. Verlaine used to call him 'Jesus Christ after three years of absinthe.'

It was when Rimbaud was camping with Cabaner that Delahaye saw him for the first time since his departure from Charleville. He found him in the dirty little lounge of the hotel surrounded by a crowd of men of letters, and he was lying, apparently asleep, on the sofa, unconscious of all who were around him. Suddenly he stretched himself, sat up rubbing his eyes and made a grimace of disgust. He was just coming round from a hashish trance which had proved most disappointing. He had lain down expecting to enjoy the loveliest of visions but all he had seen was a series of black and white moons chasing one another, at various speeds, across the sky. This must have been his first experience of drugs; it was November 1871.

Then Delahaye looked again at his school friend and saw how much he had altered during the two months he had spent in Paris. He had shot up more than a foot; he was no longer a boy, but a tall and lanky youth, and he was most distressingly thin. He looked filthy and sordid, draped as he was in an old secondhand overcoat, several sizes too large for him, which hung in tatters from his thin shoulders, and with this he wore a battered old grey felt hat. Delahaye, who was at heart a respectable bourgeois, was shocked at the appearance of his friend.

Next, when he had exhausted Cabaner's hospitality, Rimbaud slept for some weeks in the studios of those willing to grant him the charity of a night's shelter. Finally, however, Verlaine rented for him a room in a little street off the Boulevard Montparnasse, the Rue Campagne-Première, then, as now, a street of artists' studios. This was in January 1872 and Rimbaud occupied this room until he returned to Charleville for a time in March. This room, 'pleine de jour sale et de bruits d'araignées,' was the scene of many of the orgies of Rimbaud and Verlaine which led to the former's temporary exile from the capital. When he returned in May he lived in the Rue Monsieur-le-Prince and in the sordid little Hôtel dé Cluny in the Rue Victor Cousin, near the Sorbonne; he remained there until he left for Brussels in July, in company with Verlaine.

PARIS

Paris was a disappointment to Rimbaud for he was not a success with the literary people with whom he wished to stand well. Even Verlaine's boon companions, bohemians though they thought themselves to be, would never have descended to the depths of debauch to which Rimbaud was willing to descend. And moreover, there was all the difference in the world between La Bohême at the end of the Second Empire and during the first years of the Third Republic, and that of the 'nineties. In the later period dirt and depravity were considered the hallmark of genius and many a respectable 'fils de famille' ceased to wash and adopted dissolute habits in order to simulate the genius which he did not possess. Baudelaire, on the contrary, no matter to what depths of poverty he sank, always prided himself on spending at least two hours each day on his toilet, and he once fiercely arraigned his mother for daring to suggest that straitened means might have brought about a degradation of his person. In the 'nineties Baudelaire would have flaunted his poverty with pride and have gloried in it. In 1871, literature still remained a respectable and highly considered calling. The authors themselves took their position seriously as being that of men who were the depositories of truth and entrusted with the duty of helping in the 'redressment moral' of France after the disaster of the Franco-Prussian War and the tragedy of the Commune. A strange situation arose a few years later, in 1875, when Verlaine's poems were black-balled for inclusion in the third series of *Le Parnasse Contemporain* on grounds concerning only the moral character of their author. Poems from his pen had been printed in the issue of 1866 and in that of 1870 and these had been greatly admired and praised. He was in England in 1875 when he heard that a further series was being projected and he submitted certain of his verses for inclusion, some of the beautiful poems published later in *Sagesse*. However, between the second series of *Le Parnasse Contemporain* and the third, his relationship with Rimbaud had occurred, the trial in Brussels, and his subsequent term of imprisonment. As a result of this his poems were refused by the selection committee. This committee consisted of three of his former friends, Banville, Coppée and Anatole France. Banville and Coppée abstained from voting, priding themselves that in so doing they were giving proof of tolerant generosity, but they were, in fact, merely throwing the brunt of the decision on to Anatole France. He, however, was restrained by no scruples of affection, generosity or pity for his former friend and he wrote on his voting slip, 'L'auteur est indigne et ses vers sont les plus mauvais qu'on ait vus.'

Anatole France was here giving proof neither of loyal friendship nor of literary acumen for the poems were amongst the finest that Verlaine had ever written. And so it came about that the third series of *Le Parnasse Contemporain* appeared without any contribution from the pen of Verlaine.

It was literary men with similar opinions and principles whom Rimbaud met in Paris, and it could not be expected that they would approve of his professed absence of moral standards, of his dirt and of his total lack of a sense of responsibility. They could not, moreover, endure his arrogance which they considered completely unjustified. He, on his side, made no effort to hide the scorn he felt for all those whom he met, and he did not disguise from them the fact that he considered them antediluvian in their theories of art. He went amongst them with a perpetual sneer of contempt on his face.

The war and the Commune had, as yet, made little difference in the aesthetic ideals of the literary world in Paris. It was the Parnassian conception of art which generally prevailed, as it had prevailed all through the Second Empire. The writers and artists professed to worship beauty, and beauty for them meant harmony and serenity. Above all else they worshipped the beauty of the human body, particularly of the female body; not the realistic beauty portrayed in Courbet's and Manet's paintings, but an etherealized and sexless beauty which could rouse no low desires. 'Le nu harmonieux' they called it. It can be imagined that Rimbaud's *Vénus Anadyomène*, 'belle hideusement d'un ulcère à l'anus,' was not calculated to please them. Although Baudelaire had died in 1867, his work was not yet understood or appreciated, except by a few rare poets like Verlaine, and even then only imperfectly. The other poets, with their eyes turned towards the past where they considered the source of real beauty sprang, could not accept his new conception of beauty, with its urban types, city men and women instead of gods and goddesses, narrow, slummy streets instead of fresh green glades, apartment houses instead of classic palaces. The only point on which they agreed with him was in his worship for work well done. Leconte de Lisle was the leader of the poets in Paris at this time, though the most typical was perhaps Hérédia with his perfect and beautiful, cold and monotonous, verse. In Hérédia's work can most readily be seen how much poetry had lost of the freedom it had gained during the Romantic revolution. According to the Parnassian recipe it was quite possible to compose what was considered the highest poetry about almost nothing, and this led inevitably to the bankruptcy of poetry, for the conception of true poetry is not fulfilled 'by pure language and liquid versification'. Parnassian verse has been called a clever and ingenious arrangement of bric-à-brac. To these writers Rimbaud's vital and very personal form of art could not possibly make an appeal. One and all they solidly rejected him on account of what they called the chaos of his theories and his errors in grammar and syntax. In their attitude can be seen not merely dislike and disapproval but the primordial and instinctive terror of change. All the best considered poets of mature years cast him out, Leconte de Lisle and Banville; he was not even accepted by those of a generation younger, Coppée, Hérédia and Catulle Mendès, who imagined themselves progressive. Verlaine alone still had confidence in his friend's powers and his opinion was held of little account since it was believed that Rimbaud had cast an evil eye on him and had bewitched him.

By a strange coincidence, however, there had died in Paris in the previous November a poet with whom Rimbaud had much in common, a poet as fiercely individualistic and revolutionary as he, Isidore Ducasse, who wrote under the name of Comte de Lautréamont. He had died unknown and undiscovered at the age of twenty-four, but his *Chants de Maldoror* have become to-day a rich hunting-ground for Surrealist writers and painters. The richness and strangeness of Lautréamont's imagination in many ways recall that of Rimbaud, but there is less coherence in his vision and he is less of an artist. That is to say that although his imagination is in no way inferior to that of Rimbaud he possesses to a lesser degree the power of giving concrete shape to this vision, of communicating it to his readers, of taking from it what is unnecessary and which only overloads it. He did not know how to choose from amongst the wealth of visions that crowded in on him, he never learnt to separate the gold from the dross. Rimbaud's unerring artistic sense is clearly seen in the development of one draft of a poem to the next, in those poems of which several versions exist. If the rough draft of *Une Saison en Enfer*— of which only two fragments have come down to us—is compared with the final version which he himself passed for press, his method will be seen at work. In the second version he has simplified and pruned his work, ejecting what is merely exuberance of emotional feeling, the useless froth, and leaving only what is fully expressive.

It is regrettable that circumstances did not permit Rimbaud and Lautéamont to meet for they held many literary theories in common. In 1869 Lautréamont felt the same artistic needs and aspirations as Rimbaud felt in 1871, and then he wrote: 'A l'heure que j'écris, de nouveaux frissons parcourent l'atmosphère intellectuelle; il ne s'agit que d'avoir le courage de les regarder en face.' His aesthetic doctrine, expressed in *Poésies,* bears some similarity to that of Rimbaud set forth in *Les Lettres du Voyant*. It is, however, impossible for Rimbaud to have known Lautréamont's work before formulating his own theory. The first canto of *Les Chants de Maldoror,* privately printed in 1868, passed unnoticed and the complete work, published by Lacroix in 1869, was never sold, as Lautréamont refused to make the alterations which the publisher, at the very last moment, considered necessary in view of the disturbed political situation. Then came the Franco-Prussian War and, before that was over, the death of the poet.

Rimbaud was doing nothing to ingratiate himself with the literary men whom he met; on the contrary, feeling that he was not being a success, he did his utmost to make himself even more disliked. He silenced all good will amongst those prepared to be kind to him, fearing that they might be prompted by pity, and pity Rimbaud's pride was never able to accept. Restrained by no sentiments of kindness or sympathy he brutally hurt the most tender feelings of all those with whom he came into contact. Lepelletier, Verlaine's close friend, had recently lost his mother to whom he had been devoted, and Rimbaud wounded him deeply by calling him contemptuously a 'salueur de morts' when he saw him raising his hat as a funeral passed. All those who met Rimbaud thought his conduct was particularly offensive considering his extreme youth. They felt that it was not merely to be excused as the provincial awkwardness of a country bumpkin, but that it was insufferable insolence to his elders and betters. At the Café de Cluny, the meeting-place of the poets, he used to lie full length on the seats, pretending to be asleep if verses which did not please him were being read, or else emitting low grunts of disgust and scorn. If ever he opened his lips it was to let loose a torrent of revolutionary opinions which were badly received by his hearers. It was little more than six months since the Commune and the memory of those terrible weeks had burnt deeply into the minds of all Parisians.

He became the *bête noire* particularly of the kind and gentle poet

Albert Mérat. Mérat was to have figured amongst the poets in Fantin Latour's picture, *Le Coin de Table*, but at the last moment he refused to sit, saying that he did not wish to go down to posterity in company with that young hooligan Arthur Rimbaud. Finally, says Mathilde Verlaine, a vase of flowers was substituted for him. Posterity does not feel that it has greatly lost by the substitution, for who to-day remembers the name of the gentle Mérat? Indeed the only names in the picture which are known today are those of Paul Verlaine and his undesirable friend.

At this time Mérat had just published a book of verse entitled *L'Idole*, a sonnet sequence to celebrate all the physical beauties of woman. Verlaine and Rimbaud wrote a disrespectful parody of this work in the *Album Zutique*, a poem entitled *Le Sonnet du Trou du Cul*. The poem is obscene and pornographic and may have been the chief cause of Mérat's hostility to Rimbaud.

It is sad that Rimbaud should have antagonized Albert Mérat for he was one of the few poets whom, before coming to Paris, he had admired. He had said that modern literature had only two *voyants*, Paul Verlaine and Albert Mérat.

One evening at the literary dinner called *Les Vilains Bonshommes*, Rimbaud disgraced himself so that he was never again invited to attend. This dinner was held periodically at the Café du Théâtre du Bobino; it was attended by the principal writers of the day, including Banville, Hérédia, Coppée and Verlaine, and Rimbaud went several times as Verlaine's guest. This evening, however, Jean Aicard was reading a selection of his poems and Rimbaud, by the end of dinner more than a little drunk, was punctuating every line with the word *'merde'* uttered in a loud and distinct voice so that all present could hear. At first the guests pretended not to be conscious of what he was saying, thinking that he would then eventually grow tired and stop of his own accord, but it soon began to get on their nerves, especially as his voice was growing louder and drowning the voice of the poet. Then Carjat, the photographer, took it on himself to silence the impudent boy. When Rimbaud insolently replied that he would be silent for no one, Carjat shook him roughly and told him to be quiet or he would pull his ears. Rimbaud, now completely out of hand, seized hold of Verlaine's sword-stick, dashed at Carjat and would have done him bodily harm had those present not taken hold of him and reft the sword from his grasp. After this one of the other guests took him home to sleep off the effects of his intoxication.

It was decided, after the events of that evening, that he was never again to be allowed to be present at the dinners of the society.

Then Rimbaud withdrew more and more within himself, into the hot-house atmosphere of his quickly developing mind, and in that confined and unventilated space, his pride and arrogance matured with the aston-

ishing rapidity of everything else in him. Gazing with ceaseless contemplation on himself alone, he became more conscious than ever of his
own originality, of his superiority to others and of the essential soundness
of all his views. He was fast growing exasperated with everyone and
everything. Had he been a 'climber' he might have been able to curb
his expressions of disgust and to flatter those whom he considered
his inferiors, but he did not hide his contempt and soon all the men
of letters left him severely alone. There was, nevertheless, besides
Verlaine, one man who recognized his originality and promise, and this
was Léon Valade. In a letter to his friend, the literary critic, Emile
Blémont, he describes the effect that Rimbaud had on him in his first
days in Paris.

You missed a great deal in not being present at the last dinner of *Les
Affreux Bonshommes*. There a most alarming poet, not yet eighteen, was
exhibited by Paul Verlaine his inventor, and indeed his John the Baptist.
Big hands, big feet, a completely babyish face, like that of a child of thirteen,
deep blue eyes! His temperament, more wild than shy. Such is the boy,
whose imagination is a compound of great power and undreamt of corruption, who has fascinated and terrified all our friends. D'Hervilly said:
"Behold Jesus in the midst of the doctors." "More likely Satan!" replied
Maître, and so the more apt description occurred to me "Satan in the
midst of the doctors." I cannot give you the life history of our poet. Suffice
it to say that he had just come from Charleville with the firm intention of
never going home again. Come and you will be able to read his verses and
to judge for yourself.
If it were not for the millstone which Fate so often keeps in reserve to
hang about our necks, I should say that we are here beholding the birth of a
genius. This is the statement of my considered opinion, which I have reached
after three weeks of reflection and it is not merely a passing whim.

Nevertheless, by degrees Rimbaud dropped out of Paris literary life
and spent his time in the company of Verlaine, of the artist Forain,
nicknamed Gavroche, and of Richepin, all wild, anti-social creatures like
himself. With these he sat most of the day in the cafés of the *Boul'Mich*
drinking absinthe and living in a more or less permanent state of intoxication. This was the time when Verlaine was dissipating, chiefly on orgies
with him, the capital which he had inherited from his father. When the
cafés closed and finally broke up their revelry they used to repair to
Rimbaud's room in the Rue Campagne-Première, there to continue their
carousing until the following morning was far advanced.
There is no doubt that with Verlaine Rimbaud was finally able to
reach the 'long et raisonné dérèglement de tous les sens.'
'Il y a bien un lieu de boisson que je préfère,' he wrote to Delahaye,
'Vive l'Académie d'absomphe,[1] malgré la mauvaise volonté des garçons!

C'est le plus délicat et le plus tremblant des habits, que l'ivresse par la vertu de cette sauge des glaciers, l'absomphe.'

He was not, however, unconscious of the resulting physical degradation in his person through intoxication—although he considered this degradation necessary—for he added, 'Mais pour après se coucher dans la merde!'

There is a great difference between Rimbaud and Verlaine in their attitude towards drunkenness and debauch. Verlaine never asked for more than a mere momentary satisfaction of his senses and he did not question the why or the wherefore. Rimbaud, however, who had much of the puritan in his composition, considered debauch a necessary aesthetic and spiritual discipline, and for him it was no self-indulgence. It became, on the contrary, in his inverted asceticism, a form of self-maceration, a form of self-flagellation. It was the hairshirt which he always wore, the scourge he always carried stained with drops of his blood. He obtained little pleasure from the mere gratification of his senses and this the simple, less reflective and more light-hearted Verlaine could never understand. In *Comédie de la Soif,* describing intoxication, Rimbaud writes:

> J'aime, autant, mieux même,
> Pourrir dans l'étang,
> Sous l'affreuse creme,
> Près des bois flottants.

His life of debauch was for him one long martyrdom, but a martyrdom giving him all the ecstatic joys of a religious martyrdom, and to reach this sublime condition he was willing to sacrifice dignity, health and purity. When his poetic production of this period is studied it will be seen that this state of sacrifice and martyrdom was concurrent, in his case, with a state of triumph and exaltation, and that indeed the triumph and the exaltation depended on the martyrdom and the sacrifice. In later years when he realized the vanity of this form of martyrdom he treated his body as hardly, but in the opposite direction, and did not allow it even the most legitimate and necessary comforts. Now he became a *supplicié du vice* and this explains how, in the midst of depravity and vice, his face kept the look of extraordinary purity which we see in the photograph taken by Carjat at this time; the eyes and brows have in them an astonishing and spiritual beauty. 'His eyes,' said Delahaye, 'were the most beautiful that I have ever seen, with an expression of courage and gallantry, as if ready for all sacrifices, when he was serious; with an expression of child-like gentleness when he smiled; and always with an astonishing depth and tenderness.'

There was in Rimbaud's innocence and purity a platinum-like quality which no depravity could corrode. 'All the evil of the world passed through his being,' said Rivière, 'but only as a purge.' Debauch was for him a doctrine, a religious aim, and it was as stony a path to travel as that of virtue. One guesses in him at times a regret for his early uncomplicated purity, for the innocence of the days which he had spent in the open air of his native Ardennes, when he did not yet know what vice was; when he had wandered free amongst the mountains and the rivers; when he had not yet assumed this heavy burden. One feels in him a craving for rest, a weariness of the spirit in his self-imposed martyrdom and a longing that the bitter cup might be taken away from his lips. But, as long as he believed in his ideal, his fanaticism did not allow him to weaken.

NOTE
1. Absinthe.

E. M. Forster

A PASSAGE TO INDIA

Abandoning his bicycle, which fell before a servant could catch it, the young man sprang up on to the verandah. He was all animation. "Hamidullah, Hamidullah! am I late?" he cried.

"Do not apologize," said his host. "You are always late."

"Kindly answer my question. Am I late? Has Mahmoud Ali eaten all the food? If so I go elsewhere. Mr. Mahmoud Ali, how are you?"

"Thank you, Dr. Aziz, I am dying."

"Dying before your dinner? Oh, poor Mahmoud Ali!"

"Hamidullah here is actually dead. He passed away just as you rode up on your bike."

"Yes, that is so," said the other. "Imagine us both addressing you from another and happier world."

"Does there happen to be such a thing as a hookah in that happier world of yours?"

"Aziz, don't chatter. We are having a very sad talk."

The hookah had been packed too tight, as was usual in his friend's house, and bubbled sulkily. He coaxed it. Yielding at last, the tobacco jetted up into his lungs and nostrils, driving out the smoke of burning cow dung that had filled them as he rode through the bazaar. It was delicious. He lay in a trance, sensuous but healthy, through which the talk of the two others did not seem particularly sad—they were discussing as to whether or no it is possible to be friends with an Englishman. Mahmoud Ali argued that it was not, Hamidullah disagreed, but with so many reservations that there was no friction between them. Delicious indeed to lie on the broad verandah with the moon rising in front and the servants preparing dinner behind, and no trouble happening.

"Well, look at my own experience this morning."

"I only contend that it is possible in England," replied Hamidullah, who had been to that country long ago, before the big rush, and had received a cordial welcome at Cambridge.

"It is impossible here. Aziz! The red-nosed boy has again insulted me in Court. I do not blame him. He was told that he ought to insult me. Until lately he was quite a nice boy, but the others have got hold of him."

"Yes, they have no chance here, that is my point. They come out intending to be gentlemen, and are told it will not do. Look at Lesley, look at Blakiston, now it is your red-nosed boy, and Fielding will go next. Why, I remember when Turton came out first. It was in another part of the Province. You fellows will not believe me, but I have driven with Turton in his carriage—Turton! Oh yes, we were once quite intimate. He has shown me his stamp collection."

"He would expect you to steal it now. Turton! But red-nosed boy will be far worse than Turton!"

"I do not think so. They all become exactly the same, not worse, not better. I give any Englishman two years, be he Turton or Burton. It is only the difference of a letter. And I give any Englishwoman six months. All are exactly alike. Do you not agree with me?"

"I do not," replied Mahmoud Ali, entering into the bitter fun, and feeling both pain and amusement at each word that was uttered. "For my own part I find such profound differences among our rulers. Red-nose mumbles, Turton talks distinctly, Mrs. Turton takes bribes, Mrs. Red-nose does not and cannot, because so far there is no Mrs. Red-nose."

"Bribes?"

"Did you not know that when they were lent to Central India over a Canal Scheme, some Rajah or other gave her a sewing machine in solid gold so that the water should run through his state?"

"And does it?"

"No, that is where Mrs. Turton is so skillful. When we poor blacks take bribes, we perform what we are bribed to perform, and the law discovers us in consequence. The English take and do nothing. I admire them."

"We all admire them. Aziz, please pass me the hookah."

"Oh, not yet—hookah is so jolly now."

"You are a very selfish boy." He raised his voice suddenly, and shouted for dinner. Servants shouted back that it was ready. They meant that they wished it was ready, and were so understood, for nobody moved. Then Hamidullah continued, but with changed manner and evident emotion.

"But take my case—the case of young Hugh Bannister. Here is the son of my dear, my dead friends, the Reverend and Mrs. Bannister, whose goodness to me in England I shall never forget or describe. They were father and mother to me, I talked to them as I do now. In the vacations their Rectory became my home. They entrusted all their children to me—I often carried little Hugh about—I took him up to the Funeral of Queen Victoria, and held him in my arms above the crowd."

"Queen Victoria was different," murmured Mahmoud Ali.

"I learn now that this boy is in business as a leather merchant at

Cawnpore. Imagine how I long to see him and to pay his fare that this house may be his home. But it is useless. The other Anglo-Indians will have got hold of him long ago. He will probably think that I want something, and I cannot face that from the son of my old friends. Oh, what in this country has gone wrong with everything, Vakil Sahib? I ask you."

Aziz joined in. "Why talk about the English? Brrrr . . . ! Why be either friends with the fellows or not friends? Let us shut them out and be jolly. Queen Victoria and Mrs. Bannister were the only exceptions, and they're dead."

"No, no, I do not admit that, I have met others."

"So have I," said Mahmoud Ali, unexpectedly veering. "All ladies are far from alike." Their mood was changed, and they recalled little kindnesses and courtesies. "She said 'Thank you so much' in the most natural way." "She offered me a lozenge when the dust irritated my throat." Hamidullah could remember more important examples of angelic ministration, but the other, who only knew Anglo-India, had to ransack his memory for scraps, and it was not surprising that he should return to "But of course all this is exceptional. The exception does not prove the rule. The average woman is like Mrs. Turton, and, Aziz, you know what she is." Aziz did not know, but said he did. He too generalized from his disappointments—it is difficult for members of a subject race to do otherwise. Granted the exceptions, he agreed that all Englishwomen are haughty and venal. The gleam passed from the conversation, whose wintry surface unrolled and expanded interminably.

A servant announced dinner. They ignored him. The elder men had reached their eternal politics, Aziz drifted into the garden. The trees smelt sweet—green-blossomed champak—and scraps of Persian poetry came into his head. Dinner, dinner, dinner . . . but when he returned to the house for it, Mahmoud Ali had drifted away in his turn, to speak to his sais. "Come and see my wife a little then," said Hamidullah, and they spent twenty minutes behind the purdah. Hamidullah Begum was a distant aunt of Aziz, and the only female relative he had in Chandrapore, and she had much to say to him on this occasion about a family circumcision that had been celebrated with imperfect pomp. It was difficult to get away, because until they had had their dinner she would not begin hers, and consequently prolonged her remarks in case they should suppose she was impatient. Having censured the circumcision, she bethought her of kindred topics, and asked Aziz when he was going to be married.

Respectful but irritated, he answered, "Once is enough."

"Yes, he has done his duty," said Hamidullah. "Do not tease him so. He carries on his family, two boys and their sister."

"Aunt, they live most comfortably with my wife's mother, where she was living when she died. I can see them whenever I like. They are such very, very small children."

"And he sends them the whole of his salary and lives like a low-grade clerk, and tells no one the reason. What more do you require him to do?"

But this was not Hamidullah Begum's point, and having courteously changed the conversation for a few moments she returned and made it. She said, "What is to become of all our daughters if men refuse to marry? They will marry beneath them, or——" And she began the oft-told tale of a lady of Imperial descent who could find no husband in the narrow circle where her pride permitted her to mate, and had lived on unwed, her age now thirty, and would die unwed, for no one would have her now. While the tale was in progress, it convinced the two men, the tragedy seemed a slur on the whole community; better polygamy almost, than that a woman should die without the joys God has intended her to receive. Wedlock, motherhood, power in the house—for what else is she born, and how can the man who has denied them to her stand up to face her creator and his own at the last day? Aziz took his leave saying "Perhaps . . . but later . . ."—his invariable reply to such an appeal.

"You mustn't put off what you think right," said Hamidullah. "That is why India is in such a plight, because we put off things." But seeing that his young relative looked worried, he added a few soothing words, and thus wiped out any impression that his wife might have made.

During their absence, Mahmoud Ali had gone off in his carriage leaving a message that he should be back in five minutes, but they were on no account to wait. They sat down to meat with a distant cousin of the house, Mohammed Latif, who lived on Hamidullah's bounty and who occupied the position neither of a servant nor of an equal. He did not speak unless spoken to, and since no one spoke kept unoffended silence. Now and then he belched, in compliment to the richness of the food. A gentle, happy and dishonest old man; all his life he had never done a stroke of work. So long as some one of his relatives had a house he was sure of a home, and it was unlikely that so large a family would all go bankrupt. His wife led a similar existence some hundreds of miles away—he did not visit her, owing to the expense of the railway ticket. Presently Aziz chaffed him, also the servants, and then began quoting poetry, Persian, Urdu, a little Arabic. His memory was good, and for so young a man he had read largely; the themes he preferred were the decay of Islam and the brevity of Love. They listened delighted, for they took the public view of poetry, not the private which obtains in England. It never bored them to hear words, words; they breathed them with the cool night air, never stopping to analyse; the name of the poet, Hafiz, Hali, Iqbal, was sufficient guarantee. India—a hundred Indias—whispered outside beneath the indifferent moon, but for the time India seemed one and their own, and they regained their departed greatness by hearing its departure lamented, they felt young again because reminded that youth must fly. A servant in scarlet interrupted him; he was the chuprassi of the Civil Surgeon, and he handed Aziz a note.

"Old Callendar wants to see me at his bungalow," he said, not rising. "He might have the politeness to say why."

"Some case, I daresay."

"I daresay not, I daresay nothing. He has found out our dinner hour, that's all, and chooses to interrupt us every time, in order to show his power."

"On the one hand he always does this, on the other it may be a serious case, and you cannot know," said Hamidullah, considerately paving the way towards obedience. "Had you not better clean your teeth after pan?"

"If my teeth are to be cleaned, I don't go at all. I am an Indian, it is an Indian habit to take pan. The Civil Surgeon must put up with it. Mohammed Latif, my bike, please."

The poor relation got up. Slightly immersed in the realms of matter, he laid his hand on the bicycle's saddle, while a servant did the actual wheeling. Between them they took it over a tintack. Aziz held his hands under the ewer, dried them, fitted on his green felt hat, and then with unexpected energy whizzed out of Hamidullah's compound.

"Aziz, Aziz, imprudent boy. . . ." But he was far down the bazaar, riding furiously. He had neither light nor bell nor had he a brake, but what use are such adjuncts in a land where the cyclist's only hope is to coast from face to face, and just before he collides with each it vanishes? And the city was fairly empty at this hour. When his tyre went flat, he leapt off and shouted for a tonga.

He did not at first find one, and he had also to dispose of his bicycle at a friend's house. He dallied furthermore to clean his teeth. But at last he was rattling towards the civil lines, with a vivid sense of speed. As he entered their arid tidiness, depression suddenly seized him. The roads, named after victorious generals and intersecting at right angles, were symbolic of the net Great Britain had thrown over India. He felt caught in their meshes. When he turned into Major Callendar's compound he could with difficulty restrain himself from getting down from the tonga and approaching the bungalow on foot, and this not because his soul was servile but because his feelings—the sensitive edges of him—feared a gross snub. There had been a "case" last year—an Indian gentleman had driven up to an official's house and been turned back by the servants and been told to approach more suitably—only one case among thousands of visits to hundreds of officials, but its fame spread wide. The young man shrank from a repetition of it. He compromised, and stopped the driver just outside the flood of light that fell across the verandah.

The Civil Surgeon was out.

"But the sahib has left me some message?"

The servant returned an indifferent "No." Aziz was in despair. It was a servant whom he had forgotten to tip, and he could do nothing now because there were people in the hall. He was convinced that there was a message, and that the man was withholding it out of revenge. While they argued, the people came out. Both were ladies. Aziz lifted his hat. The first, who was in evening dress, glanced at the Indian and turned instinctively away.

"Mrs. Lesley, it *is* a tonga," she cried.

"Ours?" enquired the second, also seeing Aziz, and doing likewise.

"Take the gifts the gods provide, anyhow," she screeched, and both jumped in. "O Tonga wallah, club, club. Why doesn't the fool go?"

"Go, I will pay you to-morrow," said Aziz to the driver, and as they went off he called courteously, "You are most welcome, ladies." They did not reply, being full of their own affairs.

So it had come, the usual thing—just as Mahmoud Ali said. The inevitable snub—his bow ignored, his carriage taken. It might have been worse, for it comforted him somehow that Mesdames Callendar and Lesley should both be fat and weigh the tonga down behind. Beautiful women would have pained him. He turned to the servant, gave him a couple of rupees, and asked again whether there was a message. The man, now very civil, returned the same answer. Major Callendar had driven away half an hour before.

"Saying nothing?"

He had as a matter of fact said, "Damn Aziz"— words that the servant understood, but was too polite to repeat. One can tip too much as well as too little, indeed the coin that buys the exact truth has not yet been minted.

"Then I will write him a letter."

He was offered the use of the house, but was too dignified to enter it. Paper and ink were brought on to the verandah. He began: "Dear Sir,— At your express command I have hastened as a subordinate should——" and then stopped. "Tell him I have called, that is sufficient," he said, tearing the protest up. "Here is my card. Call me a tonga."

"Huzoor, all are at the club."

"Then telephone for one down to the railway station." And since the man hastened to do this he said, "Enough, enough, I prefer to walk." He commandeered a match and lit a cigarette. These attentions, though purchased, soothed him. They would last as long as he had rupees, which is something. But to shake the dust of Anglo-India off his feet! To escape from the net and be back among manners and gestures that he knew! He began a walk, an unwonted exercise.

He was an athletic little man, daintily put together, but really very strong. Nevertheless walking fatigued him, as it fatigues everyone in India except the new-comer. There is something hostile in that soil. It either yields, and the foot sinks into a depression, or else it is unexpectedly rigid and sharp, pressing stones or crystals against the tread. A series of these little surprises exhausts; and he was wearing pumps, a poor preparation for any country. At the edge of the civil station he turned into a mosque to rest.

He had always liked this mosque. It was gracious, and the arrangement pleased him. The courtyard—entered through a ruined gate—contained an ablution tank of fresh clear water, which was always in motion, being indeed part of a conduit that supplied the city. The courtyard was paved with broken slabs. The covered part of the mosque was deeper than is usual; its effect was that of an English parish church whose side has been taken out. Where he sat, he looked into three arcades whose darkness was illuminated by a small hanging lamp and by the moon. The front—in full moonlight—had the appearance of marble, and the ninety-nine names of God on the frieze stood out black, as the frieze stood out white against the sky. The contest between this dualism and the contention of shadows within pleased Aziz, and he tried to symbolize the whole into some truth of religion or love. A mosque by winning his approval let loose his imagination. The temple of another creed, Hindu, Christian, or Greek, would have bored him and failed to awaken his sense of beauty. Here was Islam, his own country, more than a Faith, more than a battle-cry, more, much more . . . Islam, an attitude towards life both exquisite and durable, where his body and his thoughts found their home.

His seat was the low wall that bounded the courtyard on the left. The ground fell away beneath him towards the city, visible as a blur of trees, and in the stillness he heard many small sounds. On the right, over in the club, the English community contributed an amateur orchestra. Elsewhere some Hindus were drumming—he knew they were Hindus, because the rhythm was uncongenial to him,—and others were bewailing a corpse—he knew whose, having certified it in the afternoon. There were owls, the Punjab mail . . . and flowers smelt deliciously in the station-master's garden. But the mosque—that alone signified, and he returned to it from the complex appeal of the night, and decked it with meanings the builder had never intended. Some day he too would build a mosque, smaller than this but in perfect taste, so that all who passed by should experience the happiness he felt now. And near it, under a low dome, should be his tomb, with a Persian inscription:

Alas, without me for thousands of years
The Rose will blossom and the Spring will bloom,
But those who have secretly understood my heart—
They will approach and visit the grave where I lie.

He had seen the quatrain on the tomb of a Deccan king, and regarded it as profound philosophy—he always held pathos to be profound. The secret understanding of the heart! He repeated the phrase with tears in his eyes, and as he did so one of the pillars of the mosque seemed to quiver. It swayed in the gloom and detached itself. Belief in ghosts ran in his blood, but he sat firm. Another pillar moved, a third, and then an Englishwoman stepped out into the moonlight. Suddenly he was furiously angry and shouted: "Madam! Madam! Madam!"

"Oh! Oh!" the woman gasped.

"Madam, this is a mosque, you have no right here at all; you should have taken off your shoes; this is a holy place for Moslems."

"I have taken them off."

"You have?"

"I left them at the entrance."

"Then I ask your pardon."

Still startled, the woman moved out, keeping the ablution-tank between them. He called after her, "I am truly sorry for speaking."

"Yes, I was right, was I not? If I remove my shoes, I am allowed?"

"Of course, but so few ladies take the trouble, especially if thinking no one is there to see."

"That makes no difference. God is here."

"Madam!"

"Please let me go."

"Oh, can I do you some service now or at any time?"

"No, thank you, really none—good night."

"May I know your name?"

She was now in the shadow of the gateway, so that he could not see her face, but she saw his, and she said with a change of voice, "Mrs. Moore."

"Mrs. ——" Advancing he found that she was old. A fabric bigger than the mosque fell to pieces, and he did not know whether he was glad or sorry. She was older than Hamidullah Begum, with a red face and white hair. Her voice had deceived him.

"Mrs. Moore, I am afraid I startled you. I shall tell my community— our friends—about you. That God is here—very good, very fine indeed. I think you are newly arrived in India."

"Yes—how did you know?"

"By the way you address me. No, but can I call you a carriage?"

"I have only come from the club. They are doing a play that I have seen in London, and it was so hot."

"What was the name of the play?"

"Cousin Kate."

"I think you ought not to walk at night alone, Mrs. Moore. There are bad characters about and leopards may come across from the Marabar Hills. Snakes also."

She exclaimed; she had forgotten the snakes.

"For example, a six-spot beetle," he continued. "You pick it up, it bites, you die."

"But you walk about yourself."

"Oh, I am used to it."

"Used to snakes?"

They both laughed. "I'm a doctor," he said. "Snakes don't dare bite me." They sat down side by side in the entrance, and slipped on their evening shoes. "Please may I ask you a question now? Why do you come to India at this time of year, just as the cold weather is ending?"

"I intended to start earlier, but there was an unavoidable delay."

"It will soon be so unhealthy for you! And why ever do you come to Chandrapore?"

"To visit my son. He is the City Magistrate here."

"Oh no, excuse me, that is quite impossible. Our City Magistrate's name is Mr. Heaslop. I know him intimately."

"He's my son all the same," she said, smiling.

"But, Mrs. Moore, how can he be?"

"I was married twice."

"Yes, now I see, and your first husband died."

"He did, and so did my second husband."

"Then we are in the same box," he said cryptically. "Then is the City Magistrate the entire of your family now?"

"No, there are the younger ones—Ralph and Stella in England."

"And the gentleman here, is he Ralph and Stella's half-brother?"

"Quite right."

"Mrs. Moore, this is all extremely strange, because like yourself I have also two sons and a daughter. Is not this the same box with a vengeance?"

"What are their names? Not also Ronny, Ralph, and Stella, surely?"

The suggestion delighted him. "No, indeed. How funny it sounds! Their names are quite different and will surprise you. Listen, please. I am about to tell you my children's names. The first is called Ahmed, the second is called Karim, the third—she is the eldest—Jamila. Three children are enough. Do not you agree with me?"

"I do."

They were both silent for a little, thinking of their respective families. She sighed and rose to go.

"Would you care to see over the Minto Hospital one morning?" he enquired. "I have nothing else to offer at Chandrapore."

"Thank you, I have seen it already, or I should have liked to come with you very much."

"I suppose the Civil Surgeon took you."

"Yes, and Mrs. Callendar."

His voice altered. "Ah! A very charming lady."

"Possibly, when one knows her better."

"What? What? You didn't like her?"

"She was certainly intending to be kind, but I did not find her exactly charming."

He burst out with: "She has just taken my tonga without my permission—do you call that being charming?—and Major Callendar interrupts me night after night from where I am dining with my friends and I go at once, breaking up a most pleasant entertainment, and he is not there and not even a message. Is this charming, pray? But what does it matter? I can do nothing and he knows it. I am just a subordinate, my time is of no value, the verandah is good enough for an Indian, yes, yes, let him stand, and Mrs. Callendar takes my carriage and cuts me dead . . ."

She listened.

He was excited partly by his wrongs, but much more by the knowledge that someone sympathized with them. It was this that led him to repeat, exaggerate, contradict. She had proved her sympathy by criticizing her fellow-countrywoman to him, but even earlier he had known. The flame that not even beauty can nourish was springing up, and though his words were querulous his heart began to glow secretly. Presently it burst into speech.

"You understand me, you know what others feel. Oh, if others resembled you!"

Rather surprised, she replied: "I don't think I understand people very well. I only know whether I like or dislike them."

"Then you are an Oriental."

She accepted his escort back to the club, and said at the gate that she wished she was a member, so that she could have asked him in.

"Indians are not allowed into the Chandrapore Club even as guests," he said simply. He did not expatiate on his wrongs now, being happy. As he strolled downhill beneath the lovely moon, and again saw the lovely mosque, he seemed to own the land as much as anyone owned it. What did it matter if a few flabby Hindus had preceded him there, and a few chilly English succeeded?

Raja Rao

THE SERPENT AND THE ROPE

I was born a Brahmin—that is, devoted to Truth and all that. "Brahmin is he who knows Brahman," etc., etc. . . . But how many of my ancestors since the excellent Yagnyavalkya, my legendary and Upanishadic ancestor, have really known the Truth excepting the Sage Mādhava, who founded an empire or, rather, helped to build an empire, and wrote some of the most profound of Vedantic texts since Sri Sankara? There were others, so I'm told, who left hearth and riverside fields, and wandered to mountains distant and hermitages "to see God face to face." And some of them did see God face to face and built temples. But when they died—for indeed they did "die"—they too must have been burnt by tank or grove or meeting of two rivers, and they too must have known they did not die. I can feel them in me, and know they knew they did not die. Who is it that tells me they did not die? Who but me.

So my ancestors went one by one and were burnt, and their ashes have gone down the rivers.

Whenever I stand in a river I remember how when young, on the day the monster ate the moon and the day fell into an eclipse, I used with *til* and kusha grass to offer the manes my filial devotion. For withal I was a good Brahmin. I even knew Grammar and the Brahma Sutras, read the Upanishads at the age of four, was given the holy thread at seven—because my mother was dead and I had to perform her funeral ceremonies, year after year, my father having married again. So with wet cloth and an empty stomach, with devotion, and sandal paste on my forehead, I fell before the rice-balls of my mother and I sobbed. I was born an orphan, and have remained one. I have wandered the world and have sobbed in hotel rooms and in trains, have looked at the cold mountains and sobbed, for I had no mother. One day, and that was when I was twenty-two, I sat in a hotel—it was in the Pyrenees—and I sobbed, for I knew I would never see my mother again.

They say my mother was very beautiful and very holy. Grandfather Kittanna said, "Her voice, son, was like a *vina* playing to itself, after evensong is over, when one has left the instrument beside a pillar in the temple. Her voice too was like those musical pillars at the Rameshwaram temple—it resonated from the depths, from some unknown space, and one felt God shone the brighter with this worship. She reminded me of

Concubine Chandramma. She had the same voice. That was long before your time," Grandfather concluded, "it was Mysore, and I have not been there these fifty years."

Grandfather Kittanna was a noble type, a heroic figure among us. It must be from him I have this natural love of the impossible—I can think that a building may just decide to fly, or that Stalin may become a saint, or that all the Japanese have become Buddhist monks, or that Mahatma Gandhi is walking with us now. I sometimes feel I can make the railway line stand up, or the elephant bear its young one in twenty-four days; I can see an aeroplane float over a mountain and sit carefully on a peak, or I could go to Fathe-Pur-Sikri and speak to the Emperor Akbar. It would be difficult for me not to think, when I am in Versailles, that I hear the uncouth voice of Roi Soleil, or in Meaux that Bossuet rubs his snuff in the palm of his hand, as they still do in India, and offers a pinch to me. I can sneeze with it, and hear Bossuet make one more of his funeral orations. For Bossuet believed—and so did Roi Soleil—that he never would die. And if they've died, I ask you, where indeed did they go?

Grandfather Kittanna was heroic in another manner. He could manage a horse, the fiercest, with a simplicity that made it go where it did not wish to go. I was brought up with the story of how Grandfather Kittanna actually pushed his horse into the Chandrapur forest one evening—the horse, Sundar, biting his lips off his face; the tiger that met him in the middle of the jungle; the leap Sundar gave, high above my Lord Sher, and the custard-apples that splashed on his back, so high he soared—and before my grandfather knew where he was, with sash and blue Maratha saddle, there he stood, Sundar, in the middle of the courtyard. The lamps were being lit, and when stableman Chowdayya heard the neigh he came and led the steed to the tank for a swish of water. Grandfather went into the bathroom, had his evening bath—he loved it to be very hot, and Aunt Seethamma had always to serve him potful after potful—and he rubbed himself till his body shone as the young of a banana tree. He washed and sat in prayer. When Atchakka asked, "Sundar is all full of scratches . . . ?" then Grandfather spoke of the tiger, and the leap. For him, if the horse had soared into the sky and landed in holy Brindavan he would not have been much surprised. Grandfather Kittanna was like that. He rode Sundar for another three years, and then the horse died—of some form of dysentery, for, you know, horses die too—and we buried him on the top of the Kittur Hill, with fife and filigree. We still make an annual pilgrimage to his tomb, and for Hyderabad reasons we cover it up with a rose-coloured muslin, like the Muslims do. Horses we think came from Arabia, and so they need a Muslim burial. Where is Sundar now? Where?

The impossible, for Grandfather, was always possible. He never—he, a Brahmin—never for once was afraid of gun or sword, and yet what depth he had in his prayers. When he came out, Aunt Seethamma used to say, "He has the shine of a Dharmaraja."

But I, I've the fright of gun and sword, and the smallest trick of violence can make me run a hundred leagues. But once having gone a hundred leagues I shall come back a thousand, for I do not really have the fear of fear. I only have fear.

I love rivers and lakes, and make my home easily by any waterside hamlet. I love palaces for their echoes, their sense of never having seen anything but the gloomy. Palaces remind me of old and venerable women, who never die. They look after others so much—I mean, orphans of the family always have great-aunts, who go on changing from orphan to orphan—that they remain ever young. One such was Aunt Lakshamma. She was married to a minister once, and he died when she was seven or eight. And since then my uncles and their daughters, my mother's cousins and their grandchildren, have always had Lakshamma to look after them, for an orphan in a real household is never an orphan. She preserved, did Lakshamma, all the clothes of the young in her eighteenth-century steel and *sheesham* trunk, in the central hall, and except when there was a death in the house these clothes never saw the light of the sun. Some of them were fifty years old, they said. The other day—that is, some seven or eight years ago—when we were told that Aunt Lakshamma, elder to my grandfather by many years, had actually died, I did not believe it. I thought she would live three hundred years. She never would complain or sigh. She never wept. We never wept when she died. For I cannot understand what death means.

My father, of course, loved me. He never let me stray into the hands of Lakshamma. He said, "Auntie smells bad, my son. I want you to be a hero and a prince." Some time before my mother died, it seems she had a strange vision. She saw three of my past lives, and in each one of them I was a son, and of course I was always her eldest born, tall, slim, deep-voiced, deferential and beautiful. In one I was a prince. That is why I had always to be adorned with diamonds—diamonds on my forehead, chest and ears. She died, they say, having sent someone to the goldsmith, asking if my hair-flower were ready. When she died they covered her with white flowers—jasmines from Coimbatore and champaks from Chamundi—and with a lot of kunkum on her they took her away to the burning ghat. They shaved me completely, and when they returned they gave me Bengal gram, and some sweets. I could not understand what had happened. Nor do I understand now. I know my mother, my Mother Gauri, is not dead, and yet I am an orphan. Am I always going to be an orphan?

That my father married for a third time—my stepmother having died leaving three children, Saroja, Sukumari, and the eldest, Kapila—is another story. My new stepmother loved me very dearly, and I could not think of a home without her bright smile and the song that shone like the copper vessels in the house. When she smiled her mouth touched her ears—and she gave me everything I wanted. I used to weep, though, thinking of my own mother. But then my father died. He died on the third of the second moon-month when the small rains had just started. I have little to tell you of my father's death, except that I did not love him; but that after he died I knew him and loved him when his body was such pure white spread ash. Even now I have dreams of him saying to me, "Son, why did you not love me, you, my Eldest Son?" I cannot repent, as I do not know what repentance is. For I must first believe there is death. And that is the central fact—I do not believe that death is. So, for whom shall I repent?

Of course, I love my father now. Who could not love one that was protection and kindness itself, though he never understood that my mother wanted me to be a prince? And since I could not be a prince—I was born a Brahmin, and so how could I be king?—I wandered my life away, and became a holy vagabond. If Grandfather simply jumped over tigers in the jungles, how many tigers of the human jungle, how many accidents to plane and car have I passed by? And what misunderstandings and chasms of hatred have lain between me and those who first loved, and then hated, me? Left to myself, I became alone and full of love. When one is alone one always loves. In fact, it is because one loves, and one is alone, one does not die.

VASSAL, SLAVE, INFERIOR

Elizabeth Hardwick

THE SUBJECTION OF WOMEN

from *A View of My Own*

A REVIEW OF *The Second Sex* BY SIMONE DE BEAUVOIR

Vassal, slave, inferior, other, thing, victim, dependent, parasite, prisoner —oh, bitter, raped, child-swollen flesh doomed to immanence! Sisyphean goddess of the dust pile! Demeter, Xantippe, Ninon de Lenclos, Marie Bashkirtsev, and "a friend of mine . . ." From cave to café, boudoir to microscope, from the knitting needles to the short story: they are all here in a potency of pages, a foreshortened and exaggerated, a mysterious and too clear relief, an eloquent lament and governessy scolding, a poem and a doctoral thesis. I suppose there is bound to be a little laughter in the wings at the mere thought of this madly sensible and brilliantly obscure tome on women by Simone de Beauvoir, *The Second Sex*.

Still the more one sinks into this very long book, turning page after page, the more clearly it seems to lack a subject with reasonable limitations and concreteness, a subject on which offered illustrations may wear some air of finality and conviction. The theme of the work is that women are not simply "women," but are, like men, in the fullest sense human beings. Yet one cannot easily write the history of people! This point may appear trivial; nevertheless, to take on this glorious and fantastic book is not like reading at all—from the first to the last sentence one has the sensation of playing some breathlessly exciting and finally exhausting game. You gasp and strain and remember; you point out and deny and agree, trying always to find some way of taking hold, of confining, defining, and understanding. What is so unbearably whirling is that the author too goes through this effort to include nearly every woman and attitude that has ever existed. There is no difference of opinion, unless it be based upon a fact of which she may be ignorant, she has not thought of also. She makes her own points and all one's objections too, often in the same sentence. The effort required for this work must have been killing. No discredit to the donkey-load undertaking is meant when one imagines Simone de Beauvoir at the end may have felt like George Eliot when she said she began *Romola* as a young woman and finished it an old one. (This touching remark did not refer to the time spent in composition, but to the wrinkling weight of the task.)

I quote a sentence about the *promises* the Soviet Union made to women: ". . . pregnancy leaves were to be paid for by the State, which would assume charge of the children, signifying not that they would be *taken away* from their parents, but they would not be *abandoned* to them." There is majesty here and the consolations of philosophy, perhaps also, in this instance, a bit of willful obfuscation; but that kind of strangeness occurs endlessly, showing, for purposes of argument at least, an oversensitivity to difficulties. A devastating dialogue goes on at this author's desk. After she has written, "the State, which would assume charge of the children," there is a comma pause. In that briefest of grammatical rests, voices assault her intelligence saying, "But suppose people don't want their children taken away by the State?" If all these disputing voices are admitted, one on top of the other, you are soon lost in incoherence and fantasy. Another instance: "It is understandable, in this perspective, that women take exeception to masculine logic. Not only is it inapplicable to her experience, but in his hands, as she knows, masculine reasoning becomes an underhanded form of force." A few pages on: "One can bank on her credulity. Woman takes an attitude of respect and faith toward the masculine universe . . ."

I take up the bewildering inclusiveness of this book, because there is hardly a thing I would want to say contrary to her thesis that Simone de Beauvoir has not said herself, including the fact, mentioned in the preface, that problems peculiar to women are not particularly pressing at the moment and that, by and large, "we have won." These acknowledgments would seem of tremendous importance, but they are a mere batting of the eye in this eternity of "oppression."

In spite of all positions being taken simultaneously, there is an unmistakable *drift* to the book. Like woman's life, *The Second Sex* is extremely repetitious and some things are repeated more often than others, although nearly every idea is repeated more than once. One is justified, then, in assuming what is repeated most often is most profoundly felt. The diction alone is startling and stabs the heart with its vigor in finding phrases of abjection and debasement. It is as though one had lived forever in that intense, shady, wretched world of *Wozzeck,* where the humor draws tears, the gaiety is fearful and children skip rope neither knowing nor caring their mother has been murdered. "Conjugal slavery, annihilation, servant, devaluation, tyranny, passive, forbidden, doomed, abused, trapped, prey, domineer, helpless, imprisoned," and so on. This immediately suggests a masochistic view of life, reinforced by the fact that for the male quite an opposite vocabulary has dug into this mind like a tick: "free, busy, active, proud, arrogant, master, existent, liberty, adventure, daring, strength, courage . . ."

Things being as they are, it is only fair to say that Simone de Beauvoir, in spite of her absorbing turn of phrase, miraculously does *not* give to me, at least, the impression of being a masochist, a Lesbian, a termagant, or a man-hater, and that this book is not "the self-pitying cry of one who resents being born a woman," as one American housewife-reviewer said. There is a nervous, fluent, rare aliveness on every page and the writer's more "earnest" qualities, her discipline, learning and doggedness, amount not only to themselves, that is, qualities which certainly help one to write long books, but to a kind of "charm" that ought to impress the most contented woman. This book is an accomplishment; on the other hand, if one is expecting something truly splendid and unique like *The Origins of Totalitarianism* by Hannah Arendt, to mention another woman, he will be disappointed.

The Second Sex begins with biological material showing that in nature there are not always two sexes and reproduction may take place asexually. I have noticed in the past that many books strongly presenting feminine claims begin in this manner, as if under a compulsion to veil the whole idea of sexual differentiation with a buzzing, watery mist of insect habits and unicellular forms of life. This is dramaturgy, meant to put one, after a heavy meal, in a receptive frame of mind. It is the dissonant, ambiguous music as the curtain rises on the all too familiar scene of man at the hunt and the woman at the steaming pot; the scene looks clear enough, but the music suggests things may not be as they appear. That woman may not have to carry those screaming brats in her womb, after all, but will, if you don't watch out, simply "divide"! And the man: it is possible in the atomic age that a pin prick may fertilize the egg and then where will he be? This material is followed by curiosities from anthropology: some primitive societies thought the woman did it all alone and the man was no more important than a dish of herbs or a draft of beet juice.

These biological and anthropological matters are of enormous fascination, but often, and a bit in this present work too, a false and dramatic use is made of them: they carry a weight of mystification and intensity quite unjustified when the subject is the modern woman. They would seem to want to throw doubt upon what is not yet doubtful: the bisexual nature of human reproduction. We are relieved when the dividing amoebas and budding sponges swim out of view.

The claim of *The Second Sex* is that what we call the feminine character is an illusion and so is feminine "psychology," both in its loose meaning and in the psychoanalytical view. None of these female traits is "given"—the qualities and incapacities women have shown rather consistently in human history are simply the result of their "situation." This situation is largely the work of men, the male sex which has sought its own convenience with undeviating purpose throughout history. The female situation does not derive, at least not sufficiently to explain it, from women's natural physical and psychological difference, but has much of its origin in economics. When man developed the idea of private property, woman's destiny was "sealed." At this time women were cut off from the more adventurous activities of war, forays, explorations, to stay at home to *protect* and *maintain* what men had achieved by their far-reaching pursuits. The woman was reduced to a state of *immanence:* stagnation, the doing of repetitive tasks, concerned with the given, with maintaining, keeping, mere functioning. Man, however, is a free being, an *existent* who makes choices, decisions, has projects which are not confined to securing the present but point to the unknown future; he dares, fails, wanders, grabs, insists. By means of his activities he *transcends* his mere animal nature. What a man gives, the woman accepts; she decides nothing, changes nothing; she polishes, mends, cleans what he has invented and shaped. The man risks life, the woman merely produces it as an unavoidable function. "That is why superiority has been accorded in humanity not to the sex that brings forth but that which kills." The man imagines, discovers religions; the women worship. He has changed the earth; she arises each morning to an expectation of stove, nursing, scrubbing, which has remained nearly as fixed as the course of our planets. Women continue in immanence not out of desire, but from "complicity." Having been robbed of economic independence, experience, substance, she clings unhappily because she has not been "allowed" to prepare for a different life.

Naturally, it is clear many women do not fit this theory and those who may be said to do so would not describe it in the words of Simone de Beauvoir. These persons' claims are admitted quite fully throughout the book, but always with the suggestion that the women who seem to be "existents" really aren't and those who insist they find fulfillment in the inferior role are guilty of "bad faith."

That is as it may be, but what, one asks at the beginning, about the man who, almost without exception in this work, is a creature of the greatest imagination, love of liberty, devotion to projects; ambitious, potent and disciplined, he scorns a life of mere "love," refuses to imprison himself in another's being, but looks toward the world, seeks to transcend himself, change the course of history. This is an exaggeration of course. For every Ophelia one remembers not only Cleopatra but poor Swann, unable, for all his taste and enthusiasm, to write his book on Vermeer, drowning his talent in the pursuit of pure pleasure which can only be given by the "other," Odette; for every excited Medea who gave up her self, her place, to follow the fickle man you remember not only Joan of Arc but that being of perfect, blowsy immanence, the Duke of Windsor, who abandoned the glories of a complex project for the sweet, repetitive, futureless domesticity of ocean liners and resorts. And Sartre has written a whole book on Baudelaire, a fascinating and immensely belligerent one, that claims Baudelaire resented responsibility for his own destiny, refused his possibilities of transcendence, would not make decisions, define himself, but flowed along on a tepid river of dependence, futility, refusal—like women, fond of scents and costumes, nostalgic, procrastinating, wishful.

It would seem then that men, even some "heroic" ones, often allow themselves to be what women are forced to be. But, of course, with the greatest will in the world a man cannot allow himself to be that most extremely doomed and chained being—the mother who must bear and raise children and whose figure naturally hangs over such a work as *The Second Sex* like Spanish moss. Simone de Beauvoir's opinion of the division of labor established in the Garden of Eden, if not as some believe earlier, is very striking:

. . . giving birth and suckling are not *activities*, they are natural functions; no projects are involved; and that is why woman found in them no reason for a lofty affirmation of her existence—she submitted passively to her biologic fate. The domestic cares of maternity imprisoned her in repetition and immanence; they were repeated from day to day in an identical form, which was perpetuated almost without change from century to century; they produced nothing new.

But what difference does it make that childbearing is not an activity, nor perhaps an instinct; it is a necessity.

The Second Sex is so briskly Utopian it fills one with a kind of shame and sadness, like coming upon old manifestoes and committee programs in the attic. It is bursting with an almost melancholy desire for women to take their possibilities *seriously,* to reject the given, the easy, the traditional. I do not, as most reviewers seem to, think the picture offered here of a woman's life is entirely false—a lifetime of chores is bad luck. But housework, child rearing, cleaning, keeping, nourishing, looking after—these must be done by someone, or worse by millions of someones day in and day out. In the home at least it would seem "custom" has not been so much capricious as observant in finding that women are fairly well adapted to this necessary routine. And they must keep at it whether they like it or not.

George Orwell says somewhere that reformers hate to admit nobody will do the tedious, dirty work of the world except under "some form of coercion." Mopping, ironing, peeling, feeding—it is not absurd to call this unvarying routine *slavery,* Simone de Beauvoir's word. But its necessity does not vanish by listing the tropical proliferation of open and concealed forms of coercion that may be necessary to make women do it. Bachelors are notoriously finicky, we have all observed. The dust pile is revoltingly real.

Most men, also, are doomed to work of brutalizing monotony. Hardly any intellectuals are willing to undertake a bit of this dreadful work their fellow beings must do, no matter what salary, what working conditions, what degree of "socialist dignity" might be attached to it. If artists could save a man from a lifetime of digging coal by digging it themselves one hour a week, most would refuse. Some would commit suicide. "It's not the time, it's the anticipation! It ruins the whole week! I can't even read, much less write!"

Childbearing and housekeeping may be repetitive and even intellectually stunting. Yet nothing so fills one with despair as those products of misplaced transcendent hope, those millions of stupid books, lunatic pamphlets, absurd editorials, dead canvases and popular songs which have clogged up the sewers and ashcans of the modern world, representing more wretched labor, dreaming, madness, vanity and waste of effort than one can bear to think of. There is an annihilating nothingness in these undertakings by comparison with which the production of one stupid, lazy, lying child is an event of some importance. Activity, transcendence, project—this is an optimistic, exhilarating vocabulary. Yet Sartre had to disown the horde of "existents" who fell to like farm hands at the table, but were not themselves able to produce so much as a carrot.

Are women "the equal" of men? This is an embarrassing subject. Women are certainly physically inferior to men and if this were not the case the whole history of the world would be different. No comradely socialist legislation on woman's behalf could accomplish a millionth of what a bit more muscle tissue, gratuitously offered by nature, might do for this "second" being.

On the average she is shorter than the male and lighter, her skeleton is more delicate . . . muscular strength is much less in women . . . she has less respiratory capacity, the lungs and trachea being smaller . . . The specific gravity of the blood is lower . . . and there is less hemoglobin; women are therefore less robust and more disposed to anemia than are males. Their pulse is more rapid, the vascular system less stable . . . Instability is strikingly characteristic of woman's organization in general . . . In comparison with her the male seems infinitely favored.

There is a kind of poetry in this description which might move a flighty person to tears. But it goes on:

These biological considerations are extremely important . . . but I deny that they establish for her a fixed and inevitable destiny. They are insufficient for setting up a hierarchy of the sexes . . . they do not condemn her to remain in a subordinate role forever.

Why doesn't this "condemn her to remain in a subordinate role forever"? In my view this poor endowment would seem to be all the answer one needs to why women don't sail the seven seas, build bridges, conquer foreign lands, lay international cables and trudge up Mount Everest. But forgetting these daring activities, a woman's physical inferiority to a man is a limiting reality every moment of her life. Because of it women are "doomed" to situations that promise reasonable safety against the more hazardous possibilities of nature, which they are too weak and easily fatigued to endure, and against the stronger man. Any woman who has ever had her wrist twisted by a man recognizes a fact of nature as humbling as a cyclone to a frail tree branch. How can *anything* be more important than this? The prodigious ramifications could occupy one for an eternity. For instance:

At eighteen T. E. Lawrence took a long bicycle tour through France by himself; no young girl would be allowed to engage in any escapade, still less to adventure on foot in a half-desert and dangerous country, as Lawrence did a year later.

Simone de Beauvoir's use of "allow" is inaccurate; she stresses "permission" where so often it is really "capacity" that is involved. For a woman a solitary bicycle tour of France would be dangerous, but not impossible; Lawrence's adventure in Arabia would be suicidal and so a woman is nearly unimaginable as the author of *The Seven Pillars of Wisdom*. First of all the Arabs would rape this unfortunate female soldier or, if they had some religious or practical reason for resisting temptation, they would certainly have to leave her behind on the march, like yesterday's garbage, as the inevitable fatigue arrived. To say that physical weakness doesn't, in a tremendous number of activities, "condemn her to a subordinate role" is a mere assertion, not very convincing to the unmuscled, light breathing, nervously unstable, blushing feminine reality.

Arabian warfare is indeed an extreme situation. But what about solitary walks through the town after midnight? It is true that a woman's freedom to enjoy this simple pleasure would be greatly increased if men had no aggressive sexual feelings toward her. Like a stray dog, also weaker than men, she might roam the world at will, arousing no more notice than a few pats on the head or an irritable kick now and then. Whether such a change is possible in the interest of the weaker sex is very doubtful.

There is the notion in *The Second Sex,* and in other radical books on the subject, that if it were not for the tyranny of custom, women's sexual life would be characterized by the same aggressiveness, greed and command as that of the male. This is by no means certain: so much seems to lead right back where we've always been. Society must, it seems, inhibit to some extent the sexuality of all human beings. It has succeeded in restraining men much less than women. Brothels, which have existed from the earliest times, are to say the least a rarity for the use of women. And yet women will patronize opium dens and are frequently alcoholic, activities wildly destructive to their home life, beauty, manners and status and far more painful and time-consuming than having children. Apparently a lot of women are dying for dope and cocktails; nearly all are somewhat thrifty, cautious and a little lazy about hunting sex. Is it necessarily an error that many people think licentious women are incapable of experiencing the slightest degree of sexual pleasure and are driven to their behavior by an encyclopedic curiosity to know if such a thing exists? A wreck of a man, tracking down girls in his Chevrolet, at least can do *that!* Prostitutes are famously cold; pimps, who must also suffer professional boredom, are not automatically felt to be impotent. Homosexual women, who have rebelled against their "conditioning" in the most crucial way, do not appear to "cruise" with that truly astonishing, ageless zest of male homosexuals. A pair seems to find each other sufficient. Drunken women who pick up a strange man look less interested in a sexual partner than in a companion for a drink the next morning. There is a staggering amount of evidence that points to the idea that women set a price of one kind or another on sexual intercourse; they are so often not in the mood.

This is not to say women aren't interested in sex *at all*. They clearly want a lot of it, but in the end the men of the world seem to want still more. It is only the quantity, the capacity in that sense, in which the sexes appear to differ. Women, in the language of sociology books, "fight very hard" to get the amount of sexual satisfaction they want—and even harder to keep men from forcing a superabundance their way. It is difficult to see how anyone can be sure that it is only man's voracious appetite for conquest which has created, as its contrary, this reluctant, passive being who has to be wooed, raped, bribed, begged, threatened, married, supported. Perhaps she really has to be. After she has been conquered she has to "pay" the man to restrain his appetite, which he is so likely to reveal at cocktail parties, and in his pitifully longing glance at the secretary—she pays with ironed shirts, free meals, the pleasant living room, a son.

And what about the arts—those womanish activities which are, in our day, mostly "done at home." For those who desire this form of tran- scendence, the other liberating activities of mankind, the office, the factory, the world of commerce, public affairs, are horrible pits where the extraordinary man is basely and casually slain.

Women have excelled in the performance arts: acting, dancing and singing—for some reason Simone de Beauvoir treats these accomplish- ments as if they were usually an extension of prostitution. Women have contributed very little to the art of painting and they are clearly weak in the gift for musical composition. (Still whole nations seem without this latter gift, which may be inherited. Perhaps even nations inherit it, the male members at least. Like baldness, women may transmit the gift of musical composition but they seldom ever suffer from it.)

Literature is the art in which women have had the greatest success. But a woman needs only to think of this activity to feel her bones rattling with violent distress. Who is to say that *Remembrance of Things Past* is "better" than the marvelous *Emma*? *War and Peace* better than *Middlemarch*? *Moby Dick* superior to *La Princesse de Clèves*? But everybody says so! It is only the whimsical, cantankerous, the eccentric critic, or those who refuse the occasion for such distinctions, who would say that any literary work by a woman, marvelous as these may be, is on a level with the very greatest accomplishments of men. Of course the *best* literature by women is superior to *most* of the work done by men and anyone who values literature at all will approach all excellence with equal enthusiasm.

The Second Sex is not whimsical about women's writing, but here again perhaps too much is made of the position in which women have been "trapped" and not enough of how "natural" and inevitable their literary limitations are. Nevertheless, the remarks on artistic women are among the most brilliant in this book. Narcissism and feelings of inferiority are, according to Simone de Beauvoir, the demons of literary women. Women want to please, "but the writer of originality, unless dead, is always shocking, scandalous; novelty disturbs and repels." Flattered to be in the world of art at all, the woman is "on her best behavior; she is afraid to disarrange, to investigate, to explode . . ." Women are timid and fall back on "ancient houses, sheepfolds, kitchen gardens, picturesque old folks, roguish children . . ." and even the best are conservative. "There are women who are mad and there are women of sound method; none has that madness in her method that we call genius."

If women's writing seems somewhat limited, I don't think it is only due to these psychological failings. Women have much less experience of life than a man, as everyone knows. But in the end are they suited to the kind of experiences men have? *Ulysses* is not just a work of genius, it is Dublin pubs, gross depravity, obscenity, brawls. Stendhal as a soldier in Napoleon's army, Tolstoy on his Cossack campaigns, Dostoevsky before the firing squad, Proust's obviously first-hand knowledge of vice, Conrad and Melville as sailors, Michelangelo's tortures on the scaffolding in the Sistine chapel, Ben Jonson's drinking bouts, dueling, his ear burnt by the authorities because of a political indiscretion in a play—these horrors and the capacity to endure them are *experience*. Experience is something more than going to law school or having the nerve to say honestly what you think in a drawing room filled with men; it is the privilege as well to endure brutality, physical torture, unimaginable sordidness, and even the privilege *to want,* like Boswell, to grab a miserable tart under Westminster Bridge. Syphilis and epilepsy —even these seem to be tragic afflictions a male writer can endure more easily than a woman. I should imagine a woman would be more depleted by epilepsy than Dostoevsky seems to have been, more ravaged by syphilis than Flaubert, more weakened by deprivation than Villon. Women live longer, safer lives than men and a man may, if he wishes, choose that life; it is hard to believe a woman could choose, like Rimbaud, to sleep in the streets of Paris at seventeen.

If you remove the physical and sexual experiences many men have made literature out of, you have carved away a great hunk of masterpieces. There is a lot left: James, Balzac, Dickens; the material in these books, perhaps not always in Balzac, is a part of women's lives too or might be "worked up"—legal practices and prison conditions in Dickens, commerce in Balzac, etc.

But the special *vigor* of James, Balzac, Dickens or Racine, the queer, remaining strength to produce masterpiece after masterpiece—that is belittling! The careers of women of prodigious productivity, like George Sand, are marked by a great amount of failure and waste, indicating that though time was spent at the desk perhaps the supreme effort was not regularly made. Who can help but feel that *some* of James's vigor is sturdily rooted in his masculine flesh and that this repeatedly success-ful creativity is less likely with the "weaker sex" even in the socialist millennium. It is not suggested that muscles write books, but there is a certain sense in which, talent and experience being equal, they may be considered a bit of an advantage. In the end, it is in the matter of ex-perience that women's disadvantage is catastrophic. It is very difficult to know how this may be extraordinarily altered.

Coquettes, mothers, prostitutes and "minor" writers—one sees these faces, defiant or resigned, still standing at the Last Judgment. They are all a little sad, like the Chinese lyric:

> *Why do I heave deep sighs?*
> *It is natural, a matter of course, all*
> *creatures have their laws.*

Robert Lowell

LIFE STUDIES

"It is the future generation that presses into being by means of these exuberant feelings and supersensible soap bubbles of ours."

—SCHOPENHAUER

"The hot night makes us keep our bedroom windows open.
Our magnolia blossoms. Life begins to happen.
My hopped up husband drops his home disputes,
and hits the streets to cruise for prostitutes,
free-lancing out along the razor's edge.
This screwball might kill his wife, then take the pledge.
Oh the monotonous meanness of his lust. . . .
It's the injustice . . . he is so unjust—
whiskey-blind, swaggering home at five.
My only thought is how to keep alive.
What makes him tick? Each night now I tie
ten dollars and his car key to my thigh. . . .
Gored by the climacteric of his want,
he stalls above me like an elephant."

Nathanael West

MISS LONELYHEARTS

MISS LONELYHEARTS IN THE DISMAL SWAMP

Soon after Mrs. Doyle left, Miss Lonelyhearts became physically sick and was unable to leave his room. The first two days of his illness were blotted out by sleep, but on the third day, his imagination began again to work.

He found himself in the window of a pawn-shop full of fur coats, diamond rings, watches, shotguns, fishing tackle, mandolins. All these things were the paraphernalia of suffering. A tortured high light twisted on the blade of a gift knife, a battered horn grunted with pain.

He sat in the window thinking. Man has a tropism for order. Keys in one pocket, change in another. Mandolins are tuned G D A E. The physical world has a tropism for disorder, entropy. Man against Nature . . . the battle of the centuries. Keys yearn to mix with change. Mandolins strive to get out of tune. Every order has within it the germ of destruction. All order is doomed, yet the battle is worth while.

A trumpet, marked to sell for $2.49, gave the call to battle and Miss Lonelyhearts plunged into the fray. First he formed a phallus of old watches and rubber boots, then a heart of umbrellas and trout flies, then a diamond of musical instruments and derby hats, after these a circle, triangle, square, swastika. But nothing proved definitive and he began to make a gigantic cross. When the cross became too large for the pawnshop, he moved it to the shore of the ocean. There every wave added to his stock faster than he could lengthen its arms. His labors were enormous. He staggered from the last wave line to his work, loaded down with marine refuse—bottles, shells, chunks of cork, fish heads, pieces of net.

Drunk with exhaustion, he finally fell asleep. When he awoke, he felt very weak, yet calm.

There was a timid knock on the door. It was open and Betty tiptoed into the room with her arms full of bundles. He made believe that he was asleep.

"Hello," he said suddenly.

Startled, she turned to explain. "I heard you were sick, so I brought some hot soup and other stuff."

He was too tired to be annoyed by her wide-eyed little mother act and let her feed him with a spoon. When he had finished eating, she opened the window and freshened the bed. As soon as the room was in order, she started to leave, but he called her back.

"Don't go, Betty."

She pulled a chair to the side of his bed and sat there without speaking.

"I'm sorry about what happened the other day," he said. "I guess I was sick."

She showed that she accepted his apology by helping him to excuse himself. "It's the Miss Lonelyhearts job. Why don't you give it up?"

"And do what?"

"Work in an advertising agency, or something."

"You don't understand, Betty, I can't quit. And even if I were to quit, it wouldn't make any difference. I wouldn't be able to forget the letters, no matter what I did."

"Maybe I don't understand," she said, "but I think you're making a fool of yourself."

"Perhaps I can make you understand. Let's start from the beginning. A man is hired to give advice to the readers of a newspaper. The job is a circulation stunt and the whole staff considers it a joke. He welcomes the job, for it might lead to a gossip column, and anyway he's tired of being a leg man. He too considers the job a joke, but after several months at it, the joke begins to escape him. He sees that the majority of the letters are profoundly humble pleas for moral and spiritual advice, that they are inarticulate expressions of genuine suffering. He also discovers that his correspondents take him seriously. For the first time in his life, he is forced to examine the values by which he lives. This examination shows him that he is the victim of the joke and not its perpetrator."

Although he had spoken soberly, he saw that Betty still thought him a fool. He closed his eyes.

"You're tired," she said. "I'll go."

"No, I'm not tired. I'm just tired of talking, you talk a while."

She told him about her childhood on a farm and of her love for animals, about country sounds and country smells and of how fresh and clean everything in the country is. She said that he ought to live there and that if he did, he would find that all his troubles were city troubles.

While she was talking, Shrike burst into the room. He was drunk and immediately set up a great shout, as though he believed that Miss Lonelyhearts was too near death to hear distinctly. Betty left without saying good-by.

Shrike had evidently caught some of her farm talk, for he said: "My friend, I agree with Betty, you're an escapist. But I do not agree that the soil is the proper method for you to use."

Miss Lonelyhearts turned his face to the wall and pulled up the covers. But Shrike was unescapable. He raised his voice and talked through the blankets into the back of Miss Lonelyhearts' head.

"There are other methods, and for your edification I shall describe them. But first let us do the escape to the soil, as recommended by Betty:

"You are fed up with the city and its teeming millions. The ways and means of men, as getting and lending and spending, you lay waste your inner world, are too much with you. The bus takes too long, while the subway is always crowded. So what do you do? So you buy a farm and walk behind your horse's moist behind, no collar or tie, plowing your broad swift acres. As you turn up the rich black soil, the wind carries the smell of pine and dung across the fields and the rhythm of an old, old work enters your soul. To this rhythm, you sow and weep and chivy your kine, not kin or kind, between the pregnant rows of corn and taters. Your step becomes the heavy sexual step of a dance-drunk Indian and you tread the seed down into the female earth. You plant, not dragon's teeth, but beans and greens. . . .

"Well, what do you say, my friend, shall it be the soil?"

Miss Lonelyhearts did not answer. He was thinking of how Shrike had accelerated his sickness by teaching him to handle his one escape, Christ, with a thick glove of words.

"I take your silence to mean that you have decided against the soil. I agree with you. Such a life is too dull and laborious. Let us now consider the South Seas:

"You live in a thatch hut with the daughter of the king, a slim young maiden in whose eyes is an ancient wisdom. Her breasts are golden speckled pears, her belly a melon, and her odor is like nothing so much as a jungle fern. In the evening, on the blue lagoon, under the silvery moon, to your love you croon in the soft sylabelew and vocabelew of her langorour tongorour. Your body is golden brown like hers, and tourists have need of the indignant finger of the missionary to point you out. They envy you your breech clout and carefree laugh and little brown bride and fingers instead of forks. But you don't return their envy, and when a beautiful society girl comes to your hut in the night, seeking to learn the secret of your happiness, you send her back to her yacht that hangs on the horizon like a nervous racehorse. And so you dream away the days, fishing, hunting, dancing, swimming, kissing, and picking flowers to twine in your hair. . . .

"Well, my friend, what do you think of the South Seas?"

Miss Lonelyhearts tried to stop him by making believe that he was asleep. But Shrike was not fooled.

"Again silence," he said, "and again you are right. The South Seas are played out and there's little use in imitating Gauguin. But don't be discouraged, we have only scratched the surface of our subject. Let us now examine Hedonism, or take the cash and let the credit go. . . .

"You dedicate your life to the pursuit of pleasure. No over-indulgence, mind you, but knowing that your body is a pleasure machine, you treat it carefully in order to get the most out of it. Golf as well as booze, Philadelphia Jack O'Brien and his chestweights as well as Spanish dancers. Nor do you neglect the pleasures of the mind. You fornicate under pictures by Matisse and Picasso, you drink from Renaissance glassware, and often you spend an evening beside the fireplace with Proust and an apple. Alas, after much good fun, the day comes when you realize that soon you must die. You keep a stiff upper lip and decide to give a last party. You invite all your old mistresses, trainers, artists and boon companions. The guests are dressed in black, the waiters are coons, the table is a coffin carved for you by Eric Gill. You serve caviar and blackberries and licorice candy and coffee without cream. After the dancing girls have finished, you get to your feet and call for silence in order to explain your philosophy of life. 'Life,' you say, 'is a club where they won't stand for squawks, where they deal you only one hand and you must sit in. So even if the cards are cold and marked by the hand of fate, play up, play up like a gentleman and a sport. Get tanked, grab what's on the buffet, use the girls upstairs, but remember, when you throw box cars, take the curtain like a dead game sport, don't squawk.'. . .

"I won't even ask you what you think of such an escape. You haven't the money, nor are you stupid enough to manage it. But we come now to one that should suit you much better. . . .

"Art! Be an artist or a writer. When you are cold, warm yourself before the flaming tints of Titian, when you are hungry, nourish yourself with great spiritual foods by listening to the noble periods of Bach, the harmonies of Brahms and the thunder of Beethoven. Do you think there is anything in the fact that their names all begin with B? But don't take a chance, smoke a 3 B pipe, and remember these immortal lines: *When to the suddenness of melody the echo parting falls the failing day*. What a rhythm! Tell them to keep their society whores and pressed duck with oranges. For you *l'art vivant*, the living art, as you call it. Tell them that you know that your shoes are broken and that there are pimples on your face, yes, and that you have buck teeth and a club foot, but that you don't care, for to-morrow they are playing Beethoven's last quartets in Carnegie Hall and at home you have Shakespeare's plays in one volume."

After art, Shrike described suicide and drugs. When he had finished with them, he came to what he said was the goal of his lecture.

"My friend, I know of course that neither the soil, nor the South Seas, nor Hedonism, nor art, nor suicide, nor drugs, can mean anything to us. We are not men who swallow camels only to strain at stools. God alone is our escape. The church is our only hope, the First Church of Christ Dentist, where He is worshiped as Preventer of Decay. The church whose symbol is the trinity new-style: Father, Son and Wire-haired Fox Terrier. . . . And so, my good friend, let me dictate a letter to Christ for you:

Dear Miss Lonelyhearts of Miss Lonelyhearts—

I am twenty-six years old and in the newspaper game. Life for me is a desert empty of comfort. I cannot find pleasure in food, drink, or women—nor do the arts give me joy any longer. The Leopard of Discontent walks the streets of my city; the Lion of Discouragement crouches outside the walls of my citadel. All is desolation and a vexation of the spirit. I feel like hell. How can I believe, how can I have faith in this day and age? Is it true that the greatest scientists believe again in you?

I read your column and like it very much. There you once wrote: 'When the salt has lost its savour, who shall savour it again?' Is the answer: 'None but the Saviour?'

Thanking you very much for a quick reply, I remain yours truly,

A Regular Subscriber"

Horace Gregory

McALPIN GARFINKEL, POET

It is enough for me to tremble,
my vital organs directed toward the sun,
toward the stars,
trembling.

It is better for me to stand at street corners
staring at women, seeing their bodies flowering
like new continents, hills warm in sunshine and
long deep rivers
(even as I am,
trembling)
than to be nothing, to fade away in grass and stone.

It is better for me to believe nothing
than to be nothing,
better for me
not to fight, to let cops and truck drivers
crash through my brains, trample my entrails,
O let me cry out my rage against millions,
carry my remains to the President,
up the steps of the White House
to be deodorized by the Department of Justice
and the Secretary of State,
thenceforth expunged
from the Congressional Record.
But I shall be intact,
no word spoken,
like laughter in my mother's womb, a pointless joke
with no beginning and no end.

And if you hear me crying: My God, my God, my God,
down streets and alleys,
I am merely trembling (afraid, my God, my God,
to be nothing, to fade away
in grass, in stone).

Clement Greenberg

AVANT-GARDE AND KITSCH
from *Art and Culture*

One and the same civilization produces simultaneously two such different things as a poem by T. S. Eliot and a Tin Pan Alley song, or a painting by Braque and a *Saturday Evening Post* cover. All four are on the order of culture, and ostensibly, parts of the same culture and products of the same society. Here, however, their connection seems to end. A poem by Eliot and a poem by Eddie Guest—what perspective of culture is large enough to enable us to situate them in an enlightening relation to each other? Does the fact that a disparity such as this within the frame of a single cultural tradition, which is and has been taken for granted—does this fact indicate that the disparity is a part of the natural order of things? Or is it something entirely new, and particular to our age?

The answer involves more than an investigation in aesthetics. It appears to me that it is necessary to examine more closely and with more originality than hitherto the relationship between aesthetic experience as met by the specific—not the generalized—individual, and the social and historical contexts in which that experience takes place. What is brought to light will answer, in addition to the question posed above, other and perhaps more important questions.

I

A society, as it becomes less and less able, in the course of its development, to justify the inevitability of its particular forms, breaks up the accepted notions upon which artists and writers must depend in large part for communication with their audiences. It becomes difficult to assume anything. All the verities involved by religion, authority, tradition, style, are thrown into question, and the writer or artist is no longer able to estimate the response of his audience to the symbols and references with which he works. In the past such a state of affairs has usually resolved itself into a motionless Alexandrianism, an academicism in which the really important issues are left untouched because they involve controversy, and in which creative activity dwindles to virtuosity in the small details of form, all larger questions being decided by the precedent of the old masters. The same themes are mechanically varied in a hundred different works, and yet nothing new is produced: Statius, mandarin verse, Roman sculpture, Beaux-Arts painting, neo-republican architecture.

It is among the hopeful signs in the midst of the decay of our present society that we—some of us—have been unwilling to accept this last phase for our own culture. In seeking to go beyond Alexandrianism, a part of Western bourgeois society has produced something unheard of heretofore:—avant-garde culture. A superior consciousness of history— more precisely, the appearance of a new kind of criticism of society, an historical criticism—made this possible. This criticism has not confronted our present society with timeless utopias, but has soberly examined in the terms of history and of cause and effect the antecedents, justifications and functions of the forms that lie at the heart of every society. Thus our present bourgeois social order was shown to be, not an eternal, "natural" condition of life, but simply the latest term in a succession of social orders. New perspectives of this kind, becoming a part of the advanced intellectual conscience of the fifth and sixth decades of the nineteenth century, soon were absorbed by artists and poets, even if unconsciously for the most part. It was no accident, therefore, that the birth of the avant-garde coincided chronologically—and geographically, too—with the first bold development of scientific revolutionary thought in Europe.

True, the first settlers of bohemia—which was then identical with the avant-garde—turned out soon to be demonstratively uninterested in politics. Nevertheless, without the circulation of revolutionary ideas in the air about them, they would never have been able to isolate their concept of the "bourgeois" in order to define what they were *not*. Nor, without the moral aid of revolutionary political attitudes, would they have had the courage to assert themselves as aggressively as they did against the prevailing standards of society. Courage indeed was needed for this, because the avant-garde's emigration from bourgeois society to bohemia meant also an emigration from the markets of capitalism, upon which artists and writers had been thrown by the falling away of aristocratic patronage. (Ostensibly, at least, it meant this—meant starving in a garret—although, as will be shown later, the avant-garde remained attached to bourgeois society precisely because it needed its money.)

Yet it is true that once the avant-garde had succeeded in "detaching" itself from society, it proceeded to turn around and repudiate revolutionary as well as bourgeois politics. The revolution was left inside society, a part of that welter of ideological struggle which art and poetry find so unpropitious as soon as it begins to involve those "precious" axiomatic beliefs upon which culture thus far has had to rest. Hence it developed that the true and most important function of the avant-garde was not to "experiment," but to find a path along which it would be possible to keep culture *moving* in the midst of ideological confusion and violence. Retiring from public altogether, the avant-garde poet or artist sought to maintain the high level of his art by both narrowing and raising it to the expression of an absolute in which all relativities and contradictions would be either resolved or beside the point. "Art for art's sake" and "pure poetry" appear, and subject matter or content becomes something to be avoided like a plague.

It has been in search of the absolute that the avant-garde has arrived at "abstract" or "nonobjective" art—and poetry, too. The avant-garde poet or artist tries in effect to imitate God by creating something valid solely on its own terms, in the way nature itself is valid, in the way a landscape—not its picture—is aesthetically valid; something *given,* increate, independent of meanings, similars or originals. Content is to be dissolved so completely into form that the work of art or literature cannot be reduced in whole or in part to anything not itself.

But the absolute is absolute, and the poet or artist, being what he is, cherishes certain relative values more than others. The very values in the name of which he invokes the absolute are relative values, the values of aesthetics. And so he turns out to be imitating, not God—and here I use "imitate" in its Aristotelian sense—but the disciplines and processes of art and literature themselves. This is the genesis of the "abstract."[1] In turning his attention away from subject matter of common experience, the poet or artist turns it in upon the medium of his own craft. The non-representational or "abstract," if it is to have aesthetic validity, cannot be arbitrary and accidental, but must stem from obedience to some worthy constraint or original. This constraint, once the world of common (extra-verted experience has been renounced, can only be found in the very processes or disciplines by which art and literature have already imitated the former. These themselves become the subject matter of art and literature. If, to continue with Aristotle, all art and literature are imitation, then what we have here is the imitation of imitating. To quote Yeats:

> Nor is there singing school but studying
> Monuments of its own magnificence.

Picasso, Braque, Mondrian, Miró, Kandinsky, Brancusi, even Klee, Matisse and Cézanne derive their chief inspiration from the medium they work in.[2] The excitement of their art seems to lie most of all in its pure preoccupation with the invention and arrangement of spaces, surfaces, shapes, colors, etc., to the exclusion of whatever is not necessarily implicated in these factors. The attention of poets like Rimbaud, Mallarmé, Valéry, Éluard, Pound, Hart Crane, Stevens, even Rilke and Yeats, appears to be centered on the effort to create poetry and on the "moments" themselves of poetic conversion, rather than on experience to be converted into poetry. Of course, this cannot exclude other pre-occupations in their work, for poetry must deal with words, and words must communicate. Certain poets, such as Mallarmé and Valéry,[3] are more radical in this respect than others—leaving aside those poets who have tried to compose poetry in pure sound alone. However, if it were easier to define poetry, modern poetry would be much more "pure" and "abstract." As for the other fields of literature—the definition of avant-garde aesthetics advanced here is no Procrustean bed. But aside from the fact that most of our best contemporary novelists have gone to school with the avant-garde, it is significant that Gide's most ambitious book is a novel about the writing of a novel, and that Joyce's *Ulysses* and *Finnegans Wake* seem to be, above all, as one French critic says, the reduction of experience to expression for the sake of expression, the expression mattering more than what is being expressed.

That avant-garde culture is the imitation of imitating—the fact itself—calls for neither approval nor disapproval. It is true that this culture contains within itself some of the very Alexandrianism it seeks to overcome. The lines quoted from Yeats referred to Byzantium, which is very close to Alexandria; and in a sense this imitation of imitating is a superior sort of Alexandrianism. But there is one most important difference: the avant-garde moves, while Alexandrianism stands still. And this, precisely, is what justifies the avant-garde's methods and makes them necessary. The necessity lies in the fact that by no other means is it possible today to create art and literature of a high order. To quarrel with necessity by throwing about terms like "formalism," "purism," "ivory tower" and so forth is either dull or dishonest. This is not to say, however, that it is to the *social* advantage of the avant-garde that it is what it is. Quite the opposite.

The avant-garde's specialization of itself, the fact that its best artists are artists' artists, its best poets, poets' poets, has estranged a great many of those who were capable formerly of enjoying and appreciating ambitious art and literature, but who are now unwilling or unable to acquire an initiation into their craft secrets. The masses have always remained more or less indifferent to culture in the process of development. But today such culture is being abandoned by those to whom it actually belongs—our ruling class. For it is to the latter that the avant-garde belongs. No culture can develop without a social basis, without a source of stable income. And in the case of the avant-garde, this was provided by an elite among the ruling class of that society from which it assumed itself to be cut off, but to which it has always remained attached by an umbilical cord of gold. The paradox is real. And now this elite is rapidly shrinking. Since the avant-garde forms the only living culture we now have, the survival in the near future of culture in general is thus threatened.

We must not be deceived by superficial phenomena and local successes. Picasso's shows still draw crowds, and T. S. Eliot is taught in the universities; the dealers in modernist art are still in business, and the publishers still publish some "difficult" poetry. But the avant-garde itself, already sensing the danger, is becoming more and more timid every day that passes. Academicism and commercialism are appearing in the strangest places. This can mean only one thing: that the avant-garde is becoming unsure of the audience it depends on—the rich and the cultivated.

Is it the nature itself of avant-garde culture that is alone responsible for the danger it finds itself in? Or is that only a dangerous liability? Are there other, and perhaps more important, factors involved?

II

Where there is an avant-garde, generally we also find a rear-guard. True enough—simultaneously with the entrance of the avant-garde, a second new cultural phenomenon appeared in the industrial West: that thing to which the Germans give the wonderful name of *Kitsch:* popular, commercial art and literature with their chromeotypes, magazine covers, illustrations, ads, slick and pulp fiction, comics, Tin Pan Alley music, tap dancing, Hollywood movies, etc., etc. For some reason this gigantic apparition has always been taken for granted. It is time we looked into its whys and wherefores.

Kitsch is a product of the industrial revolution which urbanized the masses of Western Europe and America and established what is called universal literacy.

Prior to this the only market for formal culture, as distinguished from folk culture, had been among those who, in addition to being able to read and write, could command the leisure and comfort that always goes hand in hand with cultivation of some sort. This until then had been inextricably associated with literacy. But with the introduction of universal literacy, the ability to read and write became almost a minor skill like driving a car, and it no longer served to distinguish an individual's cultural inclinations, since it was no longer the exclusive concomitant of refined tastes.

The peasants who settled in the cities as proletariat and petty bourgeois learned to read and write for the sake of efficiency, but they did not win the leisure and comfort necessary for the enjoyment of the city's traditional culture. Losing, nevertheless, their taste for the folk culture whose background was the countryside, and discovering a new capacity for boredom at the same time, the new urban masses set up a pressure on society to provide them with a kind of culture fit for their own consumption. To fill the demand of the new market, a new commodity was devised: ersatz culture, kitsch, destined for those who, insensible to the values of genuine culture, are hungry nevertheless for the diversion that only culture of some sort can provide.

Kitsch, using for raw material the debased and academicized simulacra of genuine culture, welcomes and cultivates this sensibility. It is the source of its profits. Kitsch is mechanical and operates by formulas. Kitsch is vicarious experience and faked sensations. Kitsch changes according to style, but remains always the same. Kitsch is the epitome of all that is spurious in the life of our times. Kitsch pretends to demand nothing of its customers except their money—not even their time.

The precondition for kitsch, a condition without which kitsch would be impossible, is the availability close at hand of a fully matured cultural tradition, whose discoveries, acquisitions, and perfected self-consciousness kitsch can take advantage of for its own ends. It borrows from it devices, tricks, stratagems, rules of thumb, themes, converts them into a system, and discards the rest. It draws its life blood, so to speak, from this reservoir of accumulated experience. This is what is really meant when it is said that the popular art and literature of today were once the daring, esoteric art and literature of yesterday. Of course, no such thing is true. What is meant is that when enough time has elapsed the new is looted for new "twists," which are then watered down and served up as kitsch. Self-evidently, all kitsch is academic; and conversely, all that's academic is kitsch. For what is called the academic as such no longer has an independent existence, but has become the stuffed-shirt "front" for kitsch. The methods of industrialism displace the handicrafts.

Because it can be turned out mechanically, kitsch has become an integral part of our productive system in a way in which true culture could never be, except accidentally. It has been capitalized at a tremendous investment which must show commensurate returns; it is compelled to extend as well as to keep its markets. While it is essentially its own salesman, a great sales apparatus has nevertheless been created for it, which brings pressure to bear on every member of society. Traps are laid even in those areas, so to speak, that are the preserves of genuine culture. It is not enough today, in a country like ours, to have an inclination towards the latter; one must have a true passion for it that will give him the power to resist the faked article that surrounds and presses in on him from the moment he is old enough to look at the funny papers. Kitsch is deceptive. It has many different levels, and some of them are high enough to be dangerous to the naive seeker of true light. A magazine like *The New Yorker*, which is fundamentally high-class kitsch for the luxury trade, converts and waters down a great deal of avant-garde material for its own uses. Nor is every single item of kitsch altogether worthless. Now and then it produces something of merit, something that has an authentic folk flavor; and these accidental and isolated instances have fooled people who should know better.

Kitsch's enormous profits are a source of temptation to the avant-garde itself, and its members have not always resisted this temptation. Ambitious writers and artists will modify their work under the pressure of kitsch, if they do not succumb to it entirely. And then those puzzling borderline cases appear, such as the popular novelist, Simenon, in France, and Steinbeck in this country. The net result is always to the detriment of true culture, in any case.

Kitsch has not been confined to the cities in which it was born, but has flowed out over the countryside, wiping out folk culture. Nor has it shown any regard for geographical and national-cultural boundaries. Another mass product of Western industrialism, it has gone on a triumphal tour of the world, crowding out and defacing native cultures in one colonial country after another, so that it is now by way of becoming a universal culture, the first universal culture ever beheld. Today the native of China, no less than the South American Indian, the Hindu, no less than the Polynesian, have come to prefer to the products of their native art, magazine covers, rotogravure sections and calendar girls. How is this virulence of kitsch, this irresistible attractiveness, to be explained? Naturally, machine-made kitsch can undersell the native handmade article, and the prestige of the West also helps; but why is kitsch a so much more profitable export article than Rembrandt? One, after all, can be reproduced as cheaply as the other.

In his last article on the Soviet cinema in the *Partisan Review,* Dwight Macdonald points out that kitsch has in the last ten years become the dominant culture in Soviet Russia. For this he blames the political regime—not only for the fact that kitsch is the official culture, but also that it is actually the dominant, most popular culture, and he quotes the following from Kurt London's *The Seven Soviet Arts*: ". . . the attitude of the masses both to the old and new art styles probably remains essentially dependent on the nature of the education afforded them by their respective states." Macdonald goes on to say: "Why after all should ignorant peasants prefer Repin (a leading exponent of Russian academic kitsch in painting) to Picasso, whose abstract technique is at least as relevant to their own primitive folk art as is the former's realistic style? No, if the masses crowd into the Tretyakov (Moscow's museum of contemporary Russian art: kitsch), it is largely because they have been conditioned to shun 'formalism' and to admire 'socialist realism.' "

In the first place it is not a question of a choice between merely the old and merely the new, as London seems to think—but of a choice between the bad, up-to-date old and the genuinely new. The alternative to Picasso is not Michelangelo, but kitsch. In the second place, neither in backward Russia nor in the advanced West do the masses prefer kitsch simply because their governments condition them toward it. Where state educational systems take the trouble to mention art, we are told to respect the old masters, not kitsch; and yet we go and hang Maxfield Parrish or his equivalent on our walls, instead of Rembrandt and Michelangelo. Moreover, as Macdonald himself points out, around 1925, when the Soviet regime was encouraging avant-garde cinema, the Russian masses continued to prefer Hollywood movies. No, "conditioning" does not explain the potency of kitsch.

All values are human values, relative values, in art as well as elsewhere. Yet there does seem to have been more or less of a general agreement among the cultivated of mankind over the ages as to what is good art and what bad. Taste has varied, but not beyond certain limits; contemporary connoisseurs agree with the eighteenth-century Japanese that Hokusai was one of the greatest artists of his time; we even agree with the ancient Egyptians that Third and Fourth Dynasty art was the most worthy of being selected as their paragon by those who came after. We may have come to prefer Giotto to Raphael, but we still do not deny that Raphael was one of the best painters of his time. There has been an agreement then, and this agreement rests, I believe, on a fairly constant distinction made between those values only to be found in art and the values which can be found elsewhere. Kitsch, by virtue of a rationalized technique that draws on science and industry, has erased this distinction in practice.

Let us see, for example, what happens when an ignorant Russian peasant such as Macdonald mentions stands with hypothetical freedom of choice before two paintings, one by Picasso, the other by Repin. In the first he sees, let us say, a play of lines, colors and spaces that represent a woman. The abstract technique—to accept Macdonald's supposition, which I am inclined to doubt—reminds him somewhat of the icons he has left behind him in the village, and he feels the attraction of the familiar. We will even suppose that he faintly surmises some of the great art values the cultivated find in Picasso. He turns next to Repin's picture and sees a battle scene. The technique is not so familiar—as technique. But that weighs very little with the peasant, for he suddenly discovers values in Repin's picture that seem far superior to the values he has been accustomed to find in icon art; and the unfamiliar itself is one of the sources of those values: the values of the vividly recognizable, the miraculous and the sympathetic. In Repin's picture the peasant recognizes and sees things in the way in which he recognizes and sees things outside of pictures—there is no discontinuity between art and life, no need to accept a convention and say to oneself, that icon represents Jesus because it intends to represent Jesus, even if it does not remind me very much of a man. That Repin can paint so realistically that identifications are self-evident immediately and without any effort on the part of the spectator—that is miraculous. The peasant is also pleased by the wealth of self-evident meanings which he finds in the picture: "it tells a story." Picasso and the icons are so austere and barren in comparison. What is more, Repin heightens reality and makes it dramatic: sunset, exploding shells, running and falling men. There is no longer any question of Picasso or icons. Repin is what the peasant wants, and nothing else but Repin. It is lucky, however, for Repin that the peasant is protected from the products of American capitalism, for he would not stand a chance next to a *Saturday Evening Post* cover by Norman Rockwell.

Ultimately, it can be said that the cultivated spectator derives the same values from Picasso that the peasant gets from Repin, since what the latter enjoys in Repin is somehow art too, on however low a scale, and he is sent to look at pictures by the same instincts that send the cultivated spectator. But the ultimate values which the cultivated spectator derives from Picasso are derived at a second remove, as the result of reflection upon the immediate impression left by the plastic values. It is only then that the recognizable, the miraculous and the sympathetic enter. They are not immediately or externally present in Picasso's painting, but must be projected into it by the spectator sensitive enough to react sufficiently to plastic qualities. They belong to the "reflected" effect. In Repin, on the other hand, the "reflected" effect has already been included in the picture, ready for the spectator's unreflective enjoyment.[4] Where Picasso paints *cause,* Repin paints *effect*. Repin predigests art for the spectator and spares him effort, provides him with a short cut to the pleasure of art that detours what is necessarily difficult in genuine art. Repin, or kitsch, is synthetic art.

The same point can be made with respect to kitsch literature: it provides vicarious experience for the insensitive with far greater immediacy than serious fiction can hope to do. And Eddie Guest and the *Indian Love Lyrics* are more poetic than T. S. Eliot and Shakespeare.

III

If the avant-garde imitates the processes of art, kitsch, we now see, imitates its effects. The neatness of this antithesis is more than contrived;

it corresponds to and defines the tremendous interval that separates from each other two such simultaneous cultural phenomena as the avant-garde and kitsch. This interval, too great to be closed by all the infinite gradations of popularized "modernism" and "modernistic" kitsch, corresponds in turn to a social interval, a social interval that has always existed in formal culture, as elsewhere in civilized society, and whose two termini converge and diverge in fixed relation to the increasing or decreasing stability of the given society. There has always been on one side the minority of the powerful—and therefore the cultivated—and on the other the great mass of the exploited and poor—and therefore the ignorant. Formal culture has always belonged to the first, while the last have had to content themselves with folk or rudimentary culture, or kitsch.

In a stable society that functions well enough to hold in solution the contradictions between its classes, the cultural dichotomy becomes somewhat blurred. The axioms of the few are shared by the many; the latter believe superstitiously what the former believe soberly. And at such moments in history the masses are able to feel wonder and admiration for the culture, on no matter how high a plane, of its masters. This applies at least to plastic culture, which is accessible to all.

In the Middle Ages the plastic artist paid lip service at least to the lowest common denominators of experience. This even remained true to some extent until the seventeenth century. There was available for imitation a universally valid conceptual reality, whose order the artist could not tamper with. The subject matter of art was prescribed by those who commissioned works of art, which were not created, as in bourgeois society, on speculation. Precisely because his content was determined in advance, the artist was free to concentrate on his medium. He needed not to be philosopher, or visionary, but simply artificer. As long as there was general agreement as to what were the worthiest subjects for art, the artist was relieved of the necessity to be original and inventive in his "matter" and could devote all his energy to formal problems. For him the medium became, privately, professionally, the content of his art, even as his medium is today the public content of the abstract painter's art—with that difference, however, that the medieval artist had to suppress his professional preoccupation in public—had always to suppress and subordinate the personal and professional in the finished, official work of art. If, as an ordinary member of the Christian community, he felt some personal emotion about his subject matter, this only contributed to the enrichment of the work's public meaning. Only with the Renaissance do the inflections of the personal become legitimate, still to be kept, however, within the limits of the simply and universally recognizable.

And only with Rembrandt do "lonely" artists begin to appear, lonely in their art.

But even during the Renaissance, and so long as Western art was endeavoring to perfect its technique, victories in this realm could only be signalized by success in realistic imitation, since there was no other objective criterion at hand. Thus the masses could still find in the art of their masters objects of admiration and wonder. Even the bird that pecked at the fruit in Zeuxis' picture could applaud.

It is a platitude that art becomes caviar to the general when the reality it imitates no longer corresponds even roughly to the reality recognized by the general. Even then, however, the resentment the common man may feel is silenced by the awe in which he stands of the patrons of this art. Only when he becomes dissatisfied with the social order they administer does he begin to criticize their culture. Then the plebeian finds courage for the first time to voice his opinions openly. Every man, from the Tammany alderman to the Austrian house-painter, finds that he is entitled to his opinion. Most often this resentment toward culture is to be found where the dissatisfaction with society is a reactionary dissatisfaction which expresses itself in revivalism and puritanism, and latest of all, in fascism. Here revolvers and torches begin to be mentioned in the same breath as culture. In the name of godliness or the blood's health, in the name of simple ways and solid virtues, the statue-smashing commences.

IV

Returning to our Russian peasant for the moment, let us suppose that after he has chosen Repin in preference to Picasso, the state's educational apparatus comes along and tells him that he is wrong, that he should have chosen Picasso—and shows him why. It is quite possible for the Soviet state to do this. But things being as they are in Russia—and everywhere else—the peasant soon finds that the necessity of working hard all day for his living and the rude, uncomfortable circumstances in which he lives do not allow him enough leisure, energy and comfort to train for the enjoyment of Picasso. This needs, after all, a considerable amount of "conditioning." Superior culture is one of the most artificial of all human creations, and the peasant finds no "natural" urgency within himself that will drive him toward Picasso in spite of all difficulties. In the end the peasant will go back to kitsch when he feels like looking at pictures, for he can enjoy kitsch without effort. The state is helpless in this matter and remains so as long as the problems of production have not been solved in a socialist sense. The same holds true, of course, for capitalist countries and makes all talk of art for the masses there nothing but demagogy.[5]

Where today a political regime establishes an official cultural policy, it is for the sake of demagogy. If kitsch is the official tendency of culture in Germany, Italy and Russia, it is not because their respective governments are controlled by philistines, but because kitsch is the culture of the masses in these countries, as it is everywhere else. The encouragement of kitsch is merely another of the inexpensive ways in which totalitarian regimes seek to ingratiate themselves with their subjects. Since these regimes cannot raise the cultural level of the masses—even if they wanted to—by anything short of a surrender to international socialism, they will flatter the masses by bringing all culture down to their level. It is for this reason that the avant-garde is outlawed, and not so much because a superior culture is inherently a more critical culture. (Whether or not the avant-garde could possibly flourish under a totalitarian regime is not pertinent to the question at this point.) As a matter of fact, the main trouble with avant-garde art and literature, from the point of view of fascists and Stalinists, is not that they are too critical, but that they are too "innocent," that it is too difficult to inject effective propaganda into them, that kitsch is more pliable to this end. Kitsch keeps a dictator in closer contact with the "soul" of the people. Should the official culture be one superior to the general mass-level, there would be a danger of isolation.

Nevertheless, if the masses were conceivably to ask for avant-garde art and literature, Hitler, Mussolini and Stalin would not hesitate long in attempting to satisfy such a demand. Hitler is a bitter enemy of the avant-garde, both on doctrinal and personal grounds, yet this did not prevent Goebbels in 1932-1933 from strenuously courting avant-garde artists and writers. When Gottfried Benn, an Expressionist poet, came over to the Nazis he was welcomed with a great fanfare, although at that very moment Hitler was denouncing Expressionism as *Kulturbolschewismus*. This was at a time when the Nazis felt that the prestige which the avant-garde enjoyed among the cultivated German public could be of advantage to them, and practical considerations of this nature, the Nazis being skillful politicians, have always taken precedence over Hitler's personal inclinations. Later the Nazis realized that it was more practical to accede to the wishes of the masses in matters of culture than to those of their paymasters; the latter, when it came to a question of preserving power, were as willing to sacrifice their culture as they were their moral principles; while the former, precisely because power was being withheld from them, had to be cozened in every other way possible. It was necessary to promote on a much more grandiose style than in the democracies the illusion that the masses actually rule. The literature and art they enjoy and understand were to be proclaimed the only true art and literature and any other kind was to be suppressed. Under these circumstances people like Gottfried Benn, no matter how ardently they support Hitler, become a liability; and we hear no more of them in Nazi Germany.

We can see then that although from one point of view the personal philistinism of Hitler and Stalin is not accidental to the political roles they play, from another point of view it is only an incidentally contributory factor in determining the cultural policies of their respective regimes. Their personal philistinism simply adds brutality and double-darkness to policies they would be forced to support anyhow by the pressure of all their other policies—even were they, personally, devotees of avant-garde culture. What the acceptance of the isolation of the Russian Revolution forces Stalin to do, Hitler is compelled to do by his acceptance of the contradictions of capitalism and his efforts to freeze them. As for Mussolini—his case is a perfect example of the *disponibilité* of a realist in these matters. For years he bent a benevolent eye on the Futurists and built modernistic railroad stations and government-owned apartment houses. One can still see in the suburbs of Rome more modernistic apartments than almost anywhere else in the world. Perhaps Fascism wanted to show its up-to-dateness, to conceal the fact that it was a retrogression; perhaps it wanted to conform to the tastes of the wealthy elite it served. At any rate Mussolini seems to have realized lately that it would be more useful to him to please the cultural tastes of the Italian masses than those of their masters. The masses must be provided with objects of admiration and wonder; the latter can dispense with them. And so we find Mussolini announcing a "new Imperial style." Marinetti, Chirico, *et al.,* are sent into the outer darkness, and the new railroad station in Rome will not be modernistic. That Mussolini was late in coming to this only illustrates again the relative hesitancy with which Italian Fascism has drawn the necessary implications of its role.

Capitalism in decline finds that whatever of quality it is still capable of producing becomes almost invariably a threat to its own existence. Advances in culture, no less than advances in science and industry, corrode the very society under whose aegis they are made possible. Here, as in every other question today, it becomes necessary to quote Marx word for word. Today we no longer look toward socialism for a new culture—as inevitably as one will appear, once we do have socialism. Today we look to socialism *simply* for the preservation of whatever living culture we have right now.

NOTES

1. The example of music, which has long been an abstract art, and which avant-garde poetry has tried so much to emulate, is interesting. Music, Aris-

totle said curiously enough, is the most imitative and vivid of all arts because it imitates its original—the state of the soul—with the greatest immediacy. Today this strikes us as the exact opposite of the truth, because no art seems to us to have less reference to something outside itself than music. However, aside from the fact that in a sense Aristotle may still be right, it must be explained that ancient Greek music was closely associated with poetry, and depended upon its character as an accessory to verse to make its imitative meaning clear. Plato, speaking of music, says: "For when there are no words, it is very difficult to recognize the meaning of the harmony and rhythm, or to see that any worthy object is imitated by them." As far as we know, all music originally served such an accessory function. Once, however, it was abandoned, music was forced to withdraw into itself to find a constraint or original. This is found in the various means of its own composition and performance.

2. I owe this formulation to a remark made by Hans Hofmann, the art teacher, in one of his lectures. From the point of view of this formulation, Surrealism in plastic art is a reactionary tendency which is attempting to restore "outside" subject matter. The chief concern of a painter like Dali is to represent the processes and concepts of his consciousness, not the processes of his medium.

3. See Valéry's remarks about his own poetry.

4. T. S. Eliot said something to the same effect in accounting for the shortcomings of English Romantic poetry. Indeed the Romantics can be considered the original sinners whose guilt kitsch inherited. They showed kitsch how. What does Keats write about mainly, if not the effect of poetry upon himself?

5. It will be objected that such art for the masses as folk art was developed under rudimentary conditions of production—and that a good deal of folk art is on a high level. Yes, it is—but folk art is not Athene, and it's Athene whom we want: formal culture with its infinity of aspects, its luxuriance, its large comprehension. Besides, we are now told that most of what we consider good in folk culture is the static survival of dead formal, aristocratic, cultures. Our old English ballads, for instance, were not created by the "folk," but by the post-feudal squirearchy of the English countryside, to survive in the mouths of the folk long after those for whom the ballads were composed had gone on to other forms of literature. Unfortunately, until the machine-age, culture was the exclusive prerogative of a society that lived by the labor of serfs or slaves. They were the real symbols of culture. For one man to spend time and energy creating or listening to poetry meant that another man had to produce enough to keep himself alive and the former in comfort. In Africa today we find that the culture of slave-owning tribes is generally much superior to that of the tribes that possess no slaves.

Kikuchi Kan

THE MADMAN ON THE ROOF

Characters

KATSUSHIMA YOSHITARO, the madman, twenty-four years of age
KATSUSHIMA SUEJIRO, his brother, a seventeen-year-old high school student.
KATSUSHIMA GISUKE, their father
KATSUSHIMA OYOSHI, their mother
TOSAKU, a neighbor
KICHIJI, a manservant, twenty years of age
A PRIESTESS, about fifty years of age
PLACE: A small island in the Inland Sea
TIME: 1900

The stage setting represents the backyard of the Katsushimas, who are the richest family on the island. A bamboo fence prevents one from seeing more of the house than the high roof, which stands out sharply against the rich greenish sky of the southern island summer. At the left of the stage one can catch a glimpse of the sea shining in the sunlight.

Yoshitaro, the elder son of the family, is sitting astride the ridge of the roof, and is looking out over the sea.

GISUKE (*speaking from within the house*): Yoshi is sitting on the roof again. He'll get a sunstroke—the sun's so terribly hot. (*Coming out.*) Kichiji!—Where is Kichiji?

KICHIJI (*appearing from the right*): Yes! What do you want?

GISUKE: Bring Yoshitaro down. He has no hat on, up there in the hot sun. He'll get a sunstroke. How did he get up there, anyway? From the barn? Didn't you put wires around the barn roof as I told you to the other day?

KICHIJI: Yes, I did exactly as you told me.

GISUKE (*coming through the gate to the center of the stage, and looking up to the roof*): I don't see how he can stand it, sitting on that hot slate roof. (*He calls.*) Yoshitaro! You'd better come down. If you stay up there you'll get a sunstroke, and maybe die.

KICHIJI: Young master! Come on down. You'll get sick if you stay there.

GISUKE: Yoshi! Come down quick! What are you doing up there, anyway? Come down, I say! (*He calls loudly.*) Yoshi!

YOSHITARO (*indifferently*): Wha-a-at?

GISUKE: No "whats"! Come down right away. If you don't come down, I'll get after you with a stick.

YOSHITARO (*protesting like a spoiled child*): No, I don't want to. There's something wonderful. The priest of the god Kompira is dancing in the clouds. Dancing with an angel in pink robes. They're calling to me to come (*Crying out ecstatically.*) Wait! I'm coming!

GISUKE: If you talk like that you'll fall, just as you did once before. You're already crippled and insane—what will you do next to worry your parents? Come down, you fool!

KICHIJI: Master, don't get so angry. The young master will not obey you. You should get some fried bean cake; when he sees it he will come down, because he likes it.

GISUKE: No, you had better get the stick after him. Don't be afraid to give him a good shaking-up.

KICHIJI: That's too cruel. The young master doesn't understand anything. He's under the influence of evil spirits.

GISUKE: We may have to put bamboo guards on the roof to keep him down from there.

KICHIJI: Whatever you do won't keep him down. Why, he climbed the roof of the Honzen Temple without even a ladder; a low roof like this one is the easiest thing in the world for him. I tell you, it's the evil spirits that make him climb. Nothing can stop him.

GISUKE: You may be right, but he worries me to death. If we could only keep him in the house it wouldn't be so bad, even though he is crazy; but he's always climbing up to high places. Suejiro says that everybody as far as Takamatsu knows about Yoshitaro the Madman.

KICHIJI: People on the island all say he's under the influence of a fox-spirit, but I don't believe that. I never heard of a fox climbing trees.

GISUKE: You're right. I think I know the real reason. About the time Yoshitaro was born, I bought a very expensive imported rifle, and I shot every monkey on the island. I believe a monkey-spirit is now working in him.

KICHIJI: That's just what I think. Otherwise, how could he climb trees so well? He can climb anything without a ladder. Even Saku, who's a professional climber, admits that he's no match for Yoshitaro.

GISUKE (*with a bitter laugh*): Don't joke about it! It's no laughing matter, having a son who is always climbing on the roof. (*Calling again.*) Yoshitaro, come down! Yoshitaro!—When he's up there on the roof, he doesn't hear me at all—he's so engrossed. I cut down all the trees around the house so he couldn't climb them, but there's nothing I can do about the roof.

KICHIJI: When I was a boy I remember there was a gingko tree in front of the gate.

GISUKE: Yes, that was one of the biggest trees on the island. One day Yoshitaro climbed clear to the top. He sat out on a branch, at least ninety feet above the ground, dreaming away as usual. My wife and I never expected him to get down alive, but after a while, down he slid. We were all too astonished to speak.

KICHIJI: That was certainly a miracle.

GISUKE: That's why I say it's a monkey-spirit that's working in him. (*He calls again.*) Yoshi! Come down! (*Dropping his voice.*) Kichiji, you'd better go up and fetch him.

KICHIJI: But when anyone else climbs up there, the young master gets angry.

GISUKE: Never mind his getting angry. Pull him down.

KICHIJI: Yes, Master.

(*Kichiji goes out after the ladder. Tosaku, the neighbor enters.*)

TOSAKU: Good day, sir.

GISUKE: Good day. Fine weather. Catch anything with the nets you put out yesterday?

TOSAKU: No, not much. The season's over.

GISUKE: Maybe it *is* too late now.

TOSAKU (*looking up at Yoshitaro*): Your son's on the roof again.

GISUKE: Yes, as usual. I don't like it, but when I keep him locked in a room he's like a fish out of water. Then, when I take pity on him and let him out, back he goes up on the roof.

TOSAKU: But after all, he doesn't bother anybody.

GISUKE: He bothers us. We feel so ashamed when he climbs up there and shouts.

TOSAKU: But your younger son, Suejiro, has a fine record at school. That must be some consolation for you.

GISUKE: Yes, he's a good student, and that is a consolation to me. If both of them were crazy, I don't know how I could go on living.

TOSAKU: By the way, a Priestess has just come to the island. How would you like to have her pray for your son?—That's really what I came to see you about.

GISUKE: We've tried prayers before, but it's never done any good.

TOSAKU: This Priestess believes in the god Kompira. She works all kinds of miracles. People say the god inspires her, and that's why her prayers have more effect than those of ordinary priests. Why don't you try her once?

GISUKE: Well, we might. How much does she charge?

TOSAKU: She won't take any money unless the patient is cured. If he is cured, you pay her whatever you feel like.

GISUKE: Suejiro says he doesn't believe in prayers. . . . But there's no harm in letting her try.

(*Kichiji enters carrying the ladder and disappears behind the fence.*)

TOSAKU: I'll go and bring her here. In the meantime you get your son down off the roof.

GISUKE: Thanks for your trouble. (*After seeing that Tosaku has gone, he calls again.*) Yoshi! Be a good boy and come down.

KICHIJI (*who is up on the roof by this time*): Now then, young master, come down with me. If you stay up here any longer you'll have a fever tonight.

YOSHITARO (*drawing away from Kichiji as a Buddhist might from a heathen*): Don't touch me! The angels are beckoning to me. You're not supposed to come here. What do you want?

KICHIJI: Don't talk nonsense! Please come down.

YOSHITARO: If you touch me the demons will tear you apart.

(*Kichiji hurriedly catches Yoshitaro by the shoulder and pulls him to the ladder. Yoshitaro suddenly becomes submissive.*)

KICHIJI: Don't make any trouble now. If you do you'll fall and hurt yourself.

GISUKE: Be careful!

(*Yoshitaro comes down to the center of the stage, followed by Kichiji. Yoshitaro is lame in his right leg.*)

GISUKE (*calling*): Oyoshi! Come out here a minute.

OYOSHI (*from within*): What is it?

GISUKE: I've sent for a Priestess.

OYOSHI (*coming out*): That may help. You never can tell what will.

GISUKE: Yoshitaro says he talks with the god Kompira. Well, this Priestess is a follower of Kompira, so she ought to be able to help him.

YOSHITARO (*looking uneasy*): Father! Why did you bring me down? There was a beautiful cloud of five colors rolling down to fetch me.

GISUKE: Idiot! Once before you said there was a five-colored cloud, and you jumped off the roof. That's the way you became a cripple. A Priestess of the god Kompira is coming here today to drive the evil spirit out of you, so don't you go back up on the roof.

(*Tosaku enters, leading the Priestess. She has a crafty face.*)

TOSAKU: This is the Priestess I spoke to you about.

GISUKE: Ah, good afternoon. I'm glad you've come—this boy is really a disgrace to the whole family.

PRIESTESS (*casually*): You needn't worry any more about him. I'll cure him at once with the god's help. (*Looking at Yoshitaro.*) This is the one?

GISUKE: Yes. He's twenty-four years old, and the only thing he can do is climb up to high places.

PRIESTESS: How long has he been this way?

GISUKE: Ever since he was born. Even when he was a baby, he wanted to be climbing. When he was four or five years old, he climbed onto the low shrine, then onto the high shrine of Buddha, and finally onto a very high shelf. When he was seven he began climbing trees. At fifteen he climbed to the tops of mountains and stayed there all day long. He says he talks with demons and with the gods. What do you think is the matter with him?

PRIESTESS: There's no doubt but that it's a fox-spirit. I will pray for him. (*Looking at Yoshitaro.*) Listen now! I am the messenger of the god Kompira. All that I say comes from the god.

YOSHITARO (*uneasily*): You say the god Kompira? Have you ever seen him?

PRIESTESS (*staring at him*): Don't say such sacrilegious things! The god cannot be seen.

YOSHITARO (*exultantly*): I have seen him many times! He's an old man with white robes and a golden crown. He's my best friend.

PRIESTESS (*taken aback at this assertion, and speaking to Gisuke*): This is a fox-spirit, all right, and a very extreme case. I will address the god.

(*She chants a prayer in a weird manner. Yoshitaro, held fast by Kichiji, watches the Priestess blankly. She works herself into a frenzy, and falls to the ground in a faint. Presently she rises to her feet and looks about her strangely.*)

PRIESTESS (*in a changed voice*): I am the god Kompira!

(*All except Yoshitaro fall to their knees with exclamations of reverence.*)

PRIESTESS (*with affected dignity*): The elder son of this family is under the influence of a fox-spirit. Hang him up on the branch of a tree and purify him with the smoke of green pine needles. If you fail to do what I say, you will all be punished!

(*She faints again. There are more exclamations of astonishment.*)

PRIESTESS (*rising and looking about her as though unconscious of what has taken place*): What has happened? Did the god speak?

GISUKE: It was a miracle.

PRIESTESS: You must do at once whatever the god told you, or you'll be punished. I warn you for your own sake.

GISUKE (*hesitating somewhat*): Kichiji, go and get some green pine needles.

OYOSHI: No! It's too cruel, even if it is the god's command.

PRIESTESS: He will not suffer, only the fox-spirit within him. The boy himself will not suffer at all. Hurry! (*Looking fixedly at Yoshitaro.*) Did you hear the god's command? He told the spirit to leave your body before it hurt.

YOSHITARO: That was not Kompira's voice. He wouldn't talk to a priestess like you.

PRIESTESS (*insulted*): I'll get even with you. Just wait! Don't talk back to the god like that, you horrid fox!

(*Kichiji enters with an armful of green pine boughs. Oyoshi is frightened.*)

PRIESTESS: Respect the god or be punished!

(*Gisuke and Kichiji reluctantly set fire to the pine needles, then bring Yoshitaro to the fire. He struggles against being held in the smoke.*)

YOSHITARO: Father! What are you doing to me? I don't like it! I don't like it!

PRIESTESS: That's not his own voice speaking. It's the fox within him. Only the fox is suffering.

OYOSHI: But it's cruel!

(*Gisuke and Kichiji attempt to press Yoshitaro's face into the smoke. Suddenly Suejiro's voice is heard calling within the house, and presently he appears. He stands amazed at the scene before him.*)

SUEJIRO: What's happening here? What's the smoke for?

YOSHITARO (*coughing from the smoke, and looking at his brother as at a savior*): Father and Kichiji are putting me in the smoke.

SUEJIRO (*angrily*): Father! What foolish thing are you doing now? Haven't I told you time and time again about this sort of business?

GISUKE: But the god inspired the miraculous Priestess . . .

SUEJIRO (*interrupting*): What nonsense is that? You do these insane things merely because he is so helpless.

(*With a contemptuous look at the Priestess he stamps the fire out.*)

PRIESTESS: Wait! That fire was made at the command of the god!

(*Suejiro sneeringly puts out the last spark.*)

GISUKE (*more courageously*): Suejiro, I have no education, and you have, so I am always willing to listen to you. But this fire was made at the god's command, and you shouldn't have stamped on it.

SUEJIRO: Smoke won't cure him. People will laugh at you if they hear you've been trying to drive out a fox. All the gods in the country together couldn't even cure a cold. This Priestess is a fraud. All she wants is the money.

GISUKE: But the doctors can't cure him.

SUEJIRO: If the doctors can't, nobody can. I've told you before that he doesn't suffer. If he did, we'd have to do something for him. But as long as he can climb up on the roof, he is happy. Nobody in the whole country is as happy as he is—perhaps nobody in the world. Besides, if you cure him now, what can he do? He's twenty-four years old and he knows nothing, not even the alphabet. He's had no practical experience. If he were cured, he would be conscious of being crippled, and he'se be the most miserable man alive. Is that what you want to see? It's all because you want to make him normal. But wouldn't it be foolish to become normal merely to suffer? (*Looking sidewise at the Priestess.*) Tosaku, if you brought her here, you had better take her away.

PRIESTESS (*angry and insulted*): You disbelieve the oracle of the god. You will be punished! (*She starts her chant as before. She faints, rises, and speaks in a changed voice.*) I am the great god Kompira! What the brother of the patient says springs from his own selfishness. He knows if his sick brother is cured, he'll get the family estate. Doubt not this oracle!

SUEJIRO (*excitedly knocking the Priestess down*): That's a damned lie, you old fool.

(*He kicks her.*)

PRIESTESS (*getting to her feet and resuming her ordinary voice*): You've hurt me! You savage!

SUEJIRO: You fraud! You swindler!

TOSAKU (*coming betwen them*): Wait, young man! Don't get in such a frenzy.

SUEJIRO (*still excited*): You liar! A woman like you can't understand brotherly love!

TOSAKU: We'll leave now. It was my mistake to have brought her.

GISUKE (*giving Tosaku some money*): I hope you'll excuse him. He's young and has such a temper.

PRIESTESS: You kicked me when I was inspired by the god. You'll be lucky to survive until tonight.

SUEJIRO: Liar!

OYOSHI (*soothing Suejiro*): Be still now. (*To the Priestess*): I'm sorry this has happened.

PRIESTESS (*leaving with Tosaku*): The foot you kicked me with will rot off!

(*The Priestess and Tosaku go out.*)

GISUKE (*to Suejiro*): Aren't you afraid of being punished for what you've done?

SUEJIRO: A god never inspires a woman like that old swindler. She lies about everything.

OYOSHI: I suspected her from the very first. She wouldn't do such cruel things if a real god inspired her.

GISUKE (*without any insistence*): Maybe so. But, Suejiro, your brother will be a burden to you all your life.

SUEJIRO: It will be no burden at all. When I become successful, I'll build a tower for him on top of a mountain.

GISUKE (*suddenly*): But where's Yoshitaro gone?

KICHIJI (*pointing at the roof*): He's up there.

GISUKE (*having to smile*): As usual.

(*During the preceding excitement, Yoshitaro has slipped away and climbed back up on the roof. The four persons below look at each other and smile.*)

SUEJIRO: A normal person would be angry with you for having put him in the smoke, but you see, he's forgotten everything. (*He calls.*) Yoshitaro!

YOSHITARO (*for all his madness there is affection for his brother*): Suejiro! I asked Kompira and he says he doesn't know her!

SUEJIRO (*smiling*): You're right. The god will inspire you, not a priestess like her.

(*Through a rift in the clouds, the golden light of the sunset strikes the roof.*)

SUEJIRO (*exclaiming*): What a beautiful sunset!

YOSHITARO (*his face lighted by the sun's reflection*): Suejiro, look! Can't you see a golden palace in that cloud over there? There! Can't you see? Just look! How beautiful!

SUEJIRO (*as he feels the sorrow of sanity*): Yes, I see. I see it, too. Wonderful.

YOSHITARO (*filled with joy*): There! I hear music coming from the palace. Flutes, what I love best of all. Isn't it beautiful?

(*The parents have gone into the house. The mad brother on the roof and the sane brother on the ground remain looking at the golden sunset.*)

TRANSLATED BY YOZAN T. IWASAKI AND GLENN HUGHES

LEND A MYTH TO GOD

Allen Tate

HART CRANE

The career of Hart Crane will be written by future critics as a chapter in the neo-symbolist movement.[1] An historical view of his poetry at this time would be misleading and incomplete. Like most poets of his age in America, Crane discovered Rimbaud through Eliot and the Imagists; it is certain that long before he had done any of his best work he had come to believe himself the spiritual heir of the French poet. He had an instinctive mastery of the fused metaphor of symbolism, but it is not likely that he ever knew more of the symbolist poets than he had got out of Pound's *Pavannes and Divisions*. Whether Crane's style is symbolistic, or should, in many instances, like the first six or seven stanzas of "The River," be called Elizabethan, is a question that need not concern us now.

Between "The Bridge" and "Une Saison d'Enfer" there is little essential affinity. Rimbaud achieved "disorder" out of implicit order, after a deliberate cultivation of "derangement," but in our age the disintegration of our intellectual systems is accomplished. With Crane the disorder is original and fundamental. That is the special quality of his mind that belongs peculiarly to our own time. His aesthetic problem, however, was more general; it was the historic problem of romanticism.

Harold Hart Crane, one of the great masters of the romantic movement, was born in Garrettsville, Ohio, on July 21, 1899. His birthplace is a small town near Cleveland, in the old Western Reserve, a region which, as distinguished from the lower portions of the state, where people from the Southern up-country settled, was populated largely by New England stock. He seems to have known little of his ancestry, but he frequently said that his maternal forebears had given Hartford, Connecticut, its name, and that they went "back to Stratford-on-Avon"—a fiction surely, but one that gave him distinct pleasure. His formal education was slight. After the third year at high school, when he was fifteen, it ended, and he worked in his father's candy factory in Cleveland, where the family had removed in his childhood. He repeatedly told me that money had been set aside for his education at college, but that it had been used for other purposes. With the instinct of genius he read the great poets, but he never acquired an objective mastery of any literature, or even of the history of his country—a defect of considerable interest in a poet whose most ambitious work is an American epic.

In any ordinary sense Crane was not an educated man; in many respects he was an ignorant man. There is already a Crane legend, like the Poe legend—it should be fostered because it will help to make his poetry generally known—and the scholars will decide it was a pity that so great a talent lacked early advantages. It is probable that he was incapable of the formal discipline of a classical education, and probable, too, that the eclectic education of his time would have scattered and killed his talent. His poetry not only has defects of the surface, it has a defect of vision; but its great and peculiar value cannot be separated from its limitations. Its qualities are bound up with a special focus of the intellect and sensibility, and it would be folly to wish that his mind had been better trained or differently organized.

The story of his suicide is well known. The information that I have seems authentic, but it is incomplete and subject to excessive interpretation. Toward the end of April, 1932, he embarked on the S.S. *Orizaba* bound from Vera Cruz to New York. On the night of April 26 he got into a brawl with some sailors; he was severely beaten and robbed. At noon the next day, the ship being in the Caribbean a few hours out of Havana, he rushed from his stateroom clad in pajamas and overcoat, walked through the smoking-room out onto the deck, and then the length of the ship to the stern. There without hesitation he made a perfect dive into the sea. It is said that a life-preserver was thrown to him; he either did not see it or did not want it. By the time the ship had turned back he had disappeared. Whether he forced himself down—for a moment he was seen swimming—or was seized by a shark, as the captain believed, cannot be known. After a search of thirty-five minutes his body was not found, and the *Orizaba* put back into her course.

In the summer of 1930 he had written to me that he feared his most ambitious work, *The Bridge,* was not quite perfectly "realized," that probably his soundest work was in the shorter pieces of *White Buildings,* but that his mind, being once committed to the larger undertaking, could never return to the lyrical and more limited form. He had an extraordinary insight into the foundations of his work, and I think this judgment of it will not be refuted.

From 1922 to 1928—after that year I saw him and heard from him irregularly until his death—I could observe the development of his style from poem to poem; and his letters—written always in a pure and lucid prose—provide a valuable commentary on his career. This is not the place to bring all this material together for judgment. As I look back upon his work and its relation to the life he lived, a general statement about it comes to my mind that may throw some light on the dissatisfaction that he felt with his career. It will be a judgment upon the life and works of a man whom I knew affectionately for ten years as a friend.

Suicide was the sole act of will left to him short of a profound alteration of his character. I think the evidence of this is the locked-in sensibility, the insulated egoism, of his poetry—a subject that I shall return to. The background of his death was dramatically perfect: a large portion of his finest imagery was of the sea, chiefly the Caribbean:

> O minstrel galleons of Carib fire,
> Bequeath us to no earthly shore until
> Is answered in the vortex of our grave
> The seal's wide spindrift gaze towards paradise.

His verse is full of splendid images of this order, a rich symbolism for an implicit pantheism that, whatever may be its intrinsic merit, he had the courage to vindicate with death in the end.

His pantheism was not passive and contemplative; it rose out of the collision between his own locked-in sensibility and the ordinary forms of experience. Every poem is a thrust of that sensibility into the world: his defect lay in his inability to face out the moral criticism implied in the failure to impose his will upon experience.

The Bridge is presumably an epic. How early he had conceived the idea of the poem and the leading symbolism, it is difficult to know; certainly as early as February, 1923. Up to that time, with the exception of "For the Marriage of Faustus and Helen" (1922), he had written only short poems, but most of them, "Praise for an Urn," "Black Tambourine," "Paraphrase," and "Emblems of Conduct,"[2] are among his finest work. It is a mistake then to suppose that all of *White Buildings* is early experimental writing; a large portion of that volume, and perhaps the least successful part of it, is made up of poems written after *The Bridge* was begun. "Praise for an Urn" was written in the spring of 1922—one of the finest elegies by an American poet—and although his later development gave us a poetry that the period would be much the less rich for not having, he never again had such perfect mastery of his subject—because he never again quite knew what his subject was.

Readers familiar with "For the Marriage of Faustus and Helen" admire it by passages, but the form of the poem, in its framework of symbol, is an abstraction empty of any knowable experience. The originality of the poem is in its rhythms, but it has the conventional diction that a young poet picks up in his first reading. Crane, I believe, felt that this was so; and he became so dissatisfied, not only with the style of the poem, which is heavily influenced by Eliot and Laforgue, but with the "literary" character of the symbolism, that he set about the greater task of writing *The Bridge*. He had looked upon his "Faustus and Helen" as an answer to the pessimism of the school of Eliot, and *The Bridge* was to be an even more complete answer.

There was a fundamental mistake in Crane's diagnosis of Eliot's problem. Eliot's "pessimism" grows out of an awareness of the decay of the individual consciousness and its fixed relations to the world; but Crane thought that it was due to something like pure "orneryness" an unwillingness "to share with us the breath released," the breath being a new kind of freedom that he identified emotionally with the age of the machine. This vagueness of purpose, in spite of the apparently concrete character of the Brooklyn Bridge, which became the symbol of his epic, he never succeeded in correcting. The "bridge" stands for no well-defined experience; it differs from the Helen and Faust symbols only in its unliterary origin. I think Crane was deceived by this difference, and by the fact that Brooklyn Bridge is "modern" and a fine piece of "mechanics." His more ambitious later project permitted him no greater mastery of formal structure than the more literary symbolism of his youth.

The fifteen parts of *The Bridge* taken as one poem suffer from the lack of a coherent structure, whether symbolic or narrative: the coherence of the work consists in the personal quality of the writing—in mood, feeling, and tone. In the best passages Crane has perfect mastery over the quality of his style; but the style lacks an objective pattern of ideas elaborate enough to carry it through an epic or heroic work. The single symbolic image, in which the whole poem centers, is at one moment the actual Brooklyn Bridge; at another, it is any bridge or "connection"; at still another, it is a philosophical pun and becomes the basis of a series of analogies.

In "Cape Hatteras," the aëroplane and Walt Whitman are analogous "bridges" to some transcendental truth. Because the idea is variously metaphor, symbol, and analogy, it tends to make the poem static. The poet takes it up, only to be forced to put it down again *when the poetic image of the moment is exhausted.* The idea does not, in short, fill the poet's mind; it is the starting point for a series of short flights, or inventions connected only in analogy—which explains the merely personal passages, which are obscure, and the lapses into sentimentality. For poetic sentimentality is emotion undisciplined by the structure of events or ideas of which it is ostensibly a part. The idea is not objective and articulate in itself; it lags after the poet's vision; it appears and disappears; and in the intervals Crane improvises, often beautifully, as in the flight of the aëroplane, sometimes badly, as in the passage on Whitman in the same poem.

In the great epic and philosophical works of the past, notably *The Divine Comedy,* the intellectual groundwork is not only simple philosophically; we not only know that the subject is personal salvation, just as we know that Crane's is the greatness of America: we are given also the complete articulation of the idea down to the slightest detail, and we are given it objectively apart from anything that the poet is going to say about it. When the poet extends his perception, there is a further extension of the groundwork ready to meet it and discipline it, and to compel the sensibility of the poet to stick to the subject. It is a game of chess; neither side can move without consulting the other. Crane's difficulty is that of modern poets generally: they play the game with half of the men, the men of sensibility, and because sensibility can make any move, the significance of all moves is obscure.

If we subtract from Crane's idea its periphery of sensation, we have left only the dead abstraction, the Greatness of America, which is capable of elucidation neither on the logical plane nor in terms of a generally known idea of America.

The theme of *The Bridge* is, in fact, an emotional oversimplification of a subject-matter that Crane did not, on the plane of narrative and idea, simplify at all. The poem is emotionally homogeneous and simple —it contains a single purpose; but because it is not structurally clarified it is emotionally confused. America stands for a passage into new truths. Is this the meaning of American history? The poet has every right to answer yes, and this he has done. But just what in America or about America stands for this? Which American history? The historical plot of the poem, which is the groundwork on which the symbolic bridge stands, is arbitrary and broken, where the poet would have gained an overwhelming advantage by choosing a single period or episode, a concrete event with all its dramatic causes, and by following it up minutely, and being bound to it. In short, he would have gained an advantage could he have found a subject to stick to.

Does American culture afford such a subject? It probably does not. After the seventeenth century the sophisticated history of the scholars came into fashion; our popular, legendary chronicles come down only from the remoter European past. It was a sound impulse on Crane's part to look for an American myth, some simple version of our past that lies near the center of the American consciousness; an heroic tale with just enough symbolism to give his mind both direction and play. The soundness of his purpose is witnessed also by the kind of history in the poem: it is inaccurate, and it will not at all satisfy the sticklers for historical fact. It is the history of the motion picture, of naïve patriotism. This is sound; for it ignores the scientific ideal of historical truth-in-itself, and looks for a cultural truth which might win the spontaneous allegiance of the people. It is on such simple integers of truth, not truth of fact but of religious necessity, that men unite. The American mind was formed by the eighteenth-century Enlightenment, which broke down the European "truths" and gave us a temper deeply hostile to the making of new religious truths of our own.

The impulse in *The Bridge* is religious, but the soundness of an impulse is no warrant that it will create a sound art form. The form depends on too many factors beyond the control of the poet. The age is scientific and pseudo-scientific, and our philosophy is Dewey's instrumentalism. And it is possibly this circumstance that has driven the religious attitude into a corner where it lacks the right instruments for its defense and growth, and where it is in a vast muddle about just what these instruments are. Perhaps this disunity of the intellect is responsible for Crane's unphilosophical belief that the poet, unaided and isolated from the people, can create a myth.

If anthropology has helped to destroy the credibility of myths, it has shown us how they rise: their growth is mysterious from the people as a whole. It is probable that no one man ever put myth into history. It is still a nice problem among higher critics, whether the authors of the Gospels were deliberate myth-makers, or whether their minds were simply constructed that way; but the evidence favors the latter. Crane was a myth-maker, and in an age favorable to myths he would have written a mythical poem in the act of writing an historical one.

It is difficult to agree with those critics who find his epic a single poem and as such an artistic success. It is a collection of lyrics, the best of which are not surpassed by anything in American literature. The writing is most distinguished when Crane is least philosophical, *when he writes from sensation.* "The River" has some blemishes towards the end, but by and large it is a masterpiece of order and style; it alone is enough to place Crane in the first rank of American poets, living or dead. Equally good but less ambitious are the "Proem: To Brooklyn Bridge," and "Harbor Dawn," and "The Dance" from the section called "Powhatan's Daughter."

These poems bear only the loosest relation to the symbolic demands of the theme; they contain allusions to the historical pattern or extend the slender structure of analogy running through the poem. They are primarily lyrical, and each has its complete form. The poem "Indiana," written presumably to complete the pattern of "Powhatan's Daughter," does not stand alone, and it is one of the most astonishing failures ever made by a poet of Crane's genius. "The Dance" gives us the American background for the coming white man, and "Indiana" carries the stream of history to the pioneer West. It is a nightmare of sentimentality. Crane is at his most "philosophical" in a theme in which he feels no poetic interest whatever.

The structural defect of *The Bridge* is due to this fundamental contradiction of purpose. In one of his best earlier poems, "The Wine Menagerie," he exclaims: "New thresholds, new anatomies!"—new sensation, but he could not subdue the new sensation to a symbolic form.

His pantheism is necessarily a philosophy of sensation without point of view. An epic is a judgment of human action, an implied evaluation of a civilization, a way of life. In *The Bridge* the civilization that contains the subway hell of the section called "The Tunnel" is the same civilization of the aëroplane that the poet apostrophizes in "Cape Hatteras": there is no reason why the subway should be a fitter symbol of damnation than the aëroplane: both were produced by the same mentality on the same moral plane. There is a concealed, meaningless analogy between, on the one hand, the height of the plane and the depth of the subway, and, on the other, "higher" and "lower" in the religious sense. At one moment Crane faces his predicament of blindness to any rational order of value, and knows that he is damned; but he cannot face it long, and he tries to rest secure upon the intensity of sensation.

To the vision of the abyss in "The Tunnel," a vision that Dante passed through midway of this mortal life, Crane had no alternative: when it became too harrowing he cried to his Pocahontas, a typically romantic and sentimental symbol:

> Lie to us—dance us back our tribal morn!

It is probably the perfect word of romanticism in this century. When Crane saw that his leading symbol, the bridge, would not hold all the material of his poem, he could not sustain it ironically, in the classical manner, by probing its defects; nor in the personal sections, like "Quaker Hill," does he include himself in his Leopardian denunciation of life. He is the blameless victim of a world whose impurity violates the moment of intensity, which would otherwise be enduring and perfect. He is betrayed, not by a defect of his own nature, but by the external world; he asks of nature, perfection—requiring only of himself, intensity. The persistent, and persistently defeated, pursuit of a natural absolute places Crane at the center of his age.

Alternately he asserts the symbol of the bridge and abandons it, because fundamentally he does not understand it. The idea of bridgeship is an elaborate blur leaving the inner structure of the poem confused.

Yet some of the best poetry of our generation is in *The Bridge.* Its inner confusion is a phase of the inner cross-purposes of the time. Crane was one of those men whom every age seems to select as the spokesmen of its spiritual life; they give the age away. The accidental features of their lives, their place in life, their very heredity, seem to fit them for their rôle; even their vices contribute to their preparation. Crane's biographer will have to study the early influences that confirmed him in narcissism, and thus made him typical of the rootless spiritual life of our time. The character formed by those influences represents an immense concentration, and becomes almost a symbol, of American life in this age.

Crane's poetry has incalculable moral value: it reveals our defects in their extremity. I have said that he knew little of the history of his country. It was not merely a defect of education, but a defect, in the spiritual sense, of the modern mind. Crane lacked the sort of indispensable understanding of his country that a New England farmer has who has never been out of his township. *The Bridge* attempts to include all American life, but it covers the ground with seven-league boots and, like a sightseer, sees nothing. With reference to its leading symbol, it has no subject-matter. The poem is the effort of a solipsistic sensibility to locate itself in the external world, to establish points of reference.

It seems to me that by testing out his capacity to construct a great objective piece of work, in which his definition of himself should have been articulated, he brought his work to an end. I think he knew that the structure of *The Bridge* was finally incoherent, and for that reason—as I have said—he could no longer believe even in his lyrical powers; he could not return to the early work and take it up where he had left off. Far from "refuting" Eliot, his whole career is a vindication of Eliot's major premise—that the integrity of the individual consciousness has broken down. Crane had, in his later work, no individual consciousness: the hard firm style of "Praise for an Urn," which is based upon a clear-cut perception of moral relations, and upon their ultimate inviolability, begins to disappear when the poet goes out into the world and finds that the simplicity of a child's world has no universal sanction. From then on, instead of the effort to define himself in the midst of almost overwhelming complications—a situation that might have produced a tragic poet —he falls back upon the intensity of consciousness, rather than the clarity, for his center of vision. And that is romanticism.

His world had no center, and the thrust into sensation is responsible for the fragmentary quality of his most ambitious work. This thrust took two directions—the blind assertion of the will, and the blind desire for self-destruction. The poet did not face his first problem, which is to define the limits of his personality and to objectify its moral implications in an appropriate symbolism. Crane could only assert a quality of will against the world, and at each successive failure of the will he turned upon himself. In the failure of understanding—and understanding, for Dante, was a way of love—the romantic modern poet of the age of science attempts to impose his will upon experience and to possess the world.

It is this impulse of the modern period that has given us the greatest romantic poetry: Crane instinctively continued the conception of the will that was the deliberate discovery of Rimbaud. A poetry of the will is a poetry of sensation, for the poet surrenders to his sensations of the object in his effort to identify himself with it, and to own it. Some of Crane's finest lyrics—those written in the period of *The Bridge*—carry the modern impulse as far as you will find it anywhere in the French romantics. "Lachrymae Christi" and "Passage," though on the surface made up of pure images without philosophical meaning of the explicit sort in *The Bridge,* are the lyrical equivalents of the epic: the same kind of sensibility is at work. The implicit grasp of his material that we find in "Praise for an Urn," the poet has exchanged for an external, random symbol of which there is no possibility of realization. *The Bridge* is an irrational symbol of the will, of conquest, of blind achievement in space; its obverse is "Passage," whose lack of external symbolism exhibits the poetry of the will on the plane of sensation; and this is the self-destructive return of the will upon itself.

Criticism may well set about isolating the principle upon which Crane's poetry is organized. Powerful verse overwhelms its admirers, and betrays them into more than technical imitation. That is one of the arguments of Platonism against literature; it is the immediate quality of an art rather than its whole significance that sets up schools and traditions. Crane not only ends the romantic era in his own person; he ends it logically and morally. Beyond Crane no future poet can go. (This does not mean that the romantic impulse may not rise and flourish again.) The finest passages in his work are single moments in the stream of sensation; beyond the moment he goes at his peril; for beyond it lies the discrepancy between the sensuous fact, the perception, and its organizing symbol—a discrepancy that plunges him into sentimentality and chaos. But the "bridge" is empty and static, it has no inherent content, and the poet's attribution to it of the qualities of his own moral predicament is arbitrary. That explains the fragmentary and often unintelligible framework of the poem. There was neither complete action nor ordered symbolism in terms of which the distinct moments of perception could be clarified.

This was partly the problem of Rimbaud. But Crane's problem was nearer to the problem of Keats, and *The Bridge* is a failure in the sense that "Hyperion" is a failure, and with comparable magnificence. Crane's problem, being farther removed from the epic tradition, was actually more difficult than Keats's and his treatment of it was doubtless the most satisfactory possible in our time. Beyond the quest of pure sensation and its ordering symbolism lies the total destruction of art. By attempting an extreme solution of the romantic problem Crane proved that it cannot be solved.

NOTES

1. This essay is composed of two papers written several years apart, the one in 1932, a few months after Crane's death, the other in 1937 as a review of Philip Horton's *Hart Crane: The Life of an American Poet.*

2. It is now known that this poem is an elaboration of a "sonnet" entitled "Conduct" by Samuel Greenberg. See *Poems* by Samuel Greenberg, edited by Harold Holden and Jack McManis (New York, 1947).

Hart Crane

THE BRIDGE

How many dawns, chill from his rippling rest
The seagull's wings shall dip and pivot him,
Shedding white rings of tumult, building high
Over the chained bay waters Liberty—

Then, with inviolate curve, forsake our eyes
As apparitional as sails that cross
Some page of figures to be filed away;
—Till elevators drop us from our day . . .

I think of cinemas, panoramic sleights
With multitudes bent toward some flashing scene
Never disclosed, but hastened to again,
Foretold to other eyes on the same screen;

And Thee, across the harbor, silver-paced
As though the sun took step of thee, yet left
Some motion ever unspent in thy stride,—
Implicitly thy freedom staying thee!

Out of some subway scuttle, cell or loft
A bedlamite speeds to thy parapets,
Tilting there momently, shrill shirt ballooning,
A jest falls from the speechless caravan.

Down Wall, from girder into street noon leaks,
A rip-tooth of the sky's acetylene;
All afternoon the cloud-flown derricks turn . . .
Thy cables breathe the North Atlantic still.

And obscure as that heaven of the Jews,
Thy guerdon . . . Accolade thou dost bestow
Of anonymity time cannot raise:
Vibrant reprieve and pardon thou dost show.

O harp and altar, of the fury fused,
(How could mere toil align thy choiring strings!)
Terrific threshold of the prophet's pledge,
Prayer of pariah, and the lover's cry,—

Again the traffic lights that skim thy swift
Unfractioned idiom, immaculate sigh of stars,
Beading thy path—condense eternity:
And we have seen night lifted in thine arms.

Under thy shadow by the piers I waited;
Only in darkness is thy shadow clear.
The City's fiery parcels all undone,
Already snow submerges an iron year . . .

O Sleepless as the river under thee,
Vaulting the sea, the prairies' dreaming sod,
Unto us lowliest sometime sweep, descend
And of the curveship lend a myth to God.

BOOK FOUR

SURVIVORS

Survival, if we may judge by what these gifted men say, has become a matter of courage and intelligence. We must find who we are and what we are doing, and then we must place our bets on our most intimate as well as our most objective discoveries. Survival is moral or it is nothing. When we bet in this game we bet everything we have.

Here again the variations on a theme include many kinds of men and women—philosophers, psychologists, novelists, poets, painters, architects, healers, theologians, visionaries. We see the problem of survival, the one that most directly affects each of us, with a prismatic eye.

If I were to try to put into a few words what this group wisdom means to me, I would say: I am alienated from myself, and I am also alienated from my people, when I am not true to the stern task that is imposed upon me along with the gift of life. As the recipient of more technological advantages than any of my ancestors, as a greater beneficiary of progress, I am exposed to greater temptations. I can yield to intellectual fashions, which one year see all my problems as political, next as religious, next as psychological, next as historical. I can surrender to fanatical specialists. I can also yield to a currently prevailing aestheticism-cum-affluence (or vice versa*) which would reduce everything to style.*

Or I can seek to survive as meaningfully as some of these men did. That is really what alienation is all about.

A NECROPHILOUS
AND SENSELESS CRY

Luis Portillo

UNAMUNO'S LAST LECTURE

'Unamuno died suddenly, as one who dies in war. Against whom? Perhaps against himself; and also, although many may not believe it, against the men who sold Spain and betrayed his people. Against the people itself? I have never believed that and never shall believe it.'—Antonio Machado, 'Notas de Actualidad', in the magazine *Madrid,* Valencia, February 1937.

'Some maintained, during those frantic days, their independence of mind. From the human point of view, it is a consolation; from the Spanish point of view, a hope.'—Manuel Azana, Prologue to *La Velada en Benicarlo,* Paris, May 1939.

The Ceremonial Hall in the University of Salamanca is a spacious chamber, used only on formal occasions, solemn, austere, the walls hung with tapestries. Through the huge windows enters a shimmering flood of iridescent light which deepens the amber glow of the century-old plinth stones.

This was the setting.

The play was enacted on 12 October 1936 when Spanish Fascism was in its first triumphant stage. The morning was half spent. The patriotic festival of the Hispanic Race was being celebrated.

There they were on the presidential dais: the purple calotte, the amethyst ring and the flashing pectoral cross of the Most Illustrious Doctor Plà y Daniel, Bishop of the Diocese; the lack-lustre robes of the Magistrates; the profuse glitter of military gold braid side by side with the crosses and medals exhibited on presumptuously bulging chests; the morning coat, set off by black satin lapels, of His Excellency the Civil Governor of the Province; and all these surrounded—was it to honour or to overwhelm?—the man whose pride in his incorruptible Spanish conscience was steadfast and straight: Miguel de Unamuno y Jugo, the Rector.

From the front wall, the allegorical picture of the Republic had gone, and there shone from under a canopy the Caudillo's effigy in plump insolence. To the left and right, on crimson-covered divans, the silk of the doctors' gowns and their mortar-boards with gay tassels in red, yellow, light blue and dark blue, symbolizing Law, Medicine, Letters and Science.

A few ladies were scattered among the learned men; in a prominent place, Doña Carmen Polo de Franco, the distinguished spouse of the Man of Providence.

From a packed audience which faced the dais of the elect, with its protective balustrade of dark polished wood, there rose the confused murmur of expectancy. At the far end of the long hall glinted the rounded brasses of a military band, ready to play the obligatory hymns.

The cermony began. Don Miguel opened it with the ritual formula, spoken in that unforgettable voice of his, thin and clear. Then Don Francisco Maldonado stepped onto the platform, short, fat, Professor of Literature and Salamancan landowner. With affected, baroque diction and vast erudition, he delivered a colourless and circumstantial address. At the end, he expressed his hope for a better future, with kindly and sincere emotion. He descended the steps among cheers and applause, bowed to the dais and returned to his seat. He was followed on the speaker's platform by Don José Maria Ramos Loscertales of Saragossa, tall and lean, with fluid gestures, flashing eyes, sober and precise of speech, his sensitive face in perpetual motion, expressing a subtle and enigmatic irony. He spoke of the mortal struggle raging at the time— yet another circumstantial speech. Its thesis: the energies of Spain were at white-heat in a crucible of passion—and like gold from the crucible, Spain would emerge in the end, purified and without stain, in her true colours which rejected the taints artificially imposed on her. Clamorous ovation.

And then rose General Millan Astray. With ostentatious humility, he preferred to speak from his own place. His appearance was impressive. The General is thin, of an emaciation which pretends to slimness. He has lost one eye and one arm. His face and his body bear the indelible tattoo of horrible scars. These savage mutilations and gashes evoke a sinister personality; his angry and rancorous bearing kills any compassion his mutilations might have inspired.

He had been the organizer of the *Tercio*, the Spanish Foreign Legion for operations in Africa; he had been the creator of an iron, inexorable discipline to which the reckless fugitives from other social disciplines submitted of their own free will. He had gained those wounds which to many seemed glorious, to some over-exploited, and to all horribly impressive, in those fantastic Moroccan campaigns which had been Spain's bitter nightmare under the regretted aegis of King Alfonso XIII, called 'The African' in his day. Yet the unquestionable nimbus which surrounded the figure of the General was due to the gruesome originality, to the mysterious paradox of his battlecry: *'Viva la Muerte!'*—'Long live Death!'

Barely had Millan Astray risen to his feet when his strident voice rang out, as though bursting from that heroic chest bedizened with a galaxy of crosses, the testimonials and rewards of gallantry.

First of all he said that more than one-half of all Spaniards were criminals, guilty of armed rebellion and high treason. To remove any ambiguity, he went on to explain that by these rebels and traitors he meant the citizens who were loyal to the Government.

In a sudden flash of intuition, a member of the audience was inspired so as to grasp the faultless logic of a slogan which common minds had thought the product of an epileptic brain. With fervour, he shouted: *'Viva, viva la Muerte!'*—'Long live Death!'

Impervious, the General continued his fiery speech:

'Catalonia and the Basque country—the Basque country and Catalonia —are two cancers in the body of the nation. Fascism, which is Spain's health-bringer, will know how to exterminate them both, cutting into the live, healthy flesh like a resolute surgeon free from false sentimentality. And since the healthy flesh is the soil, the diseased flesh the people who dwell on it, Fascism and the Army will eradicate the people and restore the soil to the sacred national realm . . .'

He made a pause and cast a despotic glance over the audience. And he saw that he held them in thrall, hypnotized to a man. Never had any of his harangues so subjugated the will of his listeners. Obviously, he was in his element . . . He had conquered the University! And carried away himself, he continued, blind to the subtle and withering smile of disdain on the lips of the Rector.

'Every Socialist, every Republican, every one of them without exception—and needless to say every Communist—is a rebel against the National Government which will very soon be recognized by the total-

itarian States who are aiding us, in spite of France—democratic France
—and perfidious England.

'And then, or even sooner, when Franco wants it, and with the help
of the gallant Moors who, though they wrecked my body only yesterday, today deserve the gratitude of my soul, for they are fighting for
Spain against the Spaniards . . . I mean, the bad Spaniards . . . because they are giving their lives in defence of Spain's sacred religion,
as is proved by their attending field mass, escorting the Caudillo and
pinning holy medallions and Sacred Hearts to their burnous . . .'

The General lost himself in the maze of his own vehement outburst.
He hesitated, irritated and defiant at the same time. In these straits, an
enthusiastic Fascist came to his rescue and shouted:

'*Arriba España!*'

The crowd bowed their heads in resignation. The man went on,
undaunted:

'Spain!'[1]

Mechanically, the crowd responded: 'One!'

'Spain!' he repeated.

'Great!' chorused the obedient public.

'Spain!' the Blue Shirt insisted, implacably.

'Free!' they all replied, cowed.

There was an obvious lack of warmth and listlessness in these artificially
produced responses. Several Blue Shirts rose to their feet as though
pushed by invisible springs, and raised their right arms stiffly in the
Roman salute. And they hailed the sepia-coloured photograph on the
front wall:

'Franco!'

The public rose reluctantly and chanted parrot-like:

'Franco! Franco! Franco!'

But Franco's image did not stir. Neither did the Rector.

Don Miguel did not rise to his feet. And the public fell silent and sat
down again.

All eyes were fastened in tense anxiety on the noble head, on the pale,
serene brow framed by snow-white hair. The uncertain expression of
his eyes was hidden by the glitter of his spectacles.

Between the fine curve of his nose and the silver of his Quixote-like
beard, his mouth was twisted in a bitter grimace of undisguised contempt. People began to grow uneasy. A few suddenly felt a recrudescence
of their old rancorous abhorrence. Some admired the serene fearlessness of the Master and feared for his safety. The majority were gripped
by the voluptuous thrill of imminent tragedy.

At last, Don Miguel rose slowly. The silence was an enormous void.
Into this void, Don Miguel began to pour the stream of his speech, as

though savouring each measured word. This is the essence of what he said:

'All of you are hanging on my words. You all know me, and are aware that I am unable to remain silent. I have not learnt to do so in seventy-three years of my life. And now I do not wish to learn it any more. At times, to be silent is to lie. For silence can be interpreted as acquiescence. I could not survive a divorce between my conscience and my word, always well-mated partners.

'I will be brief. Truth is most true when naked free of embellishments and verbiage.

'I want to comment on the speech—to give it that name—of General Millan Astray who is here among us.'

The General stiffened provocatively.

'Let us waive the personal affront implied in the sudden outburst of vituperation against Basques and Catalans in general. I was born in Bilbao, in the midst of the bombardments of the Second Carlist War. Later, I wedded myself to this city of Salamanca which I love deeply, yet never forgetting my native town. The Bishop, whether he likes it or not, is a Catalan from Barcelona.'

He made a pause. Faces had grown pale. The short silence was tense and dramatic. Expectation neared its peak.

'Just now, I heard a necrophilous and senseless cry: "Long live Death!" To me it sounds the equivalent of *"Muera la Vida!"*—"To Death with Life!" And I, who have spent my life shaping paradoxes which aroused the uncomprehending anger of the others, I must tell you, as an expert authority, that this outlandish paradox is repellent to me. Since it was proclaimed in homage to the last speaker, I can only explain it to myself by supposing that it was addressed to him, though in an excessively strange and tortuous form, as a testimonial to his being himself a symbol of death.

'And now, another matter. General Millan Astray is a cripple. Let it be said without any slighting undertone. He is a war invalid. So was Cervantes. But extremes do not make the rule: they escape it. Unfortunately, there are all too many cripples in Spain now. And soon, there will be even more of them if God does not come to our aid. It pains me to think that General Millan Astray should dictate the pattern of mass-psychology.

'That would be appalling. A cripple who lacks the spiritual greatness of a Cervantes—a man, not a superman, virile and complete, in spite of his mutilations—a cripple, I said, who lacks that loftiness of mind, is wont to seek ominous relief in seeing mutilation around him.'

His words rang out crystal clear. The heavy silence gave them resonance.

'General Millan Astray is not one of the select minds, even though he is unpopular, or rather, for that very reason. Because he *is* unpopular. General Millan Astray would like to create Spain anew—a negative creation—in his own image and likeness. And for that reason he wishes to see Spain crippled, as he unwittingly made clear.'

At this point General Millan Astray could stand it no longer and shouted wildly:

'*Muera la Inteligencia!*'—'To death with Intelligence!'

'No, long live intelligence! To death with bad intellectuals!' corrected Don José Maria Pemán, a journalist from Cadiz. A few voices seconded him, many hands were clenched to check an imprudent impulse to applaud the aged Rector. The Blue Shirts felt tempted to become violent, true to totalitarian procedure. But a most unusual realization of their numerical inferiority strangled this impulse at birth. Arguments flared up round the names of academicians who had disappeared or been shot. Irritated 'sh's' came from various sides. Some gowned figures had gathered round Don Miguel, some Blue Shirts round their vilified hero.

At last the clamour died down like the sound of surf on the beach, and the groups dispersed. Don Miguel again became visible to the assembly, very erect, his arms folded and his gaze fixed straight ahead, like the statue of a stoic. Once more his word dominated the hall.

'This is the temple of intellect. And I am its high priest. It is you who are profaning its sacred precincts.

'I have always, whatever the proverb may say, been a prophet in my own land. You will win, but you will not convince. You will win, because you possess more than enough brute force, but you will not convince, because to convince means to persuade. And in order to persuade you would need what you lack—reason and right in the struggle. I consider it futile to exhort you to think of Spain. I have finished.'

The controversies flamed up again, interrupted by sudden waves of unanimous silence.

Then Don Esteban Madruga, Professor of Common Law, a straightforward and truly good man, took Don Miguel by the arm, offered his other arm to Doña Carmen Polo de Franco, and led them out of the room. Unamuno walked with perfect dignity, pale and calm. Franco's wife was so stunned that she walked like an automaton.

The Junta in Burgos was consulted. Franco's orders came: they were inexorable. If the offence was considered grave enough, the Rector of Salamanca was to be executed without delay. The offence was indeed considered to be so, but somebody who was better advised realized that such an act would fatally injure the prestige of the nascent 'Movement of Salvation'. It was therefore never carried out.

Don Miguel retired to his home. His house was kept surrounded by the police.

And shortly afterwards, thus guarded, Miguel de Unamuno died suddenly on the last day of 1936, the victim of a stroke of the brain, achieving lasting peace.

NOTE

1. *España Una, Grande y Libre*—'Spain One, Great and Free'—is the obligatory Falangist slogan which is converted on all solemn occasions into chorused responses to a leading voice, as in the following scene.

Miguel de Unamuno

TRAGIC SENSE OF LIFE

Parce unicæ spes totius orbis.—TERTULLIANUS, Adversus Marcionem, 5.

IN THE DEPTHS OF THE ABYSS

We have seen that the vital longing for human immortality finds no consolation in reason and that reason leaves us without incentive or consolation in life and life itself without real finalty. But here, in the depths of the abyss, the despair of the heart and of the will and the scepticism of reason meet face to face and embrace like brothers. And we shall see it is from this embrace, a tragic—that is to say, an intimately loving—embrace, that the wellspring of life will flow, a life serious and terrible. Scepticism, uncertainty—the position to which reason, by practising its analysis upon itself, upon its own validity, at last arrives— is the foundation upon which the heart's despair must build up its hope.

Disillusioned, we had to abandon the position of those who seek to give consolation the force of rational and logical truth, pretending to prove the rationality, or at any rate the non-irrationality, of consolation; and we had to abandon likewise the position of those who seek to give rational truth the force of consolation and of a motive for life. Neither the one nor the other of these positions satisfied us. The one is at variance with our reason, the other with our feeling. These two powers can never conclude peace and we must needs live by their war. We must make of this war, of war itself, the very condition of our spiritual life.

Neither does this high debate admit of that indecent and repugnant expedient which the more or less parliamentary type of politician has devised and dubbed "a formula of agreement," the property of which is to render it impossible for either side to claim to be victorious. There is no place here for a time-serving compromise. Perhaps a degenerate and cowardly reason might bring itself to propose some such formula of agreement, for in truth reason lives by formulas; but life, which cannot be formulated, life which lives and seeks to live for ever, does not submit to formulas. Its sole formula is: all or nothing. Feeling does not compound its differences with middle terms.

Initium sapientiæ timor Domini, it is said, meaning perhaps *timor mortis,* or it may be, *timor vitæ,* which is the same thing. Always it comes about that the beginning of wisdom is a fear.

Is it true to say of this saving scepticism which I am now going to discuss, that it is doubt? It is doubt, yes, but it is much more than doubt.

Doubt is commonly something very cold, of very little vitalizing force, and above all something rather artificial, especially since Descartes degraded it to the function of a method. The conflict between reason and life is something more than a doubt. For doubt is easily resolved into a comic element.

The methodical doubt of Descartes is a comic doubt, a doubt purely theoretical and provisional—that is to say, the doubt of a man who acts as if he doubted without really doubting. And because it was a stove-excogitated doubt, the man who deduced that he existed from the fact that he thought did not approve of "those turbulent (*brouillonnes*) and restless persons who, being called neither by birth nor by fortune to the management of public affairs, are perpetually devising some new reformation," and he was pained by the suspicion that there might be something of this kind in his own writings. No, he, Descartes, proposed only to "reform his own thoughts and to build upon ground that was wholly his." And he resolved not to accept anything as true when he did not recognize it clearly to be so, and to make a clean sweep of all prejudices and received ideas, to the end that he might construct his intellectual habitation anew. But "as it is not enough, before beginning to rebuild one's dwellinghouse, to pull it down and to furnish materials and architects, or to study architecture oneself . . . but it is also necessary to be provided with some other wherein to lodge conveniently while the work is in progress," he framed for himself a provisional ethic—*une morale de provision*—the first law of which was to observe the customs of his country and to keep always to the religion in which, by the grace of God, he had been instructed from his infancy, governing himself in all things according to the most moderate opinions. Yes, exactly, a provisonal religion and even a provisional God! And he chose the most moderate opinions "because these are always the most convenient for practice." But it is best to proceed no further.

This methodical or theoretical Cartesian doubt, this philosophical doubt excogitated in a stove, is not the doubt, is not the scepticism, is not the incertitude, that I am talking about here. No! This other doubt is a passionate doubt, it is the eternal conflict between reason and feeling, science and life, logic and biotic. For science destroys the concept of personality by reducing it to a complex in continual flux from moment to moment—that is to say, it destroys the very foundation of the spiritual and emotional life, which ranges itself unyieldingly against reason.

And this doubt cannot avail itself of any provisional ethic, but has to found its ethic, as we shall see, on the conflict itself, an ethic of battle, and itself has to serve as the foundation of religion. And it inhabits a house which is continually being demolished and which continually it has to rebuild. Without ceasing the will, I mean the will never to die, the spirit of unsubmissiveness to death, labours to build up the house of life, and without ceasing the keen blasts and stormy assaults of reason beat it down.

And more than this, in the concrete vital problem that concerns us, reason takes up no position whatever. In truth, it does something worse than deny the immortality of the soul—for that at any rate would be one solution—it refuses even to recognize the problem as our vital desire presents it to us. In the rational and logical sense of the term problem, there is no such problem. This question of the immortality of the soul, of the persistence of the individual consciousness, is not rational, it falls outside reason. As a problem, and whatever solution it may receive, it is irrational. Rationally even the very propounding of the problem lacks sense. The immortality of the soul is as unconceivable as, in all strictness, is its absolute mortality. For the purpose of explaining the world and existence—and such is the task of reason—it is not necessary that we should suppose that our soul is either mortal or immortal. The mere enunciation of the problem is, therefore, an irrationality.

Let us hear what our brother Kierkegaard has to say. "The danger of abstract thought is seen precisely in respect of the problem of existence, the difficulty of which it solves by going round it, afterwards boasting that it has completely explained it. It explains immortality in general, and it does so in a remarkable way by identifying it with eternity—with the eternity which is essentially the medium of thought. But with the immortality of each individually existing man, wherein precisely the difficulty lies, abstraction does not concern itself, is not interested in it. And yet the difficulty of existence lies just in the interest of the existing being—the man who exists is infinitely interested in existing. Abstract thought besteads immortality only in order that it may kill me as an individual being with an individual existence, and so make me immortal, pretty much in the same way as that famous physician in one of Holberg's plays, whose medicine, while it took away the patient's fever, took away his life at the same time. An abstract thinker, who refuses to disclose and admit the relation that exists between his abstract thought and the fact that he is an existing being, produces a comic impression upon us, however accomplished and distinguished he may be, for he runs the risk of ceasing to be a man. While an effective man, compounded of infinitude and finitude, owes his effectiveness precisely to the conjunction of these two elements and is infinitely interested in existing, an abstract thinker, similarly compounded, is a double being, a fantastical being, who lives in the pure being of abstraction, and at times presents the sorry figure of a professor who lays aside this abstract essence as he lays aside his walking-stick. When one reads the Life of a thinker of this kind—whose writings may be excellent—one trembles at the thought of what it is to be a

man. And when one reads in his writings that thinking and being are
the same thing, one thinks, remembering his life, that that being, which
is identical with thinking, is not precisely the same thing as being a
man" (*Afsluttende uvidenskabelig Efterskrift*, chap. iii.).

What intense passion—that is to say, what truth—there is in this
bitter invective against Hegel, prototype of the rationalist!—for the
rationalist takes away our fever by taking away our life, and promises
us, instead of a concrete, an abstract immortality, as if the hunger for
immortality that consumes us were an abstract and not a concrete hunger!

It may indeed be said that when once the dog is dead there is an
end to the rabies, and that after I have died I shall no more be tortured
by this rage of not dying, and that the fear of death, or more properly, of
nothingness, is an irrational fear, but . . . Yes, but . . . *Eppur si muove!*
And it will go on moving. For it is the source of all movement!

I doubt, however, whether our brother Kierkegaard is altogether in the
right, for this same abstract thinker, or thinker of abstractions, thinks
in order that he may exist, that he may not cease to exist, or thinks perhaps in order to forget that he will have to cease to exist. This is the
root of the passion for abstract thought. And possibly Hegel was as
infinitely interested as Kierkegaard in his own concrete, individual existence, although the professional decorum of the state-philosopher compelled him to conceal the fact.

Faith in immortality is irrational. And, notwithstanding, faith, life,
and reason have mutual need of one another. This vital longing is not
properly a problem, cannot assume a logical status, cannot be formulated
in propositions susceptible of rational discussion; but it announces itself
in us as hunger announces itself. Neither can the wolf that throws itself
with the fury of hunger upon its prey or with the fury of instinct upon
the she-wolf, enunciate its impulse rationally and as a logical problem.
Reason and faith are two enemies, neither of which can maintain itself
without the other. The irrational demands to be rationalized and reason
only can operate on the irrational. They are compelled to seek mutual
support and association. But association in struggle, for struggle is a
mode of association.

In the world of living beings the struggle for life establishes an association, and a very close one, not only between those who unite together
in combat against a common foe, but between the combatants themselves. And is there any possible association more intimate than that
uniting the animal that eats another and the animal that is eaten, between
the devourer and the devoured? And if this is clearly seen in the struggle
between individuals, it is still more evident in the struggle between
peoples. War has always been the most effective factor of progress, even

more than commerce. It is through war that conquerors and conquered learn to know each other and in consequence to love each other.

Christianity, the foolishness of the Cross, the irrational faith that Christ rose from the dead in order to raise us from the dead, was saved by the rationalistic Hellenic culture, and this in its turn was saved by Christianity. Without Christianity the Renaissance would have been impossible. Without the Gospel, without St. Paul, the peoples who had traversed the Middle Ages would have understood neither Plato nor Aristotle. A purely rationalist tradition is as impossible as a tradition purely religious. It is frequently disputed whether the Reformation was born as the child of the Renaissance or as a protest against it, and both propositions may be said to be true, for the son is always born as a protest against the father. It is also said that it was the revived Greek classics that led men like Erasmus back to St. Paul and to primitive Christianity, which is the most irrational form of Christianity; but it may be retorted that it was St. Paul, that it was the Christian irrationality underlying his Catholic theology, that led them back to the classics. "Christianity is what it has come to be," it has been said, "only through its alliance with antiquity, while with the Copts and Ethiopians it is but a kind of buffoonery. Islam developed under the influence of Persian and Greek culture, and under that of the Turks it has been transformed into a destructive barbarism."[1]

We have emerged from the Middle Ages, from the medieval faith as ardent as it was at heart despairing, and not without its inward and abysmal incertitudes, and we have entered upon the age of rationalism, likewise not without its incertitudes. Faith in reason is exposed to the same rational indefensibility as all other faith. And we may say with Robert Browning,

> All we have gained, then, by our unbelief
> Is a life of doubt diversified by faith
> For one of faith diversified by doubt.
> *(Bishop Blougram's Apology.)*

And if, as I have said, faith, life, can only sustain itself by leaning upon reason, which renders it transmissible—and above all transmissible from myself to myself—that is to say, reflective and conscious—it is none the less true that reason in its turn can only sustain itself by leaning upon faith, upon life, even if only upon faith in reason, faith in its availability for something more than mere knowing, faith in its availability for living. Nevertheless, neither is faith transmissible or rational, nor is reason vital.

The will and the intelligence have need of one another, and the reverse of that old aphorism, *nihil volitum quin præcognitum,* nothing is willed but what is previously known, is not so paradoxical as at first sight it may appear—*nihil cognitur quin prævolitum,* nothing is known but what is previously willed. Vinet, in his study of Cousin's book on the *Pensées* of Pascal, says: "The very knowledge of the mind as such has need of the heart. Without the desire to see there is no seeing; in a great materialization of life and of thought there is no believing in the things of the spirit." We shall see presently that to believe is, in the first instance, to wish to believe.

The will and the intelligence seek opposite ends: that we may absorb the world into ourselves, appropriate it to ourselves, is the aim of the will; that we may be absorbed into the world, that of the intelligence. Opposite ends?—are they not rather one and the same? No, they are not, although they may seem to be so. The intelligence is monist or pantheist, the will monotheist or egoist. The intelligence has no need of anything outside it to exercise itself upon; it builds its foundation with ideas themselves, while the will requires matter. To know something is to make this something that I know myself; but to avail myself of it, to dominate it, it has to remain distinct from myself.

Philosophy and religion are enemies, and because they are enemies they have need of one another. There is no religion without some philosophic basis, no philosophy without roots in religion. Each lives by its contrary. The history of philosophy is, strictly speaking, a history of religion. And the attacks which are directed against religion from a presumed scientific or philosophical point of view are merely attacks from another but opposing religious point of view. "The opposition which professedly exists between natural science and Christianity really exists between an impulse derived from natural religion blended with the scientific investigation of nature, and the validity of the Christian view of the world, which assures to spirit its pre-eminence over the entire world of nature," says Ritschl (*Rechtfertgung und Versöhnung,* iii. chap. iv. § 28). Now this instinct is the instinct of rationality itself. And the critical idealism of Kant is of religious origin, and it is in order to save religion that Kant enlarged the limits of reason after having in a certain sense dissolved it in scepticism. The system of antitheses, contradictions, and antinomies, upon which Hegel constructed his absolute idealism, has its root and germ in Kant himself, and this root is an irrational root.

We shall see later on, when we come to deal with faith, that faith is in its essence simply a matter of will, not of reason, that to believe is to wish to believe, and to believe in God is, before all and above all, to wish that there may be a God. In the same way, to believe in the immortality of the soul is to wish that the soul may be immortal, but to wish it with such force that this volition shall trample reason under foot and pass beyond it. But reason has its revenge.

The instinct of knowing and the instinct of living, or rather of surviving, come into conflict. In his work on the *Analysis of the Sensations and the Relation of the Physical to the Psychical,*[2] Dr. E. Mach tells us that not even the investigator, the savant, *der Forscher,* is exempted from taking his part in the struggle for existence, that even the roads of science lead mouth-wards, and that in the actual conditions of the society in which we live the pure instinct of knowing, *der reine Erkenntnisstrieb,* is still no more than an ideal. And so it always will be. *Primum vivere, deinde philosophari,* or perhaps better, *primum supervivere* or *superesse.*

Every position of permanent agreement or harmony between reason and life, between philosophy and religion, becomes impossible. And the tragic history of human thought is simply the history of a struggle between reason and life—reason bent on rationalizing life and forcing it to submit to the inevitable, to mortality; life bent on vitalizing reason and forcing it to serve as a support for its own vital desires. And this is the history of philosophy, inseparable from the history of religion.

Our sense of the world of objective reality is necessarily subjective, human, anthropomorphic. And vitalism will always rise up against rationalism; reason will always find itself confronted by will. Hence the rhythm of the history of philosophy and the alternation of periods in which life imposes itself, giving birth to spiritual forms, with those in which reason imposes itself, giving birth to materialist forms, although both of these classes of forms of belief may be disguised by other names. Neither reason nor life ever acknowledges itself vanquished. But we will return to this in the next chapter.

The vital consequence of rationalism would be suicide. Kierkegaard puts it very well: "The consequence for existence[3] of pure thought is suicide. . . . We do not praise suicide but passion. The thinker, on the contrary, is a curious animal—for a few spells during the day he is very intelligent, but, for the rest, he has nothing in common with man" (*Afsluttende uvidenskabelig Efterskrift,* chap. iii., § 1).

As the thinker, in spite of all, does not cease to be a man, he employs reason in the interests of life, whether he knows it or not. Life cheats reason and reason cheats life. Scholastic-Aristotelian philosophy fabricated in the interest of life a teleologic-evolutionist system, rational in appearance, which might serve as a support for our vital longing. This philosophy, the basis of the orthodox Christian supernaturalism, whether Catholic or Protestant, was, in its essence, merely a trick on the part of life to force reason to lend it its support. But reason supported it with such pressure that it ended by pulverizing it.

I have read that the ex-Carmelite, Hyacinthe Loyson, declared that he could present himself before God with tranquillity, for he was at peace with his conscience and with his reason. With what conscience? If with his religious conscience, then I do not understand. For it is a truth that no man can serve two masters, and least of all when, though they may sign truces and armistices and compromises, these two are enemies because of their conflicting interests.

To all this someone is sure to object that life ought to subject itself to reason, to which we will reply that nobody ought to do what he is unable to do, and life cannot subject itself to reason. "Ought, therefore can," some Kantian will retort. To which we shall demur: "Cannot, therefore ought not." And life cannot submit itself to reason, because the end of life is living and not understanding.

Again, there are those who talk of the religious duty of resignation to mortality. This is indeed the very summit of aberration and insincerity. But someone is sure to oppose the idea of veracity to that of sincerity. Granted, and yet the two may very well be reconciled. Veracity, the homage I owe to what I believe to be rational, to what logically we call truth, moves me to affirm, in this case, that the immortality of the individual soul is a contradiction in terms, that it is something, not only irrational, but contra-rational; but sincerity leads me to affirm also my refusal to resign myself to this previous affirmation and my protest against its validity. What I feel is a truth, at any rate as much a truth as what I see, touch, hear, or what is demonstrated to me—nay, I believe it is more of a truth—and sincerity obliges me not to hide what I feel.

And life, quick to defend itself, searches for the weak point in reason and finds it in scepticism, which it straightway fastens upon, seeking to save itself by means of this stranglehold. It needs the weakness of its adversary.

Nothing is sure. Everything is elusive and in the air. In an outburst of passion Lamennais exclaims: "But what! Shall we, losing all hope, shut our eyes and plunge into the voiceless depths of a universal scepticism? Shall we doubt that we think, that we feel, that we are? Nature does not allow it; she forces us to believe even when our reason is not convinced. Absolute certainty and absolute doubt are both alike forbidden to us. We hover in a vague mean between these two extremes, as between being and nothingness; for complete scepticism would be the extinction of the intelligence and the total death of man. But it is not given to man to annihilate himself; there is in him something which invincibly resists destruction, I know not what vital faith, indomitable even by his will. Whether he likes it or not, he must believe, because he must act, because he must preserve himself. His reason, if he listened only to that, teaching him to doubt everything, itself included, would reduce him to a state of absolute inaction; he would perish before even he had been able to prove to himself that he existed" (*Essai sur l'indifférence en matière de religion,* iiie partie, chap. lxvii.).

Reason, however, does not actually lead us to absolute scepticism. No! Reason does not lead me and cannot lead me to doubt that I exist. Whither reason does lead me is to vital scepticism, or more properly, to vital negation—not merely to doubt, but to deny, that my consciousness survives my death. Scepticism is produced by the clash between reason and desire. And from this clash, from this embrace between despair and scepticism, is born that holy, that sweet, that saving incertitude, which is our supreme consolation.

The absolute and complete certainty, on the one hand, that death is a complete, definite, irrevocable annihilation of personal consciousness, a certainty of the same order as the certainty that the three angles of a triangle are equal to two right angles, or, on the other hand, the absolute and complete certainty that our personal consciousness is prolonged beyond death in these present or in other conditions, and above all including in itself that strange and adventitious addition of eternal rewards and punishments—both of these certainties alike would make life impossible for us. In the most secret chamber of the spirit of him who believes himself convinced that death puts an end to his personal consciousness, his memory, for ever, and all unknown to him perhaps, there lurks a shadow, a vague shadow, a shadow of shadow, of uncertainty, and while he says within himself, "Well, let us live this life that passes away, for there is no other!" the silence of this secret chamber speaks to him and murmurs, "Who knows! . . ." He may not think he hears it, but he hears it nevertheless. And likewise in some secret place of the soul of the believer who most firmly holds the belief in a future life, there is a muffled voice, a voice of uncertainty, which whispers in the ear of his spirit, "Who knows! . . ." These voices are like the humming of a mosquito when the south-west wind roars through the trees in the wood; we cannot distinguish this faint humming, yet nevertheless, merged in the clamour of the storm, it reaches the ear. Otherwise, without this uncertainty, how could we live?

"Is there?" "Is there not?"—these are the bases of our inner life. There may be a rationalist who has never wavered in his conviction of the mortality of the soul, and there may be a vitalist who has never wavered in his faith in immortality; but at the most this would only prove that just as there are natural monstrosities, so there are those who are stupid as regards heart and feeling, however great their intelligence, and those who are stupid intellectually, however great their virtue. But, in normal cases, I cannot believe those who assure me that never, not in a fleeting moment, not in the hours of direst loneliness and grief, has this murmur of uncertainty breathed upon their consciousness. I do not understand those men who tell me that the prospect of the yonder side of death has never tormented them, that the thought of their own annihilation never

disquiets them. For my part I do not wish to make peace between my heart and my head, between my faith and my reason—I wish rather that there should be war between them!

In the ninth chapter of the Gospel according to Mark it is related how a man brought unto Jesus his son who was possessed by a dumb spirit, and wheresoever the spirit took him it tore him, causing him to foam and gnash his teeth and pine away, wherefore he sought to bring him to Jesus that he might cure him. And the Master, impatient of those who sought only for signs and wonders, exclaimed: "O faithless generation, how long shall I be with you? how long shall I suffer you? bring him unto me" (ver. 19), and they brought him unto him. And when the Master saw him wallowing on the ground, he asked his father how long it was ago since this had come unto him and the father replied that it was since he was a child. And Jesus said unto him: "If thou canst believe, all things are possible to him that believeth" (ver. 23). And then the father of the epileptic or demoniac uttered these pregnant and immortal words: "Lord, I believe; help thou mine unbelief!"—Πιστεύω, κύριε, βοήθει τῇ ἀπιστίᾳ μου (ver. 24).

"Lord, I believe; help thou mine unbelief!" A contradiction seemingly, for if he believes, if he trusts, how is it that he beseeches the Lord to help his lack of trust? Nevertheless, it is this contradiction that gives to the heart's cry of the father of the demoniac its most profound human value. His faith is a faith that is based upon incertitude. Because he believes— that is to say, because he wishes to believe, because he has need that his son should be cured—he beseeches the Lord to help his unbelief, his doubt that such a cure could be affected. Of such kind is human faith; of such kind was the heroic faith that Sancho Panza had in his master, the knight Don Quijote de la Mancha, as I think I have shown in my *Vida de Don Quijote y Sancho;* a faith based upon incertitude, upon doubt. Sancho Panza was indeed a man, a whole and a true man, and he was not stupid, for only if he had been stupid would he have believed, without a shadow of doubt, in the follies of his master. And his master himself did not believe in them without a shadow of doubt, for neither was Don Quijote, though mad, stupid. He was at heart a man of despair, as I think I have shown in my above-mentioned book. And because he was a man of an heroical despair, the hero of that inward and resigned despair, he stands as the eternal exemplar of every man whose soul is the battleground of reason and immortal desire. Our Lord Don Quijote is the prototype of the vitalist whose faith is based upon uncertainty, and Sancho is the prototype of the rationalist who doubts his own reason.

Tormented by torturing doubts, August Hermann Francke resolved to call upon God, a God in whom he did not believe, or rather in whom he believed that he did not believe, imploring Him to take pity upon him, upon the poor pietist Francke, if perchance He really existed.[4] And from a similar state of mind came the inspiration of the sonnet entitled "The Atheist's Prayer," which is included in my *Rosario de Sonetos Líricos,* and closes with these lines:

> *Sufro yo a tu costa,*
> *Dios no existiente, pues si tú existieras*
> *existiería yo también de veras.*[5]

Yes, if God the guarantor of our personal immortality existed, then should we ourselves really exist. And if He exists not, neither do we exist.

That terrible secret, that hidden will of God which, translated into the language of theology, is known as predestination, that idea which dictated to Luther his *servum arbitrium,* and which gives to Calvinism its tragic sense, that doubt of our own salvation, is in its essence nothing but uncertainty, and this uncertainty, allied with despair, forms the basis of faith. Faith, some say, consists in not thinking about it, in surrendering ourselves trustingly to the arms of God, the secrets of whose providence are inscrutable. Yes, but infidelity also consists in not thinking about it. This absurd faith, this faith that knows no shadow of uncertainty, this faith of the stupid coalheaver, joins hands with an absurd incredulity, the incredulity that knows no shadow of uncertainty, the incredulity of the intellectuals who are afflicted with affective stupidity in order that they may not think about it.

And what but uncertainty, doubt, the voice of reason, was that abyss, that terrible *gouffre,* before which Pascal trembled? And it was that which led him to pronounce his terrible sentence, *il faut s'abêtir*—need is that we become fools!

All Jansenism, the Catholic adaptation of Calvinism, bears the same impress. Port-Royal, which owed its existence to a Basque, the Abbé de Saint-Cyran, a man of the same race as Iñigo de Loyola and as he who writes these lines, always preserved deep down a sediment of religious despair, of the suicide of reason. Loyola also slew his reason in obedience.

Our affirmation is despair, our negation is despair, and from despair we abstain from affirming and denying. Note the greater part of our atheists and you will see that they are atheists from a kind of rage, rage at not being able to believe that there is a God. They are the personal enemies of God. They have invested nothingness with substance and personality, and their No-God is an Anti-God.

And concerning that abject and ignoble saying, "If there were not a God it would be necessary to invent Him," we shall say nothing. It is the expression of the unclean scepticism of those conservatives who look upon religion merely as a means of government and whose interest it is that in the other life there shall be a hell for those who oppose their worldly interests in this life. The repugnant and Sadducean phrase is worthy of the time-serving sceptic to whom it is attributed.

No, with all this the deep vital sense has nothing to do. It has nothing to do with a transcendental police regimen, or with securing order—and what an order!—upon earth by means of promises and threats of eternal rewards and punishments after death. All this belongs to a lower plane—that is to say, it is merely politics, or if you like, ethics. The vital sense has to do with living.

But it is in our endeavour to represent to ourselves what the life of the soul after death really means that uncertainty finds its surest foundation. This it is that most shakes our vital desire and most intensifies the dissolvent efficacy of reason. For even if by a mighty effort of faith we overcome that reason which tells and teaches us that the soul is only a function of the physical organism, it yet remains for our imagination to conceive an image of the immortal and eternal life of the soul. This conception involves us in contradictions and absurdities, and it may be that we shall arrive with Kierkegaard at the conclusion that if the mortality of the soul is terrible, not less terrible is its immortality.

But when we have overcome the first, the only real difficulty, when we have overcome the impediment of reason, when we have achieved the faith, however painful and involved in uncertainty it may be, that our personal consciousness shall continue after death, what difficulty, what impediment, lies in the way of our imagining to ourselves this persistence of self in harmony with our desire? Yes, we can imagine it as an eternal rejuvenescence, as an eternal growth of ourselves, and as a journeying towards God, towards the Universal Consciousness, without ever an arrival, we can imagine it as . . . But who shall put fetters upon the imagination, once it has broken the chain of the rational?

I know that all this is dull reading, tiresome, perhaps tedious, but it is all necessary. And I must repeat once again that we have nothing to do with a transcendental police system or with the conversion of God into a great Judge or Policeman—that is to say, we are not concerned with heaven or hell considered as buttresses to shore up our poor earthly mortality, nor are we concerned with anything egoistic or personal. It is not I myself alone, it is the whole human race that is involved, it is the ultimate finality of all our civilization. I am but one, but all men are I's.

Do you remember the end of that *Song of the Wild Cock* which Leopardi wrote in prose?—the despairing Leopardi, the victim of reason, who never succeeded in achieving belief. "A time will come," he says, "when this Universe and Nature itself will be extinguished. And just as of the grandest kingdoms and empires of mankind and the marvellous things achieved therein, very famous in their own time, no vestige or memory remains to-day, so, in like manner, of the entire world and of the vicissitudes and calamities of all created things there will remain not a single trace, but a naked silence and a most profound stillness will fill the immensity of space. And so before ever it has been uttered or understood, this admirable and fearful secret of universal existence will be obliterated and lost." And this they now describe by a scientific and very rationalistic term—namely, *entropia*. Very pretty, is it not? Spencer invented the notion of a primordial homogeneity, from which it is impossible to conceive how any heterogeneity could originate. Well now, this *entropia* is a kind of ultimate homogeneity, a state of perfect equilibrium. For a soul avid of life, it is the most like nothingness that the mind can conceive.

To this point, through a series of dolorous reflections, I have brought the reader who has had the patience to follow me, endeavouring always to do equal justice to the claims of reason and of feeling. I have not wished to keep silence on matters about which others are silent; I have sought to strip naked, not only my own soul, but the human soul, be its nature what it may, its destiny to disappear or not to disappear. And we have arrived at the bottom of the abyss, at the irreconcilable conflict between reason and vital feeling. And having arrived here, I have told you that it is necessary to accept the conflict as such and to live by it. Now it remains for me to explain to you how, according to my way of feeling, and even according to my way of thinking, this despair may be the basis of a vigorous life, of an efficacious activity, of an ethic, of an esthetic, of a religion and even of a logic. But in what follows there will be as much of imagination as of ratiocination, or rather, much more.

I do not wish to deceive anyone, or to offer as philosopohy what it may be is only poetry or phantasmagoria, in any case a kind of mythology. The divine Plato, after having discussed the immortality of the soul in his dialogue *Phædo* (an ideal—that is to say, a lying—immortality), embarked upon an interpretation of the myths which treat of the other life, remarking that it was also necessary to mythologize. Let us, then, mythologize.

He who looks for reasons, strictly so called, scientific arguments, technically logical reflections, may refuse to follow me further. Throughout the remainder of these reflections upon the tragic sense, I am going to fish for the attention of the reader with the naked, unbaited hook; whoever wishes to bite, let him bite, but I deceive no one. Only in the conclusion I hope to gather everything together and to show that this religious despair which I have been talking about, and which is nothing other than the tragic sense of life itself, is, though more or less hidden, the very foundation of the consciousness of civilized individuals and peoples to-day—that is to say, of those individuals and those peoples who do not suffer from stupidity of intellect or stupidity of feeling.

And this tragic sense is the spring of heroic achievements.

If in that which follows you shall meet with arbitrary apothegms, brusque transitions, inconsecutive statements, veritable somersaults of thought, do not cry out that you have been deceived. We are about to enter—if it be that you wish to accompany me—upon a field of contradictions between feeling and reasoning, and we shall have to avail ourselves of the one as well as of the other.

That which follows is not the outcome of reason but of life, although in order that I may transmit it to you I shall have to rationalize it after a fashion. The greater part of it can be reduced to no logical theory or system; but like that tremendous Yankee poet, Walt Whitman, "I charge that there be no theory or school founded out of me" (*Myself and Mine*).

Neither am I the only begetter of the fancies I am about to set forth. By no means. They have also been conceived by other men, if not precisely by other thinkers, who have preceded me in this vale of tears, and who have exhibited their life and given expression to it. Their life, I repeat, not their thought, save in so far as it was thought inspired by life, thought with a basis of irrationality.

Does this mean that in all that follows, in the efforts of the irrational to express itself, there is a total lack of rationality, of all objective value? No; the absolutely, the irrevocably irrational, is inexpressible, is intransmissible. But not the contra-rational. Perhaps there is no way of rationalizing the irrational; but there is a way of rationalizing the contra-rational, and that is by trying to explain it. Since only the rational is intelligible, really intelligible, and since the absurd, being devoid of sense, is condemned to be incommunicable, you will find that whenever we succeed in giving expression and intelligibility to anything apparently irrational or absurd we invariably resolve it into something rational, even though it be into the negation of that which we affirm.

The maddest dreams of the fancy have some ground of reason, and who knows if everything that the imagination of man can conceive either has not already happened, or is not now happening or will not happen some time, in some world or another? The possible combinations are perhaps infinite. It only remains to know whether all that is imaginable is possible.

It may also be said, and with justice, that much of what I am about to set forth is merely a repetition of ideas which have been expressed a hundred times before and a hundred time refuted; but the repetition of an idea really implies that its refutation has not been final. And as I do not pretend that the majority of these fancies are new, so neither do I pretend, obviously, that other voices before mine have not spoken to the winds the same laments. But when yet another voice echoes the same eternal lament it can only be inferred that the same grief still dwells in the heart.

And it comes not amiss to repeat yet once again the same eternal lamentations that were already old in the days of Job and Ecclesiastes, and even to repeat them in the same words, to the end that the devotees of progress may see that there is something that never dies. Whosoever repeats the "Vanity of vanities" of Ecclesiastes or the lamentations of Job, even though without changing a letter, having first experienced them in his soul, performs a work of admonition. Need is to repeat without ceasing the *memento mori*.

"But to what end?" you will ask. Even though it be only to the end that some people should be irritated and should see that these things are not dead and, so long as men exist, cannot die; to the end that they should be convinced that to-day, in the twentieth century, all the bygone centuries and all of them alive, are still subsisting. When a supposed error reappears, it must be, believe me, that it has not ceased to be true in part, just as when one who was dead reappears, it must be that he was not wholly dead.

Yes, I know well that others before me have felt what I feel and express; that many others feel it to-day, although they keep silence about it. Why do I not keep silence about it too? Well, for the very reason that most of those who feel it are silent about it; and yet, though they are silent, they obey in silence that inner voice. And I do not keep silence about it because it is for many the thing which must not be spoken, the abomination of abominations—*infandum*—and I believe that it is necessary now and again to speak the thing which must not be spoken. But if it leads to nothing? Even if it should lead only to irritating the devotees of progress, those who believe that truth is consolation, it would lead to not a little. To irritating them and making them say: Poor fellow! if he would only use his intelligence to better purpose! . . . Someone perhaps will add that I do not know what I say, to which I shall reply that perhaps he may be right—and being right is such a little thing!—but that I feel what I say and I know what I feel and that suffices me. And that it is better to be lacking in reason than to have too much of it.

And the reader who perseveres in reading me will also see how out of this abyss of despair hope may arise, and how this critical position may be the well-spring of human, profoundly human, action and effort, and of solidarity and even of progress. He will see its pragmatic justification. And he will see how, in order to work, and to work efficaciously and morally, there is no need of either of these two conflicting certainties, either that of faith or that of reason, and how still less is there any need—this never under any circumstances—to shirk the problem of the immortality of the soul, or to distort it idealistically—that is to say, hypocritically. The reader will see how this uncertainty, with the suffering that accompanies it, and the fruitless struggle to escape from it, may be and is a basis for action and morals.

And in the fact that it serves as a basis for action and morals, this feeling of uncertainty and the inward struggle between reason on the one hand and faith and the passionate longing for eternal life on the other, should find their justification in the eyes of the pragmatist. But it must be clearly stated that I do not adduce this practical consequence in order to justify the feeling, but merely because I encounter it in my inward experience. I neither desire to seek, nor ought I to seek, any justification for this state of inward struggle and uncertainty and longing; it is a fact and that suffices. And if anyone finding himself in this state, in the depth of the abyss, fails to find there motives for and incentives to life and action, and concludes by committing bodily or spiritual suicide, whether he kills himself or he abandons all co-operation with his fellows in human endeavour, it will not be I who will pass censure upon him. And apart from the fact that the evil consequences of a doctrine, or rather those which we call evil, only prove, I repeat, that the doctrine is disastrous for our desires, but not that it is false in itself, the consequences themselves depend not so much upon the doctrine as upon him who deduces them. The same principle may furnish one man with grounds for action and another man with grounds for abstaining from action, it may lead one man to direct his effort towards a certain end and another man towards a directly opposite end. For the truth is that our doctrines are usually only the justification *a posteriori* of our conduct, or else they are our way of trying to explain that conduct to ourselves.

Man, in effect, is unwilling to remain in ignorance of the motives of his own conduct. And just as a man who has been led to perform a certain action by hypnotic suggestion will afterwards invent reasons which would justify it and make it appear logical to himself and others, being unaware all the time of the real cause of his action, so every man—for since "life is a dream" every man is in a condition of hypnotism—seeks to find reasons for his conduct. And if the pieces on a chessboard were endowed with consciousness, they would probably have little difficulty in ascribing their moves to freewill—that is to say, they would claim for them a finalist rationality. And thus it comes about that every philosophic theory serves to explain and justify an ethic, a doctrine of conduct, which has its real origin in the inward moral feeling of the author of the theory. But he who harbours this feeling may possibly himself have no clear consciousness of its true reason or cause.

Consequently, if my reason, which is in a certain sense a part of the reason of all my brothers in humanity in time and space, teaches me this absolute scepticism in respect of what concerns my longing for never-ending life, I think that I can assume that my feeling of life, which is the essence of life itself, my vitality, my boundless appetite for living and my abhorrence of dying, my refusal to submit to death—that it is this which suggests to me the doctrines with which I try to counter-check the working of the reason. Have these doctrines an objective value? someone will ask me, and I shall answer that I do not understand what this objective value of a doctrine is. I will not say that the more or less poetical and unphilosophical doctrines that I am about to set forth are those which make me live; but I will venture to say that it is my longing to live and to live for ever that inspires these doctrines within me. And if by means of them I succeed in strengthening and sustaining this same longing in another, perhaps when it was all but dead, then I shall have performed a man's work and, above all, I shall have lived. In a word, be it with reason or without reason or against reason, I am resolved not to die. And if, when at last I die out, I die out altogether, then I shall not have died out of myself—that is, I shall not have yielded myself to death, but my human destiny will have killed me. Unless I come to lose my head, or rather my heart, I will not abdicate from life—life will be wrested from me.

To have recourse to those ambiguous words, "optimism" and "pessimism," does not assist us in any way, for frequently they express the very contrary of what those who use them mean to express. To ticket a doctrine with the label of pessimism is not to impugn its validity, and the so-called optimists are not the most efficient in action. I believe, on the contrary, that many of the greatest heroes, perhaps the greatest of all, have been men of despair and that by despair they have accomplished their mighty works. Apart from this, however, and accepting in all their ambiguity these denominations of optimism and pessimism, that there exists a certain transcendental pessimism which may be the begetter of a temporal and terrestrial optimism, is a matter that I propose to develop in the following part of this treatise.

Very different, well I know, is the attitude of our progressives, the partisans of "the central current of contemporary European thought"; but I cannot bring myself to believe that these individuals do not voluntarily close their eyes to the grand problem of existence and that, in endeavouring to stifle this feeling of the tragedy of life, they themselves are not living a lie.

The foregoing reflections are a kind of practical summary of the criticism developed in the first six chapters of this treatise, a kind of definition of the practical position to which such a criticism is capable of leading whosoever will not renounce life and will not renounce reason and who is compelled to live and act between these upper and nether millstones which grind upon the soul. The reader who follows me further is now aware that I am about to carry him into the region of the imagination, of imagination not destitute of reason, for without reason nothing subsists, but of imagination founded on feeling. And as regards its truth, the real truth, that which is independent of ourselves, beyond the reach of our logic and of our heart—of this truth who knows aught?

NOTES

1. See Troeltsch, *Systematische christliche Religion,* in *Die Kultur der Gegenwart* series.

2. *Die Analyse der Empfindigungen und das Verhältniss des Physischen zum Psychischen,* i., § 12, note.

3. I have left the original expression here, almost without translating it— *Existents-Consequents.* It means the existential or practical, not the purely rational or logical, consequence. (Author's note.)

4. Albrecht Ritschl: *Geschichte des Pietismus,* ii., Abt. i., Bonn, 1884, p. 251.

5. Thou art the cause of my suffering, O non-existing God, for if Thou didst exist, then should I also really exist.

William Barrett

IRRATIONAL MAN

The story is told (by Kierkegaard) of the absent-minded man so abstracted from his own life that he hardly knows he exists until, one fine morning, he wakes up to find himself dead. It is a story that has a special point today, since this civilization of ours has at last got its hands on weapons with which it could easily bring upon itself the fate of Kierke-gaard's hero: we could wake up tomorrow morning dead—and without ever having touched the roots of our own existence. There is by this time widespread anxiety and even panic over the dangers of the atomic age; but the public soul-searching and stocktaking rarely, if ever, go to the heart of the matter. We do not ask ourselves what the ultimate ideas behind our civilization are that have brought us into this danger; we do not search for the human face behind the bewildering array of instruments that man has forged; in a word, we do not dare to be philosophical. Uneasy as we are over the atomic age, on the crucial question of existence itself we choose to remain as absent-minded as the man in Kierkegaard's story. One reason we do so lies in the curiously remote position to which modern society has relegated philosophy, and which philosophers them-selves have been content to accept.

If philosophers are really to deal with the problem of human existence —and no other professional group in society is likely to take over the job for them—they might very well begin by asking: How does philosophy itself exist at the present time? Or, more concretely: How do philosophers exist in the modern world? Nothing very high-flown, metaphysical, or even abstract is intended by this question; and our preliminary answer to it is equally concrete and prosy. Philosophers today exist in the Academy, as members of departments of philosophy in universities, as professional teachers of a more or less theoretical subject known as philosophy. This simple observation, baldly factual and almost statistical, does not seem to take us very deeply into the abstruse problem of exist-ence; but every effort at understanding must take off from our actual situation, the point at which we stand. "Know thyself!" is the command Socrates issued to philosophers at the beginning (or very close to it) of all Western philosophy; and contemporary philosophers might start on the journey of self-knowledge by coming to terms with the somewhat grubby and uninspiring fact of the social status of philosophy as a profession. It is in any case a fact with some interesting ambiguities.

To profess, according to the dictionary, is to confess or declare openly, and therefore publicly; consequently, to acknowledge a calling before the world. So the word bears originally a religious connotation, as when we speak of a profession of faith. But in our present society, with its elaborate subdividing of human functions, a profession is the specialized social task—requiring expertness and know-how—that one performs for pay: it is a living, one's livelihood. Professional people are lawyers, doctors, dentists, engineers—and also professors of philosophy. The profession of the philosopher in the modern world is to be a professor of philosophy; and the realm of Being which the philosopher inhabits as a living individual is no more recondite than a corner within the university.

Not enough has been made of this academic existence of the philosopher, though some contemporary Existentialists have directed searching comment upon it. The price one pays for having a profession is a *déformation professionelle,* as the French put it—a professional deformation. Doctors and engineers tend to see things from the viewpoint of their own specialty, and usually show a very marked blind spot to whatever falls outside this particular province. The more specialized a vision the sharper its focus; but also the more nearly total the blind spot toward all things that lie on the periphery of this focus. As a human being, functioning professionally within the Academy, the philosopher can hardly be expected to escape his own professional deformation, especially since it has become a law of modern society that man is assimilated more and more completely to his social function. And it is just here that a troublesome and profound ambiguity resides for the philosopher today. The profession of philosophy did not always have the narrow and specialized meaning it now has. In ancient Greece it had the very opposite: instead of a specialized theoretical discipline, philosophy there was a concrete way of life, a total vision of man and the cosmos in the light of which the individual's whole life was to be lived. These earliest philosophers among the Greeks were seers, poets, almost shamans—as well as the first thinkers. Mythological and intuitive elements permeate their thinking even where we see the first historical efforts toward conceptualization; they traffic with the old gods even while in the process of coining a new significance for them; and everywhere in the fragments of these pre-Socratic Greeks is the sign of a revelation greater than themselves which they are unveiling for the rest of mankind. Even in Plato, where the thought has already become more differentiated and specialized and where the main lines of philosophy as a theoretical discipline are being laid down, the *motive* of philosophy is very different from the cool pursuit of the savant engaged in research. Philosophy is for Plato a passionate way of life; and the imperishable example of Socrates, who lived and died for the philosophic life, was the guiding line of Plato's career for five decades after his master's death. Philosophy is the soul's search for salvation, which means for Plato deliverance from the suffering and evils of the natural world. Even today the motive for an Oriental's taking up the study of philosophy is altogether different from that of a Western student: for the Oriental the only reason for bothering with philosophy is to find release or peace from the torments and perplexities of life. Philosophy can never quite divest itself of these aboriginal claims. They are part of the past, which is never lost, lurking under the veneer of even the most sophisticatedly rational of contemporary philosophies; and even those philosophers who have altogether forsworn the great vision are called upon, particularly by the layman who may not be aware of the historical fate of specialization that has fallen upon philosophy, to give answers to the great questions.

The ancient claims of philosophy are somewhat embarrassing to the contemporary philosopher, who has to justify his existence within the sober community of professional savants and scientists. The modern university is as much an expression of the specialization of the age as is the modern factory. Moreover, the philosopher knows that everything we prize about our modern knowledge, each thing in it that represents an immense stride in certainty and power over what the past called its knowledge, is the result of specialization. Modern science was made possible by the social organization of knowledge. The philosopher today is therefore pressed, and simply by reason of his objective social role in the community, into an imitation of the scientist: he too seeks to perfect the weapons of his knowledge through specialization. Hence the extraordinary preoccupation with technique among modern philosophers, with logical and linguistic analysis, syntax and semantics; and in general with the refining away of all content for the sake of formal subtlety. The movement known as Logical Positivism, in this country (the atmosphere of humanism is probably more dominant in the European universities than here in the United States), actually trafficked upon the *guilt* philosophers felt at not being scientists; that is, at not being researchers producing reliable knowledge in the mode of science. The natural insecurity of philosophers, which in any case lies at the core of their whole uncertain enterprise, was here aggravated beyond measure by the insistence that they transform themselves into scientists.

Specialization is the price we pay for the advancement of knowledge. A price, because the path of specialization leads away from the ordinary and concrete acts of understanding in terms of which man actually lives his day-to-day life. It used to be said (I do not know whether this would still hold today) that if a dozen men were to die the meaning of Einstein's

Theory of Relativity would be lost to mankind. No mathematician today can embrace the whole of his subject as did the great Gauss little more than a century ago. The philosopher who has pursued his own specialized path leading away from the urgent and the actual may claim that his situation parallels that of the scientist, that his own increasing remoteness from life merely demonstrates the inexorable law of advancing knowledge. But the cases are in fact not parallel; for out of the abstractions that only a handful of experts can understand the physicist is able to detonate a bomb that alters—and can indeed put an end to—the life of ordinary mankind. The philosopher has no such explosive effect upon the life of his time. In fact, if they were candid, philosophers today would recognize that they have less and less influence upon the minds around them. To the degree that their existence has become specialized and academic, their importance beyond the university cloisters has declined. Their disputes have become disputes among themselves; and far from gaining the enthusiastic support needed for a strong popular movement, they now have little contact with whatever general intellectual elite still remain here outside the Academy. John Dewey was the last American philosopher to have any widespread influence on non-academic life in this country.

Such was the general philosophic situation here when, after the Second World War, the news of Existentialism arrived. It was news, which is in itself an unusual thing for philosophy these days. True, the public interest was not altogether directed toward the philosophic matters in question. It was news from France, and therefore distinguished by the particular color and excitement that French intellectual life is able to generate. French Existentialism was a kind of Bohemian ferment in Paris; it had, as a garnish for the philosophy, the cult its younger devotees had made of nightclub hangouts, American jazz, special hairdos and style of dress. All this made news for American journalists trying to report on the life that had gone on in Paris during the war and the German Occupation. Moreover, Existentialism was a literary movement as well, and its leaders —Jean-Paul Sartre, Albert Camus, Simone de Beauvoir—were brilliant and engaging writers. Nevertheless, that the American public was curious about the philosophy itself cannot altogether be denied. Perhaps the curiosity consisted in large part of wanting to know what the name, the big word, meant; nothing stirs up popular interest so much as a slogan. But there was also a genuine philosophic curiosity, however inchoate, in all this, for here was a movement that seemed to convey a message and a meaning to a good many people abroad, and Americans wanted to know about it. The desire for meaning still slumbers, though submerged, beneath the extraversion of American life.

The philosophic news from France was only a small detail in the history of the postwar years. French Existentialism, as a cult, is now as dead as last year's fad. Its leaders, to be sure, are still flourishing: Sartre and Simone de Beauvoir are still phenomenally productive, though in the case of Sartre we feel that he has already made at least his penultimate statement, so that now we have his message pretty completely; Albert Camus, the most sensitive and searching of the trio, long ago split off from the group, but has continued his exploration into themes that belonged to the original Existentialist preoccupations. As news and excitement, the movement is altogether dead; and yet it has left its mark on nearly all the writing and thinking of Europe of the last ten years. During the grim decade of the Cold War no intellectual movement of comparable importance appeared. Existentialism is the best in the way of a new and creative movement that these rather uninspired postwar years have been able to turn up. We have to say at least this in a spirit of cool critical assessment, even when we acknowledge all the frivolous and sensational elements that got attached to it.

The important thing, to repeat, was that here was a philosophy that was able to cross the frontier from the Academy into the world at large. This should have been a welcome sign to professional philosophers that ordinary mankind still could hunger and thirst after philosophy if what they were given to bite down on was something that seemed to have a connection with their lives. Instead, the reception given the new movement by philosophers was anything but cordial. Existentialism was rejected, often without very much scrutiny, as sensationalism or mere "psychologizing," a literary attitude, postwar despair, nihilism, or heaven knows what besides. The very themes of Existentialism were something of a scandal to the detached sobriety of Anglo-American philosophy. Such matters as anxiety, death, the conflict between the bogus and the genuine self, the faceless man of the masses, the experience of the death of God are scarcely the themes of analytic philosophy. Yet they are themes of life: People do die, people do struggle all their lives between the demands of real and counterfeit selves, and we do live in an age in which neurotic anxiety has mounted out of all proportion so that even minds inclined to believe that all human problems can be solved by physical techniques begin to label "mental health" as the first of our public problems. The reaction of professional philosophers to Existentialism was merely a symptom of their imprisonment in the narrowness of their own discipline. Never was the professional deformation more in evidence. The divorce of mind from life was something that had happened to philosophers simply in the pursuit of their own specialized problems. Since philosophers are only a tiny fraction of the general population, the matter would not be worth laboring were it not that this divorce of mind from life happens also to be taking place, catastrophically, in modern civilization everywhere. It happens too, as we shall see, to be one of the central themes of existential philosophy—for which we may in time owe it no small debt.

All of this has to be said even when we do concede a certain sensational and youthfully morbid side to French Existentialism. The genius of Sartre—and by this time there can scarcely be doubt that it is real genius —has an undeniably morbid side. But there is no human temperament that does not potentially reveal some truth, and Sartre's morbidity has its own unique and revelatory power. It is true also that a good deal in French Existentialism was the expression of an historical mood—the shambles of defeat after the "phony war" and the experience of utter dereliction under the German Occupation. But are moods of this kind so unimportant and trifling as to be unworthy of the philosopher's consideration? Would it not in fact be a serious and appropriate task for the philosopher to elaborate what is involved in certain basic human moods? We are living in an epoch that has produced two world wars, and these wars were not merely passing incidents but characterize the age down to its marrow; surely a philosophy that has experienced these wars may be said to have some connection with the life of its time. Philosophers who dismissed Existentialism as "merely a mood" or "a postwar mood" betrayed a curious blindness to the concerns of the human spirit, in taking the view that philosophic truth can be found only in those areas of experience in which human moods are *not* present.

Naturally enough, something very deeply American came to the surface in this initial response to Existentialism. Once again the old drama of America confronting Europe was being played out. Existentialism was so definitely a European expression that its very somberness went against the grain of our native youthfulness and optimism. The new philosophy was not a peculiarly French phenomenon, but a creation of the western European continent at the moment in history when all of its horizons— political as well as spiritual—were rapidly shrinking. The American has not yet assimilated psychologically the disappearance of his own geographical frontier, his spiritual horizon is still the limitless play of human possibilities, and as yet he has not lived through the crucial experience of human finitude. (This last is still only an abstract phrase to him.) The expression of themes like those of Existentialism was bound to strike the American as a symptom of despair and defeat, and, generally, of the declining vigor of a senescent civilization. But America, spiritually speaking, is still tied to European civilization, even though the political power lines now run the other way; and these European expressions simply point out the path that America itself will have eventually to tread; when it does it will know at last what the European is talking about.

It is necessary thus to emphasize the European—rather than the specifically French—origins of Existentialism, since in its crucial issues the whole meaning of European civilization (of which we in America are still both descendants and dependents) is radically put in question. Jean-Paul Sartre is not Existentialism—it still seems necessary to make this point for American readers; he does not even represent, as we shall see later, the deepest impulse of this philosophy. Now that French Existentialism as a popular movement (once even something of a popular nuisance) is safely dead, having left a few new reputations surviving in its wake, we can see it much more clearly for what it is—a small branch of a very much larger tree. And the roots of this larger tree reach down into the remotest depths of the Western tradition. Even in the portions of the tree more immediately visible to our contemporary eyes, we have something which is the combined product of many European thinkers, some of them operating in radically different national traditions. Sartre's immediate sources, for example, are German: *Martin Heidegger* (1889–   ) and *Karl Jaspers* (1883–   ), and for his method the great German phenomenologist, *Edmund Husserl* (1859–1938). Heidegger and Jaspers are, strictly speaking, the creators of existential philosophy in this century: they have given it its decisive stamp, brought its problems to new and more precise expression, and in general formed the model around which the thinking of all the other Existentialists revolves. Neither Heidegger nor Jaspers created their philosophies out of whole cloth; the atmosphere of German philosophy during the first part of this century had become quickened by the search for a new "philosophical anthropology"—a new interpretation of man— made necessary by the extraordinary additions to knowledge in all of the special sciences that dealt with man. Here particularly the name of *Max Scheler* (1874–1928), usually not classed as an "existentialist," must be mentioned, for his great sensitivity to this new concrete data from psychology and the social sciences, but most of all for his penetrating grasp of the fact that modern man had become in his very essence problematic. Both Scheler and Heidegger owe a great debt to Husserl, yet the relation of the latter to Existentialism is extremely paradoxical. By temperament Husserl was the anti-modernist *par excellence* among modern philosophers; he was a passionate exponent of classical rationalism, whose single and exalted aim was to ground the rationality of man upon a more adequate and comprehensive basis than the past had achieved. Yet by insisting that the philosopher must cast aside preconceptions in attending to the actual concrete data of experience, Husserl flung wide the doors of philosophy to the rich existential content that his more radical followers were to quarry. In his last writings Husserl's thought even turns slowly and haltingly in the direction of Heidegger's themes. The great rationalist is dragged slowly to earth.

But what lifted Heidegger and Jaspers above the level of their contemporary philosophic atmosphere and impelled them to give a new voice to the intellectual consciousness of the age was their decisive relation to two older nineteenth-century thinkers: *Søren Kierkegaard* (1813-1855) and *Friedrich Nietzsche* (1844-1900). Jaspers has been the more outspoken in acknowledging this filial relationship: the philosopher, he says, who has really *experienced* the thought of Kierkegaard and Nietzsche can never again philosophize in the traditional mode of academic philosophy. Neither Kierkegaard nor Nietzsche was an academic philosopher; Nietzsche, for seven years a professor of Greek at Basel in Switzerland, did his most radical philosophizing after he had fled from the world of the university and its sober community of scholars; Kierkegaard never held an academic chair. Neither developed a system; both in fact gibed at systematizers and even the possibilities of a philosophic system; and while they proliferated in ideas that were far in advance of their time and could be spelled out only by the following century, these ideas were not the stock themes of academic philosophy. Ideas are not even the real subject matter of these philosophers—and this in itself is something of a revolution in Western philosophy: their central subject is the unique experience of the single one, the individual, who chooses to place himself on trial before the gravest question of his civilization. For both Kierkegaard and Nietzsche this gravest question is Christianity, though they were driven to opposite positions in regard to it. Kierkegaard set himself the task of determining whether Christianity can still be lived or whether a civilization still nominally Christian must finally confess spiritual bankruptcy; and all his ideas were simply sparks thrown off in the fiery process of seeking to realize the truth of Christ in his own life. Nietzsche begins with the confession of bankruptcy: God is dead, says Nietzsche, and European man if he were more honest, courageous, and had keener eyes for what went on in the depths of his own soul would know that this death has taken place there, despite the lip service still paid to the old formulae and ideals of religion. Nietzsche experimented with his own life to be able to answer the question: What next? What happens to the race when at long last it has severed the umbilical cord that bound it for millennia to the gods and a transcendent world beyond this earthly world? He placed his own life on trial in order to experience this death of God to its depths. More than thinkers, Kierkegaard and Nietzsche were witnesses—witnesses who suffered for their time what the time itself would not acknowledge as its own secret wound. No concept or system of concepts lies at the center of either of their philosophies, but rather the individual human personality itself struggling for self-realization. No wonder both are among the greatest of intuitive psychologists.

Though Kierkegaard was a Dane, intellectual Denmark in his time was a cultural province of Germany, and his thought, nourished almost completely by German sources, belongs ultimately within the wider tradition of German philosophy. Modern existential philosophy is thus by and large a creation of the German genius. It rises out of that old strain of the Germanic mind which, since Meister Eckhart at the end of the Middle Ages, has sought to give voice to the deepest inwardness of European man. But this voice is also a thoroughly modern one and speaks neither with the serene mysticism of Eckhart nor with the intellectual intoxication and dreaminess of German idealism. Here introversion has come face to face with its other, the concrete actualities of life before which the older German philosophy had remained in woolgathering abstraction; face to face with historical crisis; with time, death, and personal anxiety.

Yet modern Existentialism is not of exclusively German provenance; rather it is a total European creation, perhaps the last philosophic legacy of Europe to America or whatever other civilization is now on its way to supplant Europe. The number of European thinkers of widely varying racial and national traditions who have collaborated in the fabrication of existential philosophy is much larger than the public, still somewhat bedazzled by French Existentialism, imagines. The picture of French Existentialism itself is not complete without the figure of *Gabriel Marcel* (1889–   ), Sartre's extreme opposite and trenchant critic, a devout Catholic whose philosophic sources are not German at all, but are surprisingly enough the American idealist Josiah Royce and the French intuitionist Henri Bergson. According to the record he has left in his *Metaphysical Journal,* Marcel's existentialism developed out of purely personal experience, and perhaps that is its greatest significance for us, whatever final value his philosophic formulations may have. The intimacy and concreteness of personal feeling taught Marcel the imcompleteness of all philosophies that deal purely in intellectual abstractions. But the door that opened upon this experience was Bergson's doctrine of intuition; and the figure of *Henri Bergson* (1859-1941) cannot really be omitted from any historical sketch of modern existential philosophy. Without Bergson the whole atmosphere in which Existentialists have philosophized would not have been what it was. He was the first to insist on the insufficiency of the abstract intelligence to grasp the richness of experience, on the urgent and irreducible reality of time, and—perhaps in the long run the most significant insight of all—on the inner depth of the psychic life which cannot be measured by the quantitative methods of the physical sciences; and for making all of these points the Existentialists stand greatly in his debt. Yet, from the existential point of view, there is a curious incompleteness about Bergson's thinking, as if he never came really to grips with the central subject, Man, but remained perpetually dodging and tacking about on its periphery. Certain premises of Bergson's thought—which remain, to be sure, little more than premises—are more radical than any the Existentialists have yet explored. Bergson's reputation except in France has greatly fallen off, but he is due for a revival, at which time hindsight will enable us to see that his philosophy contains much more than it seemed to, even at the height of his fame.

The Russians (White Russians, of course) have contributed three typical and interesting figures to Existentialism: *Vladimir Solovev* (1853–1900), *Leon Shestov* (1868–1938), and *Nikolai Berdyaev* (1874–1948), of whom only the last seems to be known in this country. These men are all spiritual children of Dostoevski, and they bring a peculiarly Russian vision to Existentialism: total, extreme, and apocalyptic. Solovev, primarily a theologian and religious writer, belonged to the first generation that felt the impact of Dostoevski as both prophet and novelist, and he develops the typically Dostoevskian position that there can be no compromise between the spirit of rationalism and the spirit of religion. Both Berdyaev and Shestov were Russian *émigrés,* cosmopolitans of the spirit, but nevertheless remained Russian to the core; and their writings, like those of the great Russian novelists of the nineteenth century, can show us what the mind of western Europe, the heir of classicism and rationalism, looks like to an outsider—particularly to a Russian outsider who will be satisfied with no philosophic answers that fall short of the total and passionate feelings of his own humanity.

Modern Spain has contributed two figures to existential philosophy, in *Miguel de Unamuno* (1864–1936) and *José Ortega y Gasset* (1833–1955). Unamuno, a poet first and last, wrote one of the most moving and genuine philosophic books of the whole movement; his *Tragic Sense of Life* is a work that fulfills, though in an anti-Nietzschean sense, Nietzsche's command to remain true to the earth. Unamuno had read Kierkegaard, but his thought is an expression of his own personal passion and of the Basque earth from which he sprang. Ortega, a cooler and more cosmopolitan figure, is best known in this country as the social critic of *The Revolt of the Masses.* All the basic premises of Ortega's thought derive from modern German philosophy: so far as he philosophizes, his mind is Germanic; but he was able to translate German philosophy into the language of the people, without pedantry and jargon, and particularly into the simplicity of an altogether alien language, Spanish, so that the translation itself becomes an act of creative thought. Ortega loves to hide the profundity of his thought behind the simple and casual language of a journalist or belletrist.

On the outer edge of the German tradition moves the remarkable figure of *Martin Buber* (1878–   ), a Jew whose culture is altogether Germanic but whose thought after many peregrinations has succeeded in rediscovering and anchoring itself profoundly to its Biblical and Hebraic inheritance. Buber is one of the few thinkers who has succeeded in the desperate modern search for roots, a fact with which his work continuously impresses us. The image of Biblical man moves like a shadow behind everything he writes. His thinking has the narrowness and concrete power, often the stubborn obstinacy, of Hebraism. At first glance his contribution would seem to be the slenderest of all the Existentialists, to be summed up in the title of his most moving book, *I and Thou.* It is as if Buber had sought to recast Kierkegaard's dictum, "Purity of heart is to will one thing," into: Depth of mind is to think one thought. But this one thought—that meaning in life happens in the area between person and person in that situation of contact when one says *I* to the other's *Thou*—is worth a lifetime's digging. In any case Buber is a necessary corrective to more ambitious systematizers like Heidegger and Sartre.

Thus we see that Existentialism numbers among its most powerful representatives Jews, Catholics, Protestants—as well as atheists. Contrary to the first facile journalistic reactions, the seriousness of existential thought does not arise merely out of the despair of a world from which God has departed. Such a generalization was prompted largely by the identification of existential philosophy with the school of Sartre. It should appear, from the foregoing sketch, how tiny a fragment of Existentialism the Sartrian school really does represent. So far as the central impulses of existential thought are concerned, it does not altogether matter, at least in one sense, in what religious sect a man finally finds his home. Nor is it mere heterogenous lumping-together to put Catholics, Jews, Protestants, and atheists under the rubric of one philosophy. This philosophy, as a particular mode of human thought, is single even though its practitioners wind up in different religious camps. What is common, and central, to all these philosophers is that the meaning of religion, and religious faith, is recast in relation to the individual. Each has put religion itself radically in question, and it is only to be expected that the faith, or the denial of faith, that emerges in their thought should be somewhat disconcerting to those who have followed the more public and external paths into a church. Unamuno seemed always on the verge of excommunication by the Spanish bishops; Buber is a prophet with not very much honor in his native land of Israel; and Kierkegaard fought the last battle of his life against the ordained hierarchy of the Danish Church. The atheist sect, on the other hand, sniffs the taint of heresy in Heidegger, whose thought, which he himself calls in one place a "waiting for god," has been criticized by one American philosopher as opening the back door to theology. It is evident that anyone who has passed through the depths of modern experience and strives to place religion in relation to that experience is bound to acquire the label of heretic.

Modern experience—an ambiguous enough term, to be sure, and one that will require subsequent definition—is the bond among these philosophers. The roster of names we have given is hardly complete, but surely sufficient to indicate that Existentialism is not a passing fad or a mere philosophic mood of the postwar period but a major movement of human thought that lies directly in the main stream of modern history. Over the past hundred years the development of philosophy has shown a remarkable enlargement of content, a progressive orientation toward the immediate and qualitative, the existent and the actual—toward "concreteness and adequacy," to use the words that A. N. Whitehead borrowed from William James. Philosophers can no longer attempt, as the British empiricists Locke and Hume attempted, to contruct human experience out of simple ideas and elementary sensations. The psychic life of man is not a mosaic of such mental atoms, and philosophers were able to cling to this belief so long only because they had put their own abstractions in place of concrete experience. Thus Whitehead himself, who as a Platonist can scarcely be lumped with the Existentialists, nevertheless shares in this general existential trend within modern philosophy when he describes philosophy itself as "the critique of abstractions"—the endless effort to drag the balloon of the mind back to the earth of actual experience.

Of all the non-European philosophers, William James probably best deserves to be labeled an Existentialist. Indeed, at this late date, we may very well wonder whether if would not be more accurate to call James an Existentialist than a Pragmatist. What remains of American Pragmatism today is forced to think of him as the black sheep of the movement. Pragmatists nowadays acknowledge James's genius but are embarrassed by his extremes: by the unashamedly personal tone of his philosophizing, his willingness to give psychology the final voice over logic where the two seem in conflict, and his belief in the revelatory value of religious experience. There are pages in James that could have been written by Kierkegaard, and the Epilogue to *Varieties of Religious Experience* puts the case for the primacy of personal experience over abstraction as strongly as any of the Existentialists has ever done. James's vituperation of rationalism is so passionate that latter-day Pragmatists see their own residual rationalism of scientific method thereby put in question. And it is not merely a matter of tone, but of principle, that places James among the Existentialists: he plumped for a world which contained contingency, discontinuity, and in which the centers of experience were irreducibly plural and personal, as against a "block" universe that could be enclosed in a single rational system.

Pragmatism meant something more and different for James than it did for Charles Sanders Peirce or John Dewey. The contrast between James and Dewey, particularly, sheds light on the precise point at which Pragmatism, in the strict sense, ends and Existentialism begins. A comparison between the earlier and the later writings of Dewey is almost equally illuminating on the same point. Dewey is moving in the general existential direction of modern philosophy with his insistence that the modern philosopher must break with the whole classical tradition of thought. He sees the "negative" and destructive side of philosophy (with which Existentialism has been so heavily taxed by its critics): every thinker, Dewey tells us, puts some portion of the stable world in danger as soon as he begins to think. The genial inspiration that lies behind his whole rather gangling and loose-jointed philosophy is the belief that in all departments of human experience things do not fall from heaven but grow up out of the earth. Thinking itself is only the halting and fumbling effort of a thoroughly biological creature to cope with his environment. The image of man as an earth-bound and time-bound creature permeates Dewey's writings as it does that of the Existentialists—up to a point. Beyond that point he moves in a direction that is the very opposite of Existentialism. What Dewey never calls into question is the thing he labels Intelligence, which in his last writings came to mean simply Scientific Method. Dewey places the human person securely within his biological and social context, but he never goes past this context into that deepest center of the human person where fear and trembling start. Any examination of inner experience—really inner experience—would have seemed to Dewey to take the philosopher too far away from nature in the direction of the theological. We have to remind ourselves here of the provincial and overtheologized atmosphere of the America in which Dewey started his work, and against which he had to struggle so hard to establish the validity of a secular intelligence. Given Dewey's emphasis upon the biological and sociological contexts as ultimate, however, together with his interpretation of human thought as basically an effort to transform the environment, we end with the picture of man as essentially *homo faber,* the technological animal. This belief in technique is still a supreme article of the American faith. Dewey grew up in a period in which America was still wrestling with its frontier, and the mood of his writings is unshaken optimism at the expansion of our technical mastery over nature. Ultimately, the difference between Dewey and the Existentialists is the difference between America and Europe. The philosopher cannot seriously put to himself questions that his civilization has not lived.

That is why we propose to limit the scope of our subject to Europe and consider Existentialism as a distinctly European product of this period: in fact, as the philosophy of Europe in this century. In the broadest sense of the term, no doubt, all modern thought has been touched by a greater existential emphasis than was the philosophy of the earlier modern period. This is simply the result of the stepped-up secularization of Western civilization, in the course of which man has inevitably become more attached to the promises of this earth than to the goal of a transcendent realm beyond nature. But while it is important to call attention at the outset to this broad sense of the word "existential," to carry this meaning through in detail would inevitably dilute the specific substance of Existentialism. It is Europe that has been in crisis, and it is European thinkers who have brought the existential problems to a focal expression, who have in fact dared to raise the ultimate questions. The significance of this philosophy is another matter, however, and can hardly be confined to its place of origin. Its significance is for the world and for this epoch of the world.

The reader may very well ask why, in view of this broader existential trend within modern philosophy, Existentialism should first have been greeted by professional philosophers in this country as an eccentric and sensational kind of tempest in a teapot. We should point out that Anglo-American philosophy is dominated by an altogether different and alien mode of thought—variously called analytic philosophy, Logical Positivism, or sometimes merely "scientific philosophy." No doubt, Positivism has also good claims to being the philosophy of this time: it takes as its central fact what is undoubtedly the central fact distinguishing our civilization from all others—science; but it goes on from this to take science as the ultimate ruler of human life, which it never has been and psychologically never can be. Positivist man is a curious creature who dwells in the tiny island of light composed of what he finds scientifically "meaningful," while the whole surrounding area in which ordinary men live from day to day and have their dealings with other men is consigned to the outer darkness of the "meaningless." Positivism has simply accepted the fractured being of modern man and erected a philosophy to intensify it. Existentialism, whether successfully or not, has attempted instead to gather all the elements of human reality into a total picture of man. Positivist man and Existentialist man are no doubt offspring of the same parent epoch, but, somewhat as Cain and Abel were, the brothers are divided unalterably by temperament and the initial choice they make of their own being. Of course there is on the contemporary scene a more powerful claimant to philosophic mastery than either of them: Marxism. Marxist man is a creature of technics, a busy and ingenious animal, with secular religious faith in History, of which he is the chosen collaborator. Like Positivism, Marxism has no philosophical categories for the unique facts of human personality, and in the natural course of things manages to collectivize this human personality out of existence (except where a single personality attains power, and then his personal paranoia plays havoc with the lives of two hundred million people). Both Marxism and Positivism are, intellectually speaking, relics of the nineteenth-century Enlightenment that have not yet come to terms with the shadow side of human life as grasped even by some of the nineteenth-century thinkers themselves. The Marxist and Positivist picture of man, consequently, is thin and oversimplified. Existential philosophy, as a revolt against such oversimplification, attempts to grasp the image of the whole man, even where this involves bringing to consciousness all that is dark and questionable in his existence. And in just this respect it is a much more authentic expression of our own contemporary experience.

Alfred North Whitehead

SCIENCE AND THE MODERN WORLD

The Progress of Civilisation is not wholly a uniform drift towards better things. It may perhaps wear this aspect if we map it on a scale which is large enough. But such broad views obscure the details on which rests our whole understanding of the process. New epochs emerge with comparative suddenness, if we have regard to the scores of thousands of years throughout which the complete history extends. Secluded races suddenly take their places in the main stream of events: technological discoveries transform the mechanism of human life: a primitive art quickly flowers into full satisfaction of some aesthetic craving: great religions in their crusading youth spread through the nations the peace of Heaven and the sword of the Lord.

The sixteenth century of our era saw the disruption of Western Christianity and the rise of modern science. It was an age of ferment. Nothing was settled, though much was opened—new worlds and new ideas. In science, Copernicus and Vesalius may be chosen as representative figures: they typify the new cosmology and the scientific emphasis on direct observation. Giordano Bruno was the martyr; though the cause for which he suffered was not that of science, but that of free imaginative speculation. His death in the year 1600 ushered in the first century of modern science in the strict sense of the term. In his execution there was an unconscious symbolism: for the subsequent tone of scientific thought has contained distrust of his type of general speculativeness. The Reformation, for all its importance, may be considered as a domestic affair of the European races. Even the Christianity of the East viewed it with profound disengagement. Furthermore, such disruptions are no new phenomena in the history of Christianity or of other religions. When we project this great revolution upon the whole history of the Christian Church, we cannot look upon it as introducing a new principle into human life. For good or for evil, it was a great transformation of religion; but it was not the coming of religion. It did not itself claim to be so. Reformers maintained that they were only restoring what had been forgotten.

It is quite otherwise with the rise of modern science. In every way it contrasts with the contemporary religious movement. The Reformation was a popular uprising, and for a century and a half drenched Europe in blood. The beginnings of the scientific movement were confined to a minority among the intellectual élite. In a generation which saw the Thirty Years' War and remembered Alva in the Netherlands, the worst that happened to men of science was that Galileo suffered an honourable detention and a mild reproof, before dying peacefully in his bed. The way in which the persecution of Galileo has been remembered is a tribute to the quiet commencement of the most intimate change in outlook which the human race had yet encountered. Since a babe was born in a manger, it may be doubted whether so great a thing has happened with so little stir.

The thesis which these lectures will illustrate is that this quiet growth of science has practically recoloured our mentality so that modes of thought which in former times were exceptional are now broadly spread through the educated world. This new colouring of ways of thought had been proceeding slowly for many ages in the European peoples. At last it issued in the rapid development of science; and has thereby strengthened itself by its most obvious application. The new mentality is more important even than the new science and the new technology. It has altered the metaphysical presuppositions and the imaginative contents of our minds; so that now the old stimuli provoke a new response. Perhaps my metaphor of a new colour is too strong. What I mean is just that slightest change of tone which yet makes all the difference. This is exactly illustrated by a sentence from a published letter of that adorable genius, William James. When he was finishing his great treatise on the *Principles of Psychology*, he wrote to his brother Henry James, 'I have to forge every sentence in the teeth of irreducible and stubborn facts.'

This new tinge to modern minds is a vehement and passionate interest in the relation of general principles to irreducible and stubborn facts. All the world over and at all times there have been practical men, absorbed in 'irreducible and stubborn facts': all the world over and at all times there have been men of philosophic temperament who have been absorbed in the weaving of general principles. It is this union of passionate interest in the detailed facts with equal devotion to abstract generalisation which forms the novelty in our present society. Previously it had appeared sporadically and as if by chance. This balance of mind has now become part of the tradition which infects cultivated thought. It is the salt which keeps life sweet. The main business of universities is to transmit this tradition as a widespread inheritance from generation to generation.

Another contrast which singles out science from among the European movements of the sixteenth and seventeenth centuries is its universality. Modern science was born in Europe, but its home is the whole world. In the last two centuries there has been a long and confused impact of western modes upon the civilisation of Asia. The wise men of the East have been puzzling, and are puzzling, as to what may be the regulative secret of life which can be passed from West to East without the wanton destruction of their own inheritance which they so rightly prize. More and more it is becoming evident that what the West can most readily give to the East is its science and its scientific outlook. This is transferable from country to country, and from race to race, wherever there is a rational society.

In this course of lectures I shall not discuss the details of scientific discovery. My theme is the energising of a state of mind in the modern world, its broad generalisations, and its impact upon other spiritual forces. There are two ways of reading history, forwards and backwards. In the history of thought, we require both methods. A climate of opinion —to use the happy phrase of a seventeenth century writer—requires for its understanding the consideration of its antecedents and its issues. Accordingly in this lecture I shall consider some of the antecedents of our modern approach to the investigation of nature.

In the first place, there can be no living science unless there is a widespread instinctive conviction in the existence of an *Order of Things,* and, in particular, of an *Order of Nature.* I have used the word *instinctive* advisedly. It does not matter what men say in words, so long as their activities are controlled by settled instincts. The words may ultimately destroy the instincts. But until this has occurred, words do not count. This remark is important in respect to the history of scientific thought. For we shall find that since the time of Hume, the fashionable scientific philosophy has been such as to deny the rationality of science. This conclusion lies upon the surface of Hume's philosophy. Take for example, the following passage from Section IV of his *Inquiry Concerning Human Understanding:*

In a word, then, every effect is a distinct event from its cause. It could not, therefore, be discovered in the cause; and the first invention or conception of it, *a priori,* must be entirely arbitrary.

If the cause in itself discloses no information as to the effect, so that the first invention of it must be *entirely* arbitrary, it follows at once that science is impossible, except in the sense of establishing *entirely arbitrary* connections which are not warranted by anything intrinsic to the natures either of causes or effects. Some variant of Hume's philosophy has generally prevailed among men of science. But scientific faith has risen to the occasion, and has tacitly removed the philosophic mountain.

In view of this strange contradiction in scientific thought, it is of the first importance to consider the antecedents of a faith which is impervious to the demand for a consistent rationality. We have therefore to trace the rise of the instinctive faith that there is an Order of Nature which can be traced in every detailed occurrence.

Of course we all share in this faith, and we therefore believe that the reason for the faith is our apprehension of its truth. But the formation of a general idea—such as the idea of the Order of Nature—and the grasp of its importance, and the observation of its exemplification in a variety of occasions are by no means the necessary consequences of the truth of the idea in question. Familiar things happen, and mankind does not bother about them. It requires a very unusual mind to undertake the analysis of the obvious. Accordingly I wish to consider the stages in which this analysis became explicit, and finally became unalterably impressed upon the educated minds of Western Europe.

Obviously, the main recurrences of life are too insistent to escape the notice of the least rational of humans; and even before the dawn of rationality, they have impressed themselves upon the instincts of animals. It is unnecessary to labour the point, that in broad outline certain general states of nature recur, and that our very natures have adapted themselves to such repetitions.

But there is a complementary fact which is equally true and equally obvious:—nothing ever really recurs in exact detail. No two days are identical, no two winters. What has gone, has gone forever. Accordingly the practical philosophy of mankind has been to expect the broad recurrences, and to accept the details as emanating from the inscrutable womb of things beyond the ken of rationality. Men expected the sun to rise, but the wind bloweth where it listeth.

Certainly from the classical Greek civilisation onwards there have been men, and indeed groups of men, who have placed themselves beyond this acceptance of an ultimate irrationality. Such men have endeavoured to explain all phenomena as the outcome of an order of things which extends to every detail. Geniuses such as Aristotle, or Archimedes, or Roger Bacon, must have been endowed with the full scientific mentality, which instinctively holds that all things great and small are conceivable as exemplifications of general principles which reign throughout the natural order.

But until the close of the Middle Ages the general educated public did not feel that intimate conviction, and that detailed interest, in such an idea, so as to lead to an unceasing supply of men, with ability and opportunity adequate to maintain a coördinated search for the discovery of these hypothetical principles. Either people were doubtful about the existence of such principles, or were doubtful about any success in finding them, or took no interest in thinking about them, or were oblivious to their practical importance when found. For whatever reason, search was languid, if we have regard to the opportunities of a high civilisation and the length of time concerned. Why did the pace suddenly quicken in the sixteenth and seventeenth centuries? At the close of the Middle Ages a new mentality discloses itself. Invention stimulated thought, thought quickened physical speculation, Greek manuscripts disclosed what the ancients had discovered. Finally although in the year 1500 Europe knew less than Archimedes who died in the year 212 B.C., yet in the year 1700, Newton's *Principia* had been written and the world was well started on the modern epoch.

There have been great civilisations in which the peculiar balance of mind required for science has only fitfully appeared and has produced the feeblest result. For example, the more we know of Chinese art, of Chinese literature, and of the Chinese philosophy of life, the more we admire the heights to which that civilisation attained. For thousands of years, there have been in China acute and learned men patiently devoting their lives to study. Having regard to the span of time, and to the population concerned, China forms the largest volume of civilisation which the world has seen. There is no reason to doubt the intrinsic capacity of individual Chinamen for the pursuit of science. And yet Chinese science is practically negligible. There is no reason to believe that China if left to itself would have ever produced any progress in science. The same may be said of India. Furthermore, if the Persians had enslaved the Greeks, there is no definite ground for belief that science would have flourished in Europe. The Romans showed no particular originality in that line. Even as it was, the Greeks, though they founded the movement, did not sustain it with the concentrated interest which modern Europe has shown. I am not alluding to the last generations of the European peoples on both sides of the ocean; I mean the smaller Europe of the Reformation period, distracted as it was with wars and religious disputes. Consider the world of the eastern Mediterranean, from Sicily to western Asia, during the period of about 1400 years from the death of Archimedes [in 212 B.C.] to the irruption of the Tartars. There were wars and revolutions and large changes of religion: but nothing much worse than the wars of the sixteenth and seventeenth centuries throughout Europe. There was a great and wealthy civilisation, Pagan, Christian, Mahometan. In that period a great deal was added to science. But on the whole the progress was slow and wavering; and, except in mathematics, the men of the Renaissance practically started from the position which Archimedes had reached. There had been some progress in medicine and some progress in astronomy. But the total advance was very little compared to the marvellous success of the seventeenth century. For example, compare the progress of scientific knowledge from the year 1560, just before the births of Galileo and of Kepler, up to the year 1700, when Newton was in the height of his fame, with the progress in the ancient period, already mentioned, exactly ten times as long.

Nevertheless, Greece was the mother of Europe; and it is to Greece that we must look in order to find the origin of our modern ideas. We all know that on the eastern shores of the Mediterranean there was a very flourishing school of Ionian philosophers, deeply interested in theories concerning nature. Their ideas have been transmitted to us, enriched by the genius of Plato and Aristotle. But, with the exception of Aristotle, and it is a large exception, this school of thought had not attained to the complete scientific mentality. In some ways, it was better. The Greek genius was philosophical, lucid and logical. The men of this group were primarily asking philosophical questions. What is the substratum of nature? Is it fire, or earth, or water, or some combination of any two, or of all three? Or is it a mere flux, not reducible to some static material? Mathematics interested them mightily. They invented its generality, analysed its premises, and made notable discoveries of theorems by a rigid adherence to deductive reasoning. Their minds were infected with an eager generality. They demanded clear, bold ideas, and strict reasoning from them. All this was excellent; it was genius; it was ideal preparatory work. But it was not science as we understand it. The patience of minute observation was not nearly so prominent. Their genius was not so apt for the state of imaginative muddled suspense which preceeds successful inductive generalisation. They were lucid thinkers and bold reasoners.

Of course there were exceptions, and at the very top: for example, Aristotle and Archimedes. Also for patient observation, there were the astronomers. There was a mathematical lucidity about the stars, and a fascination about the small numerable band of runaway planets.

Every philosophy is tinged with the colouring of some secret imaginative background, which never emerges explicitly into its trains of reasoning. The Greek view of nature, at least that cosmology transmitted from them to later ages, was essentially dramatic. It is not necessarily wrong for this reason: but it was overwhelmingly dramatic. It thus conceived nature as articulated in the way of a work of dramatic art, for the exemplification of general ideas converging to an end. Nature was differentiated so as to provide its proper end for each thing. There was the centre of the universe as the end of motion for those things which are heavy, and the celestial spheres as the end of motion for those things whose natures lead them upwards. The celestial spheres were for things which are impassible and ingenerable, the lower regions for things passible and generable. Nature was a drama in which each thing played its part.

I do not say that this is a view to which Aristotle would have subscribed without severe reservations, in fact without the sort of reservations which we ourselves would make. But it was the view which subsequent Greek thought extracted from Aristotle and passed on to the Middle Ages. The effect of such an imaginative setting for nature was to damp down the historical spirit. For it was the end which seemed illuminating, so why bother about the beginning? The Reformation and the scientific movement were two aspects of the revolt which was the dominant intellectual movement of the later Renaissance. The appeal to the origins of Christianity, and Francis Bacon's appeal to efficient causes as against final causes, were two sides of one movement of thought. Also for this reason Galileo and his adversaries were at hopeless cross purposes, as can be seen from his *Dialogues on the Two Systems of the World*.

Galileo keeps harping on how things happen, whereas his adversaries had a complete theory as to why things happen. Unfortunately the two theories did not bring out the same results. Galileo insists upon 'irreducible and stubborn facts,' and Simplicius, his opponent, brings forward reasons, completely satisfactory, at least to himself. It is a great mistake to conceive this historical revolt as an appeal to reason. On the contrary, it was through and through an anti-intellectualist movement. It was the return to the contemplation of brute fact; and it was based on a recoil from the inflexible rationality of medieval thought. In making this statement I am merely summarising what at the time the adherents of the old régime themselves asserted. For example, in the fourth book of Father Paul Sarpi's *History of the Council of Trent,* you will find that in the year 1551 the Papal Legates who presided over the Council ordered: 'That the Divines ought to confirm their opinions with the holy Scripture, Traditions of the Apostles, sacred and approved Councils, and by the Constitutions and Authorities of the holy Fathers; that they ought to use brevity, and avoid superfluous and unprofitable questions, and perverse contentions. . . . This order did not please the Italian Divines; who said it was a novity, and a condemning of School-Divinity, which, in all difficulties, *useth reason, and* because it was not lawful [*i.e.*, by this decree] to treat as St. Thomas [Aquinas], St. Bonaventure, and other famous men did.'

It is impossible not to feel sympathy with these Italian divines, maintaining the lost cause of unbridled rationalism. They were deserted on all hands. The Protestants were in full revolt against them. The Papacy failed to support them, and the Bishops of the Council could not even understand them. For a few sentences below the foregoing quotation, we read: 'Though many complained here-of [*i.e.*, of the Decree], yet it prevailed but little, because generally the Fathers [*i.e.*, the Bishops] desired to hear men speak with intelligible terms, not abstrusely, as in the matter of Justification, and others already handled.'

Poor belated medievalists! When they used reason they were not even intelligible to the ruling powers of their epoch. It will take centuries before stubborn facts are reducible by reason, and meanwhile the pendulum swings slowly and heavily to the extreme of the historical method.

Forty-three years after the Italian divines had written this memorial, Richard Hooker in his famous *Laws of Ecclesiastical Polity* makes exactly the same complaint of his Puritan adversaries.[1] Hooker's balanced thought—from which the appellation 'The Judicious Hooker' is derived —and his diffuse style, which is the vehicle of such thought, make his writings singularly unfit for the process of summarising by a short, pointed quotation. But, in the section referred to, he reproaches his opponents with *Their Disparagement of Reason;* and in support of his own position definitely refers to 'The greatest amongst the school-divines' by which designation I presume that he refers to St. Thomas Aquinas.

Hooker's *Ecclesiastical Polity* was published just before Sarpi's *Council of Trent.* Accordingly there was complete independence between the two works. But both the Italian divines of 1551, and Hooker at the end of that century testify to the anti-rationalist trend of thought at that epoch, and in this respect contrast their own age with the epoch of scholasticism.

This reaction was undoubtedly a very necessary corrective to the unguarded rationalism of the Middle Ages. But reactions run to extremes. Accordingly, although one outcome of this reaction was the birth of modern science, yet we must remember that science thereby inherited the bias of thought to which it owes its origin.

The effect of Greek dramatic literature was many-sided so far as concerns the various ways in which it indirectly affected medieval thought. The pilgrim fathers of the scientific imagination as it exists today are the great tragedians of ancient Athens, Aeschylus, Sophocles, Euripides. Their vision of fate, remorseless and indifferent, urging a tragic incident to its inevitable issue, is the vision possessed by science. Fate in Greek Tragedy becomes the order of nature in modern thought. The absorbing interest in the particular heroic incidents, as an example and a verification of the workings of fate, reappears in our epoch as concentration of interest on the crucial experiments. It was my good fortune to be present at the meeting of the Royal Society in London when the Astronomer Royal for England announced that the photographic plates of the famous eclipse, as measured by his colleagues in Greenwich Observatory, had verified the prediction of Einstein that rays of light are bent as they pass in the neighbourhood of the sun. The whole atmosphere of tense interest was exactly that of the Greek drama: we were the chorus commenting on the decree of destiny as disclosed in the development of a supreme incident. There was dramatic quality in the very staging:—the traditional ceremonial, and in the background the picture of Newton to remind us that the greatest of scientific generalisations was now, after more than two centuries, to receive its first modification. Nor was the personal interest wanting: a great adventure in thought had at length come safe to shore.

Let me here remind you that the essence of dramatic tragedy is not unhappiness. It resides in the solemnity of the remorseless working of things. This inevitableness of destiny can only be illustrated in terms of human life by incidents which in fact involve unhappiness. For it is only by them that the futility of escape can be made evident in the drama. This remorseless inevitableness is what pervades scientific thought. The laws of physics are the decrees of fate.

The conception of the moral order in the Greek plays was certainly not a discovery of the dramatists. It must have passed into the literary tradition from the general serious opinion of the times. But in finding this magnificent expression, it thereby deepened the stream of thought from which it arose. The spectacle of a moral order was impressed upon the imagination of a classical civilisation.

The time came when that great society decayed, and Europe passed into the Middle Ages. The direct influence of Greek literature vanished. But the concept of the moral order and of the order of nature had enshrined itself in the Stoic philosophy. For example, Lecky in his *History of European Morals* tells us 'Seneca maintains that the Divinity has determined all things by an inexorable law of destiny, which He has decreed, but which He Himself obeys.' But the most effective way in which the Stoics influenced the mentality of the Middle Ages was by the diffused sense of order which arose from Roman law. Again to quote Lecky, 'The Roman legislation was in a twofold manner the child of philosophy. It was in the first place formed upon the philosophical model, for, instead of being a mere empirical system adjusted to the existing requirements of society, it laid down abstract principles of right to which it endeavoured to conform; and, in the next place, these principles were borrowed directly from Stoicism.' In spite of the actual anarchy throughout large regions in Europe after the collapse of the Empire, the sense of legal order always haunted the racial memories of the Imperial populations. Also the Western Church was always there as a living embodiment of the traditions of Imperial rule.

It is important to notice that this legal impress upon medieval civilisation was not in the form of a few wise precepts which should permeate conduct. It was the conception of a definite articulated system which defines the legality of the detailed structure of social organism, and of the detailed way in which it should function. There was nothing vague. It was not a question of admirable maxims, but of definite procedure to put things right and to keep them there. The Middle Ages formed one long training of the intellect of Western Europe in the sense of order. There may have been some deficiency in respect to practice. But the idea never for a moment lost its grip. It was preëminently an epoch of orderly thought, rationalist through and through. The very anarchy quickened the sense for coherent system; just as the modern anarchy of Europe has stimulated the intellectual vision of a League of Nations.

But for science something more is wanted than a general sense of the order in things. It needs but a sentence to point out how the habit of definite exact thought was implanted in the European mind by the long dominance of scholastic logic and scholastic divinity. The habit remained after the philosophy had been repudiated, the priceless habit of looking for an exact point and of sticking to it when found. Galileo owes more to Aristotle than appears on the surface of his *Dialogues*: he owes to him his clear head and his analytic mind.

I do not think, however, that I have even yet brought out the greatest contribution of medievalism to the formation of the scientific movement. I mean the inexpungable belief that every detailed occurrence can be correlated with its antecedents in a perfectly definite manner, exemplifying general principles. Without this belief the incredible labours of scientists would be without hope. It is this instinctive conviction, vividly poised before the imagination, which is the motive power of research:—that there is a secret, a secret which can be unveiled. How has this conviction been so vividly implanted on the European mind?

When we compare this tone of thought in Europe with the attitude of other civilisations when left to themselves, there seems but one source for its origin. It must come from the medieval insistence on the rationality of God, conceived as with the personal energy of Jehovah and with the rationality of a Greek philosopher. Every detail was supervised and ordered: the search into nature could only result in the vindication of the faith in rationality. Remember that I am not talking of the explicit beliefs of a few individuals. What I mean is the impress on the European mind arising from the unquestioned faith of centuries. By this I mean the instinctive tone of thought and not a mere creed of words.

In Asia, the conceptions of God were of a being who was either too arbitrary or too impersonal for such ideas to have much effect on instinctive habits of mind. Any definite occurrence might be due to the fiat of an irrational despot, or might issue from some impersonal, inscrutable origin of things. There was not the same confidence as in the intelligible rationality of a personal being. I am not arguing that the European trust in the scrutability of nature was logically justified even by its own theology. My only point is to understand how it arose. My explanation is that the faith in the possibility of science, generated antecedently to the development of modern scientific theory, is an unconscious derivative from medieval theology.

But science is not merely the outcome of instinctive faith. It also requires an active interest in the simple occurrences of life for their own sake.

This qualification 'for their own sake' is important. The first phase of the Middle Ages was an age of symbolism. It was an age of vast ideas, and of primitive technique. There was little to be done with nature, except to coin a hard living from it. But there were realms of thought to be explored, realms of philosophy and realms of theology. Primitive art could symbolise those ideas which filled all thoughtful minds. The first phase of medieval art has a haunting charm beyond compare: its own intrinsic quality is enhanced by the fact that its message, which stretched beyond art's own self-justification of aesthetic achievement, was the symbolism of things lying behind nature itself. In this symbolic phase, medieval art energised in nature as its medium, but pointed to another world.

In order to understand the contrast between these early Middle Ages and the atmosphere required by the scientific mentality, we should compare the sixth century in Italy with the sixteenth century. In both centuries the Italian genius was laying the foundations of a new epoch. The history of the three centuries preceding the earlier period, despite the promise for the future introduced by the rise of Christianity, is overwhelmingly infected by the sense of the decline of civilisation. In each generation something has been lost. As we read the records, we are haunted by the shadow of the coming barbarism. There are great men, with fine achievements in action or in thought. But their total effect is merely for some short time to arrest the general decline. In the sixth century we are, so far as Italy is concerned, at the lowest point of the curve. But in that century every action is laying the foundation for the tremendous rise of the new European civilisation. In the background the Byzantine Empire, under Justinian, in three ways determined the character of the early Middle Ages in Western Europe. In the first place, its armies, under Belisarius and Narses, cleared Italy from the Gothic domination. In this way, the stage was freed for the exercise of the old Italian genius for creating organisations which shall be protective of ideals of cultural activity. It is impossible not to sympathise with the Goths: yet there can be no doubt but that a thousand years of the Papacy were infinitely more valuable for Europe than any effects derivable from a well-established Gothic kingdom of Italy.

In the second place, the codification of the Roman law established the ideal of legality which dominated the sociological thought of Europe in the succeeding centuries. Law is both an engine for government and a condition restraining government. The canon law of the Church, and the civil law of the State, owe to Justinian's lawyers their influence on the development of Europe. They established in the Western mind the ideal that an authority should be at once lawful, and law-enforcing, and should in itself exhibit a rationally adjusted system of organisation. The sixth century in Italy gave the initial exhibition of the way in which the impress of these ideas was fostered by contact with the Byzantine Empire.

Thirdly, in the non-political spheres of art and learning Constantinople exhibited a standard of realised achievement which, partly by the impulse to direct imitation, and partly by the indirect inspiration arising from the mere knowledge that such things existed, acted as a perpetual spur to Western culture. The wisdom of the Byzantines, as it stood in the imagination of the first phase of medieval mentality, and the wisdom of the Egyptians as it stood in the imagination of the early Greeks, played analogous rôles. Probably the actual knowledge of these respective wisdoms was, in either case, about as much as was good for the recipients. They knew enough to know the sort of standards which are attainable, and not enough to be fettered by static and traditional ways of thought. Accordingly, in both cases men went ahead on their own and did better. No account of the rise of the European scientific mentality can omit some notice of this influence of the Byzantine civilisation in the background. In the sixth century there is a crisis in the history of the relations between the Byzantines and the West; and this crisis is to be contrasted with the influence of Greek literature on European thought in the fifteenth and sixteenth centuries. The two outstanding men, who in the Italy of the sixth century laid the foundations of the future, were St. Benedict and Gregory the Great. By reference to them, we can at once see how absolutely in ruins was the approach to the scientific mentality which had been attained by the Greeks. We are at the zero point of scientific temperature. But the life-work of Gregory and of Benedict contributed elements to the reconstruction of Europe which secured that this reconstruction, when it arrived, should include a more effective scientific mentality than that of the ancient world. The Greeks were over-theoretical. For them science was an offshoot of philosophy. Gregory and Benedict were practical men, with an eye for the importance of ordinary things; and they combined this practical temperament with their religious and cultural activities. In particular, we owe it to St. Benedict that the monasteries were the homes of practical agriculturalists, as well as of saints and of artists and men of learning. The alliance of science with technology, by which learning is kept in contact with irreducible and stubborn facts, owes much to the practical bent of the early Benedictines. Modern science derives from Rome as well as from Greece, and this Roman strain explains its gain in an energy of thought kept closely in contact with the world of facts.

But the influence of this contact between the monasteries and the facts of nature showed itself first in art. The rise of Naturalism in the later Middle Ages was the entry into the European mind of the final ingredient necessary for the rise of science. It was the rise of interest in natural objects and in natural occurrences, for their own sakes. The natural foliage of a district was sculptured in out-of-the-way spots of the later buildings, merely as exhibiting delight in those familiar objects. The whole atmosphere of every art exhibited a direct joy in the apprehension of the things which lie around us. The craftsmen who executed the late medieval decorative sculpture, Giotto, Chaucer, Wordsworth, Walt Whitman, and, at the present day, the New England poet Robert Frost, are all akin to each other in this respect. The simple immediate facts are the topics of interest, and these reappear in the thought of science as the 'irreducible stubborn facts.'

The mind of Europe was now prepared for its new venture of thought. It is unnecessary to tell in detail the various incidents which marked the rise of science: the growth of wealth and leisure; the expansion of universities; the invention of printing; the taking of Constantinople; Copernicus; Vasco da Gama; Columbus; the telescope. The soil, the climate, the seeds, were there, and the forest grew. Science has never shaken off the impress of its origin in the historical revolt of the later Renaissance. It has remained predominantly an anti-rationalistic movement, based upon a naïve faith. What reasoning it has wanted, has been borrowed from mathematics which is a surviving relic of Greek rationalism, following the deductive method. Science repudiates philosophy. In other words, it has never cared to justify its faith or to explain its meanings; and has remained blandly indifferent to its refutation by Hume.

Of course the historical revolt was fully justified. It was wanted. It was more than wanted: it was an absolute necessity for healthy progress. The world required centuries of contemplation of irreducible and stubborn facts. It is difficult for men to do more than one thing at a time, and that was the sort of thing they had to do after the rationalistic orgy of the Middle Ages. It was a very sensible reaction; but it was not a protest on behalf of reason.

There is, however, a Nemesis which waits upon those who deliberately avoid avenues of knowledge. Oliver Cromwell's cry echoes down the ages, 'My brethren, by the bowels of Christ I beseech you, bethink you that you may be mistaken.'

The progress of science has now reached a turning point. The stable foundations of physics have broken up: also for the first time physiology is asserting itself as an effective body of knowledge, as distinct from a scrapheap. The old foundations of scientific thought are becoming unintelligible. Time, space, matter, material, ether, electricity, mechanism, organism, configuration, structure, pattern, function, all require reinterpretation. What is the sense of talking about a mechanical explanation when you do not know what you mean by mechanics?

The truth is that science started its modern career by taking over ideas derived from the weakest side of the philosophies of Aristotle's successors. In some respects it was a happy choice. It enabled the knowledge of the seventeeth century to be formularised so far as physics and chemistry were concerned, with a completeness which has lasted to the present time. But the progress of biology and psychology has probably been checked by the uncritical assumption of half-truths. If science is not to degenerate into a medley of *ad hoc* hypotheses, it must become philosophical and must enter upon a thorough criticism of its own foundations.

In the succeeding lectures of this course, I shall trace the success and the failures of the particular conceptions of cosmology with which the European intellect has clothed itself in the last three centuries. General climates of opinion persist for periods of about two to three generations, that is to say, for periods of sixty to a hundred years. There are also shorter waves of thought, which play on the surface of the tidal movement. We shall find, therefore, transformations in the European outlook, slowly modifying the successive centuries. There persists, however, throughout the whole period the fixed scientific cosmology which presupposes the ultimate fact of an irreducible brute matter, or material, spread throughout space in a flux of configurations. In itself such a material is senseless, valueless, purposeless. It just does what it does do, following a fixed routine imposed by external relations which do not spring from the nature of its being. It is this assumption that I call 'scientific materialism.' Also it is an assumption which I shall challenge as being entirely unsuited to the scientific situation at which we have now arrived. It is not wrong, if properly construed. If we confine ourselves to certain types of facts, abstracted from the complete circumstances in which they occur, the materialistic assumption expresses these facts to perfection. But when we pass beyond the abstraction, either by more subtle employment of our senses, or by the request for meanings and for coherence of thoughts, the scheme breaks down at once. The narrow efficiency of the scheme was the very cause of its supreme methodological success. For it directed attention to just those groups of facts which, in the state of knowledge then existing, required investigation.

The success of the scheme has adversely affected the various currents of European thought. The historical revolt was anti-rationalistic, because the rationalism of the scholastics required a sharp correction by contact with brute fact. But the revival of philosophy in the hands of Descartes and his successors was entirely coloured in its development by the acceptance of the scientific cosmology at its face value. The success of their ultimate ideas confirmed scientists in their refusal to modify them as the result of an enquiry into their rationality. Every philosophy was bound in some way or other to swallow them whole. Also the example of science affected other regions of thought. This historical revolt has thus been exaggerated into the exclusion of philosophy from its proper rôle of harmonising the various abstractions of methodological thought. Thought is abstract; and the intolerant use of abstractions is the major vice of the intellect. This vice is not wholly corrected by the recurrence to concrete experience. For after all, you need only attend to those aspects of your concrete experience which lie within some limited scheme. There are two methods for the purification of ideas. One of them is dispassionate observation by means of the bodily senses. But observation is selection. Accordingly, it is difficult to transcend a scheme of abstraction whose success is sufficiently wide. The other method is by comparing the various schemes of abstraction which are well founded in our various types of experience. This comparison takes the form of satisfying the demands of the Italian scholastic divines whom Paul Sarpi mentioned. They asked that *reason* should by used. Faith in reason is the trust that the ultimate natures of things lie together in a harmony which excludes mere arbitrariness. It is faith that at the base of things we shall not find mere arbitrary mystery. The faith in the order of nature which has made possible the growth of science is a particular example of a deeper faith. This faith cannot be justified by any inductive generalisation. It springs from direct inspection of the nature of things as disclosed in our own immediate present experience. There is no parting from your own shadow. To experience this faith is to know that in being ourselves we are more than ourselves: to know that our experience, dim and fragmentary as it is, yet sounds the utmost depths of reality: to know that detached details merely in order to be themselves demand that they should find themselves in a system of things: to know that this system includes the harmony of logical rationality, and the harmony of aesthetic achievement: to know that, while the harmony of logic lies upon the universe as an iron necessity, the aesthetic harmony stands before it as a living ideal moulding the general flux in its broken progress towards finer, subtler issues.

NOTE

1. Richard Hooker, *Laws of Ecclesiastical Polity,* Book III, Section viii.

C. G. Jung

MODERN MAN IN SEARCH OF A SOUL

THE SPIRITUAL PROBLEM OF MODERN MAN[1]

The spiritual problem of modern man is one of those questions which belong so intimately to the present in which we are living that we cannot judge of them fully. The modern man is a newly formed human being; a modern problem is a question which has just arisen and whose answer lies in the future. In speaking, therefore, of the spiritual problem of modern man we can at most state a question—and we should perhaps put this statement in different terms if we had but the faintest inkling of the answer. The question, moreover, seems rather vague; but the truth is that it has to do with something so universal that it exceeds the grasp of any single human being. We have reason enough, therefore, to approach such a problem with true moderation and with the greatest caution. I am deeply convinced of this, and wish it stressed the more because it is just such problems which tempt us to use high-sounding words—and because I shall myself be forced to say certain things which may sound immoderate and incautious.

To begin at once with an example of such apparent lack of caution, I must say that the man we call modern, the man who is aware of the immediate present, is by no means the average man. He is rather the man who stands upon a peak, or at the very edge of the world, the abyss of the future before him, above him the heavens, and below him the whole of mankind with a history that disappears in primeval mists. The modern man—or, let us say again, the man of the immediate present—is rarely met with. There are few who live up to the name, for they must be conscious to a superlative degree. Since to be wholly of the present means to be fully conscious of one's existence as a man, it requires the most intensive and extensive consciousness, with a minimum of unconsciousness. It must be clearly understood that the mere fact of living in the present does not make a man modern, for in that case everyone at present alive would be so. He alone is modern who is fully conscious of the present.

The man whom we can with justice call "modern" is solitary. He is so of necessity and at all times, for every step towards a fuller consciousness of the present removes him further from his original "*participation mystique*" with the mass of men—from submersion in a common unconsciousness. Every step forward means an act of tearing himself loose from that all-embracing, pristine unconsciousness which claims the bulk of mankind almost entirely. Even in our civilisations the people who form, psychologically speaking, the lowest stratum, live almost as unconsciously as primitive races. Those of the succeeding stratum manifest a level of consciousness which corresponds to the beginnings of human culture, while those of the highest stratum have a consciousness capable of keeping step with the life of the last few centuries. Only the man who is modern in our meaning of the term really lives in the present; he alone has a present-day consciousness, and he alone finds that the ways of life which correspond to earlier levels pall upon him. The values and strivings of those past worlds no longer interest him save from the historical standpoint. Thus he has become "unhistorical" in the deepest sense and has estranged himself from the mass of men who live entirely within the bounds of tradition. Indeed, he is completely modern only when he has come to the very edge of the world, leaving behind him all that has been discarded and outgrown, and acknowledging that he stands before a void out of which all things may grow.

These words may be thought to be but empty sound, and their meaning reduced to mere banality. Nothing is easier than to affect a consciousness of the present. As a matter of fact, a great horde of worthless people give themselves the air of being modern by overleaping the various stages of development and the tasks of life they represent. They appear suddenly by the side of the truly modern man as uprooted human beings, bloodsucking ghosts, whose emptiness is taken for the unenviable loneliness of the modern man and casts discredit upon him. He and his kind, few in number as they are, are hidden from the undiscerning eyes of mass-men by those clouds of ghosts, the pseudo-moderns. It cannot be helped; the "modern" man is questionable and suspect, and has always been so, even in the past.

An honest profession of modernity means voluntarily declaring bankruptcy, taking the vows of poverty and chastity in a new sense, and—what is still more painful—renouncing the halo which history bestows as a mark of its sanction. To be "unhistorical" is the Promethean sin, and in this sense modern man lives in sin. A higher level of consciousness is like a burden of guilt. But, as I have said, only the man who has outgrown the stages of consciousness belonging to the past and has amply fulfilled the duties appointed for him by his world, can achieve a full consciousness of the present. To do this he must be sound and proficient in the best sense—a man who has achieved as much as other people, and even a little more. It is these qualities which enable him to gain the next highest level of consciousness.

I know that the idea of proficiency is especially repugnant to the pseudo-moderns, for it reminds them unpleasantly of their deceits. This, however, cannot prevent us from taking it as our criterion of the modern man. We are even forced to do so, for unless he is proficient, the man who claims to be modern is nothing but an unscrupulous gambler. He must be proficient in the highest degree, for unless he can atone by creative ability for his break with tradition, he is merely disloyal to the past. It is sheer juggling to look upon a denial of the past as the same thing as consciousness of the present. "Today" stands between "yesterday" and "tomorrow", and forms a link between past and future; it has no other meaning. The present represents a process of transition, and that man may account himself modern who is conscious of it in this sense.

Many people call themselves modern—especially the pseudo-moderns. Therefore the really modern man is often to be found among those who call themselves old-fashioned. He takes this stand for sufficient reasons. On the one hand he emphasizes the past in order to hold the scales against his break with tradition and that effect of guilt of which I have spoken. On the other hand he wishes to avoid being taken for a pseudo-modern.

Every good quality has its bad side, and nothing that is good can come into the world without directly producing a corresponding evil. This is a painful fact. Now there is the danger that consciousness of the present may lead to an elation based upon illusion: the illusion, namely, that we are the culmination of the history of mankind, the fulfillment and the end-product of countless centuries. If we grant this, we should understand that it is no more than the proud acknowledgement of our destitution: we are also the disappointment of the hopes and expectations of the ages. Think of nearly two thousand years of Christian ideals followed, instead of by the return of the Messiah and the heavenly millennium, by the World War among Christian nations and its barbed-wire and poison-gas. What a catastrophe in heaven and on earth!

In the face of such a picture we may well grow humble again. It is true that modern man is a culmination, but tomorrow he will be surpassed; he is indeed the end-product of an age-old development, but he is at the same time the worst conceivable disappointment of the hopes of humankind. The modern man is aware of this. He has seen how beneficent are science, technology and organization, but also how catastrophic they can be. He has likewise seen that well-meaning governments have so thoroughly paved the way for peace on the principle "in time of peace prepare for war", that Europe has nearly gone to rack and ruin. And as for ideals, the Christian church, the brotherhood of man, international social democracy and the "solidarity" of economic interests have all failed to stand the baptism of fire—the test of reality. Today, fifteen years after the war, we observe once more the same optimism, the same organization, the same political aspirations, the same phrases and catch-words at work. How can we but fear that they will inevitably lead to further catastrophes? Agreements to outlaw war leave us sceptical, even while we wish them all possible success. At bottom, behind every such palliative measure, there is a gnawing doubt. On the whole, I believe I am not exaggerating when I say that modern man has suffered an almost fatal shock, psychologically speaking, and as a result has fallen into profound uncertainty.

These statements, I believe, make it clear enough that my being a physician has coloured my views. A doctor always spies out diseases, and I cannot cease to be a doctor. But it is essential to the physician's art that he should not discover diseases where none exists. I will therefore not make the assertion that the white races in general, and occidental nations in particular, are diseased, or that the Western world is on the verge of collapse. I am in no way competent to pass such a judgement.

It is of course only from my own experience with other persons and with myself that I draw my knowledge of the spiritual problem of modern man. I know something of the intimate psychic life of many hundreds of educated persons, both sick and healthy, coming from every quarter of the civilized, white world; and upon this experience I base my statements. No doubt I can draw only a one-sided picture, for the things I have observed are events of psychic life; they lie within us—on the *inner side,* if I may use the expression. I must point out that this is not always true of psychic life; the psyche is not always and everywhere to be found on the inner side. It is to be found on the *outside* in whole races or periods of history which take no account of psychic life as such. As examples we may choose any of the ancient cultures, but especially that of Egypt with its imposing objectivity and its naïve confession of sins that have not been committed.[2] We can no more feel the Pyramids and the Apis tombs of Sakkara to be expressions of personal problems or personal emotions, than we can feel this of the music of Bach.

Whenever there is etablished an external form, be it ritual or spiritual, by which all the yearnings and hopes of the soul are adequately expressed —as for instance in some living religion—then we may say that the psyche is outside, and no spiritual problem, strictly speaking, exists. In consonance with this truth, the development of psychology falls entirely within the last decades, although long before that man was introspective and intelligent enough to recognize the facts that are the subject-matter of psychology. The same was the case with technical knowledge. The Romans were familiar with all the mechanical principles and physical facts on the basis of which they could have constructed the steam-engine, but all that came of it was the toy made by Hero of Alexandria. There was no urgent necessity to go further. It was the division of labour and specialization in the nineteenth century which gave rise to the need to apply all available knowledge. So also a spiritual need has produced in our time our "discovery" of psychology. There has never, of course, been a time when the psyche did not manifest itself, but formerly it attracted no attention—no one noticed it. People got along without heeding it. But today we can no longer get along unless we give our best attention to the ways of the psyche.

It was men of the medical profession who were the first to notice this; for the priest is concerned only to establish an undisturbed functioning of the psyche within a recognized system of belief. As long as this system gives true expression to life, psychology can be nothing but a technical adjuvant to healthy living, and the psyche cannot be regarded as a problem in itself. While man still lives as a herd-being he has no "things of the spirit" of his own; nor does he need any, save the usual belief in the immortality of the soul. But as soon as he has outgrown whatever local form of religion he was born to—as soon as this religion can no longer embrace his life in all its fulness—then the psyche becomes something in its own right which cannot be dealt with by the measures of the Church alone. It is for this reason that we of today have a psychology founded on experience, and not upon articles of faith or the postulates of any philosophical system. The very fact that we have such a psychology is to me symptomatic of a profound convulsion of spiritual life. Disruption in the spiritual life of an age shows the same pattern as radical change in an individual. As long as all goes well and psychic energy finds its application in adequate and well-regulated ways, we are disturbed by nothing from within. No uncertainty or doubt besets us, and we *cannot* be divided against ourselves. But no sooner are one or two of the channels of psychic activity blocked, than we are reminded of a stream that is dammed up. The current flows backward to its source; the inner man wants something which the visible man does not want, and we are at war with ourselves. Only then, in this distress, do we discover the psyche; or, more precisely, we come upon something which thwarts our will, which is strange and even hostile to us, or which is incompatible with our conscious standpoint. Freud's psychoanalytic labours show this process in the clearest way. The very first thing he discovered was the existence of sexually perverse and criminal fantasies which at their face value are wholly incompatible with the conscious outlook of a civilized man. A person who was activated by them would be nothing less than a mutineer, a criminal or a madman.

We cannot suppose that this aspect of the unconscious or of the hinterland of man's mind is something totally new. Probably it has always been there, in every culture. Each culture gave birth to its destructive opposite, but no culture or civilization before our own was ever forced to take these psychic undercurrents in deadly earnest. Psychic life always found expression in a metaphysical system of some sort. But the conscious, modern man, despite his strenuous and dogged efforts to do so, can no longer refrain from acknowledging the might of psychic forces. This distinguishes our time from all others. We can no longer deny that the dark stirrings of the unconscious are effective powers—that psychic forces exist which cannot, for the present at least, be fitted in with our rational world-order. We have even enlarged our study of these forces to a science—one more proof of the earnest attention we bring to them. Previous centuries could throw them aside unnoticed; for us they are a shirt of Nessus which we cannot strip off.

The revolution in our conscious outlook, brought about by the catastrophic results of the World War, shows itself in our inner life by the shattering of our faith in ourselves and our own worth. We used to regard foreigners—the other side—as political and moral reprobates; but the modern man is forced to recognize that he is politically and morally just like anyone else. Whereas I formerly believed it to be my bounden duty to call other persons to order, I now admit that I need calling to order myself. I admit this the more readily because I realize only too well that I am losing my faith in the possibility of a rational organization of the world, that old dream of the millennium, in which peace and harmony should rule, has grown pale. The modern man's scepticism regarding all such matters has chilled his enthusiasm for politics and world-reform; more than that, it does not favour any smooth application of psychic energies to the outer world. Through his scepticism the modern man is thrown back upon himself; his energies flow towards their source and wash to the surface those psychic contents which are at all times there, but lie hidden in the silt as long as the stream flows smoothly in its course. How totally different did the world appear to mediæval man! For him the earth was eternally fixed and at rest in the centre of the universe, encircled by the course of a sun that solicitously bestowed its warmth. Men were all children of God under the loving care of the Most High, who prepared them for eternal blessedness; and all knew exactly what they should do and how they should conduct themselves in order to rise from a corruptible world to an incorruptible and joyous existence. Such a life no longer seems real to us, even in our dreams. Natural science has long ago torn this lovely veil to shreds. That age lies as far behind as childhood, when one's own father was unquestionably the handsomest and strongest man on earth.

The modern man has lost all the metaphysical certainties of his mediæval brother, and set up in their place the ideals of material security, general welfare and humaneness. But it takes more than an ordinary dose of optimism to make it appear that these ideals are still unshaken. Material security, even, has gone by the board, for the modern man begins to see that every step in material "progress" adds just so much force to the threat of a more stupendous catastrophe. The very picture terrorizes the imagination. What are we to imagine when cities today perfect measures of defence against poison-gas attacks, and practise them in "dress rehearsals"? We cannot but suppose that such attacks have been planned and provided for—again on the principle "in time of peace prepare for war". Let man but accumulate his materials of destruction and the devil within him will soon be unable to resist putting them to their fated use. It is well known that fire-arms go off of themselves if only enough of them are together.

An intimation of the law that governs blind contingency, which Heraclitus called the rule of *enantiodromia* (conversion into the opposite), now steals upon the modern man through the by-ways of his mind, chilling him with fear and paralysing his faith in the lasting effectiveness of social and political measures in the face of these monstrous forces. If he turns away from the terrifying prospect of a blind world in which building and destroying successively tip the scale, and if he then turns his gaze inward upon the recesses of his own mind, he will discover a chaos and a darkness there which he would gladly ignore. Science has destroyed even the refuge of the inner life. What was once a sheltering haven has become a place of terror.

And yet it is almost a relief for us to come upon so much evil in the depths of our own minds. We are able to believe, at least, that we have discovered the root of the evil in mankind. Even though we are shocked and disillusioned at first, we yet feel, because these things are manifestations of our own minds, that we hold them more or less in our own hands and can therefore correct or at least effectively suppress them. We like to assume that, of we succeeded in this, we should have rooted out some fraction of the evil in the world. We like to think that, on the basis of a widespread knowledge of the unconscious and its ways, no one could be deceived by a statesman who was unaware of his own bad motives; the very newspapers would pull him up: "Please have yourself analysed; you are suffering from a repressed father-complex."

I have purposely chosen this grotesque example to show to what absurdities we are led by the illusion that because something is psychic it is under our control. It is, however, true that much of the evil in the world is due to the fact that man in general is hopelessly unconscious, as it is also true that with increasing insight we can combat this evil at its source in ourselves. As science enables us to deal with injuries inflicted from without, so it helps us to treat those arising from within.

The rapid and world-wide growth of a "psychological" interest over the last two decades shows unmistakably that modern man has to some extent turned his attention from material things to his own subjective processes. Should we call this mere curiosity? At any rate, art has a way of anticipating future changes in man's fundamental outlook, and expressionist art has taken this subjective turn well in advance of the more general change.

This "psychological" interest of the present time shows that man expects something from psychic life which he has not received from the outer world: something which our religions, doubtless, ought to contain, but no longer do contain—at least for the modern man. The various forms of religion no longer appear to the modern man to come from within—to be expressions of his own psychic life; for him they are to be classed with the things of the outer world. He is vouchsafed no revelation of a spirit that is not of this world; but he tries on a number of religions and convictions as if they were Sunday attire, only to lay them aside again like worn-out clothes.

Yet he is somehow fascinated by the almost pathological manifestations of the unconscious mind. We must admit the fact, however difficult it is for us to understand that something which previous ages have discarded should suddenly command our attention. That there is a general interest in these matters is a truth which cannot be denied, their offence to good taste notwithstanding. I am not thinking merely of the interest taken in psychology as a science, or of the still narrower interest in the psychoanalysis of Freud, but of the widespread interest in all sorts of psychic phenomena as manifested in the growth of spiritualism, astrology, theosophy, and so forth. The world has seen nothing like it since the end of the seventeenth century. We can compare it only to the flowering of Gnostic thought in the first and second centuries after Christ. The spiritual currents of the present have, in fact, a deep affinity with Gnosticism. There is even a Gnostic church in France today, and I know of two schools in Germany which openly declare themselves Gnostic. The modern movement which is numerically most impressive is undoubtedly Theosophy, together with its continental sister, Anthroposophy; these are pure Gnosticism in a Hindu dress. Compared with these movements the interest in scientific psychology is negligible. What is striking about Gnostic systems is that they are based exclusively upon the manifestations of the unconscious, and that their moral teachings do not balk at the shadow-side of life. Even in the form of its European revival, the Hindu *Kundalini-Yoga* shows this clearly. And as every person informed on the subject of occultism will testify, the statement holds true in this field as well.

The passionate interest in these movements arises undoubtedly from psychic energy which can no longer be invested in obsolete forms of religion. For this reason such movements have a truly religious character, even when they pretend to be scientific. It changes nothing when Rudolf Steiner calls his Anthroposophy "spiritual science", or Mrs. Eddy discovers a "Christian Science". These attempts at concealment merely show that religion has grown suspect—almost as suspect as politics and world-reform.

I do not believe that I am going too far when I say that modern man, in contrast to his nineteenth-century brother, turns his attention to the psyche with very great expectations; and that he does so without reference to any traditional creed, but rather in the Gnostic sense of religious experience. We should be wrong in seeing mere caricature or masquerade when the movements already mentioned try to give themselves scientific airs; their doing so is rather an indication that they are actually pursuing "science" or knowledge instead of the *faith* which is the essence of Western religions. The modern man abhors dogmatic postulates taken on faith and the religions based upon them. He holds them valid only in so far as their knowledge-content seems to accord with his own experience of the deeps of psychic life. He wants to know—to experience for himself. Dean Inge of St. Paul's has called attention to a movement in the Anglican Church with similar objectives.

The age of discovery has only just come to a close in our day when no part of the earth remains unexplored; it began when men would no longer *believe* that the Hyperboreans inhabited the land of eternal sunshine, but wanted to find out and to see with their own eyes what existed beyond the boundaries of the known world. Our age is apparently bent on discovering what exists in the psyche outside of consciousness. The question asked in every spiritualistic circle is: What happens when the medium has lost consciousness? Every Theosophist asks: What shall I experience at higher levels of consciousness? The question which every astrologer puts is this: What are the effective forces and determinants of my fate beyond the reach of my conscious intention? And every psychoanalyst wants to know: What are the unconscious drives behind the neurosis?

Our age wishes to have actual experiences in psychic life. It wants to experience for itself, and not to make assumptions based on the experience of other ages. Yet this does not preclude its trying anything in a hypothetical way—for instance, the recognized religions and the genuine sciences. The European of yesterday will feel a slight shudder run down his spine when he gazes at all deeply into these delvings. Not only does he consider the subject of this research all too obscure and uncanny, but even the methods employed seem to him a shocking misuse of man's finest intellectual attainments. What can we expect an astronomer to say when he is told that at least a thousand horoscopes are drawn today to one three hundred years ago? What will the educator and the advocate of philosophical enlightenment say to the fact that the world has not been freed of one single superstition since Greek antiquity? Freud himself, the founder of psychoanalysis, has thrown a glaring light upon the dirt, darkness and evil of the psychic hinterland, and has presented these things as so much refuse and slag; he has thus taken the utmost pains to discourage people from seeking anything behind them. He did not succeed, and his warning has even brought about the very thing he wished to prevent: it has awakened in many people an admiration for all this filth. We are tempted to call this sheer perversity; and we could hardly explain it save on the ground that it is not a love of dirt, but the fascination of the psyche, which draws these people.

There can be no doubt that from the beginning of the nineteenth century—from the memorable years of the French Revolution onwards—man has given a more and more prominent place to the psyche, his increasing attentiveness to it being the measure of its growing attraction for him. The enthronement of the Goddess of Reason in Nôtre Dame seems to have been a symbolic gesture of great significance to the Western world—rather like the hewing down of Wotan's oak by the Christian missionaries. For then, as at the Revolution, no avenging bolt from heaven struck the blasphemer down.

It is certainly more than an amusing coincidence that just at that time a Frenchman, Anquetil du Perron, was living in India, and, in the early eighteen-hundreds, brought back with him a translation of the *Oupnek'-hat*—a collection of fifty *Upanishads*—which gave the Western world its first deep insight into the baffling mind of the East. To the historian this is mere chance without any factors of cause and effect. But in view of my medical experience I cannot take it as accident. It seems to me rather to satisfy a psychological law whose validity in personal life, at least, is complete. For every piece of conscious life that loses its importance and value—so runs the law—there arises a compensation in the unconscious. We may see in this an analogy to the conservation of energy in the physical world, for our psychic processes have a quantitative aspect also. No psychic value can disappear without being replaced by another of equivalent intensity. This is a rule which finds its pragmatic sanction in the daily practice of the psychotherapist; it is repeatedly verified and never fails. Now the doctor in me refuses point blank to consider the life of a people as something that does not conform to psychological law. A people, in the doctor's eyes, presents only a somewhat more complex picture of psychic life than the individual. Moreover, taking it the other way round, has not a poet spoken of the "nations" of his soul? And quite correctly, as it seems to me, for in one of its aspects the psyche is not individual, but is derived from the nation, from collectivity, or from humanity even. In some way or other we are part of an all-embracing psychic life, of a single "greatest" man, to quote Swedenborg.

And so we can draw a parallel: just as in me, a single human being, the darkness calls forth the helpful light, so does it also in the psychic life of a people. In the crowds that poured into Nôtre Dame, bent on destruction, dark and nameless forces were at work that swept the individual off his feet; these forces worked also upon Anquetil du Perron, and provoked an answer which has come down in history. For he brought the Eastern mind to the West, and its influence upon us we cannot as yet measure. Let us beware of underestimating it! So far, indeed, there is little of it to be seen in Europe on the intellectual surface: some orientalists, one or two Buddhist enthusiasts, and a few sombre celebrities like Madame Blavatsky and Annie Besant. These manifestations make us think of tiny, scattered islands in the ocean of mankind; in reality they are like the peaks of submarine mountain-ranges of considerable size. The Philistine believed until recently that astrology had been disposed of long since, and was something that could be safely laughed at. But today, rising out of the social deeps, it knocks at the doors of the universities from which it was banished some three hundred years ago. The same is true of the thought of the East; it takes root in the lower social levels and slowly grows to the surface. Where did the five or six million Swiss francs for the Anthroposophist temple at Dornach come from? Certainly not from one individual. Unfortunately there are no statistics to tell us the exact number of avowed Theosophists today, not to mention the unavowed. But we can be sure that there are several millions of them. To this number we must add a few million Spiritualists of Christian or Theosophic leanings.

Great innovations never come from above; they come invariably from below; just as trees never grow from the sky downward, but upward from the earth, however true it is that their seeds have fallen from above. The upheaval of our world and the upheaval in consciousness is one and the same. Everything becomes relative and therefore doubtful. And while man, hesitant and questioning, contemplates a world that is distracted with treaties of peace and pacts of friendship, democracy and dictatorship, capitalism and Bolshevism, his spirit yearns for an answer that will allay the turmoil of doubt and uncertainty. And it is just people of the lower social levels who follow the unconscious forces of the psyche; it is the much-derided, silent folk of the land—those who are less infected with academic prejudices than great celebrities are wont to be. All these people, looked at from above, present mostly a dreary or laughable comedy; and yet they are as impressively simple as those Galileans who were once called blessed. Is it not touching to see the refuse of man's psyche gathered together in compendia a foot thick? We find recorded in *Anthropophyteia* with scrupulous care the merest babblings, the most absurd actions and the wildest fantasies, while men like Havelock Ellis and Freud have dealt with the like matters in serious treatises which have been accorded all scientific honours. Their reading public is scattered over the breadth of the civilized, white world. How are we to explain this zeal, this almost fanatical worship of repellent things? In this way: the repellent things belong to the psyche, they are of the substance of the psyche and therefore as precious as fragments of manuscript salvaged from ancient ruins. Even the secret and noisome things of the inner life are valuable to modern man because they serve his purpose. But what purpose?

Freud has prefixed to his *Interpretation of Dreams* the citation: *Flectere si nequeo superos Acheronta movebo*—"If I cannot bend the gods on high, I will at least set Acheron in uproar". But to what purpose?

The gods whom *we* are called to dethrone are the idolized values of our conscious world. It is well known that it was the love-scandals of the ancient deities which contributed most to their discredit; and now history is repeating itself. People are laying bare the dubious foundations of our belauded virtues and incomparable ideals, and are calling out to us in triumph: "There are your man-made gods, mere snares and delusions tainted with human baseness—whited sepulchres full of dead men's bones and of all uncleanness". We recognize a familiar strain, and the Gospel words, which we never could make our own, now come to life again.

I am deeply convinced that these are not vague analogies. There are too many persons to whom Freudian psychology is dearer than the Gospels, and to whom the Russian Terror means more than civic virtue. And yet all these people are our brothers, and in each of us there is at least *one* voice which seconds them—for in the end there is a psychic life which embraces us all.

The unexpected result of this spiritual change is that an uglier face is put upon the world. It becomes so ugly that no one can love it any longer—we cannot even love ourselves—and in the end there is nothing in the outer world to draw us away from the reality of the life within. Here, no doubt, we have the true significance of this spiritual change. After all, what does Theosophy, with its doctrines of *karma* and reincarnation, seek to teach except that this world of appearance is but a temporary health-resort for the morally unperfected? It depreciates the present-day world no less radically than does the modern outlook, but with the help of a different technique; it does not vilify our world, but grants it only a relative meaning in that it promises other and higher worlds. The result is in either case the same.

I grant that all these ideas are extremely "unacademic", the truth being that they touch modern man on the side where he is least conscious. Is it again a mere coincidence that modern thought has had to come to terms with Einstein's relativity theory and with ideas about the structure of the atom which lead us away from determinism and visual representation? Even physics volatilizes our material world. It is no wonder, then, in my opinion, if the modern man falls back upon the reality of psychic life and expects from it that certainty which the world denies him.

But spiritually the Western world is in a precarious situation—and the danger is greater the more we blind ourselves to the merciless truth with illusions about our beauty of soul. The Occidental burns incense to himself, and his own countenance is veiled from him in the smoke. But how do we strike men of another colour? What do China and India think of us? What feelings do we arouse in the black man? And what is the opinion of all those whom we deprive of their lands and exterminate with rum and venereal disease?

I have a Red Indian friend who is the governor of a pueblo. When we were once speaking confidentially about the white man, he said to me: "We don't understand the whites; they are always wanting something—always restless—always looking for something. What is it? We don't know. We can't understand them. They have such sharp noses, such thin, cruel lips, such lines in their faces. We think they are all crazy."

My friend had recognized, without being able to name it, the Aryan bird of prey with his insatiable lust to lord it in every land—even those that concern him not at all. And he had also noted that megalomania of ours which leads us to suppose, among other things, that Christianity is the only truth, and the white Christ the only Redeemer. After setting the whole East in turmoil with our science and technology, and exacting tribute from it, we send our missionaries even to China. The stamping out of polygamy by the African missions has given rise to prostitution on such a scale that in Uganda alone twenty thousand pounds sterling is spent yearly on preventatives of venereal infection, not to speak of the moral consequences, which have been of the worst. And the good European pays his missionaries for these edifying achievements! No need to mention also the story of suffering in Polynesia and the blessings of the opium trade.

That is how the European looks when he is extricated from the cloud of his own moral incense. No wonder that to unearth buried fragments of psychic life we have first to drain a miasmal swamp. Only a great idealist like Freud could devote a lifetime to the unclean work. This is the beginning of our psychology. For us acquaintance with the realities of psychic life could start only at this end, with all that repels us and that we do not wish to see.

But if the psyche consisted for us only of evil and worthless things, no power in the world could induce a normal man to pretend to find it attractive. This is why people who see in Theosophy nothing but regrettable intellectual superficiality, and in Freudian psychology nothing but sensationalism, prophesy an early and inglorious end for these movements. They overlook the fact that they derive their force from the fascination of psychic life. No doubt the passionate interest that is aroused by them may find other expressions; but it will certainly show itself in these forms until they are replaced by something better. Superstition and preversity are after all one and the same. They are transitional or embryonic stages from which new and riper forms will emerge.

Whether from the intellectual, the moral or the æsthetic viewpoint, the undercurrents of the psychic life of the West present an uninviting picture. We have built a monumental world around about us, and have slaved for it with unequaled energy. But it is so imposing only because we have spent upon the outside al that is imposing in our natures—and what we find when we look within must necesarily be as it is, shabby and insufficient.

I am aware that in saying this I somewhat anticipate the actual growth of consciousness. There is as yet no general insight into these facts of psychic life. Westerners are only on the way to a recognition of these facts, and for quite understandable reasons they struggle violently against it. Of course Spengler's pessimism has exerted some influence, but this has been safely confined to academic circles. As for psychological insight, it always trespasses upon personal life, and therefore meets with personal resistances and denials. I am far from considering these resistances meaningless; on the contrary I see in them a healthy reaction to something which threatens destruction. Whenever relativism is taken as a fundamental and final principle it has a destructive effect. When, therefore, I call attention to the dismal undercurrents of the psyche, it is not in order to sound a pessimistic note; I wish rather to emphasize the fact that the unconscious has a strong attraction not only for the sick, but for healthy, constructive minds as well—and this in spite of its alarming aspect. The psychic depths are nature, and nature is creative life. It is true that nature tears down what she has herself built up—yet she builds it once again. Whatever values in the visible world are destroyed by modern relativism, the psyche will produce their equivalents. At first we cannot see beyond the path that leads downward to dark and hateful things—but no light or beauty will ever come from the man who cannot bear this sight. Light is always born of darkness, and the sun never yet stood still in heaven to satisfy man's longing or to still his fears. Does not the example of Anquetil du Perron show us how psychic life survives its own eclipse? China hardly believes that European science and technology are preparing her ruin. Why should we believe that we must be destroyed by the secret, spiritual influence of the East?

But I forget that we do not yet realize that while we are turning upside down the material world of the East with our technical proficiency, the East with its psychic proficiency is throwing our spiritual world into confusion. We have never yet hit upon the thought that while we are overpowering the Orient from without, it may be fastening its hold upon us from within. Such an idea strikes us as almost insane, because we have eyes only for gross material connections, and fail to see that we must lay the blame for the intellectual confusion of our middle class at the doors of Max Müller, Oldenberg, Neumann, Deussen, Wilhelm and others like them. What does the example of the Roman Empire teach us? After the conquest of Asia Minor, Rome became Asiatic; even Europe was infected by Asia, and remains so today. Out of Cilicia came the Mithraic cult—the religion of the Roman army—and it spread from Egypt to fogbound Britain. Need I point to the Asiatic origin of Christianity?

We have not yet clearly grasped the fact that Western Theosophy is an amateurish imitation of the East. We are just taking up astrology again, and that to the Oriental is his daily bread. Our studies of sexual life, originating in Vienna and in England, are matched or surpassed by Hindu teachings on this subject. Oriental texts ten centuries old introduce us to philosophical relativism, while the idea of indetermination, newly broached in the West, furnishes the very basis of Chinese science. Richard Wilhelm has even shown me that certain complicated processes discovered by analytical psychology are recognizably described in ancient Chinese texts. Psychoanalysis itself and the lines of thought to which it gives rise—surely a distinctly Western development—are only a beginner's attempt compared to what is an immemorial art in the East. It should be mentioned that the parallels between psychoanalysis and yoga have already been traced by Oskar A. H. Schmitz.

The Theosophists have an amusing idea that certain Mahatmas, seated somewhere in the Himalayas or Tibet, inspire or direct every mind in the world. So strong, in fact, can be the influence of the Eastern belief in magic upon Europeans of a sound mind, that some of them have assured me that I am unwittingly inspired by the Mahatmas with every good thing I say, my own inspirations being of no account whatever. This myth of the Mahatmas, widely circulated and firmly believed in the West, far from being nonsense, is—like every myth—an important psychological truth. It seems to be quite true that the East is at the bottom of the spiritual change we are passing through today. Only this East is not a Tibetan monastery full of Mahatmas, but in a sense lies within us. It is from the depths of our own psychic life that new spiritual forms will arise; they will be expressions of psychic forces which may help to subdue the boundless lust for prey of Aryan man. We shall perhaps come to know something of that circumscription of life which has grown in the

East into a dubious quietism; also something of that stability which human existence acquires when the claims of the spirit become as imperative as the necessities of social life. Yet in this age of Americanization we are still far from anything of the sort, and it seems to me that we are only at the threshold of a new spiritual epoch. I do not wish to pass myself off as a prophet, but I cannot outline the spiritual problem of modern man without giving emphasis to the yearning for rest that arises in a period of unrest, or to the longing for security that is bred of insecurity. It is from need and distress that new forms of life take their rise, and not from mere wishes or from the requirements of our ideals.

To me, the crux of the spiritual problem of today is to be found in the fascination which psychic life exerts upon modern man. If we are pessimists, we shall call it a sign of decadence; if we are optimistically inclined, we shall see in it the promise of a far-reaching spiritual change in the Western world. At all events, it is a significant manifestation. It is the more noteworthy because it shows itself in broad sections of every people; and it is the more important because it is a matter of those imponderable psychic forces which transform human life in ways that are unforeseen and—as history shows—unforeseeable. These are the forces, still invisible to many persons today, which are at the bottom of the present "psychological" interest. When the attractive power of psychic life is so strong that man is neither repelled nor dismayed by what he is sure to find, then it has nothing of sickliness or perversion about it.

Along the great highroads of the world everything seems desolate and outworn. Instinctively the modern man leaves the trodden ways to explore the by-paths and lanes, just as the man of the Græco-Roman world cast off his defunct Olympian gods and turned to the mystery-cults of Asia. The force within us that impels us to the search, turning outward, annexes Eastern Theosophy and magic; but it also turns inward and leads us to give our thoughtful attention to the unconscious psyche. It inspires in us the self-same scepticism and relentlessness with which a Buddha swept aside his two million gods that he might come to the pristine experience which alone is convincing.

And now we must ask a final question. Is what I have said of the modern man really true, or is it perhaps the result of an optical illusion? There can be no doubt whatever that the facts I have cited are wholly irrelevant contingencies in the eyes of many millions of Westerners, and seem only regrettable errors to a large number of educated persons. But I may ask: What did a cultivated Roman think of Christianity when he saw it spreading among the people of the lowest classes? The biblical God is still a living person in the Western world—as living as Allah beyond the Mediterranean. One kind of believer holds the other an ignoble heretic, to be pitied and tolerated if he cannot be changed. What is more, a clever European is convinced that religion and such things are good enough for the masses and for women, but are of little weight compared to economic and political affairs.

So I am refuted all along the line, like a man who predicts a thunderstorm when there is not a cloud in the sky. Perhaps it is a storm beneath the horizon that he senses—and it may never reach us. But what is significant in psychic life is always below the horizon of consciousness, and when we speak of the spiritual problem of modern man we are dealing with things that are barely visible—with the most intimate and fragile things—with flowers that open only in the night. In daylight everything is clear and tangible; but the night lasts as long as the day, and we live in the night-time also. There are persons who have bad dreams which even spoil their days for them. And the day's life is for many people such a bad dream that they long for the night when the spirit awakes. I even believe that there are nowadays a great many such people, and this is why I maintain that the spiritual problem of modern man is much as I have presented it. I must plead guilty, indeed, to the charge of one-sidedness, for I have not mentioned the modern spirit of commitment to a practical world about which everyone has much to say because it lies in such full view. We find it in the ideal of internationalism or supernationalism which is embodied in the League of Nations and the like; and we find it also in sport and, very expressively, in the cinema and in jazz music.

These are certainly characteristic symptoms of our time; they show unmistakably how the ideal of humanism is made to embrace the body also. Sport represents an exceptional valuation of the human body, as does also modern dancing. The cinema, on the other hand, like the detective story, makes it possible to experience without danger all the excitement, passion and desirousness which must be repressed in a humanitarian ordering of life. It is not difficult to see how these symptoms are connected with the psychic situation. The attractive power of the psyche brings about a new self-estimation—a re-estimation of the basic facts of human nature. We can hardly be surprised if this leads to the rediscovery of the body after its long depreciation in the name of the spirit. We are even tempted to speak of the body's revenge upon the spirit. When Keyserling sarcastically singles out the chauffeur as the culture-hero of our time, he has struck, as he often does, close to the mark. The body lays claim to equal recognition; like the psyche, it also exerts a fascination. If we are still caught by the old idea of an antithesis between mind and matter, the present state of affairs means an unbearable contradiction; it may even divide us against ourselves. But if we can reconcile ourselves with the mysterious truth that spirit is the living body seen from within, and the body the outer manifestation of the living spirit—the two being really one

—then we can understand why it is that the attempt to transcend the present level of consciousness must give its due to the body. We shall also see that belief in the body cannot tolerate an outlook that denies the body in the name of the spirit. These claims of physical and psychic life are so pressing compared to similar claims in the past, that we may be tempted to see in this a sign of decadence. Yet it may also signify a rejuvenation, for as Hölderlin says:

> Danger itself
> Fosters the rescuing power.[3]

What we actually see is that the Western world strikes up a still more rapid tempo—the American tempo—the very opposite of quietism and resigned aloofness. An enormous tension arises between the opposite poles of outer and inner life, between objective and subjective reality. Perhaps it is a final race between ageing Europe and young America; perhaps it is a desperate or a wholesome effort of conscious man to cheat the laws of nature of their hidden might and to wrest a yet greater, more heroic victory from the sleep of the nations. This is a question which history will answer.

In coming to a close after so many bold assertions, I would like to return to the promise made at the outset to be mindful of the need for moderation and caution. Indeed, I do not forget that my voice is but one voice, my experience a mere drop in the sea, my knowledge no greater than the visual field in a microscope, my mind's eye a mirror that reflects a small corner of the world, and my ideas—a subjective confession.

NOTES

1. The author has made some changes in this essay since its publication in German. (*Trans.*)

2. According to Egyptian tradition, when the dead man meets his judges in the underworld, he makes a detailed confession of the crimes he has *not* committed, but leaves unmentioned his actual sins. (*Trans.*)

3. *Wo Gefahr ist,*
Wächst das Rettende auch. (Hölderlin.)

Seami Motokiyo

ON ATTAINING THE STAGE OF YŪGEN

Yūgen is considered to be the mark of supreme attainment in all the arts and accomplishments. In the art of the *Nō* in particular, the manifestation of *yūgen* is of the first importance. When *yūgen* in the *Nō* is displayed, it is generally apparent to the eye, and it is the one thing which audiences most admire, but actors who possess *yūgen* are few and far between. This is because they do not know its true meaning and so do not reach that stage.

In what kind of place is the stage of *yūgen* to be found? Let us begin by examining the various classes of people on the basis of the appearance that they made in society. May we not say of the courtiers whose behavior is distinguished and whose appearance far surpasses that of other men, that they are at the stage of *yūgen*? From this we may see that the essence of *yūgen* is true beauty and gentleness. Tranquillity and elegance make for *yūgen* in personal appearance. In the same way, the *yūgen* of discourse lies in a grace of language and a complete mastery of the speech of the nobility and the gentry so that even the most casual utterance will be graceful. A musical performance may be said to possess *yūgen* when the melody flows beautifully and sounds smooth and sensitive. A dance will possess *yūgen* when the discipline has been thoroughly mastered and the audience is delighted by the performer's movements and by his serene appearance. Acting possesses *yūgen* when the performance of the Three Roles[1] is beautiful. If the characterization calls for a display of anger or for the representation of a devil, the actions may be somewhat forceful, but as long as the actor never loses sight of the beauty of the effect and bears in mind always the correct balance between his mental and physical actions and between the movements of his body and feet,[2] his appearance will be so beautiful that it may be called the "*yūgen* of a devil."

All these aspects of *yūgen* must be kept in mind and made a part of the actor's body, so that whatever part he may be playing *yūgen* will never be absent. Whether the character he portrays be of high or low birth, man or woman, priest, peasant, rustic, beggar, or outcast, he should think of each of them as crowned with a wreath of flowers. Although their positions in society differ, the fact that they can all appreciate the beauty of flowers makes flowers of all of them.[3] Their particular flower is shown by their outward appearance. An actor, through the use of his intelligence, makes his presentation seem beautiful. It is his intelligence which permits him to grasp the above principles; to learn poetry so as to impart *yūgen* to his discourse; and to study the most elegant costuming so as to give *yūgen* to his bearing. Though the characterization varies according to the different parts, the actor should realize that the ability to appear beautiful is the seed of *yūgen*. It is all too apt to happen that an actor, believing that once he has mastered the characterization of the different parts he has attained the highest stage of excellence, forgets his appearance and is therefore unable to enter the realm of *yūgen*. Unless, however, he enters that realm he will not attain to the highest achievements, and will therefore not become a great master. That is why there are so few masters. The actor must consider *yūgen* as the most important aspect of his art, and study to perfect his understanding of it.

The "highest achievements" of which I have spoken are beauty of form and manner. The most careful attention must be given to the appearance presented. When the form is beautiful, whether in dancing, singing, or in any type of characterization, it may be called a "highest achievement." When the form is ugly, the performance will be inferior. The actor should realize that *yūgen* is attained when all different forms of visual and aural expression are beautiful. It is when the actor himself has worked out these principles and made himself their master that he may be said to have entered the realm of *yūgen*. If he fails to work out these principles for himself, he will not master them, and however much he may aspire to attain *yūgen,* he will never in all his life do so.

NOTES

1. Seami considered the Three Basic Roles to be those of the old person, the woman, and the warrior.

2. Seami elsewhere discusses the relation between what the actor expresses with his body and what he knows but does not overtly express. At first an actor who has studied with a master does not know any more than what he has learned and what he expresses, but as he himself acquires mastery there are things which he comes to understand beyond what he has been taught, and which he suggests rather than expresses. The relation between the movements of the body and feet refers to a theory of Seami's that if the body and the feet move in the same manner the effect will be crude. Thus, in an agitated passage when the feet are stamping wildly, the movements of the body should be gentle or a disorderly effect will be produced which will mar the spectator's enjoyment.

3. That is, their love of beauty makes them beautiful, irrespective of their station.

AN EARTHLY STORY WITH A HELLISH MEANING

D. H. Lawrence

STUDIES IN CLASSIC AMERICAN LITERATURE

NATHANIEL HAWTHORNE AND THE SCARLET LETTER

Nathaniel Hawthorne writes romance.

And what's romance? Usually, a nice little tale where you have everything As You Like It, where rain never wets your jacket and gnats never bite your nose and it's always daisy-time. *As You Like It* and *Forest Lovers*, etc. *Morte D'Arthur*.

Hawthorne obviously isn't this kind of romanticist: though nobody has muddy boots in *The Scarlet Letter*, either.

But there is more to it. *The Scarlet Letter* isn't a pleasant, pretty romance. It is a sort of parable, an earthly story with a hellish meaning.

All the time there is this split in the American art and art-consciousness. On the top it is as nice as pie, goody-goody and lovey-dovey. Like Hawthorne being such a blue-eyed darling, in life, and Longfellow and the rest such sucking-doves. Hawthorne's wife said she "never saw him in time," which doesn't mean she saw him too late. But always in the "frail effulgence of eternity."

Serpents they were. Look at the inner meaning of their art and see what demons they were.

You *must* look through the surface of American art, and see the inner diabolism of the symbolic meaning. Otherwise it is all mere childishness.

That blue-eyed darling Nathaniel knew disagreeable things in his inner soul. He was careful to send them out in disguise.

Always the same. The deliberate consciousness of Americans so fair and smooth-spoken, and the under-consciousness so devilish. *Destroy! destroy! destroy!* hums the under-consciousness. *Love and produce! Love and produce!* cackles the upper consciousness. And the world hears only the love-and-produce cackle. Refuses to hear the hum of destruction underneath. Until such time as it will *have* to hear.

The American has got to destroy. It is his destiny. It is his destiny to destroy the whole corpus of the white psyche, the white consciousness. And he's got to do it secretly. As the growing of a dragonfly inside a chrysalis or cocoon destroys the larva grub, secretly.

Though many a dragonfly never gets out of the chrysalis case: dies inside. As America might.

So the secret chrysalis of *The Scarlet Letter,* diabolically destroying the old psyche inside.

Be good! Be good! warbles Nathaniel. *Be good, and never sin! Be sure your sins will find you out.*

So convincingly that his wife never saw him "as in time."

Then listen to the diabolic undertone of *The Scarlet Letter.*

Man ate of the tree of knowledge, and became ashamed of himself.

Do you imagine Adam had never lived with Eve before that apple episode? Yes, he had. As a wild animal with his mate.

It didn't become "sin" till the knowledge-poison entered. That apple of Sodom.

We are divided in ourselves, against ourselves. And that is the meaning of the cross symbol.

In the first place, Adam knew Eve as a wild animal knows its mate, momentaneously, but vitally, in blood-knowledge. Blood-knowledge, not mind-knowledge. Blood-knowledge, that seems utterly to forget, but doesn't. Blood-knowledge, instinct, intuition, all the vast vital flux of knowing that goes on in the dark, antecedent to the mind.

Then came that beastly apple, and the other sort of knowledge started.

Adam began to look at himself. "My hat!" he said. "What's this? My Lord! What the deuce!—And Eve! I wonder about Eve."

Thus starts KNOWING. Which shortly runs to UNDERSTANDING, when the devil gets his own.

When Adam went and took Eve, *after* the apple, he didn't do any more than he had done many a time before, in act. But in consciousness he did something very different. So did Eve. Each of them kept an eye on what they were doing, they watched what was happening to them. They wanted to KNOW. And that was the birth of sin. Not *doing* it, but KNOWING about it. Before the apple, they had shut their eyes and their minds had gone dark. Now, they peeped and pried and imagined. They watched themselves. And they felt uncomfortable after. They felt self-conscious. So they said, "The *act* is sin. Let's hide. We've sinned."

No wonder the Lord kicked them out of the Garden. Dirty hypocrites.

The sin was the self-watching, self-consciousness. The sin, and the doom. Dirty understanding.

Nowadays men do hate the idea of dualism. It's no good, dual we are. The cross. If we accept the symbol, then, virtually, we accept the fact. We are divided against ourselves.

For instance, the blood *hates* being KNOWN by the mind. It feels itself destroyed when it is KNOWN. Hence the profound instinct of privacy.

And on the other hand, the mind and the spiritual consciousness of man simply *hates* the dark potency of blood-acts: hates the genuine dark sensual orgasms, which do, for the time being, actually obliterate the mind and the spiritual consciousness, plunge them in a suffocating flood of darkness.

You can't get away from this.

Blood-consciousness overwhelms, obliterates, and annuls mind-consciousness.

Mind-consciousness extinguishes blood-consciousness, and consumes the blood.

We are all of us conscious in both ways. And the two ways are antagonistic in us.

They will always remain so.

That is our cross.

The antagonism is so obvious, and so far-reaching, that it extends to the smallest thing. The cultured, highly-conscious person of today *loathes* any form of physical, "menial" work: such as washing dishes or sweeping a floor or chopping wood. This menial work is an insult to the spirit. "When I see men carrying heavy loads, doing brutal work, it always makes me want to cry," said a beautiful, cultured woman to me.

"When you say that, it makes me want to beat you," said I, in reply. "When I see you with your beautiful head pondering heavy thoughts, I just want to hit you. It outrages me."

My father hated books, hated the sight of anyone reading or writing.

My mother hated the thought that any of her sons should be condemned to manual labor. Her sons must have something higher than that.

She won. But she died first.

He laughs longest who laughs last.

There is a basic hostility in all of us between the physical and the mental, the blood and the spirit. The mind is "ashamed" of the blood. And the blood is destroyed by the mind, actually. Hence pale-faces.

At present the mind-consciousness and the so-called spirit triumphs. In America supremely. In America, nobody does anything from the blood. Always from the nerves, if not from the mind. The blood is chemically reduced by the nerves, in American activity.

When an Italian laborer labors, his mind and nerves sleep, his blood acts ponderously.

Americans, when they are *doing* things, never seem really to be doing them. They are "busy about" it. They are always busy "about" something. But truly *immersed* in *doing* something, with the deep blood-consciousness active, that they never are.

They *admire* the blood-conscious spontaneity. And they want to get it in their heads. "Live from the body," they shriek. It is their last mental shriek. Co-*ordinate*.

It is a further attempt still to rationalize the body and blood. "Think about such and such a muscle," they say, "and relax there."

And every time you "conquer" the body with the mind (you can say "heal" it, if you like) you cause a deeper, more dangerous complex or tension somewhere else.

Ghastly Americans, with their blood no longer blood. A yellow spiritual fluid.

The Fall.

There have been lots of Falls.

We *fell* into *knowledge* when Eve bit the apple. Self-conscious knowledge. For the first time the mind put up a fight against the blood. Wanting to UNDERSTAND. That is to intellectualize the blood.

The blood must be *shed*, says Jesus.

Shed on the cross of our own divided psyche.

Shed the blood, and you become mind-conscious. Eat the body and drink the blood, self-cannibalizing, and you become extremely conscious, like Americans and some Hindus. Devour yourself, and God knows what a lot you'll know, what a lot you'll be conscious of.

Mind you don't choke yourself.

For a long time men *believed* that they could be perfected through the mind, through the spirit. They believed, passionately. They had their ecstasy in pure consciousness. They *believed* in purity, chastity, and the wings of the spirit.

America soon plucked the bird of the spirit. America soon killed the *belief* in the spirit. But not the practice. The practice continued with a sarcastic vehemence. America, with a perfect inner contempt for the spirit and the consciousness of man, practices the same spirituality and universal love and KNOWING all the time, incessantly, like a drug habit. And inwardly gives not a fig for it. Only for the *sensation*. The pretty-pretty *sensation* of love, loving all the world. And the nice fluttering aeroplane *sensation* of knowing, knowing, knowing. Then the prettiest of all sensations, the sensation of UNDERSTANDING. Oh, what a lot they understand, the darlings! *So* good at the trick, they are. Just a trick of self-conceit.

The Scarlet Letter gives the show away.

You have your pure-pure young parson Dimmesdale.

You have the beautiful Puritan Hester at his feet.

And the first thing she does is to seduce him.

And the first thing he does is to be seduced.

And the second thing they do is to hug their sin in secret, and gloat over it, and try to understand.

Which is the myth of New England.

Deerslayer refused to be seduced by Judith Hutter. At least the Sodom apple of sin didn't fetch him.

But Dimmesdale was seduced gloatingly. Oh, luscious Sin!

He was such a pure young man.

That he had to make a fool of purity.

The American psyche.

Of course, the best part of the game lay in keeping up pure appearances.

The greatest triumph a woman can have, especially an American woman, is the triumph of seducing a man: especially if he is pure.

And he gets the greatest thrill of all, in falling.—"Seduce me, Mrs. Hercules."

And the pair of them share the subtlest delight in keeping up pure appearances, when everybody knows all the while. But the power of pure appearances is something to exult in. All America gives in to it. *Look* pure!

To seduce a man. To have everybody know. To keep up appearances of purity. Pure!

This is the great triumph of woman.

A. The Scarlet Letter. Adulteress! The great Alpha, Alpha! Adulteress! The new Adam and Adama! American!

A. Adulteress! Stitched with gold thread, glittering upon the bosom. The proudest insignia.

Put her upon the scaffold and worship her there. Worship her there. The Woman, the Magna Mater. *A*. Adulteress! Abel!

Abel! Abel! Abel! Admirable!

It becomes a farce.

The fiery heart. *A*. Mary of the Bleeding Heart. Mater Adolerata! *A*. Capital *A*. Adulteress. Glittering with gold thread. Abel! Adultery. Admirable!

It is, perhaps, the most colossal satire ever penned. *The Scarlet Letter*. And by a blue-eyed darling of a Nathaniel.

Not Bumppo, however.

The human spirit, fixed in a lie, adhering to a lie, giving itself perpetually the lie.

All begins with *A*.

Adulteress. Alpha. Abel, Adam. *A*. America.

The Scarlet Letter.

"Had there been a Papist among the crowd of Puritans, he might have seen in this beautiful woman, so picturesque in her attire and mien, and with the infant at her bosom, an object to remind him of the image of Divine Maternity, which so many illustrious painters have vied with one another to represent; something which should remind him, indeed, but only by contrast, of that sacred image of sinless Motherhood, whose infant was to redeem the world."

Whose infant was to redeem the world indeed! It will be a startling redemption the world will get from the American infant.

"Here was a taint of deepest sin in the most sacred quality of human life, working such effect that the world was only the darker for this woman's beauty, and more lost for the infant she had borne."

Just listen to the darling. Isn't he a master of apology?

Of symbols, too.

His pious blame is a chuckle of praise all the while.

Oh, Hester, you are a demon. A man *must* be pure, just that you can seduce him to a fall. Because the greatest thrill in life is to bring down the Sacred Saint with a flop into the mud. Then when you've brought him down, humbly wipe off the mud with your hair, another Magdalen. And then go home and dance a witch's jig of triumph, and stitch yourself a Scarlet Letter with gold thread, as duchesses used to stitch themselves coronets. And then stand meek on the scaffold and fool the world. Who will all be envying you your sin, and beating you because you've stolen an advantage over them.

Hester Prynne is the great nemesis of woman. She is the KNOWING Ligeia risen diabolic from the grave. Having her own back. UNDERSTANDING.

This time it is Mr. Dimmesdale who dies. She lives on and is Abel.

His spiritual love was a lie. And prostituting the woman to his spiritual love, as popular clergymen do, in his preachings and loftiness, was a tall white lie. Which came flop.

We are so pure in spirit. Hi-tiddly-i-ty!

Till she tickled him in the right place, and he fell.

Flop.

Flop goes spiritual love.

But keep up the game. Keep up appearances. Pure are the pure. To the pure all things, etc.

Look out, Mister, for the Female Devotee. Whatever you do, don't let her start tickling you. She knows your weak spot. Mind your Purity.

When Hester Prynne seduced Arthur Dimmesdale it was the beginning of the end. But from the beginning of the end to the end of the end is a hundred years or two.

Mr. Dimmesdale also wasn't at the end of his resources. Previously, he had lived by governing his body, ruling it, in the interests of his spirit. Now he has a good time all by himself torturing his body, whipping it, piercing it with thorns, macerating himself. It's a form of masturbation. He wants to get a mental grip on his body. And since he can't quite manage it with the mind, witness his fall—he will give it what for, with whips. His will shall *lash* his body. And he enjoys his pains. Wallows in them. To the pure all things are pure.

It is the old self-mutilation process, gone rotten. The mind wanting to get its teeth in the blood and flesh. The ego exulting in the tortures of the mutinous flesh. I, the ego, I *will* triumph over my own flesh. Lash! Lash! I am a grand free spirit. *Lash!* I am the master of my soul! *Lash! Lash!* I am the captain of my soul. *Lash!* Hurray! "In the fell clutch of circumstance," etc., etc.

Good-by Arthur. He depended on women for his Spiritual Devotees, spiritual brides. So, the woman just touched him in his weak spot, his Achilles Heel of the flesh. Look out for the spiritual bride. She's after the weak spot.

It is the battle of wills.

"For the will therein lieth, which dieth not——"

The Scarlet Woman becomes a Sister of Mercy. Didn't she just, in the late war. Oh, Prophet Nathaniel!

Hester urges Dimmesdale to go away with her, to a new country, to a new life. He isn't having any.

He knows there is no new country, no new life on the globe today. It is the same old thing, in different degrees, everywhere. *Plus ça change, plus c'est la même chose.*

Hester thinks, with Dimmesdale for her husband, and Pearl for her child, in Australia, maybe, she'd have been perfect.

But she wouldn't. Dimmesdale had already fallen from his integrity as a minister of the Gospel of the Spirit. He had lost his manliness. He didn't see the point of just leaving himself between the hands of a woman and going away to a "new country," to be her thing entirely. She'd only have despised him more, as every woman despises a man who has "fallen" to her; despises him with her tenderest lust.

He stood for nothing any more. So let him stay where he was and dree out his weird.

She had dished him and his spirituality, so he hated her. As Angel Clare was dished, and hated Tess. As Jude in the end hated Sue: or should have done. The women make fools of them, the spiritual men. And when, as men, they've gone flop in their spirituality, they can't pick themselves up whole any more. So they just crawl, and die detesting the female, or the females, who made them fall.

The saintly minister gets a bit of his own back, at the last minute, by making public confession from the very scaffold where she was exposed. Then he dodges into death. But he's had a bit of his own back, on everybody.

"Shall we not meet again?" whispered she, bending her face down close to him. "Shall we not spend our immortal life together? Surely, surely we have ransomed one another with all this woe! Thou lookest far into eternity with those bright dying eyes. Tell me what thou seest!"

"Hush, Hester—hush," said he, with tremulous solemnity. "The law we broke!—the sin here so awfully revealed! Let these alone be in thy thoughts. I fear! I fear!"

So he dies, throwing the "sin" in her teeth, and escaping into death.

The law we broke, indeed. You bet!

Whose law?

But it is truly a law, that man must either stick to the belief he has grounded himself on, and obey the laws of that belief, or he must admit the belief itself to be inadequate, and prepare himself for a new thing.

There was no change in belief, either in Hester or in Dimmesdale or in Hawthorne or in America. The same old treacherous belief, which was really cunning disbelief, in the Spirit, in Purity, in Selfless Love, and in Pure Consciousness. They would go on following this belief, for the sake of the sensationalism of it. But they would make a fool of it all the time. Like Woodrow Wilson, and the rest of modern Believers. The rest of modern Saviors.

If you meet a Savior today, be sure he is trying to make an innermost fool of you. Especially if the savior be an UNDERSTANDING WOMAN, offering her love.

Hester lives on, pious as pie, being a public nurse. She becomes at last an acknowledged saint, Abel of the Scarlet Letter.

She would, being a woman. She has had her triumph over the individual man, so she quite loves subscribing to the whole spiritual life of society. She will make herself as false as hell, for society's sake, once she's had her real triumph over Saint Arthur.

Blossoms out into a Sister-of-Mercy Saint.

But it's a long time before she really takes anybody in. People kept on thinking her a witch, which she was.

As a matter of fact, unless a woman is held, by man, safe within the bounds of belief, she becomes inevitably a destructive force. She can't help herself. A woman is almost always vulnerable to pity. She can't bear to see anything *physically* hurt. But let a woman loose from the bounds and restraints of man's fierce belief, in his gods and in himself, and she becomes a gentle devil. She becomes subtly diabolic. The colossal evil of the united spirit of Woman. WOMAN, German woman or American woman, or every other sort of woman, in the last war, was something frightening. As every *man* knows.

Woman becomes a helpless, would-be-loving demon. She is helpless. Her very love is a subtle poison.

Unless a man believes in himself and his gods, *genuinely*: unless he fiercely obeys his own Holy Ghost: his woman will destroy him. Woman is the nemesis of doubting man. She can't help it.

And with Hester, after Ligeia, woman becomes a nemesis to man. She bolsters him up from the outside, she destroys him from the inside. And he dies hating her, as Dimmesdale did.

Dimmesdale's spirituality had gone on too long, too far. It had become a false thing. He found his nemesis in woman. And he was done for.

Woman is a strange and rather terrible phenomenon, to man. When the subconscious soul of woman recoils from its creative union with man, it becomes a destructive force. It exerts, willy-nilly, an invisible destructive influence. The woman herself may be as nice as milk, to all appearance, like Ligeia. But she is sending out waves of silent destruction of the faltering spirit in men, all the same. She doesn't know it. She can't even help it. But she does it. The devil is in her.

The very women who are most busy saving the bodies of men, and saving the children: these women doctors, these nurses, these educationalists, these public-spirited women, these female saviors: they are all, from the inside, sending out waves of destructive malevolence which eat out the inner life of a man, like a cancer. It is so, it will be so, till men realize it and react to save themselves.

God won't save us. The women are so devilish godly. Men must save themselves in this strait, and by no sugary means either.

A woman can use her sex in sheer malevolence and poison, while she is *behaving* as meek and good as gold. Dear darling, she is really snow-white in her blamelessness. And all the while she is using her sex as a she-devil, for the endless hurt of her man. She doesn't know it. She will never believe it if you tell her. And if you give her a slap in the face for her fiendishness, she will rush to the first magistrate, in indignation. She is so *absolutely* blameless, the she-devil, the dear, dutiful creature.

Give her the great slap, just the same, just when she is being most angelic. Just when she is bearing her cross most meekly.

Oh, woman out of bounds is a devil. But it is man's fault. Woman never *asked,* in the first place, to be cast out of her bit of an Eden of belief and trust. It is man's business to bear the responsibility of belief. If he becomes a spiritual fornicator and liar, like Ligeia's husband and Arthur Dimmesdale, how *can* a woman believe in him? Belief doesn't go by choice. And if a woman doesn't believe in a *man,* she believes, essentially, in nothing. She becomes, willy-nilly, a devil.

A devil she is, and a devil she will be. And most men will succumb to her devilishness.

Hester Prynne was a devil. Even when she was so meekly going round as a sick-nurse. Poor Hester. Part of her wanted to be saved from her own devilishness. And another part wanted to go on and on in devilishness, for revenge. Revenge! REVENGE! It is this that fills the unconscious spirit of woman today. Revenge against man, and against the spirit of man, which has betrayed her into unbelief. Even when she is most sweet and a salvationist, she is her most devilish, is woman. She gives her man the sugar-plum of her own submissive sweetness. And when he's taken this sugar-plum in his mouth, a scorpion comes out of it. After he's taken this Eve to his bosom, oh, so loving, she destroys him inch by inch. Woman and her revenge! She will have it, and go on having it, for decades and decades, unless she's stopped. And to stop her you've got to believe in yourself and your gods, your own Holy Ghost, Sir Man; and then you've got to fight her, and never give in. She's a devil. But in the long run she is conquerable. And just a tiny bit of her wants to be conquered. You've got to fight three quarters of her, in absolute hell, to get at the final quarter of her that wants a release, at last, from the hell of her own revenge. But it's a long last. And not yet.

"She had in her nature a rich, voluptuous, oriental characteristic—a taste for the gorgeously beautiful." This is Hester. This is American. But she repressed her nature in the above direction. She would not even allow herself the luxury of laboring at fine, delicate stitching. Only she dressed her little sin-child Pearl vividly, and the scarlet letter was gorgeously embroidered. Her Hecate and Astarte insignia.

"A voluptuous, oriental characteristic——" That lies waiting in American women. It is probable that the Mormons are the forerunners of the coming real America. It is probable that men will have more than one wife, in the coming America. That you will have again a half-Oriental womanhood, and a polygamy.

The gray nurse, Hester. The Hecate, the hell-cat. The slowly evolving, voluptuous female of the new era, with a whole new submissiveness to the dark, phallic principle.

But it takes time. Generation after generation of nurses and political women and salvationists. And in the end, the dark erection of the images of sex-worship once more, and the newly submissive women. That kind of depth. Deep women in that respect. When we have at last broken this insanity of mental-spiritual consciousness. And the women *choose* to experience again the great submission.

"The poor, whom she sought out to be the objects of her bounty, often reviled the hand that was stretched to succor them."

Naturally. The poor hate a salvationist. They smell the devil underneath.

"She was patient—a martyr indeed—but she forbore to pray for her enemies, lest, in spite of her forgiving aspirations, the words of the blessing should stubbornly twist themselves into a curse."

So much honesty, at least. No wonder the old witch-lady Mistress Hibbins claimed her for another witch.

"She grew to have a dread of children; for they had imbibed from their parents a vague idea of something horrible in this dreary woman gliding silently through the town, with never any companion but only one child."

"A vague idea!" Can't you see her "gliding silently"? It's not a question of a vague idea imbibed, but a definite feeling directly received.

"But sometimes, once in many days, or perchance in many months, she felt an eye—a human eye—upon the ignominious brand, that seemed to give a momentary relief, as if half her agony were shared. The next instant, back it all rushed again, with a still deeper throb of pain; for in that brief interval she had sinned again. Had Hester sinned alone?"

Of course not. As for sinning again, she would go on all her life silently, changelessly "sinning." She never repented. Not she. Why should she? She had brought down Arthur Dimmesdale, that too-too snow-white bird, and that was her life-work.

As for sinning again when she met two dark eyes in a crowd, why of course. Somebody who understood as she understood.

I always remember meeting the eyes of a gipsy woman, for one moment, in a crowd, in England. She knew; and I knew. What did we know? I was not able to make out. But we knew.

Probably the same fathomless hate of this spiritual-conscious society in which the outcast woman and I both roamed like meek-looking wolves. Tame wolves waiting to shake off their tameness. Never able to.

And again, that "voluptuous, oriental" characteristic that knows the mystery of the ithyphallic gods. She would not betray the ithyphallic gods to this white, leprous-white society of "lovers." Neither will I, if I can help it. These leprous-white, seducing, spiritual women, who "understand" so much. One has been too often seduced, and "understood." "I can read him like a book," said my first lover of me. The book is in several volumes, dear. And more and more comes back to me the gulf of dark hate and *other* understanding, in the eyes of the gipsy woman. So different from the hateful white light of understanding which floats like scum on the eyes of white, oh, so white English and American women, with their understanding voices and their deep, sad words, and their profound, *good* spirits. Pfui!

Hester was scared only of one result of her sin: Pearl. Pearl, the scarlet letter incarnate. The little girl. When women bear children, they produce either devils or sons with gods in them. And it is an evolutionary process. The devil in Hester produced a purer devil in Pearl. And the devil in Pearl will produce—she married an Italian count—a piece of purer devilishness still.

And so from hour to hour we ripe and ripe.

And then from hour to hour we rot and rot.

There was that in the child "which often impelled Hester to ask in bitterness of heart, whether it were for good or ill that the poor little creature had been born at all."

For ill, Hester. But don't worry. Ill is as necessary as good. Malevolence is as necessary as benevolence. If you have brought forth, spawned, a young malevolence, be sure there is a rampant falseness in the world against which this malevolence must be turned. Falseness has to be bitten and bitten, till it is bitten to death. Hence Pearl.

Pearl. Her own mother compares her to the demon of plague, or scarlet fever, in her red dress. But then, plague is necessary to destroy a rotten, false humanity.

Pearl, the devilish girl-child, who can be so tender and loving and *understanding,* and then, when she has understood, will give you a hit across the mouth, and turn on you with a grin of sheer diabolic jeering.

Serves you right, you shouldn't be *understood.* That is your vice. You shouldn't want to be loved, and then you'd not get hit across the mouth. Pearl will love you: marvelously. And she'll hit you across the mouth: oh, so neatly. And serves you right.

Pearl is perhaps the most modern child in all literature.

Old-fashioned Nathaniel, with his little-boy charm, he'll tell you what's what. But he'll cover it with smarm.

Hester simply *hates* her child, from one part of herself. And from another, she cherishes her child as her one precious treasure. For Pearl is the continuing of her female revenge on life. But female revenge hits both ways. Hits back at its own mother. The female revenge in Pearl hits back at Hester, the mother, and Hester is simply livid with fury and "sadness," which is rather amusing.

"The child could not be made amenable to rules. In giving her existence a great law had been broken; and the result was a being whose elements were perhaps beautiful and brilliant, but all in disorder, or with an order peculiar to themselves, amidst which the point of variety and arrangement was difficult or impossible to discover."

Of course, the order is peculiar to themselves. But the point of variety is this: "Draw out the loving, sweet soul, draw it out with marvelous understanding; and then spit in its eye."

Hester, of course, didn't at all like it when her sweet child drew out her motherly soul, with yearning and deep understanding: and then spit in the motherly eye, with a grin. But it was a process the mother had started.

Pearl had a peculiar look in her eyes: "a look so intelligent, yet so inexplicable, so perverse, sometimes so malicious, but generally accompanied by a wild flow of spirits, that Hester could not help questioning at such moments whether Pearl was a human child."

A little demon! But her mother, and the saintly Dimmesdale, had borne her. And Pearl, by the very openness of her perversity, was more straightforward than her parents. She flatly refuses any Heavenly Father, seeing the earthly one such a fraud. And she has the pietistic Dimmesdale on toast, spits right in his eye: in both his eyes.

Poor, brave, tormented little soul, always in a state of recoil, she'll be a devil to men when she grows up. But the men deserve it. If they'll let themselves be "drawn" by her loving understanding, they deserve that she shall slap them across the mouth the moment they *are* drawn. The chickens! Drawn and trussed.

Poor little phenomenon of a modern child, she'll grow up into the devil of a modern woman. The nemesis of weak-kneed modern men, craving to be love-drawn.

The third person in the diabolic trinity, or triangle, of the Scarlet Letter, is Hester's first husband, Roger Chillingworth. He is an old Elizabethan physician, with a gray beard and a long-furred coat and a twisted shoulder. Another healer. But something of an alchemist, a magician. He is a magician on the verge of modern science, like Francis Bacon.

Roger Chillingworth is of the old order of intellect, in direct line from the mediaeval Roger Bacon alchemists. He has an old, intellectual belief in the dark sciences, the Hermetic philosophies. He is no Christian, no selfless aspirer. He is not an aspirer. He is the old authoritarian in man.

The old male authority. But without passional belief. Only intellectual belief in himself and his male authority.

Shakespeare's whole tragic wail is because of the downfall of the true male authority, the ithyphallic authority and masterhood. It fell with Elizabeth. It was trodden underfoot with Victoria.

But Chillingworth keeps on the *intellectual* tradition. He hates the new spiritual aspirers, like Dimmesdale, with a black, crippled hate. He is the old male authority, in intellectual tradition.

You can't keep a wife by force of an intellectual tradition. So Hester took to seducing Dimmesdale.

Yet her only marriage, and her last oath, is with the old Roger. He and she are accomplices in pulling down the spiritual saint.

"Why dost thou smile so at me?" she says to her old, vengeful husband. "Art thou not like the Black Man that haunts the forest around us? Hast thou not enticed me into a bond which will prove the ruin of my soul?"

"Not thy soul!" he answered with another smile. "No, not thy soul!"

It is the soul of the pure preacher, that false thing, which they are after. And the crippled physician—this other healer—blackly vengeful in his old, distorted male authority, and the "loving" woman, they bring down the saint between them.

A black and complementary hatred, akin to love, is what Chillingworth feels for the young, saintly parson. And Dimmesdale responds, in a hideous kind of love. Slowly the saint's life is poisoned. But the black old physician smiles, and tries to keep him alive. Dimmesdale goes in for self-torture, self-lashing, lashing his own white, thin, spiritual savior's body. The dark old Chillingworth listens outside the door and laughs, and prepares another medicine, so that the game can go on longer. And the saint's very soul goes rotten. Which is the supreme triumph. Yet he keeps up appearances still.

The black, vengeful soul of the crippled, masterful male, still dark in his authority: and the white ghastliness of the fallen saint! The two halves of manhood mutually destroying one another.

Dimmesdale has a *"coup"* in the very end. He gives the whole show away by confessing publicly on the scaffold, and dodging into death, leaving Hester dished, and Roger, as it were, doubly cuckolded. It is a neat last revenge.

Down comes the curtain, as in Ligeia's poem.

But the child Pearl will be on in the next act, with her Italian count and a new brood of vipers. And Hester grayly Abelling, in the shadows, after her rebelling.

It is a marvelous allegory. It is to me one of the greatest allegories in all literature, *The Scarlet Letter*. Its marvelous under-meaning! And its perfect duplicity.

The absolute duplicity of that blue-eyed *Wunderkind* of a Nathaniel. The American wonder-child, with his magical allegorical insight.

But even wonder-children have to grow up in a generation or two.

And even SIN becomes stale.

Rainer Maria Rilke

THE NOTEBOOKS OF MALTE LAURIDS BRIGGE

It will be difficult to persuade me that the story of the Prodigal Son is not the legend of him who did not want to be loved. When he was a child, everybody in the house loved him. He grew up knowing nothing else and came to feel at home in their softness of heart, when he was a child.

But as a boy he sought to lay aside such habits. He could not have put it into words, but when he wandered about outside all day and did not even want to have the dogs along, it was because they too loved him; because in their glances there was observation and sympathy, expectancy and solicitude; because even in their presence one could do nothing without gladdening or giving pain. But what he meant in those days was that profound indifference of his heart, which sometimes, of an early morning in the fields, seized him with such purity that he began to run, in order to have neither time nor breath to be more than an airy moment in which the morning comes to consciousness.

The secret of that life of his which never yet had been, spread out before him. Involuntarily he forsook the footpath and ran on into the fields, with arms outstretched, as if in this wide reach he could master several directions at once. And then he would throw himself down behind some hedge, and mattered to no one. He peeled himself a willow flute, flung a stone at some little wild animal, bent over and compelled a beetle to turn round: all this became no destiny, and the skies passed on as over nature. At last came afternoon with all its inspirations; one was a buccaneer on the island of Tortuga, and there was no obligation in being that; one besieged Campêche, one took Vera Cruz by storm; it was possible to be the whole army or a commander on horseback or a ship on the ocean, according to the way one felt. But if it entered one's head to kneel, then swiftly one became Deodatus of Gozon and had slain the dragon and, learned, all hot, that this heroism was arrogant, without obedience. For one spared oneself nothing that belonged to the business. But however numerous the imaginings that came to one, in between there was always time to be nothing but a bird, uncertain what kind. Only then came the return home.

Heavens, how much there was then to cast off and forget; for it was necessary to forget thoroughly; otherwise one betrayed oneself when they pressed one. However one lingered and looked about, the gable always did loom up at last. The first window up there kept its eye on one; somebody might very well be standing there. The dogs, in whom expectation had been growing all day, scurried through the bushes and drove one together into the person they believed one to be. And the house did the rest. Once one entered into the full smell of it, most things were already decided. Details might still be changed; in the main one was the person for whom they took one here; the person for whom, out of his little past and their own wishes, they had long fashioned a life; the creature belonging to them all, who stood day and night under the suggestion of their love, between their hope and their suspicion, before their blame or praise.

Useless for such a person to go upstairs with indescribable caution. They will all be in the sitting-room, and if the door merely opens they will look his way. He remains in the dark, he wants to wait for their questioning. But then comes the worst. They take him by the hands, they draw him toward the table, and all of them, as many as are present, stretch inquisitively into the lamplight. They have the best of it; they keep in the shadow, while on him alone falls, with the light, all the shame of having a face.

Shall he stay, imitating with a lie the vague life they ascribe to him, and grow to resemble them all in his every feature? Shall he divide himself between the delicate truthfulness of his will and the clumsy deceit that spoils it for himself? Shall he give up trying to become the thing that might hurt those of his family who have nothing left but a weak heart?

No, he will go away. For example, while they are all busy setting out on his birthday table those badly conceived gifts meant, once again, to compensate for everything. Go away for ever. Not until long afterward was it to become clear to him how much he had then intended never to love, in order not to put anyone in the terrible position of being loved. It occurred to him years later and, like other projects, this too had been impossible. For he had loved and loved again in his solitude; each time with waste of his whole nature and with unspeakable fear for the liberty of the other. Slowly he learned to penetrate the beloved object with the rays of his feeling, instead of consuming it in them. And he was spoiled by the fascination of recognizing through the ever more transparent form of his beloved, the expanses it opened to his desire infinitely to possess.

How he could weep for nights then with yearning to be himself penetrated by such rays. But a woman loved, who yields, is still far from being a woman who loves. O disconsolate nights, when he received back again his flooding gifts, in pieces, heavy with transience. How he thought then of the troubadours who feared nothing more than being answered. All his money, acquired and increased, he gave in order not to experience this too. He hurt them with his gross paying, anxious from day to day lest they try to enter into his love. For he no longer had hope of experiencing the lover who should pierce him.

Even at the time when poverty terrified him daily with new hardnesses, when his head was the favorite toy of misery and utterly worn bare, when ulcers opened all over his body like auxiliary eyes against the blackness of tribulation, when he shuddered at the rubbish upon which he had been abandoned because he himself was like it: even then still, when he reflected, his greatest terror was lest anyone should respond to him. What were all obscurities since, compared to the opaque sadness of those embraces in which everything lost itself? Did one not wake feeling one had no future? Did one not go about, meaningless, without right to any danger whatever? Had not one had a hundred times to promise not to die? Perhaps it was the stubbornness of this bitter memory, which wanted to keep itself a place to return to again and again, that made his life endure amid the refuse. Finally he was found again. And not till then, not till his shepherd years, did all his past find calm.

Who shall describe what befell him then? What poet has the persuasiveness to reconcile the length of the days he now lived with the brevity of life? What art is vast enough to evoke simultaneously his slight, cloaked figure and the whole high spaciousness of his gigantic nights?

That was the time which began with his feeling of being general, anonymous, like a slowly recovering convalescent. He did not love, unless it were that he loved to be. The lowly affection of his sheep lay not too close to him; like light falling through clouds it dispersed about him and shimmered softly on the meadows. In the innocent track of their hunger he strode silently over the pastures of the world. Strangers saw him on the Acropolis, and perhaps he was for a long time one of the shepherds in Les Baux, and saw petrified time outlast that lofty race which, with all the conquests of seven and three, could not get the better of the sixteen rays of its own star. Or should I imagine him at Orange, resting against the rustic triumphal arch? Should I see him in the soul-accustomed shade of Aliscamps as, among graves that stand open like the graves of the resurrected, his eyes pursue a dragon-fly?

It is all the same. I see more than himself: I see his life, which at that time began its long love to God, that silent, aimless labor. For over him, who had wanted to withhold himself for always, there came once more the growing and undeviating urge of his heart. And this time he hoped to be answered. His whole nature, grown prescient and poised while he had been so long alone, promised him that he whom he now meant, knew how to love with penetrating, radiant love. But while he longed to be loved at last in so masterly a way, his senses, accustomed to far distances, grasped the extreme remoteness of God. Nights came when he thought to fling himself toward him into space; hours full of discovery, when he felt strong enough to dive for the earth and pull it upward on the storm tide of his heart. He was like one who hears a glorious language and feverishly conceives plans to write, to create in it. He had still to experience the dismay of learning how difficult this language was; he was unwilling to believe at first that a long life could pass away in forming the first short fictitious phrases that have no sense. He flung himself into this study like a runner into a race; but the density of what had to be mastered slowed him up. Nothing more humiliating could be thought out than this apprenticeship. He had found the philosopher's stone, and now he was being forced ceaselessly to transmute the swiftly made gold of his happiness into the lumpy lead of patience. He, who had adapted himself to space, like a worm traced crooked passages without outlet or direction. Now that with so much labor and sorrow he was learning to love, it was shown him how trivial and careless up to now all the love had been which he thought to have achieved. How none of it could have come to anything, because he had not begun to work at it and make it real.

During those years the great changes were going on in him. He almost forgot God over the hard work of drawing near him, and all that he hoped perhaps to attain with him in time was "sa patience de supporter une âme." The accidents of fate, which men hold important, had long ago deserted him, but now even whatever of pleasure and pain were necessary lost their spicy by-taste and became pure and nourishing for him. From the roots of his being developed the sturdy, evergreen plant of a fertile joy. He became wholly engrossed in learning to master what constituted his inner life; he wanted to omit nothing, for he did not doubt that his love was in all this and growing. Indeed, his inward composure went so far that he resolved to retrieve the most important of the things he had hitherto been unable to accomplish, those that had simply been waited through. He thought above all of his childhood, and, the more calmly he reflected, the more unachieved did it seem to him; all its memories had about them the vagueness of premonitions, and their counting as past made them almost future. To take all this once more, and this time really, upon himself—this was the reason he, the estranged, turned home. We do not know whether he remained; we only know that he came back.

Those who have told the story try at this point to remind us of the house as it then was; for there only a short time has passed, a little counted time, everyone in the house can say how much. The dogs have grown old, but they are still alive. It is reported that one of them let out a howl. An interruption cuts through the whole day's work. Faces appear at the windows, faces that have aged and faces that have grown up, touching in their resemblance. And in one quite old face recognition suddenly breaks through, pale. Recognition? Really only recognition?— Forgiveness. Forgiveness of what?—Love. My God: love.

He, the recognized, had not even been thinking, preoccupied as he was, that love could still exist. It is easy to understand how, of all that now happened, only this should have been transmitted to us: his gesture, the incredible gesture that had never before been seen—the gesture of supplication with which he threw himself at their feet, imploring them not to love. Scared and wavering, they lifted him to themselves. They interpreted his outburst in their own fashion, forgiving. It must have been an indescribable release for him that, despite the desperate evidence of his attitude, they all misunderstood him. Probably he was able to remain. For he recognized more clearly from day to day that the love of which they were so vain and to which they secretly encouraged one another, had nothing to do with him. He almost had to smile at their exertions, and it became clear how little they could have him in mind.

What did they know of him? He was now terribly difficult to love, and he felt that One alone was able for the task. But He was not yet willing.

Franz Kafka

THE CASTLE

When by a turn in the road K. recognised that they were near the inn, he was greatly surprised to see that darkness had already set in. Had he been gone for such a long time? Surely not for more than an hour or two, by his reckoning. And it had been morning when he left. And he had not felt any need for food. And just a short time ago it had been uniform daylight, and now the darkness of night was upon them. "Short days, short days," he said to himself, slipped off the sledge, and went towards the inn.

At the top of the little flight of steps leading into the house stood the landlord, a welcome figure, holding up a lighted lantern. Remembering his conductor for a fleeting moment K. stood still, there was a cough in the darkness behind him, that was he. Well, he would see him again soon. Not until he was level with the landlord, who greeted him humbly, did he notice two men, one on either side of the doorway. He took the lantern from his host's hand and turned the light upon them; it was the men he had already met, who were called Arthur and Jeremiah. They now saluted him. That reminded him of his soldiering days, happy days for him, and he laughed. "Who are you?" he asked, looking from one to the other. "Your assistants," they answered. "It's your assistants," corroborated the landlord in a low voice. "What?" said K. "are you my old assistants whom I told to follow me and whom I am expecting?" They answered in the affirmative. "That's good," observed K. after a short pause. "I'm glad you've come." "Well," he said, after another pause, "you've come very late, you're very slack." "It was a long way to come," said one of them. "A long way?" repeated K., "but I met you just now coming from the Castle." "Yes," said they, without further explanation. "Where is the apparatus?" asked K. "We haven't any," said they. "The apparatus I gave you?" said K. "We haven't any," they reiterated. "Oh, you are fine fellows!" said K., "do you know anything about surveying?" "No," said they. "But if you are my old assistants you must know something about it," said K. They made no reply. "Well, come in," said K. pushing them before him into the house.

They sat down then all three together over their beer at a small table, saying little, K. in the middle with an assistant on each side. As on the other evening, there was only one other table occupied by a few peasants.

"You're a difficult problem," said K., comparing them, as he had already done several times, "how am I to know one of you from the other? The only difference between you is your names, otherwise you're as like as. . . ." He stopped, and then went on involuntarily, "you're as like as two snakes." They smiled. "People usually manage to distinguish us quite well," they said in self-justification. "I am sure they do," said K., "I was a witness of that myself, but I can only see with my own eyes, and with them I can't distinguish you. So I shall treat you as if you were one man and call you both Arthur, that's one of your names, yours, isn't it?" he asked one of them. "No," said the man, "I'm Jeremiah." "It doesn't matter," said K. "I'll call you both Arthur. If I tell Arthur to go anywhere you must both go, if I give Arthur something to do you must both do it, that has the great disadvantage for me of preventing me from employing you on separate jobs, but the advantage that you will both be equally responsible for anything I tell you to do. How you divide the work between you doesn't matter to me, only you're not to excuse yourselves by blaming each other, for me you're only one man." They considered this, and said: "We shouldn't like that at all." "I don't suppose so," said K.; "of course you won't like it, but that's how it has to be." For some little time one of the peasants had been sneaking round the table and K. had noticed him; now the fellow took courage and went up to one of the assistants to whisper something. "Excuse me," said K., bringing his hand down on the table and rising to his feet, "these are my assistants and we're discussing private business. Nobody is entitled to disturb us." "Sorry, sir, sorry," muttered the peasant anxiously, retreating backwards towards his friends. "And this is my most important charge to you," said K., sitting down again. "You're not to speak to anyone without my permission. I am a stranger here, and if you are my old assistants you are strangers too. We three strangers must stand by each other therefore, give me your hands on that." All too eagerly they stretched out their hands to K. "Never mind the trimming," said he, "but remember that my command holds good. I shall go to bed now, and I recommend you to do the same. To-day we have missed a day's work, and to-morrow we must begin very early. You must get hold of a sleigh for taking me to the Castle and have it ready outside the house at six o'clock." "Very well," said one. But the other interrupted him. "You say 'very well,' and yet you know it can't be done." "Silence," said K. "You're trying already to dissociate yourselves from each other." But then the first man broke in: "He's right, it can't be done, no stranger can get into the Castle without a permit." "Where does one apply for a permit?" "I don't know, perhaps to the Castellan." "Then we'll apply by telephone, go and telephone to the Castellan at once, both of you." They rushed to the instrument, asked for the connection—how eager

they were about it! in externals they were absurdly docile—and enquired if K. could come with them next morning into the Castle. The
"No" of the answer was audible even to K. at his table. But the answer
went on and was still more explicit, it ran as follows: "Neither to-morrow
nor at any other time." "I shall telephone myself," said K., and got up.
While K. and his assistants hitherto had passed nearly unremarked except for the incident with the one peasant, his last statement aroused
general attention. They all got up when K. did, and although the landlord tried to drive them away, crowded round him in a close semicircle
at the telephone. The general opinion among them was that K. would
get no answer at all. K. had to beg them to be quiet, saying he did not
want to hear their opinion.

The receiver gave out a buzz of a kind that K. had never before heard
on a telephone. It was like the hum of countless children's voices—but yet
not a hum, the echo rather of voices singing at an infinite distance—
blended by sheer impossibility into one high but resonant sound which
vibrated on the ear as if it were trying to penetrate beyond mere hearing.
K. listened without attempting to telephone, leaning his left arm on the
telephone shelf.

He did not know how long he had stood there, but he stood until the
landlord pulled at his coat saying that a messenger had come to speak
with him. "Go away!" yelled K. in an access of rage, perhaps into the
mouthpiece, for someone immediately answered from the other end.
The following conversation ensued: "Oswald speaking, who's there?"
cried a severe, arrogant voice with a small defect in its speech, as seemed
to K., which its owner tried to cover by an exaggerated severity. K. hesitated to announce himself, for he was at the mercy of the telephone, the
other could shout him down or hang up the receiver, and that might mean
the blocking of a not unimportant way of access. K.'s hesitation made
the man impatient. "Who's there?" he repeated, adding, "I should be
obliged if there was less telephoning from down there, only a minute ago
somebody rang up." K. ignored this remark, and announced with sudden
decision: "The Land Surveyor's assistant speaking." "What Land Surveyor? What assistant?" K. recollected yesterday's telephone conversation,
and said briefly, "Ask Fritz." This succeeded, to his own astonishment.
But even more than at his success he was astonished at the organisation of the Castle service. The answer came: "Oh, yes. That everlasting Land Surveyor. Quite so. What about it? What assistant?"
"Joseph," said K. He was a little put out by the murmuring of the
peasants behind his back, obviously they disapproved of his ruse. He
had no time to bother about them, however, for the conversation absorbed all his attention. "Joseph?" came the question. "But the assistants are called . . ." there was a short pause, evidently to enquire the

names from somebody else, "Arthur and Jeremiah." "These are the new assistants," said K. "No, they are the old ones." "They are the new ones, I am the old assistant; I came to-day after the Land Surveyor." "No," was shouted back. "Then who am I?" asked K. as blandly as before.

And after a pause the same voice with the same defect answered him, yet with a deeper and more authoritative tone: "You are the old assistant."

K. was listening to the new note, and almost missed the question: "What is it you want?" He felt like laying down the receiver. He had ceased to expect anything from this conversation. But being pressed, he replied quickly: "When can my master come to the Castle?" "Never," was the answer. "Very well," said K., and hung the receiver up.

Behind him the peasants had crowded quite close. His assistants, with many side glances in his direction, were trying to keep them back. But they seemed not to take the matter very seriously, and in any case the peasants, satisfied with the result of the conversation, were beginning to give ground. A man came cleaving his way with rapid steps through the group, bowed before K. and handed him a letter. K. took it, but looked at the man, who for the moment seemed to him the more important. There was a great resemblance between this new-comer and the assistants, he was slim like them and clad in the same tight-fitting garments, had the same suppleness and agility, and yet he was quite different. How much K. would have preferred him as an assistant! He reminded K. a little of the girl with the infant whom he had seen at the tanner's. He was clothed nearly all in white, not in silk, of course; he was in winter clothes like all the others, but the material he was wearing had the softness and dignity of silk. His face was clear and frank, his eyes larger than ordinary. His smile was unusually joyous; he drew his hand over his face as if to conceal the smile, but in vain. "Who are you?" asked K. "My name is Barnabas," said he, "I am a messenger." His lips were strong and yet gentle as he spoke. "Do you approve of this kind of thing?" asked K., pointing to the peasants for whom he was still an object of curiosity, and who stood gaping at him with their open mouths, coarse lips, and literally tortured faces—their heads looked as if they had been beaten flat on top and their features as if the pain of the beating had twisted them to the present shape—and yet they were not exactly gaping at him, for their eyes often flitted away and studied some indifferent object in the room before fixing on him again, and then K. pointed also to his assistants who stood linked together, cheek against cheek, and smiling, but whether submissively or mockingly could not be determined, all these he pointed out as if presenting a train of followers forced upon him by circumstances, and as if he expected Barnabas— that indicated intimacy, it occurred to K.—always to discriminate between him and them. But Barnabas—quite innocently, it was clear—ignored the question, letting it pass as a well-bred servant ignores some remark of his master only apparently addressed to him, and merely surveyed the room in obedience to the question, greeting by a pressure of the hand various acquaintances among the peasants and exchanging a few words with the assistants, all with a free independence which set him apart from the others. Rebuffed but not mortified, K. returned to the letter in his hand and opened it. Its contents were as follows: "My dear Sir, As you know, you have been engaged for the Count's service. Your immediate superior is the Superintendent of the village, who will give you all particulars about your work and the terms of your employment, and to whom you are responsible. I myself, however, will try not to lose sight of you. Barnabas, the bearer of this letter, will report himself to you from time to time to learn your wishes and communicate them to me. You will find me always ready to oblige you, in so far as that is possible. I desire my workers to be contented." The signature was illegible, but stamped beside it was "Chief of Department X." "Wait a little!" said K. to Barnabas, who bowed before him, then he commanded the landlord to show him to his room, for he wanted to be alone with the letter for a while. At the same time he reflected that Barnabas, although so attractive, was still only a messenger, and ordered a mug of beer for him. He looked to see how Barnabas would take it, but Barnabas was obviously quite pleased and began to drink the beer at once. Then K. went off with the landlord. The house was so small that nothing was available for K. but a little attic room, and even that had caused some difficulty, for two maids who had hitherto slept in it had had to be quartered elsewhere. Nothing indeed had been done but to clear the maids out, the room was otherwise quite unprepared, no sheets on the single bed, only some pillows and a horseblanket still in the same rumpled state as in the morning. A few sacred pictures and photographs of soldiers were on the walls, the room had not even been aired; obviously they hoped that the new guest would not stay long, and were doing nothing to encourage him. K. felt no resentment, however, wrapped himself in the blanket, sat down at the table, and began to read the letter again by the light of a candle.

It was not a consistent letter; in part it dealt with him as with a free man whose independence was recognised, the mode of address, for example, and the reference to his wishes. But there were other places in which he was directly or indirectly treated as a minor employee, hardly visible to the Heads of Departments; the writer would try to make an effort "not to lose sight" of him, his superior was only the village superintendent to whom he was actually responsible, probably his sole colleague would be the village policeman. These were inconsistencies, no doubt about it. They were so obvious that they had to be faced. It hardly occurred to K. that they might be due to indecision; that seemed a mad idea in connection with such an organisation. He was much more inclined to read into them a frankly offered choice, which left it to him to make what he liked out of the letter, whether he preferred to become a village worker with a distinctive but merely apparent connection with the Castle, or an ostensible village worker whose real occupation was determined through the medium of Barnabas. K. did not hesitate in his choice, and would not have hesitated even had he lacked the experience which had befallen him since his arrival. Only as a worker in the village, removed as far as possible from the sphere of the Castle, could he hope to achieve anything in the Castle itself; the village folk, who were now so suspicious of him, would begin to talk to him once he was their fellow-citizen, if not exactly their friend; and if he were to become indistinguishable from Gerstäcker or Lasemann—and that must happen as soon as possible, everything depended on that—then all kinds of paths would be thrown open to him, which would remain not only for ever closed to him but quite invisible were he to depend merely on the favour of the gentlemen in the Castle. There was of course a danger, and that was sufficiently emphasised in the letter, even elaborated with a certain satisfaction, as if it were unavoidable. That was sinking to the workman's level—service, superior, work, terms of employment, responsible, workers—the letter fairly reeked of it, and even though more personal messages were included they were written from the standpoint of an employer. If K. were willing to become a workman he could do so, but he would have to do it in grim earnest, without any other prospect. K. knew that he had no real compulsory discipline to fear, he was not afraid of that, and in this case least of all, but the pressure of a discouraging environment, of a growing resignation to disappointment, the pressure of the imperceptible influences of every moment, these things he did fear, but that was a danger he would have to guard against. Nor did the letter pass over the fact that if it should come to a struggle K. had had the hardihood to make the first advances; it was very subtly indicated and only to be sensed by an uneasy conscience—an uneasy conscience, not a bad one—it lay in the three words "as you know," referring to his engagement in the Count's service. K. had reported his arrival, and only after that, as the letter pointed out, had he known that he was engaged.

K. took down a picture from the wall and stuck the letter on the nail, this was the room he was to live in and the letter should hang there.

Then he went down to the inn parlour. Barnabas was sitting at a table with the assistants. "Oh, there you are," said K. without any reason, only because he was glad to see Barnabas, who jumped to his feet at once.

Hardly had K. shown his face when the peasants got up and gathered round him, it had become a habit of theirs to follow him round. "What are you always following me about for?" cried K. They were not offended, and slowly drifted back to their seats again. One of them in passing said casually in apology, with an enigmatic smile which was reflected on several of the other's faces: "There's always something new to listen to," and he licked his lips as if news were meat and drink to him. K. said nothing conciliatory, it was good for them to have a little respect for him, but hardly had he reached Barnabas when he felt a peasant breathing down the back of his neck. He had only come, he said, for the salt-cellar, but K. stamped his foot with rage and the peasant scuttled away without the salt-cellar. It was really easy to get at K., all one had to do was to egg on the peasants against him, their persistent interference seemed much more objectionable to him than the reserve of the others, nor were they free from reserve either, for if he had sat down at their table they would not have stayed. Only the presence of Barnabas restrained him from making a scene. But he turned round to scowl at them, and found that they too were all looking at him. When he saw them sitting like that, however, each man in his own place, not speaking to one another and without any apparent mutual understanding, united only by the fact that they were all gazing at him, he concluded that it was not out of malice that they pursued him, perhaps they really wanted something from him and were only incapable of expressing it, if not that, it might be pure childishness, which seemed to be in fashion at the inn; was not the landlord himself childish, standing there stock-still gazing at K. with a glass of beer in his hand which he should have been carrying to a customer, and oblivious of his wife, who was leaning out of the kitchen hatch calling to him?

With a quieter mind K. turned to Barnabas; he would have liked to dismiss his assistants, but could not think of an excuse. Besides, they were brooding peacefully over their beer. "The letter," began K., "I have read it. Do you know the contents?" "No," said Barnabas, whose look seemed to imply more than his words. Perhaps K. was as mistaken in Barnabas's goodness as in the malice of the peasants, but his presence remained a comfort. "You are mentioned in the letter, too, you are supposed to carry messages now and then from me to the Chief, that's why I thought you might know the contents." "I was only told," said Barnabas, "to give you the letter, to wait until you had read it, and then to bring back a verbal or written answer if you thought it needful." "Very well," said K., "there's no need to write anything; convey to the Chief—by the way, what's his name? I couldn't read his signature." "Klamm," said Barnabas. "Well, convey to Herr Klamm my thanks for his recognition and for his great kindness, which I appreciate, being as I am one who has not yet proved his worth here. I shall follow his instructions faithfully. I have no particular requests to make for to-day." Barnabas, who had listened with close attention, asked to be allowed to recapitulate the message. K. assented, Barnabas repeated it word for word. Then he rose to take his leave.

K. had been studying his face the whole time, and now he gave it a last survey. Barnabas was about the same height as K., but his eyes seemed to look down on K., yet that was almost in a kind of humility, it was impossible to think that this man could put anyone to shame. Of course he was only a messenger, and did not know the contents of the letters he carried, but the expression in his eyes, his smile, his bearing, seemed also to convey a message, however little he might know about it. And K. shook him by the hand, which seemed obviously to surprise him, for he had been going to content himself with a bow.

As soon as he had gone—before opening the door he had leaned his shoulder against it for a moment and embraced the room generally in a final glance—K. said to the assistants: "I'll bring down the plans from my room, and then we'll discuss what work is to be done first." They wanted to accompany him. "Stay here," said K. Still they tried to accompany him. K. had to repeat his command more authoritatively. Barnabas was no longer in the hall. But he had only just gone out. Yet in front of the house—fresh snow was falling—K. could not see him either. He called out: "Barnabas!" No answer. Could he still be in the house? Nothing else seemed possible. None the less K. yelled the name with the full force of his lungs. It thundered through the night. And from the distance came a faint response, so far away was Barnabas already. K. called him back, and at the same time went to meet him; the spot where they encountered each other was no longer visible from the inn.

"Barnabas," said K., and could not keep his voice from trembling. "I have something else to say to you. And that reminds me that it's a bad arrangement to leave me dependent on your chance comings for sending a message to the Castle. If I hadn't happened to catch you just now—how you fly along, I thought you were still in the house—who knows how long I might have had to wait for your next appearance." "You can ask the Chief," said Barnabas, "to send me at definite times appointed by yourself." "Even that would not suffice," said K., "I might have nothing to say for a year at a time, but something of urgent importance might occur to me a quarter of an hour after you had gone."

"Well," said Barnabas, "shall I report to the Chief that between him and you some other means of communication should be established instead of me?" "No, no," said K., "not at all, I only mention the matter in passing, for this time I have been lucky enough to catch you." "Shall we go back to the inn," said Barnabas, "so that you can give me the new message there?" He had already taken a step in the direction of the inn. "Barnabas," said K., "it isn't necessary, I'll go a part of the way with you." "Why don't you want to go to the inn?" asked Barnabas. "The people there annoy me," said K., "you saw for yourself how persistent the peasants are." "We could go into your room," said Barnabas. "It's the maids' room," said K., "dirty and stuffy—it's to avoid staying there that I want to accompany you for a little, only," he added, in order finally to overcome Barnabas' reluctance, "you must let me take your arm, for you are surer of foot than I am." And K. took his arm. It was quite dark, K. could not see Barnabas' face, his figure was only vaguely discernible, he had had to grope for his arm a minute or two.

Barnabas yielded and they moved away from the inn. K. realised, indeed, that his utmost efforts could not enable him to keep pace with Barnabas, that he was a drag on him, and that even in ordinary circumstances this trivial accident might be enough to ruin everything, not to speak of side-streets like the one in which he had got stuck that morning, out of which he could never struggle unless Barnabas were to carry him. But he banished all such anxieties, and was comforted by Barnabas' silence; for if they went on in silence then Barnabas, too, must feel that their excursion together was the sole reason for their association.

They went on, but K. did not know whither, he could discern nothing, not even whether they had already passed the church or not. The effort which it cost him merely to keep going made him lose control of his thoughts. Instead of remaining fixed on their goal they strayed. Memories of his home kept recurring and filled his mind. There, too, a church stood in the market-place, partly surrounded by an old graveyard which was again surrounded by a high wall. Very few boys had managed to climb that wall, and for some time K., too, had failed. It was not curiosity which had urged them on. The graveyard had been no mystery to them. They had oftened entered it through a small wicket-gate, it was only the smooth high wall that they had wanted to conquer. But one morning—the empty, quiet market-place had been flooded with sunshine, when had K. ever seen it like that either before or since? —he had succeeded in climbing it with astonishing ease; at a place where he had already slipped down many a time he had clambered with a small flag between his teeth right to the top at the first attempt. Stones were still rattling down under his feet, but he was at the top. He stuck the flag in, it flew in the wind, he looked down and round about him, over his shoulder, too, at the crosses mouldering in the ground, nobody was greater than he at that place and that moment. By chance the teacher had come past and with a stern face had made K. descend. In jumping down he had hurt his knee and had found some difficulty in getting home, but still he had been on the top of the wall. The sense of that triumph had seemed to him then a victory for life, which was not altogether foolish, for now so many years later on the arm of Barnabas in the snowy night the memory of it came to succour him.

He took a firmer hold, Barnabas was almost dragging him along, the silence was unbroken. Of the road they were following all that K. knew was that to judge from its surface they had not yet turned aside into a by-street. He vowed to himself that however difficult the way and however doubtful even the prospect of his being able to get back, he would not cease from going on. He would surely have strength enough to let himself be dragged. And the road must come to an end some time. By day the Castle had looked within easy reach, and, of course, the messenger would take the shortest cut.

At that moment Barnabas stopped. Where were they? Was this the end? Would Barnabas try to leave him? He wouldn't succeed. K. clutched his arm so firmly that it almost made his hand ache. Or had the incredible happened, and were they already in the Castle or at its gates? But they had not done any climbing so far as K. could tell. Or had Barnabas taken him up by an imperceptibly mounting road? "Where are we?" said K. in a low voice, more to himself than to Barnabas. "At home," said Barnabas in the same tone. "At home?" "Be careful now, sir, or you'll slip. We go down here." "Down?" "Only a step or two," added Barnabas, and was already knocking at a door.

A girl opened it, and they were on the threshold of a large room almost in darkness, for there was no light save for a tiny oil lamp hanging over a table in the background. "Who is with you, Barnabas?" asked the girl. "The Land Surveyor," said he. "The Land Surveyor," repeated the girl in a louder voice, turning towards the table. Two old people there rose to their feet, a man and a woman, as well as another girl. They greeted K. Barnabas introduced the whole family, his parents and his sisters Olga and Amalia. K. scarcely glanced at them and let them take his wet coat off to dry at the stove.

So it was only Barnabas who was at home, not he himself. But why had they come here? K. drew Barnabas aside and asked: "Why have you come here? Or do you live in the Castle precincts?" "The Castle precincts?" repeated Barnabas, as if he did not understand. "Barnabas," said K., "you left the inn to go to the Castle." "No," said Barnabas, "I left it to come home, I don't go to the Castle till the early morning, I never sleep there." "Oh," said K., "so you weren't going to the Castle, but only here"—the man's smile seemed less brilliant, and his person more insignificant—"Why didn't you say so?" "You didn't ask me, sir," said Barnabas, "you only said you had a message to give me, but you wouldn't give it in the inn parlour, or in your room, so I thought you could speak to me quietly here in my parents' house. The others will all leave us if you wish—and, if you prefer, you could spend the night here. Haven't I done the right thing?" K. could not reply. It had been simply a misunderstanding, a common, vulgar misunderstanding, and K. had been completely taken in by it. He had been bewitched by Barnabas' close-fitting, silken-gleaming jacket, which, now that it was unbuttoned, displayed a coarse dirty grey shirt patched all over, and beneath that the huge muscular chest of a labourer. His surroundings not only corroborated all this but even emphasized it, the old gouty father who progressed more by the help of his groping hands than by the slow movements of his stiff legs, and the mother with her hands folded on her bosom, who was equally incapable of any but the smallest steps by reason of her stoutness. Both of them, father and mother, had been advancing from their corner towards K. ever since he had come in, and were still a long way off. The yellow-haired sisters, very like each other and very like Barnabas, but with harder features than their brother, great strapping wenches, hovered round their parents and waited for some word of greeting from K. But he could not utter it. He had been persuaded that in this village everybody meant something to him, and indeed he was not mistaken, it was only for these people here that he could feel not the slightest interest. If he had been fit to struggle back to the inn alone he would have left at once. The possibility of accompanying Barnabas to the Castle early in the morning did not attract him. He had hoped to penetrate into the Castle unremarked in the night on the arm of Barnabas, but on the arm of the Barnabas he had imagined, a man who was more to him than anyone else, the Barnabas he had conceived to be far above his apparent rank and in the intimate confidence of the Castle. With the son of such a family, however, a son who integrally belonged to it, and who was already sitting at table with the others, a man who was not even allowed to sleep in the Castle, he could not possibly go to the Castle in the broad light of day, it would be a ridiculous and hopeless undertaking.

K. sat down on a window-seat where he determined to pass the night without accepting any other favour. The other people in the village, who turned him away or were afraid of him, seemed much less dangerous, for all that they did was to throw him back on his own resources, helping him to concentrate his powers, but such ostensible helpers as these who on the strength of a petty masquerade brought him into their homes instead of into the Castle, deflected him, whether intentionally or not, from his goal and only helped to destroy him. An invitation to join the family at table he ignored completely, stubbornly sitting with bent head on his bench.

Then Olga, the gentler of the sisters, got up, not without a trace of maidenly embarrassment, came over to K. and asked him to join the family meal of bread and bacon, saying that she was going to fetch some beer. "Where from?" asked K. "From the inn," she said. That was welcome news to K. He begged her instead of fetching beer to accompany him back to the inn, where he had important work waiting to be done. But the fact now emerged that she was not going so far as his inn, she was going to one much nearer, called the Herrenhof. None the less K. begged to be allowed to accompany her, thinking that there perhaps he might find a lodging for the night; however wretched it might be he would prefer it to the best bed these people could offer him. Olga did not reply at once, but glanced towards the table. Her brother stood up, nodded obligingly, and said: "If the gentleman wishes." This assent was almost enough to make K. withdraw his request, nothing could be of much value if Barnabas assented to it. But since they were already wondering whether K. would be admitted into that inn and doubting its possibility, he insisted emphatically upon going, without taking the trouble to give a colourable excuse for his eagerness; this family would have to accept him as he was, he had no feeling of shame where they were concerned. Yet he was somewhat disturbed by Amalia's direct and serious gaze, which was unflinching and perhaps a little stupid.

On their short walk to the inn—K. had taken Olga's arm and was leaning his whole weight on her as earlier on Barnabas, he could not get along otherwise—he learned that it was an inn exclusively reserved for gentlemen from the Castle, who took their meals there and sometimes slept there whenever they had business in the village. Olga spoke to K. in a low and confidential tone, to walk with her was pleasant, almost as pleasant as walking with her brother. K. struggled against the feeling of comfort she gave him, but it persisted.

From outside, the new inn looked very like the inn where K. was staying. All the houses in the village resembled one another more or less, but still a few small differences were immediately apparent here; the front steps had a balustrade, and a fine lantern was fixed over the doorway. Something fluttered over their heads as they entered, it was a flag with the Count's colours. In the hall they were at once met by the landlord, who was obviously on a tour of inspection; he glanced at K. in passing with small eyes that were either screwed up critically or half-asleep, and said: "The Land Surveyor mustn't go anywhere but into the bar." "Certainly," said Olga, who took K.'s part at once, "he's only escorting me." But K. ungratefully let go her arm and drew the landlord aside. Olga meanwhile waited patiently at the end of the hall. "I should like to spend the night here," said K. "I'm afraid that's impossible," said the landlord. "You don't seem to be aware that this house is reserved exclusively for gentlemen from the Castle." "Well, that may be the rule," said K., "but it's surely possible to let me sleep in a corner somewhere." "I should be only too glad to oblige you," said the landlord, "but besides the strictness with which the rule is enforced— and you speak about it as only a stranger could—it's quite out of the question for another reason; the Castle gentlemen are so sensitive that I'm convinced they couldn't bear the sight of a stranger, at least unless they were prepared for it; and if I were to let you sleep here, and by some chance or other—and chances are always on the side of the gentlemen—you were discovered, not only would it mean my ruin but yours too. That sounds ridiculous, but it's true." This tall and closely-buttoned man who stood with his legs crossed, one hand braced against the wall and the other on his hip, bending down a little towards K. and speaking confidentially to him, seemed to have hardly anything in common with the village, even although his dark clothes looked like a peasant's finery. "I believe you absolutely," said K., "and I didn't mean to belittle the rule, although I expressed myself badly. Only there's something I'd like to point out, I have some influence in the Castle, and shall have still more, and that secures you against any danger arising out of my stay here overnight, and is a guarantee that I am able fully to recompense any small favour you may do me." "Oh, I know," said the landlord, and repeated again, "I know all that." Now was the time for K. to state his wishes more clearly, but this reply of the landlord's disconcerted him, and so he merely asked, "Are there many of the Castle gentlemen staying in the house to-night?" "As far as that goes, to-night is favourable," returned the landlord, as if in encouragement, "there's only one gentleman." Still K. felt incapable of urging the matter, but being in hopes that he was as good as accepted, he contented himself by asking the name of the gentleman. "Klamm," said the landlord casually, turning meanwhile to his wife who came rustling towards them in a remarkably shabby, old-fashioned gown overloaded with pleats and frills, but of a fine city cut. She came to summon the landlord, for the Chief wanted something or other. Before the landlord complied, however, he turned once more to K., as if it lay with K. to make the decision about staying all night. But K. could not utter a word, overwhelmed as he was by the discovery that it was his patron who was in the house. Without being able to explain it completely to himself he did not feel the same freedom of action in relation to Klamm as he did to the rest of the Castle, and the idea of being caught in the inn by Klamm, although it did not terrify him as it did the landlord, gave him a twinge of uneasiness, much as if he were thoughtlessly to hurt the feelings of someone to whom he was bound by gratitude; at the same time, however, it vexed him to recognise already in these qualms the obvious effects of that degradation to an inferior status which he had feared, and to realise that although they were so obvious he was not even in a position to counteract them. So he stood there biting his lips and said nothing. Once more the landlord looked back at him before disappearing through a doorway, and K. returned the look without moving from the spot, until Olga came up and drew him away. "What did you want with the landlord?" she asked. "I wanted a bed for the night," said K. "But you're staying with us!" said Olga in surprise. "Of course," said K., leaving her to make what she liked of it.

W. B. Yeats

THE SECOND COMING

Turning and turning in the widening gyre
The falcon cannot hear the falconer;
Things fall apart; the centre cannot hold;
Mere anarchy is loosed upon the world,
The blood-dimmed tide is loosed, and everywhere
The ceremony of innocence is drowned;
The best lack all conviction, while the worst
Are full of passionate intensity.

Surely some revelation is at hand;
Surely the Second Coming is at hand.
The Second Coming! Hardly are those words out
When a vast image out of *Spiritus Mundi*
Troubles my sight: somewhere in sands of the desert
A shape with lion body and the head of a man,
A gaze blank and pitiless as the sun,
Is moving its slow thighs, while all about it
Reel shadows of the indignant desert birds.
The darkness drops again; but now I know
That twenty centuries of stony sleep
Were vexed to nightmare by a rocking cradle,
And what rough beast, its hour come round at last,
Slouches towards Bethlehem to be born?

Paul Klee

CREATIVE CREDO

I.

Since graphic art tends of its own accord to abstraction, it is only natural that it should be receiving higher appreciation today. From the first it can present the object in a more patterned, more imaginative, more nonobjective manner, and hence with incomparably greater precision than any other form of art. The more purely we work graphically, that is to say, the more we accept the elements underlying graphic art, the less equipped we are for a realistic representation of things. A prestidigitator, of course, violating the elements, will create certain illusions. But that is no longer pure art, because it is at the expense of the real elements. Pure art arises when the element of design and the expression of the formal organism are in real correspondence with the spirit of the content. And in any organism the parts stand in a logical proportion to the whole. Small integers underlie the proportion.

We should not be misled into thinking, for example, that the picture of a naked man is organic only because the fingers are in correct proportion to the hands, the hands to the forearm and biceps, and so on. That is another side of art; it can, however, serve as an example of how to achieve analogous results when we are working with pure elements of form.

II.

The formal elements of graphic art are dot, line, plane and space, the last three charged with energy of various kinds. A planar element is not composed of dots and lines. Rather it comes about when we use a blunt crayon with unvarying intensity. An example of a spatial element would be a cloudlike, misty dab of a full brush, applied with varying intensities. As has already been suggested, dots and lines placed in relationship to one another can also generate planar and spatial shapes.

Let us develop these principles by taking a little jaunt into the land of better insight. Our first act is to move beyond the lifelessness of the dot. Soon we stop to catch our breath. This is rendered by a *broken line, or one articulated by repeated stops*. We look back to see how far we have come. This is "countermovement." We pause and consider the paths in various directions—this gives us a *sheaf of lines*. A river gets in our way and we must use a boat. This is a *wavy line*. Further upstream there might be a bridge: *series of curves*. Across the river we meet someone who shares our views, who also wishes to reach greater insight. For a while we are in agreement about everything down to the smallest detail: this is *convergence*. But agreement will soon cease: *divergence*. Soon we are all flustered, though he more than I: *difference in expressiveness of two lines*. We cross a freshly plowed field: *plane traversed by lines*. Then a forest. My companion loses his way, looks here and there, and even sniffs the ground like a hunting dog.

I too am no longer so cool-headed. There is another river and a thick mist rising above the bottomlands: "spatial element." By and by the atmosphere clears somewhat. We encounter some basket weavers: *texture of lines*. They have a baby with them, with lovely curly hair: *corkscrew motif*. Later on it grows sultry and dark: *spatial element*. A flash of lightning on the horizon: *zigzag line*. But there are still stars overhead: *scattered dots*. Soon we come to an inn and put up for the night. Before we fall asleep a good many memories bob to the surface, for a little walking tour of this sort is full of impressions: all sorts of lines, dots, dabs, smooth planes, planes animated by dabs, cross-hatchings; wavy movements, articulated and obstructed movements, countermovements, textures, tissues, masonry effects, scales, solo lines, duet lines, lines fading out and lines that gain strength because they are in the fog—*dynamism*. The blithe evenness of the first stretch, then the inhibitions, the uncertainty. Faint tremblings; the caresses of cool breezes. At the approach of the thunderstorm, the sudden buzz of gadflies. Fury. Killing. The aim in view as a guideline, even in the underbrush, even in the dusk. Fortunately the night did not descend too soon. Anxiety. Fear comes seldom. Keep healthy, don't take on too many burdens. The lightning flash reminded me of the fever chart of a sick child, some years ago. I felt fear, then. Now we sleep. Tomorrow we continue.

III.

I defined the concept of element as something integral in itself. We enrich the formal harmony by using structures composed of elements, as for example surfaces represented by lines entering into relationships —the view of flowing streams, for instance. Or else we may proceed from dots to lines, or create spatial structures out of lines and dots in third-dimensional relationships—for example, fish darting past, above and below one another. In this way the organism becomes more richly articulated, and the number of potential variations becomes infinite.

IV.

Movement underlies the growth and decay of all things. In Lessing's *Laokoon*, which in our piety we still go on tormenting our brains over, a great fuss is made about the difference between temporal and spatial art. But look more closely into the matter and the whole problem turns out to be a pedant's delusion. For space too is a temporal concept.

When a dot begins to move and becomes a line, the process takes time; likewise, when a line is displaced and becomes a surface; likewise when moving surfaces become spaces. Is a work of pictorial art created all at once? Not at all—it is built up bit by bit, just like a house. How long does it take to build a house? And what about the beholder—is he finished with the work at one glance? Unfortunately, he often is. Feuerbach has remarked that to understand a picture, a chair is needed. Why a chair? So that the mind will not be distracted by tired legs. And what usually makes legs tired? Prolonged standing. So the mind needs space in which to spread itself—in other words, time.

Character is movement. Only the dot is timeless, and in itself it is lifeless. The universe, too, is all movement. On earth stasis is a chance obstruction of matter. It is an illusion to take this cessation of movement as primary.

The Scripture story of Creation is an excellent parable of movement. The work of art, too, is primarily creation; it is never experienced as a mere product.

A creative fire flares, is transmitted by the hand, flashes to the canvas, and on the canvas a spark leaps up to the eye, forming the third dimension, and then, closing the circle, returns to its source.

The essential activity of the beholder is also temporal. He moves part after part into his retina. In order to fix upon a new section, he must abandon the old one. Sooner or later he stops, and takes his leave, like the artist. If what he saw was enjoyable and promises more enjoyment, if he thinks it was worthwhile, he comes back—exactly as the artist does.

In the work of art paths are made for the eye of the beholder which moves along from patch to patch like an animal grazing. In music there are channels conducting sound to the ear; in the drama there are both sight and sound. The work of art arose out of movement, is itself congealed movement, and is perceived by movement—the movement of the eye muscles.

The beholder suffers from the disadvantage of being presented with an end-product; as far as the creative process is concerned, he appears to be going at the work the wrong way round. We do wrong to offer him obstacles instead of pleasure. The artist therefore should try for a certain transparent simplicity in the construction of his work of art; but this simplicity must not be confounded with poverty. The artist's sureness, skill and deeper knowledge are in no way at cross purposes with this simplicity. A musical work has the advantage that it is received by the hearer exactly in the order of its conception; but when it is heard many times, the senses are dulled by the very evenness of the impression. For the nonspecialist a pictorial work has the virtue that the order of its perception may be strongly varied, and thus its ambiguity more richly appreciated.

V.

In the past artists represented things they had seen on earth, things they liked seeing or might have liked to see. Today they reveal the relativity of visible things; they express their belief that the visible is only an isolated aspect in relation to the universe as a whole, and that other, invisible truths are the overriding factors. Things appear to assume a broader and more diversified meaning, often seeming to contradict the rational experience of yesterday. The artist strives to express the essential character of the accidental.

By including the elements of good and evil a moral sphere is created. Evil is viewed not as an enemy whom we conquer or are conquered by, but as a force which has its share in the making of the Whole, an essential factor in creation and evolution. The presence of the masculine principle (evil, disturbing, passionate), and the feminine principle (good, serene, growing), results in the forging of an ethical balance.

Corresponding to this is the dialectic of forms, movement and countermovement, or—if we want to put this in more elementary terms—colorism, as in Delaunay's analysis of forms by color. Every energy calls for its complement, for art is always seeking the equilibrium that arises out of the play of forces, a state in which abstract forms can become meaningful objects, or else pure symbols as constant as numbers and letters of the alphabet. Taken all together, these may become symbols of the cosmos; that is to say, they become a form of religious expression.

A few examples:

I. A sailor of classical antiquity in a boat, greatly pleased with the clever contrivance which such a boat is. The ancients would represent him in those terms. By contrast, modern man strolling over the deck of a steamer is aware of quite other factors:

1. His own motion.
2. The motion of the ship, which may be contrary to his.
3. The speed and direction of the current.
4. The rotation of the earth.
5. The earth's motion in its orbit.
6. The orbits of stars and moons around it.

Resultant: a system of movements in the universe, with the ego on the steamer as the center.

II. An apple tree in blossom: its character, its roots, the rising sap in its trunk, a cross section with its annual rings, the blossom with its various parts and sexual functions, the fruit, the core with its seeds. The whole is a structure of states of growth.

III. A man sleeping: the circulation of his blood, the measured respiration of his lungs, the delicate operations of his kidneys, and in his brain a world of dreams, with all their ties to the powers of destiny. The whole is a structure of functions united in the most peaceful repose.

Art is a parable of Creation; it is an example, as the terrestrial is an example of the cosmos. But all these matters we have been speaking of are not yet art. The release of the elements, the grouping of them in subdivisions composed of parts, the articulation of the whole by building up several aspects simultaneously, pictorial polyphony, the achievement of equilibrium between the various movements, all higher and still higher questions of form, are vital factors in artistic communication; but they do not in themselves produce art of the highest level. For at that level, mystery begins and the intellect counts for nothing. At the highest level, imagination is guided by instinctual stimuli, and illusions are created which buoy us up and stir us more than do the familiar things of earth. In that realm are borne the symbols which comfort the mind, which perceives that it need not be chained to the potentialities of terrestrial things. Up there, ethical seriousness reigns, and along with it impish laughter at the learned apparatus of scholars and parsons.

Neither higher potentiality nor reality can be of any avail to us. Away with everyday things and away with the occult sciences—they are barking up the wrong tree. Art goes beyond both the real and the imaginary object. Art plays an unknowing game with things. Just as a child at play imitates us, so we at play imitate the forces which created and are creating the world.

Art should be at home everywhere, like a fairy tale; and it should know how to deal in good and evil, like the Almighty. To man art should be like a vacation in the country, an opportunity for him to change his point of view and see himself transplanted into a world of diversions which offers only pleasant things, and from which he returns, strengthened, to the routine of daily life. Still more, it should help him put off his shell, to imagine himself God for a few moments, and, remembering the possibility of repeating such a transformation, to look forward to evening after work when the soul sits down at table to nourish its famished nerves and replenish its weary organs with fresh juices. All art should lead to this, both the broad rivers and charming, aphoristic, many-branched rivulet of graphic art.

Frank Lloyd Wright

GENIUS AND THE MOBOCRACY

MOBOCRACY AND GENIUS

Demoralization of the creative instinct—O Lord, be merciful—lies in this universified, governmentalized substitution of a falsely decorated *mobocracy* for the thought-built *democracy* we might have. This wretched graft of which we are inordinately proud has so blinded us that already it is difficult for us even to recognize the dishonesty from which we spring and in which we live, and from which we will have suffered the greatest of all losses in this passing era of the omnipresent borrower, arrant physicist, and this ismic salesman—the artist. It is he who is primarily to blame! The weakling has not been equal to his true place. He has been a coward when and wherever his people needed his vision and courage most. Throw him in with the professionals, journalists, and the art critic (with his camera) and for good measure throw in the "history of art" as usually taught. They all belong together. Of such sham are the implements by which we work our intolerable waste: the misuse or abuse of our bravest and best; the chronic substitution of quantity for quality; guesswork instead of interior discipline and no instruction in organic construction on a good foundation, all down the line! These add up to the ruin of the creative instinct of any nation. This defect is now either the entertainment or the popular punishment meted out to the fire-born by our false success-ideal. By odious comparison genius is today just about where Louis H. Sullivan was yesterday; the life of the human spirit is wasted more securely than ever: waste sustained by authority for our already enormously increasing masses of "ownership." Even as in that day the stronger the property habit in the life of the masses—the more our bias is totalitarian. Ownership unless unusually natural and enlightened does not tend democratic. Our young men are not urged, they are hunger-driven by false standards of success toward standardization, first, and ideas based on principle—if any— afterward. *To oppose this trend toward makeshift lives more and more standardized* is where we find the same old human frontier upon which organic architecture as great art must now go to work. Science—as inspiration—is through. In any long view science cannot substitute for Nature. It may take Nature apart but cannot put Nature together again for the growth of the human soul.

A dense conspiracy of the matter-of-fact against the human spirit is what monitors this science mentality we are calling a civilization—one which science has presented and promoted. Meantime we are miscalling our confused art and sterilized education "culture" when both destroyed by science are mainly tools for money-making. Invention? Only another tool for the same purpose. As a matter of course, such "art," "education," and "invention" allow us no fundamental architecture of our own. How, then, can democracy build? We have brains enough. We have the tools. But we have no true mind at this crucial moment in this matter of the structure of a native architecture natural to us. An affair of genuine culture, it lies far beyond the cowardly revival of the classics versus the two-dimensional patterns of the "modernist" and we have little deep conviction concerning the reality of anything if *we can't see* it work by being taught to see only in the "flat"; spiritual integrity— *depth*—always the unwelcome intruder. We do not dare to think for fear we might feel our insignificance? We are afraid to feel for fear of our thought otherwise. Nor have we deep enough faith in ourselves as ourselves to realize that the basis of democracy is—teaching men, or allowing them "to know themselves." No. Wherever the deeper essentials of life are concerned, we are craven cowards. A rat-like perspicacity? We have it, and the same courage.

It has always been difficult for me to see the grandeur of promiscuity. The horse there, too, is behind the cart. Honor hides behind the barn.

But at least so long as we are not yet committed to the mobocrat's idea of "the common man" there is hope. I have never yet met this "common man." In a democracy it is you and it is I who are the protagonists of any future that is now—democratic or fascist. And that means no future for us as a democratic nation is to be found by condoning imitations by disciples, to live in, or in sending youth to standardized schools; perfectly good plums to get back prunes.

THE SENSE OF GUILT

Now, to say that the ideal disciple—man or nation—is hard to find may of course be only a way of saying that the ideal master does not exist?

Somehow I've always felt that were the master ideal his disciple would be so—even if in spite of himself. Does the disciple not reflect the master and exaggerate his mortality just as he does his immortality?

Did not Judas personify these forces? Probably he did.

Is there no ideal discipleship because the relationship is wrong? Is it all too human to be ideal discipline for the son of a technocracy without soul so far going, going, gone from democracy as this one of ours? To look to *any* disciple for *his own integrity* due to experience by interior discipline? Is this like looking for light in a place inevitably in the dark shadow of false eminence? But if not false, why dark; eminence should be luminous? Why is it not so for the youths of our modern world? It is because we continue to propagate them and murder them by conscription, vast mass-education, and bad politics? Where does the faith of the neophyte lie now? I don't know . . . of course, the mechanical pace is fast; competition in this and that, meum and tuum, is more and more keen. The higher the education, the more grossly expedient it is. Life by imitation like a sickness spreads wide and thin over the vast surface of a continent. Government is becoming enormity, mostly burdensome bureaucratic expropriation, punishment, or propaganda for the business of war and the preservation of the "to-have-and-to-hold" we call "security." Such intensity as we know is mostly the voracity we call speed and the desperation we call "efficiency." Both are objectionable just as light on a purposely hidden crime would be.

But I do know by the flippant attitudes of arrant, national egotism that nobility of spirit is condemned to die by unimaginative reason or worse—the arrogant humility of our very best people. In what we call production and success there is no longer the spirit of youth because there is no firm platform nor any springboard at all for truly creative imagination. In this civilization, premature by way of science and sudden riches—probably proceeding from barbarism to degeneracy with stunning waste of power—genius is a sin against the mob! It is the calamity of our time that no master, were he to come to us today, could survive to enjoy true, that is to say, secure fame. Notoriety—no end —would be all he could hope for during his lifetime. If any post-mortem "halo" for him, dead, it would have to be carefully adjusted, by experts, to shed agreeable light on the establishments endorsed by the canonizers themselves. Their name is legion.

Something very like this massacre upon the life of imaginative reason, an assassination of which I write with unsympathetic patience and moderated invective, lieber-meister had many times more bitterly described to me. Some day some other original, wishful lover of a liberal architecture for the coming of age of our democracy, will be writing of it all as happening to him.

In due course when some *qualified* historian—a barbarian perhaps now that we hoard and hide the atom bomb—may refer to the architecture of the late nineteenth and early twentieth centuries, what honor it has will be found so far as the life of architecture is new—not renewed—to stem directly from one Louis H. Sullivan of Adler and Sullivan, Architects, Chicago, Illinois, say, in the late eighteen-nineties?

As a matter of course, only the higher discipleship which it is fair to say education is could have missed the master's own good book, "The Autobiography of an Idea." I find many high-school boys have read it, also the Mayor of Louisville, Kentucky. His name is Farnsley.

Now, as for my place in the practice of that idea—with my inside eyes wide-open I chose to go with Louis H. Sullivan at the proper time to be "the pencil in his hand." Later I left him to carry on my work in my way as I best could. I came back to him as an architect and a friend about twenty years later, not long enough before he dropped by the wayside. Leaving that wayside with contempt, but hope, I have persistently worked. I remember the master once saying to me, sadly (he was writing something about the apparently miraculous survival of the Imperial Hotel in the Tokio temblor of 1922): "Frank, you have never been my disciple—but you are the only one who ever worked with me who understood. I couldn't do what you've done, nor could you have done what you've done but for me!"

What did the master mean? He meant that though inspired by him I had not copied his work. I have never imitated him or anyone. He was great enough to be proud of me because I wasn't his disciple. He had no more respect for disciples than for a draughtsman.

I am proud to have worked by his side inspired to this day by him. A master! Yes. But no more mine than yours or anyone's who will *understand* what he understood and be faithful to that comprehension. This entire aftermath we call history, and are taught to teach to teachers to teach, must have been mis-made in some such equivocal fashion as I have seen history made of his work and my own in architecture. More hapless "text" mis-made to be mis-read. I have seen the whole "movement" since inception trickle in little by little, the mere "look-of-the-thing" meantime so manipulated as to confuse and confound the simple truth because to some unqualified but all the more presumptuous writer it seemed unpleasant, or expedient, to disagree. I have seen the long arm of coincidence manipulated to reflect borrowed credit where it could not belong—and lived to see this expedient remouthed as prejudiced propaganda. Pretentious or ignorant personalities writing in the name of art in all nations have taken a fling at the subject, all professing advanced perspective from bad matter-of-fact or none. I have seen this "civilization" of ours itself excel in such conscienceless equivocation and by way of unlimited exercises of equivocal character become unanimously exterior, quite satisfied to be merely careerist. More shameless evasion or shallow pretense characterizes the phase of our mentality we call "art" than any I know—but perhaps only because I have seen this phase of our disgrace grow up.

Sophisticates obsessed by the notion that culture with a capital C for our lives must come from "abroad," play upon this weakness of ours. The exhibitionist criticism of the museum seems unaware that most of the modernist movements it presents, imagining them good for a sensation, derive from monarchy and are consciously or unconsciously bound to the roots of fascism. A bitter smile from me—to see the "trend" wherever the driver spoke with suitable foreign accent. I have come to see for myself—finally—what the master himself said with extreme disgust (and unusual profanity): "Wright! . . . why are they [the American people] so g—— d—— credulous?" Many years later when he always called me "Frank" he would say wearily, "Frank, our people don't think any more." But let me here confess: imported endorsements are nearer the truth than our own authorities ever were on the subject. But if our own crop of disciples is without honor, what of the country itself that produces them in school, in art, in politics, in religion, "ad libitum ad nauseam"? Such a state would have to die not as Louis H. Sullivan died with honor, unsuccessful, alone, but dishonored in the mass by its own kind of "success."

Now, why all this attention to the specious disciple? For one thing, reflections from the master to whom I listened a half-century ago now verified by my own experience.

For another (maybe an attempt to unscramble eggs), on account of the way I have seen history "scrambled" by disciples and come down the line deformed in respect to Louis H. Sullivan, myself, and the new architecture. In books, pamphlets, magazines, newspapers, and in all languages it has come until all history—for me—assumes a spurious aspect. With complete skepticism I now read whatever is written not only on the new architecture but any other subject. I want to know "written by whom," then "what about the writer"? When I feel I know the thing as pretentious or the usual posterior-personal slant, I throw the equivocal mass away and try to form an opinion from between the lines. I suggest that you, kind reader, do the same here. No self-portrait or portrayal of one person by another nor any report of a cause however great or small—or of both put together—as is the case here—can be impersonal. Nor should be. As for fame—fame will always mean more to posterity than it can ever mean to the recipient alive or dead. Thought by callow youth to be fun—to the famous man fame is likely to be only funny.

CONCERNING THE APPRENTICE

Now that we have looked this gift horse, the disciple, in the mouth—the apprentice! What about the volunteer apprentice? It is my feeling and experience that the volunteer apprentice is a better basis for a future architecture for democracy than the selective disciple. Probably the only way we will achieve a great architecture. We can make best use of our best youth that way. The apprentice comes next to the doing of the thing to put his hand to it. What quality he has is soon put to test. He makes good or he loses out. As he is situated, next to spirit, character counts most. He has a chance to develop kindness, understanding, encouragement, and companionship by way of sacrifice to his ideal. Pretense is vain. Presumption is upset. By his performance he is known, and the shirker is soon shown up by the worker. In quality the apprentice is likely to remain fresh and honest because he shares by his own ability in creative effort of unquestioned superiority or else he would be no voluntary apprentice.

A GOOD APPRENTICE IS ABLE TO SERVE WITHOUT BECOMING A VASSAL

As distinguished from the disciple the apprentice confronts his preference and is in position to serve reality. But he may become a disciple, lose contact with his conscience, and so lower his character in selfish pursuit of his own consequence at expense to his art. But as a creative force his chance of survival in his chosen field is far greater than any chance due the ambiguous disciple. There may be infinite disciples but comparatively few apprentices. The psychology of the modern apprentice therefore differs radically from that of the disciple although the apprentice may become a disciple, deceive himself, and disintegrate. To the apprentice belongs the responsible, direct approach; the approach of the disciple is intuitive, mainly selfish, and irresponsible. The apprentice works with direct responsibility to and for his inspiration. The disciple presumes upon whatever relationship he has to the master. Of the two—the apprentice has foundation in actual service to his ideal. The disciple has at best assumed elevation without any sacrificial foundation. He has tried to take the short-cut. Hence the apprentice will realize what the disciple may only surmise. Withal the apprentice is straightforward, proceeding by experience from Nature to ethics and back again to the drawing board. The disciple is equivocal and knows no ethics. If and when both are men these comparisons are fair enough. The disciple has already sold his exemplar to his client in his own name. The apprentice will not so sell until he becomes a disciple. He would lose his credit and so his self-respect. To license him to build eventually would build up a profession being torn down now by favored sons with paper degrees.

The apprentice in a democracy does not differ so much from the apprentice of *"le moyen âge,"* except that, instead of the slave he then was, he is the comrade of his master, and to any extent he is able to live up to.

To detach oneself from the nature of the doing is the greatest calamity that can befall an apprentice. But the apprentice also is "loaded." The man who takes one is either brave or an incorrigible egoist. But his duty is clear. He must share himself with those who admire and trust him.

At the height of his power I knew Louis H. Sullivan—Master—as his right-hand man. And it is in the nature of what I have said that all I could honestly tell of him is personal to me. I can give the master to you only by way of his draughtsman, myself. Inasmuch as you can only see him here through me, if intimately of him this "writing" is inevitably intimate of me. So you know him by way of this willing pencil in his hand for nearly seven years. Who, then, was this Louis H. Sullivan I still call lieber-meister so long after he is gone because he is still an inspiration to me? How did this "pencil" come to his hand? This book is my attempt to answer.

From me at this time the first-person singular will offend many, surprise some, and disappoint more. But in this whole matter, at risk of rousing resentment among skeptical or unwilling readers (becoming myself liable to the charge of bad "taste" by hurting the feelings of others), wherever lieber-meister is concerned with me or I with him I have repeated complimentary or condemnatory words, both, as I well remember them. Because while this work is authentic it is no documentary treatise. I prefer the humble arrogance of sincerity to the arrogant humility of self-deception; so hypercriticism averse to the first-person singular would better not try to read it. I am more concerned with truth than fact. But when I use a fact the fact is fact.

This book is "in memoriam" because of a promise.

I do not like to write it because—but for the promise—it should be unnecessary to do so. Louis H. Sullivan—lyric poet—no functionalist—should, by now, be well known and cherished *for what his gift truly was;* his "gift" at the same time so much more (and other) than is on the record.

The profound naturalness of one's own being is the essential condition of a great architect, and the condition of greatness in the man. It has been the ambition of my life to achieve it with glass and steel—bricks, boards, a hod of mortar, a "client," and "the union."

So, wherever the practice of architecture today rises to the dignity of an idea in harmony with place and time, independent of ism, ist, or ite, the origin of that practice is middle-West to our courageous national experiment in freedom and stems from one, Louis H. Sullivan—beginning about 1889. But the pen is a tricky tool—fascinating but treacherous.

John Marin

TO MY PAINT CHILDREN

To you who have been in the
making—these many years—
and who are now made to the
best of my making
and do now find yourselves
hung in all your seeming nakedness—on
these walls
bear yourselves well and
disclose no more than can be disclosed by
your being what you are
Hold yourselves aloof—hold
yourselves—strange—with a strange
strangeness
Tempt those who can be tempted
and for those—cease not to tempt—but if
one says "he has you" go you into hiding
Now—my Paint Kids—Poppa—
knows you are Splayed in parts—are weak
in parts
with here and there—of a part
missing—inarticulate—but not so much so
but that Poppa gets a meaning
yes you are incomplete—you are
not quite rigged up—there'll be here and there
a—missing—to complete your balanced order
that's where your Poppa hasn't
quite clicked—your baffled Poppa—still you
have each and every one *somewhat* clicked—some
few of you *somehow* clicked
so that Even the most crippled of
you—well he loves you all—you're his
love-paint-children—and
however you are looked at—don't change yourselves—just keep—being yourselves—

you ask no questions—you
answer no questions—

you move in your own movings
Content to play in your own little yards
he—your Poppa—has surrounded you with
each a little fence—

each fence perhaps hurriedly
made perhaps not too well made—just like
yourselves—

your fence now becomes a part
of you—I hope it won't hinder your playing—
I trust it will serve to make you play the
harder within yourselves—knowing your
boundaries—

and if your fence does keep
them—who would see—from seeing you too
intimately—it will make to tantalize—
so that they will be made—as it were—
to take peeps through the pickets—

your Poppa had quite a job
in the making of you—

We will give them quite a job
if they really want to see you

Now there have been Somethings
said about the which I will now speak

you see—you my—water paint
kids and you my—Oilpaint—Kids are different

but you were made each and every
one of you by that same old Codger—your
Poppa—

I would say you are neither the
one or the other to be jealous of one another

to you my Oil Kids—your Poppa—
got a somewhat reputation a making your *water*
sisters

but you Seem to be a Coming along—
tolerably well—tolerably well—maybe a little
haltingly but still a moving I hope—as to why
I speak of this there be those who have said—
may still say—You should never have been born—

Give them not a thought—
You are not if you are not

but you *Are* if you *are* and *that's that*
Now to all of you *again be yourselves*

> behave as individuals—
to the Extent that you have these ingredients
within you—as healthy—well balanced
individuals should behave

> Wherever you go—and Poppa
hopes that those of you who—go—won't
become lonesome—will have a warm habitation—
will be allowed to live—will be in good
Company—deserving good company and for
those of you who return back to him

> well—Poppa too knows where
a few fatted calves are to be found

> now to all of you *don't forget*
—thank warmly—the man who's made it
possible your being where you are

> *So long* Kids—Poppa salutes
you—again don't meddle in other people's
affairs—if they love our AFFAIR—dance to
them Kids—DANCE—your loving Poppa

JOHN MARIN

Herbert Read

ART NOW

BACKGROUND FROM REYNOLDS TO BERGSON:
REVOLUTION IN THE THEORETICAL CONCEPTION OF ART

I want, in this first chapter, to trace that gradual change in the philosophy of beauty which has, so to speak, prepared the way for the practice of modern art. We must go back a long way—back, in fact, to the beginnings of the empirical method in criticism generally. We shall then find a growing awareness of the diversity of art, and as more and more manifestations of the artist's will come under the review of philosophers, the old *a priori* method becomes inadequate, and finally fails: a new science is born, the science of art. It is a science which admits evidence from many fields hitherto not associated with the philosophy of beauty—evidence from history and anthropology, from religion and psychology, from morphology and philology—from every science that deals with the spirit of man and the modes of its expression. The difference which exists between the modern science of art and what passed for the science of art in the eighteenth century—in the writings, for example, of our own Hogarth, Richardson and Reynolds—is almost total. It seems even more distinct than the difference between the actual arts themselves.

REYNOLDS AND THE GRAND MANNER

The art of the eighteenth century, as represented by Reynolds and codified in his *Discourses,* is a most curious dead-end in human development. Until the close of the eighteenth century we can say that every period had its style, however obscure and however unworthy. But after this time the spirit of man apparently ceased to express itself in direct and original modes; it began instead to conform to previous modes of expression: and so we get that series of revivals of style—the neo-Gothic, the neo-classic, the debased eclecticism of the Great Exhibitions —ending with the end of the nineteenth century in a general bankruptcy of the academic tradition.

The seeds of the decay were inherent in that secondary but finally predominant aspect of the Renaissance known as The Classical Revival.

How far the ideas of the Classical Revival conform to the principles and practice of the artists of ancient Greece I will not attempt to estimate; but we may say that that aspect of Greek art which emphasized its intellectual or rational structure was seized on and made the canon of all aesthetic expression. 'There is (in Greek art) an almost metaphysical belief that beauty and the ideal type for sculptural representation are characterised by an almost supersensual, because intellectual and mathematical, structure.'[1] This notion of a canon of beauty, a type-form which should satisfy the reason in its quest for perfection, is the dominant characteristic of the whole classical tradition. When most justified (by the judgment of successive ages—a pragmatic test, I admit) this ideal reconciles the vitality of organic life, especially as represented by the human form, with the stability and universality of an intellectual concept. Natural facts are given a rational interpretation; the organic is lifted to the plane of the intellect; the vital seeks a point of equilibrium in physical law. But the virtue of an equilibrium is that it is easily upset: the thrill it communicates comes from its delicate tension. It was inevitable that the eighteenth century, with the gradual triumph of the Cartesian philosophy and the consequent degradation of instinct and imagination, should overweight the balance on the side of reason. And precisely *that* eventuality is fatal to the existence of art. Art may flourish in a rank and barbaric manner from an excess of animal vitality; but it withers and dies in the arid excesses of reason. And it is because, not for the first time in the history of man, reason became predominant in the philosophy of art, that art in the eighteenth century suffered such a complete eclipse.

The obsequies are, appropriately enough, celebrated with pomp and circumstance in the *Discourses* of Sir Joshua Reynolds; there the classical ideal is finally devitalised in the doctrine of the Grand Manner, or the Great Style. We shall best realise the distance modern art has travelled if we take this style as our point of departure. But it is not easy, as Reynolds himself realised, to define in what the Great Style consists; and Reynolds' own training had been too empirical for him to acquiesce in the notion that taste or genius could be taught by rules. 'Experience is all in all,' he said, 'but it is not everyone who profits by experience; and most people err, not so much from want of capacity to find their object, as from not knowing what object to pursue. . . . The power of discovering what is deformed in Nature, or, in other words, what is particular and uncommon, can be acquired only by experience; and the whole beauty and grandeur of Art consists . . . in being able to get above all singular forms, local customs, particularities, and details of every kind. All the objects which are exhibited to our view by Nature, upon close examination will be found to have their blemishes and defects. The most beautiful forms have something about them like weakness, minuteness, or imperfection. But it is not every eye that perceives these blemishes. It must be an eye long used to the contemplation and comparison of these forms. The Painter who aims at the greatest style . . . corrects Nature by herself, her imperfect state by her more perfect. His eye being enabled to distinguish the accidental deficiencies, excrescences, and deformities of things, from their general figures, *he makes out an abstract idea* of their forms more perfect than any one original. . . . This idea of the perfect state of Nature, which the artist calls the Ideal beauty, is the great leading principle by which works of genius are conducted.[2]

Here we have the final formulation of the classical doctrine in art, and this final formulation does not differ essentially from that of Dryden at the end of the seventeenth century, or, for that matter, from that of Alberti in the fifteenth century. Common to them all is the notion that the artist 'makes out an abstract idea'; and that is the feature of the classical ideal to be kept in mind for purposes of contrast with the emergence of a new ideal. Further, the classical ideal is a static ideal, an ideal based on the *status quo* of a particular civilisation, that civilisation established in Greece and continued in Mediterranean Europe until the present day.

VICO AND THE RISE OF THE GENETIC CONCEPT OF ART

If I were to select a single word to characterise the opposing ideal which already in the eighteenth century had made its obscure appearance, that word would be *genetic*. And if I were to select a single name as the originator of this ideal, that name would be *Vico*. Within two years of Reynolds's birth, there was published in Italy the *Scienza Nuova* of Giambattista Vico, a work which, though its title makes a claim for novelty, was in effect a return to the principles and methods of the Scholastic philosophy, which in their turn were based on the principles and methods of Aristotle. This 'new science' involved a conception of society as a developing organism, and Vico's aim, as it concerns us now, was to determine the place of art in the history of such an organism. This led him to the formulation of a theory of poetry totally distinct from the prevailing classical ideal, and distinct, therefore, from those principles of poetry which the seventeenth century regarded as for all times 'laid down by Plato and confirmed by Aristotle'. Vico identifies poetry with the primitive phase in the history of man: poetry is the first form of history, it is the metaphysic of man whilst he is still living in a direct sensuous relation to his environment, before he has learned to form universals and to reflect. Imagination is clearly differentiated from intellect, and all forms of poetic activity are shown to depend on the imagination; in civilised epochs poetry can only be written by those who have the capacity to suspend the operation of the intellect, to put the mind in fetters and to return to the unreflecting mode of thought characteristic of the childhood of the race.

I must not expatiate too much on Vico's theory of poetry, though I believe it to be of profound significance: I can only refer to Croce's exposition of the subject, to Vico himself, and throw out the prediction that we are going to hear a great deal more about Vico in the immediate[3] future, and that, in short, his theories are going to play a predominant part in the development of modern criticism. Meanwhile I want to emphasise as significant the method employed by Vico: the return to origins. His theory is based on a study of mythology and particularly of Homer. And that is what I mean by the *genetic* method—a method which studies art in relation to its origins, its history and distribution—in brief, the empirical method itself. The whole of the modern tradition in art is a direct result of such an approach to art: art no longer conceived as a rational ideal, a painful striving towards an intellectual perfection; but art conceived as a stage in the ideal history of mankind, as a pre-logical mode of expression, as something necessary and inevitable and organic, the language of the Heroic age, the expression of imaginative heroism in the life of the artist in any age.

METAPHYSICAL AESTHETICS

The next name I would like to mention is that of *Herder,* though I ought to refer in passing to his master Baumgarten, who has perhaps gained a rather fictitious importance by inventing the name *aesthetics,* and by making the first attempt to claim the subject as a science. He defined aesthetics as 'the science of sensuous knowledge', and gave birth to that great school of metaphysical aesthetic represented by Kant and Hegel—an idealistic, aprioristic approach to our subject which has little relevance to our practical enquiry. I cannot see that the course of art has in any way been influenced by the *Critique of Judgment.* But Herder, unlike Kant but like Vico, went back to the sources, to objective things, to primitive poetry and folk-song, and his conclusions are the same as Vico's. Again I only want to insist on the method: it was applied in the main to the study of language and poetry, and its relevance to the visual or plastic arts was still unobserved.

After Kant the world, as Jean Paul Richter said, swarmed with aestheticians. I have never been able to believe that the idealistic conception of art, developed on the basis of Kant's aesthetic by writers like Schiller, Fichte and Schelling, and given a more popular romantic expression by poets like Richter and Novalis, is worth the time that would be involved in mastering its mysteries. It is all based on the discussion of abstract categories like imagination and fancy, form and idea, which are rarely, if ever, related to objective works of art. There is no critical method involved, no correlation of facts. To describe the Homeric epic, as Schelling does, as 'the very identity conditioning the foundation of history in the Absolute', is a deplorable departure from the precision of Vico's Homeric criticism. I do not wish this to be construed as a reflection on philosophy in general, for philosophy properly conceived is the highest of all mental disciplines; but science is prior to philosophy; science must establish its facts before philosophy can make use of them. Philosophers have in general ignored the possibility of a science of art and have proceeded blissfully on *a priori* assumptions as to its nature. That is why I think we are entitled boldly to ignore the aesthetic of idealism. I have some compunction in applying such a sweeping statement to *Hegel*, in whom this aesthetic reaches its final and most definitive expression. Hegel shows throughout his *Philosophy of Fine Art* a real sensibility towards all forms of art—a sensibility often in advance of his time. I might instance, as examples of his acuity, his defence of the librettos of Mozart's operas; his perception that the superiority of Dante's epic over all other epics was due to the element of sympathy; and in the sphere of the plastic arts, a passage like the following, which betrays a habit of accurate observation:

'It is, therefore, *colour,* and the art of colouring, which make the painter a painter. We dwell with pleasure, no doubt, on the drawing, and exceptionally so on the study or sketch, as on that which preeminently betrays the quality of genius; but however rich with invention and imagination, with whatever directness the soul of an artist may assert itself in such studies by reason of the more transparent and mobile shell of their form, yet the fact remains that to be painting we must have colour, if the work is not to continue abstract from the point of view of its sensuous material in the vital individuality and articulation of its objects. We must, however, at the same time admit that drawings and dry point drawings from the hand of great masters such as Raphael and Albrecht Dürer are of real importance. In fact from a certain point of view we may say that it is just these hand drawings which carry with them the finest interest. We find here the wonderful result that the entire spirit of the master is expressed directly in such manual facility, a facility which places with the greatest ease, in instantaneous work, without any preliminary essays, the essential substance of the master's conception. The border drawings of Dürer, for example, in the Prayer-book of the Munich library, are of indescribable ideality and freedom. Idea and execution appear in such a case to be one and the same thing, whereas in finished pictures we cannot avoid the sense that the consummate result is only secured after repeated over-paintings, a continuous process of advance and finish.'[4]

But all Hegel's experience of art was of no avail against the over-ruling necessities of his system, for, as Croce has pointed out, 'the principles of Hegel's system are at bottom rationalistic and hostile to religion, and hostile no less to art.' Art for Hegel was only a stage, and a lower stage, in the progress of the mind towards truth. Art can only represent truth in sensible form, but, he thought, we have passed beyond the stage when the mind can be satisfied with such representations. The absolute must now be apprehended by the spirit, that is to say, by philosophy, and art must be discarded like the toys of a childhood we have outgrown. Obviously, a philosopher who puts art so firmly in the past cannot be of use to anyone who is trying to find a philosophy of art in the present.

For similar reasons we shall pass by the names of Schopenhauer, Herbart and Schleiermacher; in spite of the many brilliant things they have to say about art as a general concept, they are all engaged in the philosophical game of system-building, and we feel that their theories of art have no essential connection with works of art. Fundamentally they are neither critically nor historically minded: they accept the taste and cultural traditions of their own time as infallible and are content to quote as illustrations a few hackneyed types like the Apollo of the Belvedere. The famous philologist, Wilhelm von Humboldt, is a much more significant figure. His specifically aesthetic works seem to be of no great originality, being mere commentaries on the classical canons: but his main work is based on an objective study of language and in this field he came to exactly the same conclusions as Vico—that language, for example, is a product of the struggle to reach an intutition of things, that poetry precedes prose and gives us reality in its sensible appearance. But he never seems to have thought of applying this same objective method to the plastic arts, confining himself to vague analogies and comparisons.

THE EMPIRICAL APPROACH

This long and increasingly complicated movement of *a priori* aesthetics continued far past the middle of the nineteenth century, but its very excesses produced a reaction. The first to react were the positivists—Herbert Spencer and Grant Allen in England, and Taine in France—but in its first violence this reaction was extremely crude: we come down from

the clouds but we do not find ourselves in the region of art. I defy anyone to associate aesthetic sensibility with the mentality of Herbert
Spencer. But it is a different matter with Gustav Theodor *Fechner,* whose
Vorschule der Ästhetik was first published in 1876. Fechner is the real
founder of the modern science of art, the first philosopher to study art
'von unten', to base an aesthetic on an empirical or inductive study of
works of art. He inaugurated those experimental methods with a statistical aim which are still being pursued in psychological laboratories all over
the world, in spite of Croce's contemptuous dismissal of them as 'a
pastime or hobby neither more nor less important than playing Patience
or collecting stamps'. Regarded separately these methods may often
seem ridiculous enough and irrelevant; but in their aggregate, and as
summarised, for example, in the survey made by O. Külpe,[5] there can
be no doubt that they have taught us a lot about the physical character of
objects commonly accepted as beautiful, and a lot about the psychological
reactions of various types of people to such objects. It is the philosopher's
own fault if he is not able to assimilate such facts into his general theory
of art.

I attach much more importance to the type of empirical study represented by names like Gottfried Semper, Konrad Fiedler, and Ernest
Grosse. *Semper* is the historical materialist in the sphere of art; he accepts (and this in itself is an original step for which he cannot be given
too much credit) the whole evidence presented by works of art surviving
from any epoch and asks: what are the universal and typical forms which
we can discern in all this multiplicity? He surveys all his material and
points out the recurring forms and motives; he then asks whether these
are determined by the purpose which the object has to serve, the material
from which it is made, or the nature of the tools and technical methods
used in its making. Semper's principal work[6] appeared in 1860 and has
continued to exercise considerable influence, not only on direct disciples
in the method like Alois Riegl in his study of late Roman art, but on
artists (the present-day emphasis on the doctrine that the artist must
respect the nature of his material derives directly from it) and on the
arrangement of museums. There is no doubt that Semper's method is an
extremely fertile one, and when it is used, as he used it, with unfailing
sensibility and soundness, it must lead to a much better comprehension of
the nature of the artistic activity in man, and the conditions which determine its forms throughout history—the conditions, we might add, which
are determining its forms to-day.

Semper's ideas have been developed with great subtlety and intelligence
by Konrad *Fiedler,* an aesthetician who is sadly neglected in England and
grossly under-rated by writers like Croce. Fiedler holds fast to the idea

that art is the will creative in the terms of a material: the artist considers his material and solves, not a technical problem, but a formal one. 'The artist (he says) is not differentiated from other people by any special perceptive faculty enabling him to perceive more or with greater intensity, or endowing his eye with any special power of selecting, collecting, transforming, ennobling or illuminating; but rather by his peculiar gift of being able to pass immediately from perception to intuitive expression; his relation to nature is not perceptive, but expressive'—and expressive, we might add, in tangible and sensible objects, objects which conform to their material essence. The artist speaks in stone, in wood, in bronze, in colour, just as the poet speaks in words: the artist makes thought visible, without the intermediary of verbal concepts. This is a very significant theory, one of the main theories underlying the practice of contemporary artists.[7] Fiedler, who was active in the eighties and nineties of the last century, was in close contact with the most original artists of his day— with Hans von Marées and Adolf von Hildebrand—and his doctrine, with its striking insistence on the necessity of originality (for there is no proper artistic activity in the use of hackneyed forms, as there would be no proper poetic expression in the use of hackneyed metaphors), is peculiarly relevant to our present purpose. Fiedler, in fact, was ready to admit that the new and significant in art can only arise out of direct opposition to the past, and in relation to modern architecture, for example, he would have insisted on the necessity of thinking within the terms of the materials, steel and concrete, to the exclusion of all ideas derived from the utilisation of wood and stone.

The third name I mentioned as particularly significant in the foundation of an aesthetic of modern art was that of Ernst *Grosse*. In 1894, whilst still in his twenties, he published his first book, *Die Anfänge der Kunst* (The Beginnings of Art). Grosse, more decisively than anyone else, breaks away from the idea that art is confined to the products of the Graeco-Roman tradition, and insists on the science of art incorporating, in the manner of any other humanistic science, the whole genesis and scope of the artistic activity. And just as science in general, in so far as it is concerned with organic life, is almost inconceivable on any but a genetic and evolutionary basis, so this facet of human life must be studied in its origins and development. Thus began that research into prehistoric and primitive art which is still progressing, and which, by bringing to our attention the works of primitive and prehistoric peoples, and pointing out their aesthetic significance, has been one of the most powerful influences in modern art. For in primitive art we see so clearly, what is so difficult to perceive in the complex products of highly cultured civilisations—the directly expressive quality of the artist's vision, its objectification in solid shapes.

THE SIGNIFICANCE OF PRIMITIVE ART

Parallel to this line of approach, and on the principle that ontogenesis repeats phylogenesis, we have had a serious study of the art of children, culminating in the comparatively recent works of Bühler, Wulff and Eng. I shall say no more about it than that it has fully confirmed the general validity of the genetic method in aesthetics, and again, by drawing attention to the positive qualities of chidren's art, has had a direct influence on the practice of modern artists—there has been a deliberate attempt to reach back to the naivety and fresh simplicity of the childlike outlook— a retrograde step, of course, if you regard 'the march of intellect' with complacency or satisfaction.[8] It is not claimed that the art of savages, prehistoric men and children can be given the same value as the art of civilised men: in the humanistic scale of values, such art is almost negligible. But our present enquiry is concerned, not with the problem of values, but with the nature and development of art, and from this point of view it is impossible to exaggerate the significance of primitive art. The virtue of a plant is in its seed: its form is implicit in its first shoot. We can learn more of the essential nature of art from its earliest manifestations in primitive man (and in children) than from its intellectual elaboration in great periods of culture. For in its later stages art is overlaid by modes of life and manners that are not of its essence. Primitive man and the child do not distinguish in our ratiocinative manner between the real and the ideal. Art for them is perhaps not so disinterested: it is not extraneous and complementary to life, but an intensification of life: a stirring of the pulse, a heightening of the heart's beat, a tautening of the muscles, a necessary and exigent mode of expression. Art, indeed, is regarded by primitive man as of such practical importance that its use is socialised; an artist for art's sake would probably be killed as a dangerous devil, but an artist for the community's sake becomes priest and king, for he is the maker of magic, the voice of the spirits, the inspired oracle, the intermediary through whom the tribe secures fertility for their crops or success for their hunters. His hand is veritably the hand of God.

Art from this point of view, let us frankly admit, has nothing to do with polite culture or intelligence. In its origins it is an exercise or activity of the senses, the plastic expression of elementary intuitions. As such, it is not the possession of one people, but is diffused over the whole world. But in its creative aspect it is a limited activity—that is to say, it is confined to special individuals who have special faculties—not of feeling or of thought—but of expression, of objectification. With these faculties, the favoured individual can appeal to the senses, to the aesthetic emotions, of the community. Art is therefore closely related to skill—not only because all visual or plastic arts depend on learning the use of some tool, but also because one cannot otherwise describe the ability to fashion objects to the will, to the heart's desire. But art is more than skill, because skill is purely functional. Art begins where function ends: it is a refinement on function, though it should not interfere with function. Where functional forms are equal in operative efficiency, there is still room for the aesthetic sensibility to make a choice—to say that one spear-head is *more beautiful* than another, one axe *more beautiful* than another. And this brings us down to the root-problem of aesthetics—what do we imply by this preference? That one shape is more pleasing than another—but why? If it had done nothing else, the genetic method in aesthetics would have justified itself by finally isolating this question. In order to answer it, another method was necessary—the psychological method. It is not possible to explain the pleasure or satisfaction we derive from the formal elements in art until we have laid bare the physiology of instinctive responses, explained the part played by pattern in the stimulation of visual acuteness, the relation of rhythm to bodily and perhaps (as the Chinese would have us believe) to cosmic movements, the unconscious appeal of concrete and abstract symbolism, the emotive effect of pure colours and tones, and so on.

THE PSYCHOLOGY OF ART, THE RECEPTIVE ASPECT

To give any adequate account of modern psychological theories of art is beyond the scope of this essay. We owe the establishment of a scientific psychology of art mainly to four Germans—Karl Groos, Theodor Lipps, J. Volkelt, and Max Dessoir—and their enquiries revolve for the most part round what is known as the theory of Einfühlung, or *empathy*. This theory tends to become so generalised that it loses a good deal of its specific application to works of art. Primarily it is a theory of aesthetic appreciation, in contrast to the theories which we have just been considering, which were more concerned with the object and the conditions of its creation. It is a theory which finds the explanation of aesthetic pleasure in the nature of the sympathetic relation established between the spectator and the work of art. This is revealed as no mere fellow-feeling, of feeling *with,* but rather a form of imaginative identification of the self with the object, a feeling *into.* It is an immediate, direct, intuitive relation of perception to the *form* of the object. Lipps, who is the classical exponent of the theory, describes it in this way:

'The object of sympathy is our objectified ego, transposed into others and therefore discovered in them. We feel ourselves in others and we feel others in ourselves. In others, or by means of them, we feel ourselves happy, free, enlarged, elevated, or the contrary of all these. The aesthetic feeling of sympathy is not a mere mode of aesthetic enjoyment, it is that enjoyment itself. All aesthetic enjoyment is founded, in the last analysis, singly and wholly upon sympathy: even that caused by geometrical, architectonic, and other abstract lines and forms.'

But it would be an abuse of the word to describe the latter mode of feeling as sympathy: we do not necessarily humanise the rising column or the graceful vase which we contemplate: we feel into their shape, conform to it, and react to its limits, its mass, its rhythmic convolution; and so we invent the word *empathy*. Further, it is possible to say that empathy is a vitally different thing according as the object of contemplation is human, organic, or abstract; Lipps himself distinguishes between simple and symbolic empathy. What I want to make clear, and I think my statement is warranted by Lipps and Volkelt, is that the initial stage in this process is not one of feeling: it is not merely a sentimental association of the self with the object. There is a direct intuitive awareness of form, an unconscious identification, and the specifically aesthetic *feeling* follows. This is made particularly clear by certain types of contemporary abstract art.

We must, in fact, distinguish three stages in the complete aesthetic experience before a work of art: (1) the immediate perception or apprehension of the object, (2) the reaction of the affective system to the form of the apprehended object, and (3) the reaction of the spectator's mind to the conceptual nature of the object, to the 'content', that is to say, of the work of art, and to all its secondary associations.

THE CREATIVE ASPECT

The creative aspect of art, according to this theory, is a more complicated process. Here I do not propose to follow any particular lead, but I think the general theory of the psychological school I have mentioned would allow us to distinguish the following stages of the creative process in the visual arts: they correspond very closely with the stages in other arts, such as poetry and music:

1. There is first a predisposing emotional mood, a state of readiness or awareness, perhaps a sense of the momentary availability of the unconscious levels of the mind.

2. Whilst he is in this state there come to the artist the first premonitions of a symbol, or thought to be expressed, not in words, but in visible and tangible material shape—perhaps 'this landscape', 'this dish of fruit', perhaps only an abstract adumbration of planes and masses.

3. Then, as a third step, we have the mental elaboration of this symbol,

the introduction or selection of images which the mind intuitively associates with the symbol, the determination of the emotional value or pressure of the images.

4. Next the artist seeks an appropriate method, including an appropriate material, by means of which he can represent the symbol.

5. Finally, there is the actual technical process of translating the mental perception into objective form—a process during which the original symbol may receive considerable modifications.

It should be observed, however, that what we in this psychological manner analyse into five consecutive and distinct stages, in actual practice takes place as an integral and inseparable activity. Moreover, the artist does not necessarily always begin at the beginning, with a vague emotional mood. He may begin at almost any stage and go backwards before going forwards—he may, and very often does, begin with the material, paint or stone, and from a concentration on this, and perhaps from a playful preliminary activity with his tools, he induces the preliminary mood. But fundamental to all exact psychology of the creative process is the notion that art is the expression through the senses of states of intuition, perception or emotion, peculiar to the individual. Nowhere, in the modern psychology of art, will you find any justification for the notion that art is primarily an intellectual activity concerned with the formulation of absolute or ideal types. That art has been and still is occupied with human and spiritual values, the psychologist is willing to admit; but these have nothing to do with the nature of the aesthetic process itself. They are questions of value—values in ethics, sociology, religion or philosophy, not aesthetic values. On that dogma, supported as it is by the whole force of the modern science of art, the practice of contemporary art stands or falls.

THE PRESENT PHILOSOPHY OF ART

It is natural to ask, in conclusion, whether the very diverse speculations and discoveries of the modern science of art which I have so cursorily surveyed, have received any integration within a modern system of philosophy. No contemporary philosopher can now safely neglect this sphere of the human spirit, but it is to be doubted whether any one has given it an adequate or just place within a unified view of the universe. Croce, of course, has made the attempt, but it is an attempt which rests on a rejection of the evidence of the empirical and psychological approach I have described, and which resorts instead to a species of solipsism that attempts to identify aesthetics and linguistics. It is the last flicker of a defunct idealism, and I do not propose to stop to examine it. It is daily earning discredit and will not for long embarrass us with its terminological confusions. It is only in the work of Henri Bergson that I personally have found any treatment of art which is at once scientific in its basis and philosophical in its aim. But Bergson, alas, has never given us an aesthetic: we are left to gather together for ourselves the incidental wisdom on this subject which lies scattered through his various books. As an example of this wisdom, and as a definition of art which seems to me to be reconcilable, not only with the vast range of artistic expression in the past and in our present time, but also with the objective theories of art which I have described, I would like to quote a passage from his book on *Laughter*:

'From time to time, in a fit of absent-mindedness, nature raises up souls that are more detached from life. Not with that intentional, logical, systematical detachment—the result of reflection and philosophy, but rather with a natural detachment, one innate in the structure of sense or consciousness, which at once reveals itself by a virginal manner, so to speak, of seeing, hearing, or thinking. . . .

'One man applies himself to colours and forms, and since he loves colour for colour and form for form, since he perceives them for their sake and not for his own, it is the inner life of things that he sees appearing through their forms and colours. Little by little he insinuates it into our own perception, baffled though we may be at the outset. For a few moments at least, he diverts us from the prejudices of form and colour that come between ourselves and reality. And thus he realises the loftiest ambition of art, which here consists in revealing to us nature. Others, again, retire within themselves. Beneath the thousand rudimentary actions which are the outward and visible signs of an emotion, behind the common-place, conventional expression that both reveals and conceals an individual mental state, it is the emotion, the original mood, to which they attain in its undefiled essence. And then, to induce us to make the same effort ourselves, they contrive to make us see something of what they have seen: by rhythmical arrangement of words, which thus become organised and animated with a life of their own, they tell us—or rather suggest—things that speech was not calculated to express. Others delve yet deeper still. Beneath these joys and sorrows which can, at a pinch, be translated into language, they grasp something that has nothing in common with language, certain rhythms of life and breath that are closer to man than his inmost feelings, being the living law—varying with each individual—of his enthusiasm and despair, his hopes and regrets. By setting free and emphasising this music, they force it upon our attention; they compel us, willy-nilly, to fall in with it, like passers-by who join in a dance. And thus they impel us to set in motion, in the depths of our being, some secret chord which was only waiting to thrill. . . .'[9]

There are many terms in such a statement that would need defining in an exact aesthetic, but alike in the loftiness of its conception and the truth of its observation, these words adequately summarise that revolution in thought which has accompanied and which sanctions the revolution in contemporary art.

NOTES

1. Rhys Carpenter: *The Esthetic Basis of Greek Art* (1921).

2. The Third Discourse (delivered December 14, 1770).

3. This word was too optimistic. But, in spite of the war, translations of Vico's works have been proceeding and certain critical studies are due for publication which may still bear out my prediction (1947).

4. *The Philosophy of Fine Art* by G. W. F. Hegel. Trans. by F. P. B. Osmaston. 4 vols, 1920. Vol. iii, p. 275.

5. *Der gegenwärtige Stand der experimentellen Ästhetik* (1906).

6. *Der Stil in den technischen und tektonischen Künsten, oder praktische Ästhetik.*

7. It has been further developed by Henri Focillon in *The Life of Forms in Art* (Trans. by C. Beecher Hogan and George Kubler. Yale Univ. Press, 1942), one of the most precise and beautiful works in the realm of aesthetics.

8. I have dealt fully with this aspect of the subject in *Education Through Art* (London: 1st Edn., 1943).

9. *Laughter* (1900) by Henri Bergson, trans. by Brereton and Rothwell.

Vincent Van Gogh

LETTER TO EMILE BERNARD

[ARLES: MID-AUGUST 1888]

My dear Bernard,

I want to do figures, figures and more figures. It's stronger than I am this race of bipeds, from the baby to Socrates, from the woman with raven black hair and white skin to the woman with yellow hair and a brick-red face baked by the sun.

Meanwhile I am doing mostly other things.

Thanks for your letter. This time I am writing in great haste, and absolutely worn out.

I am very pleased you have gone to join Gauguin.

All the same I have a new figure study, which is absolutely a continuation of certain studies of heads I did in Holland. I showed them to you one day with a large picture of that period, *The Potato Eaters*: I wish you could see the new one. It's still a study, but colour plays such an important part that a black and white drawing wouldn't give you any impression of it.

I wanted to send you a very large and careful drawing of it. But then it was really something quite different, accurate though it was. For the colour again suggests the burning heat of harvest-time in the south, right in the middle of the dog-days; without that it's quite another picture.

I like to think you and Gauguin would understand it: but the others will find it ugly all right!

You know what peasants are like, how much of the wild beast there is about the genuine article.

I have also a *Men Unloading a Sand-Barge*. That is to say there are two boats, purplish pink in emerald green water, with grey sand, barrows, planks and a little chap in blue and yellow. All that seen from a quay above, in other words a bird's eye view. No sky: it's only a study, or rather a very rough sketch, done in the teeth of the *mistral*. Further, I am attempting some dusty thistles with a big swarm of butterflies fluttering around them.

The full summer sun here is lovely. It beats down on one's head and I am sure it makes one crazy. But as I was that before, anyhow, I can revel in it.

I am thinking of decorating my studio with half-a-dozen pictures of

Sunflowers: a decoration in which chrome yellow, crude or broken, shall blaze forth against various backgrounds of *blue*, ranging from the very palest emerald up to *royal blue* and framed with thin strips of wood painted *orange*.

The sort of effect of Gothic stained glass windows.

Ah! dear friends, we crazy ones get pleasure through our eyes all right, don't we?

Unfortunately Nature takes her toll of the beasts, our bodies are disgusting and frequently a heavy charge. But ever since Giotto, who suffered a lot, it has been thus.

And, all the same, what pleasure he took in his sight, what a smile, the toothless smile of that old lion Rembrandt wearing his white cotton nightcap and with his palette in his hand.

I would love to be able to come and spend a few days at Pont-Aven: however, I seek consolation by looking at the sunflowers.

A cordial handshake: and till soon again.

Vincent.

THIS IS ALL VERY BAFFLING TO MAN

Florida Scott-Maxwell

WOMEN AND SOMETIMES MEN

THE MASCULINE AND FEMININE PRINCIPLE

This talk of masculine sides and feminine sides of the character as though both were clearly defined, and everyone could see and feel them distinctly both in ourselves and in others, may well arouse some protest. The protest would be justified, for the more one ponders this subject the more it is seen as a constant exchange. Men and women pass strength and weakness back and forth to each other. Hardness and softness appear and disappear in both. We live the truth that every quality is sometimes good and sometimes bad, until our wits are addled and we are driven to seek further understanding.

There might be further protest expressing the general distaste aroused by the crude labeling of psychologists, who with far too much assurance trample among the mysteries of human personality. This sense of outrage is understandable, having reason and taste on its side, yet I am convinced by many years of psychological work that experience of the structure of the psyche can bring about a new integration of personality. Analytical psychology has shown that man is masculine outside, with his unconscious personified as feminine, while woman is feminine outside, but with so much of the masculine in her unconscious that it can and does blow her about with the passion of a gale. These findings have now been widely tested and can be taken as a starting point in a search for knowledge of ourselves.

We do not have to go far afield to see that the less a woman recognizes and honors her masculine side the more primitive it is; often explosive and violently unreasonable, sometimes withering her into an arid pedantry, yet often gallantly if excessively heroic. While a man's unadmitted feminine side can keep him evasive of hard reality, making him childish and clamant for ease, seeking everywhere the indulgent mother who will let him remain unborn. Inertia is his greatest problem, and in that stillness he avoids the differentiation he has turned from.

Both men and women are acutely sensitive in these matters, as both imagine they should be completely masculine or feminine, and could be if the other sex would let them; each is outraged to have a doubt cast that this is less than true. But if we do not admit the duality of our natures, then inevitably the unadmitted side is only too apt to be inferior, and we are rightly humiliated when it lives us in spite of ourselves. This is a very prickly subject, involving the frank admission of owning that part of ourselves of which we are least conscious, that part that lies greatly in the unconscious. Only a conviction of the rewards that clarity may bring make one dare to approach it all.

Since there seems no escape from using the terms masculine side and feminine side as though they were definite things, things on which we all agreed—which is true in a profound and widely inclusive way—these terms must be defined. It may be foolhardy, winning small agreement, but it can hardly be avoided. So—fully conscious that I skirt the morass of ambiguity—I take my first step by saying that masculinity moves toward a goal. I follow other psychologists here. Masculinity gives life. One can say that masculinity acts, so a change takes place, and something new has been defined. Then he who acts has to become responsible for his act, opposition must be faced, because a former pattern has been broken. Standing by his act he has to become an individual, one against many, capable of the thought and force that are required by the new thing he has defined.

The taut bow and pointed arrow of the masculine principle were needed if civilizations were to be born, and life was to move forward. Perhaps man's greatest need was to separate himself from the feminine, the maternal oneness. In order to create himself he had to discriminate the masculine from the feminine, to discriminate against the feminine, knowing its formlessness to be his greatest enemy.

This struggle took many forms in many periods. The beginning, the preconscious, could be called feminine, but slowly men evolved laws making sharp definitions, and laws became sacrosanct. Vices and virtues separated, and the spirit was above us, and our instincts were beneath. The body born to die sought the immortality of the spirit, and the division between the two was a clarity, perhaps the great victory. Slowly the power of the instincts was half surmounted, until painfully though incompletely the division between the soul and body was accomplished.

This division occurred in the soul of man. He fought for and found the spirit, and in his religions all heavenly things, the sky, the sun, and even God himself were seen as masculine. Man needed it to be so, and perhaps life needed it to be so. It is certain that the division of two such great opposites created a center where thought became possible; a center where one could withdraw from the dangerous encroachment of the instincts. This meant that man had begun to know his own opposites in his own nature, and could grow strong in his own individuality.

But this had a laming effect on woman, and it may be that she still carries the wound. As the patriarchal religions gained ascendancy over the matriarchal religions, she became the lower half of life. She even became the temptress of man; she could not approach the spirit, and man was the intermediary between her and God. Man's need to see woman as a source of evil for man, and so near to evil in herself, could not help but play a decisive part in forming the character of woman, and influencing her attitude toward herself. She still quivers under it, and seems to be still dazed by the contradictions it implies.

It would not be surprising if this were one of the deep wells which feeds woman's anger, and contrariness and doubt, for these are the qualities of the excluded and dishonored. From this well may also arise the spring of woman's compassion, her patience, selflessness, and insight, the qualities of those who know need, and who answer need; who watch and succor the life and death struggle of men, knowing that all woman has to give is needed.

While women helped they did something more, for they contrived to ignore the paradox they had to live. The paradox that is rooted in sexuality. For she was taught that the sexuality she represented was evil, while the man who loved her said that her sexuality was his greatest good. She was urged by those in authority to be most virtuous, as the body was a vile thing, and woman was the body. She was the body all alone, as it were. This contradiction, this meeting of joy and sin in woman, is part of her essential quality. Women accept it and live it, but somewhere it creates a discord in us, a discord in our blood that makes us ill at ease with ourselves. It puts a drop of poison in us, and will, until we take on this great contradiction both for our own sakes and for that of men.

It is of course the universal wound in the human soul caused by the conflict between the body and the spirit, as real for men as for women, but it has a special bearing on women. If I have come quickly down the ages, merging times and periods, it would have helped but little to pause for accuracy; the way is scattered with records of this discord in life, the discord at the very point where women enter life.

It is a conflict so great that it amounts to nothing less than the struggle between good and evil as it is played out between men and women. It is a struggle where the animal in either can make them both lower than animals, plunging them into self-hatred and self-disgust. But it is also the struggle where tenderness and love create happiness, and an indescribable oneness. These heights and depths are represented by woman, and she typifies the painful doubt as to whether each will be at his best or his worst. It is she who calls out good or bad as though she was the very touchstone of meaning, until this great conflict is almost considered her fault, as though she had created it.

Woman's view of the conflict differs from that of man. What we see from our view almost arrests thought, arresting above all thought about man, for we know that he asks us to surmount the conflict, but also asks us not to step outside it. If man is to be consciousness, then woman must—apparently—be life. So she is wanted to remain at the place of greatest vitality, alive in her body and in her heart. Receiving man and— this is almost his deepest claim—so receiving him that he can think well of himself. For it is not only man's body that woman receives, it is his sense of his essential value that is so often in her care. His idea of himself may make him ask her to deny her own existence, and sometimes he asks her to deny that he is what he is. It is what man asks woman to do to truth itself that paralyzes her power of thought. She is stunned by the difference between personal life and public life, between personal truth and public truth, and how can this contradiction be thought out to clarity? It is hard enough to live it.

But in spite of everything the feminine principle has supported the masculine principle, for the struggle was great even when the protagonists were small. Woman has believed in man even when he did not warrant it, and she has endured the further paradox that man needed woman's aid even when he said he was strength and she was weakness. Because of his need and his dearness she has believed in him, though sometimes it was for life's sake more than for his own.

She learned that she is a danger to him because of the weakness that he finds in himself when with her. He comes to her at his peril for she can soften him, she can expose him to his passions, and his childishness, and to all that is most primitive and most formless in him. She exposes him to the unconscious, so how natural if she has been feared for her power over man; feared and scorned and ruthlessly suppressed, she was then left to carry both his sins and her own. While he, much lightened by what he had left with her, went forward to clarify all those impersonal things in which we have half our being.

Man left woman far behind, and he left her almost incapable of thought. Yet it must never be forgotten that love binds some men and women together, contradicting all other contradictions. While women in general were called inferior, any individual woman might carry the symbol of the man's soul, which he said she was. And this was true, for his unknown feminine side in all its rich life was projected onto her, whether as lust or as love. He saw himself in his image of her, and calling it her, feared or revered it.

When woman was man's ideal he asked her to help him live his ideal, which could mean that he at once left her to perform valiant deeds under her banner. The faulty, indissoluble partnership between man and woman has been lived in many ways, the most constant pattern being that he worked outside the home, while she worked inside; she bore his children for him, formed their characters, respected his work, and sometimes did it for him when he could not. It is almost true to say that while man developed specialized interests woman has carried the wholeness that man could not bear to live. Though it is also true that when he is many-sided, she is sometimes the nothingness he does not know he has.

Woman has always been taught that she must respect man's reason, that it is indeed his great gift of reason that marks him as her superior. But here an odd impasse is reached and a revolt occurs. She knows that the reason of man is one of the glories of clarity. But it is this that inflames her, until any approach to reason can seem a thing outraging to woman.

This is not so surprising as it seems, for man's reasoning can, and often does, go over into its opposite where it concerns women. Religions and philosophies say such strange things about woman, that she sees the weakness in the man who could say such things and doubts the validity of his reason. She is frequently astounded at the human outcome of man's reason and is amazed at the jugglery he permits himself to perform with it. Combined with all this is her daily experience of the unreasonableness of man in his relation to her. It is true that a woman seldom follows abstract reason, and her own role being so poignantly irrational, she becomes wary of all reason as though reason itself were her natural enemy.

This knot is so tightly drawn that one hesitates to touch it further, but it may be safe to suggest that there is some sense in woman's enmity to the ordered processes of thought. For thought sometimes has the inevitable fault of ignoring feeling, and when this happens feeling says truly that thought is incomplete, and almost unreal.

· This is all very baffling to man, and can make him feel helpless and hopeless, which has its own sadness and irony. Woman knows that in private she can defeat man's gift of reason with the strength of her unreason, and may she not be forgiven the pleasure this sometimes gives her?

One has to admit that the position into which nature and man has put woman is outside reason. She makes it work, how often and how well, but that is because she can harmonize the irrational, out of high spirits and out of tenderness. She can make the irrational transcend reason, resolving all contradictions, melting all opposites into a contained whole; and too often she has to carry the refuse of reason, shamed and entangled by its results. It has to be admitted that she can also live the tangle without a gleam of awareness of what she is doing. Or she protests, for she knows at first hand the dangerous power of the idea.

Her home can be destroyed by the ardor of an idea. We have long been told that Madame Pélissier, the wife of the French potter, saw the floor boards of her home torn up to fire her husband's kiln. Her children were hungry and she had turned into a fury because of her husband's obsession with the making of a hard glaze. She might be taken as typical of the women who only knew that the life of the family was being ruined by an idea. And men have had strange ideas, ideas against life, horrifying, eccentric, and abortive. So wives often fear ideas in their husbands and they fear thought in themselves, for thought can make devotion impossible. So there has been a tendency in women to avoid mental processes, and nature has seconded them here.

But tendencies follow great principles while individuals are small and uncertain, prone to wide differences, making nonsense of laws. So any individual man may very well live in a constant predicament. For life requires great qualities of him and it is his pride to represent them, even when he prefers not to live them. Yet it must be trying for him when women claim it as their natural right that he should always maintain order, and produce his greatness on demand. Many a woman assumes that as masculinity is in charge of the world it should allow nothing to go amiss, and she blames the man nearest if it does. For though we give our lives into the care of men, we forget the sorry truth that men cannot always be strong in character, or clear in thought. Who could? If a man sometimes plays his role greatly, and is the very apex of life, how fortunate! At other times he can be the first to say: "Have a heart!"

After this flickering glance at masculinity, and what it seems to stand for, and at how man's needs and accomplishments have affected women, dare I now try to encircle femininity? Not as it is perhaps, because of that we are still uncertain, but as it has been expected to be. This could be taken as the second step in search of our subject; not forgetting that we must look for woman both as a mirage in the eyes of men, and as she feels her reality to be.

I would then say that life, and men, ask mercy of women. They ask for generosity, and for the compassion of acceptance. They ask for joy, kindness and blindness, work and forgetfulness. Too often they ask for variety in indulgence. In short they ask for many aspects of love. They also ask to be allowed to stop being strong, and they enjoy not being clear. They assume at times—their bad times—that all these things are nothing less than their right, easy to give, costing nothing; and too often they are blind to the contradiction at the heart of their demands.

Women must for their own sake, and for life's sake, accept and respect men, and we have to agree forthrightly that as a whole men are more highly differentiated than women. Men have gone far in impersonal achievement and in codified thought, and they have created many specialized worlds. It has to be said that they have done nothing less than create the entire outer scene, which makes what goes on behind the scenes such a surprising contrast.

One of the most poignant paradoxes in the life of a woman is that when a man comes to her, he so often comes to recover his simple humanity, and to rest from being at his best. So a woman frequently has to forego his better side, taking it on trust as a matter of hearsay, and she accepts his lesser side as her usual experience of him. This is hard for her, and here her protests can make him feel a need for her mercy. For while she wishes to admire him she may lack the knowledge, and perhaps the intelligence, to understand the side by which he wins acclaim. She sees his collapse into his home, accepts his need of collapse, indeed receives him with every antenna alert, yet she may forego his superiority with regret. She longs to see his greatness, but has to meet the claim of his smallness.

This contrast between what women hear men can be, and what they sometimes know they are, can be a source of woman's destructive doubt. She is so often split between devotion and rebellion that she sometimes plays the role of the modern Michal who laughed when she saw David dancing before the Ark of the Lord, and whose punishment was being made sterile for mocking when she saw David transcend himself.

Can we take it then that man is sometimes less than wholly masculine, and shall we now ask if woman is always feminine? Does she always show mercy and compassion? But these are love, and at its highest level. If these are expected of woman she is greatly honored, for mercy is a divine attribute. Our Lady is merciful, Kwan Yin is merciful. Few religions are without their Goddess of mercy; so somewhere men and women revere each other, hope for, ask, and blindly expect greatness in each other. Seeing what we exchange in our daily life, let us be glad and even awestruck if we sometimes seek a divine completeness in each other.

Once more we would do well to leave great principles, and this time we must take a look at any individual woman. If she is willing to watch herself live an ordinary day, she must admit how seldom she is merciful; how infrequently she gives any hint of knowing love, and how often it is her own masculinity that drives her roughly until she is nearer a dark avenging fury, than she is to an angel of mercy.

We are now almost impelled to believe that there is no knowing when either men or women may be found living from the side of their natures they forget they possess. We may find out more about these latent sides, and why people choose to live them; that both sides exist in each of us is now regarded as a commonplace of human character and we see it lived wherever we look. It used to be said that when the biological side of life had been fulfilled women took on greater firmness of character, and that men softened markedly, so that each by the process of living rounded out their dual natures. But education for women, and the hard conditions of our times, even some new impulse toward wholeness not yet understood, have given the two sides of man and woman a new prominence.

When men or women are hard pressed, tried beyond their strength, then we may see women summon dogged energy, hardening themselves to deny their hurts, and we may see men caught by their own weakness, trapped by too great difficulty, and sinking into what can seem a long sulk. So our duality becomes more obvious and we are seen to live every aspect of our opposing qualities. But when a quality is an asset and when it is a liability—this needs insight and hardihood to discover.

A man's hurt heart and spiritual wound, as well as his childish evasion and moral cowardice, may make him recoil into his feminine side as his final shelter from the danger of living. Or he may do it from greater and different motives. He may, almost unwittingly, seek to explore and expand his own nature, so that he sinks almost gladly into his latent side, needing to claim it, half realizing that he is a cripple until he finds his creative feeling in his own depths.

Many men today show unmistakably that their feeling is withdrawn from the arid aspects of our modern world; and this is true of the best as well as the worst. The split between thought and feeling is a symptom of our times. For feeling has gone down into the undefinable places where the fresh life lies that is so desperately needed. Many men are suffering the ordeal of loss of feeling. They become stark in their abstract thought, hardly able to endure their own bleak detachment or their rudimentary materialism. While those of a softer nature may live their femininity in its poorest aspects, caught in a travesty of all that femininity stands for. But the perceptive man deprived of his feeling, may after much unhappy frustration come to honor it, learning to know it as the true assessment of living value, and essential half of his own wholeness.

While some men are caught in the latent side of their own natures, many women show a barely smothered anger that is perhaps a just protest at our modern plight. For countless women are carrying heavy burdens hitherto unattempted. They are giving great service to society, but they do it by drawing on qualities which they have only recently made their own, and which one might say they have made incompletely their own. So that in many circles of society both men and women play an uncertain role.

Emily Brontë

WUTHERING HEIGHTS

1801.—

I have just returned from a visit to my landlord—the solitary neighbour that I shall be troubled with. This is certainly a beautiful country! In all England, I do not believe that I could have fixed on a situation so completely removed from the stir of society. A perfect misanthropist's heaven; and Mr. Heathcliff and I are such a suitable pair to divide the desolation between us. A capital fellow! He little imagined how my heart warmed towards him when I beheld his black eyes withdraw so suspiciously under their brows, as I rode up, and when his fingers sheltered themselves, with a jealous resolution, still further in his waistcoat, as I announced my name.

"Mr. Heathcliff!" I said.

A nod was the answer.

"Mr. Lockwood, your new tenant, sir. I do myself the honour of calling as soon as possible after my arrival, to express the hope that I have not inconvenienced you by my perseverance in soliciting the occupation of Thrushcross Grange: I heard yesterday you had had some thoughts"——

"Thrushcross Grange is my own, sir," he interrupted, wincing. "I should not allow any one to inconvenience me, if I could hinder it—walk in!"

The "walk in" was uttered with closed teeth, and expressed the sentiment, "Go to the deuce": even the gate over which he leant manifested no sympathising movement to the words; and I think that circumstance determined me to accept the invitation: I felt interested in a man who seemed more exaggeratedly reserved than myself.

When he saw my horse's breast fairly pushing the barrier, he did put out his hand to unchain it, and then suddenly preceded me up the causeway, calling, as we entered the court—"Joseph, take Mr. Lockwood's horse; and bring up some wine."

"Here we have the whole establishment of domestics, I suppose," was the reflection suggested by this compound order. "No wonder the grass grows up between the flags, and cattle are the only hedge-cutters."

Joseph was an elderly, nay an old man: very old, perhaps, though hale and sinewy. "The Lord help us!" he soliloquised in an undertone of peevish displeasure, while relieving me of my horse: looking, meantime, in my face so sourly that I charitably conjectured he must have need of divine aid to digest his dinner, and his pious ejaculation had no reference to my unexpected advent.

Wuthering Heights is the name of Mr. Heathcliff's dwelling. "Wuthering" being a significant provincial adjective, descriptive of the atmospheric tumult to which its station is exposed in stormy weather. Pure, bracing ventilation they must have up there at all times, indeed; one may guess the power of the north wind blowing over the edge, by the excessive slant of a few stunted firs at the end of the house; and by a range of gaunt thorns all stretching their limbs one way, as if craving alms of the sun. Happily, the architect had foresight to build it strong: the narrow windows are deeply set in the wall, and the corners defended with large jutting stones.

Before passing the threshold, I paused to admire a quantity of grotesque carving lavished over the front, and especially about the principal door; above which, among a wilderness of crumbling griffins and shameless little boys, I detected the date "1500," and the name "Hareton Earnshaw." I would have made a few comments, and requested a short history of the place from the surly owner; but his attitude at the door appeared to demand my speedy entrance, or complete departure, and I had no desire to aggravate his impatience previous to inspecting the penetralium.

One step brought us into the family sitting-room, without any introductory lobby or passage: they call it here "the house" pre-eminently. It includes kitchen and parlour, generally; but I believe at Wuthering Heights the kitchen is forced to retreat altogether into another quarter: at least I distinguished a chatter of tongues, and a clatter of culinary utensils, deep within; and I observed no signs of roasting, boiling, or baking, about the huge fire-place; nor any glitter of copper saucepans and tin cullenders on the walls. One end, indeed, reflected splendidly both light and heat from ranks of immense pewter dishes, interspersed with silver jugs and tankards, towering row after row, on a vast oak dresser, to the very roof. The latter had never been underdrawn: its entire anatomy lay bare to an inquiring eye, except where a frame of wood laden with oatcakes and clusters of legs of beef, mutton, and ham, concealed it. Above the chimney were sundry villainous old guns, and a couple of horse-pistols: and, by way of ornament, three gaudily-painted canisters disposed along its ledge. The floor was of smooth white stone; the chairs, high-backed, primitive structures, painted green: one or two heavy black ones lurking in the shade. In an arch under the dresser, reposed a huge, liver-coloured bitch pointer, surrounded by a swarm of squealing puppies; and other dogs haunted other recesses.

The apartment and furniture would have been nothing extraordinary as belonging to a homely, northern farmer, with a stubborn countenance, and stalwart limbs set out to advantage in knee-breeches and gaiters. Such an individual seated in his arm-chair, his mug of ale frothing on the round table before him, is to be seen in any circuit of five or six miles among these hills, if you go at the right time after dinner. But Mr. Heathcliff forms a singular contrast to his abode and style of living. He is a dark-skinned gypsy in aspect, in dress and manners a gentleman: that is, as much a gentleman as many a country squire: rather slovenly, perhaps, yet not looking amiss with his negligence, because he has an erect and handsome figure; and rather morose. Possibly, some people might suspect him of a degree of underbred pride; I have a sympathetic chord within that tells me it is nothing of the sort: I know, by instinct, his reserve springs from an aversion to showy displays of feeling—to manifestations of mutual kindliness. He'll love and hate equally under cover, and esteem it a species of impertinence to be loved or hated again. No, I'm running on too fast: I bestow my own attributes over liberally on him. Mr. Heathcliff may have entirely dissimilar reasons for keeping his hand out of the way when he meets a would-be acquaintance, to those which actuate me. Let me hope my constitution is almost peculiar: my dear mother used to say I should never have a comfortable home; and only last summer I proved myself perfectly unworthy of one.

While enjoying a month of fine weather at the sea-coast, I was thrown into the company of a most fascinating creature: a real goddess in my eyes, as long as she took no notice of me. I "never told my love" vocally; still, if looks have language, the merest idiot might have guessed I was over head and ears: she understood me at last, and looked a return—the sweetest of all imaginable looks. And what did I do? I confess it with shame—shrunk icily into myself, like a snail; at every glance retired colder and farther; till finally the poor innocent was led to doubt her own senses, and, overwhelmed with confusion at her supposed mistake, persuaded her mamma to decamp. By this curious turn of disposition I have gained the reputation of deliberate heartlessness; how undeserved, I alone can appreciate.

I took a seat at the end of the hearthstone opposite that towards which my landlord advanced, and filled up an interval of silence by attempting to caress the canine mother, who had left her nursery, and was sneaking wolfishly to the back of my legs, her lip curled up, and her white teeth watering for a snatch. My caress provoked a long, guttural snarl.

"You'd better let the dog alone," growled Mr. Heathcliff in unison, checking fiercer demonstrations with a punch of his foot. "She's not accustomed to be spoiled—not kept for a pet." Then, striding to a side door, he shouted again, "Joseph!"

Joseph mumbled indistinctly in the depths of the cellar, but gave no intimation of ascending; so his master dived down to him, leaving me *vis-à-vis* the ruffianly bitch and a pair of grim shaggy sheep-dogs, who shared with her a jealous guardianship over all my movements. Not anxious to come in contact with their fangs, I sat still; but, imagining they would scarcely understand tacit insults, I unfortunately indulged in winking and making faces at the trio, and some turn of my physiognomy so irritated madam, that she suddenly broke into a fury and leapt on my knees. I flung her back, and hastened to interpose the table between us. This proceeding roused the whole hive: half-a-dozen four-footed fiends, of various sizes and ages, issued from hidden dens to the common centre. I felt my heels and coat-laps peculiar subjects of assault; and parrying off the larger combatants as effectually as I could with the poker, I was constrained to demand, aloud, assistance from some of the household in re-establishing peace.

Mr. Heathcliff and his man climbed the cellar steps with vexatious phlegm: I don't think they moved one second faster than usual, though the hearth was an absolute tempest of worrying and yelping. Happily, an inhabitant of the kitchen made more despatch: a lusty dame, with tucked-up gown, bare arms, and fire-flushed cheeks, rushed into the midst of us flourishing a frying-pan: and used that weapon, and her tongue, to such purpose, that the storm subsided magically, and she only remained, heaving like a sea after a high wind, when her master entered on the scene.

"What the devil is the matter?" he asked, eyeing me in a manner that I could ill endure after this inhospitable treatment.

"What the devil, indeed!" I muttered. "The herd of possessed swine could have had no worse spirits in them than those animals of yours, sir. You might as well leave a stranger with a brood of tigers!"

"They won't meddle with persons who touch nothing," he remarked, putting the bottle before me, and restoring the displaced table. "The dogs do right to be vigilant. Take a glass of wine?"

"No, thank you."

"Not bitten, are you?"

"If I had been, I would have set my signet on the biter." Heathcliff's countenance relaxed into a grin.

"Come, come," he said, "you are flurried, Mr. Lockwood. Here, take a little wine. Guests are so exceedingly rare in this house that I and my dogs, I am willing to own, hardly know how to receive them. Your health, sir!"

I bowed and returned the pledge; beginning to perceive that it would be foolish to sit sulking for the misbehaviour of a pack of curs: besides, I felt loath to yield the fellow further amusement at my expense; since the humour took that turn. He—probably swayed by prudential consideration of the folly of offending a good tenant—relaxed a little in the laconic style of chipping off his pronouns and auxiliary verbs, and introduced what he supposed would be a subject of interest to me,—a discourse on the advantages and disadvantages of my present place of retirement. I found him very intelligent on the topics we touched; and before I went home, I was encouraged so far as to volunteer another visit to-morrow. He evidently wished no repetition of my intrusion. I shall go, notwithstanding. It is astonishing how sociable I feel myself compared with him.

Yesterday afternoon set in misty and cold. I had half a mind to spend it by my study fire, instead of wading through heath and mud to Wuthering Heights. On coming up from dinner however (N.B.—I dine between twelve and one o'clock; the housekeeper, a matronly lady, taken as a fixture along with the house, could not, or would not, comprehend my request that I might be served at five), on mounting the stairs with this lazy intention, and stepping into the room, I saw a servant-girl on her knees surrounded by brushes and coal-scuttles, and raising an infernal dust as she extinguished the flames with heaps of cinders. This spectacle drove me back immediately; I took my hat, and, after a four miles' walk arrived at Heathcliff's garden gate just in time to escape the first feathery flakes of a snowshower.

On that bleak hill-top the earth was hard with a black frost, and the air made me shiver through every limb. Being unable to remove the chain, I jumped over, and, running up the flagged causeway bordered with straggling gooseberry bushes, knocked vainly for admittance, till my knuckles tingled and the dogs howled.

"Wretched inmates!" I ejaculated mentally, "you deserve perpetual isolation from your species for your churlish inhospitality. At least, I would not keep my door barred in the day-time. I don't care—I will get in!" So resolved, I grasped the latch and shook it vehemently. Vinegar-faced Joseph projected his head from a round window of the barn.

"What are ye for?" he shouted. "T' maister's down i' t' fowld. Go round by th' end ot' laith, if ye went to spake to him."

"Is there nobody inside to open the door?" I hallooed, responsively.

"There's nobbut t' missis; and shoo'll not oppen't an ye mak yer flaysome dins till neeght."

"Why? Cannot you tell her who I am, eh, Joseph?"

"Nor-ne me! I'll hae no hend wi't," muttered the head, vanishing.

The snow began to drive thickly. I seized the handle to essay another trial; when a young man without coat, and shouldering a pitchfork, appeared in the yard behind. He hailed me to follow him, and, after marching through a washhouse, and a paved area containing a coal-shed, pump, and pigeon-cot, we at length arrived in the huge, warm cheerful apartment, where I was formerly received. It glowed delightfully in the radiance of an immense fire, compounded of coal, peat, and wood; and near the table, laid for a plentiful evening meal, I was pleased to observe the "missis," an individual whose existence I had never previously suspected. I bowed and waited, thinking she would bid me take a seat. She looked at me, leaning back in her chair, and remained motionless and mute.

"Rough weather!" I remarked. "I'm afraid, Mrs. Heathcliff, the door must bear the consequence of your servants' leisure attendance: I had hard work to make them hear me."

She never opened her mouth. I stared—she stared also: at any rate, she kept her eyes on me in a cool, regardless manner, exceedingly embarrassing and disagreeable.

"Sit down," said the young man gruffly. "He'll be in soon."

I obeyed; and hemmed, and called the villain Juno, who deigned, at this second interview, to move the extreme tip of her tail, in token of owning my acquaintance.

"A beautiful animal!" I commented again. "Do you intend parting with the little ones, madam?"

"They are not mine," said the amiable hostess, more repellingly than Heathcliff himself could have replied.

"Ah, your favourites are among these?" I continued, turning to an obscure cushion full of something like cats.

"A strange choice of favourites!" she observed scornfully.

Unluckily, it was a heap of dead rabbits. I hemmed once more, and drew closer to the hearth, repeating my comment on the wildness of the evening.

"You should not have come out," she said, rising and reaching from the chimney-piece two of the painted canisters.

Her position before was sheltered from the light; now, I had a distinct view of her whole figure and countenance. She was slender, and apparently scarcely past girlhood: an admirable form, and the most exquisite little face that I have ever had the pleasure of beholding; small features, very fair; flaxen ringlets, or rather golden, hanging loose on her delicate neck; and eyes, had they been agreeable in expression, that would have been irresistible: fortunately for my susceptible heart, the only sentiment they evinced hovered between scorn, and a kind of desperation, singularly unnatural to be detected there. The canisters were almost out of her reach; I made a motion to aid her; she turned upon me as a miser might turn if anyone attempted to assist him in counting his gold.

"I don't want your help," she snapped; "I can get them for myself."

"I beg your pardon!" I hastened to reply.

"Were you asked to tea?" she demanded, tying an apron over her neat black frock, and standing with a spoonful of the leaf poised over the pot.

"I shall be glad to have a cup," I answered.

"Were you asked?" she repeated.

"No," I said, half smiling. "You are the proper person to ask me."

She flung the tea back, spoon and all, and resumed her chair in a pet; her forehead corrugated, and her red underlip pushed out, like a child's ready to cry.

Meanwhile, the young man had slung on to his person a decidedly shabby upper garment, and, erecting himself before the blaze, looked down on me from the corner of his eyes, for all the world as if there were some mortal feud unavenged between us. I began to doubt whether he were a servant or not: his dress and speech were both rude, entirely devoid of the superiority observable in Mr. and Mrs. Heathcliff; his thick, brown curls were rough and uncultivated, his whiskers encroached bearishly over his cheeks, and his hands were embrowned like those of a common labourer: still his bearing was free, almost haughty, and he showed none of a domestic's assiduity in attending on the lady of the house. In the absence of clear proofs of his condition, I deemed it best to abstain from noticing his curious conduct; and, five minutes afterwards, the entrance of Heathcliff relieved me, in some measure, from my uncomfortable state.

"You see, sir, I am come, according to promise!" I exclaimed, assuming the cheerful; "and I fear I shall be weather-bound for half an hour, if you can afford me shelter during that space."

"Half-an-hour?" he said, shaking the white flakes from his clothes; "I wonder you should select the thick of a snowstorm to ramble about in. Do you know that you run a risk of being lost in the marshes? People familiar with these moors often miss their road on such evenings; and I can tell you there is no chance of a change at present."

"Perhaps I can get a guide among your lads, and he might stay at the Grange till morning—could you spare me one?"

"No, I could not."

"Oh, indeed! Well, then, I must trust to my own sagacity."

"Umph!"

"Are you going to make th' tea?" demanded he of the shabby coat, shifting his ferocious gaze from me to the young lady.

"Is _he_ to have any?" she asked, appealing to Heathcliff.

"Get it ready, will you?" was the answer, uttered so savagely that I started. The tone in which the words were said revealed a genuine bad nature. I no longer felt inclined to call Heathcliff a capital fellow. When the preparations were finished, he invited me with—"Now, sir, bring forward your chair." And we all, including the rustic youth, drew round the table: an austere silence prevailing while we discussed our meal.

I thought, if I had caused the cloud, it was my duty to make an effort to dispel it. They could not every day sit so grim and taciturn; and it was impossible, however ill-tempered they might be, that the universal scowl they wore was their every-day countenance.

"It is strange," I began, in the interval of swallowing one cup of tea and receiving another—"it is strange how custom can mould our tastes and ideas: many could not imagine the existence of happiness in a life of such complete exile from the world as you spend, Mr. Heathcliff; yet I'll venture to say, that, surrounded by your family, and with your amiable lady as the presiding genius over your home and heart"——

"My amiable lady!" he interrupted, with an almost diabolical sneer on his face. "Where is she—my amiable lady?"

"Mrs. Heathcliff, your wife, I mean."

"Well, yes— Oh, you would intimate that her spirit has taken the post of ministering angel, and guards the fortunes of Wuthering Heights even when her body is gone. Is that it?"

Perceiving myself in a blunder, I attempted to correct it. I might have seen there was too great a disparity between the ages of the parties to make it likely that they were man and wife. One was about forty: a period of mental vigour at which men seldom cherish the delusion of being married for love by girls: that dream is reserved for the solace of our declining years. The other did not look seventeen.

Then it flashed upon me—"The clown at my elbow, who is drinking his tea out of a basin and eating his bread with unwashed hands, may be her husband: Heathcliff, junior, of course. Here is the consequence of being buried alive: she has thrown herself away upon that boor from sheer ignorance that better individuals existed! A sad pity—I must beware how I cause her to regret her choice." The last reflection may seem conceited; it was not. My neighbour struck me as bordering on repulsive; I knew, through experience, that I was tolerably attractive.

"Mrs. Heathcliff is my daughter-in-law," said Heathcliff, corroborating my surmise. He turned, as he spoke, a peculiar look in her direction: a look of hatred; unless he has a most perverse set of facial muscles that will not, like those of other people, interpret the language of his soul.

"Ah, certainly—I see now: you are the favoured possessor of the beneficent fairy," I remarked, turning to my neighbour.

This was worse than before: the youth grew crimson, and clenched his fist, with every appearance of a meditated assault. But he seemed to recollect himself presently, and smothered the storm in a brutal curse, muttered on my behalf: which, however, I took care not to notice.

"Unhappy in your conjectures, sir," observed my host; "we neither of us have the privilege of owning your good fairy; her mate is dead. I said she was my daughter-in-law, therefore, she must have married my son."

"And this young man is"——

"Not my son, assuredly."

Heathcliff smiled again, as if it were rather too bold a jest to attribute the paternity of that bear to him.

"My name is Hareton Earnshaw," growled the other; "and I'd counsel you to respect it!"

"I've shown no disrespect," was my reply, laughing internally at the dignity with which he announced himself.

He fixed his eye on me longer than I cared to return the stare, for fear I might be tempted either to box his ears or render my hilarity audible. I began to feel unmistakably out of place in that pleasant family circle. The dismal spiritual atmosphere overcame, and more than neutralised, the glowing physical comforts round me; and I resolved to be cautious how I ventured under those rafters a third time.

The business of eating being concluded, and no one uttering a word of sociable conversation, I approached a window to examine the weather. A sorrowful sight I saw: dark night coming down prematurely, and sky and hills mingled in one bitter whirl of wind and suffocating snow.

"I don't think it possible for me to get home now without a guide," I could not help exclaiming. "The roads will be buried already; and, if they were bare, I could scarcely distinguish a foot in advance."

"Hareton, drive those dozen sheep into the barn porch. They'll be covered if left in the fold all night: and put a plank before them," said Heathcliff.

"How must I do?" I continued, with rising irritation.

There was no reply to my question; and on looking round I saw only Joseph bringing in a pail of porridge for the dogs, and Mrs. Heathcliff leaning over the fire, diverting herself with burning a bundle of matches which had fallen from the chimney-piece as she restored the tea canister to its place. The former, when he had deposited his burden, took a critical survey of the room, and in cracked tones, grated out:

"Aw wonder how yah can faishion to stand thear i' idleness un war, when all on 'em's goan out! Bud yah're a nowt, and it's no use talking— yah'll niver mend o' yer ill ways, but goa raight to t' devil, like yer mother afore ye!"

I imagined, for a moment, that this piece of eloquence was addressed to me; and, sufficiently enraged, stepped towards the aged rascal with an intention of kicking him out of the door. Mrs. Heathcliff, however, checked me by her answer.

"You scandalous old hypocrite!" she replied. "Are you not afraid of being carried away bodily, whenever you mention the devil's name? I warn you to refrain from provoking me, or I'll ask your abduction as a special favour. Stop! look here, Joseph," she continued, taking a long, dark book from a shelf; "I'll show you how far I've progressed in the Black Art: I shall soon be competent to make a clear house of it. The red cow didn't die by chance; and your rheumatism can hardly be reckoned among providential visitations!"

"Oh, wicked, wicked!" gasped the elder; "may the Lord deliver us from evil!"

"No, reprobate! you are a castaway—be off, or I'll hurt you seriously! I'll have you all modelled in wax and clay; and the first who passes the limits I fix, shall—I'll not say what he shall be done to—but, you'll see! Go, I'm looking at you!"

The little witch put a mock malignity into her beautiful eyes, and Joseph, trembling with sincere horror, hurried out praying and ejaculating "wicked" as he went. I thought her conduct must be prompted by a species of dreary fun; and, now that were alone, I endeavoured to interest her in my distress.

"Mrs. Heathcliff," I said earnestly, "you must excuse me for troubling you. I presume, because, with that face, I'm sure you cannot help being good-hearted. Do point out some landmarks by which I may know my way home: I have no more idea how to get there than you would have how to get to London!"

"Take the road you came," she answered, ensconcing herself in a chair, with a candle, and the long book open before her. "It is brief advice, but as sound as I can give."

"Then, if you hear of me being discovered dead in a bog or a pit full of snow, your conscience won't whisper that it is partly your fault?"

"How so? I cannot escort you. They wouldn't let me go to the end of the garden-wall."

"*You!* I should be sorry to ask you to cross the threshold, for my convenience, on such a night," I cried. "I want you to *tell* me my way, not to *show* it; or else to persuade Mr. Heathcliff to give me a guide."

"Who? There is himself, Earnshaw, Zillah, Joseph and I. Which would you have?"

"Are there no boys at the farm?"

"No; those are all."

"Then, it follows that I am compelled to stay."

"That you may settle with your host. I have nothing to do with it."

"I hope it will be a lesson to you to make no more rash journeys on these hills," cried Heathcliff's stern voice from the kitchen entrance. "As to staying here, I don't keep accommodations for visitors: you must share a bed with Hareton or Joseph, if you do."

"I can sleep on a chair in this room," I replied.

"No, no! A stranger is a stranger, be he rich or poor; it will not suit me to permit any one the range of the place while I am off guard!" said the unmannerly wretch.

With this insult, my patience was at an end. I uttered an expression of disgust, and pushed past him into the yard, running against Earnshaw in my haste. It was so dark that I could not see the means of exit; and, as I wandered round, I heard another specimen of their civil behaviour amongst each other. At first the young man appeared about to befriend me.

"I'll go with him as far as the park," he said.

"You'll go with him to hell!" exclaimed his master, or whatever relation he bore. "And who is to look after the horses, eh?"

"A man's life is of more consequence than one evening's neglect of the horses: somebody must go," murmured Mrs. Heathcliff, more kindly than I expected.

"Not at your command!" retorted Hareton. "If you set store on him, you'd better be quiet."

"Then I hope his ghost will haunt you; and I hope Mr. Heathcliff will never get another tenant till the Grange is a ruin!" she answered sharply.

"Hearken, hearken, shoo's cursing on 'em!" muttered Joseph, towards whom I had been steering.

He sat within earshot, milking the cows by the light of a lantern, which I seized unceremoniously, and, calling out that I would send it back on the morrow, rushed to the nearest postern.

"Maister, maister, he's staling t' lanthern!" shouted the ancient, pursuing my retreat. "Hey, Gnasher! Hey, dog! Hey, Wolf, holld him, holld him!"

On opening the little door, two hairy monsters flew at my throat, bearing me down and extinguishing the light; while a mingled guffaw from Heathcliff and Hareton, put the copestone on my rage and humiliation. Fortunately, the beasts seemed more bent on stretching their paws and yawning and flourishing their tails, than devouring me alive; but they would suffer no resurrection, and I was forced to lie till their malignant masters pleased to deliver me: then, hatless and trembling with wrath, I ordered the miscreants to let me out—on their peril to keep me one minute longer—with several incoherent threats of retaliation that, in their indefinite depth of virulency, smacked of King Lear.

The vehemence of my agitation brought on a copious bleeding at the nose, and still Heathcliff laughed, and still I scolded. I don't know what would have concluded the scene, had there not been one person at hand rather more rational than myself, and more benevolent than my entertainer. This was Zillah, the stout housewife; who at length issued forth to inquire into the nature of the uproar. She thought that some of them had been laying violent hands on me; and, not daring to attack her master, she turned her vocal artillery against the younger scoundrel.

"Well, Mr. Earnshaw," she cried, "I wonder what you'll have agait next! Are we going to murder folk on our very doorstones? I see this house will never do for me—look at t' poor lad, he's fair choking! Wisht, wisht! you mun'n't go on so. Come in, and I'll cure that: there now, hold ye still."

With these words she suddenly splashed a pint of icy water down my neck, and pulled me into the kitchen. Mr. Heathcliff followed, his accidental merriment expiring quickly in his habitual moroseness.

I was sick exceedingly, and dizzy and faint; and thus compelled perforce to accept lodgings under his roof. He told Zillah to give me a glass of brandy, and then passed on to the inner room; while she condoled with me on my sorry predicament, and having obeyed his orders, whereby I was somewhat revived, ushered me to bed.

While leading the way upstairs, she recommended that I should hide the candle, and not make a noise; for her master had an odd notion about the chamber she would put me in, and never let anybody lodge there willingly. I asked the reason. She did not know, she answered: she had only lived there a year or two; and they had so many queer goings on, she could not begin to be curious.

Too stupefied to be curious myself, I fastened the door and glanced round for the bed. The whole furniture consisted of a chair, a clothespress, and a large oak case, with squares cut out near the top resembling coach windows. Having approached this structure I looked inside, and perceived it to be a singular sort of old-fashioned couch, very conveniently designed to obviate the necessity for every member of the family having a room to himself. In fact, it formed a little closet, and the ledge of a window, which it enclosed, served as a table. I slid back the panelled sides, got in with my light, pulled them together again, and felt secure against the vigilance of Heathcliff, and every one else.

The ledge, where I placed my candle, had a few mildewed books piled up in one corner; and it was covered with writing scratched on the paint. This writing, however, was nothing but a name repeated in all kinds of characters, large and small—*Catherine Earnshaw,* here and there varied to *Catherine Heathcliff,* and then again to *Catherine Linton.*

In vapid listlessness I leant my head against the window, and con-

tinued spelling over Catherine Earnshaw—Heathcliff—Linton, till my
eyes closed; but they had not rested five minutes when a glare of white
letters started from the dark as vivid as spectres—the air swarmed with
Catherines; and rousing myself to dispel the obtrusive name, I discovered
my candle wick reclining on one of the antique volumes, and perfuming
the place with an odour of roasted calf-skin. I snuffed it out, and, very
ill at ease under the influence of cold and lingering nausea, sat up and
spread open the injured tome on my knee. It was a Testament, in lean
type, and smelling dreadfully musty: a fly-leaf bore the inscription—
"Catherine Earnshaw, her book," and a date some quarter of a century
back. I shut it, and took up another, and another, till I had examined
all. Catherine's library was select, and its state of dilapidation proved it
to have been well used; though not altogether for a legitimate purpose:
scarcely one chapter had escaped a pen-and-ink commentary—at least,
the appearance of one—covering every morsel of blank that the printer
had left. Some were detached sentences; other parts took the form of a
regular diary, scrawled in an unformed childish hand. At the top of an
extra page (quite a treasure, probably, when first lighted on) I was
greatly amused to behold an excellent caricature of my friend Joseph,—
rudely, yet powerfully sketched. An immediate interest kindled within me
for the unknown Catherine, and I began forthwith to decipher her faded
hieroglyphics.

"An awful Sunday!" commenced the paragraph beneath. "I wish my
father were back again. Hindley is a detestable substitute—his conduct
to Heathcliff is atrocious—H. and I are going to rebel—we took our
initiatory step this evening.

"All day had been flooding with rain; we could not go to church, so
Joseph must needs get up a congregation in the garret; and, while
Hindley and his wife basked downstairs before a comfortable fire—doing
anything but reading their Bibles, I'll answer for it—Heathcliff, myself,
and the unhappy plough-boy, were commanded to take our Prayerbooks,
and mount: were ranged in a row, on a sack of corn, groaning and
shivering, and hoping that Joseph would shiver too, so that he might
give us a short homily for his own sake. A vain idea! The service lasted
precisely three hours; and yet my brother had the face to exclaim, when
he saw us descending, 'What, done already?' On Sunday evenings we
used to be permitted to play, if we did not make much noise; now a
mere titter is sufficient to send us into corners!

" 'You forget you have a master here,' says the tyrant. 'I'll demolish
the first who puts me out of temper! I insist on perfect sobriety and
silence. Oh, boy! was that you? Frances, darling, pull his hair as you go
by: I heard him snap his fingers.' Frances pulled his hair heartily, and

then went and seated herself on her husband's knee; and there they were, like two babies, kissing and talking nonsense by the hour—foolish palaver that we should be ashamed of. We made ourselves as snug as our means allowed in the arch of the dresser. I had just fastened our pinafores together, and hung them up for a curtain, when in comes Joseph on an errand from the stables. He tears down my handiwork, boxes my ears and croaks—

" 'T' maister nobbut just buried, and Sabbath no o'ered, und t' sound o' t' gospel still i' yer lugs, and ye darr be laiking! Shame on ye! sit ye down, ill childer! there's good books enough if ye'll read 'em! sit ye down, and think o' yer sowls!'

"Saying this, he compelled us so to square our positions that we might receive from the far-off fire a dull ray to show us the text of the lumber he thrust upon us. I could not bear the employment. I took my dingy volume by the scroop, and hurled it into the dog-kennel, vowing I hated a good book. Heathcliff kicked his to the same place. Then there was a hubbub!

" 'Maister Hindley!' shouted our chaplain. 'Maister, coom hither! Miss Cathy's riven th' back off "Th' Helmet o' Salvation," un' Heathcliff's pawsed his fit into t' first part o' "T' Brooad Way to Destruction!" It's fair flaysome that ye let 'em go on this gait. Ech! th' owd man wad ha' laced 'em properly—but he's goan!'

"Hindley hurried up from his paradise on the hearth, and seizing one of us by the collar, and the other by the arm, hurled both into the back kitchen; where, Joseph asseverated, 'owd Nick' would fetch us as sure as we were living: and, so comforted, we each sought a separate nook to await his advent. I reached this book, and a pot of ink from a shelf, and pushed the house-door ajar to give me light, and I have got the time on with writing for twenty minutes; but my companion is impatient, and proposes that we should appropriate the dairywoman's cloak, and have a scamper on the moors, under its shelter. A pleasant suggestion—and then, if the surly old man come in, he may believe his prophecy verified—we cannot be damper, or colder, in the rain than we are here."

. . . . . .

I suppose Catherine fulfilled her project, for the next sentence took up another subject; she waxed lachrymose.

"How little did I dream that Hindley would ever make me cry so!" she wrote. "My head aches, till I cannot keep it on the pillow; and still I can't give over. Poor Heathcliff! Hindley calls him a vagabond, and won't let him sit with us, nor eat with us any more; and, he says, he and I must not play together, and threatens to turn him out of the house if we break his orders. He has been blaming our father (how dared he?) for treating H. too liberally; and he swears he will reduce him to his right place"——

·   ·   ·   ·   ·   ·

I began to nod drowsily over the dim page: my eye wandered from manuscript to print. I saw a red ornamented title—"Seventy Times Seven, and the First of the Seventy-First. A Pious Discourse delivered by the Reverend Jabes Branderham, in the Chapel of Gimmerdon Sough." And while I was, half consciously, worrying my brain to guess what Jabes Branderham would make of his subject, I sank back in bed, and fell asleep. Alas, for the effects of bad tea and bad temper! what else could it be that made me pass such a terrible night? I don't remember another that I can at all compare with it since I was capable of suffering.

I began to dream, almost before I ceased to be sensible of my locality. I thought it was morning; and I had set out on my way home, with Joseph for a guide. The snow lay yards deep in our road; and, as we floundered on, my companion wearied me with constant reproaches that I had not brought a pilgrim's staff: telling me that I could never get into the house without one, and boastfully flourishing a heavy-headed cudgel, which I understood to be so denominated. For a moment I considered it absurd that I should need such a weapon to gain admittance into my own residence. Then a new idea flashed across me. I was not going there: we were journeying to hear the famous Jabes Branderham preach from the text—"Seventy Times Seven"; and either Joseph, the preacher, or I had committed the "First of the Seventy-First," and were to be publicly exposed and excommunicated.

We came to the chapel. I have passed it really in my walks, twice or thrice; it lies in a hollow, between two hills: an elevated hollow, near a swamp, whose peaty moisture is said to answer all the purposes of embalming on the few corpses deposited there. The roof has been kept whole hitherto; but as the clergyman's stipend is only twenty pounds per annum, and a house with two rooms, threatening speedily to determine into one, no clergyman will undertake the duties of pastor: especially as it is currently reported that his flock would rather let him starve than increase the living by one penny from their own pockets. However, in my dream, Jabes had a full and attentive congregation; and he preached —good God! what a sermon: divided into *four hundred and ninety* parts, each fully equal to an ordinary address from the pulpit, and each discussing a separate sin! Where he searched for them, I cannot tell. He had his private manner of interpreting the phrase, and it seemed necessary the brother should sin different sins on every occasion. They were of the most curious character: odd transgressions that I never imagined previously.

Oh, how weary I grew. How I writhed, and yawned, and nodded, and revived! How I pinched and pricked myself, and rubbed my eyes, and stood up, and sat down again, and nudged Joseph to inform me if he would *ever* have done. I was condemned to hear all out: finally, he reached the "*First of the Seventy-First.*" At that crisis, a sudden inspiration descended on me; I was moved to rise and denounce Jabes Branderham as the sinner of the sin that no Christian need pardon.

"Sir," I exclaimed, "sitting here within these four walls, at one stretch, I have endured and forgiven the four hundred and ninety heads of your discourse. Seventy times seven times have I plucked up my hat and been about to depart—Seventy times seven times have you preposterously forced me to resume my seat. The four hundred and ninety first is too much. Fellow-martyrs, have at him! Drag him down, and crush him to atoms, that the place which knows him may know him no more!"

"*Thou art the man!*" cried Jabes, after a solemn pause, leaning over his cushion. "Seventy times seven times didst thou gapingly contort thy visage—seventy times seven did I take counsel with my soul—Lo, this is human weakness: this also may be absolved! The First of the Seventy-First is come. Brethren, execute upon him the judgment written. Such honour have all His saints!"

With that concluding word, the whole assembly, exalting their pilgrim's staves, rushed round me in a body; and I, having no weapon to raise in self-defence, commenced grappling with Joseph, my nearest and most ferocious assailant, for his. In the confluence of the multitude, several clubs crossed; blows, aimed at me, fell on other sconces. Presently the whole chapel resounded with rappings and counter-rappings: every man's hand was against his neighbour; and Branderham, unwilling to remain idle, poured forth his zeal in a shower of loud taps on the boards of the pulpit, which responded so smartly that, at last, to my unspeakable relief, they woke me. And what was it that had suggested the tremendous tumult? What had played Jabes's part in the row? Merely, the branch of a fir-tree that touched my lattice, as the blast wailed by, and rattled its dry cones against the panes! I listened doubtingly an instant; detected the disturber, then turned and dozed, and dreamt again: if possible, still more disagreeably than before.

This time, I remembered I was lying in the oak closet, and I heard distinctly the gusty wind, and the driving of the snow; I heard, also, the fir-bough repeat its teasing sound, and ascribed it to the right cause: but it annoyed me so much, that I resolved to silence it, if possible; and, I thought, I rose and endeavoured to unhasp the casement. The hook was soldered into the staple: a circumstance observed by me when awake, but forgotten. "I must stop it, nevertheless!" I muttered, knocking my knuckles through the glass, and stretching an arm out to seize the importunate branch; instead of which, my fingers closed on the fingers of a little, ice-cold hand! The intense horror of nightmare came over me: I tried to draw back my arm, but the hand clung to it, and a most melancholy voice sobbed, "Let me in—let me in!" "Who are you?" I asked, struggling, meanwhile, to disengage myself. "Catherine Linton," it replied, shiveringly (why did I think of *Linton?* I had read *Earnshaw* twenty times for Linton); "I'm come home: I'd lost my way on the moor!" As it spoke, I discerned, obscurely, a child's face looking through the window. Terror made me cruel; and, finding it useless to attempt shaking the creature off, I pulled its wrist on to the broken pane, and rubbed it to and fro till the blood ran down and soaked the bedclothes: still it wailed, "Let me in!" and maintained its tenacious gripe, almost maddening me with fear. "How can I?" I said at length. "Let *me* go, if you want me to let you in!" The fingers relaxed, I snatched mine through the hole, hurriedly piled the books up in a pyramid against it, and stopped my ears to exclude the lamentable prayer. I seemed to keep them closed above a quarter of an hour; yet, the instant I listened again, there was the doleful cry moaning on! "Begone!" I shouted, "I'll never let you in, not if you beg for twenty years." "It is twenty years," mourned the voice: "twenty years. I've been a waif for twenty years!" Thereat began a feeble scratching outside, and the pile of books moved as if thrust forward. I tried to jump up; but could not stir a limb; and so yelled aloud, in a frenzy of fright. To my confusion, I discovered the yell was not ideal: hasty footsteps approached my chamber door; somebody pushed it open, with a vigorous hand, and a light glimmered through the squares at the top of the bed. I sat shuddering yet, and wiping the perspiration from my forehead: the intruder appeared to hesitate, and muttered to himself. At last, he said in a half-whisper, plainly not expecting an answer, "Is anyone here?" I considered it best to confess my presence; for I knew Heathcliff's accents, and feared he might search further, if I kept quiet. With this intention, I turned and opened the panels. I shall not soon forget the effect my action produced.

Heathcliff stood near the entrance, in his shirt and trousers: with a candle dripping over his fingers, and his face as white as the wall behind him. The first creak of the oak startled him like an electric shock! the light leaped from his hold to a distance of some feet, and his agitation was so extreme, that he could hardly pick it up.

"It is only your guest, sir," I called out, desirous to spare him the humiliation of exposing his cowardice further. "I had the misfortune to scream in my sleep, owing to a frightful nightmare. I'm sorry I disturbed you."

"Oh, God confound you, Mr. Lockwood! I wish you were at the——" commenced my host, setting the candle on a chair, because he found it impossible to hold it steady. "And who showed you up into this room?" he continued, crushing his nails into his palms, and grinding his teeth to subdue the maxillary convulsions. "Who was it? I've a good mind to turn them out of the house this moment!"

"It was your servant, Zillah," I replied, flinging myself on to the floor, and rapidly resuming my garments. "I should not care if you did, Mr. Heathcliff; she richly deserves it. I suppose that she wanted to get another proof that the place was haunted, at my expense. Well, it is— swarming with ghosts and globlins! You have reason in shutting it up, I assure you. No one will thank you for a doze in such a den!"

"What do you mean?" asked Heathcliff, "and what are you doing? Lie down and finish out the night, since you *are* here; but, for Heaven's sake! don't repeat that horrid noise; nothing could excuse it, unless you were having your throat cut!"

"If the little fiend had got in at the window, she probably would have strangled me!" I returned. "I'm not going to endure the persecutions of your hospitable ancestors again. Was not the Reverend Jabes Branderham akin to you on the mother's side? And that minx, Catherine Linton, or Earnshaw, or however she was called—she must have been a changeling—wicked little soul! She told me she had been walking the earth those twenty years: a just punishment for her mortal transgressions, I've no doubt!"

Scarcely were these words uttered, when I recollected the association of Heathcliff's with Catherine's name in the book, which had completely slipped from my memory, till thus awakened. I blushed at my inconsideration; but, without showing further consciousness of the offence, I hastened to add—"The truth is, sir, I passed the first part of the night in"—Here I stopped afresh—I was about to say "perusing those old volumes," then it would have revealed my knowledge of their written, as well as their printed contents: so, correcting myself, I went on, "in spelling over the name scratched on that window-ledge. A monotonous occupation, calculated to set me asleep, like counting, or"——

"What *can* you mean by talking in this way to *me?*" thundered Heathcliff with savage vehemence. "How—how *dare* you, under my roof?—God! he's mad to speak so!" And he struck his forehead with rage.

I did not know whether to resent this language or pursue my explanation; but he seemed so powerfully affected that I took pity and proceeded with my dreams; affirming I had never heard the appellation of

"Catherine Linton" before, but reading it often over produced an impression which personified itself when I had no longer my imagination under control. Heathcliff gradually fell back into the shelter of the bed, as I spoke; finally sitting down almost concealed behind it. I guessed, however, by his irregular and intercepted breathing, that he struggled to vanquish an excess of violent emotion. Not liking to show him that I had heard the conflict, I continued my toilette rather noisily, looked at my watch, and soliloquised on the length of the night: "Not three o'clock yet! I could have taken oath it had been six. Time stagnates here: we must surely have retired to rest at eight!"

"Always at nine in winter, and rise at four," said my host, suppressing a groan: and, as I fancied by the motion of his arm's shadow, dashing a tear from his eyes. "Mr. Lockwood," he added, "you may go into my room: you'll only be in the way, coming downstairs so early; and your childish outcry has sent sleep to the devil for me."

"And for me, too," I replied. "I'll walk in the yard till daylight, and then I'll be off; and you need not dread a repetition of my intrusion. I'm now quite cured of seeking pleasure in society, be it country or town. A sensible man ought to find sufficient company in himself."

"Delightful company!" muttered Heathcliff. "Take the candle, and go where you please. I shall join you directly. Keep out of the yard, though, the dogs are unchained; and the house—Juno mounts sentinel there, and—nay, you can only ramble about the steps and passages. But, away with you! I'll come in two minutes!"

I obeyed, so far as to quit the chamber; when, ignorant where the narrow lobbies led, I stood still, and was witness, involuntarily, to a piece of superstition on the part of my landlord, which belied, oddly, his apparent sense. He got on to the bed, and wrenched open the lattice, bursting, as he pulled at it, into an uncontrollable passion of tears. "Come in! come in!" he sobbed. "Cathy, do come. Oh do—*once* more! Oh! my heart's darling; hear me *this* time, Catherine, at last!" The spectre showed a spectre's ordinary caprice: it gave no sign of being; but the snow and wind whirled wildly through, even reaching my station, and blowing out the light.

There was such an anguish in the gush of grief that accompanied this raving, that my compassion made me overlook its folly, and I drew off, half angry to have listened at all, and vexed at having related my ridiculous nightmare, since it produced that agony; though *why,* was beyond my comprehension. I descended cautiously to the lower regions, and landed in the back kitchen, where a gleam of fire, raked compactly together, enabled me to rekindle my candle. Nothing was stirring except a brindled, grey cat, which crept from the ashes, and saluted me with a querulous mew.

Two benches, shaped in sections of a circle, nearly enclosed the hearth; on one of these I stretched myself, and Grimalkin mounted the other. We were both of us nodding, ere any one invaded our retreat, and then it was Joseph, shuffling down a wooden ladder that vanished in the roof, through a trap: the ascent to his garret, I suppose. He cast a sinister look at the little flame which I had enticed to play between the ribs, swept the cat from its elevation, and bestowing himself in the vacancy, commenced the operation of stuffing a three-inch pipe with tobacco. My presence in his sanctum was evidently esteemed a piece of impudence too shameful for remark: he silently applied the tube to his lips, folded his arms, and puffed away. I let him enjoy the luxury unannoyed; and after sucking out his last wreath, and heaving a profound sigh, he got up, and departed as solemnly as he came.

A more elastic footstep entered next; and now I opened my mouth for a "good morning," but closed it again, the salutation unachieved; for Hareton Earnshaw was performing his orisons *sotto voce,* in a series of curses directed against every object he touched, while he rummaged a corner for a spade or shovel to dig through the drifts. He glanced over the back of the bench, dilating his nostrils, and thought as little of exchanging civilities with me as with my companion the cat. I guessed, by his preparations, that egress was allowed, and, leaving my hard couch, made a movement to follow him. He noticed this, and thrust at an inner door with the end of his spade, intimating by an inarticulate sound that there was the place where I must go, if I changed my locality.

It opened into the house, where the females were already astir. Zillah urging flakes of flame up the chimney with a colossal bellows; and Mrs. Heathcliff, kneeling on the hearth, reading a book by the aid of the blaze. She held her hand interposed between the furnace-heat and her eyes, and seemed absorbed in her occupation; desisting from it only to chide the servant for covering her with sparks, or to push away a dog, now and then, that snoozled its nose over forwardly into her face. I was surprised to see Heathcliff there also. He stood by the fire, his back towards me, just finishing a stormy scene to poor Zillah; who ever and anon interrupted her labour to pluck up the corner of her apron, and heave an indignant groan.

"And you, you worthless"—he broke out as I entered, turning to his daughter-in-law, and employing an epithet as harmless as duck, or sheep, but generally represented by a dash——. "There you are, at your idle tricks again! The rest of them do earn their bread—you live on my charity! Put your trash away, and find something to do. You shall pay me for the plague of having you eternally in my sight—do you hear, damnable jade?"

"I'll put my trash away, because you can make me, if I refuse," answered the young lady, closing her book, and throwing it on a chair. "But I'll not do anything, though you should swear your tongue out, except what I please!"

Heathcliff lifted his hand, and the speaker sprang to a safer distance, obviously acquainted with its weight. Having no desire to be entertained by a cat-and-dog combat, I stepped forward briskly, as if eager to partake the warmth of the hearth, and innocent of any knowledge of the interrupted dispute. Each had enough decorum to suspend further hostilities: Heathcliff placed his fists, out of temptation, in his pockets; Mrs. Heathcliff curled her lip, and walked to a seat far off, where she kept her word by playing the part of a statue during the remainder of my stay. That was not long. I declined joining their breakfast, and, at the first gleam of dawn, took an opportunity of escaping into the free air, now clear, and still, and cold as impalpable ice.

My landlord hallooed for me to stop, ere I reached the bottom of the garden, and offered to accompany me across the moor. It was well he did, for the whole hill-back was one billowy, white ocean; the swells and falls not indicating corresponding rises and depressions in the ground: many pits, at least, were filled to a level; and entire ranges of mounds, the refuse of the quarries, blotted from the chart which my yesterday's walk left pictured in my mind. I had remarked on one side of the road, at intervals of six or seven yards, a line of upright stones, continued through the whole length of the barren: these were erected, and daubed with lime on the purpose to serve as guides in the dark; and also when a fall, like the present, confounded the deep swamps on either hand with the firmer path: but, excepting a dirty dot pointing up here and there, all traces of their existence had vanished: and my companion found it necessary to warn me frequently to steer to the right or left, when I imagined I was following, correctly, the windings of the road. We exchanged little conversation, and he halted at the entrance of Thrushcross Park, saying, I could make no error there. Our audieux were limited to a hasty bow, and then I pushed forward, trusting to my own resources; for the porter's lodge is untenanted as yet. The distance from the gate to the Grange is two miles: I believe I managed to make it four; what with losing myself among the trees, and sinking up to the neck in snow: a predicament which only those who have experienced it can appreciate. At any rate, whatever were my wanderings, the clock chimed twelve as I entered the house; and that gave me exactly an hour for every mile of the usual way from Wuthering Heights.

My human fixture and her satellites rushed to welcome me; exclaiming, tumultuously, they had completely given me up; everybody conjectured that I had perished last night; and they were wondering how they must set about the search for my remains. I bid them be quiet, now that they saw me returned, and, benumbed to my very heart, I dragged upstairs; whence, after putting on dry clothes, and pacing to and fro thirty or forty minutes, to restore the animal heat, I am adjourned to my study, feeble as a kitten: almost too much so to enjoy the cheerful fire and smoking coffee which the servant has prepared for my refreshment.

What vain weather-cocks we are! I, who had determined to hold myself independent of all social intercourse, and thanked my stars that, at length, I had lighted on a spot where it was next to impracticable—I, weak wretch, after maintaining till dusk a struggle with low spirits and solitude, was finally compelled to strike my colours; and, under pretense of gaining information concerning the necessities of my establishment, I desired Mrs. Dean, when she brought in supper, to sit down while I ate it; hoping sincerely she would prove a regular gossip, and either rouse me to animation or lull me to sleep by her talk.

"You have lived here a considerable time," I commenced; "did you not say sixteen years?"

"Eighteen, sir: I came, when the mistress was married, to wait on her; after she died, the master retained me for his housekeeper."

"Indeed."

There ensued a pause. She was not a gossip, I feared; unless about her own affairs, and those could hardly interest me. However, having studied for an interval, with a fist on either knee, and a cloud of meditation over her ruddy countenance, she ejaculated:

"Ah, times are greatly changed since then!"

"Yes," I remarked, "you've seen a good many alterations, I suppose?"

"I have: and troubles too," she said.

"Oh, I'll turn the talk on my landlord's family!" I thought to myself. "A good subject to start! And that pretty girl-widow, I should like to know her history: whether she be a native of the country, or, as is more probable, an exotic that the surly *indigenæ* will not recognize for kin." With this intention I asked Mrs. Dean why Heathcliff let Thrushcross Grange, and preferred living in a situation and residence so much inferior. "Is he not rich enough to keep the estate in good order?" I inquired.

"Rich, sir!" she returned. "He has, nobody knows what money, and every year it increases. Yes, yes, he's rich enough to live in a finer house than this: but he's very near—close-handed; and, if he had meant to flit to Thrushcross Grange, as soon as he heard of a good tenant he could not have borne to miss the chance of getting a few hundreds more. It is strange people should be so greedy, when they are alone in the world!"

"He had a son, it seems?"

"Yes, he had one—he is dead."

"And that young lady, Mrs. Heathcliff, is his widow?"

"Yes."

"Where did she come from originally?"

"Why, sir, she is my late master's daughter: Catherine Linton was her maiden name. I nursed her, poor thing! I did wish Mr. Heathcliff would remove here, and then we might have been together again."

"What! Catherine Linton?" I exclaimed, astonished. But a minute's reflection convinced me it was not my ghostly Catherine. "Then," I continued, "my predecessor's name was Linton?"

"It was."

"And who is that Earnshaw: Hareton Earnshaw, who lives with Mr. Heathcliff? are they relations?"

"No; he is the late Mrs. Linton's nephew."

"The young lady's cousin, then?"

"Yes; and her husband was her cousin also: one on the mother's, the other on the father's side: Heathcliff married Mr. Linton's sister."

"I see the house at Wuthering Heights has 'Earnshaw' carved over the front door. Are they an old family?"

"Very old, sir; and Hareton is the last of them, as our Miss Cathy is of us—I mean of the Lintons. Have you been to Wuthering Heights? I beg pardon for asking; but I should like to hear how she is!"

"Mrs. Heathcliff? She looked very well, and very handsome; yet, I think, not very happy."

"O dear, I don't wonder! And how did you like the master?"

"A rough fellow, rather, Mrs. Dean. Is not that his character?"

"Rough as a saw-edge, and hard as whinstone! The less you meddle with him the better."

"He must have had some ups and downs in life to make him such a churl. Do you know anything of his history?"

"It's a cuckoo's, sir—I know all about it: except where he was born, and who were his parents, and how he got his money, at first. And Hareton has been cast out like an unfledged dunnock! The unfortunate lad is the only one in all this parish that does not guess how he has been cheated."

"Well, Mrs. Dean, it will be a charitable deed to tell me something of my neighbours: I feel I shall not rest, if I go to bed; so be good enough to sit and chat an hour."

"Oh, certainly, sir! I'll just fetch a little sewing, and then I'll sit as long as you please. But you've caught cold: I saw you shivering, and you must have some gruel to drive it out."

The worthy woman bustled off, and I crouched nearer the fire; my head felt hot, and the rest of me chill: moreover, I was excited, almost to a pitch of foolishness, through my nerves and brain. This caused me to feel, not uncomfortable, but rather fearful (as I am still) of serious effects from the incidents of to-day and yesteday. She returned presently, bringing a smoking basin and a basket of work; and, having placed the former on the hob, drew in her seat, evidently pleased to find me so companionable.

Before I came to live here, she commenced—waiting no farther invitation to her story—I was almost always at Wuthering Heights; because my mother had nursed Mr. Hindley Earnshaw, that was Hareton's father, and I got used to playing with the children: I ran errands too, and helped to make hay, and hung about the farm ready for anything that anybody would set me to. One fine summer morning—it was the beginning of harvest, I remember—Mr. Earnshaw, the old master, came downstairs, dressed for a journey; and after he had told Joseph what was to be done during the day, he turned to Hindley, and Cathy, and me—for I sat eating my porridge with them—and he said, speaking to his son, "Now my bonny man, I'm going to Liverpool to-day, what shall I bring you? You may choose what you like: only let it be little, for I shall walk there and back: sixty miles each way, that is a long spell!" Hindley named a fiddle, and then he asked Miss Cathy; she was hardly six years old, but she could ride any horse in the stable, and she chose a whip. He did not forget me; for he had a kind heart, though he was rather severe sometimes. He promised to bring me a pocketful of apples and pears, and then he kissed his children, said good-bye, and set off.

It seemed a long while to us all—the three days of his absence—and often did little Cathy ask when he would be home. Mrs. Earnshaw expected him by supper-time on the third evening, and she put the meal off hour after hour; there were no signs of his coming, however, and at last the children got tired of running down to the gate to look. Then it grew dark; she would have had them to bed, but they begged sadly to be allowed to stay up; and, just about eleven o'clock, the door-latch was raised quietly and in stepped the master. He threw himself into a chair, laughing and groaning, and bid them all stand off, for he was nearly killed—he would not have such another walk for the three kingdoms.

"And at the end of it, to be flighted to death!" he said, opening his great-coat, which he held bundled up in his arms. "See here, wife! I was never so beaten with anything in my life: but you must e'en take it as a gift of God; though it's as dark almost as if it came from the devil."

We crowded round, and over Miss Cathy's head, I had a peep at a dirty, ragged, black-haired child; big enough both to walk and talk: indeed, its face looked older than Catherine's; yet, when it was set on its feet, it only stared round, and repeated over and over again some gibberish, that nobody could understand. I was frightened, and Mrs. Earnshaw was ready to fling it out of doors: she did fly up, asking how he could fashion to bring that gypsy brat into the house, when they had their own bairns to feed and fend for? What he meant to do with it, and whether he were mad? The master tried to explain the matter; but he was really half dead with fatigue, and all that I could make out, amongst her scolding, was a tale of his seeing it starving, and houseless, and as good as dumb, in the streets of Liverpool, where he picked it up and inquired for its owner. Not a soul knew to whom it belonged, he said; and his money and time being both limited, he thought it better to take it home with him at once, than run into vain expenses there: because he was determined he would not leave it as he found it. Well, the conclusion was that my mistress grumbled herself calm; and Mr. Earnshaw told me to wash it, and give it clean things, and let it sleep with the children.

Hindley and Cathy contented themselves with looking and listening till peace was restored: then, both began searching their father's pockets for the presents he had promised them. The former was a boy of fourteen, but when he drew out what had been a fiddle crushed to morsels in the great-coat, he blubbered aloud; and Cathy, when she learned the master had lost her whip in attending on the stranger, showed her humour by grinning and spitting at the stupid little thing; earning for her pains a sound blow from her father to teach her cleaner manners. They entirely refused to have it in bed with them, or even in their room; and I had no more sense, so I put it on the landing of the stairs, hoping it might be gone on the morrow. By chance, or else attracted by hearing his voice, it crept to Mr. Earnshaw's door, and there he found it on quitting his chamber. Inquiries were made as to how it got there; I was obliged to confess, and in recompense for my cowardice and inhumanity was sent out of the house.

This was Heathcliff's first introduction to the family. On coming back a few days afterwards (for I did not consider my banishment perpetual) I found they had christened him "Heathcliff": it was the name of a son who died in childhood, and it has served him ever since, both for Christian and surname. Miss Cathy and he were now very thick; but Hindley hated him! and to say the truth I did the same; and we plagued and went on with him shamefully: for I wasn't reasonable enough to feel my injustice, and the mistress never put in a word on his behalf when she saw him wronged.

He seemed a sullen, patient child; hardened, perhaps, to ill-treatment: he would stand Hindley's blows without winking or shedding a tear, and my pinches moved him only to draw in a breath and open his eyes, as if he had hurt himself by accident and nobody was to blame. This en-

durance made old Earnshaw furious, when he discovered his son perse-
cuting the poor, fatherless child, as he called him. He took to Heathcliff
strangely, believing all he said (for that matter, he said precious little,
and generally the truth), and petting him up far above Cathy, who was
too mischievous and wayward for a favourite.

So, from the very beginning, he bred bad feeling in the house; and at
Mrs. Earnshaw's death, which happened in less than two years after,
the young master had learned to regard his father as an oppressor rather
than a friend, and Heathcliff as a usurper of his parent's affections and
his privileges; and he grew bitter with brooding over these injuries. I sym-
pathised a while; but when the children fell ill of the measles, and I
had to tend them, and take on me the cares of a woman at once, I
changed my ideas. Heathcliff was dangerously sick: and while he lay at
the worst he would have me constantly by his pillow: I suppose he felt
I did a good deal for him, and he hadn't wit to guess that I was compelled to do it. However, I will say this, he was the quietest child that
ever a nurse watched over. The difference between him and the others
forced me to be less partial. Cathy and her brother harassed me terribly:
he was as uncomplaining as a lamb; though hardness, not gentleness,
made him give little trouble.

He got through, and the doctor affirmed it was in a great measure owing to me, and praised me for my care. I was vain of his commendations,
and softened towards the being by whose means I earned them, and
thus Hindley lost his last ally: still I couldn't dote on Heathcliff, and I
wondered often what my master saw to admire so much in the sullen boy,
who never, to my recollection, repaid his indulgence by any sign of
gratitude. He was not insolent to his benefactor, he was simply insensible;
though knowing perfectly the hold he had on his heart, and conscious
he had only to speak and all the house would be obliged to bend to his
wishes. As an instance, I remember Mr. Earnshaw once bought a couple
of colts at the parish fair, and gave the lads each one. Heathcliff took
the handsomest, but it soon fell lame, and when he discovered it, he said
to Hindley—

"You must exchange horses with me: I don't like mine; and if you
won't I shall tell your father of the three thrashings you've given me this
week, and show him my arm, which is black to the shoulder." Hindley
put out his tongue and cuffed him over the ears. "You'd better do it at
once," he persisted, escaping to the porch (they were in the stable):
"you will have to; and if I speak of these blows, you'll get them again
with interest." "Off, dog!" cried Hindley, threatening him with an iron
weight used for weighing potatoes and hay. "Throw it," he replied,
standing still, "and then I'll tell how you boasted that you would turn
me out of doors as soon as he died, and see whether he will not turn you

out directly." Hindley threw it, hitting him on the breast, and down he fell, but staggered up immediately, breathless and white; and, had not I prevented it, he would have gone just so to the master, and got full revenge by letting his condition plead for him, intimating he had caused it. "Take my colt, gypsy, then!" said young Earnshaw. "And I pray that he may break your neck: take him, and be damned, you beggarly interloper! and wheedle my father out of all he has: only afterwards show him what you are, imp of Satan.—And after that, I hope he'll kick out your brains!"

Heathcliff had gone to loose the beast, and shift it to his own stall; he was passing behind it, when Hindley finished his speech by knocking him under its feet, and without stopping to examine whether his hopes were fulfilled, ran away as fast as he could. I was surprised to witness how coolly the child gathered himself up, and went on with his intention; exchanging saddles and all, and then sitting down on a bundle of hay to overcome the qualm which the violent blow occasioned, before he entered the house. I persuaded him easily to let me lay the blame for his bruises on the horse: he minded little what tale was told since he had what he wanted. He complained so seldom, indeed, of such stirs as these, that I really thought him not vindictive: I was deceived completely, as you will hear.

In the course of time, Mr. Earnshaw began to fail. He had been active and healthy, yet his strength left him suddenly; and when he was confined to the chimney-corner he grew grievously irritable. A nothing vexed him; and suspected slights of his authority nearly threw him into fits. This was especially to be remarked if any one attempted to impose upon, or domineer over, his favourite: he was painfully jealous lest a word should be spoken amiss to him; seeming to have got into his head the notion that, because he liked Heathcliff, all hated, and longed to do him an ill turn. It was a disadvantage to the lad; for the kinder among us did not wish to fret the master, so we humoured his partiality; and that humouring was rich nourishment to the child's pride and black tempers. Still it became in a manner necessary; twice, or thrice, Hindley's manifestation of scorn, while his father was near, roused the old man to a fury: he seized his stick to strike him, and shook with rage that he could not do it.

At last, our curate (we had a curate then who made the living answer by teaching the little Lintons and Earnshaws, and farming his bit of land himself) advised that the young man should be sent to college; and Mr. Earnshaw agreed, though with a heavy spirit, for he said—"Hindley was nought, and would never thrive as where he wandered."

I hoped heartily we should have peace now. It hurt me to think the master should be made uncomfortable by his own good deed. I fancied the discontent of age and disease arose from his family disagreements: as he would have it that it did: really, you know, sir, it was in his sinking frame. We might have got on tolerably, notwithstanding, but for two people, Miss Cathy and Joseph, the servant: you saw him I daresay, up yonder. He was, and is yet most likely, the wearisomest self-righteous Pharisee that ever ransacked a Bible to rake the promises to himself and fling the curses to his neighbours. By his knack of sermonising and pious discoursing, he contrived to make a great impression on Mr. Earnshaw; and the more feeble the master became, the more influence he gained. He was relentless in worrying him about his soul's concerns, and about ruling his children rigidly. He encouraged him to regard Hindley as a reprobate; and, night after night, he regularly grumbled out a long string of tales against Heathcliff and Catherine: always minding to flatter Earnshaw's weakness by heaping the heaviest blame on the latter.

Certainly, she had ways with her such as I never saw a child take up before; and she put all of us past our patience fifty times and oftener in a day: from the hour she came downstairs till the hour she went to bed, we had not a minute's security that she wouldn't be in mischief. Her spirits were always at high-water mark, her tongue always going—singing, laughing, and plaguing everybody who would not do the same. A wild, wicked slip she was—but she had the bonniest eye, the sweetest smile, and lightest foot in the parish; and, after all, I believe she meant no harm; for when once she made you cry in good earnest, it seldom happened that she would not keep you company, and oblige you to be quiet that you might comfort her. She was much too fond of Heathcliff. The greatest punishment we could invent for her was to keep her separate from him: yet she got chided more than any of us on his account. In play, she liked exceedingly to act the little mistress: using her hands freely, and commanding her companions: she did so to me, but I would not bear shopping and ordering; and so I let her know.

Now, Mr. Earnshaw did not understand jokes from his children: he had always been strict and grave with them; and Catherine, on her part, had no idea why her father should be crosser and less patient in his ailing condition, than he was in his prime. His peevish reproofs wakened in her a naughty delight to provoke him: she was never so happy as when we were all scolding her at once, and she defying us with her bold, saucy look, and her ready words; turning Joseph's religious curses into ridicule, baiting me, and doing just what her father hated most—showing how her pretended insolence, which he thought real, had more power over Heathcliff than his kindness: how the boy would do *her* bidding in anything, and *his* only when it suited his own inclination. After behaving as badly as possible all day, she sometimes came fondling to make it up at night. "Nay, Cathy," the old man would say, "I cannot love thee; thou'rt worse than thy brother. Go say thy prayers, child, and ask God's pardon. I doubt thy mother and I must rue that we ever reared thee!" That made her cry, at first: and then being repulsed continually hardened her, and she laughed if I told her to say she was sorry for her faults, and beg to be forgiven.

But the hour came, at last, that ended Mr. Earnshaw's troubles on earth. He died quietly in his chair one October evening, seated by the fireside. A high wind blustered round the house, and roared in the chimney: it sounded wild and stormy, yet it was not cold, and we were all together—I, a little removed from the hearth, busy at my knitting, and Joseph reading his Bible near the table (for the servants generally sat in the house then, after their work was done). Miss Cathy had been sick, and that made her still; she leant against her father's knee, and Heathcliff was lying on the floor with his head in her lap. I remember the master, before he fell into a doze, stroking her bonny hair—It pleased him rarely to see her gentle—and saying—"Why canst thou not always be a good lass, Cathy?" And she turned her face up to his, and laughed, and answered, "Why cannot you always be a good man, father?" But as soon as she saw him vexed again, she kissed his hand, and said she would sing him to sleep. She began singing very low, till his fingers dropped from hers, and his head sank on his breast. Then I told her to hush, and not stir, for fear she should wake him. We all kept as mute as mice a full half-hour, and should have done so longer, only Joseph, having finished his chapter, got up and said that he must rouse the master for prayers and bed. He stepped forward, and called him by name, and touched his shoulder; but he would not move, so he took the candle and looked at him. I thought there was something wrong as he set down the light; and seizing the children each by an arm, whispered them to "frame upstairs, and make little din—they might pray alone that evening—he had summut to do."

"I shall bid father good-night first," said Catherine, putting her arms round his neck, before we could hinder her. The poor thing discovered her loss directly—she screamed out—"Oh, he's dead, Heathcliff! he's dead!" And they both set up a heart-breaking cry.

I joined my wail to theirs, loud and bitter; but Joseph asked what we could be thinking of to roar in that way over a saint in heaven. He told me to put on my cloak and run to Gimmerton for the doctor and the parson. I could not guess the use that either would be of, then. However, I went, through wind and rain, and brought one, the doctor, back with me; the other said he would come in the morning. Leaving Joseph to explain matters, I ran to the children's room: their door was ajar, I saw they had never laid down, though it was past midnight; but they were calmer, and did not need me to console them. The little souls were comforting each other with better thoughts than I could have hit on: no parson in the world ever pictured heaven so beautifully as they did, in their innocent talk: and, while I sobbed and listened, I could not help wishing we were all there safe together.

Mr. Hindley came home to the funeral; and—a thing that amazed us, and set the neighbours gossiping right and left—he brought a wife with him. What she was, and where she was born, he never informed us: probably she had neither money nor name to recommend her, or he would scarcely have kept the union from his father.

She was not one that would have disturbed the house much on her own account. Every object she saw, the moment she crossed the threshold, appeared to delight her; and every circumstance that took place about her: except the preparing for the burial, and the presence of the mourners. I thought she was half silly, from her behaviour while that went on: she ran into her chamber, and made me come with her, though I should have been dressing the children; and there she sat shivering and clasping her hands, and asking repeatedly: "Are they gone yet?" Then she began describing with hysterical emotion the effect it produced on her to see black; and started, and trembled, and, at last, fell a-weeping—and when I asked what was the matter? answered, she didn't know; but she felt so afraid of dying! I imagined her as little likely to die as myself. She was rather thin, but young, and fresh-complexioned, and her eyes sparkled as bright as diamonds. I did remark, to be sure, that mounting the stairs made her breathe very quick: that the least sudden noise set her all in a quiver, and that she coughed troublesomely sometimes: but I knew nothing of what these symptoms portended, and had no impulse to sympathise with her. We don't in general take to foreigners here, Mr. Lockwood, unless they take to us first.

Young Earnshaw was altered considerably in the three years of his absence. He had grown sparer, and lost his colour, and spoke and dressed quite differently; and, on the very day of his return, he told Joseph and me we must thenceforth quarter ourselves in the back-kitchen, and leave the house for him. Indeed, he would have carpeted and papered a small spare room for a parlour; but his wife expressed such pleasure at the white floor and huge glowing fire-place, at the pewter dishes and delft-case, and dog-kennel, and the wide space there was to move about in where they usually sat, that he thought it unnecessary to her comfort, and so dropped the intention.

She expressed pleasure, too, at finding a sister among her new acquaintances; and she prattled to Catherine, and kissed her, and ran about with her, and gave her quantities of presents, at the beginning. Her affection tired very soon, however, and when she grew peevish, Hindley became tyrannical. A few words from her, evincing a dislike to Heathcliff, were enough to rouse in him all his old hatred of the boy. He drove him from their company to the servants, deprived him of the instructions of the curate, and insisted that he should labour out of doors instead; compelling him to do so as hard as any other hand on the farm.

Heathcliff bore his degradation pretty well at first, because Cathy taught him what she learnt, and worked or played with him in the fields. They both promised fair to grow up as rude as savages; the young master being entirely negligent how they behaved, and what they did, so they kept clear of him. He would not even have seen after their going to church on Sundays, only Joseph and the curate reprimanded his carelessness when they absented themselves; and that reminded him to order Heathcliff a flogging, and Catherine a fast from dinner or supper. But it was one of their chief amusements to run away to the moors in the morning and remain there all day, and the after punishment grew a mere thing to laugh at. The curate might set as many chapters as he pleased for Catherine to get by heart, and Joseph might thrash Heathcliff till his arm ached; they forgot everything the minute they were together again: at least the minute they had contrived some naughty plan of revenge; and many a time I've cried to myself to watch them growing more reckless daily, and I not daring to speak a syllable, for fear of losing the small power I still retained over the unfriended creatures. One Sunday evening, it chanced that they were banished from the sitting-room, for making a noise, or a light offence of the kind; and when I went to call them to supper, I could discover them nowhere. We searched the house, above and below, and the yard and stables; they were invisible: and at last, Hindley in a passion told us to bolt the doors, and swore nobody should let them in that night. The household went to bed; and I, too anxious to lie down, opened my lattice and put my head out to hearken, though it rained: determined to admit them in spite of the prohibition, should they return. In a while, I distinguished steps coming up the road, and the light of a lantern glimmered through the gate. I threw a shawl over my head and ran to prevent them from waking Mr. Earnshaw by knocking. There was Heathcliff by himself: it gave me a start to see him alone.

"Where is Miss Catherine?" I cried hurriedly. "No accident, I hope?" "At Thrushcross Grange," he answered; "and I would have been there too, but they had not the manners to ask me to stay." "Well, you will catch it!" I said: "you'll never be content till you're sent about your business. What in the world led you wandering to Thrushcross Grange?" "Let me get off my wet clothes, and I'll tell you all about it, Nelly," he replied. I bid him beware of rousing the master, and while he undressed and I waited to put out the candle, he continued—"Cathy and I escaped from the wash-house to have a ramble at liberty, and getting a glimpse of the Grange lights, we thought we would just go and see whether the Lintons passed their Sunday evenings standing shivering in corners, while their father and mother sat eating and drinking, and singing and laughing, and burning their eyes out before the fire. Do you think they do? Or reading sermons, and being catechised by their man-servant, and set to learn a column of Scripture names, if they don't answer properly?" "Probably not," I responded. "They are good children, no doubt, and don't deserve the treatment you receive, for your bad conduct." "Don't cant, Nelly," he said: "nonsense! We ran from the top of the Heights to the park, without stopping—Catherine completely beaten in the race; because she was barefoot. You'll have to seek for her shoes in the bog tomorrow. We crept through a broken hedge, groped our way up the path, and planted ourselves on a flower-plot under the drawing-room window. The light came from thence; they had not put up the shutters, and the curtains were only half closed. Both of us were able to look in by standing on the basement, and clinging to the ledge, and we saw—ah! it was beautiful—a splendid place carpeted with crimson, and crimson-covered chairs and tables, and a pure white ceiling bordered by gold, a shower of glassdrops hanging in silver chains from the centre, and shimmering with little soft tapers. Old Mr. and Mrs. Linton were not there; Edgar and his sister had it entirely to themselves. Shouldn't they have been happy? We should have thought ourselves in heaven! And now, guess what your good children were doing? Isabella—I believe she is eleven, a year younger than Cathy—lay screaming at the farther end of the room, shrieking as if witches were running red-hot needles into her. Edgar stood on the hearth weeping silently, and in the middle of the table sat a little dog, shaking its paw and yelping; which, from their mutual accusations, we understood they had nearly pulled in two between them. The idiots! That was their pleasure! to quarrel who should hold a heap of warm hair, and each begin to cry because both, after struggling to get it, refused to take it. We laughed outright at the petted things; we did despise them! When would you catch me wishing to have what Catherine wanted? or find us by ourselves, seeking entertainment in yelling, and sobbing, and rolling on the ground, divided by the whole room? I'd not exchange, for a thousand lives, my condition here, for Edgar Linton's at Thrushcross Grange— not if I might have the privilege of flinging Joseph off the highest gable, and painting the house-front with Hindley's blood!"

"Hush, hush!" I interrupted. "Still you have not told me, Heathcliff, how Catherine is left behind?"

"I told you we laughed," he answered. "The Lintons heard us, and with one accord, they shot like arrows to the door; there was silence, and then a cry, 'Oh, mamma, mamma! Oh, papa! Oh, mamma, come here, Oh, papa, oh!' They really did howl out something in that way. We made frightful noises to terrify them still more, and then we dropped off the ledge, because somebody was drawing the bars, and we felt we had better flee. I had Cathy by the hand, and was urging her on, when all at once she fell down. 'Run, Heathcliff, run!' she whispered. 'They have let the bull-dog loose, and he holds me!' The devil had seized her ankle, Nelly: I heard his abominable snorting. She did not yell out—no! she would have scorned to do it, if she had been spitted on the horns of a mad cow. I did, though! I vociferated curses enough to annihilate any fiend in Christendom; and I got a stone and thrust it between his jaws, and tried with all my might to cram it down his throat. A beast of a servant came up with a lantern, at last, shouting—'Keep fast, Skulker, keep fast!' He changed his note, however, when he saw Skulker's game. The dog was throttled off; his huge, purple tongue hanging half a foot out his mouth, and his pendant lips streaming with bloody slaver. The man took Cathy up: she was sick: not from fear, I'm certain, but from pain. He carried her in; I followed, grumbling execrations and vengeance. 'What prey, Robert?' hallooed Linton from the entrance. 'Skulker has caught a little girl, sir,' he replied; 'and there's a lad here,' he added making a clutch at me, 'who looks an out-and-outer! Very like, the robbers were for putting them through the window to open the doors to the gang after all were asleep, that they might murder us at their ease. Hold your tongue, you foul-mouthed thief, you! you shall go to the gallows for this. Mr. Linton, sir, don't lay by your gun.' 'No, no, Robert,' said the old fool. 'The rascals knew that yesterday was my rent day: they thought to have me cleverly. Come in; I'll furnish them a reception. There, John, fasten the chain. Give Skulker some water, Jenny. To beard a magistrate in his stronghold, and on the Sabbath, too! Where will their insolence stop? Oh, my dear Mary, look here! Don't be afraid, it is but a boy—yet the villain scowls so plainly in his face; would it not be a kindness to the country to hang him at once, before he shows his nature in acts as well as features?' He pulled me under the chandelier, and Mrs. Linton placed her spectacles on her nose and raised her hands in horror. The cowardly children crept nearer also, Isabella lisping—'Frightful thing! Put him in the cellar, papa. He's exactly like the son of the fortune-teller that stole my tame pheasant. Isn't he, Edgar?'

"While they examined me, Cathy came round; she heard the last speech, and laughed. Edgar Linton, after an inquisitive stare, collected sufficient wit to recognise her. They see us at church, you know, though we seldom meet them elsewhere. 'That's Miss Earnshaw!' he whispered to his mother, 'and look how Skulker has bitten her—how her foot bleeds!'

" 'Miss Earnshaw? Nonsense!' cried the dame; 'Miss Earnshaw scouring the country with a gypsy! And yet, my dear, the child is in mourning —surely it is—and she may be maimed for life!'

" 'What culpable carelessness in her brother!' exclaimed Mr. Linton, turning from me to Catherine. I've understood from Shielders' (that was the curate, sir) 'that he lets her grow up in absolute heathenism. But who is this? Where did she pick up this companion? Oho! I declare he is that strange acquisition my late neighbour made, in his journey to Liverpool—a little Lascar, or an American or Spanish castaway.'

" 'A wicked boy, at all events,' remarked the old lady, 'and quite unfit for a decent house! Did you notice his language, Linton? I'm shocked that my children should have heard it.'

"I recommenced cursing—don't be angry, Nelly—and so Robert was ordered to take me off. I refused to go without Cathy; he dragged me into the garden, pushed the lantern into my hand, assured me that Mr. Earnshaw should be informed of my behaviour, and, bidding me march directly, secured the door again. The curtains were still looped up at one corner, and I resumed my station as spy; because, if Catherine had wished to return, I intended shattering their great glass panes to a million of fragments, unless they let her out. She sat on a sofa quietly. Mrs. Linton took off the grey cloak of the dairymaid which we had borrowed for our excursion, shaking her head and expostulating with her, I suppose: she was a young lady, and they made a distinction between her treatment and mine. Then the woman-servant brought a basin of warm water, and washed her feet; and Mr. Linton mixed a tumbler of negus, and Isabella emptied a plateful of cakes into her lap, and Edgar stood gaping at a distance. Afterwards, they dried and combed her beautiful hair, and gave her a pair of enormous slippers, and wheeled her to the fire; and I left her, as merry as she could be, dividing her food between the little dog and Skulker, whose nose she pinched as he ate; and kindling a spark of spirit in the vacant blue eyes of the Lintons—a dim reflection from her own enchanting face. I saw they were full of stupid admiration; she is so immeasurably superior to them—to everybody on earth, is she not, Nelly?"

"There will more come of this business than you reckon on," I answered, covering him up and extinguishing the light. "You are incurable, Heathcliff; and Mr. Hindley will have to proceed to extremities, see if he won't!" My words came truer than I desired. The luckless adventure made Earnshaw furious. And then Mr. Linton, to mend matters, paid us a visit himself on the morrow; and read the young master such a lecture on the road he guided his family, that he was stirred to look about him, in earnest. Heathcliff received no flogging, but he was told that the first word he spoke to Miss Catherine should ensure a dismissal; and Mrs. Earnshaw undertook to keep her sister-in-law in due restraint when she returned home; employing art, not force: with force she would have found it impossible.

Emily Dickinson

POEMS

A narrow fellow in the grass
Occasionally rides;
You may have met him,—did you not?
His notice sudden is.

The grass divides as with a comb,
A spotted shaft is seen;
And then it closes at your feet
And opens further on.

He likes a boggy acre,
A floor too cool for corn.
Yet when a child, and barefoot,
I more than once, at morn,

Have passed, I thought, a whip-lash
Unbraiding in the sun,—
When, stooping to secure it,
It wrinkled, and was gone.

Several of nature's people
I know, and they know me;
I feel for them a transport
Of cordiality;

But never met this fellow,
Attended or alone,
Without a tighter breathing,
And zero at the bone.

I died for beauty, but was scarce
Adjusted in the tomb,
When one who died for truth was lain
In an adjoining room.

He questioned softly why I failed?
"For beauty," I replied.
"And I for truth,—the two are one;
We brethren are," he said.

And so, as kinsmen met a night,
We talked between the rooms,
Until the moss had reached our lips,
And covered up our names.

Because I could not stop for Death,
He kindly stopped for me;
The carriage held but just ourselves
And Immortality.

We slowly drove, he knew no haste,
And I had put away
My labor, and my leisure too,
For his civility.

We passed the school where children played
At wrestling in a ring;
We passed the fields of gazing grain,
We passed the setting sun.

We paused before a house that seemed
A swelling of the ground;
The roof was scarcely visible,
The cornice but a mound.

Since then 'tis centuries; but each
Feels shorter than the day
I first surmised the horses' heads
Were toward eternity.

PRIMARY WORDS ARE SPOKEN FROM THE BEING

Martin Buber

I AND THOU

To man the world is twofold, in accordance with his twofold attitude.

The attitude of man is twofold, in accordance with the twofold nature of the primary words which he speaks.

The primary words are not isolated words, but combined words.

The one primary word is the combination *I–Thou*.

The other primary word is the combination *I–It;* wherein, without a change in the primary word, one of the words *He* and *She* can replace *It*.

Hence the *I* of man is also twofold.

For the *I* of the primary word *I-Thou* is a different *I* from that of the primary word *I-It*.

Primary words do not signify things, but they intimate relations.

Primary words do not describe something that might exist independently of them, but being spoken they bring about existence.

Primary words are spoken from the being.

If *Thou* is said, the *I* of the combination *I–Thou* is said along with it.

If *It* is said, the *I* of the combination *I–It* is said along with it.

The primary word *I–Thou* can only be spoken with the whole being.

The primary word *I–It* can never be spoken with the whole being.

There is no *I* taken in itself, but only the *I* of the primary word *I–Thou* and the *I* of the primary word *I–It*.

When a man says *I* he refers to one or other of these. The *I* to which he refers is present when he says *I*. Further, when he says *Thou* or *It,* the *I* of one of the two primary words is present.

The existence of *I* and the speaking of *I* are one and the same thing.

When a primary word is spoken the speaker enters the word and takes his stand in it.

The life of human beings is not passed in the sphere of transitive verbs alone. It does not exist in virtue of activities alone which have some *thing* for their object.

I perceive something. I am sensible of something. I imagine something. I will something. I feel something. I think something. The life of human beings does not consist of all this and the like alone.

This and the like together establish the realm of *It*.

But the realm of *Thou* has a different basis.

When *Thou* is spoken, the speaker has no thing for his object. For where there is a thing there is another thing. Every *It* is bounded by others; *It* exists only through being bounded by others. But when *Thou* is spoken, there is no thing. *Thou* has no bounds.

When *Thou* is spoken, the speaker has no *thing*; he has indeed nothing. But he takes his stand in relation.

It is said that man experiences his world. What does that mean?

Man travels over the surface of things and experiences them. He extracts knowledge about their constitution from them: he wins an experience from them. He experiences what belongs to the things.

But the world is not presented to man by experiences alone. These present him only with a world composed of *It* and *He* and *She* and *It* again.

I experience something.—If we add "inner" to "outer" experiences, nothing in the situation is changed. We are merely following the uneternal division that springs from the lust of the human race to whittle away the secret of death. Inner things or outer things, what are they but things and things!

I experience something.—If we add "secret" to "open" experiences, nothing in the situation is changed. How self-confident is that wisdom which perceives a closed compartment in things, reserved for the initiate and manipulated only with the key. O secrecy without a secret! O accumulation of information! It, always It!

The man who experiences has not part in the world. For it is "in him" and not between him and the world that the experience arises.

The world has no part in the experience. It permits itself to be experienced, but has no concern in the matter. For it does nothing to the experience, and the experience does nothing to it.

As experience, the world belongs to the primary word *I–It*.
The primary word *I–Thou* establishes the world of relation.

The spheres in which the world of relation arises are three.

First, our life with nature. There the relation sways in gloom, beneath the level of speech. Creatures live and move over against us, but cannot come to us, and when we address them as *Thou,* our words cling to the threshold of speech.

Second, our life with men. There the relation is open and in the form of speech. We can give and accept the *Thou.*

Third, our life with spiritual beings. There the relation is clouded, yet it discloses itself; it does not use speech, yet begets it. We perceive no *Thou,* but none the less we feel we are addressed and we answer—forming, thinking, acting. We speak the primary word with our being, though we cannot utter *Thou* with our lips.

But with what right do we draw what lies outside speech into relation with the world of the primary word?

In every sphere in its own way, through each process of becoming that is present to us we look out toward the fringe of the eternal *Thou*; in each we are aware of a breath from the eternal *Thou*; in each *Thou* we address the eternal *Thou.*

I consider a tree.

I can look on it as a picture: stiff column in a shock of light, or splash of green shot with the delicate blue and silver of the background.

I can perceive it as movement: flowing veins on clinging, pressing pith, suck of the roots, breathing of the leaves, ceaseless commerce with earth and air—and the obscure growth itself.

I can classify it in a species and study it as a type in its structure and mode of life.

I can subdue its actual presence and form so sternly that I recognise it only as an expression of law—of the laws in accordance with which a

constant opposition of forces is continually adjusted, or of those in accordance with which the component substances mingle and separate.

I can dissipate it and perpetuate it in number, in pure numerical
relation.

In all this the tree remains my object, occupies space and time, and
has its nature and constitution.

It can, however, also come about, if I have both will and grace, that
in considering the tree I become bound up in relation to it. The tree is
now no longer *It*. I have been seized by the power of exclusiveness.

To effect this it is not necessary for me to give up any of the ways
in which I consider the tree. There is nothing from which I would have
to turn my eyes away in order to see, and no knowledge that I would
have to forget. Rather is everything, picture and movement, species and
type, law and number, indivisibly united in this event.

Everything belonging to the tree is in this: its form and structure,
its colours and chemical composition, its intercourse with the elements
and with the stars, are all present in a single whole.

The tree is no impression, no play of my imagination, no value depending on my mood; but it is bodied over against me and has to do
with me, as I with it—only in a different way.

Let no attempt be made to sap the strength from the meaning of the
relation: relation is mutual.

The tree will have a consciousness, then, similar to our own? Of that
I have no experience. But do you wish, through seeming to succeed in
it with yourself, once again to disintegrate that which cannot be disin-
tegrated? I encounter no soul or dryad of the tree, but the tree itself.

If I face a human being as my *Thou,* and say the primary word *I–Thou*
to him, he is not a thing among things, and does not consist of things.

Thus human being is not *He* or *She*, bounded from every other *He* and
She, a specific point in space and time within the net of the world; nor
is he a nature able to be experienced and described, a loose bundle
of named qualities. But with no neighbour, and whole in himself, he
is *Thou* and fills the heavens. This does not mean that nothing exists
except himself. But all else lives in *his* light.

Just as the melody is not made up of notes nor the verse of words
nor the statue of lines, but they must be tugged and dragged till their
unity has been scattered into these many pieces, so with the man to
whom I say *Thou*. I can take out from him the colour of his hair, or
of his speech, or of his goodness. I must continually do this. But each
time I do it he ceases to be *Thou*.

And just as prayer is not in time but time in prayer, sacrifice not in
space but space in sacrifice, and to reverse the relation is to abolish

the reality, so with the man to whom I say *Thou*. I do not meet with him at some time and place or other. I can set him in a particular time and place; I must continually do it: but I set only a *He* or a *She*, that is an *It*, no longer my *Thou*.

So long as the heaven of *Thou* is spread out over me the winds of causality cower at my heels, and the whirlpool of fate stays its course.

I do not experience the man to whom I say *Thou*. But I take my stand in relation to him, in the sanctity of the primary word. Only when I step out of it do I experience him once more. In the act of experience *Thou* is far away.

Even if the man to whom I say *Thou* is not aware of it in the midst of his experience, yet relation may exist. For *Thou* is more than *It* realises. No deception penetrates here; here is the cradle of the Real Life.

This is the eternal source of art: a man is faced by a form which desires to be made through him into a work. This form is no offspring of his soul, but is an appearance which steps up to it and demands of it the effective power. The man is concerned with an act of his being. If he carries it through, if he speaks the primary word out of his being to the form which appears, then the effective power streams out, and the work arises.

The act includes a sacrifice and a risk. This is the sacrifice: the endless possibility that is offered up on the altar of the form. For everything which just this moment in play ran through the perspective must be obliterated; nothing of that may penetrate the work. The exclusiveness of what is facing it demands that it be so. This is the risk: the primary word can only be spoken with the whole being. He who gives himself to it may withhold nothing of himself. The work does not suffer me, as do the tree and the man, to turn aside and relax in the world of *It*; but it commands. If I do not serve it aright it is broken, or it breaks me.

I can neither experience nor describe the form which meets me, but only body it forth. And yet I behold it, splendid in the radiance of what confronts me, clearer than all the clearness of the world which is experienced. I do not behold it as a thing among the "inner" things nor as an image of my "fancy," but as that which exists in the present. If test is made of its objectivity the form is certainly not "there." Yet what is actually so much present as it is? And the relation in which I stand to it is real, for it affects me, as I affect it.

To produce is to draw forth, to invent is to find, to shape is to discover. In bodying forth I disclose. I lead the form across—into the world of *It*. The work produced is a thing among things, able to be experienced and described as a sum of qualities. But from time to time it can face the receptive beholder in its whole embodied form.

Etienne Gilson

PAINTING AND REALITY

THE SIGNIFICANCE OF MODERN PAINTING

By the "significance of modern painting" we mean all that the preceding considerations can suggest to a philosopher concerning the ultimate nature of reality. Such views of the mind are limited in a twofold way. First, they hang on the nature of the particular problem from which they are taken: only a limited number of determined questions can be asked about the world from the point of view of the art of painting. Next, such considerations are still more limited by the particular approach of the philosopher to this particular problem. The fact that the art of painting seems to have reached a critical point in its history can be said, in a sense, to dominate the discussion of the whole problem. An observer asking the same questions two centuries from now will find himself confronted with new forms of the same problem, even perhaps with new problems. Another observer living in our own times and asking the same questions would probably consider them in the light of different facts. But may we not hope that, in the last analysis, all these different approaches and all these differently formulated conclusions will ultimately point out a common truth?

The significance of modern painting is perhaps better seen when painting is compared with other arts, such as music, in which, because it consists of sounds only, imitation is practically impossible. Imitative music is immediately recognized for what it is. In the "Pastoral Symphony, it occupies about the same place and fulfills the same function as that of certain "collages" in cubist paintings. In both cases the creative nature of art is emphasized by the insertion, in the musical piece or in the painting, of a fragment of reality. But even among what have often been called the "arts of design," there is at least one that has never been submitted to the servitude of imitation—namely, architecture. There is nothing in the material used by architects that is not likewise included in sculpture or painting. Solid materials, such as those used by sculptors, are assembled by architects in a certain order and according to certain proportions; architecture has lines, volumes, geometrical intelligibility immediately perceptible to sight, tone values due to the ceaselessly changing way in which light plays over the accidents of its surface; architecture can even make use of color if it chooses, and still architecture is not, has never been, and is not even now in danger of becoming an art of imitation.

Some painters, wholly unrelated to the nonimitational school, have clearly discerned this eminent dignity of architecture.[1] Their remarks give full meaning to the old tradition, mostly Greek in origin, that associated music with the birth of certain famous architectural masterpieces. And, indeed, in a sense architecture is a sort of solidified music. A building is like a stone symphony whose parts coexist in space instead of succeeding one another in time. In neither one of these two arts is there any direct imitation of nature. There are caves in nature, but there are no houses, still less temples, community centers, or commemorative buildings of any kind. True enough, architecture, too, has its own artistic limitations. Functional architecture, which comes under the heading of engineering rather than of the fine arts, is a perfectly legitimate and necessary type of architecture; there is hardly a building in which functional considerations do not play a determining part; only, to the extent that they do, architecture pursues another end than beauty— that is to say, that quality which enables an object to please the eyes.

Since they are man-made realities without any model in nature, buildings can be considered so many additions to the world of natural objects. This is so true that one of the latest additions to the body of scientific disciplines, human geography, has often incorporated the study of human habitations in the general description of the face of the earth, which is geography. In the beginning to build houses, man was simply continuing the natural process by which nature evolves animal shells. The process is different, and shells are usually more beautiful than houses, but, in both cases, the result is an increase in the number of existing beings, not the duplicating of some of them by a set of images whose only end is to be their imitations. There is therefore a possible use of lines, surfaces, and colors other than the imitational use that is still so often considered coessential with painting.

Strangely enough, it seems that primitive arts exhibit the same lack of interest in the imitational reproduction of visual appearances. The reason usually given for this is that primitive artisans could not, and still cannot, achieve the perfect resemblance that is supposed to be the ideal of sculpture and painting. This is tantamount to saying that the *Iliad* and the *Odyssey* were written in verse because their authors could not have written them in prose. It does not take into consideration another possibility—that as soon as they undertake to create, men go straightway not to that which is more useful or more obvious, but to that which is noble, more beautiful, and therefore more important. It is more important to create a being whose justification is in itself than to turn out endless clever images of such beings. If it is a true painting, a simple still life creates a new pattern of plastic forms well calculated to please the eye. Images add nothing to existing reality; artistic creations do increase the sum total of the objects whose reality is as certain as their intelligibility.

An obvious fact should suffice to convince us all of this truth. The development of art history and art criticism parallels the admirable development of modern science. Neither art criticism nor science would exist if art and nature did not first provide them with an objective reality to study. Being comes before knowledge; because it is art, painting stands on the side of being.

This applies to the history of painting from the early Middle Ages to our own times. The unanimous admiration for Giotto expressed by practically all painters who ever wrote probably can be attributed to a felicitous blending of incipient imitation with a large proportion of the artistic creativity of Byzantine art. Up to Giotto, paintings continue to be, like human dwellings, so many products of the human power to add artifacts to the number of natural beings. Such artifacts are beings produced by nature through the agency of man, himself a product of nature. Petrarch and Laura never lived in Pistoia, but if an artist puts them there, they will eternally be passing before its cathedral. We beg to suggest that the art of painting always keeps faith with its own essence when, whatever its date, local origin, and style, it fulfills this creative function.[2]

But man has other functions to fulfill. Besides that of making, he also fulfills those of doing and knowing. This assertion, which probably sounds metaphysical to the ears of our contemporaries, would have been maintained as strictly biological by Aristotle, as indeed it is. Leaving aside the order of morality, which is that of doing, we can state as a bare fact that, if there were no men in the world of nature, reality would no more be aware of its own existence and of its own intelligibility than of its power to increase the sum total of beauty in the cosmos. It is now customary, in certain circles, to poke fun at the simplicity with which the Greeks, then the Christians, expressed their admiration for that peerless natural being, man, but this admiration was much more justified than the present tendency to vilify human nature by reducing it to the common level of brute life. Even apart from any theological assumption, it remains a scientifically objective fact that, through man, and through him alone, nature finally achieved self-awareness. Science is the name for this outstanding achievement.

During the long episode that lasted from the end of the fifteenth century to the beginning of nonrepresentational art, painters, instead of remaining firmly established on the ground of nature, progressively or regressively shifted over to the ground of imitation, representation, and, in short, exchanged making for knowing. Imitation—that is, representation of reality as it appears to be—stands on the side of science or, to use a more modest word, knowledge. Reduced to its simplest expression, the function of modern art has been to restore painting to its primitive and true function, which is to continue through man the creative activity of nature. In so doing, modern painting has destroyed nothing and condemned nothing that belongs in any one of the legitimate activities of man; it has simply regained the clear awareness of its own nature and recovered its own place among the creative activities of man.[3]

The evolution of modern painting entails consequences that go beyond the boundaries of pure art. Because these consequences are philosophical in nature, no painter should be made responsible for them. As to philosophers, it is too easy to forsee that, even if they agreed to discuss these problems in the light of what precedes, each of them would draw a different set of conclusions from the same facts. We shall therefore content ourselves with pointing out the main lines of thought that, as far as we can see, would best agree with the suggestions made by painters themselves in those of their writings which we have read.

Starting from the last conclusion to which modern painters have led us, one seems to be well founded in saying that their common ambition is to bring art closer to nature than it seems to have been ever since, considering itself a sort of speculative approach to truth, it began to take sides with knowing against making. Many painters now tend to consider themselves natural forces sharing in the fecundity of nature and their works so many beings produced by nature through their own art. Everything invites them to adopt such an attitude—first of all, their recent rediscovery of the nonimitational character of painting qua painting, but also their increasing awareness of the biological affinities between the conception and birth of a painting and those of any living being. In Herbert Read's words: "Aesthetic activity is biological in its nature and functions."[4] If we remember that the life of man is that of an animal endowed with intellectual knowledge, we shall not fail to use the term "biological" in the fullness of its meaning. To make works of art is proper to man, and it differentiates human evolution from common animal evolution precisely because the life of an intellectual animal is essentially different from that of any other known species of living beings.

The peril that threatens this recent orientation in the field of aesthetics is precisely to forget that, if the study of intellectual life belongs to biology, as could be gathered from the study of Aristotle's treatise *On the Soul,* biology itself has to broaden its field to make room for the disciplines that deal with the problems related to knowledge, action, and creation. In the present case, a deep difference separates the natural production of things and beings from the production of works of art by man. The fact that all artists designated it by the word "creation," which is borrowed from Christian theology, clearly shows that the biological process by virtue of which paintings come to be is somewhat different from the natural evolution of animals from their conception to their birth. The distinction of the two biological levels that has just been suggested finds here its necessary application.

In speaking of creation, no artist normally imagines himself a rival of the supreme being Paul Cézanne used to call *Deus Pater Omnipotens.* Some artists may have been tempted by pride, but few succumbed to the temptation. Yet the sole fact that such an illusion was at least possible proves that the making of works of art implies a feeling of power and of domination over matter analogous to those which religion attributed to God. We have noted several expressions of this creative exaltation written by various painters, but some of them have carried their observation deeper and attempted to say in what sense, although the formula could not be taken as literally true, they felt justified in describing their work as creation.

Seen from without, works of art are characterized by their amazing diversity. Civilizations, countries, schools, individual artists, all leave behind paintings recognizable by their styles and bearing the marks of their various origins. Seen from within—that is, from the point of view of their authors—these paintings are characterized by their imprevisibility. Naturally, history does not hesitate to explain how, and for what reasons, the art of painting has followed the evolution that it has taken. What has not yet been seen is a painter able to foretell the future evolution of his art or the probable development of his own career, or even, when he begins a new painting, what this particular work will look like after being completed. Unless we are mistaken, what the term "creation" expresses in the writings of artists is precisely that character of "novelty" which is so typical of artistic production. Far from proceeding with the mechanical previsibility of natural operations, whose effects are always more or less previsible and, as they say, determined, art is full of ignorances, uncertainties, and surprises for the artist himself, who sometimes sees his work docilely following his decisions, sometimes entering ways he had not foreseen.

These two characteristics of imprevisibility and liberty are the more remarkable in that, according to the unanimous consent of painters, nothing is more dangerous for them than to trust to luck. The kind of imprevisibility that characterizes the work of art is very different from that which attends chance. No true artist will leave anything to chance; only, when everything has been foreseen, prepared, and calculated, the creative painter still does not know what his work is going to be. What he has calculated is less his work than the way he is going to do it. An artist somewhat resembles a man who, before making a decision of vital importance, collects all the facts relevant to the case, weighs the various decisions that are possible, calculates their probable consequences, and still does not know how his will ultimately will decide. These are the classical moments of the philosophical description of a free act. Just as previsibility attends determination, imprevisibility attends liberty. The true meaning of the word "creation" in the writings of painters is practically the same as that of the word "liberty" when it is understood in this sense. As Eric Gill once said, the artist does not create *de nihilo*, but he does create *de novo*. This is so true that when we want to say of an artist that he has had his day, we simply say that he is unable to renew himself. A self-repeating artist has reached the end of his creative activity.[5]

Remarkably enough, the questions we ask about the probable future of a painter's career, or, for that matter, about the probable future of the art of painting in general, are similar to the questions an observer could have asked, many millenniums ago, concerning the probable development of life on the surface of the earth. Even now, confronted with the results of these millenniums of change, modern science does not find it too easy to explain how this change took place. The word "evolution" remains a symbol for a demonstrated explanation still to come. We simply do not know.[6] But if it is true that man is part and parcel of nature, and that artists are men, then their personal experience of artistic creativity should be able to unveil to us some of the secrets of the inventiveness of nature. Unless we decide that man is unrelated to the cosmos in which he lives, what happens in him must bear some relationship to what is happening to the whole of which he is a part. What happens in painters suggests the presence, at the origin of universal becoming, of an inner force of invention and creativity that, everywhere at work in the world of matter, achieves self-awareness in the mind of artists.

This approach to the cosmic problems discussed by scientists and philosophers is neglected by almost all philosophers. The reason for this is that philosophy itself is knowledge, and since knowledge must be true to exist, philosophical problems are usually related to the truth of certain propositions. Now, truth is the conformity of intellection with its object. Consequently, where there is no object, there is no truth. This consequence entails another one. If there are forces or energies in the world whose operations cause effects that are new in both existence and nature, philosophers feel naturally inclined to disregard them as irrelevant to their own discipline. In this, science in no way differs from philosophy. Always ready to account for works of art, and even for artists, once artists have already produced their works, science is unable to say anything sensible about the very act by which works of art are being produced by artists. Some painters have been so acutely aware of the opposition between the respective attitudes of artists and scientists toward reality that they expressed their dislike of scientists in somewhat crude terms.[7] But there is no opposition between art and science; there simply is a real distinction between their functions. The very possibility of science presupposes the existence of realities produced by art, or by a still higher power than that of artists and of art. By definition, science is not qualified to deal with what it presupposes. When science attempts to deal with what it itself naturally presupposes, it simply denies the existence of such problems or of such realities. The natural tendency of science and speculative philosophy is to consider their intellectual formulations of reality equivalent to reality itself. True enough, philosophers and scientists are well aware of the fact that they do not know everything; on the contrary, they often declare that what they know is little in comparison with what still remains to be known; but they also believe that what remains to be known will be found to be homogeneous in nature with what they already know.

If there are forces or energies in the world productive of novelty, the only discipline that can directly communicate with them is art, any art, provided only it keeps faith with its own essence, which is that of a creative activity in the order of formal being. When approached from the point of view of art, reality becomes very different from what it seems to be when seen from the point of view of speculation. It is being only to the extent that becoming is being. Art introduces us to a world of forms whose final completion is the outcome of a sort of biological growth.[8] But even this is not quite true, for biological growth does not seem to have any choice, whereas artists are in quest of forms that only their own free choice is able to determine. Nor should we feel surprised to hear some of them describe their attitude as one of obedience to an "internal necessity," for, indeed, the long and ascetic preparation that precedes artistic creation has precisely for its object to eliminate the obstacles—perceptions, images, imitational urges, acquired habits, and even skill—that stand in the way of the new germinal form and impede its materialization. The internal necessity to which an artist must submit is not a necessity for his will. The internal necessity by which creative artists often feel bound is that of the very form to which their own free will chooses to give actual existence in a matter fittingly disposed to receive it. Other disciplines, such as, for instance, ethics, can introduce philosophers to the problems related to the freedom of doing; art is the only approach we have to the freedom of making.

This is to say that art invites philosophy to take into serious consideration problems for which philosophers exhibit little interest.[9] In Plato's doctrine, all questions related to existence as well as to the causes and origins of things are kept out of the domain of science properly so called and reserved for probable opinion, which expresses itself under the form of narratives, or myths. Plato's *Timaeus* is the best example of such an approach to these problems. In the philosophy of Aristotle, on the contrary, there are no such things as myths, so all problems related to origins disappear at once. The world of Aristotle is eternal, indestructible, as well as uncreated, and all the fleeting beings that ceaselessly come to be and pass away are nothing more than temporary embodiments of their eternal and immutable species. Only the accidental is new in the world of Aristotle; is is no wonder, then, that when the time came for him to define art, he found nothing better to say about it than to reduce it to imitation. What else could he have done? Both philosophy and science are hostile to becoming, except, of course, to the becoming that brings nothing really new into the world and does not endanger previsibility.

Theology has often favored similar views, for the simple reason that, since they had to credit God with science, many theologians naturally conceived him by analogy with a perfect human scientist. But there were difficulties. The first one was that, since Aristotle had not had to solve any problem of origins, he had had no use for the notion of Ideas. It thus became imperative for theologians to supplement Aristotle with Plato. Now, this simply cannot be done. Philosophies just are not that way. One cannot possibly retain ninety-five per cent of Aristotle and add five per cent of Plato to it. If one does, the resulting mixture is plain incoherence. So theologians have had no other choice than to evolve their own notion of the creative power of God and of the way in which this power has been exercised. This has led them to two conclusions that, rather hard to reconcile from the point of view of man, must needs be actually reconciled, in fact, if there is a God. One of these conclusions is that, since the divine science must needs be perfect, the future of the universe must eternally remain an open book before the sight of God. The second one is that, since there are freedom and contingency in the universe, the perfect knowledge that God has of the future does not prevent contingency and freedom from playing their parts in the general history of the world. Various theological answers have been given to this essentially theological problem; the only point we are concerned with, as philosophers, is the fact that an exclusively speculative approach to the problem is bound to minimize the elements of novelty and natural imprevisibility which must be present in a world created by the free will of an all-powerful God. The reason for this assertion can be stated in a few words: if all effects resemble their causes, a freely created world must exhibit at least some traces of the free creative power of its Author.

This is the reason why, despite resemblances in terminologies, the created universe of Christian theologians has never been identical with the uncreated universe of Aristotle; but the same reason probably accounts for this other fact, that when modern artists undertook to investigate the nature of their own activity, they spontaneously resorted to the creationist terminology of Christian theologians. As often happens, while speculating in the light of its own principles, theology is here acting as a guiding star for philosophers considering the nature of the world as well as for artists considering the nature of art.

If there is such a thing as a divine art, it must be very different from our own. First of all, our own art never creates in the proper sense of the word. It does not create its matter; it does not even properly create its forms. Human art simply assembles the elements of composites that, once made, are possessed of their own forms for the sole reason that they *are*.[10] Moreover, if one can speak of God as of the supreme Artist, his art is certainly innocent of any groping and of any becoming due to what would be for him the incomplete previsibility of his own works. Unlike the Ideas of Plato, those of Christian theology are one with the very being of the Creator; unlike the Prime Mover of Aristotle, the Christian Creator of the world has Ideas of all things known by him and creatable by his power. For this very reason, nothing that happens can possibly be new in the sight of God. Yet, when all is said and done, the God of the Jews and of the Christians did create the universe, and if this was nothing new in him, it certainly was the beginning of all newness in the created world itself. According to Christian theology, creative power belongs to God alone, and the world of creation owns no parcel of it. But it does not take a divine power to achieve novelty in the communication of existence and in the forming of man-made beings. This is what artists do. It is what modern painting has done in the highest degree, and, be it for this reason only, it deserves the careful consideration of philosophers, even perhaps of theologians.

Metaphysicians and theologians usually say that, since effects resemble their causes, created beings resemble their Creator. Because his very essence is to be the pure act of being, the world created by God is, or exists. Because this existence of the world is due to the efficacy of the divine power acting as a cause, we see all the beings included in God's creation causing, acting, and operating in their diverse ways and according to their different natures. Things, Thomas Aquinas liked to say, imitate God in that they are and in that they are causes. Such are the painters, whose works add to the beauty of the world. Painters are the makers of new visual forms whose proper function is to make intelligibility perceptible to human sight.

This is the most solid ground there is for speaking of a religious art. In a created universe whatever exists is religious because it imitates God in its operations as well as in its being. If what precedes is true, art, too, is religious in its very essence, because to be creative is to imitate, in a finite and analogical way, the divine prerogative, exclusively reserved for HE WHO IS, of making things to be. Now, as has already been seen, to make things be and to make them beautiful are one and the same thing.[11] Each artist, then, while exerting his often anguished effort to add new types of beings to those which make up the world of nature, should be conscious of the resemblance between his finite art and the infinitely perfect efficacy of the divine power. All truly creative art is religious in its own right.

By the same token, the meaning of the words "Christian art" becomes at once apparent. The problem does not arise in connection with picturing conceived as an art distinct from painting properly so called. Some religions exclude images; others do not hesitate to appeal to them as to visual aids in the teaching of religious truth. Christianity has always done so, the more willingly as, upholding the truth of the substantial unity of man, the Church has always associated, in both cult and prayer, the mind of man, his affectivity, and his activity. It seems therefore evident that picturing fulfills in Christian worship an important function, whose proper end is inscribed in its very nature and which cannot possibly reach this end without resorting to imitational art. The subject here is of primary importance, and nothing is more legitimate in it than to do what most creative artists would consider an abomination: to rely upon the subject more than upon the art as a source of emotion. In religious imagery, this is not only legitimate; it is necessarily required by its very end. He to whom a bare wooden cross does not suffice is perhaps not so wholly Christian as he should be; he who sees in a crucifix the thing of beauty it may well be, but nothing else, is not a Christian at all. The art of doing Christian pictures does not exclude the possibility of doing Christian paintings; by itself, however, it necessarily is representational art.[12]

This answer is but indirectly related to the problem of creative Christian art. On the contrary, the fact that all the main moments of human life have a religious significance lies at the very center of the question. Ever since the birth of Our Lord, the birth of every child is a nativity. There is, in a Christian universe made up of created beings, a direct invitation to artists to join in the praise of God by co-operating with his creative power and by increasing, to the extent that man can do so, the sum total of being and beauty in the world. This is the more instantly required when the works to be produced by human art are primarily destined to a specifically religious use. There then is an inner affinity between the intended end and the means to be employed to reach it. Religion can survive without art; it even survives in spite of the fact that its churches have largely become so many temples dedicated to the exhibition of industrialized ugliness and to the veneration of painted nonbeing. But when Christian artists are called upon to celebrate the glory of God by cooperating, in their modest human manner, with the work of creation, it becomes imperative that their own works be things of beauty. Otherwise, these works would not truly *be,* and the artists themselves would contribute nothing.

Philosophers, too, have something to learn from a careful examination of art under all its forms. In the case of painting, we find ourselves enriched with privileged information concerning the way physical beings come to be. It would be somewhat naïve to imagine nature acting as an artist—that is to say, as a man—but the fear of this kind of anthropomorphism should not make us fall into another error, which consists in believing that man is in himself a separate being, self-sufficient and wholly different from the universe that includes him. The physical energies that move the world of matter crop up, so to speak, in man's self-awareness of himself as well as of his operations.

It is difficult for us, who are not sharing in their creative power, to formulate inferences based upon what artists say. There would be no excuse for taking such liberties if they themselves were not so often found struggling for words in an effort to go beyond the limits of their own personal experience and to reach conclusions valid for all men. They do not all use the same formulas, but the diversity of their language points out a common truth for which perhaps there are no adequate words. The world in which creative painters live appears to them, not at all as an obstacle, but as something that must be transcended. Assuredly, for them as men, the world of nature is the very same reality it is for us and that we share in common with them, but for them as painters, it is not in the world of nature that ultimate reality lies. They feel that there is still another reality hidden behind the appearances of nature and that it is their own function to discover it in order to express it, or, rather, to express it in order to discover it; for, indeed, this metareality has to be made to be before being made to be known. The constantly recurring opposition of painters of all schools to the literal imitation of nature finds its deepest justification in this feeling. Nor is this conviction peculiar to painters alone. The "poetic principle" invoked by Edgar Allan Poe, which he simply calls "a sense of the Beautiful," seems to obey only one law—namely, not to be a mere repetition of the forms, the sounds, the odors of nature as well as of the common feelings with which they inspire all men.[13] When Poe says that "mere repetition is not poetry," he wholly agrees with the conviction expressed by so many painters that to initiate new realities, not to repeat already existing ones, is the proper end of the art of painting.

The universe in which painters live is therefore a still incomplete one. With a heart full of misgivings, the artist sees himself as one of those whom destiny has elected to enrich the world with new beings. Others before him have been honored with the same mission, and their works are there to witness their success in fulfilling it. But this is no reason he himself should evade his duty, for just as he could not have done the works of his predecessors, nobody else could possibly do the works he seems to be called upon to produce.

The force that will cause their existence is, first of all, an irresistible urge to paint probably akin to the fundamental forces that have given rise to the impressive procession of the vegetal and animal species since the first appearance of life upon earth. Despite its intensity, this force is neither a blind impulse nor a lucid progression toward a clearly seen goal. It could be more justly compared to the groping of primitive forms, if the forms of nature possessed an awareness of their own becoming. A sort of inner sense of direction, not always immune to error, seems to direct both nature and artists toward their respective goals, which are the perfecting of one more being of nature or one more work of art.[14]

The most remarkable feature about this universe of creative artists is the particular relationship it reveals between being and intelligibility. The mechanically conceived universe of René Descartes, and all those which followed it to the end of the last century, were very different from the world in whose existence creative artists invite us to believe. Given a certain quantity of extended matter and the elementary laws of motion, Descartes could make bold to reconstruct a priori just such a universe as the one we live in. No artist ever lived in such a world. Not that there is less intelligibility in the universe of a modern painter than there was in the world of Descartes, but instead of preceding being, as it naturally does in a world for knowledge, intelligibility attends it and finds in it its very foundation in the world of intelligible qualities familiar to creative artists. It is a universe that is always trying to say more than has already been said, or, at least, to say it otherwise; but it does not yet know the sense of what it is about to say; the sense will be clear as soon as the words are found to say it. Yet there is surely going to be a sense; otherwise there would be no words. So also with paintings. All significant works of art, however much they may at first surprise the eye, the ear, or the mind, ultimately reveal the inner intelligibility without which they would not *be*. But it is in giving being to their works that painters themselves realize their intelligibility.

However we may interpret them—and artists are not responsible for the reflections inspired by their art—the facts on which these remarks are founded should remain present in our mind, be it only as so many invitations to pursue the dialogue with the discoveries of modern art as eagerly as we do with the discoveries of modern science. It would be difficult to say which ones are the more important, not indeed in the order of practical life, where applied science reigns supreme, but in the disinterested order of philosophical speculation. A lifetime is not too long to understand the message of so many paintings waiting for us everywhere on the surface of the earth, but one cannot begin too soon to listen to what it says. Nor should one be afraid to embark on the somewhat strange adventures to which we are invited by some of these masterpieces. It is only too possible that some of them will always remain for us like those secret domains of which, in dreams, we vainly try to find the key. In such cases, we shall never know who was at fault, but the odds are on genius. He who sincerely exposes himself to creative art and agrees to share in its ventures will often be rewarded by the discovery, made in joy, that an endlessly increasing accumulation of beauty is, even now, in progress on this man-inhabited planet. As a still higher level, he will know the exhilarating feeling of finding himself in contact with the closest analogue there is, in human experience, to the creative power from which all the beauties of art as well as those of nature ultimately proceed. Its name is Being.

NOTES

1. *"On architecture.* It is itself the ideal, for everything in architecture is idealized by men. Even the straight line is man's invention; it exists nowhere in nature. . . . Architecture, unlike sculpture and painting, takes nothing directly from nature, and here it resembles the art of music—unless it be claimed that just as music recalls the noises of the outside world, so architecture echoes the dens of animals, the caves and the forest. But this is never direct imitation as we understand the word when we speak of the two arts that copy the exact forms to be found in nature." (*Journal of Eugène Delacroix*, p. 160 [September 20, 1852].)

2. "Actually, plastic art is manifested in two principal tendencies, the 'realistic' and the 'abstract.' The first is viewed as an expression of our aesthetic feelings evoked by the appearance of nature and life. The latter is an abstract expression of color, form and space by means of more abstract and often geometric forms or planes; it does not follow nature's aspect and its intention is to create a new reality." (Piet Mondrian, "Liberation from Oppression in Art and Life," *Plastic Art and Pure Plastic Art*, p. 43.) The new reality at stake is what Mondrian calls "universal beauty" (universal, as liberated from the particular limiting forms); here again, the notion of creation in art excludes that of imitation (p. 50).

3. "This is an age in which the glories are shared by the money makers & the literary men. It is an age of money & an age of print. This is inevitable (vide *Game*, Dec. 1922, article 'Idiocy or Ill-Will') & one of the results is that the literary critic of works of art always seeks for and belauds only 'literary content' in such works &, where he finds none, weeps or howls. The painting of Giotto is admirable and the more remarkable because it is great painting in spite of his preoccupation with illustration or story telling. The painting of Cimabue is upon a higher plane, a more exalted plane, a plane more removed from representation & one upon which the painter finds himself face to face with God. It may well be maintained that the great Byzantine school deserves

even greater honour for here was not simply one individual bathing in the vision of God but, as it seems, a whole people, & for several centuries, filled with the Holy Ghost. Their works are indeed the evidence—to the Jews a stumbling block, to the Gentiles foolishness, & to Mr. Chesterton & Sir William Orpen ugliness and dullness." (*Letters of Eric Gill,* pp. 179–80.)

4. *The Philosophy of Modern Art,* p. 13. We apologize for borrowing this perfect formula without subscribing to all the consequences that it entails in the mind of its author. It is important, however, that two authors whose general philosophies are so different should meet on such an important point, and that they should do so on the strength of two distinct analyses of the meaning of modern art considered as a sort of collective experiment. We would willingly subscribe to the following sentence (pp. 13–14): "There is no phase of art, from the palaeolithic cave-paintings to the latest developments of constructivism, that does not seem to be an illustration of the biological and teleological significance of the aesthetic activity in man." This view has been more fully developed in the Conway Memorial Lecture for 1951, given by the same author under the title of *Art and the Evolution of Man.*—By "constructivism," Read seems to mean the position maintained by Naum Gabo in "A Retrospective View of Constructive Art," included in *Three Lectures on Modern Art.*

5. "Plato's theory is right enough but does not go *all* the way. The word 'type' suggests one thing which is typical of many things. No doubt this is an important department of 'art'—the discovery of the *type,* the weeding out of the accidental & extraneous so that, as in a Hindu sculpture of a tree, all trees are resumed. But this job is only one department & not I think the *most* important—it is one of the arts but not the highest or most specifically artistic art so to say. The art which is art specifically & at its highest is that of pure creation—*de novo, ad hoc & ex nihilo.* This is God's art & not man's. But man, in the second degree, by virtue of 'free will' can create (not out of nothing but, *de novo & ad hoc,* out of what God has made). Thus he makes not types but *uniques*—things that represent nothing but themselves & of which there is & cannot be another example in the whole Universe of created beings." (*Letters of Eric Gill,* p. 235; cf. pp. 275–76.)

6. Biological evolution is a fact; what still remains obscure are the limits of this fact as well as the reasons that make it different from mere change. There is, as biologists say, "orthogenesis"—that is, "the process by which a certain number of characteristics are modified in evolution in the same direction and according to a principle of increasing unity" (Jean-Paul Aron, "The Problem of Evoluton," *Diogenes,* VII [1954], 94, n. 5). This is what remains to be accounted for— namely, the very fact, known to all those who ever considered the most elementary facts in embryogeny, and which Aristotle explained by the notion of final cause.—On the present scientific formulation of these problems, see L. Cuenot, *L'Évolution biologique.* His conclusions are summed up in Jean-Paul Aron, p. 96.

7. See the comic hostility of Delacroix toward scientists in general, *Journal,* pp. 155–56 (May 6, 1852), quoted above, p. 138, n. 5.

8. Art imitates nature (Aristotle, *Physics,* II, 2, 194a, 21). This saying is usually understood in the sense that the works of art strive to imitate the visual appearance of the works of nature. This is not what it means in Aristotle; the art he has in mind is medicine, which works as nature does. As Thomas Aquinas understands it, this famous saying means that art is to its operations and its works in the same relationship as nature is to its own operations and its own works. The whole doctrine has been summarized as follows: "The origin of what is made by art is the human intellect, itself derived, as some sort of resemblance, from the divine intellect, which is the origin of natural things. Whence it necessarily follows that the operations of art imitate the operations of nature, and also that the products of art imitate the products of nature." Man looks at the way God does things in nature in order to learn, as a good pupil, how to do his own works; but the two domains remain distinct because the works of nature are no works of art. "If art had to make things of nature, it would operate as nature does. But, on the one hand, nature does not bring any work of art to completion; it simply prepares certain of their elements and places

under the eyes of artists, so to speak, a model of the way to operate. On the other hand, art may well examine the products of nature; it even can make use of them in order to perform its own works, but it cannot produce the works of nature. Whence it appears that with respect to the things of nature, human reason does nothing more than to *know;* but with respect to works of art, human reason both *knows* and *makes* ["est et cognoscitiva et factiva"]. Thus, those among the human sciences which are about natural objects are speculative, whereas those which are about man made things are practical, and about operations carried in imitation of nature." (Thomas Aquinas, *In libros politicorum Aristotelis expositio,* Prooemium, 1–2 [ed. Spiazzi, p. 1].)—The doctrine is sometimes expressed in saying that art imitates nature in operation rather than in representation: "ars imitatur naturam in operando, non in repraesentando."

9. Our own views on this philosophical problem are to be found in *Being and Some Philosophers.*

10. Thomas Aquinas, *Summa theologiae,* I, 45, 5, 1st obj. and answer.

11. The perfect formula is given by Eric Gill (*Beauty Looks After Herself,* p. 66): "Beauty—the word is a stumbling block. Do not let us stumble over it. Beauty is *the Splendour of Being.* The primary constituent of visible Being is Order."

12. In his *Théories,* Denis strongly protested against the excesses of the "expression by the subject" in religious art. In 1896, he did not hesitate to write that, although a masterpiece, it was with Vinci's *Last Supper* that religious painting "entered the way to perdition." If he represents a subject endowed with an emotional value of its own, as was here the case, the painter does not act upon our emotions through his work, but through his subject. The way was then open to Munkácsy, Tissot, "and all that is worse in religious art." From then on, it was going to be the subject alone that, in religious painting, would invite to worship (pp. 41–42). This perhaps is the shortest definition of the art Philistine: "He does not look at the painting; he sees nothing but the subject."

13. *The Complete Tales and Poems,* p. 893.

14. See Eric Gill's letter to William Rothenstein, February 25, 1917 (in *Letters,* pp. 88–89): "I am speaking only of the actual work—the paint or the stone— and not at all of its significance or meaning or value in the abstract, what it's 'worth to God,' but simply what it *is.* On the one side are e.g.: Giotto, etc.; Persian Rugs; Bricks & Iron Girders; Tools, Steam engines; Folk Song; Plain Song; Caligraphy [*sic*]; Toys (not some few modern ones tho.); Animals; Men & Women physically regarded; Hair; Lines; String; Plaited Straw; Beer & so on. On the other are Velázquez, Rembrandt, etc. No, this second list is too difficult —what I wish to convey is that such things as I name in the 1st. list & such things as young children's drawings & the works of savages are themselves actually a part of nature, organically one with nature and in no sense outside her—while, on the other hand, the work of Rembrandt & most moderns (the modern contribution—the renaissance) is not a part of nature but is apart from nature—is in fact an appreciation & a criticism of nature—a reviewing of nature as of something to be loved or hated. Good criticism is an excellent thing—why not? Well, it's no good trying to write all this—I wish we could meet & thrash it out." We intentionally preserve these last lines, as a symbol of the discouragement artists experience when they try to talk about art. Cf. the letter to Walter Shewring, March 28, 1933 (pp. 275–76), and to *The Friend,* July 14, 1933 (p. 277), where Gill forcibly restates his distinction between interpretative and creative art—that is, "between the works which 'hold a mirror up to nature' and those which are themselves *part* of nature. It is clear that the characteristic works of post-Renaissance painters and sculptors are of the interpretative kind, while the works of the European and Indian middle ages and those of China, Mexico, Egypt and all 'primitive' and 'savage' peoples are of the other kind. They are 'natural' objects in the sense that they are the natural product of the kind of being that man is—a creature that needs things for use, who delights in making what he needs and who can only with difficulty be prevented from making things in such a way as that they please him when made."—Cf. Braque, *Le Jour et la nuit,* p. 13: "The painter does not strive to reconstitute an anecdote, but to constitute a pictorial fact."

Paul Tillich

THE PROTESTANT ERA

KAIROS

The ideas here set forth present a summons to a thinking that is conscious of history, to a consciousness of history whose roots reach down into the depth of the unconditional,[1] whose conceptions are created from the primordial concerns of the human spirit, and whose ethos is an inescapable responsibility for the present moment in history. The form of this summons will not be that of a sermon; it will not be propaganda or romanticism or poetry but serious intellectual work, striving for a philosophy of history that is more than a logic of the cultural sciences and yet does not lag behind it in sharpness and objectivity. It would be a meaningless beginning to wish to undertake such a task in the brief limits of an essay if more were intended than to bring *one* concrete conception into a sharp light, a conception that, if it alone has been made to stand out clearly, can be illuminating for many others—the conception of "kairos." A summons to a consciousness of history in the sense of the kairos, a striving for an interpretation of the meaning of history on the basis of the conception of kairos, a demand for a consciousness of the present and for action in the present in the spirit of kairos—that is what is intended here.

I

It was a fine feeling that made the spirit of the Greek language signify *chronos*, "formal time," with a different word from *kairos,* "the right time," the moment rich in content and significance. And it is no accident that this word found its most pregnant and most frequent usage when the Greek language became the vessel for the dynamic spirit of Judaism and primitive Christianity—in the New Testament. His "kairos" had not yet come, is said of Jesus; and then it had once at some time or other come, *en kairo,* in the moment of the fulness of time. Time is an empty form only for abstract, objective reflection, a form that can receive any kind of content; but to him who is conscious of an ongoing creative life it is laden with tensions, with possibilities and impossibilities, it is qualitative and full of significance. Not everything is possible at every time, not everything is true at every time, nor is everything demanded at every moment. Various "rulers," that is different cosmic powers, rule at different times, and the "ruler," conquering all the other angels and powers, reigns in the time that is full of destiny and tension between the Resurrection and the Second Coming, in the "present time," which in its essence is different from every other time of the past. In this tremendous, most profoundly stirred consciousness of history is rooted the idea of the kairos; and from this beginning it will be molded into a conception purposely adapted to a philosophy of history.

It is no superfluous undertaking if a summons to a consciousness of history is made, for it is by no means obvious to the human mind and spirit that they are historical; rather, a spiritual outlook that is unaware of history is far more frequent, not only beacuse of dulness and lack of spirit—these we have always had and always will have—but also because of deep instincts of a psychic and metaphysical kind. This outlook that is unconscious of history has two main roots. It may be rooted in the awareness of what is beyond time, the eternal. This type of mentality knows no change and no history. Or it may be rooted in the bondage of all time to this world, to nature and to her eternally recurrent course and change, to the ever continuing return of times and things. There is a mystical unawareness of history which views everything temporal as a transparent cover, as a deceptive veil and image of the eternal, and which wants to rise above such distractions to a timeless contemplation of the timeless; and then there is what we may call a naturalistic unawareness of history, which persists in a bondage to the course of nature and lets it be consecrated in the name of the eternal by priest and cult. For wide areas of Asiatic culture mystical unawareness of history is the basic spiritual attitude. In contrast to this, consciousness of history is relatively rare. In principle, it is a characteristic element in the development of the Semitic-Persian and Christian-occidental outlook. But even there it appears only at those times when a new vitality has emerged, in the supreme moments of the creative apprehension of the world. All the more important is it for the whole development of mankind at large that this consciousness should in the Occident again and again emerge in full vigor and depth. For one thing is certain: Once it has definitely emerged, it will by degrees bring all nations under its spell; for an action conscious of history can be countered only by an action conscious of history; and if Asia in proud self-consciousness because of an age-old possession defends itself against the Occident, then, to the extent in which this opposition takes place consciously, it is already transported to the soil of historical thinking, and therefore it is by virtue of the very struggle itself brought into the domain of historical consciousnesss.

But in the Occident itself an opponent has risen against historical thinking, an opponent issuing from the mystical view of the world, nourished by the naturalistic attitude, and shaped by the rational, mathematical method of thinking—the technical-mathematical explanation of the world by means of natural science, the rational conception of reality as a machine with eternally constant laws of movement manifest in an infinitely recurring and predictable natural process. The mentality that has produced this conceptual framework as its creation has, in turn, come so much under its spell that it has made itself into a part of this machine, into a piece of this eternally identical process. It has so surrendered itself to its own creation that it has considered itself as a mechanism and has forgotten that this machine was created by it. This is a great threat to occidental culture. It means the loss of a precious possession, a greater catastrophe than that of never having had it. These words are directed to the materialistically minded among the socialists, and they are needed in order to reveal the contradiction in which the socialists stand if, as heirs of a powerful philosophy of history and as bearers of the present consciousness of history, they turn to worship a philosophy that excludes meaningful history and accepts a meaningless natural process. A "materialistic interpretation of history" would be a contradiction in itself, if it were meant to be anything other than an "economic" interpretation of history or if it were meant to have anything to do with metaphysical materialism. Unfortunately, the word has here often become a deception, hiding the actual situation. No system has a better right to raise a protest against the late bourgeois materialism that has no consciousness of history than does socialism, a movement that is unprecedently aware of history. The stronger it raises this protest and the more it gives evidence of the kairos, the further it gets away from all metaphysical materialism, and the more clearly it reveals its belief in the creative power of life.

II

The first great philosophy of history was born out of a keen sense of duality and conflict. The struggle between light and darkness, between good and evil, is its essence. World history is the effect of this conflict; in history the entirely new occurs, the unique, the absolutely decisive; defeats may be suffered on the way, but in the end comes the victory of the light. Thus did Zarathustra, the Persian prophet, interpret history. Jewish prophecy brought into this picture the ethical drive of its God of justice. The epochs of the struggle are the epochs of history. History is determined by supra-historical events. The most important period is the final one, that of the struggle for the ultimate decision, an epoch beyond which no new epoch can be imagined. This type of historical consciousness thinks in conceptions of an absolute character: the absolute opposition between light and darkness, between good and evil; the final decision; the unconditional "No" and the unconditional "Yes" which are struggling with each other. It is an attitude toward history which is moved by a tremendous spiritual tension and by an ultimate responsibility on the part of the individual. This is the great, early expression of man's historical consciousness: the philosophy of history expressed in absolute terms.

It can take on two basic forms. The first form of the absolute philosophy of history is defined by a tense feeling that the end of time is near: the Kingdom of God is at hand, the time of decision is imminent, the great, the real kairos is appearing which will transform everything. This is the revolutionary-absolute type. It sees the goal of history in the "kingdom from above" or in the victory of reason within this world. In both cases an absolute "No" is pronounced upon all the past, and an absolute "Yes" is pronounced upon the future. This interpretation of history is fundamental for all strong historical consciousness, as is the interpretation in which the conception of the kairos was first grasped.

The second form of the absolute philosophy of history can be called a conservative transformation of the revolutionary form as it was achieved by Augustine in his struggle against the chiliastic revivals of the early Christian belief in the imminent coming of the Kingdom of God in history. The background of this type is the same as that of the revolutionary type: the vision of a struggle between two forces in all epochs of history. But, according to the conservative type, the decisive event has already happened. The new is victoriously established in history, although it is still attacked by the forces of darkness. The church in its hierarchical structure represents this new reality. There are still improvements, partial defeats, and partial victories to be expected and, of course, the final catastrophe, in which the evil is destroyed and history will come to an end. But nothing really new can be expected within history. A conservative attitude toward the given is demanded.

The dangerous element in both forms of the absolute philosophy of history, in the conservative as well as in the revolutionary form, is the fact that a special historical reality is set up as absolute, whether it be an existing church or the expected rational society. This, of course, brings a continuous tension into the historical consciousness; but, at the same time, it depreciates all other historical realities. In the Augustinian interpretation, which in principle corresponds with the inner feeling and self-consciousness of all predominantly sacramental churches, only the history of a special church is, in the strict sense, significant for the philosophy of history. Her inner conflicts and their resolution, her fights against external enemies—these are the viewpoints under which all other events are envisaged and estimated. The fight for God and against the world, which is the present historical task, means, in practice, a fight for the church, for a pure doctrine, for a hierarchy. Against this ecclesiastical interpretation of history we must conceive of the kairos in universal terms, and we must not limit it to the past but raise it to a general principle of history, to a principle that is also relevant to the present.

Again and again sectarian revolutionary impulses have opposed the ecclesiastical-conservative mentality, in religious or in secular terms. Whether the great revolution is thought of as from beyond and is expected through the action of God exclusively, or as prepared for by human action, or as being a creation of the human spirit and an act of political revolution; whether the utopias are based on ideas of natural law, such as democracy, socialism, and anarchism (heirs of the religious utopias) or on a transcendent myth, the consciousness of the kairos is equally strong and equally unconditional in all of them. But, in contrast to the conservative interpretation, the kairos in this view lies in the present: "The kingdom is at hand." This excitement, however, about the present and the exclusive orientation toward the future in the revolutionary movements blinds them with respect to the past. The sects are opposed to the ecclesiastical traditions, the *bourgeoisie* destroys the aristocratic forms of life, socialism fights against the bourgeois heritage. The history of the past disappears in the dynamic thrust toward the future. This is the reason why a strong historical consciousness has often accompanied ignorance about past history—for instance, in the proletarian masses—and this is the reason why, on the other hand, a tremendous amount of historical knowledge has not overcome an attitude of detachment and misapprehension with respect to the present moment of history, for instance, in the bourgeois historians of the last decades (in contrast to the great bourgeois historians of the eighteenth century, with their revolutionary visions). For these scholars history was an object of causal explanation or of exact descriptions, but it did not concern them existentially. It was not a place of actual decisions (in spite of their great achievements in historical research). But oppressed and ignorant people, and those few from the educated classes who identified themselves with the people, created the revolutionary-absolute interpretation of history. So it was in early Christianity, in most of the medieval sects, and in our own period. But the lack of a sense of tradition was also the reason for the strong elements of utopianism in all these movements. Their ignorance of the past betrayed them into the feeling that the period of perfection had already started, that the absolute transformation was only a matter of days or of a few years, and that they were its representatives and bearers.

Both forms of an absolute philosophy of history are judged by the absolute itself. The unconditional cannot be identified with any given reality, whether past or future; there is no absolute church, there is no absolute kingdom of reason and justice in history. A conditional reality set up as something unconditional, a finite reality to which divine predicates are attributed, is antidivine; it is an "idol." This prophetic criticism, launched in the name of the unconditional, breaks the absolute church and the absolute society; conservative ecclesiasticism and revolutionary utopianism are alike idolatry.

This is the message of the so-called "theology of crisis," represented by Karl Barth in his powerful commentary on Paul's Epistle to the Romans. No finite reality can claim an absolute status. Everything conditioned is judged by the unconditional in terms of "Yes" and "No." There is a permanent crisis going on in history, a crisis in the double sense of the Greek word: judgment and separation. No moment of history is without this tension, the tension between the unconditional and the conditional. The crisis is permanent. The kairos is always given. But there are no outstanding moments in history with respect to the manifestation of the unconditional (except the *one* moment which is called "Jesus Christ" and which has a supra-historical character). History as such loses its absolute significance; hence it loses the tremendous weight it has in the revolutionary interpretations of history. From the absolute point of view, history becomes indifferent. A third type of absolute philosophy of history appears in this doctrine of "crisis," the "indifference" type. It is indifferent to the special heights and depths of the historical process. A kind of "divine humor" toward history is praised, reminding one of romantic irony or of Luther's understanding of history as the realm of God's strange acting. In this attitude the concept of crisis has no actuality; it remains abstract, beyond every special criticism and judgment. But this is not the way in which the crisis can be effective and the negative can be overcome. The latter is possible only by a new creation. Not negation but affirmation conquers the negative. The appearance of the new is the concrete crisis of the old, the historical judgment against it. The new creation may be worse than the old one which is brought into crisis by it; and, whether better or worse, it is subjected to judgment itself. But in the special historical moment it is *en kairo* ("at the right time") while the old creation is not. In this way history receives the weight and seriousness which belong to it. The absolute—to vary a famous saying of Hegel—is not so impotent as to remain in separation from the relative. It appears in the relative as judgment and creation. This leads to the description of relative interpretations of history.

III

We may distinguish three types in the relative form of philosophy of history: the classical, the progressive, and the dialectical type. The common characteristic of relative interpretations of history is their relativizing attitude toward historical events and, accordingly, the loss of absolute tensions. Instead of absolute judgments, there appears a uniform and universal evaluation of all phenomena on the basis of a historical understanding which is able to have an intuitive feeling for the meaning of every single phenomenon. Thus the relative interpretations comprehend the richness and abundance of historical reality, and they offer the possibility of integrating it into a universal philosophy of history.

The classical philosophy of history can be subsumed under the motto that "every epoch is immediately under God." In every epoch human nature develops the fulness of its possibilities; in every epoch, in every nation, an eternal idea of God is realized. History is the great process of growth of the tree of mankind. This is the vision of people like Leibniz, Goethe, and Ranke. But epochs and nations are not revelations of human nature in the same way in all times. There are differences between blossom and decay, between creative and sterile periods; the vitality of the creative process is the criterion according to which the various periods are judged. This links the classical interpretation of history to the nonhistorical naturalism of the Greeks, as is especially obvious in Spengler's physiognomy of the cultural cycles. Here every culture is a tree by itself with a thousand-year span of life and a final disappearance. History is torn into separate processes originating in different geographical areas and having nothing to do with one another. Crisis is in a rather negative sense the transition from the creative to the technical period of development, which leads to inescapable self-destruction. In spite of this relationship between the classical and the naturalistic interpretation of history, they are different in their basic attitude. The modern form of the classical philosophy of history belongs to Christian humanism and betrays its Christian background in spite of its longing for the Greek way of life. In contrast to the tragic pessimism of the ancient world, it maintains the independent meaning of history.

This is the point of contact which it has with the progressive-relative philosophy of history. Just as the religious enthusiasm of early Christian (and many sectarian) expectations of the end became weakened after the continuous delay of the end and the establishment of the church in the world (or of the sect as a large denomination), so also the secular revolutionary movements become relativistic after their political victory and after the necessary disappointment about the gap between expectation and reality. At this moment "crisis" becomes restricted criticism, radical change becomes slow transformation, the ideal is projected into a remote future, the enthusiasm is replaced by the clever calculation of possibilities, the belief that the turning-point has arrived is exchanged for the certainty of a continuous progress. The religious idea of a history of revelation in several stages is secularized into the idea of a progressive education of the human race (Lessing).

The progressive-relative attitude can emphasize the restricting elements of the idea of progress. Then it tends to become more and more conservative, defending the status quo, clinging to the given, praising the positive against the negative and critical, developing a positivistic behavior and philosophy. If, on the contrary, progressivism emphasizes the negative-critical element of the idea of progress, two ways are open to it. Either it becomes an attitude of, so to speak, professional criticism which is unable to accept anything positive and to express any affirmation—an empty, often cynical, often oversophisticated, often desperate criticism. Or it becomes an attitude of an intensive will to create something new, not to accept the "positively given." In this case it easily loses its relative character and becomes absolute and revolutionary. The consciousness of a kairos becomes possible. Thus the ambiguity of the progressive interpretation of history is its danger and its power.

A connecting of the classical with the progressive interpretation of history results in the dialectical interpretation: this is the highest type of the relative interpretations. It operates in three forms, the theological, the logical, and the sociological, each depending in many respects upon the others.

The theological form is anticipated in the proclamation of the three eras of the Father, the Son, and the Spirit by the Abbé Joachim of Floris in the twelfth century; it is taken up in the idea of the three ages expounded by the leaders of the Enlightenment and of German idealism; and it appears again in the three stages (the theological, the metaphysical, and the positivistic stages) of Comte's philosophy of history. The logical form of the dialectical philosophy of history is so typically and impressively represented by Hegel that it is sufficient merely to mention him, while the sociological form is represented in the French socialistic romanticism with its distinction between the critical and the organic periods and, above all, in the economic interpretation of history by Karl Marx.

A common element in these three forms of the dialectical interpretation of history is their positive valuation of all periods. Every period is more than a transitory moment in the historical process. It has a meaning of its own, an eternal significance. But, besides its relation to the absolute, it is related to the other periods. It is more or less perfect in relation to them. There is "immediacy" with respect to the unconditional, and, at the same time, there is progress with respect to other periods in every period of history. The classical and the progressive philosophy of history are united in the dialectical method.

The dialectical interpretations of history (theological, logical, and sociological) betray an ambiguity similar to that of the progressive interpretation. They can be understood in absolute and in relative terms. According to Joachim, Hegel, Marx, and Comte, the last period of history is "at hand." It can already be recognized in the womb of the present period. (For Hegel his own philosophy is the moment of its birth.) The epoch of the Holy Spirit, the stage of perfect self-consciousness, the classless society, the foundation of the religion of positive science, are final stages; they are *kairoi* in the absolute sense. A revolutionary impulse is visible in all these dialecticians of history, even in Hegel, in his principle of negation. From this side of their thinking they belong to the revolutionary-absolute interpreters of history. Joachim and Marx were so esteemed by their revolutionary followers. But there is another side to the picture. Dialectical thinking subjects every moment of time to its "Yes and No." It does not negate the past unconditionally, and it does not affirm the future unconditionally. The period of the Spirit, in Joachim's vision, is prepared for by the periods of the Father and the Son. But what prevents the history of salvation from preparing something new in the womb of the period of the Spirit? The Germanic nations, according to Hegel, are the last bearers of the process in which the absolute idea actualizes itself. But why should the principle of negation be impotent in face of the Germanic peoples alone? The alternation of organic and critical periods in French socialism gives a high valuation to the Middle Ages. But why should the next organic period, socialism, be protected against a new "critical" period? And why should the period of positive sciences, which is an offspring of religion and metaphysics, not produce another higher period?—a question directed to Comte. And why, finally, should the classless society, which Marx expects, be the end of historical dialectics? Why should the proletariat, after its victory, not succumb to cleavages similar to those experienced by the victorious *bourgeosie?* An absolute stage as the end of the dialectical process is a contradiction of the dialectical principle. It is an idea taken from the revolutionary-absolute interpretations of history. In this ambiguity the limits of the dialectical interpretation of history become manifest: either it must stop the dialectical process arbitrarily, or it must fall back to a doctrine of infinite repetition.

IV

The last considerations have shown us the struggle for an interpretation of history which is in accord with the meaning of the kairos. We have described and schematized the different interpretations in order to draw from them the demands that the idea of kairos poses for any interpretation of history. There are, first of all, two demands that can be derived from the two main groups of interpretations of history. From the absolute types we derive the demand for an absolute tension in the historical consciousness; from the relative types we derive the demand for a universal historical consciousness; from the relative types we derive the demand for a universal historical thinking. We reject any attempt to absolutize *one* historical phenomenon over against all the others, challenging, at the same time, the leveling of all epochs into a process of endless repetition of relativities. A twofold demand may therefore be made upon a philosophy of history that is aware of the kairos. The tension characteristic of the absolute interpretation of history must be united with the universalism of the relative interpretations. But this demand contains a paradox. What happens in the kairos should be absolute, and yet not absolute, but under judgment of the absolute.

This demand is fulfilled when the conditioned surrenders itself to become a vehicle for the unconditional.

The relation of the conditioned to the unconditional, in individual as well as in social life, is either an openness of the conditioned to the dynamic presence of the unconditional or a seclusion of the conditioned within itself. The finite life is either turned toward the infinite or turned away from it toward itself. Where there is an acceptance of the eternal manifesting itself in a special moment of history, in a kairos, there is openness to the unconditional. Such openness can be expressed in religious as well as in secular symbols as the expectation of the transcendent Kingdom of God, or the thousand years of the reign of Christ, or the third epoch of world history, or the final stage of justice and peace. However different the historical consciousness involved in the use of the one or the other of these symbols may be, the consciousness of the kairos, of the outstanding moment in history, can express itself in each of them.

Openness to the unconditional, turning toward it, receiving and bearing it, are metaphors that all express the same reality. But they express it only in a highly abstract way and require a much more concrete interpretation of their meaning. An age that is open to the unconditional and is able to accept a kairos is not necessarily an age in which a majority of people are actively religious. The number of actively religious people can be greater in a so-called "irreligious" than in a religious period. But an age that is turned toward, and open to, the unconditional is one in which the consciousness of the presence of the unconditional permeates and guides all cultural functions and forms. The divine, for such a state of mind, is not a problem but a presupposition. Its "givenness" is more certain than that of anything else. This situation finds expression, first of all, in the dominating power of the religious sphere, but not in such a way as to make religion a special form of life ruling over the other forms. Rather, religion is the life-blood, the inner power, the ultimate meaning of all life. The "sacred" or the "holy" inflames, imbues, inspires, all reality and all aspects of existence. There is no profane nature or history, no profane ego, and no profane world. All history is sacred history, everything that happens bears a mythical character; nature and history are not separated. Equally, the separation of subject and object is missing; things are considered more as powers than as things. Therefore, the relation of them is not that of technical manipulation but that of immediate spiritual communion and of "magical" (in the larger sense of the word) influence. And the knowledge of things has not the purpose of analyzing them in order to control them; it has the purpose of finding their inner meaning, their mystery, and their divine significance. Obviously, in such a situation, the arts play a much greater role than in a scientific or technical age. They reveal the meaning of the myth on the basis of which everybody lives. In the same way social and political acts cannot be imagined without the powers of the divine sphere. The individual is entirely surrounded and carried by this all-penetrating spiritual substance out of which blessedness (and also curse) comes to him. He cannot escape it. Only in extreme cases of vocation or revolt can the individual extricate himself from the whole to which he belongs. Merely individual religion, individual culture, individual emotional life, and individual economic interests are impossible in such a social and spiritual situation. We shall call such a situation "theonomous," not in the sense that in it God lays down the laws but in the sense that such an age, in all its forms, is open to and directed toward the divine. How could such a stage of history disappear? What has destroyed primitive theonomy? The answer is the always present, always driving, always restless principle of "autonomy." Just as theonomy does not mean a situation in which God gives laws, so autonomy does not mean lawlessness. It means the acceptance of the structures and laws of reality as they are present in human mind and in its structures and laws. Autonomy means obedience to reason, i.e., to the "logos" immanent in reality and mind. Autonomy operates in the theoretical, as well as in the practical, spheres of culture. It replaces mystical nature with rational nature; it puts in the place of mythical events historical happenings, and in the place of the magical sense of communion it sets up technical control. It constitutes communities on the basis of purpose, and morality on the basis of individual perfection. It analyzes everything in order to put it together rationally. It makes religion a matter of personal decision and makes the inner life of the individual dependent upon itself. It releases also the forces of an autonomous political and economic activity.

Autonomy is always present as a tendency; it acts under the surface of every theonomy. "The secret impressionist that lives in every true artist" (Hartlaub) is the model for the secret astronomer in every true astrologer, and the secret physician in every true medicine man. The power of scientific and technical needs, in war and in industry and agriculture; the rationalizing energy inherent in the centralization of religion and government; the individualizing power of all strong piety; the struggle of ethical as against ritualistic "holiness"—all these forces are at work every moment, and they try to break through the bonds of the theonomous situation. The outcome of this struggle varies greatly. The theonomous situation can be so strong that autonomy cannot even start, as in many primitive cultures. Or it can achieve a certain degree of rationalization, at which point it comes to a standstill, and the forms thus created receive a final sanction, as, for example, in China. Or the rationalization can pierce directly through the finite world and become an all-devouring principle, as in Indian mysticism. Or autonomy can remain in the religious realm, as in Protestantism. Or it can achieve a complete victory, as in ancient Greece and in the modern Enlightenment. Or it can, after a victorious period, be partly conquered again, as at the end of the ancient world and in the anti-autonomous attitudes of Protestant orthodoxy and of the Counter Reformation. Each of these events is a turning-point in history. It was felt so by the contemporaries, and it appears as such in the historical tradition. Each of them can be called a "kairos," an outstanding moment in the temporal process, a moment in which the eternal breaks into the temporal, shaking and transforming it and creating a crisis in the depth of human existence.

Autonomy is the dynamic principle of history. Theonomy, on the other hand, is the substance and meaning of history. How are they related to each other? First of all, it must be stated that autonomy is not necessarily a turning-away from the unconditional. It is, so to speak, the obedient acceptance of the unconditional character of the form, the logos, the universal reason in world and mind. It is the acceptance of the norms of truth and justice, of order and beauty, of personality and community. It is obedience to the principles that control the realms of individual and social culture. These principles have unconditional validity. Obedience to them is obedience to the logos-element in the unconditional. The difference, however, between autonomy and theonomy is that in an autonomous culture the cultural forms appear only in their finite relationship, while in a theonomous culture they appear in their relation to the unconditional. Autonomous science, for instance, deals with the logical forms and the factual material of things; theonomous science deals, beyond this, with their ultimate meaning and their existential significance. Autonomy is not "irreligious," although it is not a vehicle of religion. It is indirectly religious through the form; it is not directly religious. The humility of the scientific empiricist is religious, but it does not appear as such; it is not theonomous. The heroism of Stoic self-control is religious, but it is not theonomous. The mystery of Leonardo's "Mona Lisa" is religious, but it does not show that it is. If both theonomy and autonomy are related to the unconditional, can we choose between them according to our taste, our psychological inclination, or our sociological tradition? This question is itself its own answer. Where it can be raised, theonomy already has been lost. As long as theonomy is in power, no alternative is open. If its power is broken, it cannot be re-established as it was, the autonomous road must be traveled to its very end, namely, to the moment in which a new theonomy appears in a new kairos.

A new theonomy is not the negation of autonomy, nor is it the attempt to suppress it and its freedom of creativity. For such attempts, which often have been made, with or without success, we use the term "heteronomous." Heteronomy imposes an alien law, religious or secular, on man's mind. It disregards the logos structure of mind and world. It destroys the honesty of truth and the dignity of the moral personality. It undermines creative freedom and the humanity of man. Its symbol is the "terror" exercised by absolute churches or absolute states. Religion, if it acts heteronomously, has ceased to be the substance and life-blood of a culture and has itself become a section of it, which, forgetting its theonomous greatness, betrays a mixture of arrogance and defeatism.

Theonomy does not stand against autonomy as heteronomy does. Theonomy is the answer to the question implied in autonomy, the question concerning a religious substance and an ultimate meaning of life and culture. Autonomy is able to live as long as it can draw from the religious tradition of the past, from the remnants of a lost theonomy. But more and more it loses this spiritual foundation. It becomes emptier, more formalistic, or more factual and is driven toward skepticism and cynicism, toward the loss of meaning and purpose. The history of autonomous cultures is the history of a continuous waste of spiritual substance. At the end of this process autonomy turns back to the lost theonomy with impotent longing, or it looks forward to a new theonomy in the attitude of creative waiting until the kairos appears.

Kairos in its *unique* and universal sense is, for Christian faith, the appearing of Jesus as the Christ. Kairos in its *general* and special sense for the philosopher of history is every turning-point in history in which the eternal judges and transforms the temporal. Kairos in its *special* sense, as decisive for our present situation, is the coming of a new theonomy on the soil of a secularized and emptied autonomous culture.

In these concepts and their dialectical relations the answer is given to the basic question of the philosophy of history: How can the absolute categories which characterize a genuine kairos be united with the relativity of the universal process of history? The answer is: History comes from and moves toward periods of theonomy, i.e., periods in which the conditioned is open to the unconditional without claiming to be unconditioned itself. Theonomy unites the absolute and the relative element in the interpretation of history, the demand that everything relative become the vehicle of the absolute and the insight that nothing relative can ever become absolute itself.

This solution concedes a limited truth to the interpretations of history discussed before.

The conservative-absolute philosophy of history is right in tracing the fight for and against theonomy, the "struggle between belief and unbelief," as it has been called, through all history. But it is wrong in identifying theonomy with a historical church.

The revolutionary-absolute philosophy of history is right in emphasizing the absolute tension toward absolute fulfilment, experienced in every kairos. In each kairos the "Kingdom of God is at hand," for it is a world-historical, unrepeatable, unique decision for and against the unconditional. Every kairos is, therefore, implicitly the universal kairos and an actualization of the unique kairos, the appearance of the Christ. But no kairos brings the fulfilment in time.

The warning against the idolatrous elevation of *one* moment in history, given by the indifferent-absolute philosophy of history, has a decisive influence on the solution: Everything can be a vessel of the unconditional, but nothing can be unconditioned itself. This, however, does not produce indifference toward history; it creates an attitude that takes history absolutely seriously.

The classical-relative philosophy of history is right in its idea of humanity as a whole, in its emphasis on autonomy, and in its recognition of the national, regional, and traditional differentiations within mankind. It understands the universality and individuality of human history and the special conditions of each kairos; but it fails in not accepting the absolute categories and absolute decisions connected with the experience of the kairos.

In every transforming activity a belief in progress is implied. Progressivism is the philosophy of action. Acting out of the kairos means acting in the direction of theonomy. And there is progress from what is not yet or no longer true theonomy toward its realization. In this the progressive-relative philosophy of history is right. But it is wrong in making the law of acting a law of being, for there is no law of universal progress. The fight between theonomy and its foes always goes on and grows more refined and more disastrous, the more the technical progress changes the surface of the earth, binding together all nations for common creation and common destruction at the same time.

The philosophy of the kairos is closely related to the dialectical interpretations of history. Theonomy, autonomy, and heteronomy are dialectically related to one another, since each of these ideas drives beyond itself. But there are some important differences. There is, in the doctrine of the kairos, no final stage in which dialectics, against its nature, ceases to operate. There is, in the doctrine of the kairos, not only the horizontal dialectic of the historical process but also the vertical dialectic operating between the unconditional and the conditioned. And, finally, there is no logical, physical, or economic necessity in the historical process, according to the doctrine of the kairos. It moves through that unity of freedom and fate which distinguishes history from nature.

V

We are convinced that today a kairos, an epochal moment of history, is visible. This is not the place to give reasons for this conviction, although we should refer to the ever growing literature that is critical of our culture and to movements in which the consciousness of the crisis has taken a living form. These may not be proofs that are objectively convincing; proofs of that sort cannot exist. Indeed, the consciousness of the kairos is dependent on one's being inwardly grasped by the fate and destiny of the time. It can be found in the passionate longing of the masses; it can become clarified and take form in small circles of conscious intellectual and spiritual concern; it can gain power in the prophetic word; but it cannot be demonstrated and forced; it is deed and freedom, as it is also fate and grace.

The movement most strongly conscious of the kairos seems to us today to be socialism. "Religious socialism" is our attempt at interpreting and shaping socialism from the viewpoint of theonomy, from the vision of the kairos. It proceeds from the presupposition that in present-day socialism there are certain elements that are incompatible with the idea of the kairos, that are "untimely elements" in which originally creative ideas are perverted or corrupted. Religious socialism for that reason energetically carries on the cultural criticism characteristic of all socialism and seeks to lead the latter to its own real depth, while directing this criticism also against socialism itself.

In present-day socialism are brought together the revolutionary-absolute type in the this-worldly form and the dialectical-relative type in the form of an economic interpretation of history. But a balancing of the two has not been achieved. The unconditional is not grasped in its positive and negative power. It is not grasped in its positive significance as the principle of theonomy, judging and transforming *all* sides of our industrial civilization, including economics and politics. And the negative power of the unconditional is not appreciated, which brings the bearers of the crisis under judgment along with those who are criticized by them, and which judges also every future state of society. The reason for this twofold failure is that socialism, in spite of all its criticism of the bourgeois epoch, has been unable to keep itself free from its negative element, namely, its attempt to exclude the unconditional from the spheres of thought and action and, accordingly, to create the new epoch merely through technology and strategy. Socialism was not aware that precisely in this fashion it was prolonging the old epoch. Socialism saw the kairos, but it did not see its depth; it did not recognize the extent to which it stood itself under the crisis. When it fought against "bourgeois" science, it did not see how it itself shared the basic presupposition of this science, the purely objectifying relationship to the world, to spirit, and to history; and it did not see how, in spite of a different basic impulse, it was fettered within the bonds of that attitude. When it rejected the aesthetic aristocratic practice of art, it was not aware of the fact that, in its promotion of an art determined by its content and oriented to a particular type of ethics and politics, it stood simply at the other pole of the same axis. If in its theory of education it made its focal point the "enlightenment" and the technical discipline of intellect and will for the purpose of an economic and political acquisition of power, it did not realize that it was thereby adopting the basic attitude of its enemies or that it was trying to resist them by the very weapons with the help of which their enemies had deadened the souls of men and had made their bodies into mere cogs in a machine. If it made the highest possible increase of economic welfare into the all-determining and foremost aim, it did not see that it became thereby a mere competitor of capitalism, which believed that it could better accomplish the same thing through social welfare and technical progress. If socialism intended to deprive the spiritual and religious life of its intrinsic value, considering it as a mere ideology, it did not sense that it thereby strengthened the attitude toward economics and life in general that is characteristic of materialistic capitalism. When socialism viewed the atomistic individual as an ultimate reality and then tried to unite him with others through the solidarity of mere interests, it was not aware of its dependence upon the decomposition of "liberal" society and upon the false assumption that human groups may be ultimately motivated by the "struggle for existence." If socialism fought against religion in its ecclesiastical and dogmatic forms, and for that purpose took over all the means of combat and the slogans of the old liberal struggle against the churches, it did not see that it thereby came into the danger of cutting off the roots out of which alone enthusiasm, consecration, "holiness," and unconditional devotion can flow into it: the unconditional "Yes" to the unconditional, regardless of what its forms or symbols might be.

In all these things religious socialism is willing to push the criticism further, to carry it through deeper, to bring it to its ultimate and decisive point. It strives to be more radical, more revolutionary, than socialism, because it wishes to reveal the crisis from the viewpoint of the unconditional. It wishes to make socialism conscious of the present kairos.

With this aim, it follows that religious socialism is always ready to place itself under the criticism of the unconditional. By far the greatest danger for the religious-socialist movement seems to me to be where "religion" is used as a matter of strategy. Here the bourgeois element which socialism drags along with it is in a fateful way encouraged. A merging between the present-day socialism and the churches of our day impedes the coming of the kairos by mutually strengthening the very elements that must be eliminated. Religious socialism must not, for the present, become either a church-political movement or a state-political party, since it loses thereby the unrestricted power to bring both the churches and the parties under judgment.

Religious socialism should, in any case, avoid considering socialism as a religious law, by appealing to the authority of Jesus or to the primitive Christian community. There exists no direct way from the unconditional to any concrete solution. The unconditional is never a law or a promoter of a definite form of the spiritual or social life. The contents of the historical life are tasks and ventures of the creative spirit. The truth is a living truth, a creative truth, and not a law. What we are confronted with is never and nowhere an abstract command; it is living history, with its abundance of new problems whose solution occupies and fulfills every speech.

One question may still be raised, and we offer a brief answer to it: "Is it possible that the message of the kairos is an error?"

The answer is not difficult to give. The message is always an error; for it sees something immediately imminent which, considered in its ideal aspect, will never become a reality and which, considered in its real aspect, will be fulfilled only in long periods of time. And yet the message of the kairos is never an error; for where the kairos is proclaimed as a prophetic message, it is already present; it is impossible for it to be proclaimed in power without its having grasped those who proclaim it.

NOTE

1. The term "unconditional" which is often used in this book points to that element in every religious experience which makes it religious. In every symbol of the divine an unconditional claim is expressed, most powerfully in the command: "Thou shalt love the Lord thy God with *all* thy heart and with all thy soul, and with all thy mind." No partial, restricted, conditioned love of God is admitted. The term "unconditioned" or the adjective made into the substantive, "the unconditional," is an abstraction from such sayings which abound in the Bible and in great religious literature. The unconditional is a quality, not a being. It characterizes that which is our ultimate and, consequently, unconditional concern, whether we call it "God" or "Being as such" or the "Good as such" or the "True as such," or whether we give it any other name. It would be a complete mistake to understand the unconditional as a being the existence of which can be discussed. He who speaks of the "existence of the unconditional" has thoroughly misunderstood the meaning of the term. Unconditional is a quality which we experience in encountering reality, for instance, in the unconditional character of the voice of the conscience, the logical as well as the moral. In this sense, as a quality and not as a being, the term is used in all the following articles.

S. Radhakrishnan

EAST AND WEST

TECHNOLOGY A SERVANT, NOT MASTER

We are tempted to assume that technological progress is real progress and that material success is the criterion of civilisation. If the Eastern peoples become fascinated by machines and techniques and use them, as Western nations do, to build huge industrial organisations, large military establishments, they would get involved in power politics and drift into the danger of death. Scientific and technological civilisation brings great opportunities and great rewards but also great risks and temptations. If machines get into the saddle, all our progress will have been in vain. The problem facing us is a universal one. Both East and West are threatened with the same danger and face the same destiny. Science and technology are neither good nor bad. They are not to be tabooed but tamed and assigned their proper place. They become dangerous only if they become idols.

From that dim and distant date when a human creature struck out the first flint instrument, through all the ages until now, when man belts the globe with the radio and plans to annihilate whole cities with bombs from the sky, the course of human life has been a career of material conquest and mechanical achievement. The pen, the brush, the wheel, the spade, the plough, the boat, the lever, the pulley, the locomotive and the internal combustion engine form a continuous ascent. Nuclear fission is not anything new in principle from, say, the discovery of fire. The machine is an expression of the victory of mind over matter. It is not an end in itself. It is a tool devised by man to give practical effect to his ideals. If our ideals are wrong, the fault is in ourselves, not in the machines. If our ideals are right, machines could be used to remove injustice, improve the lot of mankind, and help the spirit to grow into maturity. There is nothing in a motor car which requires us to drive it so fast as to kill innocent pedestrians. There is nothing in an aeroplane which compels us to drop bombs on fellowmen. There is nothing wrong with the machines as such. If they turn out to be evil, it is because we are evil.

Those who declare that the danger of our situation is the increase of machines in daily use point to the excessive *tempo* of modern civilisation, the anxiety connected with the competition of living, the precariousness of life, the drabness and monotony of the lives of many workers who are required to repeat the same movement hour after hour mechanically, the exciting nature of our amusements and the love for blinding speed and deafening noise.

The old labour-saving devices were utilised within the province of the human world. When technology is released from human control it loses its meaning and we have a triumph of the means over the end. Before the Industrial Revolution, men controlled the instruments and made complete objects. They took pleasure in the exercise of their skill. Their work was sacramental. About such work, Hegel says: 'from the merely bodily movement of the dance to the stupendous and gigantic works of architecture . . . all these works fall into the category of sacrifice . . . the very activity is an offering; no longer of a purely external thing but of the inner subjectivity . . . in this producing the sacrifice is spiritual activity and the effort which, as a negation of the particular self-consciousness, holds fast to the purpose that lives within and in imagination, and brings it forth to outward view'.

In the technological civilisation, where we concentrate on one minute part of the whole, our work is deprived of the breath of soul. In the race to speed up production, work in the factories is reduced to such tiny components that no skill or intelligence is needed. This repetitive work has brought to millions of workers boredom, fatigue and monotony. The workers lose their personal character and live on the surface of consciousness. We do not bring out the best in the human being. Besides in an age anxious for higher standards, we are overlooking the essential value of a simple and austere life. The importance of an individual does not depend on his possessions but on his way of living. India has stressed the values of contentment and self-control in regard to material needs and worldly ambition. Any one who is lost in this technological civilisation whether as a producer or a consumer is depersonalised, deprived of his roots, torn out of his natural context, thrown as it were into an empty space. To preserve the infinite value of the individual, the dignity and rights of man, the freedom of the spirit in an age of technology is not easy. This is possible only with the revival of faith, which is the fulfilling of the spirit in the depths of man, in which man is linked above and beyond himself with the origin of his being.

Unfortunately, some of the leaders of our age who are fascinated by the triumphs of science and technology speak of man as a purely mechanical material being, a creature made up of automatic reflexes. They emphasize the more earthly propensities of human beings and seem to be unaware of the higher sanctity that lives in them. Many of our age suffer from loss of faith. They are the spiritually displaced, the culturally uprooted, the traditionless. Being rooted nowhere they suffer an intense loneliness and so seek comradeship anywhere. They become tribal; only the modern tribe is larger than any country. It embraces continents. The unsheltered beings who are in a mood of defiance or in the despair of nihilism are exploited by the new prophets of earthly paradise.

Our boundless ability in mastering our material environment is of infinitely less importance to us than our relations with ourselves and our fellowmen. The possession of reason is not a guarantee of our humanity. To become truly human, we need something more than reason.

We cannot base the new civilisation on science and technology alone. They do not furnish a reliable foundation. We must learn to live from a new basis, if we wish to avoid the catastrophe that threatens us. We must discover the reserves of spirituality, respect for human personality, the sense of the sacred found in all religious traditions and use them to fashion a new type of man who uses the instruments he has invented with a renewed awareness that he is capable of greater things than mastery of nature. The service to which man must return is man himself, the spirit in him. It is not enough to feed the human animal, or to train the human mind. We must also attend to the human spirit.[1]

CREATIVE RELIGION

While Europe is threatened with new dangers, Asia and Africa are being transformed by the impact on them of Western ideas and technical skill. The world is becoming increasingly interconnected and cultures and civilisations are mingling. To think that any one way of life is the only way seems to be the height of egocentricity. The different geniuses of the people need not be reduced to a dead level of uniformity. They reveal different qualities. Our task is not to displace one way of life by another but to share the treasures of which each is the guardian.

There are no fundamental distinctions between the East and the West. Each one of us is both Eastern and Western. East and West are not two historical and geographical concepts. They are two possibilities which every man in every age carries within himself, two movements of the human spirit. There is tension in the nature of man between his scientific and religious impulses. This tension or tumult is not a disaster but a challenge and an opportunity.

Each one of us is both religious and rational. There have been outstanding scientific contributions from the East and notable religious gifts from the West. At best it is only a difference of emphasis. Mind and spirit are both qualities of human nature. They have not yet attained an equilibrium.[2] There is today a schism in the soul between mind and spirit. A society is stable when its different components, economic and political, cultural and social, are in harmony. If these elements fall into discord, the social order disintegrates.

The hopeful and the distressing features of our age are worldwide and not peculiar to the East or the West. If the purpose of the world is to be realised, all nations require to go through a process of inner renewal. World unity cannot be achieved only through the United Nations Organisation and its agencies. Local solutions are not enough. Everything hangs together. Only total peace can prevent total war. There is the religious view for which the East has stood, and which is not unknown in the West, that man with his sense of values is the most concrete embodiment of the divine on earth. This view has suffered from a misunderstanding of the spirit of science which has resulted in the intellectual devastation of spiritual life, the drying out of creative energies.

Great spiritual revivals occur through the fusion of different traditions. In Clement's metaphor the Christian Church itself was the confluence of two rivers, the Hellenistic and the Jewish. The impact of Christianity converted the disintegrating Græco-Roman world into a new community. The common enclosure of all beings in space and time, through the occupation of the earth's surface gives us the physical basis and makes possible the unity of mankind. This latter is not a fact but a task. The diffusion of ideas and implements is making for intellectual unity. But human solidarity and coherence are possible only through the radiant moments of the profound revelations of spirit which work like a ferment in the course of history. They constitute the goal and justification of the human endeavour for world coherence. The meeting of East and West today may produce a spiritual renaissance and a world community that is struggling to be born.

The present conditions of the world, the universal acceptance of the scientific method, studies in comparative religion, the challenge of world unity are producing in all religions a movement of religious creativity. Progressive thinkers of different faiths are getting together in a common endeavour to realise the good life through truth and love. The world is groping not for the narrow, stunted religion of the dogmatic schools, not one of fanaticism that is afraid of the light but for a creative spiritual religion. It should not be inconsistent with the spirit of science. It should foster humanist ideals and make for world unity.

A true understanding of science supports a religion of spirit. Science is not an entirely self-moving process; or an unconscious instrument of historical change. The development of science is due to the genius of the individual who has knowledge, skill and values. Man is not master of the universe because he can split the atom. He can split the atom because he has that in him which is far superior to the atom. The material achievements stand as witnesses to what the human spirit can accomplish. Again, these achievements are the outcome of severe mental and moral discipline, disinterested devotion to truth, a spirit of dedication as well as creative imagination.

The conflict between science and religion is due to historical circumstances. In the past scientists have suffered from religious and political tyrannies. Giordano Bruno was burnt at the stake, Galileo was imprisoned and threatened, and even today scientists are discouraged by threats of political inquisition or moral ostracism from speaking the truth. If the release of nuclear energy is not welcomed as opening a new era in man's mastery of nature and its powers for the common good but is looked upon as a new threat to mankind, it is because of the overpowering influence of nationalist dogmas. Scientists must stand against all tyranny, determined to preserve the integrity of science and prevent its perversion from its proper beneficent use and save civilisation from misusing science for its own destruction. God is truth and the service of truth is the service of God.[3]

Both religion and science affirm the unity of nature. The central assumption of science is the intuition of religion that nature is intelligible. When we study the processes of nature we are impressed by their order and harmony and are led to a belief in the divine reality. St. Thomas put it, 'By considering what God has made we can—first of all—catch a glimpse of the divine wisdom which has in some measure impressed a certain likeness to itself upon them'. We should see in the order and constancy, the beauty and pattern of nature, the divine wisdom and not in the exceptional and the bizarre. To suggest that the whole course of history is bound up with some unique event which happened at one time and in one place in a universe which has had nearly 6,000 million years of existence may strain the scientific conscience of even ordinary people. Heaven mingles with earth from the very start.

Goethe tells us that Faust investigated all branches of human knowledge, found no answers that would satisfy him and reached the place of *nothing* in his quest for truth. He exclaims: 'And here I am at last, a very fool, with useless learning curst, no wiser than at first'. His learning proves useless, his quest meaningless. He is faced with despair. He opens an ancient book and his eyes fall on the seal of Solomon —the two triangles placed upside down, signifying the interpenetration of lower and higher nature. A change comes over him and he exclaims:

'Ha, what new life divine, intense, floods in a moment every sense. I feel the dawn of youth again. . . . Was it a God who wrote these signs?' Earth and heaven are intermingled.[4] He has a new understanding of the visible world. Even at the moment when his journey had led him to darkness, a new light is revealed.

Science is empirical; it is non-dogmatic. It is openminded. Religious truths which are commended to us should not be mixed up with incredible dogmas. They must be based on experience, not of the physical world but of the religious reality. Even the concepts of science acquire their validity in experience. Experience is not limited to perceptual experience or the date of introspection. It should take into account para-normal phenomena and spiritual insights.

If scientific truth is what works in experience, religious truth also can be put to the same test. If we take the raw material of human nature and process it through detachment, humility and love, knowledge of God is attained. Religious exercises are intended to produce religious results. Albert Schweitzer observes: 'Rational thinking which is free from assumptions ends in mysticism'.[5]

The Eastern emphasis on religion as experience or life is being increasingly accepted by the religious people of all denominations. It is not faith but works that are needed. Not all those who say Lord, Lord, but those who do the will of God.[6] Talmud has it: 'Would that they had forgotten my name and done that which I commanded of them'. The utterly superficial character of our religious faith was given a practical demonstration in the Second World War when adherents of religions dragged themselves down to incredible depths.

To conform to the will of the Supreme, personal sanctification is necessary. The flame of spirit must be kindled in each human soul. 'Thus saith the Lord God . . . I will put a new spirit within you; and I will take the stony heart out of their flesh and will give them an heart of flesh'.[7] The way to this spiritual change is through detachment which develops the qualities of truth and honesty, chastity and sobriety, mercy and forgiveness. So long as we are dominated by our own passions and desires we will flout our neighbour, never leave him in peace, build institutions and societies which mirror our violent impulses, aggression and greed. The change from self-centredness to God-centredness brings with it a peace and radiance of living. We reach the deepest vision into the nature of the Real by devotion, contemplation and detachment. The basic element in religion is not the intellectual acceptance of dogmatic principles or historic events. These are but the preparation for the experience which affects our entire being, which ends our disquiet, our anguish, the sense of the aimlessness of our fragile and fugitive existence. St. Ambrose says 'Not by dialectic did it please the Lord God to save His people'.[8] Religion is not mere contemplation of the truth but suffering for it. The human mind is sadly crippled in its religious thinking by the belief that truth has been found, embodied, standardised, and nothing remains for man to do but to reproduce feebly some precious features of an immutable perfection. Such a view of rationalistic self-sufficiency overlooks the quality of religion as spiritual adventure. In the Eastern religions, the fulfilment of man's life is an experience in which every aspect of his being is raised to its highest extent. We pass from darkness to light. We feel caught up in a universal purpose. Our being is integrated, our solitude is ended. We are no longer the victims of the world around us but its masters. Every religious seer from the moment he has the vision and is moved to the depths of his being launches on a new path. The Buddha or Jesus is a redeemer or saviour only in so far as he calls upon us to be born anew. In their life and teaching they set us examples of conversion whereby we break the bonds that are laid on us by our first birth and by nature and rise above our original imperfection. When our consciousness is raised above the normal, when *meta-noia* occurs, we apprehend the unknowable and experience a joy so extreme that no language is adequate to describe the ravishment of the soul, when it meets in its own depths the ground of its own life and of all reality.

This awareness of Absolute Being which the seers speak of is ineffable.[9] The Ineffable which we encounter can be *shown* but not said, in the words of Ludwig Wittgenstein.[10] Whitehead has some excellent words on this subject: 'It is characteristic of the learned mind to exalt words. Yet mothers can ponder many things which their lips cannot express. These many things which are thus known constitute the ultimate religious evidence beyond which there is no appeal'.[11] When the experience is communicated through symbols, there is variety in the latter which are shaped by the knowledge and beliefs of the seers. The basic experience is, however, the same whether we deal with Hindu, Buddhist, Christian and Sufi mystics. The late Dean Inge said that 'whatever their creed, date or nationality, the witness of the mystics is wonderfully unanimous'.[12]

When the integral insight or the experience of the whole self is interpreted for purposes of communication by intellectual symbols, the latter are only symbolic. Eternity cannot be translated fully into categories of time, awareness of being cannot be adequately expressed in terms of existence, in spatio-temporal symbols. Yet they are not unrelated. Some of the religious ideas are results of profound insight. The symbols and images are used as aids to the worship of God, though they are not objects of worship themselves.

When we frame theories of religion we turn the being of the soul

into the having of a thing. We transform what originally comprehended our being into some object which we ourselves comprehend.
The total experience becomes an item of knowledge. The notions of God
formed by men are not God Himself. The theories of God are tested
by the facts or experiences of religion which prompted them. We should
not take them as final and universally binding.

The Absolute which is beyond the distinctions of subject and object, as the divine subject illumines the plane of cosmic objectiva-
tion, sustains and absorbs it. The world which science studies is the
revelation of spirit. All nature and life are sacramental.

When we say that God wills this world, it does not mean that
His will is capricious. It only suggests that universal possibility is
limitless and unpredictable. It also means that the created world cannot assume an absolute character. Were it so, then the relative would
be absolute. Even as human beings are conformed to God, made in
His image—otherwise they would not exist,—the world is the reflection of God. Even as we are different from God, the world is different
from God.

Love of neighbour is taught by all religions but the capacity to
love is difficult to attain. Growth in spiritual life is the only force
which gives us the capacity to love our neighbour, even when we
are not naturally inclined to do so. In the *Epistle of St. James,* it
says: 'Whence come wars and fightings among you? Come they not
hence, even of your desires, that war in your members'. Conflicting
desires within men lead to strains and conflicts among men. We must
be at harmony within ourselves. The words of St. Teresa are full of
meaning. 'Christ has no body now on earth but yours; yours are the
feet with which He goes about doing good; yours are the hands with
which He blesses'. William Law, the great eighteenth century mystic
said: 'By love I do not mean any natural tenderness, which is more
or less in people according to their constitution; but I mean a larger
principle of soul, founded in reason and piety which makes us tender,
kind and gentle to all our fellow creatures as creatures of God and
for His sake'.[13] This world has long suffered and bled from religious
intolerance. Even the political intolerance of our time which has
become as despotic, as universal and as bitter as any religious conflict
has assumed a religious garb reminding us of the Crusades of the
Middle Ages. The motive that impelled the Christian armies to
march eastward was faith. But sincerity of faith is not a security
against wild intolerance. The Crusaders thought that they were fighting
for the Christian God against the Muslim God. They could not
conceive it to be possible that the God of Islam might be the same
God on whom they themselves relied.[14] All too often men feel that

their loyalty to their religious society absolves them from the restraints they would impose on their private actions. We become ambitious not for ourselves but for our religious organisations. The phenomenon is described by William Law as 'turning to God without turning from self'. All the lusts and prejudices of the heart are retained but identified with some supposedly religious cause. 'Pride, self-exaltation, hatred and persecution, under a cloak of religious zeal will sanctify actions which nature, left to itself, would be ashamed to own'. We are prepared to burn and torture in the name of the love of God. Mankind seems to be involved in a corporate system of evil to which it seems to be in bondage. It appears as though some monster had taken charge of it, which possesses men and situations, making the best endeavours of honest men and using their good impulses for evil purposes. If God is love,[15] He cannot be a jealous God. With jealous God goes the doctrine of the chosen people. If God's light is the light that lighteth every man[16] that He left not Himself without witness[17] the adherents of religions other than our own are not shut out from the love of God. There are alternative approaches to the mystery of God.

At its depth, religion in its silences and expressions is the same. There is a common ground on which the different religious traditions rest. This common ground belongs of right to all of us, as it has its source in the non-historical, the eternal. The same elements appear in the experiences of the seers of the different religions. We all seek the same goal under different banners. When we get across the frontiers of formulas and the rigidities of regulations, the same spiritual life is to be found. The universality of fundamental ideas which historical studies demonstrate is the hope of the future. It emphasises the profound truth which Eastern religions had always stressed, the transcendent unity underlying the empirical diversity of religions.

There have been in the Christian world too, many profound thinkers who did not believe in spiritual exclusiveness. Nicholas of Cusa was prepared to recognise elements of truth in non-Christian religions. According to him Christianity should give as well as receive. He believed in the *coincidentia oppositorum,* i.e. everything lives and takes effect by reason of being the point of intersection of two opposite forces. God is all-embracing infinity and is found in even the smallest thing.[18] Professor Arnold J. Toynbee[19] writes that he would 'express his personal belief that the four higher religions that were alive in the age in which he was living were four variations on a single theme, and that, if all the four components of this heavenly music of the spheres could be audible on earth simultaneously, and with equal clarity, to one pair of human ears, the happy hearer would find himself listening, not to a discord, but to a harmony'. He does not believe that any one religion is an exclusive and definitive revelation of spiritual truth. To deny to other religions that they may be 'God's chosen and sufficient channels for revealing Himself to some human souls, is for me, to be guilty of blasphemy'. He quotes Symmachus who says: 'the heart of so great a mystery can never be reached by following one road only'.[20] Archbishop William Temple puts it in a different way: 'All that is noble in the non-Christian systems of thought or conduct or worship is the work of Christ upon them and within them. By the Word of God—that is to say, by Jesus Christ— Isaiah and Plato and Zoroaster and (the) Buddha and Confucius conceived and uttered such truths as they declared. There is only one divine light, and every man in his measure is enlightened by it. Yet, each has only a few rays of that light, which needs all the wisdom of all the human traditions to manifest the entire compass of its spectrum'.[21]

The history of Christianity shows how in its great days it was capable of giving as well as receiving. It has been perpetually changing its emphasis and even surrendering its dogmas. It adapted itself to the needs of the Roman Empire when it converted it, of the barbarian world which had its own cultural traditions and social institutions. The medieval Catholic belief in the impossibility of salvation outside the Church has faded away. I do not think there are many today who support the clear cut ruling of Lateran IV, *De Fide Catholica*: 'There is only one universal Church of the faithful and outside it none at all can be saved'. In this changing world even dogmas change. Take, for example, the medieval doctrine of the eternal perdition of unbaptised infants. Take Augustine's words: 'Hold fast to this truth, that not only men of rational age but even babes who die without the sacrament of baptism in the name of Father, Son and Holy Ghost, pass from this world to be punished in eternal fire'.[22] According to the Catholic *Encyclopædia,* as late as A.D. 1100, 'St. Anselm was at one with St. Augustine in holding that unbaptised children share in the positive sufferings of the damned'. The authoritative 'Catechism of the *Council of Trent*' (1566) holds that unbaptised children are 'born to eternal misery and perdition'. Catholics do not accept this dogma today.

We should not insist on an objective, universally valid doctrinal content. Where everybody thinks alike nobody thinks at all. In a world community each individual will have freedom to evolve his own realisation of the Supreme and the historical faiths will remain free to grow according to their own genius. Each religion contributes to the richness of the whole even as each note contributes to the complexity and harmony of the music of the symphony. In the present crisis, the spiritual forces of the world must come together and the great religious traditions should transcend their differences of form, underline their basic unity and draw from it the strength necessary to counter materialistic determinism. The type of religion here outlined is scientific, empirical and humanistic. It fosters the full development of man which includes the spirit in man. It will not be silent in the face of man's inhumanity to man.

Islam attracted attention because it complained about the theological controversies in which Christians lost themselves neglecting the social problems. Communism again is attracting attention because it condemned the other-worldly and reactionary character of religion. Truly religious souls will identify themselves with the social and human revolution that is afoot and guide the aspirations of mankind for a better and fuller life.

Christ is the second Adam, the first born of a new race of men, who, as the spiritual kingdom is spread on earth, will achieve a unity of nature and supernature, comparable to our present union of mind and animal nature but transcending it as rational life transcends the sentient life below it. The effort of man to remake himself and remake the world in the pattern of a divine order gives greatness and significance to his failures. The Christian hope is the creation of a new species of spiritual personality of which the first fruits had already been manifested in Jesus and the saints. They are the heralds of truth on earth, the instruments of the Divine for the spread of spiritual religion. The process of creation is still going on. It is not complete. It is in the process of completion.[23]

CONCLUSION

We are living at the dawn of a new era of universal humanity. There is a thrill of hope, a flutter of expectation as when the first glimmer of dawn awakens the earth. Whether we like it or not we live in one world[24] and require to be educated to a common conception of human purpose and destiny. The different nations should live together as members of the human race, not as hostile entities but as friendly partners in the endeavour of civilisation. The strong shall help the weak and all shall belong to the one world federation of free nations. If we escape from the dangers attendant on the control by irresponsible men, of sources of power hitherto unimaginable, we will unite the peoples of all races in a community, catholic, comprehensive and co-operative. We will realise that no people or group of peoples has had a monopoly in contributing to the development of civilisation. We will recognise and celebrate the achievements of all nations and thus promote universal brotherhood. Especially in matters of religion we must understand the valuable work of the sages of other countries and ages.

Peace is not the mere absence of war; it is the development of a strong fellow-feeling, an honest appreciation of other people's ideas and values. Distinctions of a physical character diminish in importance as the understanding of the significance of the inner life of man increases. We need, not merely a closer contact between East and West but a closer union, a meeting of minds and a union of hearts.

Mankind stems from one origin from which it has figured out in many forms. It is now striving toward the reconciliation of that which has been split up. The separation of East and West is over. The history of the new world, the one world, has begun. It promises to be large in extent, varied in colour, rich in quality.

NOTES

1. For St. Paul, man is 'spirit and soul and body', I *Thessalonians* V: 23.

2. H. G. Wood, in his contribution to the book, *Has the Church Failed?* writes: 'In spite of the contribution of many profound, honest and courageous Christian thinkers and teachers during the last hundred years, in general, the Christian mind has not yet adequately come to terms with the scientific temper and with modern knowledge'. p. 153.

3. 'It is to him who masters our minds by the force of truth and not to those who enslave them by violence that we owe our reverence' said Voltaire. 'Minds are conquered not by arms but by greatness of soul' said Spinoza. Satyam eva jayate nānṛtam. Truth alone conquers, not untruth. This is the motto of the Indian nation.

4. Eternity enters into time, and it is in time that all movement takes place. . . . Eternity is not limited by the conditions of time and is eternal in virtue of its cyclical recurrence'. *Hermetica* Asclepius III.

5. *Philosophy of Civilisation* (1923).

6. Oliver Cromwell in a letter to his son from Ireland on April 2, 1650 writes: 'The true knowledge is not literal or speculative, but the inward transforming the mind to it'. See G. M. Trevelyan, *An Autobiography and Other Essays* (1949) p. 170.

7. *Ezekiel* XI: 16 and 19.

8. Non in dialectica complacuit Domino Deo salvum facere populum suum. *De Fide* I. 5.42.

9. Goethe in *Faust* says: 'With the people and especially with the clergy, who have him daily upon their tongues, God becomes a phrase, a mere name which they utter without any accompanying idea. But if they were penetrated with this greatness, they would rather be dumb, for very reverence would not dare to name him'.

10. *Tractatus logico philosophicus,* E.T. 56. 522, p. 187.

11. *Religion in the Making,* p. 67.

12. *The Philosophy of Plotinus,* Vol. II, p. 143.

13. yatra kvāpi sthito dharme sadācāraparo yadi,
yāyād avaśyam kalyāṇam iti dṛṣṭiḥ sudarśanam.

To whatever system of religion one may belong, if he is inclined towards good conduct, he will certainly attain happiness. This view is the right one. *Subodhavānīprakāśa* (1938) p. 25.

14. The historian of the Crusades, Mr. Steven Runciman, concludes his account with very significant words which have a bearing on the contemporary world situation: 'In the long sequence of interaction and fusion between Orient and Occident out of which our civilisation has grown, the Crusades were a tragic and destructive episode. The historian, as he gazes back across the centuries, must find his admiration overcast by sorrow at the witness that it bears to the limitations of human nature. There was so much courage and so little honour, so much devotion and so little understanding. High ideals were besmirched by cruelty and greed, enterprise and endurance by a blind and narrow self-righteousness; and the Holy War itself was nothing more than a long act of

intolerance in the name of God, which is the sin against the Holy Ghost'.
A History of the Crusades, Vol. III (1954) p. 480.

15. I *John* IV:16.　　　　16. *John* I:9.　　　　17. *Acts* XIV:17.

18. Cyrus, the Persian Emperor, when he overthrew the Babylonians under whom Judaea was, gave the Jews all possible help for rebuilding Jerusalem and its temple. It is interesting to know that in Hungary, under the leadership of its ruler, Prince Sigismund, the Diet of Torda in 1557 issued a decree 'that everyone may freely embrace the religion and faith that he has preferred and may support preachers of his own religion, and that neither party shall disturb the other's worship or do harm or inflict injury on the other' quoted in *Hibbert Journal,* January 1954, p. 157.

19. *A Study of History,* Vol. II (1954) p. 428.

20. Professor Toynbee explains his position in clear terms: In our spiritual struggle, he says 'I guess that both the West and the world are going to turn away from man—worshipping ideologies—Communism and secular individualism alike—and become converted to an Oriental religion coming neither from Russia nor from the West. I guess that this will be the Christian religion that came to the Greeks and the Romans from Palestine, with one of two elements in traditional Christianity discarded and replaced by a new element from India. I expect and hope that this avatar of Christianity will include the vision of God as being Love. But I also expect and hope that it will discard the other traditional Christian vision of God as being a jealous god, and that it will reject the self-glorification of this jealous god's "chosen people" as being unique. This is where India comes in, with her belief (complementary to the vision of God as Love) that there may be more than one illuminating and saving approach to the mystery of the universe.' *Times Literary Supplement* (April 16, 1954) p. 249.

21. *Readings in Saint John's Gospel,* First Series (1939).

22. De hoc saeculo transeunt sempiterna igne puniendos.

23. *Colossians* I:18.

24. Gone are the days when madness was confined
　　By seas or hills from spreading through Mankind:
　　When, though a Nero fooled upon a string,
　　Wisdom still reigned unruffled in Peking;
　　And God in welcome smiled from Buddha's face,
　　Though Calvin in Geneva preached of grace.
　　For now our linked-up globe has shrunk so small,
　　One Hitler in it means mad days for all.
　　Through the whole World each wave of worry spreads,
　　And Ipoh dreads the war that Ipsden dreads.

　　　　Martyn Skinner: *Letters to Malaya,* I and II, 1941, pp. 34–5.

JUST EASE THESE DARBIES TO THE WEST

Herman Melville

MOBY DICK

THE GRAND ARMADA

The long and narrow peninsula of Malacca, extending south-eastward from the territories of Birmah, forms the most southerly point of all Asia. In a continuous line from that peninsula stretch the long islands of Sumatra, Java, Bally, and Timor; which, with many others, form a vast mole, or rampart, lengthwise connecting Asia with Australia, and dividing the long unbroken Indian ocean from the thickly studded oriental archipelagoes. This rampart is pierced by several sally-ports for the convenience of ships and whales; conspicuous among which are the straits of Sunda and Malacca. By the straits of Sunda, chiefly, vessels bound to China from the west, emerge into the China seas.

Those narrow straits of Sunda divide Sumatra from Java; and standing midway in that vast rampart of islands, buttressed by that bold green promontory, known to seamen as Java Head; they not a little correspond to the central gateway opening into some vast walled empire: and considering the inexhaustible wealth of spices, and silks, and jewels, and gold, and ivory, with which the thousand islands of that oriental sea are enriched, it seems a significant provision of nature, that such treasures, by the very formation of the land, should at least bear the appearance, however ineffectual, of being guarded from the all-grasping western world. The shores of the Straits of Sunda are unsupplied with those domineering fortresses which guard the entrances to the Mediterranean, the Baltic, and the Propontis. Unlike the Danes, these Orientals do not demand the obsequious homage of lowered top-sails from the endless procession of ships before the wind, which for centuries past, by night and by day, have passed between the islands of Sumatra and Java, freighted with the costliest cargoes of the east. But while they freely waive a ceremonial like this, they do by no means renounce their claim to more solid tribute.

Time out of mind the piratical proas of the Malays, lurking among the low shaded coves and islets of Sumatra, have sallied out upon the vessels sailing through the straits, fiercely demanding tribute at the point of their spears. Though by the repeated bloody chastisements they have received at the hands of European cruisers, the audacity of these corsairs has of late been somewhat repressed; yet, even at the present day, we occasionally hear of English and American vessels, which, in those waters, have been remorselessly boarded and pillaged.

With a fair, fresh wind, the Pequod was now drawing nigh to these straits; Ahab purposing to pass through them into the Javan sea, and thence, cruising northwards, over waters known to be frequented here and there by the Sperm Whale, sweep inshore by the Philippine Islands, and gain the far coast of Japan, in time for the great whaling season there. By these means, the circumnavigating Pequod would sweep almost all the known Sperm Whale cruising grounds of the world, previous to descending upon the Line in the Pacific; where Ahab, though everywhere else foiled in his pursuit, firmly counted upon giving battle to Moby Dick, in the sea he was most known to frequent; and at a season when he might most reasonably be presumed to be haunting it.

But how now? in this zoned quest, does Ahab touch no land? does his crew drink air? Surely, he will stop for water. Nay. For a long time, now, the circus-running sun had raced within his fiery ring, and needs no sustenance but what's in himself. So Ahab. Mark this, too, in the whaler. While other hulls are loaded down with alien stuff, to be transferred to foreign wharves; the world-wandering whale-ship carries no cargo but herself and crew, their weapons and their wants. She has a whole lake's contents bottled in her ample hold. She is ballasted with utilities; not altogether with unusable pig-lead and kentledge. She carries years' water in her. Clear old prime Nantucket water; which, when three years afloat, the Nantucketer, in the Pacific, prefers to drink before the brackish fluid, but yesterday rafted off in casks, from the Peruvian or Indian streams. Hence it is, that, while other ships may have gone to China from New

York, and back again, touching at a score of ports, the whale-ship, in all that interval, may not have sighted one grain of soil; her crew having seen no man but floating seamen like themselves. So that did you carry them the news that another flood had come; they would only answer— "Well, boys, here's the ark!"

Now, as many Sperm Whales had been captured off the western coast of Java, in the near vicinity of the Straits of Sunda; indeed, as most of the ground, roundabout, was generally recognised by the fishermen as an excellent spot for cruising; therefore, as the Pequod gained more and more upon Java Head, the look-outs were repeatedly hailed, and admonished to keep wide awake. But though the green palmy cliffs of the land soon loomed on the starboard bow, and with delighted nostrils the fresh cinnamon was snuffed in the air, yet not a single jet was descried. Almost renouncing all thought of falling in with any game hereabouts, the ship had well nigh entered the straits, when the customary cheering cry was heard from aloft, and ere long a spectacle of singular magnificence saluted us.

But here be it premised, that owing to the unwearied activity with which of late they have been hunted over all four oceans, the Sperm Whales, instead of almost invariably sailing in small detached companies, as in former times, are now frequently met with in extensive herds, sometimes embracing so great a multitude, that it would almost seem as if numerous nations of them had sworn solemn league and covenant for mutual assistance and protection. To this aggregation of the Sperm Whale into such immense caravans, may be imputed the circumstance that even in the best cruising grounds, you may now sometimes sail for weeks and months together, without being greeted by a single spout; and then be suddenly saluted by what sometimes seems thousands on thousands.

Broad on both bows, at the distance of some two or three miles, and forming a great semicircle, embracing one half of the level horizon, a continuous chain of whale-jets were up-playing and sparkling in the noon-day air. Unlike the straight perpendicular twin-jets of the Right Whale, which, dividing at top, fall over in two branches, like the cleft drooping boughs of a willow, the single forward-slanting spout of the Sperm Whale presents a thick curled bush of white mist, continually rising and falling away to leeward.

Seen from the Pequod's deck, then, as she would rise on a high hill of the sea, this host of vapory spouts, individually curling up into the air, and beheld through a blending atmosphere of bluish haze, showed like the thousand cheerful chimneys of some dense metropolis, descried of a balmy autumnal morning, by some horseman on a height.

As marching armies approaching an unfriendly defile in the mountains, accelerate their march, all eagerness to place that perilous passage in their rear, and once more expand in comparative security upon the plain; even so did this vast fleet of whales now seem hurrying forward through the straits; gradually contracting the wings of their semicircle, and swimming on, in one solid, but still crescentic centre.

Crowding all sail the Pequod pressed after them; the harpooneers handling their weapons, and loudly cheering from the heads of their yet suspended boats. If the wind only held, little doubt had they, that chased through these Straits of Sunda, the vast host would only deploy into the Oriental seas to witness the capture of not a few of their number. And who could tell whether, in that congregated caravan, Moby Dick himself might not temporarily be swimming, like the worshipped white-elephant in the coronation procession of the Siamese! So with stun-sail piled on stun-sail, we sailed along, driving these leviathans before us; when, of a sudden, the voice of Tashtego was heard, loudly directing attention to something in our wake.

Corresponding to the crescent in our van, we beheld another in the rear. It seemed formed of detached white vapors, rising and falling something like the spouts of the whales; only they did not so completely come and go; for they constantly hovered, without finally disappearing. Levelling his glass at this sight, Ahab quickly revolved in his pivot-hole, crying, "Aloft there, and rig whips and buckets to wet the sail;—Malays, sir, and after us!"

As if too long lurking behind the headlands, till the Pequod should fairly have entered the straits, these rascally Asiatics were now in hot pursuit, to make up for their over-cautious delay. But when the swift Pequod, with a fresh leading wind, was herself in hot chase; how very kind of these tawny philanthropists to assist in speeding her on to her own chosen pursuit,—mere riding-whips and rowels to her, that they were. As with glass under arm, Ahab to-and-fro paced the deck; in his forward turn beholding the monsters he chased, and in the after one the blood-thirsty pirates chasing *him;* some such fancy as the above seemed his. And when he glanced upon the green walls of the watery defile in which the ship was then sailing, and bethought him that through that gate lay the route to his vengeance, and beheld, how that through that same gate he was now both chasing and being chased to his deadly end; and not only that, but a herd of remorseless wild pirates and inhuman atheistical devils were infernally cheering him on with their curses;—when all these conceits had passed through his brain, Ahab's brow was left gaunt and ribbed, like the black sand beach after some stormy tide had been gnawing it, without being able to drag the firm thing from its place.

But thoughts like these troubled very few of the reckless crew; and when, after steadily dropping and dropping the pirates astern, the Pequod at last shot by the vivid green Cockatoo Point on the Sumatra side, emerging at last upon the broad waters beyond; then, the harpooneers seemed more to grieve that the swift whales had been gaining upon the ship, than to rejoice that the ship had so victoriously gained upon the Malays. But still driving on in the wake of the whales, at length they seemed abating their speed; gradually the ship neared them; and the wind now dying away, word was passed to spring to the boats. But no sooner did the herd, by some presumed wonderful instinct of the Sperm Whale, become notified of the three keels that were after them,—though as yet a mile in their rear,—than they rallied again, and forming in close ranks and battalions, so that their spouts all looked like flashing lines of stacked bayonets, moved on with redoubled velocity.

Stripped to our shirts and drawers, we sprang to the white-ash, and after several hours' pulling were almost disposed to renounce the chase, when a general pausing commotion among the whales gave animating tokens that they were now at last under the influence of that strange perplexity of inert irresolution, which, when the fishermen perceive it in the whale, they say he is gallied. The compact martial columns in which they had been hitherto rapidly and steadily swimming, were now broken up in one measureless rout; and like King Porus' elephants in the Indian battle with Alexander, they seemed going mad with consternation. In all directions expanding in vast irregular circles, and aimlessly swimming hither and thither, by their short thick spoutings, they plainly betrayed their distraction of panic. This was still more strangely evinced by those of their number, who, completely paralysed as it were, helplessly floated like water-logged dismantled ships on the sea. Had these Leviathans been but a flock of simple sheep, pursued over the pasture by three fierce wolves, they could not possibly have evinced such excessive dismay. But this occasional timidity is characteristic of almost all herding creatures. Though banding together in tens of thousands, the lion-maned buffaloes of the West have fled before a solitary horseman. Witness, too, all human beings, how when herded together in the sheepfold of a theatre's pit, they will, at the slightest alarm of fire, rush helter-skelter for the outlets, crowding, trampling, jamming, and remorselessly dashing each other to death. Best, therefore, withhold any amazement at the strangely gallied whales before us, for there is no folly of the beast of the earth which is not infinitely outdone by the madness of men.

Though many of the whales, as has been said, were in violent motion, yet it is to be observed that as a whole the herd neither advanced nor retreated, but collectively remained in one place. As is customary in those cases, the boats at once separated, each making for some one lone whale on the outskirts of the shoal. In about three minutes' time, Queequeg's harpoon was flung; the stricken fish darted blinding spray in our faces, and then running away with us like light, steered straight for the heart of the herd. Though such a movement on the part of the whale struck under such circumstances, is in no wise unprecedented; and indeed is almost always more or less anticipated; yet does it present one of the more perilous vicissitudes of the fishery. For as the swift monster drags you deeper and deeper into the frantic shoal, you bid adieu to circumspect life and only exist in a delirious throb.

As, blind and deaf, the whale plunged forward, as if by sheer power of speed to rid himself of the iron leech that had fastened to him; as we thus tore a white gash in the sea, on all sides menaced as we flew, by the crazed creatures to and fro rushing about us; our beset boat was like a ship mobbed by ice-isles in a tempest, and striving to steer through complicated channels and straits, knowing not at what moment it may be locked in and crushed.

But not a bit daunted, Queequeg steered us manfully; now sheering off from this monster directly across our route in advance; now edging away from that, whose colossal flukes were suspended overhead, while all the time, Starbuck stood up in the bows, lance in hand, pricking out of our way whatever whales he could reach by short darts, for there was no time to make long ones. Nor were the oarsmen quite idle, though their wonted duty was now altogether dispensed with. They chiefly attended to the shouting part of the business. "Out of the way, Commodore!" cried one, to a great dromedary that of a sudden rose bodily to the surface, and for an instant threatened to swamp us. "Hard down with your tail, there!" cried a second to another, which, close to our gunwale, seemed calmly cooling himself with his own fan-like extremity.

All whale-boats carry certain curious contrivances, originally invented by the Nantucket Indians, called druggs. Two thick squares of wood of equal size are stoutly clenched together, so that they cross each other's grain at right angles; a line of considerable length is then attached to the middle of this block, and the other end of the line being looped, it can in a moment be fastened to a harpoon. It is chiefly among gallied whales that this drugg is used. For then, more whales are close round you than you can possibly chase at one time. But sperm whales are not every day encountered; while you may, then, you must kill all you can. And if you cannot kill them all at once, you must wing them, so that they can be afterwards killed at your leisure. Hence it is, that at times like these the drugg comes into requisition. Our boat was furnished with three of them. The first and second were successfully darted, and we saw the whales staggeringly running off, fettered by the enormous sidelong resistance of the towing drugg. They were cramped like malefactors with the chain and ball. But upon flinging the third, in the act of tossing overboard the clumsy wooden block, it caught under one of the seats of the boat, and in an instant tore it out and carried it away, dropping the oarsman in the boat's bottom as the seat slid from under him. On both sides the sea came in at the wounded planks, but we stuffed two or three drawers and shirts in, and so stopped the leaks for the time.

It had been next to impossible to dart these drugged-harpoons, were it not that as we advanced into the herd, our whale's way greatly diminished; moreover, that as we went still further and further from the circumference of commotion, the direful disorders seemed waning. So that when at last the jerking harpoon drew out, and the towing whale sideways vanished; then, with the tapering force of his parting momentum, we glided between two whales into the innermost heart of the shoal, as if from some mountain torrent we had slid into a serene valley lake. Here the storms in the roaring glens between the outermost whales, were heard but not felt. In this central expanse the sea presented that smooth satin-like surface, called a sleek, produced by the subtle moisture thrown off by the whale in his more quiet moods. Yes, we were now in that enchanted calm which they say lurks at the heart of every commotion. And still in the distracted distance we beheld the tumults of the outer concentric circles, and saw successive pods of whales, eight or ten in each, swiftly going round and round, like multiplied spans of horses in a ring; and so closely shoulder to shoulder, that a Titanic circus-rider might easily have over-arched the middle ones, and so have gone round on their backs. Owing to the density of the crowd of reposing whales, more immediately surrounding the embayed axis of the herd, no possible chance of escape was at present afforded us. We must watch for a breach in the living wall that hemmed us in; the wall that had only admitted us in order to shut us up. Keeping at the centre of the lake, we were occasionally visited by small tame cows and calves; the women and children of this routed host.

Now, inclusive of the occasional wide intervals between the revolving outer circles, and inclusive of the spaces between the various pods in any one of those circles, the entire area at this juncture, embraced by the whole multitude, must have contained at least two or three square miles. At any rate—though indeed such a test at such a time might be deceptive—spoutings might be discovered from our low boat that seemed playing up almost from the rim of the horizon. I mention this circumstance, because, as if the cows and calves had been purposely locked up in this innermost fold; and as if the wide extent of the herd had hitherto prevented them from learning the precise cause of its stopping; or, possibly, being so young, unsophisticated, and every way innocent and inexperienced; however it may have been, these smaller whales—now and then visiting our becalmed boat from the margin of the lake—evinced a wondrous fearlessness and confidence, or else a still becharmed panic which it was impossible not to marvel at. Like household dogs they came snuffing round us, right up to our gunwales, and touching them; till it almost seemed that some spell had suddenly domesticated them. Queequeg patted their foreheads; Starbuck scratched their backs with his lance; but fearful of the consequences, for the time refrained from darting it.

But far beneath this wondrous world upon the surface, another and still stranger world met our eyes as we gazed over the side. For, suspended in those watery vaults, floated the forms of the nursing mothers of the whales, and those that by their enormous girth seemed shortly to become mothers. The lake, as I have hinted, was to a considerable depth exceedingly transparent; and as human infants while suckling will calmly and fixedly gaze away from the breast, as if leading two different lives at the time; and while yet drawing mortal nourishment, be still spiritually feasting upon some unearthly reminiscence;—even so did the young of these whales seem looking up towards us, but not at us, as if we were but a bit of Gulf-weed in their new-born sight. Floating on their sides, the mothers also seemed quietly eyeing us. One of these little infants, that from certain queer tokens seemed hardly a day old, might have measured some fourteen feet in length, and some six feet in girth. He was a little frisky; though as yet his body seemed scarce yet recovered from that irksome position it had so lately occupied in the maternal reticule; where, tail to head, and all ready for the final spring, the unborn whale lies bent like a Tartar's bow. The delicate side-fins, and the palms of his flukes, still freshly retained the plaited crumpled appearance of a baby's ears newly arrived from foreign parts.

"Line! line!" cried Queequeg, looking over the gunwale; "him fast! him fast!—Who line him! Who struck?—Two whale; one big, one little!"

"What ails ye, man?" cried Starbuck.

"Look-e here," said Queequeg pointing down.

As when the stricken whale, that from the tub has reeled out hundreds of fathoms of rope; as, after deep sounding, he floats up again, and shows the slackened curling line buoyantly rising and spiralling towards the air; so now, Starbuck saw long coils of the umbilical cord of Madame Leviathan, by which the young cub seemed still tethered to its dam. Not seldom in the rapid vicissitudes of the chase, this natural line, with the maternal end loose, becomes entangled with the hempen one, so that the cub is thereby trapped. Some of the subtlest secrets of the seas seemed divulged to us in this enchanted pond. We saw young Leviathan amours in the deep.[1]

And thus, though surrounded by circle upon circle of consternations and affrights, did these inscrutable creatures at the centre freely and fearlessly indulge in all peaceful concernments; yes, serenely revelled in dalliance and delight. But even so, amid the tornadoed Atlantic of my being, do I myself still for ever centrally disport in mute calm; and while ponderous planets of unwaning woe revolve round me, deep down and deep inland there I still bathe me in eternal mildness of joy.

Meanwhile, as we thus lay entranced, the occasional sudden frantic spectacles in the distance evinced the activity of the other boats, still engaged in drugging the whales on the frontier of the host; or possibly carrying on the war within the first circle, where abundance of room and some convenient retreats were afforded them. But the sight of the enraged drugged whales now and then blindly darting to and fro across the circles, was nothing to what at last met our eyes. It is sometimes the custom when fast to a whale more than commonly powerful and alert, to seek to hamstring him, as it were, by sundering or maiming his gigantic tail-tendon. It is done by darting a short-handled cutting-spade, to which is attached a rope for hauling it back again. A whale wounded (as we afterwards learned) in this part, but not effectually, as it seemed, had broken away from the boat, carrying along with him half of the harpoon line; and in the extraordinary agony of the wound, he was now dashing among the revolving circles like the lone mounted desperado Arnold, at the battle of Saratoga, carrying dismay wherever he went.

But agonizing as was the wound of this whale, and an appalling spectacle enough, any way; yet the peculiar horror with which he seemed to inspire the rest of the herd, was owing to a cause which at first the intervening distance obscured from us. But at length we perceived that by one of the unimaginable accidents of the fishery, this whale had become entangled in the harpoon-line that he towed; he had also run away with the cutting-spade in him; and while the free end of the rope attached to that weapon, had permanently caught in the coils of the harpoon-line round his tail, the cutting-spade itself had worked loose from his flesh. So that tormented to madness, he was now churning through the water, violently flailing with his flexible tail, and tossing the keen spade about him, wounding and murdering his own comrades.

This terrific object seemed to recall the whole herd from their stationary fright. First, the whales forming the margin of our lake began to crowd a little, and tumble against each other, as if lifted by half spent billows from afar; then the lake itself began faintly to heave and swell; the submarine bridal-chambers and nurseries vanished; in more and more contracting orbits the whales in the more central circles began to swim in thickening clusters. Yes, the long calm was departing. A low advancing hum was soon heard; and then like to the tumultuous masses of block-ice when the great river Hudson breaks up in Spring, the entire host of whales came tumbling upon their inner centre, as if to pile themselves up in one common mountain. Instantly Starbuck and Queequeg changed places; Starbuck taking the stern.

"Oars! Oars!" he intensely whispered, seizing the helm—"gripe your oars, and clutch your souls, now! My God, men, stand by! Shove him off, you Queequeg—the whale there!—prick him!—hit him! Stand up— stand up, and stay so! Spring men—pull, men; never mind their backs— scrape them!—scrape away!"

The boat was now all but jammed between two vast black bulks, leaving a narrow Dardanelles between their long lengths. But by desperate endeavor we at last shot into a temporary opening; then giving way rapidly, and at the same time earnestly watching for another outlet. After many similar hair-breadth escapes, we at last swiftly glided into what had just been one of the outer circles, but now crossed by random whales, all violently making for one centre. This lucky salvation was cheaply purchased by the loss of Queequeg's hat, who, while standing in the bows to prick the fugitive whales, had his hat taken clean from his head by the air-eddy made by the sudden tossing of a pair of broad flukes close by.

Riotous and disordered as the universal commotion now was, it soon resolved itself into what seemed a systematic movement; for having clumped together at last in one dense body, they then renewed their onward flight with augmented fleetness. Further pursuit was useless; but the boats still lingered in their wake to pick up what drugged whales might be dropped astern, and likewise to secure one which Flask had killed and waifed. The waif is a pennoned pole, two or three of which are carried by every boat; and when, when additional game is at hand, are inserted upright into the floating body of a dead whale, both to mark its place on the sea, and also as token of prior possession, should the boats of any other ship draw near.

The result of this lowering was somewhat illustrative of that sagacious saying in the Fishery,—the more whales the less fish. Of all the drugged whales only one was captured. The rest contrived to escape for the time, but only to be taken, as will hereafter be seen, by some other craft than the Pequod.

NOTE

1. The sperm whale, as with all other species of the Leviathan, but unlike most other fish, breeds indifferently at all seasons; after a gestation which may probably be set down at nine months, producing but one at a time; though in some few known instances giving birth to an Esau and Jacob:—a contingency provided for in suckling by two teats, curiously situated, one on each side of the anus; but the breasts themselves extend upwards from that. When by chance these precious parts in a nursing whale are cut by the hunter's lance, the mother's pouring milk and blood rivallingly discolor the sea for rods. The milk is very sweet and rich; it has been tasted by man; it might do well with strawberries. When overflowing with mutual esteem, the whales salute *more hominum*.

Herman Melville

PIERRE

PIERE JUST EMERGING FROM HIS TEENS

I.

There are some strange summer mornings in the country, when he who is but a sojourner from the city shall early walk forth into the fields, and be wonder-smitten with the trance-like aspect of the green and golden world. Not a flower stirs; the trees forget to wave; the grass itself seems to have ceased to grow; and all Nature, as if suddenly become conscious of her own profound mystery, and feeling no refuge from it but silence, sinks into this wonderful and indescribable repose.

Such was the morning in June, when, issuing from the embowered and high-gabled old home of his fathers, Pierre, dewily refreshed and spirit-ualized by sleep, gayly entered the long, wide, elm-arched street of the village, and half unconsciously bent his steps toward a cottage, which peeped into view near the end of the vista.

The verdant trance lay far and wide; and through it nothing came but the brindled kine, dreamily wandering to their pastures, followed, not driven, by ruddy-cheeked, white-footed boys.

As touched and bewitched by the loveliness of this silence, Pierre neared the cottage, and lifted his eyes, he swiftly paused, fixing his glance upon one upper, open casement there. Why now this impassioned, youthful pause? Why this enkindled check and eye? Upon the sill of the casement, a snow-white glossy pillow reposes, and a trailing shrub has softly rested a rich, crimson flower against it.

Well, mayst thou seek that pillow, thou odoriferous flower, thought Pierre; not an hour ago, her own cheek must have rested there. "Lucy!"

"Pierre!"

As heart rings to heart those voices rang, and for a moment, in the bright hush of the morning, the two stood silently but ardently eying each other, beholding mutual reflections of a boundless admiration and love.

"Nothing but Pierre," laughed the youth, at last; "thou hast forgotten to bid me good-morning."

"That would be little. Good-mornings, good-evenings, good days, weeks, months, and years to thee, Pierre;—bright Pierre!—Pierre!"

Truly, thought the youth, with a still gaze of inexpressible fondness; truly the skies do ope, and this invoking angel looks down.—"I would return thee thy manifold good-mornings, Lucy, did not that presume thou had'st lived through a night; and by Heaven, thou belong'st to the regions of an infinite day!"

"Fie, now, Pierre; why should ye youths always swear when ye love?"

"Because in us love is profane, since it mortally reaches toward the heaven in ye!"

"There thou fly'st again, Pierre; thou art always circumventing me so. Tell me, why should ye youths ever show so sweet an expertness in turning all trifles of ours into trophies of yours?"

"I know not how that is, but ever was it our fashion to do." And shaking the casement shrub, he dislodged the flower, and conspicuously fastened it in his bosom.—"I must away now, Lucy; see! under these colors I march."

"Bravissimo! oh, my only recruit!"

II.

Pierre was the only son of an affluent, and haughty widow; a lady who externally furnished a singular example of the preservative and beautifying influences of unfluctuating rank, health, and wealth, when joined to a fine mind of medium culture, uncankered by any inconsolable grief, and never worn by sordid cares. In mature age, the rose still miraculously clung to her cheek; litheness had not yet completely uncoiled itself from her waist, nor smoothness unscrolled itself from her brow, nor diamondness departed from her eyes. So that when lit up and bediademed by ballroom lights, Mrs. Glendinning still eclipsed far younger charms, and had she chosen to encourage them, would have been followed by a train of infatuated suitors, little less young than her own son Pierre.

But a reverential and devoted son seemed lover enough for this widow Bloom; and besides all this, Pierre when namelessly annoyed, and sometimes even jealously transported by the too ardent admiration of the handsome youths, who now and then, caught in unintended snares, seemed to entertain some insane hopes of wedding this unattainable being; Pierre had more than once, with a playful malice, openly sworn, that the man—gray-beard, or beardless—who should dare to propose marriage to his mother, that man would by some peremptory unrevealed agency immediately disappear from the earth.

This romantic filial love of Pierre seemed fully returned by the triumphant maternal pride of the widow, who in the clearcut lineaments and noble air of the son, saw her own graces strangely translated into the opposite sex. There was a striking personal resemblance between them; and as the mother seemed to have long stood still in her beauty, heedless of the passing years; so Pierre seemed to meet her half-way, and by a splendid precocity of form and feature, almost advanced himself to that mature stand-point in Time, where his pedestaled mother so long had stood. In the playfulness of their unclouded love, and with that strange license which a perfect confidence and mutual understanding at all points, had long bred between them, they were wont to call each other brother and sister. Both in public and private this was their usage; nor when thrown among strangers, was this mode of address ever suspected for a sportful assumption; since the amaranthiness of Mrs. Glendinning fully sustained this youthful pretension.— Thus freely and lightsomely for mother and son flowed on the pure joined current of life. But as yet the fair river had not borne its waves to those side-ways repelling rocks, where it was thenceforth destined to be forever divided into two unmixing streams.

An excellent English author of these times enumerating the prime advantages of his natal lot, cites foremost, that he first saw the rural light. So with Pierre. It had been his choice fate to have been born and nurtured in the country, surrounded by scenery whose uncommon loveliness was the perfect mould of a delicate and poetic mind; while the popular names of its finest features appealed to the proudest patriotic and family associations of the historic line of Glendinning. On the meadows which sloped away from the shaded rear of the manorial mansion, far to the winding river, an Indian battle had been fought, in the earlier days of the colony, and in that battle the paternal great-grandfather of Pierre, mortally wounded, had sat unhorsed on his saddle in the grass, with his dying voice, still cheering his men in the fray. This was Saddle-Meadows, a name likewise extended to the mansion and the village. Far beyond these plains, a day's walk for Pierre, rose the storied heights, where in the Revolutionary War his grandfather had for several months defended a rude but all-important stockaded fort, against the repeated combined assaults of Indians, Tories, and Regulars. From before that fort, the gentlemanly, but murderous half-breed, Brandt, had fled, but had survived to dine with General Glendinning, in the amicable times which followed that vindictive war. All the associations of Saddle-Meadows were full of pride to Pierre. The Glendinning deeds by which their estate had so long been held, bore the cyphers of three Indian kings, the aboriginal and only conveyancers of those noble woods and plains. Thus loftily, in the days of his circumscribed youth, did Pierre glance along the background of his race; little recking of that maturer and larger interior development, which should forever deprive these things of their full power of pride in his soul.

But the breeding of Pierre would have been unwisely contracted, had his youth been unintermittingly passed in these rural scenes. At a very early period he had begun to accompany his father and mother—and afterwards his mother alone—in their annual visits to the city; where naturally mingling in a large and polished society, Pierre had insensibly formed himself in the airier graces of life, without enfeebling the vigor derived from a martial race, and fostered in the country's clarion air.

Nor while thus liberally developed in person and manners, was Pierre deficient in a still better and finer culture. Not in vain had he spent long summer afternoons in the deep recesses of his father's fastidiously picked and decorous library; where the Spenserian nymphs had early led him into many a maze of all-bewildering beauty. Thus, with a graceful glow on his limbs, and soft, imaginative flames in his heart, did this Pierre glide toward maturity, thoughtless of that period of remorseless insight, when all these delicate warmths should seem frigid to him, and he should madly demand more ardent fires.

Nor had that pride and love which had so bountifully provided for the youthful nurture of Pierre, neglected his culture in the deepest element of all. It had been a maxim with the father of Pierre, that all gentleman-hood was vain; all claims to it preposterous and absurd, unless the primeval gentleness and golden humanities of religion had been so thoroughly wrought into the complete texture of the character, that he who pronounced himself gentleman, could also rightfully assume the meek, but kingly style of Christian. At the age of sixteen, Pierre partook with his mother of the Holy Sacraments.

It were needless, and more difficult, perhaps, to trace out precisely the absolute motives which prompted these youthful vows. Enough, that as to Pierre had descended the numerous other noble qualities of his ancestors; and as he now stood heir to their forests and farms; so by the same insensible sliding process, he seemed to have inherited their docile homage to a venerable Faith, which the first Glendinning had brought over sea, from beneath the shadow of an English minister. Thus in Pierre was the complete polished steel of the gentleman, girded with Religion's silken sash; and his great-grandfather's soldierly fate had taught him that the generous sash should, in the last bitter trial, furnish its wearer with Glory's shroud; so that what through life had been worn for Grace's sake, in death might safely hold the man. But while thus all alive to the beauty and poesy of his father's faith, Pierre little foresaw that this world hath a secret deeper than beauty, and Life some burdens heavier than death.

So perfect to Pierre had long seemed the illuminated scroll of his life thus far, that only one hiatus was discoverable by him in that sweetly-writ manuscript. A sister had been omitted from the text. He mourned that so delicious a feeling as fraternal love had been denied him. Nor could the fictitious title, which he so often lavished upon his mother, at all supply the absent reality. This emotion was most natural; and the full cause and reason of it even Pierre did not at that time entirely appreciate. For surely a gentle sister is the second best gift to a man; and it is first in point of occurrence; for the wife comes after. He who is sisterless, is as a bachelor before his time. For much that goes to make up the deliciousness of a wife, already lies in the sister.

"Oh, had my father but had a daughter!" cried Pierre; "some one whom I might love, and protect, and fight for, if need be. It must be a glorious thing to engage in a mortal quarrel on a sweet sister's behalf! Now, of all things, would to heaven, I had a sister!"

Thus, ere entranced in the gentler bonds of a lover; thus often would Pierre invoke heaven for a sister; but Pierre did not then know, that if there be any thing a man might well pray against, that thing is the responsive gratification of some of the devoutest prayers of his youth.

It may have been that this strange yearning of Pierre for a sister, had part of its origin in that still stranger feeling of loneliness he sometimes experienced, as not only the solitary head of his family, but the only surnamed male Glendinning extant. A powerful and populous family had by degrees run off into the female branches; so that Pierre found himself surrounded by numerous kinsmen and kinswomen, yet companioned by no surnamed male Glendinning, but the duplicate one reflected to him in the mirror. But in his more wonted natural mood, this thought was not wholly sad to him. Nay, sometimes it mounted into an exultant swell. For in the ruddiness, and flushfulness, and vaingloriousness of his youthful soul, he fondly hoped to have a monopoly of glory in capping the fame-column, whose tall shaft had been erected by his noble sires.

In all this, how unadmonished was our Pierre by that foreboding and prophetic lesson taught, not less by Palmyra's quarries, than by Palmyra's ruins. Among those ruins is a crumbling, uncompleted shaft, and some leagues off, ages ago left in the quarry, is the crumbling corresponding capital, also incomplete. These Time seized and spoiled; these Time crushed in the egg; and the proud stone that should have stood among the clouds, Time left abased beneath the soil. Oh, what quenchless feud is this, that Time hath with the sons of Men!

III.

It has been said that the beautiful country round about Pierre appealed to very proud memories. But not only through the mere chances of things, had that fine country become ennobled by the deeds of his sires, but in Pierre's eyes, all its hills and swales seemed as sanctified through their very long uninterrupted possession by his race.

That fond ideality which, in the eyes of affection, hallows the least trinket once familiar to the person of a departed love; with Pierre that talisman touched the whole earthly landscape about him; for remembering that on those hills his own fine fathers had gazed; through those woods, over these lawns, by that stream, along these tangled paths, many a grand-dame of his had merrily strolled when a girl; vividly recalling these things, Pierre deemed all that part of the earth a love-token; so that his very horizon was to him as a memorial ring.

The monarchical world very generally imagines, that in demagoguical America the sacred Past hath no fixed statues erected to it, but all things irreverently seethe and boil in the vulgar caldron of an everlasting uncrystalizing Present. This conceit would seem peculiarly applicable to the social condition. With no chartered aristocracy, and no law of entail, how can any family in America imposingly perpetuate itself? Certainly that common saying among us, which declares, that be a family conspicuous as it may, a single half-century shall see it abased; that maxim undoubtedly holds true with the commonalty. In our cities families rise and burst like bubbles in a vat. For indeed the democratic element operates as a subtile acid among us; forever producing new things by corroding the old; as in the south of France verdigris, the primitive material of one kind of green paint, is produced by grape-vinegar poured upon copper plates. Now in general nothing can be more significant of decay than the idea of corrosion; yet on the other hand, nothing can more vividly suggest luxuriance of life, than the idea of green as a color; for green is the peculiar signet of all-fertile Nature herself. Hereinby apt analogy we behold the marked anomalousness of America; whose character abroad, we need not be surprised, is misconceived, when we consider how strangely she contradicts all prior notions of human things; and how wonderfully to her, Death itself becomes transmuted into Life. So that political institutions, which in other lands seem above all things intensely artificial, with America seem to possess the divine virtue of a natural law; for the most mighty of nature's laws is this, that out of Death she brings Life.

Still, are there things in the visible world, over which ever-shifting Nature hath not so unbounded a sway. The grass is annually changed; but the limbs of the oak, for a long term of years, defy that annual decree. And if in America the vast mass of families be as the blades of grass, yet some few there are that stand as the oak; which, instead of decaying, annually puts forth new branches; whereby Time, instead of subtracting, is made to capitulate into a multiple virtue.

In this matter we will—not superciliously, but in fair spirit—compare pedigrees with England, and strange as it may seem at the first blush, not without some claim to equality. I dare say, that in this thing the Peerage Book is a good statistical standard whereby to judge her; since the compilers of that work can not be entirely insensible on whose patronage they most rely; and the common intelligence of our own people shall suffice to judge us. But the magnificence of names must not mislead us as to the humility of things. For as the breath in all our lungs is hereditary, and my present breath at this moment, is further descended than the body of the present High Priest of the Jews, so far as he can assuredly trace it; so mere names, which are also but air, do likewise revel in this endless descendedness. But if Richmond, and St. Albans, and Grafton, and Portland, and Buccleugh, be names almost old as England herself, the present Dukes of those names stop in their own genuine pedigrees at Charles II., and there find no very fine fountain; since what we would deem the least glorious parentage under the sun, is precisely the parentage of a Buccleugh, for example; whose ancestress could not well avoid being a mother, it is true, but had accidentally omitted the preliminary rite. Yet a king was the sire. Then only so much the worse; for if it be small insult to be struck by a pauper but mortal offense to receive a blow from a gentleman, then of all things the bye-blows of kings must be signally unflattering. In England the Peerage is kept alive by incessant restorations and creations. One man, George III., manufactured five hundred and twenty-two peers. An earldom, in abeyance for five centuries, has suddenly been assumed by some commoner, to whom it had not so much descended, as through the art of the lawyers been made flexibly to bend in that direction. For not Thames is so sinuous in his natural course, not the Bridgewater Canal more artificially conducted, than blood in the veins of that winding or manufactured nobility. Perishable as stubble, and fungous as the fungi, those grafted families successively live and die on the eternal soil of a name. In England this day, twenty-five hundred peerages are extinct; but the names survive. So that the empty air of a name is more endurable than a man, or than dynasties of men; the air fills man's lungs and puts life into a man, but man fills not the air, nor puts life into that.

All honor to the names then, and all courtesy to the men; but if St. Albans tell me he is all-honorable and all-eternal, I must still politely refer him to Nell Gwynne.

Beyond Charles II. very few indeed—hardly worthy of note—are the present titled English families which can trace any thing like a direct unvitiated blood-descent from the thief knights of the Norman. Beyond Charles II. their direct genealogies seem vain as though some Jew clothesman, with a tea-canister on his head, turned over the first chapter of St.

Matthew to make out his unmingled participation in the blood of King Saul, who had long died ere the career of the Cæsar began.

Now, not preliminarily to enlarge upon the fact that, while in England an immense mass of state-masonry is brought to bear as a buttress in upholding the hereditary existence of certain houses, while with us nothing of that kind can possibly be admitted; and to omit all mention of the hundreds of unobtrusive families in New England who, nevertheless, might easily trace their uninterrupted English lineage to a time before Charles the Blade: not to speak of the old and oriental-like English planter families of Virginia and the South; the Randolphs for example, one of whose ancestors, in King James' time, married Pocahontas the Indian Princess, and in whose blood therefore an underived aboriginal royalty was flowing over two hundred years ago; consider those most ancient and magnificent Dutch Manors at the North, whose perches are miles—whose meadows overspread adjacent countries—and whose haughty rent-deeds are held by their thousand farmer tenants, so long as grass grows and water runs; which hints of a surprising eternity for a deed, and seem to make lawyer's ink unobliterable as the sea. Some of those manors are two centuries old; and their present patrons or lords will show you stakes and stones on their estates put there—the stones at least—before Nell Gwynne the Duke-mother was born, and genealogies which, like their own river, Hudson, flow somewhat farther and straighter than the Serpentine brooklet in Hyde Park.

These far-descended Dutch meadows lie steeped in a Hindooish haze; an eastern patriarchalness sways its mild crook over pastures, whose tenant flocks shall there feed, long as their own grass grows, long as their own water shall run. Such estates seem to defy Time's tooth, and by conditions which take hold of the indestructible earth seem to contemporize their fee-simples with eternity. Unimaginable audacity of a worm that but crawls through the soil he so imperially claims!

In midland counties of England they boast of old oaken dining-halls where three hundred men-at-arms could exercise of a rainy afternoon, in the reign of the Plantagenets. But our lords, the Patroons, appeal not to the past, but they point to the present. One will show you that the public census of a county, is but part of the roll of his tenants. Ranges of mountains, high as Ben Nevis or Snowdon, are their walls; and regular armies, with staffs of officers, crossing rivers with artillery, and marching through primeval woods, and threading vast rocky defiles, have been sent out to distrain upon three thousand farmer-tenants of one landlord, at a blow. A fact most suggestive two ways; both whereof shall be nameless here.

But whatever one may think of the existence of such mighty lordships in the heart of a republic, and however we may wonder at their thus surviving, like Indian mounds, the Revolutionary flood; yet survive and exist they do, and are now owned by their present proprietors, by as good nominal title as any peasant owns his father's old hat, or any duke his great-uncle's old coronet.

For all this, then, we shall not err very widely if we humbly conceive, that—should she choose to glorify herself in that inconsiderable way— our America will make out a good general case with England in this short little matter of large estates, and long pedigrees—pedigrees I mean, wherein is no flaw.

IV.

In general terms we have been thus decided in asserting the great genealogical and real-estate dignity of some families in America, because in so doing we poetically establish the richly aristocratic condition of Master Pierre Glendinning, for whom we have before claimed some special family distinction. And to the observant reader the sequel will not fail to show, how important is this circumstance, considered with reference to the singularly developed character and most singular life-career of our hero. Nor will any man dream that the last chapter was merely intended for a foolish bravado, and not with a solid purpose in view.

Now Pierre stands on this noble pedestal; we shall see if he keeps that fine footing; we shall see if Fate hath not just a little bit of a small word or two to say in this world. But it is not laid down here that the Glendinnings dated back beyond Pharaoh, or the deeds of Saddle-Meadows to the Three Magi in the Gospels. Nevertheless, those deeds, as before hinted, did indeed date back to three kings—Indian kings—only so much the finer for that.

But if Pierre did not date back to the Pharaohs, and if the English farmer Hampdens were somewhat the seniors of even the oldest Glendinning; and if some American manors boasted a few additional years and square miles over his, yet think you that it is at all possible, that a youth of nineteen should—merely by way of trial of the thing—strew his ancestral kitchen hearth-stone with wheat in the stalk, and there standing in the chimney thresh out that grain with a flail, whose aerial evolutions had free play among all that masonry; were it not impossible for such a flailer so to thresh wheat in his own ancestral kitchen chimney without feeling just a little twinge or two of what one might call family pride? I should say not.

Or how think you it would be with this youthful Pierre, if every day descending to breakfast, he caught sight of an old tattered British banner or two, hanging over an arched window in his hall; and those banners captured by his grandfather, the general, in fair fight? Or how think you it would be if every time he heard the band of the military company of the village, he should distinctly recognize the peculiar tap of a British kettle-drum also captured by his grandfather in fair fight, and afterwards suitably inscribed on the brass and bestowed upon the Saddle-Meadows Artillery Corps? Or how think you it would be, if sometimes of a mild meditative Fourth of July morning in the country, he carried out with him into the garden by way of ceremonial cane, a long majestic, silver-tipped staff, a Major-General's baton, once wielded on the plume-nodding and musket-flashing review by the same grandfather several times here-in-before mentioned? I should say that considering Pierre was quite young and very unphilosophical as yet, and withal rather high-blooded; and sometimes read the History of the Revolutionary War, and possessed a mother who very frequently made remote social allusions to the epaulettes of the Major-General his grandfather;—I should say that upon all of these occasions, the way it must have been with him, was a very proud, elated sort of way. And if this seem but too fond and foolish in Pierre; and if you tell me that this sort of thing in him showed him no sterling Democrat, and that a truly noble man should never brag of any arm but his own; then I beg you to consider again that this Pierre was but a youngster as yet. And believe me you will pronounce Pierre a thorough-going Democrat in time; perhaps a little too Radical altogether to your fancy.

In conclusion, do not blame me if I here make repetition, and do verbally quote my own words in saying that *it had been the choice fate of Pierre to have been born and bred in the country.* For to a noble American youth this indeed—more than in any other land—this indeed is a most rare and choice lot. For it is to be observed, that while in other countries, the finest families boast of the country as their home; the more prominent among us, proudly cite the city as their seat. Too often the American that himself makes his fortune, builds him a great metropolitan house, in the most metropolitan street of the most metropolitan town. Whereas a European of the same sort would thereupon migrate into the country. That herein the European hath the better of it, no poet, no philosopher, and no aristocrat will deny. For the country is not only the most poetical and philosophical, but it is the most aristocratic part of this earth, for it is the most venerable, and numerous bards have en-nobled it by many fine titles. Whereas the town is the more plebeian portion: which, besides many other things, is plainly evinced by the dirty unwashed face perpetually worn by the town; but the country, like any Queen, is ever attended by scrupulous lady's maids in the guise of the seasons, and the town hath but one dress of brick turned up with stone; but the country hath a brave dress for every week in the year;

sometimes she changes her dress twenty-four times in the twenty-four hours; and the country weareth her sun by day as a diamond on a Queen's brow; and the stars by night as necklaces of gold beads; whereas the town's sun is smoky paste, and no diamond, and the town's stars are pinchbeck and not gold.

In the country then Nature planted our Pierre; because Nature intended a rare and original development in Pierre. Never mind if hereby she proved ambiguous to him in the end; nevertheless, in the beginning she did bravely. She blew her wind-clarion from the blue hills, and Pierre neighed out lyrical thoughts, as at the trumpet-blast, a war-horse paws himself into a lyric of foam. She whispered through her deep groves at eve, and gentle whispers of humanness, and sweet whispers of love, ran through Pierre's thought-veins, musical as water over pebbles. She lifted her spangled crest of a thickly-starred night, and forth at that glimpse of their divine Captain and Lord, ten thousand mailed thoughts of heroicness started up in Pierre's soul, and glared round for some insulted good cause to defend.

So the country was a glorious benediction to young Pierre; we shall see if that blessing pass from him as did the divine blessing from the Hebrews; we shall yet see again, I say, whether Fate hath not just a little bit of a word or two to say in this world; we shall see whether this wee little bit scrap of latinity be very far out of the way—*Nemo contra Deum nisi Deus ipse.*

V.

"Sister Mary," said Pierre, returned from his sunrise stroll, and tapping at his mother's chamber door:—"do you know, sister Mary, that the trees which have been up all night, are all abroad again this morning before you?—Do you not smell something like coffee, my sister?"

A light step moved from within toward the door; which opened, showing Mrs. Glendinning, in a resplendently cheerful morning robe, and holding a gay wide ribbon in her hand.

"Good morning, madam," said Pierre, slowly, and with a bow, whose genuine and spontaneous reverence amusingly contrasted with the sportive manner that had preceded it. For thus sweetly and religiously was the familiarity of his affections bottomed on the profoundest filial respect.

"Good afternoon to you, Pierre, for I suppose it is afternoon. But come, you shall finish my toilette;—here, brother—" reaching the ribbon—"now acquit yourself bravely—" and seating herself away from the glass, she awaited the good offices of Pierre.

"First Lady in waiting to the Dowager Duchess Glendinning," laughed Pierre, as bowing over before his mother, he gracefully passed the ribbon round her neck, simply crossing the ends in front.

"Well, what is to hold it there, Pierre?"

"I am going to try and tack it with a kiss, sister,—there!—oh, what a pity that sort of fastening won't always hold!—where's the cameo with the fawns, I gave you last night?—Ah! on the slab—you were going to wear it then?—Thank you, my considerate and most politic sister— there!—but stop—here's a ringlet gone romping—so now, dear sister, give that Assyrian toss to your head."

The haughtily happy mother rose to her feet, and as she stood before the mirror to criticize her son's adornings, Pierre, noticing the straggling tie of her slipper, knelt down and secured it. "And now for the urn," he cried, "madam!" and with a humorous gallantry, offering his arm to his mother, the pair descended to breakfast.

With Mrs. Glendinning it was one of those spontaneous maxims, which women sometimes act upon without ever thinking of, never to appear in the presence of her son in any dishabille that was not eminently becoming. Her own independent observation of things, had revealed to her many very common maxims, which often become operatively lifeless from a vicarious reception of them. She was vividly aware how immense was that influence, which, even in the closest ties of the heart, the merest appearances make upon the mind. And as in the admiring love and grace-ful devotion of Pierre lay now her highest joy in life; so she omitted no slightest trifle which could possibly contribute to the preservation of so sweet and flattering a thing.

Besides all this, Mary Glendinning was a woman, and with more than the ordinary vanity of women—if vanity it can be called—which in a life of nearly fifty years had never betrayed her into a single published impropriety, or caused her one known pang at the heart. Moreover, she had never yearned for admiration; because that was her birthright by the eternal privilege of beauty; she had always possessed it; she had not to turn her head for it, since spontaneously it always encompassed her. Vanity, which in so many women approaches to a spiritual vice, and therefore to a visible blemish; in her peculiar case—and though possessed in a transcendent degree—was still the token of the highest health; in-asmuch as never knowing what it was to yearn for its gratification, she was almost entirely unconscious of possessing it at all. Many women carry this light of their lives flaming on their foreheads; but Mary Glendinning unknowingly bore hers within. Through all the infinite traceries of feminine art, she evenly glowed like a vase which, internally illuminated, gives no outward sign of the lighting flame, but seems to shine by the very virtue of the exquisite marble itself. But that bluff corporeal admiration, with which some ball-room women are content, was no admiration to the mother of Pierre. Not the general homage of men, but the selected homage of the noblest men, was what she felt to be her appropriate right. And as her own material partialities were added to, and glorified the rare and absolute merits of Pierre; she considered the voluntary allegiance of his affectionate soul, the representative fealty of the choicest guild of his race. Thus, though replenished through all her veins with the subtlest vanity, with the homage of Pierre alone she was content.

But as to a woman of sense and spirit, the admiration of even the noblest and most gifted man, is esteemed as nothing, as long as she remains conscious of possessing no directly influencing and practical sorcery over his soul; and as notwithstanding all his intellectual superiority to his mother, Pierre, through the unavoidable weakness of inexperienced and unexpanded youth, was strangely docile to the maternal tuitions in nearly all the things which thus far had any ways interested or affected him; therefore it was, that to Mary Glendinning this reverence of Pierre was invested with all the proudest delights and witcheries of self-complacency, which it is possible for the most conquering virgin to feel. Still more. That nameless and infinitely delicate aroma of inexpressible tenderness and attentiveness which, in every refined and honorable attachment, is cotemporary with the courtship, and precedes the final banns and the rite; but which, like the *bouquet* of the costliest German wines, too often evaporates upon pouring love out to drink, in the disenchanting glasses of the matrimonial days and nights; this highest and airiest thing in the whole compass of the experience of our mortal life; this heavenly evanescence—still further etherealized in the filial breast—was for Mary Glendinning, now not very far from her grand climacteric, miraculously revived in the courteous lover-like adoration of Pierre.

Altogether having its origin in a wonderful but purely fortuitous combination of the happiest and rarest accidents of earth; and not to be limited in duration by that climax which is so fatal to ordinary love; this softened spell which still wheeled the mother and son in one orbit of joy, seemed a glimpse of the glorious possibility, that the divinest of those emotions, which are incident to the sweetest season of love, is capable of an indefinite translation into many of the less signal relations of our many chequered life. In a detached and individual way, it seemed almost to realize here below the sweet dreams of those religious enthusiasts, who paint to us a Paradise to come, when etherealized from all drosses and stains, the holiest passion of man shall unite all kindreds and climes in one circle of pure and unimpairable delight.

VI.

There was one little uncelestial trait, which, in the opinion of some, may mar the romantic merits of the gentlemanly Pierre Glendinning. He always had an excellent appetite, and especially for his breakfast. But when we consider that though Pierre's hands were small, and his ruffles white, yet his arm was by no means dainty, and his complexion inclined to brown; and that he generally rose with the sun, and could not sleep without riding his twenty, or walking his twelve miles a day, or felling a fair-sized hemlock in the forest, or boxing, or fencing, or boating, or performing some other gymnastical feat; when we consider these athletic habitudes of Pierre, and the great fullness of brawn and muscle they built round about him; all of which manly brawn and muscle, three times a day loudly clamored for attention; we shall very soon perceive that to have a bountiful appetite, was not only no vulgar reproach, but a right royal grace and honor to Pierre; attesting him a man and a gentleman; for a thoroughly developed gentleman is always robust and healthy; and Robustness and Health are great trencher-men.

So when Pierre and his mother descended to breakfast, and Pierre had scrupulously seen her supplied with whatever little things were convenient to her; and had twice or thrice ordered the respectable and immemorial Dates, the servitor, to adjust and re-adjust the window-sashes, so that no unkind current of air should take undue liberties with his mother's neck; after seeing to all this, but in a very quiet and in-conspicuous way; and also after directing the unruffled Dates, to swing out, horizontally into a particular light, a fine joyous painting, in the good-fellow, Flemish style (which painting was so attached to the wall as to be capable of that mode of adjusting), and furthermore after darting from where he sat a few invigorating glances over the river-meadows to the blue mountains beyond; Pierre made a masonic sort of mysterious motion to the excellent Dates, who in automaton obedience thereto, brought from a certain agreeable little side-stand, a very prominent-looking cold pasty; which, on careful inspection with the knife, proved to be the embossed savory nest of a few uncommonly tender pigeons of Pierre's own shooting.

"Sister Mary," said he, lifting on his silver trident one of the choicest of many fine pigeon morsels; "Sister Mary," said he, "in shooting these pigeons, I was very careful to bring down one in such a manner that the breast is entirely unmarred. It was intended for you! and here it is. Now Sergeant Dates, help hither your mistress' plate. No?—nothing but the crumbs of French rolls, and a few peeps into a coffee-cup—is that a breakfast for the daughter of yonder bold General?"—pointing to a full-length of his gold-laced grandfather on the opposite wall. "Well, pitiable is my case when I have to breakfast for two. Dates!"

"Sir."

"Remove that toast-rack, Dates; and this plate of tongue, and bring the rolls nearer, and wheel the stand farther off, good Dates."

Having thus made generous room for himself, Pierre commenced operations, interrupting his mouthfuls by many sallies of mirthfulness.

"You seem to be in prodigious fine spirits this morning, brother Pierre," said his mother.

"Yes, very tolerable; at least I can't say, that I am low-spirited exactly, sister Mary;—Dates, my fine fellow, bring me three bowls of milk."

"One bowl, sir, you mean," said Dates, gravely and imperturbably.

As the servitor left the room, Mrs. Glendinning spoke. "My dear Pierre, how often have I begged you never to permit your hilariousness to betray you into overstepping the exact line of propriety in your intercourse with servants. Dates' look was a respectful reproof to you just now. You must not call Dates, *My fine fellow*. He *is* a fine fellow, a very fine fellow, indeed; but there is no need of telling him so at my table. It is very easy to be entirely kind and pleasant to servants, without the least touch of any shade of transient good-fellowship with them."

"Well, sister, no doubt you are altogether right; after this I shall drop the *fine,* and call Dates nothing but *fellow;*—Fellow, come here!—how will that answer?"

"Not at all, Pierre—but you are a Romeo, you know, and so for the present I pass over your nonsense."

"Romeo! oh, no. I am far from being Romeo—" sighed Pierre. "I laugh, but he cried; poor Romeo! alas Romeo! woe is me, Romeo! he came to a very deplorable end, did Romeo, sister Mary."

"It was his own fault though."

"Poor Romeo!"

"He was disobedient to his parents."

"Alas Romeo!"

"He married against their particular wishes."

"Woe is me, Romeo!"

"But you, Pierre, are going to be married before long, I trust, not to a Capulet, but to one of our own Montagues; and so Romeo's evil fortune will hardly be yours. You will be happy."

"The more miserable Romeo!"

"Don't be so ridiculous, brother Pierre; so you are going to take Lucy that long ride among the hills this morning? She is a sweet girl; a most lovely girl."

"Yes, that is rather my opinion, sister Mary.—By heavens, mother, the five zones hold not such another! She is—yes—though I say it—Dates!—he's a precious long time getting that milk!"

"Let him stay.—Don't be a milk-sop, Pierre!"

"Ha! my sister is a little satirical this morning. I comprehend."

"Never rave, Pierre; and never rant. Your father never did either; nor is it written of Socrates; and both were very wise men. Your father was profoundly in love—that I know to my certain knowledge—but I never heard him rant about it. He was always exceedingly gentlemanly: and gentlemen never rant. Milk-sops and Muggletonians rant, but gentlemen never."

"Thank you, sister.—There, put it down, Dates; are the horses ready?"

"Just driving round, sir, I believe."

"Why, Pierre," said his mother, glancing out at the window, "are you going to Santa Fe De Bogota with that enormous old phaeton;—what do you take that Juggernaut out for?"

"Humor, sister, humor; I like it because it's old-fashioned, and because the seat is such a wide sofa of a seat, and finally because a young lady by the name of Lucy Tartan cherishes a high regard for it. She vows she would like to be married in it."

"Well, Pierre, all I have to say, is, be sure that Christopher puts the coach-hammer and nails, and plenty of cords and screws into the box. And you had better let him follow you in one of the farm wagons, with a spare axle and some boards."

"No fear, sister; no fear;—I shall take the best of care of the old phaeton. The quaint old arms on the panel, always remind me who it was that first rode in it."

"I am glad you have that memory, brother Pierre."

"And who it was that *next* rode in it."

"Bless you!—God bless you, my dear son!—always think of him and you can never err; yes, always think of your dear perfect father, Pierre."

"Well, kiss me now, dear sister, for I must go."

"There; this is my cheek, and the other is Lucy's; though now that I look at them both, I think that hers is getting to be the most blooming; sweeter dews fall on that one, I suppose."

Pierre laughed, and ran out of the room, for old Christopher was getting impatient. His mother went to the window and stood there.

"A noble boy, and docile"—she murmured—"he has all the frolicsomeness of youth, with little of its giddiness. And he does not grow vain-glorious in sophomorean wisdom. I thank heaven I sent him not to college. A noble boy, and docile. A fine, proud, loving, docile, vigorous boy. Pray God, he never becomes otherwise to me. His little wife, that is to be, will not estrange him from me; for she too is docile,—beautiful, and reverential, and most docile. Seldom yet have I known such blue eyes as hers, that were not docile, and would not follow a bold black one, as two meek blue-ribboned ewes, follow their martial leader. How glad am I that Pierre loves her so, and not some dark-eyed haughtiness, with whom I could never live in peace; but who would be ever setting her young married state before my elderly widowed one, and claiming all the homage of my dear boy—the fine, proud, loving, docile, vigorous boy!—the lofty-minded, well-born, noble boy; and with such sweet docilities! See his hair! He does in truth illustrate that fine saying of his father's, that as the noblest colts, in three points—abundant hair, swelling chest, and sweet docility—should resemble a fine woman, so should a noble youth. Well, good-bye, Pierre, and a merry morning to ye!"

So saying she crossed the room, and—resting in a corner—her glad proud eye met the old General's baton, which the day before in one of his frolic moods Pierre had taken from its accustomed place in the pictured-bannered hall. She lifted it, and musingly swayed it to and fro; then paused, and staff-wise rested with it in her hand. Her stately beauty had ever somewhat martial in it; and now she looked the daughter of a General, as she was; for Pierre's was a double revolutionary descent. On both sides he sprung from heroes.

"This is his inheritance—this symbol of command! and I swell out to think it. Yet but just now I fondled the conceit that Pierre was so sweetly docile! Here sure is a most strange inconsistency! For is sweet docility a general's badge? and is this baton but a distaff then?—Here's something widely wrong. Now I almost wish him otherwise than sweet and docile to me, seeing that it must be hard for man to be an uncompromising hero and a commander among his race, and yet never ruffle any domestic brow. Pray heaven he show his heroicness in some smooth way of favoring fortune, not be called out to be a hero of some dark hope forlorn;—of some dark hope forlorn, whose cruelness makes a savage of a man. Give him, O God, regardful gales! Fan him with unwavering prosperities! So shall he remain all docility to me, and yet prove a haughty hero to the world!"

Herman Melville

BARTLEBY THE SCRIVENER

I am a rather elderly man. The nature of my avocations for the last thirty years has brought me into more than ordinary contact with what would seem an interesting and somewhat singular set of men, of whom as yet nothing that I know of has ever been written:—I mean the law-copyists or scriveners. I have known very many of them, professionally and privately, and if I pleased, could relate divers histories, at which good-natured gentlemen might smile, and sentimental souls might weep. But I waive the biographies of all other scriveners for a few passages in the life of Bartleby, who was a scrivener the strangest I ever saw or heard of. While of other law-copyists I might write the complete life, of Bartleby nothing of that sort can be done. I believe that no materials exist for a full and satisfactory biography of this man. It is an irreparable loss to literature. Bartleby was one of those beings of whom nothing is ascertainable, except from the original sources, and in his case those are very small. What my own astonished eyes saw of Bartleby, *that* is all I know of him, except, indeed, one vague report which will appear in the sequel.

Ere introducing the scrivener, as he first appeared to me, it is fit I make some mention of myself, my *employés,* my business, my chambers, and general surroundings; because some such description is indispensable to an adequate understanding of the chief character about to be presented.

Imprimis: I am a man who, from his youth upward, has been filled with a profound conviction that the easiest way of life is the best. Hence, though I belong to a profession proverbially energetic and nervous, even to turbulence, at times, yet nothing of that sort have I ever suffered to invade my peace. I am one of those unambitious lawyers who never addresses a jury, or in any way draws down public applause; but in the cool tranquillity of a snug retreat, do a snug business among rich men's bonds and mortgages and title-deeds. All who know me, consider me an eminently *safe* man. The late John Jacob Astor, a personage little given to poetic enthusiasm, had no hesitation in pronouncing my first grand point to be prudence; my next, method. I do not speak it in vanity, but simply record the fact, that I was not unemployed in my profession by the late John Jacob Astor; a name which, I admit, I love to repeat, for it hath a rounded and orbicular sound to it, and rings like unto bullion. I will freely add, that I was not insensible to the late John Jacob Astor's good opinion.

Some time prior to the period at which this little history begins, my avocations had been largely increased. The good old office, now extinct in the State of New York, of a Master in Chancery, had been conferred upon me. It was not a very arduous office, but very pleasantly remunerative. I seldom lose my temper; much more seldom indulge in dangerous indignation at wrongs and outrages; but I must be permitted to be rash here and declare, that I consider the sudden and violent abrogation of the office of Master in Chancery, by the new Constitution, as a —— premature act; inasmuch as I had counted upon a life-lease of the profits, whereas I only received those of a few short years. But this is by the way.

My chambers were upstairs at No. —— Wall Street. At one end they looked upon the white wall of the interior of a spacious sky-light shaft, penetrating the building from top to bottom. This view might have been considered rather tame than otherwise, deficient in what landscape painters call "life." But if so, the view from the other end of my chambers offered, at least, a contrast, if nothing more. In that direction my windows commanded an unobstructed view of a lofty brick wall, black by age and everlasting shade; which wall required no spy-glass to bring out its lurking beauties, but for the benefit of all near-sighted spectators, was pushed up to within ten feet of my window panes. Owing to the great height of the surrounding buildings, and my chambers being on the second floor, the interval between this wall and mine not a little resembled a huge square cistern.

At the period just preceding the advent of Bartleby, I had two persons as copyists in my employment, and a promising lad as an office-boy. First, Turkey; second, Nippers; third, Ginger Nut. These may seem names, the like of which are not usually found in the Directory. In truth they were nicknames, mutually conferred upon each other by my three clerks, and were deemed expressive of their respective persons or characters. Turkey was a short, pursy Englishman of about my own age, that is, somewhere not far from sixty. In the morning, one might say, his face was of a fine florid hue, but after twelve o'clock, meridian—his dinner hour—it blazed like a grate full of Christmas coals; and continued blazing—but, as it were, with a gradual wane—till 6 o'clock P.M. or thereabouts, after which I saw no more of the proprietor of the face, which, gaining its meridian with the sun, seemed to set with it, to rise, culminate, and decline the following day, with the like regularity and undiminished glory. There are many singular coincidences I have known in the course of my life, not the least among which was the fact, that exactly when Turkey displayed his fullest beams from his red and radiant countenance, just then, too, at that critical moment, began the daily period when I considered his business capacities as seriously disturbed for the remainder of the twenty-four hours. Not that he was absolutely idle, or averse to business then; far from it. The difficulty was, he was apt to be altogether too energetic. There was a strange, inflamed, flurried, flighty recklessness of activity about him. He would be incautious in dipping his pen into his inkstand. All his blots upon my documents, were dropped there after twelve o'clock meridian. Indeed, not only would he be reckless and sadly given to making blots in the afternoon, but some days he went further, and was rather noisy. At such times, too, his face flamed with augmented blazonry, as if cannel coal had been heaped on anthracite. He made an unpleasant racket with his chair; spilled his sand-box; in mending his pens, impatiently split them all to pieces, and threw them on the floor in a sudden passion; stood up and leaned over his table, boxing his papers about in a most indecorous manner, very sad to behold in an elderly man like him. Nevertheless, as he was in many ways a most valuable person to me, and all the time before twelve o'clock, meridian, was the quickest, steadiest creature, too, accomplishing a great deal of work in a style not easy to be matched—for these reasons, I was willing to overlook his eccentricities, though indeed, occasionally, I remonstrated with him. I did this very gently, however, because, though the civilest, nay, the blandest and most reverential of men in the morning, yet in the afternoon he was disposed, upon provocation, to be slightly rash with his tongue, in fact, insolent. Now, valuing his morning services as I did, and resolving not to lose them—yet, at the same time, made uncomfortable by his inflamed ways after twelve o'clock; and being a man of peace, unwilling by my admonitions to call forth unseemly retorts from him— I took upon me, one Saturday noon (he was always worse on Saturdays), to hint to him, very kindly, that perhaps now that he was growing old, it might be well to abridge his labours; in short, he need not come to my chambers after twelve o'clock, but, dinner over, had best go home to his lodgings and rest himself till tea-time. But no; he insisted upon his afternoon devotions. His countenance became intolerably fervid, as he oratorically assured me—gesticulating, with a long ruler, at the other side of the room—that if his services in the morning were useful, how indispensable, then, in the afternoon?

"With submission, sir," said Turkey on this occasion, "I consider myself your right-hand man. In the morning I but marshal and deploy my columns; but in the afternoon I put myself at their head, and gallantly charge the foe, thus!"—and he made a violent thrust with the ruler.

"But the blots, Turkey," intimated I.

"True,—but, with submission, sir, behold these hairs! I am getting old. Surely, sir, a blot or two of a warm afternoon is not to be severely urged against grey hairs. Old age—even if it blot the page—is honourable. With submission, sir, we *both* are getting old."

This appeal to my fellow-feeling was hardly to be resisted. At all events, I saw that go he would not. So I made up my mind to let him stay, resolving, nevertheless, to see to it, that during the afternoon he had to do with my less important papers.

Nippers, the second on my list, was a whiskered, sallow, and, upon the whole, rather piratical-looking young man of about five and twenty. I always deemed him the victim of two evil powers—ambition and indigestion. The ambition was evinced by a certain impatience of the duties of a mere copyist—an unwarrantable usurpation of strictly professional affairs, such as the original drawing up of legal documents. The indigestion seemed betokened in an occasional nervous testiness and grinning irritability, causing the teeth to audibly grind together over mistakes committed in copying; unnecessary maledictions, hissed, rather than spoken, in the heat of business; and especially by a continual discontent with the height of the table where he worked. Though of a very ingenious mechanical turn, Nippers could never get this table to suit him. He put chips under it, blocks of various sorts, bits of pasteboard, and at last went so far as to attempt an exquisite adjustment by final pieces of folded blotting-paper. But no invention would answer. If, for the sake of easing his back, he brought the table lid at a sharp angle well up toward his chin, and wrote there like a man using the steep roof of a Dutch house for his desk—then he declared that it stopped the circulation in his arms. If now he lowered the table to his waistbands, and stooped over it in writing, then there was a sore aching in his back. In short, the truth of the matter was, Nippers knew not what he wanted. Or, if he wanted anything, it was to be rid of a scrivener's table altogether. Among the manifestations of his diseased ambition was a fondness he had for receiving visits from certain ambiguous-looking fellows in seedy coats, whom he called his clients. Indeed I was aware that not only was he, at times, considerable of a ward-politician, but he occasionally did a little business at the Justices' courts, and was not unknown on the steps of the Tombs. I have good reason to believe, however, that one individual who called upon him at my chambers, and who, with a grand air, he insisted was his client, was not other than a dun, and the alleged title-deed, a bill. But with all his failings, and the annoyances he caused me, Nippers, like his compatriot Turkey, was a very useful man to me; wrote a neat, swift hand; and, when he chose, was not deficient in a gentlemanly sort of deportment. Added to this, he always dressed in a gentlemanly sort of way; and so, incidentally, reflected credit upon my chambers. Whereas with respect to Turkey, I had much ado to keep him from being a reproach to me. His clothes were apt to look oily and smell of eating-houses. He wore his pantaloons very loose and baggy in summer. His coats were execrable; his hat not to be handled. But while the hat was a thing of indifference to me, inasmuch as his natural civility and deference, as a dependent Englishman, always led him to doff it the moment he entered the room, yet his coat was another matter. Concerning his coats, I reasoned with him; but with no effect. The truth was, I suppose, that a man with so small an income, could not afford to sport such a lustrous face and a lustrous coat at one and the same time. As Nippers once observed, Turkey's money went chiefly for red ink. One winter day I presented Turkey with a highly-respectable looking coat of my own, a padded grey coat, of a most comfortable warmth, and which buttoned straight up from the knee to the neck. I thought Turkey would appreciate the favour, and abate his rashness and obstreperousness of afternoons. But no. I verily believe that buttoning himself up in so downy and blanket-like a coat had a pernicious effect upon him; upon the same principle that too much oats are bad for horses. In fact, precisely as a rash, restive horse is said to feel his oats, so Turkey felt his coat. It made him insolent. He was a man whom prosperity harmed.

Though concerning the self-indulgent habits of Turkey I had my own private surmises, yet touching Nippers I was well persuaded that whatever might be his faults in other respects, he was, at least, a temperate young man. But, indeed, nature herself seemed to have been his vintner, and at his birth charged him so thoroughly with an irritable, brandy-like disposition, that all subsequent potations were needless. When I consider how, amid the stillness of my chambers, Nippers would sometimes impatiently rise from his seat, and stooping over his table, spread his arms wide apart, seize the whole desk, and move it, and jerk it, with a grim, grinding motion on the floor, as if the table were a perverse voluntary agent, intent on thwarting and vexing him; I plainly perceive that for Nippers, brandy and water were altogether superfluous.

It was fortunate for me that, owing to its peculiar cause—indigestion—the irritability and consequent nervousness of Nippers, were mainly observable in the morning, while in the afternoon he was comparatively mild. So that Turkey's paroxysms only coming on about twelve o'clock, I never had to do with their eccentricities at one time. Their fits relieved each other like guards. When Nipper's was on, Turkey's was off; and *vice versa*. This was a good natural arrangement under the circumstances.

Ginger Nut, the third on my list, was a lad some twelve years old. His father was a carman, ambitious of seeing his son on the bench instead of a cart, before he died. So he sent him to my office as student at law, errand boy, and cleaner and sweeper, at the rate of one dollar a week. He had a little desk to himself, but he did not use it much. Upon inspection, the drawer exhibited a great array of the shells of various sorts of nuts. Indeed, to this quick-witted youth the whole noble science of the law was contained in a nut-shell. Not the least among the employments of Ginger Nut, as well as one which he discharged with the most alacrity, was his duty as cake and apple purveyor for Turkey and Nippers. Copying law papers being proverbially a dry, husky sort of business, my two scriveners were fain to moisten their mouths very often with Spitzenbergs to be had at the numerous stalls nigh the Custom House and Post Office. Also, they sent Ginger Nut very frequently for that peculiar cake—small, flat, round, and very spicy—after which he had been named by them. Of a cold morning, when business was but dull, Turkey would gobble up scores of these cakes, as if they were mere wafers—indeed they sell them at the rate of six or eight for a penny—the scrape of his pen blending with the crunching of the crisp particles in his mouth. Of all the fiery afternoon blunders and flurried rashness of Turkey, was his once moistening a ginger-cake between his lips, and clapping it on to a mortgage for a seal. I came within an ace of dismissing him then. But he mollified me by making an oriental bow and saying—"With submission, sir, it was generous of me to find you in stationery on my own account."

Now my original business—that of a conveyancer and title hunter, and drawer-up of recondite documents of all sorts—was considerably increased by receiving the master's office. There was now great work for scriveners. Not only must I push the clerks already with me, but I must have additional help. In answer to my advertisement, a motionless young man one morning stood upon my office threshold, the door being open, for it was summer. I can see that figure now— pallidly neat, pitiably respectable, incurably forlorn! It was Bartleby.

After a few words touching his qualifications, I engaged him, glad to have among my corps of copyists a man of so singularly sedate an aspect, which I thought might operate beneficially upon the flighty temper of Turkey, and the fiery one of Nippers.

I should have stated before that ground glass folding doors divided my premises into two parts, one of which was occupied by my scriveners, the other by myself. According to my humour I threw open these doors, or closed them. I resolved to assign Bartleby a corner by the folding-doors, but on my side of them, so as to have this quiet man within easy call, in case any trifling thing was to be done. I placed his desk close up to a small side window in that part of the room, a window which originally had afforded a lateral view of certain grimy back-yards and bricks, but which, owing to subsequent erections, commanded at present no view at all, though it gave some light. Within three feet of the panes was a wall, and the light came down from far above, between two lofty buildings, as from a very small opening in a dome. Still further to a satisfactory arrangement, I procured a high green folding screen, which might entirely isolate Bartleby from my sight, though not remove him from my voice. And thus, in a manner, privacy and society were conjoined.

At first Bartleby did an extraordinary quantity of writing. As if long famishing for something to copy, he seemed to gorge himself on my documents. There was no pause for digestion. He ran a day and night line, copying by sun-light and by candle-light. I should have been quite delighted with his application, had he been cheerfully industrious. But he wrote on silently, palely, mechanically.

It is, of course, an indispensable part of a scrivener's business to verify the accuracy of his copy, word by word. Where there are two or more scriveners in an office, they assist each other in this examination, one reading from the copy, the other holding the original. It is a very dull, wearisome, and lethargic affair. I can readily imagine that to some sanguine temperaments it would be altogether intolerable. For example, I cannot credit that the mettlesome poet Byron would have contentedly sat down with Bartleby to examine a law document of, say five hundred pages, closely written in a crimpy hand.

Now and then, in the haste of business, it had been my habit to assist in comparing some brief document myself, calling Turkey or Nippers for this purpose. One object I had in placing Bartleby so handy to me behind the screen, was to avail myself of his services on such trivial occasions. It was on the third day, I think, of his being with me, and before any necessity had arisen for having his own writing examined, that, being much hurried to complete a small affair I had in hand, I abruptly called to Bartleby. In my haste and natural expectancy of instant compliance, I sat with my head bent over the original on my desk, and my right hand sideways, and somewhat nervously extended with the copy, so that immediately upon emerging from his retreat, Bartleby might snatch it and proceed to business without the least delay.

In this very attitude did I sit when I called to him, rapidly stating what it was I wanted him to do—namely, to examine a small paper with me. Imagine my surprise, nay, my consternation, when without moving from his privacy, Bartleby in a singularly mild, firm voice, replied, "I would prefer not to."

I sat awhile in perfect silence, rallying my stunned faculties. Immediately it occurred to me that my ears had deceived me, Bartleby had entirely misunderstood my meaning. I repeated my request in the clearest tone I could assume. But in quite as clear a one came the previous reply, "I would prefer not to."

"Prefer not to," echoed I, rising in high excitement, and crossing the room with a stride. "What do you mean? Are you moon-struck? I want you to help me compare this sheet here—take it," and I thrust it toward him.

"I would prefer not to," said he.

I looked at him steadfastly. His face was leanly composed; his grey eye dimly calm. Not a wrinkle of agitation rippled him. Had there been the least uneasiness, anger, impatience or impertinence in his manner; in other words, had there been anything ordinarily human about him; doubtless I should have violently dismissed him from the premises. But as it was, I should have as soon thought of turning my pale plaster-of-paris bust of Cicero out of doors. I stood gazing at him awhile, as he went on with his own writing, and then reseated myself at my desk. This is very strange, thought I. What had one best do? But my business hurried me. I concluded to forget the matter for the present, reserving it for my future leisure. So calling Nippers from the other room, the paper was speedily examined.

A few days after this, Bartleby concluded four lengthy documents, being quadruplicates of a week's testimony taken before me in my High Court of Chancery. It became necessary to examine them. It was an important suit, and great accuracy was imperative. Having all things arranged, I called Turkey, Nippers and Ginger Nut from the next room, meaning to place the four copies in the hands of my four clerks, while I should read from the original. Accordingly Turkey, Nippers and Ginger Nut had taken their seats in a row, each with his document in hand, when I called to Bartleby to join this interesting group.

"Bartleby! quick, I am waiting."

I heard a slow scrape of his chair legs on the uncarpeted floor, and soon he appeared standing at the entrance of his hermitage.

"What is wanted?" said he mildly.

"The copies, the copies," said I hurriedly. "We are going to examine them. There"—and I held toward him the fourth quadruplicate.

"I would prefer not to," he said, and gently disappeared behind the screen.

For a few moments I was turned into a pillar of salt, standing at the head of my seated column of clerks. Recovering myself, I advanced toward the screen, and demanded the reason for such extraordinary conduct.

"*Why* do you refuse?"

"I would prefer not to."

With any other man I should have flown outright into a dreadful passion, scorned all further words, and thrust him ignominiously from my presence. But there was something about Bartleby that not only strangely disarmed me, but in a wonderful manner touched and disconcerted me. I began to reason with him.

"These are your own copies we are about to examine. It is labour saving to you, because one examination will answer for your four papers.

It is common usage. Every copyist is bound to help examine his copy. Is it not so? Will you not speak? Answer!"

"I prefer not to," he replied in a flute-like tone. It seemed to me that while I had been addressing him, he carefully revolved every statement that I made; fully comprehended the meaning; could not gainsay the irresistible conclusion; but, at the same time, some paramount consideration prevailed with him to reply as he did.

"You are decided, then, not to comply with my request—a request made according to common usage and common sense?"

He briefly gave me to understand that on that point my judgment was sound. Yes: his decision was irreversible.

It is not seldom the case that when a man is browbeaten in some unprecedented and violently unreasonable way, he begins to stagger in his own plainest faith. He begins, as it were, vaguely to surmise that, wonderful as it may be, all the justice and all the reason are on the other side. Accordingly, if any disinterested persons are present, he turns to them for some reinforcement for his own faltering mind.

"Turkey," said I, "what do you think of this? Am I not right?"

"With submission, sir," said Turkey, with his blandest tone, "I think that you are."

"Nippers," said I, "what do *you* think of it?"

"I think I should kick him out of the office."

(The reader of nice perceptions will here perceive that, it being morning, Turkey's answer is couched in polite and tranquil terms but Nippers's reply in ill-tempered ones. Or, to repeat a previous sentence, Nippers's ugly mood was on duty, and Turkey's off.)

"Ginger Nut," said I, willing to enlist the smallest suffrage in my behalf, "what do *you* think of it?"

"I think, sir, he's a little *luny,*" replied Ginger Nut, with a grin.

"You hear what they say," said I, turning towards the screen, "come forth and do your duty."

But he vouchsafed no reply. I pondered a moment in sore perplexity. But once more business hurried me. I determined again to postpone the consideration of this dilemma to my future leisure. With a little trouble we made out to examine the papers without Bartleby, though at every page or two, Turkey deferentially dropped his opinion that this proceeding was quite out of the common; while Nippers, twitching in his chair with a dyspeptic nervousness, ground out between his set teeth occasional hissing maledictions against the stubborn oaf behind the screen. And for his (Nippers's) part, this was the first and the last time he would do another man's business without pay.

Meanwhile Bartleby sat in his hermitage, oblivious to everything but his own peculiar business there.

Some days passed, the scrivener being employed upon another lengthy work. His late remarkable conduct led me to regard his ways narrowly. I observed that he never went to dinner; indeed that he never went any where. As yet I had never of my personal knowledge known him to be outside of my office. He was a perpetual sentry in the corner. At about eleven o'clock though, in the morning, I noticed that Ginger Nut would advance towards the opening in Bartleby's screen, as if silently beckoned thither by a gesture invisible to me where I sat. The boy would then leave the office jingling a few pence, and reappear with a handful of ginger-nuts which he delivered in the hermitage, receiving two of the cakes for his trouble.

He lives, then, on ginger-nuts, thought I; never eats a dinner, properly speaking; he must be a vegetarian then; but no; he never eats even vegetables, he eats nothing but ginger-nuts. My mind then ran on in reveries concerning the probable effects upon the human constitution of living entirely on ginger-nuts. Ginger-nuts are so called because they contain ginger as one of their peculiar constituents, and the final flavour-ing one. Now what was ginger? A hot, spicy thing. Was Bartleby hot and spicy? Not at all. Ginger, then, had no effect upon Bartleby. Probably he preferred it should have none.

Nothing so aggravates an earnest person as a passive resistance. If the individual so resisted be of a not inhumane temper, and the resisting one perfectly harmless in his passivity; then, in the better moods of the former, he will endeavour charitably to construe to his imagination what proves impossible to be solved by his judgment. Even so, for the most part, I regarded Bartleby and his ways. Poor fellow! thought I, he means no mischief; it is plain he intends no insolence; his aspect sufficiently evinces that his eccentricities are involuntary. He is useful to me. I can get along with him. If I turn him away, the chances are he will fall in with some less indulgent employer, and then he will be rudely treated, and perhaps driven forth miserably to starve. Yes. Here I can cheaply purchase a delicious self-approval. To befriend Bartleby; to humour him in his strange wilfulness, will cost me little or nothing, while I lay up in my soul what will eventually prove a sweet morsel for my conscience. But this mood was not invariable with me. The passiveness of Bartleby sometimes irritated me. I felt strangely goaded on to encounter him in new opposition, to elicit some angry spark from him answerable to my own. But indeed I might as well have essayed to strike fire with my knuckles against a bit of Windsor soap. But one afternoon the evil im-pulse in me mastered me, and the following little scene ensued:

"Bartleby," said I, "when those papers are all copied, I will compare them with you."

"I would prefer not to."

"How? Surely you do not mean to persist in that mulish vagary?"

No answer.

I threw open the folding-doors near by, and turning upon Turkey and Nippers, exclaimed in an excited manner:

"He says, a second time, he won't examine his papers. What do you think of it, Turkey?"

It was afternoon, be it remembered. Turkey sat glowing like a brass boiler, his bald head steaming, his hands reeling among his blotted papers.

"Think of it?" roared Turkey; "I think I'll just step behind his screen, and black his eyes for him!"

So saying, Turkey rose to his feet and threw his arms into a pugilistic position. He was hurrying away to make good his promise, when I detained him, alarmed at the effect of incautiously rousing Turkey's combativeness after dinner.

"Sit down, Turkey," said I, "and hear what Nippers has to say. What do you think of it, Nippers? Would I not be justified in immediately dismissing Bartleby?"

"Excuse me, that is for you to decide, sir. I think his conduct quite unusual, and indeed unjust, as regards Turkey and myself. But it may only be a passing whim."

"Ah," exclaimed I, "you have strangely changed your mind then— you speak very gently of him now."

"All beer," cried Turkey; "gentleness is effects of beer—Nippers and I dined together to-day. You see how gentle *I* am, sir. Shall I go and black his eyes?"

"You refer to Bartleby, I suppose. No, not to-day, Turkey," I replied; "pray, put up your fists."

I closed the doors, and again advanced towards Bartleby. I felt additional incentives tempting me to my fate. I burned to be rebelled against again. I remembered that Bartleby never left the office.

"Bartleby," said I, "Ginger Nut is away; just step round to the Post Office, won't you? (it was but a three minutes' walk), and see if there is anything for me."

"I would prefer not to."

"You *will* not?"

"I *prefer* not."

I staggered to my desk, and sat there in a deep study. My blind inveteracy returned. Was there any other thing in which I could procure myself to be ignominiously repulsed by this lean, penniless wight?—my hired clerk? What added thing is there, perfectly reasonable, that he will be sure to refuse to do?

"Bartleby!"

No answer.

"Bartleby," in a louder tone.

No answer.

"Bartleby," I roared.

Like a very ghost, agreeably to the laws of magical invocation, at the third summons, he appeared at the entrance of his hermitage.

"Go to the next room, and tell Nippers to come to me."

"I prefer not to," he respectfully and slowly said, and mildly disappeared.

"Very good, Bartleby," said I, in a quiet sort of serenely severe self-possessed tone, intimating the unalterable purpose of some terrible retribution very close at hand. At the moment I half intended something of the kind. But upon the whole, as it was drawing towards my dinner-hour, I thought it best to put on my hat and walk home for the day, suffering much from perplexity and distress of mind.

Shall I acknowledge it? The conclusion of this whole business was, that it soon became a fixed fact of my chambers, that a pale young scrivener, by the name of Bartleby, had a desk there; that he copied for me at the usual rate of four cents a folio (one hundred words); that he was permanently exempt from examining the work done by him, that duty being transferred to Turkey and Nippers, out of compliment doubtless to their superior acuteness; moreover, said Bartleby was never on any account to be despatched on the most trivial errand of any sort; and that even if entreated to take upon him such a matter, it was generally understood that he would prefer not to—in other words, that he would refuse point-blank.

As days passed on, I became considerably reconciled to Bartleby. His steadiness, his freedom from all dissipation, his incessant industry (except when he chose to throw himself into a standing revery behind his screen), his great stillness, his unalterableness of demeanour under all circumstances, made him a valuable acquisition. One prime thing was this,—*he was always there;*—first in the morning, continually through the day, and the last at night. I had a singular confidence in his honesty. I felt my most precious papers prefectly safe in his hands. Sometimes to be sure I could not, for the very soul of me, avoid falling into sudden spasmodic passions with him. For it was exceeding difficult to bear in mind all the time those strange peculiarities, privileges, and unheard of exemptions, forming the tacit stipulations on Bartleby's part under which he remained in my office. Now and then, in the eagerness of despatching pressing business, I would inadvertently summon Bartleby, in a short, rapid tone, to put his finger, say, on the incipient tie of a bit of red tape with which I was about compressing some papers. Of course, from behind the screen the usual answer, "I prefer not to," was sure to come; and then, how could a human creature with the common infirmities of our nature, refrain from bitterly exclaiming upon such perverseness— such unreasonableness. However, every added repulse of this sort which I received only tended to lessen the probability of my repeating the inadvertence.

Here it must be said, that according to the custom of most legal gentlemen occupying chambers in densely-populated law buildings, there were several keys to my door. One was kept by a woman residing in the attic, which person weekly scrubbed and daily swept and dusted my apartments. Another was kept by Turkey for convenience sake. The third I sometimes carried in my own pocket. The fourth I knew not who had.

Now, one Sunday morning I happened to go to Trinity Church, to hear a celebrated preacher, and finding myself rather early on the ground, I thought I would walk round to my chambers for awhile. Luckily I had my key with me; but upon applying it to the lock, I found it resisted by something inserted from the inside. Quite surprised, I called out; when to my consternation a key was turned from within; and thrusting his lean visage at me, and holding the door ajar, the apparition of Bartleby appeared, in his shirt sleeves, and otherwise in a strangely tattered dishabille, saying quietly that he was sorry, but he was deeply engaged just then, and—preferred not admitting me at present. In a brief word or two, he moreover added, that perhaps I had better walk round the block two or three times, and by that time he would probably have concluded his affairs.

Now, the utterly unsurmised appearance of Bartleby, tenanting my law-chambers of a Sunday morning, with his cadaverously gentlemanly *nonchalance*, yet withal firm and self-possessed, had such a strange effect upon me, that incontinently I slunk away from my own door, and did as desired. But not without sundry twinges of impotent rebellion against the mild effrontery of this unaccountable scrivener. Indeed, it was his wonderful mildness chiefly, which not only disarmed me, but unmanned me, as it were. For I consider that one, for the time, is in a way unmanned when he tranquilly permits his hired clerk to dictate to him, and order him away from his own premises. Furthermore, I was full of uneasiness as to what Bartleby could possibly be doing in my office in his shirt sleeves, and in an otherwise dismantled condition of a Sunday morning. Was anything amiss going on? Nay, that was out of the question. It was not to be thought of for a moment that Bartleby was an immoral person. But what could he be doing there—copying? Nay again, whatever might be his eccentricities, Bartleby was an eminently decorous person. He would be the last man to sit down to his desk in any state approaching to nudity. Besides, it was Sunday; and there was something about Bartleby that forbade the supposition that he would by any secular occupation violate the proprieties of the day.

Nevertheless, my mind was not pacified; and full of a restless curiosity, at last I returned to the door. Without hindrance I inserted my key, opened it, and entered. Bartleby was not to be seen. I looked round anxiously, peeped behind his screen; but it was very plain that he was gone. Upon more closely examining the place, I surmised that for an indefinite period Bartleby must have ate, dressed, and slept in my office, and that too without plate, mirror, or bed. The cushioned seat of a ricketty old sofa in one corner bore the faint impress of a lean, reclining form. Rolled away under his desk, I found a blanket; under the empty grate, a blacking box and brush; on a chair, a tin basin, with soap and a ragged towel; in a newspaper a few crumbs of ginger-nuts and a morsel of cheese. Yes, thought I, it is evident enough that Bartleby has been making his home here, keeping bachelor's hall all by himself. Immediately then the thought came sweeping across me, What miserable friendlessness and loneliness are here revealed! His poverty is great; but his solitude, how horrible! Think of it. Of a Sunday, Wall street is deserted as Petra; and every night of every day it is an emptiness. This building too, which of week-days hums with industry and life, at nightfall echoes with sheer vacancy, and all through Sunday is forlorn. And here Bartleby makes his home; sole spectator of a solitude which he has seen all populous—a sort of innocent and transformed Marius brooding among the ruins of Carthage!

For the first time in my life a feeling of overpowering stinging melancholy seized me. Before, I had never experienced aught but a not-unpleasing sadness. The bond of a common humanity now drew me irresistibly to gloom. A fraternal melancholy! For both I and Bartleby were sons of Adam. I remembered the bright silks and sparkling faces I had seen that day, in gala trim, swan-like sailing down the Mississippi of Broadway; and I contrasted them with the pallid copyist, and thought to myself, Ah, happiness courts the light, so we deem the world is gay; but misery hides aloof, so we deem that misery there is none. These sad fancyings—chimeras, doubtless, of a sick and silly brain—led on to other and more special thoughts, concerning the eccentricities of Bartleby. Presentiments of strange discoveries hovered round me. The scrivener's pale form appeared to me laid out, among uncaring strangers, in its shivering winding sheet.

Suddenly I was attracted by Bartleby's closed desk, the key in open sight left in the lock.

I mean no mischief, seek the gratification of no heartless curiosity, thought I; besides, the desk is mine, and its contents, too, so I will make bold to look within. Everything was methodically arranged, the papers smoothly placed. The pigeon holes were deep, and, removing the files of documents, I groped into their recesses. Presently I felt something there, and dragged it out. It was an old bandana handkerchief, heavy and knotted. I opened it, and saw it was a savings' bank.

I now recalled all the quiet mysteries which I had noted in the man. I remembered that he never spoke but to answer; that though at intervals he had considerable time to himself, yet I had never seen him reading— no, not even a newspaper; that for long periods he would stand looking out, at his pale window behind the screen, upon the dead brick wall; I was quite sure he never visited any refectory or eating-house; while his pale face clearly indicated that he never drank beer like Turkey, or tea and coffee even, like other men; that he never went anywhere in particular that I could learn; never went out for a walk, unless indeed that was the case at present; that he had declined telling who he was, or whence he came, or whether he had any relatives in the world; that though so thin and pale, he never complained of ill health. And more than all, I remembered a certain unconscious air of pallid—how shall I call it?—of pallid haughtiness, say, or rather an austere reserve about him, which had positively awed me into my tame compliance with his eccentricities, when I had feared to ask him to do the slightest incidental thing for me, even though I might know, for his long-continued motionlessness, that behind his screen he must be standing in one of those deadwall reveries of his.

Revolving all these things, and coupling them with the recently discovered fact that he made my office his constant abiding place and home, and not forgetful of his morbid moodiness; revolving all these things, a prudential feeling began to steal over me. My first emotions had been those of pure melancholy and sincerest pity; but just in proportion as the forlornness of Bartleby grew and grew to my imagination, did that same melancholy merge into fear, that pity into repulsion. So true it is, and so terrible, too, that up to a certain point the thought or sight of misery enlists our best affections; but, in certain special cases, beyond that point it does not. They err who would assert that invariably this is owing to the inherent selfishness of the human heart. It rather proceeds from a certain hopelessness of remedying excessive and organic ill. To a sensitive being, pity is not seldom pain. And when at last it is perceived that such pity cannot lead to effectual succour, common sense bids the soul be rid of it. What I saw that morning persuaded me that the scrivener was the victim of innate and incurable disorder. I might give alms to his body; but his body did not pain him; it was his soul that suffered, and his soul I could not reach.

I did not accomplish the purpose of going to Trinity Church that morning. Somehow, the things I had seen disqualified me for the time from church-going. I walked homeward, thinking what I would do with Bartleby. Finally, I resolved upon this:—I would put certain calm questions to him the next morning, touching his history, &c., and if he declined to answer them openly and unreservedly (and I supposed he would prefer not), then to give him a twenty dollar bill over and above whatever I might owe him, and tell him his services were no longer required; but that if in any other way I could assist him, I would be happy to do so, especially if he desired to return to his native place, wherever that might be, I would willingly help to defray the expenses. Moreover, if, after reaching home, he found himself at any time in want of aid, a letter from him would be sure of a reply.

The next morning came.

"Bartleby," said I, gently calling to him behind his screen.

No reply.

"Bartleby," said I, in a still gentler tone, "come here; I am not going to ask you to do anything you would prefer not to do—I simply wish to speak to you."

Upon this he noiselessly slid into view.

"Will you tell me, Bartleby, where you were born?"

"I would prefer not to."

"Will you tell me *anything* about yourself?"

"I would prefer not to."

"But what reasonable objection can you have to speak to me? I feel friendly towards you."

He did not look at me while I spoke, but kept his glance fixed upon my bust of Cicero, which, as I then sat, was directly behind me, some six inches above my head.

"What is your answer, Bartleby?" said I, after waiting a considerable time for a reply, during which his countenance remained immovable, only there was the faintest conceivable tremor of the white attenuated mouth.

"At present I prefer to give no answer," he said, and retired into his hermitage.

It was rather weak in me I confess, but his manner on this occasion nettled me. Not only did there seem to lurk in it a certain calm disdain, but his perverseness seemed ungrateful, considering the undeniable good usage and indulgence he had received from me.

Again I sat ruminating what I should do. Mortified as I was at his behaviour, and resolved as I had been to dismiss him when I entered my office, nevertheless I strangely felt something superstitious knocking at my heart, and forbidding me to carry out my purpose, and denouncing me for a villain if I dared to breathe one bitter word against this forlornest of mankind. At last, familiarly drawing my chair behind his screen, I sat down and said: "Bartleby, never mind then about revealing your history; but let me entreat you, as a friend, to comply as far as may be with the usages of this office. Say now you will help to examine papers to-morrow or next day: in short, say now that in a day or two you will begin to be a little reasonable:—say so, Bartleby."

"At present I would prefer not to be a little reasonable," was his mildly cadaverous reply.

Just then the folding-doors opened, and Nippers approached. He seemed suffering from an unusually bad night's rest, induced by severer indigestion than common. He overheard those final words of Bartleby.

"*Prefer not,* eh?" gritted Nippers—"I'd *prefer* him, if I were you, sir," addressing me—"I'd *prefer* him; I'd give him preferences, the stubborn mule! What is it, sir, pray, that he *prefers* not to do now?"

Bartleby moved not a limb.

"Mr. Nippers," said I, "I'd prefer that you would withdraw for the present."

Somehow, of late I had got into the way of involuntarily using this word "prefer" upon all sorts of not exactly suitable occasions. And I trembled to think that my contact with the scrivener had already and seriously affected me in a mental way. And what further and deeper aberration might it not yet produce? This apprehension had not been without efficacy in determining me to summary means.

As Nippers, looking very sour and sulky, was departing, Turkey blandly and deferentially approached.

"With submission, sir," said he, "yesterday I was thinking about Bartleby here, and I think that if he would but prefer to take a quart of good ale every day, it would do much towards mending him, and en-abling him to assist in examining his papers."

"So you have got the word, too," said I, slightly excited.

"With submission, what word, sir," asked Turkey, respectfully crowd-ing himself into the contracted space behind the screen, and by so doing, making me jostle the scrivener. "What word, sir?"

"I would prefer to be left alone here," said Bartleby, as if offended at being mobbed in his privacy.

"*That's* the word, Turkey," said I—"*that's* it."

"Oh, *prefer?* oh, yes—queer word. I never use it myself. But, sir, as I was saying, if he would but prefer—"

"Turkey," interrupted I, "you will please withdraw."

"Oh certainly, sir, if you prefer that I should."

As he opened the folding-door to retire, Nippers at his desk caught a glimpse of me, and asked whether I would prefer to have a certain paper copied on blue paper or white. He did not in the least roguishly accent the word prefer. It was plain that it involuntarily rolled from his tongue. I thought to myself, surely I must get rid of a demented man, who already has in some degree turned the tongues, if not the heads, of myself and clerks. But I thought it prudent not to break the dismission at once.

The next day I noticed that Bartleby did nothing but stand at his window in his dead-wall revery. Upon asking him why he did not write, he said that he had decided upon doing no more writing.

"Why, how now? what next?" exclaimed I, "do no more writing?"

"No more."

"And what is the reason?"

"Do you not see the reason for yourself?" he indifferently replied.

I looked steadfastly at him, and perceived that his eyes looked dull and glazed. Instantly it occurred to me, that his unexampled diligence in copying by his dim window for the first few weeks of his stay with me might have temporarily impaired his vision.

I was touched. I said something in condolence with him. I hinted that, of course, he did wisely in abstaining from writing for a while, and urged him to embrace that opportunity of taking wholesome exercise in the open air. This, however, he did not do. A few days after this, my other clerks being absent, and being in a great hurry to despatch certain letters by the mail, I thought that, having nothing else earthly to do, Bartleby would surely be less inflexible than usual, and carry these letters to the Post Office. But he blankly declined. So, much to my inconvenience, I went myself.

Still added days went by. Whether Bartleby's eyes improved or not, I could not say. To all appearance, I thought they did. But when I asked him if they did, he vouchsafed no answer. At all events, he would do no copying. At last, in reply to my urgings, he informed me that he had permanently given up coyping.

"What!" exclaimed I; "suppose your eyes should get entirely well— better than ever before—would you not copy then?"

"I have given up copying," he answered and slid aside.

He remained, as ever, a fixture in my chamber. Nay—if that were possible—he became still more of a fixture than before. What was to be done? He would do nothing in the office: why should he stay there? In plain fact, he had now become a millstone to me, not only useless as a necklace, but afflictive to bear. Yet I was sorry for him. I speak less than truth when I say that, on his own account, he occasioned me uneasiness. If he would but have named a single relative or friend, I would instantly have written, and urged their taking the poor fellow away to some convenient retreat. But he seemed alone, absolutely alone in the universe. A bit of wreckage in the mid-Atlantic. At length, necessities connected with my business tyrannized over all other considerations. Decently as I could, I told Bartleby that in six days' time he must unconditionally leave the office. I warned him to take measures, in the interval, for procuring some other abode. I offered to assist him in this endeavour, if he himself would take the first step towards a removal. "And when you finally quit me, Bartleby," added I, "I shall see that you go away not entirely unprovided. Six days from this hour, remember."

At the expiration of that period, I peeped behind the screen, and lo! Bartleby was there.

I buttoned up my coat, balanced myself; advanced slowly towards him, touched his shoulder, and said, "The time has come; you must quit this place; I am sorry for you; here is money; but you must go."

"I would prefer not," he replied, with his back still towards me.

"You *must*."

He remained silent.

Now I had an unbounded confidence in this man's common honesty. He had frequently restored to me sixpences and shillings carelessly dropped upon the floor, for I am apt to be very reckless in such shirt-button affairs. The proceeding then which followed will not be deemed extraordinary.

"Bartleby," said I, "I owe you twelve dollars on account; here are thirty-two; the odd twenty are yours.—Will you take it?" and I handed the bills towards him.

But he made no motion.

"I will leave them here then," putting them under a weight on the table. Then taking my hat and cane and going to the door, I tranquilly turned and added—"After you have removed your things from these offices, Bartleby, you will of course lock the door—since every one is now gone for the day but you—and if you please, slip your key underneath the mat, so that I may have it in the morning. I shall not see you again; so good-bye to you. If hereafter in your new place of abode I can be of any service to you, do not fail to advise me by letter. Good-bye, Bartleby, and fare you well."

But he answered not a word; like the last column of some ruined temple, he remained standing mute and solitary in the middle of the otherwise deserted room.

As I walked home in a pensive mood, my vanity got the better of my pity. I could not but highly plume myself on my masterly management in getting rid of Bartleby. Masterly I call it, and such it must appear to any dispassionate thinker. The beauty of my procedure seemed to consist in its perfect quietness. There was no vulgar bullying, no bravado of any sort, no choleric hectoring, no striding to and fro across the apartment, jerking out vehement commands for Bartleby to bundle himself off with his beggarly traps. Nothing of the kind. Without loudly bidding Bartleby depart—as an inferior genius might have done—I *assumed* the ground that depart he must; and upon that assumption built all I had to say. The more I thought over my procedure, the more I was charmed with it. Nevertheless, next morning, upon awakening, I had my doubts,—I had somehow slept off the fumes of vanity. One of the coolest and wisest hours a man has, is just after he awakes in the morning. My procedure seemed as sagacious as ever,—but only in theory. How it would prove in practice— there was the rub. It was truly a beautiful thought to have assumed Bartleby's departure; but, after all, that assumption was simply my own, and none of Bartleby's. The great point was, not whether I had assumed that he would quit me, but whether he would prefer so to do. He was more a man of preferences than assumptions.

After breakfast, I walked down town, arguing the probabilities *pro* and *con*. One moment I thought it would prove a miserable failure, and Bartleby would be found all alive at my office as usual; the next moment it seemed certain that I should see his chair empty. And so I kept veering about. At the corner of Broadway and Canal Street, I saw quite an excited group of people standing in earnest conversation.

"I'll take odds he doesn't," said a voice as I passed.

"Doesn't go?—done!" said I, "put up your money."

I was instinctively putting my hand in my pocket to produce my own, when I remembered that this was an election day. The words I had overheard bore no reference to Bartleby, but to the success or non-success of some candidate for the mayoralty. In my intent frame of mind, I had, as it were, imagined that all Broadway shared in my excitement, and were debating the same question with me. I passed on, very thankful that the uproar of the street screened my momentary absent-mindedness.

As I had intended, I was earlier than usual at my office door. I stood listening for a moment. All was still. He must be gone. I tried the knob. The door was locked. Yes, my procedure had worked to a charm; he indeed must be vanished. Yet a certain melancholy mixed with this: I was almost sorry for my brilliant success. I was fumbling under the door mat for the key, which Bartleby was to have left for me, when accidentally my knee knocked against a panel, producing a summoning sound, and in response a voice came to me from within—"Not yet; I am occupied."

It was Bartleby.

I was thunderstruck. For an instant I stood like the man who, pipe in mouth, was killed one cloudless afternoon long ago in Virginia, by summer lightning; at his own warm open window he was killed, and remained leaning out there upon the dreamy afternoon, till some one touched him, and he fell.

"Not gone!" I murmured at last. But again obeying that wondrous ascendency which the inscrutable scrivener had over me—and from which ascendency, for all my chafing, I could not completely escape—I slowly went down stairs and out into the street, and while walking round the block, considered what I should next do in this unheard-of perplexity. Turn the man out by an actual thrusting I could not; to drive him away by calling him hard names would not do; calling in the police was an unpleasant idea; and yet, permit him to enjoy his cadaverous triumph over me,—this too I could not think of. What was to be done? or, if nothing could be done, was there anything further that I could *assume* in the matter? Yes, as before I had prospectively assumed that Bartleby would depart, so now I might retrospectively assume that departed he was. In the legitimate carrying out of this assumption, I might enter my office in a great hurry, and pretending not to see Bartleby at all, walk straight against him as if he were air. Such a proceeding would in a singular degree have the appearance of a home-thrust. It was hardly possible that Bartleby could withstand such an application of the doctrine of assumptions. But, upon second thought, the success of the plan seemed rather dubious. I resolved to argue the matter over with him again.

"Bartleby," said I, entering the office, with a quietly severe expression, "I am seriously displeased. I am pained, Bartleby. I had thought better of you. I had imagined you of such a gentlemanly organization, that in any delicate dilemma a slight hint would suffice—in short, an assumption; but it appears I am deceived. Why," I added, unaffectedly starting, "you have not even touched that money yet," pointing to it, just where I had left it the evening previous.

He answered nothing.

"Will you, or will you not, quit me?" I now demanded in a sudden passion, advancing close to him.

"I would prefer *not* to quit you," he replied, gently emphasizing the *not*.

"What earthly right have you to stay here? Do you pay any rent? Do you pay my taxes? Or is this property yours?"

He answered nothing.

"Are you ready to go on and write now? Are your eyes recovered? Could you copy a small paper for me this morning? or help examine a few lines? or step round to the Post Office? In a word, will you do any thing at all, to give a colouring to your refusal to depart the premises?"

He silently retired into his hermitage.

I was now in such a state of nervous resentment that I thought it but prudent to check myself, at present, from further demonstrations. Bartleby and I were alone. I remembered the tragedy of the unfortunate Adams and the still more unfortunate Colt in the solitary office of the latter; and how poor Colt, being dreadfully incensed by Adams, and imprudently permitting himself to get wildly excited, was at unawares hurried into his fatal act—an act which certainly no man could possibly deplore more than the actor himself. Often it had occurred to me in my ponderings upon the subject, that had that altercation taken place in the public street, or at a private residence, it would not have terminated as it did. It was the circumstance of being alone in a solitary office, upstairs, of a building entirely unhallowed by humanizing domestic associations—an uncarpeted office, doubtless, of a dusty, haggard sort of appearance;—this it must have been, which greatly helped to enhance the irritable desperation of the hapless Colt.

But when this old Adam of resentment rose in me and tempted me concerning Bartleby, I grappled him and threw him. How? Why, simply by recalling the divine injunction: "A new commandment give I unto you, that ye love one another." Yes, this it was that saved me. Aside from higher considerations, charity often operates as a vastly wise and prudent principle—a great safeguard to its possessor. Men have committed murder for jealousy's sake, and anger's sake, and hatred's sake, and selfishness' sake, and spiritual pride's sake; but no man that ever I heard of, ever committed a diabolical murder for sweet charity's sake. Mere self-interest, then, if no better motive can be enlisted, should, especially with high-tempered men, prompt all beings to charity and philanthropy. At any rate, upon the occasion in question, I strove to drown my exasperated feelings toward the scrivener by benevolently construing his conduct. Poor fellow, poor fellow! thought I, he doesn't mean any thing; and besides, he has seen hard times, and ought to be indulged.

I endeavoured also immediately to occupy myself, and at the same time to comfort my despondency. I tried to fancy that in the course of the morning, at such time as might prove agreeable to him, Bartleby, of his own free accord, would emerge from his hermitage, and take up some decided line of march in the direction of the door. But no. Half-past twelve o'clock came; Turkey began to glow in the face, overturn his inkstand, and become generally obstreperous; Nippers abated down into quietude and courtesy; Ginger Nut munched his noon apple; and Bartleby remained standing at his window in one of his profoundest dead-wall reveries. Will it be credited? Ought I to acknowledge it? That afternoon I left the office without saying one further word to him.

Some days now passed, during which at leisure intervals I looked a little into "Edwards on the Will," and "Priestley on Necessity." Under the circumstances, those books induced a salutary feeling. Gradually I slid into the persuasion that these troubles of mine, touching the scrivener, had been all predestinated from eternity, and Bartleby was billeted upon me for some mysterious purpose of an all-wise Providence, which is was not for a mere mortal like me to fathom. Yes, Bartleby, stay there behind your screen, thought I; I shall persecute you no more; you are harmless and noiseless as any of these old chairs; in short, I never feel so private as when I know you are here. At least I see it, I feel it; I penetrate to the predestinated purpose of my life. I am content. Others may have loftier parts to enact; but my mission in this world, Bartleby, is to furnish you with office room for such period as you may see fit to remain.

I believe that this wise and blessed frame of mind would have continued with me had it not been for the unsolicited and uncharitable remarks obtruded upon me by my professional friends who visited the rooms. But thus it often is, that the constant friction of illiberal minds wears out at last the best resolves of the more generous. Though to be sure, when I reflected upon it, it was not strange that people entering my office should be struck by the peculiar aspect of the unaccountable Bartleby, and so be tempted to throw out some sinister observations concerning him. Sometimes an attorney having business with me, and calling at my office, and finding no one but the scrivener there, would undertake to obtain some sort of precise information from him touching my whereabouts; but without heeding his idle talk, Bartleby would remain standing immovable in the middle of the room. So, after contemplating him in that position for a time, the attorney would depart, no wiser than he came.

Also, when a Reference was going on, and the room full of lawyers and witnesses and business was driving fast, some deeply occupied legal gentleman present, seeing Bartleby wholly unemployed, would request him to run round to his (the legal gentleman's) office and fetch some papers for him. Thereupon, Bartleby would tranquilly decline, and yet remain idle as before. Then the lawyer would give a great stare, and turn to me. And what could I say? At last I was made aware that all through the circle of my professional acquaintance, a whisper of wonder was running round, having reference to the strange creature I kept at my office. This worried me very much. And as the idea came upon me of his possibly turning out a long-lived man, and keep occupying my chambers, and denying my authority; and perplexing my visitors; and scandalizing my professional reputation; and casting a general gloom over the premises; keeping soul and body together to the last upon his savings (for doubtless he spent but half a dime a day), and in the end perhaps outlive me, and claim possession of my office by right of his perpetual occupancy: as all these dark anticipations crowded upon me more and more, and my friends continually intruded their relentless remarks upon the apparition in my room, a great change was wrought in me. I resolved to gather all my faculties together, and for ever rid me of this intolerable incubus.

Ere revolving any complicated project, however, adapted to this end, I first simply suggested to Bartleby the propriety of his permanent departure. In a calm and serious tone, I commended the idea to his careful and mature consideration. But having taken three days to meditate upon it, he apprised me that his original determination remained the same; in short, that he still preferred to abide with me.

What shall I do? I now said to myself, buttoning up my coat to the last button. What shall I do? what ought I to do? what does conscience say I *should* do with this man, or rather ghost? Rid myself of him, I must; go, he shall. But how? You will not thrust him, the poor, pale, passive mortal,—you will not thrust such a helpless creature out of your door? you will not dishonour yourself by such cruelty? No, I will not, I cannot do that. Rather would I let him live and die here, and then mason up his remains in the wall. What then will you do? For all your coaxing, he will not budge. Bribes he leaves under your own paper-weight on your table; in short, it is quite plain that he prefers to cling to you.

Then something severe, something unusual must be done. What! surely you will not have him collared by a constable, and commit his innocent pallor to the common jail? And upon what ground could you procure such a thing to be done?—a vagrant, is he? What! he a vagrant, a wanderer, who refuses to budge? It is because he will *not* be a vagrant, then, that you seek to count him *as* a vagrant. That is too absurd. No visible means of support: there I have him. Wrong again: for indubitably he *does* support himself, and that is the only unanswerable proof that any man can show of his possessing the means so to do. No more then. Since he will not quit me, I must quit him. I will change my offices; I will move elsewhere; and give him fair notice, that if I find him on my new premises I will then proceed against him as a common trespasser.

Acting accordingly, next day I thus addressed him: "I find these chambers too far from the City Hall; the air is unwholesome. In a word, I propose to remove my offices next week, and shall no longer require your services. I tell you this now, in order that you may seek another place."

He made no reply, and nothing more was said.

On the appointed day I engaged carts and men, proceeded to my chambers, and having but little furniture, everything was removed in a few hours. Throughout all, the scrivener remained standing behind the screen, which I directed to be removed the last thing. It was withdrawn; and being folded up like a huge folio, left him the motionless occupant of a naked room. I stood in the entry watching him a moment, while something from within me upbraided me.

I re-entered, with my hand in my pocket—and—and my heart in my mouth.

"Good-bye, Bartleby; I am going—good-bye, and God some way bless you; and take that," slipping something in his hand. But it dropped upon the floor and then—strange to say—I tore myself from him whom I had so longed to be rid of.

Established in my new quarters, for a day or two I kept the door locked, and started at every footfall in the passages. When I returned to my rooms after any little absence, I would pause at the threshold for an instant, and attentively listen, ere applying my key. But these fears were needless. Bartleby never came nigh me.

I thought all was going well, when a perturbed looking stranger visited me, inquiring whether I was the person who had recently occupied rooms at No. —— Wall street.

Full of forebodings, I replied that I was.

"Then sir," said the stranger, who proved a lawyer, "you are responsible for the man you left there. He refuses to do any copying, he refuses to do anything; and he says he prefers not to; and he refuses to quit the premises."

"I am very sorry, sir," said I, with assumed tranquillity, but an inward tremor, "but, really, the man you allude to is nothing to me—he is no relation or apprentice of mine, that you should hold me responsible for him."

"In mercy's name, who is he?"

"I certainly cannot inform you. I know nothing about him. Formerly I employed him as a copyist; but he has done nothing for me now for some time past."

"I shall settle him then,—good morning, sir."

Several days passed, and I heard nothing more; and though I often felt a charitable prompting to call at the place and see poor Bartleby, yet a certain squeamishness of I know not what withheld me.

All is over with him, by this time, thought I at last, when through another week no further intelligence reached me. But coming to my room the day after, I found several persons waiting at my door in a high state of nervous excitement.

"That's the man—here he comes," cried the foremost one, whom I recognized as the lawyer who had previously called upon me alone.

"You must take him away, sir, at once," cried a portly person among them, advancing upon me, and whom I knew to be the landlord of No. —— Wall street. "These gentlemen, my tenants, cannot stand it any longer; Mr. B——," pointing to the lawyer, "has turned him out of his room, and he now persists in haunting the building generally, sitting upon the banisters of the stairs by day, and sleeping in the entry by night. Everybody here is concerned; clients are leaving the offices; some fears are entertained of a mob; something you must do, and that without delay."

Aghast at this torrent, I fell back before it, and would fain have locked myself in my new quarters. In vain I persisted that Bartleby was nothing to me—no more than to any one else there. In vain:—I was the last person known to have anything to do with him, and they held me to the terrible account. Fearful then of being exposed in the papers (as one person present obscurely threatened) I considered the matter, and at length said, that if the lawyer would give me a confidential interview with the scrivener, in his (the lawyer's) own room, I would that afternoon strive my best to rid them of the nuisance they complained of.

Going up stairs to my old haunt, there was Bartleby silently sitting upon the banister at the landing.

"What are you doing here, Bartleby?" said I.

"Sitting upon the banister," he mildly replied.

I motioned him into the lawyer's room, who then left us.

"Bartleby," said I, "are you aware that you are the cause of great tribulation to me, by persisting in occupying the entry after being dismissed from the office?"

No answer.

"Now one of two things must take place. Either you must do something, or something must be done to you. Now what sort of business would you like to engage in? Would you like to re-engage in copying for some one?"

"No; I would prefer not to make any change."

"Would you like a clerkship in a dry-goods store?"

"There is too much confinement about that. No, I would not like a clerkship; but I am not particular."

"Too much confinement," I cried, "why you keep yourself confined all the time!"

"I would prefer not to take a clerkship," he rejoined, as if to settle that little item at once.

"How would a bartender's business suit you? There is no trying of the eyesight in that."

"I would not like it at all; though, as I said before, I am not particular."

His unwonted wordiness inspirited me. I returned to the charge.

"Well then, would you like to travel through the country collecting bills for the merchants? That would improve your health."

"No, I would prefer to be doing something else."

"How then would going as a companion to Europe to entertain some young gentleman with your conversation,—how would that suit you?"

"Not at all. It does not strike me that there is anything definite about that. I like to be stationary. But I am not particular."

"Stationary you shall be then," I cried, now losing all patience, and for the first time in all my exasperating connection with him fairly flying into a passion. "If you do not go away from these premises before night, I shall feel bound—indeed I *am* bound—to—to—to quit the premises myself!" I rather absurdly concluded, knowing not with what possible threat to try to frighten his immobility into compliance. Despairing of all further efforts, I was precipitately leaving him, when a final thought occurred to me—one which had not been wholly unindulged before.

"Bartleby," said I, in the kindest tone I could assume under such exciting circumstances, "will you go home with me now—not to my office, but my dwelling—and remain there till we can conclude upon some convenient arrangement for you at our leisure? Come, let us start now, right away."

"No: at present I would prefer not to make any change at all."

I answered nothing; but effectually dodging every one by the suddenness and rapidity of my flight, rushed from the building, ran up Wall street toward Broadway, and then jumping into the first omnibus was soon removed from pursuit. As soon as tranquillity returned I distinctly perceived that I had now done all that I possibly could, both in respect to the demands of the landlord and his tenants, and with regard to my own desire and sense of duty, to benefit Bartleby, and shield him from rude persecution. I now strove to be entirely care-free and quiescent; and my conscience justified me in the attempt; though indeed it was not so successful as I could have wished. So fearful was I of being again hunted out by the incensed landlord and his exasperated tenants, that, surrendering my business to Nippers, for a few days I drove about the upper part of the town and through the suburbs, in my rockaway; crossed over to Jersey City and Hoboken, and paid fugitive visits to Manhattanville and Astoria. In fact I almost lived in my rockaway for the time.

When again I entered my office, lo, a note from the landlord lay upon the desk. I opened it with trembling hands. It informed me that the writer had sent to the police, and had Bartleby removed to the Tombs as a vagrant. Moreover, since I knew more about him than any one else, he wished me to appear at that place, and make a suitable statement of the facts. These tidings had a conflicting effect upon me. At first I was indignant; but at last almost approved. The landlord's energetic, summary disposition had led him to adopt a procedure which I do not think I would have decided upon myself; and yet as a last resort, under such peculiar circumstances, it seemed the only plan.

As I afterwards learned, the poor scrivener, when told that he must be conducted to the Tombs, offered not the slightest obstacle, but in his own pale, unmoving way silently acquiesced.

Some of the compassionate and curious bystanders joined the party; and headed by one of the constables, arm-in-arm with Bartleby the silent procession filed its way through all the noise, and heat, and joy of the roaring thoroughfares at noon.

The same day I received the note I went to the Tombs, or, to speak more properly, the Halls of Justice. Seeking the right officer, I stated the purpose of my call, and was informed that the individual I described was indeed within. I then assured the functionary that Bartleby was a perfectly honest man, and greatly to be a compassionated (however unaccountable) eccentric. I narrated all I knew, and closed by suggesting the idea of letting him remain in as indulgent confinement as possible till something less harsh might be done—though indeed I hardly knew what. At all events, if nothing else could be decided upon, the alms-house must receive him. I then begged to have an interview.

Being under no disgraceful charge, and quite serene and harmless in all his ways, they had permitted him freely to wander about the prison, and especially in the inclosed grass-platted yards thereof. And so I found him there, standing all alone in the quietest of the yards, his face toward a high wall—while all around, from the narrow slits of the jail windows, I thought I saw peering out upon him the eyes of murderers and thieves.

"Bartleby!"

"I know you," he said, without looking round,—"and I want nothing to say to you."

"It was not I that brought you here, Bartleby," said I, keenly pained at his implied suspicion. "And to you, this should not be so vile a place. Nothing reproachful attaches to you by being here. And see, it is not so sad a place as one might think. Look, there is the sky and here is the grass."

"I know where I am," he replied, but would say nothing more, and so I left him.

As I entered the corridor again a broad, meat-like man in an apron accosted me, and jerking his thumb over his shoulder said—"Is that your friend?"

"Yes."

"Does he want to starve? If he does, let him live on the prison fare, that's all."

"Who are you?" asked I, not knowing what to make of such an unofficially speaking person in such a place.

"I am the grub-man. Such gentlemen as have friends here, hire me to provide them with something good to eat."

"Is this so?" said I, turning to the turnkey.

He said it was.

"Well then," said I, slipping some silver into the grubman's hands (for so they called him), "I want you to give particular attention to my friend there; let him have the best dinner you can get. And you must be as polite to him as possible."

"Introduce me, will you?" said the grub-man, looking at me with an expression which seemed to say he was all impatience for an opportunity to give a specimen of his breeding.

Thinking it would prove of benefit to the scrivener, I acquiesced; and asking the grub-man his name, went up with him to Bartleby.

"Bartleby, this is Mr. Cutlets; you will find him very useful to you."

"Your sarvant, sir, your sarvant," said the grub-man, making a low salutation behind his apron. "Hope you find it pleasant here, sir;—spacious grounds—cool apartments, sir—hope you'll stay with us some time—try to make it agreeable. May Mrs. Cutlets and I have the pleasure of your company to dinner, sir, in Mrs. Cutlets' private room?"

"I prefer not to dine to-day," said Bartleby, turning away. "It would disagree with me; I am unused to dinners." So saying, he slowly moved to the other side of the inclosure and took up a position fronting the dead-wall.

"How's this?" said the grub-man, addressing me with a stare of astonishment. "He's odd, ain't he?"

"I think he is a little deranged," said I, sadly.

"Deranged? deranged is it? Well now, upon my word, I thought that friend of yourn was a gentleman forger; they are always pale and genteel-like, them forgers. I can't help pity 'em—can't help it, sir. Did you know Monroe Edwards?" he added touchingly, and paused. Then, laying his hand pityingly on my shoulder, sighed, "he died of the consumption at Sing-Sing. So you weren't acquainted with Monroe?"

"No, I was never socially acquainted with any forgers. But I cannot stop longer. Look to my friend yonder. You will not lose by it. I will see you again."

Some few days after this, I again obtained admission to the Tombs, and went through the corridors in quest of Bartleby; but without finding him.

"I saw him coming from his cell not long ago," said a turnkey, "maybe he's gone to loiter in the yards."

So I went in that direction.

"Are you looking for the silent man?" said another turnkey passing me. "Yonder he lies—sleeping in the yard there. 'Tis not twenty minutes since I saw him lie down."

The yard was entirely quiet. It was not accessible to the common prisoners. The surrounding walls, of amazing thickness, kept off all sounds behind them. The Egyptian character of the masonry weighed upon me with its gloom. But a soft imprisoned turf grew under foot. The heart of the eternal pyramids, it seemed, wherein by some strange magic, through the clefts grass-seed, dropped by birds, had sprung.

Strangely huddled at the base of the wall—his knees drawn up, and lying on his side, his head touching the cold stones—I saw the wasted Bartleby. But nothing stirred. I paused; then went close up to him; stooped over, and saw that his dim eyes were open; otherwise he seemed profoundly sleeping. Something prompted me to touch him. I felt his hand, when a tingling shiver ran up my arm and down my spine to my feet.

The round face of the grub-man peered upon me now. "His dinner is ready. Won't he dine to-day, either? Or does he live without dining?"

"Lives without dining," said I, and closed the eyes.

"Eh!—He's asleep, ain't he?"

"With kings and counsellors," murmured I.

.   .   .   .   .   .

There would seem little need for proceeding further in this history. Imagination will readily supply the meagre recital of poor Bartleby's interment. But ere parting with the reader, let me say, that if this little narrative has sufficiently interested him, to awaken curiosity as to who Bartleby was, and what manner of life he led prior to the present narrator's making his acquaintance, I can only reply, that in such curiosity I fully share—but am wholly unable to gratify it. Yet here I hardly know whether I should divulge one little item of rumour, which came to my ear a few months after the scrivener's decease. Upon what basis it rested, I could never ascertain; and hence, how true it is I cannot now tell. But inasmuch as this vague report has not been without a certain strange suggestive interest to me, however sad, it may prove the same with some others; and so I will briefly mention it. The report was this: that Bartleby had been a subordinate clerk in the Dead Letter Office at Washington, from which he had been suddenly removed by a change in the administration. When I think over this rumour I cannot adequately express the emotions which seize me. Dead letters! does it not sound like dead men? Conceive a man by nature and misfortune prone to a pallid hopelessness: can any business seem more fitted to heighten it than that of continually handling these dead letters, and assorting them for the flames? For by the cartload they are annually burned. Sometimes from out the folded paper the pale clerk takes a ring:—the finger it was meant for, perhaps, moulders in the grave; a bank-note sent in swiftest charity:—he whom it would relieve, nor eats nor hungers any more; pardon for those who died despairing; hope for those who died unhoping; good tidings for those who died stifled by unrelieved calamities. On errands of life, these letters speed to death.

Ah Bartleby! Ah humanity!

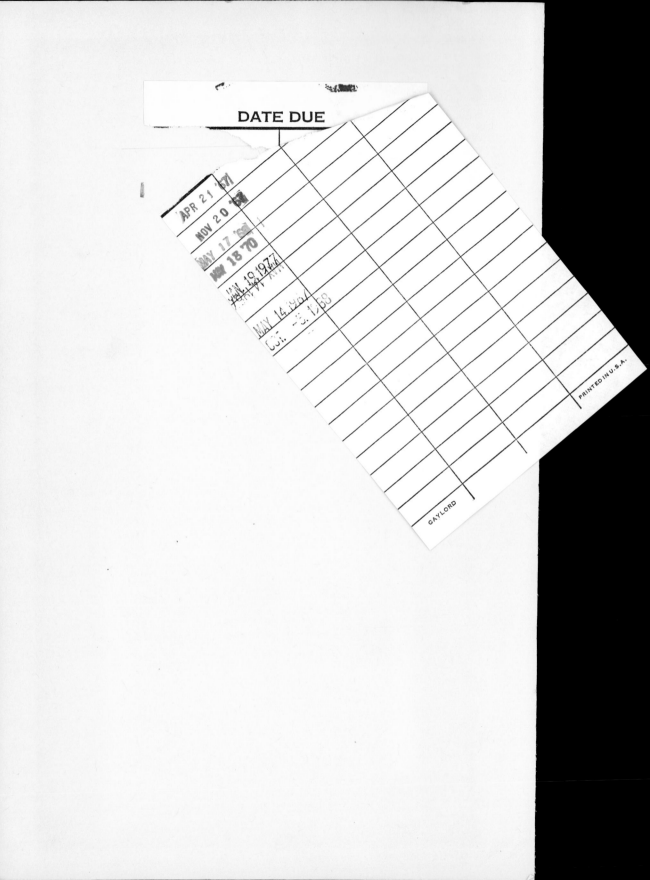